BIBLICAL WORLDVIEW

CREATION
FALL
REDEMPTION

Greenville, South Carolina

Note: The fact that a given writer is cited or quoted in this textbook does not mean that BJU Press endorses that writer (or his or her book, article, etc.) from the standpoint of morals, philosophy, theology, or scientific hypotheses. The nature of a worldview book is such that we must cite and quote people with whom we have fundamental disagreements. In some cases we quote or cite positively people with whom we strongly disagree on other issues—because they do an excellent job saying what's true about the issue at hand. Part of developing a Christian worldview is cultivating the ability to discern between the good and problematic views even of other Christians. This textbook itself is not flawless; it was produced by fallen and finite human beings. It is the privilege and responsibility of every teacher and student to test the claims of *Biblical Worldview: Creation, Fall, Redemption*—and of the writers this book cites—against God's infallible revelation in Scripture.

BIBLICAL WORLDVIEW:
CREATION, FALL, REDEMPTION

Lead Author & General Editor
Mark L. Ward Jr., PhD

Contributing Authors
Brian Collins, PhD
Bryan Smith, PhD
Gregory Stiekes, PhD

Editor
Dennis Cone, MA

Advisory Board
Jim Berg, MA
Brenton Cook, PhD
Eric Newton, PhD
Lesa Seibert, EdD

Consultants
Brad Batdorf, EdD
Wesley Barley, MDiv
Don Congdon, MA
Kevin Collins, MDiv
Terry Egolf
Zachary Franzen
Michelle Radford, MFA
Rachel Santopietro
Steve Skaggs, MEd
Esther Wilkison

Project Coordinator
Matthew Ryan

Cover & Book Design
Michael Asire

Page Layout
Bonnijean Marley
Jessica Johnson

Cover Illustration
Chris Koelle

Illustrators
Zachary Franzen
Chris Koelle
Del Thompson

Permissions
Sylvia Gass
Sarah Gundlach
Brenda Hansen
Carrie Walker

Photograph credits appear on page 473.

ISBN 978-1-60682-727-7

15 14 13 12 11 10 9 8 7 6 5 4 3 2 1

CONTENTS

7 SCIENCE

8 HISTORY

9 ARTS & CULTURE

"Quite unknown to myself, I was, while a boy, under *A HOPELESS DISADVANTAGE* in studying nature. I was very near-sighted, so that the only things I could study were those I ran against or stumbled over. . . . It was this summer that I got my first gun, and it puzzled me to find that my companions seemed to see things to shoot at which I could not see at all. One day they read aloud an advertisement in huge letters on a distant billboard, and I then realized that *SOMETHING WAS THE MATTER,* for not only was I unable to read the sign but I could not even see the letters. I spoke of this to my father, and soon afterwards got my first pair of spectacles, which literally opened *AN ENTIRELY NEW WORLD* to me. I had no idea how beautiful the world was until I got those spectacles. I had been a clumsy and awkward little boy, and while much of my clumsiness and awkwardness was doubtless due to general characteristics, a good deal of it was due to the fact that I could not see and yet *WAS WHOLLY IGNORANT THAT I WAS NOT SEEING.*"[1]

—THEODORE ROOSEVELT

1

WORLDVIEW

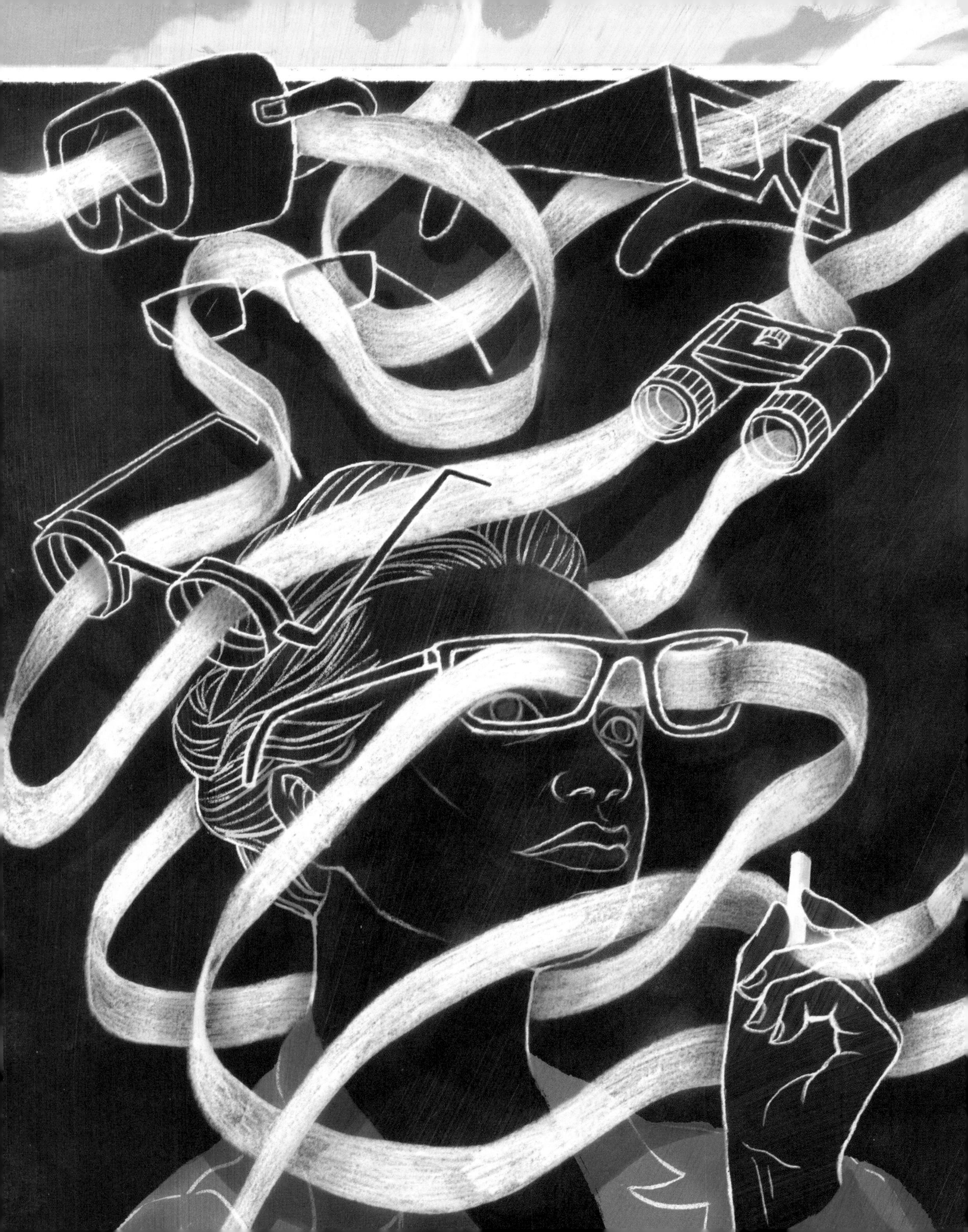

Chapter One WORLDVIEWS

For the weapons of our warfare are not of the flesh but have divine power to destroy strongholds. We destroy arguments and every lofty opinion raised against the knowledge of God, and take every thought captive to obey Christ.

Scripture Memory
2 Corinthians 10:4–5

1.1 WORLDVIEW LENSES

"By faith we understand that the universe was created by the word of God, so that what is seen was not made out of things that are visible" (Heb. 11:3).

By faith *we* understand this, we followers of Jesus Christ (if you are such a follower). But not everyone sees the world that way.

PROJECT STEVE

Take the National Center for Science Education. A few years ago, the NCSE began Project Steve. And you have to hand it to them—it was very clever. They rounded up a thousand or so scientists named Steve to sign a statement expressing their support for evolution:

> Evolution is a vital, well-supported, unifying principle of the biological sciences, and the scientific evidence is overwhelmingly in favor of the idea that all living things share a common ancestry. . . . It is scientifically inappropriate and pedagogically* irresponsible for creationist pseudoscience* . . . to be introduced into the science curricula of our nation's public schools.[1]

The implication of Project Steve is clear. If they found this many pro-evolution scientists who all shared the same name, then just think how many scientists must be out there wishing their names were Steve so they could sign the statement too. Project Steve was a way of saying to Bible-believing Christians, "You're a small, ignorant, and cultish group."

To the Steves, biblical Christianity is scientifically out of date. The Bible may describe ancient miracles, but scientists see themselves as ones who put miracles into our hands today. In an age of amazing scientific and technological advances, the Steves think it's irrational to believe the mutterings of long-dead prophets.

HEART REASONS

Not everyone who rejects Christianity does so for intellectual reasons, however—not even the intel-

pedagogically: *educationally, having to do with teaching*

pseudoscience: *(pseudo: false) a theory or methodology that claims to be scientific but isn't really*

PROJECT BILL

Where Project Steve was subtle and even humorous, other prominent voices in Western culture are blunt and insulting:

> You can't be a rational person six days of the week and put on a suit and make rational decisions and go to work and, on one day of the week, go to a building and think you're drinking the blood of a 2,000-year-old space god. That doesn't make you a person of faith. That makes you a schizophrenic.[2]

That was comedian and political commentator Bill Maher speaking on a popular late-night network TV show. (And just to be clear, Christians don't believe we're drinking blood at the Lord's table, and Jesus isn't a "space god.")

lectuals. One of the big points of this first unit on worldview will be that people tend to use superficial, head-level arguments to cover up deeper, heart-level reasons for turning from God.

And those heart reasons can be very powerful. People in this world are hurting, and many blame God. If He's so powerful and so good, why does He let such evil and painful things happen to me? That argument is probably at least as common (if not more common) among unbelievers than the pro-evolution arguments used by the Steves. In an age of deep despair, many victims of other people's sins find it offensive to be told that they are sinners too.

SMART PEOPLE

Western society (the "West" basically means the nations of Western Europe and some of the countries colonized by them, such as the United States and Canada) has a sometimes awkward, sometimes adversarial relationship with religion. Hurting people sense that they need "spirituality," but Christianity is too exclusive and too demanding for them. And among cultural elites,* religion—especially Christianity—is thought to pose a threat to the social order. Those elites will let you have your religion if you really must—as long as you keep it out of politics and the laboratory. But the boundaries around religion keep shrinking ever tighter, squeezing it out of journalism, the arts, and education (in a process called secularization*).

cultural elites: *the recognized leaders in all aspects of a culture, from politics to academics to the arts*

secularization: *the process of a society turning away from religion or faith in anything supernatural*

We might as well admit it because the Bible does. Many of the very smart people out there—smarter than you, smarter even than *Biblical Worldview* textbook authors—think that your religion is not just mere opinion, but mere foolish opinion. Paul admitted about the Corinthian Christians long ago, "Not many of you were wise according to worldly standards, not many were powerful, not many were of noble birth" (1 Cor. 1:26).

NOMA

One of the most famous scientists named Steve was Stephen Jay Gould (1941–2002), a paleontologist and evolutionary biologist who wrote many popular books about science. Dr. Gould is known for proposing an idea about the relationship between religion and science that he calls "NOMA"—Non-Overlapping Magisteria.[3] Gould is willing to grant some kind of authority (that's what *magisterium* means) to religion, but it's an authority that does not overlap with scientific authority.

But take heart because that's not where Paul stops. Instead, he continues, "God chose what is foolish in the world to shame the wise; God chose what is weak in the world to shame the strong" (1 Cor. 1:27).

How, then, do you respond to these smart people? There are three major options:

Option 1: Give in. Give up your faith completely.

Regarding this option, this whole book is one big "Don't do that." It's totally unnecessary, not to mention that it's an offense against your Creator.

Option 2: Give in a little—but only on the really disputed issues like evolution and homosexual marriage. Admit that the Bible may be wrong in just a few places.

Don't do this, either. Either God spoke clearly in His Word about these issues or He didn't. If He spoke clearly, giving in even a little will lead to giving in a lot anytime someone puts enough pressure on you.

Option 3: Don't give in at all if someone contradicts Scripture, no matter how smart or how numerous the Steves are. Instead, argue back—lovingly and graciously, but powerfully and confidently—knowing that God's reason for using the weak to shame the wise is "so that no human being might boast in the presence of God" (1 Cor 1:29).

OPTION 3

Option 3 is, obviously, this book's recommendation. The Bible speaks about all of life—not just about morals and church. God speaks through Scripture in ways that ought to influence even a college biology class. So there's good reason to go for option 3.

But it raises some immediate practical problems.

Let's imagine a Steve-versus-You scenario: Dr. Steve at his lectern versus you in your fold-down, wooden seat in a massive lecture hall during your freshman year at college. Steve with his hard-earned PhD (give him some real credit for that) versus you with your hard-earned high school diploma.

Scene: Biology 101, State University in Dodge, Dakota. One-hundred thirty-six 18-year-olds (you're sitting on the tenth row) watching ugly but informative PowerPoints that Steve has put together to lead his young charges from ignorance to scientific light.

Dialogue: Not much, really. It's just Steve talking. And he's good at it. He's smart and engaging—nerdy but only in a cool way. He knows his phyla and his genera. You, as one who's always enjoyed science, are really liking this class.

Internal dialogue: But you're ready. You know he's going to deny the Bible's account of creation; you just don't know how or when. But you won't give in. No matter what. You promised Mom.

But three autumn weeks pass, and you haven't heard anything you believe you're supposed to disagree with. You're pretty overwhelmed by the vast store of scientific knowledge between Steve's two ears. And then, finally, Steve hits the evolution lesson.

Steve is very disarming. He's not nasty toward creationists. He doesn't make you stand up to proclaim your faith and then laugh derisively at you. He doesn't even know you're there. Nonetheless he makes you feel dumb, dumber than you already feel after almost a month listening to his intellect sing.

He simply points to the evidence: there those trilobites* are, sitting in exactly the sedimentary stratum* that the evolutionary model* predicts. Look at the picture. They're just hanging out, doing whatever it is fossilized trilobites like to do while they're waiting millions of years to be discovered by paleontologists. You can't deny your senses. Suddenly you can't think of a way to make the evidence fit Scripture.

trilobite: *extinct sea creature often found fossilized*

stratum: *rock layer*

model: *a simplified description of vast amounts of data*

You've got an immediate, practical problem.

OPTIONS 3.1 AND 3.2

As it turns out, Option 3 has two sub-options, each of which is valid in its own way.

Option 3.1: Argue back based on your own superior understanding of the evidence.

There are Christian geologists and biologists in the world (some of them are even named Steve) who can offer competing explanations of the scientific data—or who have access to additional data that might revise the picture described by your university professor.

This is part of why you have a high school science class: to learn these explanations and amass this data—and to learn how to come up with your own explanations and find your own data via scientific methodology.

But believing scientists haven't yet persuaded the non-Christian ones (or vice versa). And you? You're eighteen. Your professor has been teaching the evolutionary history of apes and men since the days when you were learning to make monkey sounds. You simply don't know as much as he knows. That's why you're sitting in his class. You're hoping he'll teach you.

Arguments based on evidence have a definite place, and we'll talk a lot more about them. But right now, as you're sitting in that class, they're not going to help you very much—even if you were the top science student in high school.

What do you need to help you answer the questions that Dr. Steve put into your head—so that you stay true to your Christian beliefs and live according to them when you reach college? You need the other sub-option.

Option 3.2: Argue back, perhaps initially only in your own mind, based on the concept of "worldview."

COMING TO TERMS

The word *worldview* appears to have come into English as a translation of the German word *Weltanschauung*. *Welt* (velt) means "world," and *anschauung* (ON-shao-ung) means "point of view," "opinion," or "perception."

Christian thinkers have used or proposed different terms. The prime minister of the Netherlands at the turn of the twentieth century, Abraham Kuyper, was a strong Christian and strong proponent of worldview thinking. He liked to call the biblical worldview the "Christian world and life view." But that's unwieldy, like a couch being carried through a narrow door. Most people have settled on *worldview*.

WORLDVIEW

It certainly seems like Dr. Steve has a mountain of evidence on his side. But if you look at what he says more closely, you'll find that evidence is not the only ingredient in his thinking. The evidence he cites sounds convincing only because he looks at that evidence in a certain way—in a way that is colored by his **worldview**.

What exactly is a worldview? Let's start with a few illustrations; a little later in this chapter, we'll move to a definition.

- A chain: Every chain of reasoning has to start somewhere.
- A building: Every brick of your knowledge has to be built on some ultimate foundation. It can't just be bricks all the way down.
- A lens: A worldview is like a set of lenses through which you see everything around you.

Lenses may be the most helpful illustration of what a worldview does. If you wear glasses or contacts, you might remember when you first put them on. The world looked sharper, but your new seeing apparatus felt awkward. You were very aware of it. Maybe the contacts made your eyes water or the frames on your glasses distracted you by their shape and color. But it's unlikely that this feeling lasted very long. By now, you're so used to your lenses that you don't see them at all. Instead you see through them.

That's what a worldview is like—a set of lenses through which you view the world. But because you got it so long ago and it grew on you so naturally, you may never have looked at your worldview at all.

And let's extend this metaphor a little bit: you really can't look at your glasses distinctly while they're on your face. At most you see a fuzzy rim and the very edges of the lenses. You can't look at the lenses themselves unless you take them off, and that is very difficult to do. They're stuck on there pretty well.

Dr. Steve, trained biology expert, wears glasses just like you do—except your glasses (if you're a Christian) are different from his, or at least they ought to be. Most scientists in Project Steve see the world through atheistic lenses in which every evidence for God's existence is twisted into an evidence for His absence. But it's not the evidence that's different. It's the lenses through which Dr. Steve sees it.

FOR REAL?

A website publicizes a program for teaching science and claims that it is "the only worldview-neutral curriculum that supports both Christian and secular values."[4] Evaluate the claim this advertisement makes. Can a science curriculum be worldview neutral?

Look at the Grand Canyon through biblical lenses, and you'll see results of a worldwide flood. Look at the same 277-mile stretch of beauty through evolutionist glasses, and you'll probably see millions of years of erosion. But the canyon stays the same.

THINKING IT THROUGH 1.1

1. What claim(s) did Project Steve make in expressing its support for evolution?
2. List the three major options for responding when your faith is challenged.
3. Identify the two distinct approaches you can take when seeking to carry out the third option.
4. What are the three illustrations the book provides regarding how a worldview functions?
5. Briefly explain why it is biblically invalid to respond with Option 1 or Option 2 to those who challenge your faith.

1.2 WORLDVIEW INGREDIENTS

This book will suggest that every worldview—whether Dr. Steve's or yours—has three ingredients:

1. A worldview contains a "head-heart system" of basic beliefs, assumptions, and values.
2. A worldview tells a big story about the world.
3. A worldview produces action.

INGREDIENT 1: HEAD-HEART SYSTEM

Most definitions of worldview start here: a worldview is a set of **basic beliefs**, a more or less organized (and most people's worldviews are less organized) system of assumptions and values. People's thoughts tend to develop patterns and fit into systems. Even if they are content with numerous inconsistencies, their thoughts are never completely random—none of us can bear to live in total mental chaos. God made us to be like Himself; that's what it means to be made in God's own image (Gen. 1:27). God thinks logically, and we can't help but want to as well.

There is a difference between functional beliefs and basic beliefs. You may believe that Reykjavik is the capital of Iceland, but this is not a basic belief. Worldview thinker Al Wolters suggests that basic beliefs answer questions like "Can violence ever be right? Are there any absolute, unchanging moral rules for human life? Is there a point to suffering? Do we survive death?"[5]

A Head System

Think again of that chain metaphor. Why do you think, if you do, that a mass murderer such as Hitler deserved death? Probably because you believe that taking numerous innocent human lives—like Hitler did—is wrong. That's one chain link back. Why is taking six million Jewish lives (and perhaps five million other civilians' lives) wrong? Because taking even one human life is wrong. That's one more chain link. But why is that wrong? Because human life should not be taken without just cause. Why? Because human life is intrinsically valuable.

That's the last link in the chain for most people like Steve. It seems totally obvious to them that this is the case. When American Founding Father Thomas Jefferson wanted to argue that every person has equal value, he wrote, "We hold these truths to be self-evident, that all men are created equal." But he added something: "They are endowed by their Creator with certain unalienable Rights." By saying that, Jefferson added one more link to the chain: humanity gets its value from its Creator.

So what if Steve's set of beliefs and system of assumptions includes no Creator? What if, when Steve looks through his worldview lenses at another person, he sees a fellow survivor of the evolutionary process rather than one who bears the image of the one true God? What if his chain of reasoning only goes as far as the big bang?

This is the Western (remember: European and American) world we live in, a world where every chain hangs, ultimately, from a large explosion 13.8 billion years ago. Suppose you ask, "What is the big bang hanging on?" You're likely to be told you're talking nonsense. As one famous scientist named Steve (Stephen Hawking) reportedly put it, asking what happened before the big bang is like asking what's north of the North Pole.

But Westerners don't tend to see their set of beliefs as a worldview precisely because they don't think they have any mere "beliefs"—not about what's important, at least. They frequently fail to recognize, as two particular worldview thinkers put it, that "world views are founded on ultimate faith commitments."[7]

Dr. Steve isn't a geologist, but he's pretty smart. What would he say about the Grand Canyon? How old is it? He might respond that there are several theories: 5–6 million years, 17 million, maybe even 70 million. The middle figure seems to be the most popular right now. And those numbers are arrived at via a combination of various "data sets." We know, Steve will say, how much erosion the Colorado River has created in the last hundred years or so—since records began to be kept. We can also locate fossils and study rock deposition layers.

JEFFERSONIAN TRUTH

Thomas Jefferson spoke of a Creator in the American Declaration of Independence, but he didn't mean by this quite the same thing the Bible means. Neither was he a deist, exactly, though the Founding Fathers are often thought to be deists. Christian historian Gregg Frazer suggests that Jefferson—and Ben Franklin, and John Adams—are best described as "theistic rationalists."[6] They believed in a god, but a god who served reason—and not the other way around. Notice that he said truths can be "self-evident," that is, drawn from within rather than revealed by God.

WHAT'S NORTH OF THE NORTH POLE?

World-renowned scientist Stephen Hawking, a believer in macro-evolution,* reportedly commented, "What happened before the big bang? Well, what's north of the North Pole?"

But is this a legitimate comparison? We know there is a North Pole. You can go there and stand on it. But no one has seen the big bang. You can't go there. It seems like a necessary conclusion from the evidence only if you look at the evidence from a certain worldview—a strange worldview in which natural things (like big bangs) can happen without causes.[8]

macro-evolution: *the scientific model which proposes that living species evolved from lower forms of life*

Stephen Hawking
(1942–)

Putting all these data sets together is a very demanding and complex process. Let's focus on only one. If Steve studies just erosion, he can calculate how long it would take for the Colorado River to cut the canyon from top to bottom (though one theory, at least, thinks it was cut at different rates on either side of a divide).

But if Steve uses erosion rates to arrive at an age for the Grand Canyon, where's fact and where's assumption? Where's evidence and where's belief? Fact and evidence are limited to a mere century of data, and they tend to hide an essential layer of Steve's assumptions and beliefs: that erosion rates have been more or less constant—that no cataclysmic floods, for example, have come through town (but not all scientists assume this regarding the Grand Canyon).

Steve can't come to the Grand Canyon without any preconceived notions; we've all been conceiving notions since not too long after we ourselves were conceived, and we will necessarily carry them with us on our trip. All "facts" come with theories attached. Steve can't and won't ever see "facts" without his worldview lenses on.

In fact, as we'll discuss later, no understanding can ever happen without believing. The fear of the Lord (which certainly implies belief in His existence) is the beginning of all knowledge, according to Proverbs 1:7. It's the first principle. It's the ABCs, the basics, without which we don't have any knowledge worth calling knowledge.

A Heart System

This connection between the fear of the Lord and knowledge points to a key truth: a worldview isn't just a "head" system. One reason a person's worldview can be inconsistent, wrong, and even evil is that worldviews grow ultimately from the heart.

A man on the street in a downtown area (true story) once told a Christian who was handing out tracts, "I used to be a Christian. I went to church with my grandma pretty much all the time. But I wanted to have sex whenever I wanted it, and I couldn't see how a God who wants me to be happy would tell me to stop."

PEOPLE WHO WANT FREEDOM FROM GOD ARE LIKE FISH THAT WANT FREEDOM FROM WATER.[9]

That was not a head system speaking—a careful, logical analysis of the benefits and detriments of sexual promiscuity. It was a heart system saying, "I want what I want [pleasure via immorality, in this case], and I'm going to adopt a belief system which allows it—and drop the belief system that doesn't."

The Bible speaks of the heart as the center of the person. Jesus said, "Out of the abundance of the heart the mouth speaks"—in other words, whatever fills your heart will tend to flow out of your mouth (Matt. 12:34). And right after that, Jesus said that the nature of your heart determines what kind of fruit you produce, good or bad (12:35). You say what you say and you do what you do because you love what you love—because of what's in your heart.

After Adam's Fall, the human heart became "deceitful above all things, and desperately sick" (Jer. 17:9). So one of the most precious promises of the Bible is that through Jesus' death and resurrection God not only cleanses our hearts (1 John 1:7) but also gives us new ones:

> I will give you a new heart, and a new spirit I will put within you. And I will remove the heart of stone from your flesh and give you a heart of flesh. (Ezek. 36:26)

EVIDENCE AGENDA

Nobody has to guess what evolutionary biologist and Oxford professor Richard Dawkins thinks about God. He is far from subtle; his most popular book is entitled *The God Delusion*. And Dawkins will let you make no mistake about it: he disbelieves God solely because he lacks the evidence. Dawkins claims to take an objective, unbiased view of all evidence:

> If all the evidence in the universe turned in favor of creationism, I would be the first to admit it, and would immediately change my mind. As things stand, however, all available evidence (and there is a vast amount of it) favors evolution. It is for this reason and this reason alone that I argue for evolution with a passion that matches the passion of those who argue against it. My passion is based on evidence.[10]

Modern scientists like Dawkins frequently claim to have no agenda except finding out the truth. If they admit to having assumptions, they claim that those assumptions are themselves based on evidence. But this is impossible because, as we've seen, every human being brings preformed ideas into every situation.

This is a display of omnipotence; God can clean up and replace the dirtiest and most unredeemable thing in the universe, the human heart. God alone has the power to reach inside you and alter you at your very root, your innermost heart desires and loves. And by giving you a new heart, God sets into motion a lifelong process whereby He reshapes you into the image of Jesus Christ (Rom. 8:28–29). This is a process in which you must "make every effort," Peter says (2 Pet. 1:5), but in the end you'll find that only "divine power" can explain why you went from loving evil things to loving good (1:3).

Modern, rationalistic* humans tend to believe that what they love does not matter—that a soccer player, for example, who cheats on his taxes and sleeps around a lot can be just as good a goalie as the next guy; all that matters is that the neurons in his brain and the tendons in his arms are in proper working order. But the Bible points to a deeper reality underneath our reasoning and our cognitive* skills. Even non-Christian philosopher and public intellectual* Stanley Fish has said, "Sometimes the principled reasons people give for taking a position are just window dressing, good for public display but only incidental to the heart of the matter, which is the state of their hearts."[11]

Dr. Steve likes to say that he's just taking an unbiased look at the evidence. He'll believe in God when he sees God, like the Soviet cosmonaut who reportedly informed ground controllers that God didn't exist because He wasn't visible from space. But especially when it comes to life's significant questions, an unbiased view is not possible. If Steve doesn't love the loveliest Being in the universe, how can his head-heart system really be expected to lead him to truth?

rationalism: *the belief that reason, and not religion or experience, provides the only firm foundation for knowledge*

cognitive: *having to do with the mind and thinking*

public intellectual: *an academic or other member of the intelligentsia who takes his message public rather than keeping his debates stuck in places where only other intellectuals will read them*

THINKING IT THROUGH 1.2A

1. What are the three ingredients of *worldview* that are mentioned in the definition given in this section?
2. Why do humans seek to have systems of thought with logical consistency?
3. How does Proverbs 1:7 express the connection of basic beliefs with values in the head-heart system?
4. What is at the center of a person, determining beliefs and behaviors?
5. When evaluating the chain of reasoning for the most popular systems of thought (i.e., head systems) in Western culture, what is the first link in the chain (the ultimate faith commitment) for Christianity versus the first link for secularism?

INGREDIENT 2: MASTER STORY

The second major element in worldviews is story. A worldview tells a *master story*, a big story that begins in the beginning (like Genesis 1:1) and tells what happened afterwards to shape the world into what it is. (Such a "big story" is sometimes called a **metanarrative**.)

The story of the world that Project Steve is promoting goes something like this: "Once upon a time, the big bang happened. We all evolved by random, undirected processes from non-life through lower forms of life to reach the top of the evolutionary heap (at least here on earth). Our problems exist because our evolution is incomplete. Our purpose is to evolve and progress still further toward . . . well, future extinction as the energy in the universe burns out."

Some scientists have recognized that this master story is, to put it mildly, uninspiring. It does little to bring purpose to individual cultures or peace to individual people who find themselves hurting on the bottom of the heap. Those on top might even use this story to conclude that survival of the fittest justifies whatever violent choices they make. So some scientists have worked to turn the results of modern science into what they call "a story for our times," a big story that will inspire us and guide us all morally on life's path.

PBS: *Public Broadcasting Service, a nationwide network that produces documentaries that are generally respected*

cosmologist: *a scientist who focuses on the big story of the universe*

Two of these scientists produced a PBS* documentary called *The Journey of the Universe*. Host Brian Swimme, an evolutionary cosmologist,* opens the film with the following comments, as stirring music plays in the background:

> Many of the world's greatest stories begin with a journey, a quest to answer life's most intimate questions: Where do we come from? Why are we here? From the dawn of time, all cultures have created stories to help explain the ultimate nature of things. And perhaps a new story is emerging in our time, one grounded in contemporary science and yet nourished by the ancient religious wisdom of our planet.[12]

In something of an odd twist, Swimme actually teaches at a Catholic university (the coauthor of the documentary, Mary Evelyn Tucker, is a scientist at Yale who also teaches at the divinity school there). But despite Swimme's apparent respect for "religious wisdom," God never shows up in this story of the universe's journey:

> The universe began as a great outpouring of cosmic breath, of cosmic energy, that then swirled and twisted and complexified until it could burst forth into flowers, and animals, and fish—all of these elegant explosions of energy. . . . These deep discoveries of science are leading to a new story of the universe: over the course of 14 billion years hydrogen gas transformed itself into mountains, butterflies, the music of Bach, and you and me. . . . The universe has a story: a beginning; a middle, where we are now; and perhaps in some far distant future, an end.[13]

The Power of Story

Swimme and Tucker recognize that human beings need stories to organize their lives and their ideas. The beliefs, assumptions, and loves found in Worldview Ingredient 1, the head-heart system, make sense because of the story into which they fit. It makes sense to believe that humans are valuable within a story that starts with God making them in His image—just like it makes sense for animal-rights activists to refuse to eat meat in a story that portrays humans as just another kind of animal.

On the other hand, it doesn't make sense to believe that this world is going to get better and better forever (an assumption if there ever was one) if the story you believe about the world begins with a big bang and ends with the dissipation of all matter and energy.

It doesn't make sense to call anything in this world "right" or "wrong" if we are all random atom collections. What does it matter if I hate my sister or I ate all your candy? Or if I love porn? So what? That's just what protoplasm does at this elevation above sea level.

It also doesn't make sense to get upset about injustice if your big story has only two characters, matter and energy. North Koreans are starving to death? Hey, their matter and energy will go back into circulation after they're done with it. Your dad screams at you or gets drunk (or both)? Hey, as long as the species survives, we can handle some collateral damage.*

collateral damage: *accidental, unintended negative consequences—such as civilians dying when a military target gets bombed from a drone*

It simply isn't true that atheists and evolutionists are all openly horrible people who use natural selection* as an excuse to rape and pillage. None of them would talk this way. But, given the story they tell about the world, how can they justify getting so publicly upset about rapists and pillagers?

natural selection: *the evolutionary process by which the "fittest" survive the clash of organisms, regional populations, or even whole species*

The true story about the world will work. It won't tell you to believe what your everyday experiences tell you is false. It won't tell you that God doesn't exist when, in actual fact, "the heavens declare the glory of God" (Ps. 19:1). It won't tell you morals are up for grabs when, in actual fact, every "conscience also bears witness" that God's law has been written on the human heart (Rom 2:14–15). It won't tell you there's no hope when your whole heart knows that there is, somewhere (Eccles. 3:11).

Death Is Wrong

In *Surprised by Oxford*, Carolyn Weber tells the story of how she became a Christian at an unlikely place: Oxford University in England. One experience that was instrumental in her conversion was a formal dinner party at which a renowned surgeon spoke of an experience he had while poised over a beating heart, scalpel in hand.

> "As I was standing there, all the uncertainty of my life, the absurdity of all this death, and all our attempts to ward it off, came down to a pinprick of light." His hands began to tremble—a serious problem for a surgeon—until something clicked. "When I see death, I know it is *wrong*," he said. "*Really, really wrong.* In-my-gut wrong. It was not meant to be. It was not meant for us. We were not built for it. Everything in my body . . . twists against it. Not just my death, but the death of every living thing. . . . I don't know how one can go to medical school and not be in greater awe of a Creator than ever before."[14]

You also know, as every atheist does on some level, that death was not meant to be. Don't ever believe a big story that tells you otherwise.

Alternate Stories

Swimme's is not the only big story that people in our world find persuasive. Many other stories have told whole nations and cultures where they came from, who they are, and where they're going:

• *Secularism* tells a story that goes like this: "However we got here, we're here now. And the one unchanging fact about humanity is that we won't all agree why we're here anyway because we all believe different things about the gods—or lack thereof. Our societal problems come from the way religion heats up simple, solvable conflicts

POSTMAN ON POSTMODERNISM

Look at what public intellectual Neil Postman had to say about the effects of the postmodern worldview combined with the unbelievable amount of data spraying at us in this information age:

> Like the Sorcerer's Apprentice, we are awash in information, without even a broom to help us get rid of it. The tie between information and human purpose has been severed. Information is now a commodity that is bought and sold; it comes indiscriminately, whether asked for or not, directed at no one in particular, in enormous volume, at high speeds, disconnected from meaning and import. It comes unquestioned and uncombined, and we do not have . . . a loom to weave it all into fabric. No transcendent narratives to provide us with moral guidance, social purpose, intellectual economy. No stories to tell us what we need to know, and especially what we do not need to know.[15]

into holy wars. Because we just can't know who's right, religion should stay out of education, law, politics, and the marketplace. Humanity will improve if people can just learn to keep their religion private."

• *Marxism's* big story, which once ruled much of the world, goes like this: "As the proletarians* begin to notice that the bourgeois* are getting rich off their labor, they stage a revolt. This revolution ushers in a new socialist society in which everyone owns the means of production and benefits fairly from it."

• *Postmodernism* has a fuzzy big story which basically boils down to a deep skepticism that anyone can even tell big stories. How can we claim to view the whole world when each of us is rooted so firmly to the ground? Postmodernism's story is this: "Once upon a time, there were no big stories, only local ones. So don't pretend you know the big story of the world because you might start to believe yourself and therefore begin oppressing people who disagree with your story."

proletarian: *member of the proletariat (working class); a person who has no money and must therefore "sell" his labor*

bourgeois: *(boor-ZHWA) members of the middle class; owners of industrial factories*

Like the story Brian Swimme tells, none of these stories works. Secularism's story can't be right: politics and education are always full of religious assumptions—neutrality is a myth. Marxism's story can't be right, either. Its record of mass murder, corruption, and poverty at least puts that story into grave doubt. And postmodernism's story can't be right. Some people are being oppressed by other people's big stories, but without the ability to tell a story about the way the world *really should be*, how can the oppressed people fight back?

The Christian Story

Christianity, of course, must be added to the list of powerful big stories (metanarratives) that people tell themselves about our world. The argument of this book is that biblical Christianity tells the only big story that works, the only one that is true. We'll talk a great deal more about the Christian metanarrative, but here's a short summary: *the Bible is the story of what God is doing to glorify Himself by redeeming His fallen creation.* This is the story of Creation, Fall, and Redemption—**CFR**.*

CFR: *an acronym for Creation, Fall, Redemption*

Every little story in the world, from the Bible's stories to your own life story, makes the right sense only when seen within this big story. Choose anything God put in this world, and you can be certain that (C) it is fundamentally good because God created it, (F) the Fall of Adam has tarnished it in some way, and (R) it can be restored to its original purpose by Christ, the rightful ruler of this planet.

Take music. Music is, at its heart, good like its Creator. Notes are good. Tones are good. It's the same with pitches, timbres, and rhythms. Every one of these things was programmed by God into His "very good" creation. Every one of them will be present in the new earth, where the "glory and the honor of the nations" will shine (Rev. 21:26). But in between Creation and full Redemption, there's the Fall. And music, like every other good thing created by God, has been touched by the Fall. We can still use it for good, but now it's often hijacked for all sorts of wicked purposes. Good things God created are twisted every day into things that dishonor Him.

The same is true of every subject you study in school, like science and history. It's true of sports, of business, of politics, of journalism, of marriage. If you don't have a Christian master story, a biblical metanarrative, to guide you in evaluating what you see, you'll tend to get confused about what's good and what's bad in this world. But with that story you will know who you are, where you came from, where you're going, what's wrong with the world, and who can fix it—all the basic worldview questions.

> ***"We should want to live our chapters well, but doing so requires that we know the chapters that led up to us in our time and our moment; it requires that we open our eyes and consciously begin to shape those chapters that are coming after."*** [16]
>
> —NATHAN WILSON

Every worldview contains a master story that answers questions about our world.

INGREDIENT 3: MAKING SOMETHING OF THE WORLD

If, after reading *Biblical Worldview: Creation, Fall, Redemption*, you start to see the power of our world's various head-heart systems, this book will have achieved only partial success. If you are skilled at seeing the importance of the Bible's metanarrative to a truly Christian worldview, success will still be incomplete. The goal of this book is to be God's tool to move you to live out the Christian worldview. This is the third aspect of our definition of worldview: action.

Worldview talk can sound like useless intellectual discussion to some Christians. But if you will use the Christian worldview to influence and shape your life—your job choices, your family size, your community involvement, your use of media—you can have an impact on your world.

Salt and Light

Jesus Christ Himself, a masterful teacher, used two metaphors to make this point. He urged His followers to be "salt" and told them to shine as "light."

> You are the salt of the earth, but if salt has lost its taste, how shall its saltiness be restored? It is no longer good for anything except to be thrown out and trampled under people's feet. You are the light of the world. A city set on a hill cannot be hidden. Nor do people light a lamp and put it under a basket, but on a stand, and it gives light to all in the house. In the same way, let your light shine before others, so that they may see your good works and give glory to your Father who is in heaven. (Matt. 5:13–16)

Light shines. That's its job. Jesus' disciples are supposed to shine a light through doing good works, a light everyone can see. There may be places of great influence available to you in this world, and it is not wrong to stand in those places: a taller lampstand can give light to more people. Film, education, journalism, sociology—all of these fields are open to Christians with the right knowledge and skills. All of them are powerful tools for spreading light. No Western nation, at least currently, bars Christians completely from positions of shining influence.

Light shines, but salt flavors. If salt loses its sharp, distinct taste, it's worthless. Some positions of influence will be available to you only if you are willing to diminish the unique taste of your biblical views. You can have the job only if you agree to be a little less salty.

But Jesus says you have to be influential and distinct at the same time. You have to be light and salt. Don't drop your Christianity in order to gain more influence; then what will you be influencing people to do? And don't pass up opportunities for legitimate influence (state senator, TV journalist) out of some fear that it's wrong for a Christian to have influence.

Jesus' call here is, at the very least, a call to bring glory to God by living out the Christian worldview. Keeping your Christian worldview inside the class you're now taking will be like covering your headlights with duct tape. You won't see where you're going, and people won't notice your presence. So let this book be a call to you to go live out what you learn.

Dominion over the Earth

This call has deep roots in the Bible, going all the way back to the first page. God created Adam and Eve with several purposes, according to Genesis 1:

- be fruitful and multiply
- fill the earth
- subdue the earth and have dominion over it

We'll explore these commands in much greater detail in the next unit, but for now simply notice that powerful word *dominion*. Who has dominion? Kings, queens. God wanted mankind to be kings and queens over His planet, to fill and rule the world as His representatives. That's one reason we are, according to that same chapter, made "in God's image." We are, in other words, to be like God and to represent Him. He is a ruler, and so are we supposed to be.

But the territory God made man and woman to rule over is not merely spiritual; it is physical. To subdue the earth and have dominion over it is to press it toward its ideal, to maximize its usefulness for humanity. It means taking whatever little section of this world God gives you and making the most of it.

supernaturalism: *the idea that there is something above or outside of nature, such as a divine being*

apologist: *defender; often refers to one who commends and defends the Christian faith*

Interestingly, this kind of dominion is just what the scientists in Project Steve are good at. And in this they're really on to something. Many of them, even the most atheistic, admit having a certain eager awe that pushed them into science at a young age. Listen to what Dawkins, as a scientist and one of the world's most influential atheists, has said about his own response to nature: "The fact that I do not subscribe to supernaturalism* doesn't mean that I don't respond [to the discoveries of science] in an emotional way that one might almost describe as spiritual."[17] (This calls to mind a comment reportedly made by apologist* G. K. Chesterton: "The worst moment for an atheist is when he has a profound sense of gratitude and has no one to thank.")

A desire to obey Genesis 1:28 is not what motivates most scientists, but they are, in fact, subduing the earth and having dominion over it. They are making something of this world. They are living out their worldview, inconsistent though it may be, in such a way that it overlaps with the Christian faith. Scientists—along with musicians, artists, writers, engineers, chefs, and people in nearly any other profession—have inherited a tradition of doing their jobs a certain way. Previous generations have made advances and improvements in all these areas, and that's a good thing. That fits well with God's command to have dominion.

The call of the Christian worldview is for you to become a "creative cultivator," someone who takes the traditions of your calling (history, politics, literature, art, computers, or whatever) and cultivates those traditions in a faithfully Christian way. This book, then, will end up being something of a waste if you don't ever take your worldview into the real world.

Culture

One last note: You'll find that as you work out your worldview, you won't be alone. You will naturally find yourself aligned with (and influenced by) other people. You will be part of a "culture." **Culture** is what you and others together make of the world. Your worldview will unite you with others, and the things and ideas you all produce will change and develop the culture you've inherited from previous generations. Culture is a good thing. God built culture into this world.

But not everyone who fills the earth, subdues it, and takes dominion over it does so in a God-honoring way. Great artists and scientists take dominion, but so do dictators and mad Nazi doctors who experiment on living children. So let's end with two warnings about the work of creating and cultivating:

- "Engaging the culture" is a common catch phrase. If it means taking part in our God-ordained work of taking wise dominion over the world He gave us, then fine. But for some Christians it seems to mean going to sexually explicit movies in order, somehow, to gain a platform for telling others about Jesus (a platform that rarely seems to materialize). This is a world created by God, but it's also a world that has fallen into sin. Some elements of a given culture may be too twisted by sin for you to get involved in them. We will discuss this in much greater detail later on.
- "Changing the world" is another buzzword you might have heard. And again, if God lets you do some world-changing, then fine. But because of the sinful twisting the world has undergone, God warns you not to love it (1 John 2:15–17) and not to let it shape you (Rom. 12:2). It is naive to assume that you can change Hollywood without Hollywood changing you. Though you should make every effort to represent God as a creative cultivator who bears His image, there will be some aspects of nature, culture, and your own life that will not be made right until Jesus, God's Son, comes back to rule in person on earth (Rom. 8:23; Phil. 3:20–21; Rev. 19:11–16).

So be careful how you view your role in this world. God will one day triumph over all His enemies, but this triumph does not give Christians the right to be "triumphalist"—full of arrogance about our supposed virtue and future success compared to others'. Your life's calling may be a humble one that makes a difference that only God and your own family notices. That's up to God, not you.

Make it your life's ambition to be faithful to God's words in Scripture, and—despite all the ways every Christian is inconsistent with his or her own worldview—you will find that the Christian worldview will bring contentment. Only people who live God's way will feel satisfied with God's plan for the world He made.

EVERYONE HAS A WORLDVIEW

This all adds up to a definition of *worldview* that goes something like this:

A worldview is

1. a set of basic beliefs, assumptions, and values,
2. which arises from a big story about the world and
3. produces individual and group action—human culture.

All three of these things are visible daily in the lives of every human on earth. What do you say when you're at the graveside of a friend? How about when you vote? How will you respond when someone deeply wounds you? What set of values will guide you as you raise your children? Having a worldview is simply part of being an adult.

Many modern liberals, influenced by the secularist worldview, don't like to be upfront about their deepest beliefs, values, and commitments. They hide behind a veneer of neutrality that often deceives even those liberals themselves. But one reason Christians can see the world with clarity is that we can be upfront. In the secularist worldview, everyone's beliefs have equal value. There is no authority to appeal to apart from other humans—humans who disagree, who all have their own biases, who are finite.* But Christians have access, through the Bible, to the one Person who has a true worldview—He can see everything. By faith we understand.

finite: *limited by space, time, and gifting; the opposite of* infinite

This does not mean we know everything or that other worldviews are always wrong and Christians are always right. Christians are sinful and limited too. You are holding a "worldview" textbook in your hands because you need to know what God says to you about your world and what it contains. "The earth is the Lord's," after all, "and the fullness thereof"—that means everything in it (Ps. 24:1). God has a plan for this world. And He views it from a perspective that you're going to learn more about.

There have been times when Christians apparently understood God's viewpoint—and God's "big story"—a little better than they do now. It's always a mistake to think that some previous era in history was the ideal one (Eccles. 7:10), but there's no denying that Christianity used to be salt and light on a grander cultural scale than it is today. For all the sins and errors of the church through the centuries (times when its salt was way too bland and it hid its light under a basket), Christians still had a big impact on education, politics, art, science, and music. Christians truly made something of this world, just as God intended. They did heady, intellectual things like analyzing and evaluating, but they also acted. They did something with the biblical worldview. They proclaimed Christ's gospel, and they wielded great societal influence.

In fact, that influence is the very reason so many scientists are named Steve (did Project Steve ever think of that?). *Stephen* is a name from the Bible, and its popularity stems directly from Christianity's past cultural dominance in European countries. It's ironic that a thousand unbelieving scientists bear the name of the first Christian to die for his faith—all because Christians in the past were salt and light, used by God to influence the pagan world around them.

There's no reason that can't happen again.

And no reason you shouldn't take part.

WHAT'S IN A NAME?

Why is *Stephen* (*Stefan, Etienne, Esteban, Steffen, Steponas*) such a common name throughout the modern West?

THINKING IT THROUGH 1.2B

1. What is the technical term for the second worldview ingredient, a big or master story?
2. Why do humans need big stories?
3. What are the three main points of the big story of the Bible?
4. What biblical command should motivate you to be engaged as a creative cultivator in your culture?
5. What two metaphors did Jesus use to illustrate the third worldview ingredient (putting into action what you believe)?
6. Explain what it means for a Christian to be salt and light.

1 CHAPTER REVIEW

TERMS TO REMEMBER

worldview
basic beliefs
metanarrative
CFR
culture

Scripture Memory

2 Corinthians 10:4–5

Making Connections

1. Which option does this chapter recommend you should take when your faith is challenged? Why should you respond this way?
2. Explain how the illustration of a lens communicates the way a worldview functions.
3. Explain the head and heart systems and how they are related.
4. How does Genesis 1:28 relate to culture?

Developing Skills in Apologetics and Worldview

5. If you were called upon to defend a biblical view of creation in a conversation with a non-Christian science professor, would you choose Option 3.1 or Option 3.2? Why?
6. How do you think telling the "big story" of Creation, Fall, and Redemption could help your non-Christian neighbor better understand your presentation of the gospel?

Examining Assumptions and Evidence

7. Are the scientists in Project Steve looking at the world through worldview lenses? How do you know?
8. How did the affections of the Soviet cosmonaut (page 9) influence his interpretation of what he saw in space?
9. Why are metanarratives necessary?
10. What is the danger of ignoring your responsibility to be salt? What is the danger of ignoring your responsibility to be light?

Becoming a Creative Cultivator

11. Brainstorm to come up with a list of three ways you can be salt and three ways you can be light in your community.

Chapter Two **PRESUPPOSITIONS**

By faith we understand that the universe was created by the word of God, so that what is seen was not made out of things that are visible.

Scripture Memory
Hebrews 11:3

2.1 PRESUPPOSITIONS

Whenever you go on a mission to prove something—to find the truth—you have to make a distinction between two different kinds of ideas. Some ideas will be new to you, things you discover on your truth mission. But other ideas will already be there in your head. You can't start a truth mission without them (every chain of reasoning hangs on something previous). In fact, you wouldn't seek truth if you didn't already have some ideas in your head (and some desires in your heart) motivating you to go seeking and letting you know where to begin.

PRESUPPOSITIONS MAKE IT POSSIBLE (AND IMPOSSIBLE) TO SEE

J. Warner Wallace was thirty-five years old before he ever realized that there was one idea in his head guiding and shaping all his other ideas—namely, the idea that "nature is all there is." It was then, he says, "I recognized how unreasonable it was for me to reject the possibility of anything supernatural before I even began to investigate the supernatural claims of Christianity."[1]

Wallace was an atheist at the time and a homicide detective. And he tells an interesting story about how **presuppositions** can influence someone's thinking. While training to figure out real-life whodunits, Wallace and his mentor* were investigating the murder of a woman in her own home.

"It was her husband," announced the more experienced detective. "Find him for me, and we'll have our killer." The older man pointed out to Wallace a picture of a man and the murdered woman that had been turned over on the bedside table. He pointed to men's clothes in the closet. In his mind, the evidence was conclusive. Mystery solved.

Or was it? Police later discovered that the woman had no husband or even a boyfriend. The picture and male clothing were evidence not of a spouse but of a brother. This brother lived in another country but visited occasionally, so he kept some clothes at his sister's home. The murderer, as it turns out, was a neighbor she didn't even know.

The older detective had what's called a "presupposition"—an idea you have in your head even before you look at the evidence. He presupposed (and in many cases he would have been right) that murdered women were often killed by men they loved, and this presupposition guided his interpretation of what he saw. He didn't even consider other possibilities because the lenses he was looking through kept him from seeing them.

EVIDENTIALISM

The apparent solution to this detective's problem is to try to eliminate all presuppositions, attempting to come to the evidence with total neutrality, complete objectivity, no bias or opinion.

---

mentor: *a respected and experienced teacher or trainer*

And this is precisely how most modern defenders of the Bible operate. One philosopy professor, for example, says that when studying the claims of the Bible, the "subjective* element" needs to be "offset as much as possible." He admits that "biases can never be completely eliminated," but he insists that we can know what happened in the past if we follow the evidence of history according to the rules. This is the way he argues for Christianity when debating non-Christians.[2]

This viewpoint is called evidentialism. **Evidentialists** tend to think that the way to persuade unbelievers that Christ died for them or that God created the universe is to list all the evidence. If only unbelievers could be persuaded that there is a mountain of evidence for our position and very little, if any, for theirs, they'd believe. We need, they say, to get unbelievers to set aside their worldviews for just an hour and take an honest look at the evidence. Some evidentialists make it a policy not to use the Bible at all in public debates with non-Christians. An evidentialist may say to the unbeliever, "I recognize that you don't believe the Bible, so I'm going to set it aside and step onto some common ground, some neutral territory where we can both talk peacefully. Then you'll see that my position is the more reasonable one."

A VERDICT THAT DEMANDS EVIDENCE

An apologist who has authored dozens of books summarizes well the evidentialist viewpoint: "I prefer a method that I call the 'minimal facts' approach. The major idea is to utilize data that have two characteristics: they are well-evidenced, usually for multiple reasons, and they are generally admitted by critical scholars who research this particular area."[3]

AS A MATTER OF FACT

Evidentialism is "a method of defending the Christian faith (apologetics) that assumes that data drawn from history and experience (facts) can demonstrate the reasonableness of Christian claims and can therefore help to prepare a person for faith in Christ by removing obstacles to belief. Thus evidentialism attempts to give as much 'evidence' as possible to substantiate crucial facts of the Christian faith such as the resurrection of Christ or the historical accuracy of the biblical accounts."

—*Pocket Dictionary of Theological Terms*[4]

subjective: *based on someone's personal knowledge, opinions, and desires*

THE MORALITY OF KNOWLEDGE

Maybe that's good advice for a Sherlock Holmes working on a murder case. But when it comes to life's most important questions, is that even possible? Can you be neutral and objective about God?

The Bible says you can't. Early in his letter to the Romans, Paul says very clearly that unbelieving people "suppress" the truth about God that they can see all around them in creation—and inside themselves through the moral laws God has written on their hearts (Rom. 1:18–21; 2:14–15). Despite that knowledge, they have "exchanged the truth about God for a lie" (Rom. 1:25).

People who suppress their knowledge of God's existence and their innate knowledge of God's moral law are not neutral and objective. Paul says that "*although they knew God*, they did not honor him as God or give thanks to him, but they became futile in their thinking, and their foolish hearts were darkened" (Rom. 1:21).

People, in other words, don't start off neutral. We're all born knowing about God and His moral law at some level. Being an unbeliever requires many acts of willful suppression of the knowledge that God put inside us. People can't claim ignorance of Him. They are morally responsible for what they know. Paul says, "They are without excuse" (Rom. 1:20).

This is so true that Solomon is willing to say in Scripture, "The fear of the Lord is the beginning of knowledge" (Prov. 1:7). You don't have knowledge of the world as it really is till you have something else first—the fear of the Lord. Not just our actions, not just our emotions, but even our knowledge is supposed to be submitted to God. As Paul puts it, we are to "take every *thought* captive to obey Christ" (2 Cor. 10:5).

According to the Bible, knowledge is moral; you know either obediently or rebelliously. The answer, then, is not to get rid of your presuppositions but to have good ones.

FINITUDE AND MODEL-MAKING

Even if you could be a neutral fact-evaluating machine, you'd still have to deal with your limits. Humans can't know everything, and they can't be everywhere at once. They can't travel back in time.

In the absence of firsthand eyewitness experience (and even that can get twisted in a person's memory, as any courtroom cross-examination can show you), you are stuck putting together a good theory—or **model**—with the available data. It's just like the way an aeronautical engineer might build a scale model of a new jet to test it in a wind tunnel. And it's not just engineers that make models. Economists and others do it too. The real-life facts about economics in a country of 320 million people are unbelievably complicated, so much so that only one Person can hold them all in His mind, let alone understand them. But economists at the US Federal Reserve still have to make decisions that affect every single one of those people (and, truly, countless more around the globe). So they simplify. They have to. They boil down trillions of facts—payroll numbers in Portland, sugar sales in Sarasota, the housing market in Hartford—into a much simpler "model" of all the data. Without a model to hang new facts on, the facts become an impenetrable jumble, like earbuds in your pocket.

That's why most scientists, when making new discoveries in the biological field, immediately attempt to fit those discoveries into the evolutionary model. For example, paleontologist Mary Schweitzer of North Carolina State University discovered something that captured the world's attention: she found soft tissue inside a *T. rex* bone—blood, cartilage. "What we found was unusual, because it was still soft and still transparent and still flexible," Schweitzer said.[5]

This find was unusual because the currently accepted scientific model says that (1) the *T. rex* became extinct sixty-five million years ago and (2) soft tissue doesn't last anywhere near that long.

When evolutionary scientists can't explain how soft tissue could have lasted millions of years, they have a conundrum, facts that don't fit well into their model.

But let's be clear: there's nothing wrong with trying to fit new facts into your model. It's a necessary process for all human knowing. If the new facts don't fit well, then the question is whether the model itself is accurate and self-consistent (and, as we'll see in the science unit, the evolutionary model is not).

After Schweitzer's discovery, researchers looked for soft tissue in other fossils, and they found a lot of it, in fossils going back (allegedly) as much as 200 million years. "The problem is, for 300 years we thought, 'Well, the organics [like soft tissue] are all gone, so why should we look for something that's not going to be there?' and nobody looks," she says.

In other words, paleontologists went on a truth mission with certain ideas (a certain model) already in their heads, and those ideas both guided and shaped their inquiry. Those ideas actually blinded them for decades to facts sitting right in front

THE IRONY OF IT ALL

Evolutionary scientists now think iron in a dinosaur's blood may explain the soft tissue's survival; they've preserved tissue in a lab for two years using iron. It's hard to call this proof of their view; two years is a good deal less than 65 million. More finds like this may someday overturn the evolutionary model, even among non-Christians.

of them. Because they presupposed that these bones were countless years old, they never stopped to look for soft tissue inside. The solution is not for scientists to shove all their knowledge out of their heads and start over with complete objectivity; it's to start with the right model, the right presuppositions.

WORLDVIEW APOLOGETICS

The morality of knowledge, human finitude, and model-making all point us back to the value—actually, the *necessity*—of presuppositions. We can only take in so many facts at a time, so we build models. And those models are based on presuppositions. And those presuppositions are either submitted to God's Word or they are not. No one can serve two masters (Matt. 6:24).

Even homicide detectives can't set aside all theories and become completely neutral and objective while working on a murder case. And when it comes to life's most important questions, it's even more obvious that complete objectivity is simply not possible.

So evidentialists, despite all the good they do, are wrong about something very important. There is no neutral territory that believers and unbelievers can step onto for purposes of discussion. If a Christian says to an atheist, "I won't quote the Bible in my debate with you," the Christian has already given up the debate—because the main point being debated is whether or not people can know ultimate truth without God revealing it to them in Scripture. You can't build a ladder up to God made out of good reasons when, without God, there's nothing to put the ladder on.

There's got to be a way to debate the claims of the Bible with non-Christians that doesn't start with denying certain claims of the Bible, an approach that doesn't act like *God's* words are somehow proven true by *your* words.

There is a way, and it goes back to what we discussed in the previous chapter on worldview. Christians need to gently, graciously, but confidently show unbelievers their own lenses, their presuppositions. Christians—in reliance on the Holy Spirit who alone can open people's eyes—should use the claims of the Bible to help non-Christians see the role their head-heart systems and their master stories play in what they make of the world. (We'll call this **worldview apologetics**.)

> ***"It seems to me that . . . the current orthodoxy about the cosmic order is the product of governing assumptions that are unsupported, and that it flies in the face of common sense."***[6]
>
> —THOMAS NAGEL

We're back to the idea of worldview lenses. If you believe that the earth is billions of years old and that humans evolved by chance from lower forms of life, you will see all of the evidence you encounter through those lenses. If you believe, as some ancient cultures did, that men were created because the gods got tired of doing manual labor, your view of your own job will be distorted by that lens. Even if you believe that God was too weak or too uncaring to give you a better family—or body, or brain—it will be impossible for you to see the world as it really is.

A lot of people in the West (Christians included) talk as if the worldview with the biggest bucket of evidence wins. But it's not as if there is a bunch of evidence for Creationism in the world, a bunch of evidence for evolution, some for a spiritist/animist viewpoint, and a little for a cyclical Hindu worldview. Instead, everybody has access to the same data. Think of some of the simple facts of our experience: the salinity levels in sea water, the properties of aluminum, even the personality tendencies of kids with Down syndrome. These are not **proof** of anyone's worldview; no, they are interpreted by your worldview. You see these facts through the lenses made up of your beliefs about the world.

ARE YOU AN EVIDENTIALIST?

You might be a kind of evidentialist even though you may never have realized it. Have you come to this worldview book thinking something like the following? "I'm only in high school, so I don't have all the evidence in hand yet. Hopefully this book will give me the ammo I need to prove that Christianity is true—or else if it fails to convince me, maybe I'm outta here."

Don't think this way. This is only your evidentialism putting you in a difficult spot. What if evidence comes out that appears to almost everybody to disprove the Christian faith? (*National Geographic* and other major American magazines seem to put out an article saying something like that every Easter.) It's hard to have faith anywhere close to the size of a mustard seed if you're always waiting for the next archaeological dig in Israel to prove or disprove your biblical beliefs. Evidentialism never ends. Abraham, one of the Bible's greatest examples of faith, never would have left Ur if he had been this kind of evidentialist.

This book is not recommending that you turn a blind eye to the evidence. God offers evidence even in Scripture (as Paul did in 1 Corinthians 15:6 when he appealed to the number of people who saw Jesus alive after the resurrection). So sticking your head in the sand will not be necessary. It sometimes takes some hard work and rigorous study to combine the evidence and the Bible into a harmonious story, but since God is the one who made both, they will harmonize. You simply have to recognize that all evidence gets fed through your model, your worldview lenses, your presuppositions before it becomes "knowledge." Christians are just people who use a biblical model, biblical lenses, and biblical presuppositions.

THINKING IT THROUGH 2.1

1. What must every truth mission start with and why?
2. Why do evidentialists attempt to set aside their worldview lenses when they interpret evidence?
3. What three realities point to the necessity and value of presuppositions?
4. What's wrong with holding to your Christianity loosely until all the evidence is in?
5. What is the worldview apologetics approach to using evidence?

2.2 PROOF

Evidence is important, because Christianity is a religion rooted firmly in history. Unlike, say, Buddhism, the life and teachings of the founder of our religion (Jesus Christ) would be worthless if He never really existed. It matters a lot whether a flesh-and-blood man named Jesus of Nazareth really lived and really died in Palestine two thousand years ago—and really lives again. If He doesn't live, we Christians should be pitied more than anyone (1 Cor. 15:19). Historical evidence for Christ's death, therefore, has real value.

But it has equally real limits. Many sites on the internet list a lot of evidences that Jesus really and truly rose from the dead, evidence such as ancient historians who mention Jesus.

But even if the valuable academic discipline of history were able to "prove" to everyone's satisfaction that Christ really died and lived again, could it ever demonstrate what Christ's death and resurrection *meant*? How can any historical or scientific evidence prove that Christ's crucifixion on a Roman cross in AD 29 paid for the sins of the whole world, the way the Bible claims (1 Cor. 15:3)? Evidence has limits. And "proof" is not as simple a concept as you might think.

WHAT COUNTS AS PROOF?

We often talk as if proof is obvious. We fight instead over evidence—whether or not the evidence really "proves" our assertions. But how often have you stopped and asked yourself, "What counts as proof?" And better yet, "Who says?"

The kind of proof demanded by a lot of people in the educated West is empirical,* scientific proof. "If I can't prove God's existence, I won't believe in Him!" Other people instead demand miracles: "If God gets me a new car and a new job, I'll believe." This is nothing new. Two thousand years ago Paul observed, "Jews demand signs, and Greeks seek wisdom." And what was Paul's solution? Miracles? Rational debates? He did use those things. But ultimately his solution was simple: "We preach Christ crucified" (1 Cor. 1:22–23).

empirical: *able to be seen, heard, smelled, tasted, or felt*

And notice what Paul says next: preaching Christ was "a stumbling block to Jews and folly to Gentiles" (1:23). Paul purposefully preached a message he knew most people would reject. He knew that his "proofs" would not be sufficient for them. But he also knew that there were some people who would listen: "To those who are called, both Jews and Greeks, Christ [is] the power of God and the wisdom of God" (1:24). Christ Himself was the sign the Jews were looking for; He is the wisdom that educated Greeks wanted to find—even if many refused to see it.

It is appropriate to use reason and argumentation and evidence when presenting the Christian faith to others—and when you are struggling with your own doubts. But the Christian message has at its heart the message, "Christ died for our sins and rose again," and many people won't accept any miracles or any argument as proof of that. Even within the pages of the Bible, miracles have a pretty poor track record of convincing people of the truth. Just think about the Israelites bitterly demanding to go back to Egypt very shortly after God parted an ocean to rescue them!

And what scientific or historical "proof" could possibly be offered for the assertion that Jesus died for our sins? Even if credible witnesses saw a man named Jesus of Nazareth die (and they did), how could they possibly know that His shoulders were truly bent by the weight of the world's sin? That's not something any human can see. And even if credible witnesses saw Christ resurrected (and they did), how could they possibly know that He was "raised for

PERSUADING OTHERS

The apostle Paul himself "reasoned in the synagogue every Sabbath, and tried to persuade Jews and Greeks" about the truths of the gospel (Acts 18:4). The art of persuasion was also of interest to the ancient Greek philosopher Aristotle, who defined rhetoric as "the ability in any particular case to see the available means of persuasion."

Whereas Paul's writing offers more warnings about evil means of persuasion than it offers suggestions on how to persuade, Aristotle outlined three major factors involved in persuading others through speech: *pathos*, *logos*, and *ethos*. Your *pathos* includes your feeling as well as your read of the audience. Your *logos* is your reason and your structure. Your *ethos*, lastly, is your character. Character is an especially important part of the defense of the Christian message because the gospel claims to save people from the power of sin. Anybody, Christian or not, can memorize a list of proofs for the existence of God. But Christians should make every effort to ensure that their *ethos* is as powerful an argument as their *logos* is.

our justification" (Rom. 4:25)? Justification, one of the most precious realities in the Bible, is completely invisible, weightless, and odorless. You can't "prove" these things via the scientific method.

Are Christians stuck, then, when it comes to rational debate? Do we have no way to answer the demand to "prove it"?

GOD'S UNDENIABLE PROOF

Some evidentialists (not all) do talk as if the Christian faith can be rationally proved to the satisfaction of anyone who will listen. Many websites boast that they present "undeniable proof that the Bible is true!"

But these presentations typically ignore very direct statements of Scripture: Paul said in Romans that the truth about God's power and existence can be "clearly seen" in the creation (Rom. 1:20 KJV), and yet some people deny it every day of their lives. Paul says they "suppress" it:

> The wrath of God is revealed from heaven against all ungodliness and unrighteousness of men, who by their unrighteousness suppress the truth. For what can be known about God is plain to them, because God has shown it to them. For his invisible attributes, namely, his eternal power and divine nature, have been clearly perceived, ever since the creation of the world, in the things that have been made. So they are without excuse. (Rom. 1:18–20)

If you can't "prove" the Christian faith to your atheist aunt, don't assume the trouble is with your command of the evidence. She's already denying the best evidence there is, the evidence God gave her. Creation is "undeniable proof." But because people's minds and hearts are fallen, they do in fact deny it. Paul says so. One day God will bring a proof so undeniable that "every tongue [will] confess that Jesus Christ is Lord" (Phil. 2:11). But for now He allows His image-bearers—breathing air He provides using lungs He designed—to deny that He exists.

Christians should point to evidence; God does. But they shouldn't have high hopes that their evidence and their arguments will be successful in winning over people who are determined not to believe. And that's most people, most of the time.

So one answer to the non-Christian's demand that we "prove it" is that God is already doing it, right now, everywhere, and yet people aren't listening.

GOD PROVES GOD

Jesus talked to a gathering of Jews about proof: "The Father who sent me has himself borne witness about me. His voice you have never heard, his form you have never seen, and you do not have his word abiding in you, for you do not believe the one whom he has sent" (John 5:37–38). Even God in flesh, Jesus Christ, ultimately appealed to the Father's authority when arguing that He was telling the truth. If people believe God, they'll believe His Son.

BY FAITH WE ALL UNDERSTAND

Some of the central claims of Christianity are impossible to "prove" if science (including the historical sciences) is the only way to achieve proof. Christians ought to feel free to admit that no scientific or historical test could ever confirm that Jesus died for our sins. We know that He did, but it is "by faith we understand" (Heb. 11:3). Ultimately, however, faith is how everyone understands anything. It's not just Christians who must rely, ultimately, on faith. It's scientists, atheists, spiritualists—everybody.

Some people are **empiricists**. In their view, only experience, regulated by the scientific method, can discover truth. But how can empiricists prove this? What experiment can they run to verify that the scientific method is the only way to know anything? How can the scientific method prove the validity of the scientific method?

This is not to deny that science is useful; it's only to note that empiricists have a very definite faith lying at the foundation of their worldview. They believe that true knowledge comes only through the five senses, aided by scientific tools.

Or take a worldview we could call "rationalism." **Rationalists** trust reason. For them, reason is the bedrock that all human knowledge rests on. And if you ask them how they know that reason determines what counts as proof, all they can do is give you a reason. But how could reason ever prove that reason is the only way to prove things? How can reason prove reason? It takes blind faith to be a rationalist.

Empiricists and rationalists are guilty of a vicious form of circular reasoning. It's like they are looking in a mirror with a mirror behind them. They see an infinite regression, and in the end all they're looking at is themselves.

Christians are not alone in basing their worldview on faith, but at least Christians can be honest about it. Christians believe that God counts as His own proof, and that He has spoken in the Bible. In the end, the worldview approach in this book is only saying that God doesn't need character references. He's the ultimate foundation for truth, a foundation not resting on anything else. This is an argument the Bible itself uses. "When God made a promise to Abraham, since he had no one greater by whom to swear, he swore by himself, saying, 'Surely I will bless you and multiply you'" (Heb. 6:13–14).

Every worldview is based ultimately on a foundation that is taken by faith. If you appeal to reason but refuse to appeal ultimately to God, then reason is the faith-based foundation that God (in your mind) rests on. If you think that experience can prove God independently from His Word, then the five senses are more ultimate than God is. If God really did speak in Scripture, what higher authority can we appeal to in order to tell us that God really did speak and that what He said was true?

Philosopher Bertrand Russell was once asked what he would say if, after death, he was questioned by God about why he hadn't believed. The famous atheist's reply? "Not enough evidence."[7] But if every worldview is based on faith, even Russell's materialist view, then the demand for more evidence is an insult to our Creator.

THE ROLE OF REASON AND EVIDENCE

Does the role of faith in Christianity—and in every worldview—eliminate the need for reason and evidence? Definitely not.

Reason

Reason is an incredibly valuable tool that God has given us for better understanding His Word and His world. Human reason is only problematic when it tries to become a judge standing above God's Word.

But even people whose intellects are not submitted to God often use their powers of reason to spot falsehood. For example, agnostic* philosopher Thomas Nagel demonstrates several logical problems with Neo-Darwinism in his book *Mind and Cosmos*.[8] Nagel simply points out that materialist explanations for human consciousness and values actually undermine our ability to have confidence in our reason—including the reasoning for Neo-Darwinism.

agnostic: *someone who says he does not know whether God exists*

Nagel's critique of Neo-Darwinism does not prove that Christianity is true, but it does point out serious problems with a worldview that has been a powerful enemy to the biblical one.

A Christian is totally free to use his reasoning powers to step into another worldview like Neo-Darwinism and ask questions like Nagel's. How is it that you can feel such strong moral opposition to genocide or child labor given your worldview? How can you say, if the world is a closed system of cause and effect, that anything is "wrong"? You can say you don't like it. You can say it's not likely to help humanity win the great battle of the survival of the fittest. But how can you justify calling anything truly "evil"? Surely a worldview in which you can't call something evil is not a worldview you want to live in.

Then invite unbelievers to look at the world from the Christian point of view. Encourage them to see how human values and morality flow from the fact that God created us out of love. This is a biblically faithful way to use reason.

Evidence

There are biblically faithful ways to use evidence too. Christians should believe God's Word because God is trustworthy, not (ultimately) because the evidence points to it being true. That would make evidence an authority over Scripture. But Christians should expect the world to be full of evidence for Scripture and the Christian worldview.

For instance, critics of the Bible used to see Daniel's claim that Belshazzar was king of Babylon as an error. All the historical records, the critics said, indicated that Nabonidus was the last king of Babylon prior to the Persians' arrival. Belshazzar's name didn't even appear in any Babylonian records. But then in 1854 (as well as again in the 1960s), archaeologists discovered documents that identify Belshazzar as Nabonidus's son. These documents in the form of clay cylinders mentioned that he participated in governing Babylon. The critics were silenced, sort of. They came up with new objections to Daniel, but at least they dropped that one.

Notice three little things about the use of evidence that we can learn from this story (and many others like it):

1. Evidence can play an important role in defending Scripture against attacks.
2. Evidence does not "prove" that the Bible is true. The Bible was true in its statements about Belshazzar long before 1854. The archaeologists' discoveries made that truth easier to defend, but they didn't "prove" the Bible.
3. The Bible's critics are like moles in a whack-a-mole game. Bop one on the head and another one will pop up instantly. Bop that one, and the first one is back up again. Evidence alone cannot persuade those who want to disbelieve. Nonetheless, God's Holy Spirit sometimes uses evidence from archaeology or history to diminish a person's resistance to accepting God's Word.

PROOF AND PERSUASION

There isn't one single method of proving the truth to every person. Paul used more than one approach to preach the one gospel (compare Acts 14:13–52 with Acts 17:22–34). The arguments you offer for the truth of Scripture can differ depending on your situation. There will be times when it's appropriate to tell stories of Christ's power over alcohol addiction. That might be a wise "proof" to offer. And there will be times—depending on your gifting, your training, and the situation—when it will be wise to mention the work of a contemporary historian or archaeologist. But ultimately, the best thing is just to let God speak. At the very least, don't agree to silence Him before a discussion even begins. Go ahead and quote Scripture to non-Christians. God's Spirit goes with His Word. He is the only one, in the end, who can really persuade. He can use you as His tool to defend the Bible, but ultimately He is the only one who can reach into a person's heart and "prove it."

THINKING IT THROUGH 2.2

1. Why is evidence important even though it is limited?
2. What evidence for God's existence are all atheists denying even before they ever hear the gospel?
3. Why is faith a necessary element in every worldview?
4. What positive role can historical and scientific evidence play in the defense of the Christian faith?
5. What might be a wise "proof" of the Christian faith to offer to a wealthy businessperson who has no time for God? Or to a lonely widow?

2.3 DOUBT YOUR DOUBTS

Do you ever find yourself having doubts about the Christian faith?

Like personal, emotional doubts: *How could a loving God let this happen to me? How could I possibly be a true Christian when I just can't ever seem to win the battle against my lusts or my anger?*

Or like intellectual doubts: *How could the Bible be true when most of the smart, influential people out there think it's a myth or out of date? How come I can't get answers to all my questions?*

One wise Christian author has this advice for doubters: "Doubt your doubts."[9] And here's why you should: If you could find out all the facts about the young adults who have left your church or Christian school and then abandoned the Christian faith entirely, you'd likely notice something about them. They tend to fit in pretty well with the outside world. They might be hipsters* instead of goth* or preppy* instead of grunge,* but not one of them would have adopted the ancient animistic* beliefs of the Uyghur people of northwestern China.

hipster, goth, preppy, grunge: *four different subcultures each with its own fashion style*

animistic (*n.* animism): *believing that inanimate objects such as rocks, trees, and rivers have souls or spirits*

This is not an accident, so doubt your doubts. If Americans leaving the church find TV-saturated, pop-music-inebriated atheistic secularism to be more attractive than Christianity, it's not because that worldview is truly a more intelligent choice than a biblical one. It's attractive to young people in the American church because so many people around them find it attractive—and because a heart with an agenda to live its own way will find a way to throw off God's authority. If they had been born into a Christian family in the Tarim Basin, surrounded by those Uyghurs, they'd probably find Uyghur animism attractive and plausible. So doubt your doubts.

But the truth can't be determined by majority vote—there are too many competing worldviews out there. No single one would be the clear winner.

This observable fact—that people believe all sorts of different things about the world—can be unsettling when you first encounter it. But trust the truth and doubt your doubts. This is exactly the situation the Bible would lead you to expect: when people suppress their knowledge of the one true God, they come up with all sorts of other idols to replace Him (Rom. 1:18–32).

YOU WANT PROOF?

People who doubt want proof. But it's precisely what you presuppose about God that determines what counts as "proof" for you. Do you want proof that the Bible is true? Proof that God exists? The author of the epistle to the Hebrews wrote,

> By faith we understand that the universe was created by the word of God, so that what is seen was not made out of things that are visible. (Heb. 11:3)

This is the Christian way of knowing truth: "by faith we understand." Faith comes before knowledge.

counterintuitive: *something that seems absurd at first glance*

This seems totally counterintuitive* to most Western people. You believe and then you understand? Isn't that backwards? Don't we understand and then believe? We look for evidence, and then we believe what we see. It seems wrong, even, to believe something before we see the evidence and make a judgment for ourselves. Atheist Richard Dawkins said, "Faith is the great cop-out, the great excuse to evade the need to think and evaluate evidence."[10]

But as this chapter has tried to persuade you to see, Richard Dawkins has faith-based presuppositions just like everyone else. And, interestingly enough, that phrase in Hebrews 11:3—"by faith we understand"—follows shortly after another phrase in which we see the Greek word for "evidence," "demonstration," or "proof." It's in a sentence you may have memorized:

> Now faith is the substance of things hoped for, the evidence of things not seen. (Heb. 11:1 KJV)

Note carefully what this verse is saying: "faith is . . . evidence." Another accurate way to translate the Greek here is, "Faith is . . . proof."

WE WALK BY FACT

A secularist will typically say that Christians live by faith while he lives by fact. But everyone lives by faith—the difference is what they have their faith in. The secularist has his faith, ultimately, in human reason. The Christian sees reason as a valuable tool, but only if it's submitted to its Creator.

It's a fact that the universe was created by the word of God—a knowable fact we can have evidence and proof for. But, ultimately speaking, faith is the means by which we get this all-important knowledge. The experience of your five senses (the basis of the scientific method) is important, but it's not enough. Neither is mere logic. Your five senses are very useful in bringing you all kinds of data, but they can't build you a tower all the way to heaven and give you some kind of scientific "proof" that God exists. There does come a point at which you must simply believe what Romans 1 says you already know: that God exists. If you want to understand—if you want proof—the Bible says, "Believe." And the chapter that says "by faith we understand," Hebrews 11, is called "The Hall of Faith" because it lists dozens of people who bucked their cultures and maintained a rock-solid belief in realities they couldn't see.

Abraham lived in a day when belief in one God seemed implausible to everyone—as implausible as the idea that science is the only way to achieve certainty (almost certainly, *nobody* in Abraham's day believed that). Abraham moved into a tiny minority in his world when he decided to believe what just about no one else did: "the Lord, he is God" (Ps. 100:3). What proof of God's existence could Abraham offer that would satisfy all the idol worshipers around him?

And what does it mean to "prove" that God is what He says He is, anyway? If He's omniscient (all-knowing) and omnipotent (all-powerful)—then how can this be proved? If such a being exists, humans are too limited to discover if there are any limits to His knowledge. We're too weak to even be able to find out if He has all power. We're just going to have to take His word for it. We're going to have to believe.

TAKING TRUTH ON AUTHORITY

Modern Americans (and other heirs of the European intellectual tradition) simply must recognize that, when it comes to many, many truths we accept, we are all believing without seeing. It isn't just Christians who have presuppositions; it's everybody.

Take climate change. Is the earth warming? If so, are people causing it to warm? If it's warming because of human activities, is that bad? If the earth is warming and if this is bad, can humans do anything to cool it back down—or are we in the middle of some big global cycle we didn't cause and can't stop?

Now another question (answer honestly!): are you qualified to judge?

Are you a climate scientist with extensive knowledge of the complex computer-based weather modeling necessary to speak with authority on global climate change? Are you even one of the small minority of people in the world who have enough scientific knowledge to follow and evaluate those experts' arguments?

TRUSTING THE TRUTH

One of the authors of this textbook faced a crisis in his own faith during his senior year of college. He didn't doubt that, if the Bible is true, he himself was a child of God. He just began to doubt that the Bible is truly God's Word. It was largely Romans 1 that helped him to reestablish a firm faith in the God of the sixty-six books of the Bible. Romans 1 says that God's eternal power and divine nature are clearly visible in the creation. And indeed, it seemed obvious to this doubter that the beautiful, awesome creation—from the biggest redwood tree to the smallest microbe on its bark—simply could not have come from nothing as many modern scientists believe.

There are educated people who make good-faith efforts to read credible publications and reach informed decisions on these issues. But that's probably not most of us. Most people's belief or disbelief in climate change does not come from careful reading and study. Instead, asking people if they believe whether humans are responsible for global climate change really boils down to asking, "Which authorities do you accept?" In the United States, for example, belief in global climate change tends to follow political party lines.

You can, of course, go to the library, do some intensive Googling, or even travel around the world and look at the evidence for yourself. And these are important research skills you're now learning in school. But how long will it take you to have a truly informed opinion? Probably a good while: years of schooling and lots of hard study on your own. No one person can do that kind of work for every major issue facing society. There's not enough time in the day.

C. S. Lewis has a classic paragraph about this in his influential book *Mere Christianity*.

> Ninety-nine per cent of the things you believe are believed on authority. I believe there is such a place as New York. I have not seen it myself. I could not prove by abstract reasoning that there must be such a place. I believe it because reliable people have told me so. . . . A man who jibbed* at authority in other things as some people do in religion would have to be content to know nothing all his life.[11]

C.S. Lewis

jib: *to draw back like a harnessed horse that doesn't want to move forward*

In the end, on many significant issues, you're going to have to look to some experts. You're going to have to take answers to important questions on someone else's authority. If we have to accept truth on authority all the time anyway, what is so strange about accepting God's authority?

You don't defend a lion. You just let it out of its cage. So said the eloquent preacher Charles Spurgeon. He was talking, of course, about the Bible.

Now this is a book defending the Bible. And the Bible itself calls on us to be ready to answer non-Christians' questions—and to be as persuasive as we can be (1 Pet. 3:15). But Spurgeon was on to something important. Quite frequently the Bible needs no defense; it just needs to be let out of its cage. The Bible carries the authority of its Author, and He can answer—or silence—objections as He sees fit.

When we have hard questions about the world, about our own pain, about truth, the Bible is not shy in giving us answers. And faithful men and women in the Bible were not too shy to ask God hard questions.

Think about Job. If anyone had good reasons to ask, "Why, God?" it was Job. As one author put it, "Job believes in the moral order, but in his case God has repaid good with evil, and this throws his worldview into crisis."[12]

God could have provided Job with reasons to trust His goodness and power. He does this, in fact, in many places in Scripture: "God is our refuge and strength, a very present help in trouble" (Ps. 46:1).

But God doesn't have to do this, or at least not in the way we demand. And in Job's case, He didn't. At the end of the book of Job, God basically said, "I am Creator; you are creature. That should be reason enough to trust My power and goodness." Then in the New Testament, Paul raises what is probably the most difficult question in theology: "[If God] hardens whomever he wills . . . , 'Why does he still find fault?'" (Rom. 9:18–19). And God's answer is similar to what He said to Job: "Who are you, O man, to answer back to God? Will what is molded say to its molder, 'Why have you made me like this?'" (Rom. 9:20). These are reasons to trust God, but they don't explain everything we might want to know—Job presumably died without ever knowing why he had suffered so much.

ULTIMATE AUTHORITY

"I'll believe it when I see it" may sound like a pretty defensible, unobjectionable thing to say. But as our Creator, God is allowed to determine what counts as proof. He's allowed to demand that we simply trust Him, that we take truth ultimately on His authority. He's allowed to expect us to make His words our starting presupposition. The fear of the Lord *is* the beginning of knowledge.

THINKING IT THROUGH 2.3

1. If young people in your church or Christian school abandon the Christian faith, which worldview do you think they're likely to adopt instead?
2. Biblically speaking, is seeing believing, or is believing seeing?
3. Why is faith in some authority unavoidable?
4. How did God confront Job's faltering faith?
5. List five things that most people in your culture believe on the authority of others rather than from their own direct experience.

2 CHAPTER REVIEW

TERMS TO REMEMBER

presupposition
evidentialists
model
worldview apologetics
proof
empiricists
rationalists

Scripture Memory

Hebrews 11:3

Making Connections

1. What do evidentialists seek to eliminate? Why?
2. Explain why presuppositions are inescapable.
3. Explain why truth must be taken on authority.
4. What's the first step, according to the Bible, in getting true knowledge?

Developing Skills in Apologetics and Worldview

5. How could sharing your personal testimony of the Holy Spirit's work in your life add to your conversation with an unbeliever?
6. How could you help friends who believe in evolution to recognize ways their worldview lenses are influencing their interpretation of the scientific evidence?

Examining Assumptions and Evidence

7. Why must all knowledge be moral?
8. What authority source do empiricists presuppose? What about rationalists?
9. What role does evidence play in the pursuit of truth? What can and can't it do?
10. Is there anyone who has merely intellectual objections to the gospel? Explain.

Becoming a Creative Cultivator

11. Listen to a debate between a Christian and an unbeliever. Write a one-page paper in which you do the following:
    - ☐ identify the apologetic approach the Christian most closely exemplified
    - ☐ evaluate the benefits of that approach
    - ☐ evaluate the drawbacks of that approach
    - ☐ offer any alternative or additional arguments the Christian could have used

Chapter Three THE TWO-STORY VIEW

For in [Christ] all the fullness of God was pleased to dwell, and through him to reconcile to himself all things, whether on earth or in heaven, making peace by the blood of his cross.

Scripture Memory
Colossians 1:19–20

3.1 THE TWO-STORY VIEW

There are various ways to win an intellectual debate. The good ways all involve diligently researching the topic and carefully listening to your opponent(s). But there are other ways to win—like diligently knocking your opponent down and carefully taking his lunch. Playground bullies typically employ the latter approach. And so, sometimes, do worldviews.

Minority worldviews are the ones that can expect to experience bullying, and right now, despite large numbers of people claiming to be Christians around the world, the biblical worldview is a minority pretty much everywhere. So, along with other minorities, it sometimes finds itself lunchless.

One example is Nathaniel Abraham, a Christian biologist (an expert on zebrafish) who says he was fired by Woods Hole Oceanographic Institute because he refused to admit that Darwinian evolution was scientific fact. In similar cases major universities have denied career advancement to Christians, and sometimes it can be difficult to figure out whether their belief in creationism was a factor or not. But Woods Hole, a federally funded research center, didn't deny Abraham's claim; they admitted that he was fired for his creationism. They simply alleged that belief in evolution was a necessary component of his job.

Don't get *too* alarmed. Christians in the Western world are not facing violent persecution, or at least not yet. Few are losing their jobs because of their faith. But the intellectual climate in most places is not friendly to biblical Christianity. If Christians aren't being fired from high-profile academic or political jobs, it may be because they're not getting them in the first place (or because they aren't working in a way that's distinctively Christian).

This is not new. Christians have always faced challenges to their worldview. The ancient Romans actually accused Christians of being atheists because they didn't believe in the gods of the Roman pantheon.* Greek philosophers laughed at the idea that God became man, died for human sin, and rose from the dead. Christians today should not be surprised when the biblical worldview creates friction with the popular worldviews around it—or when that friction makes sparks fly.

THE MORAL MINORITY

The biblical worldview is a minority position all around the globe (though not necessarily in all portions of history), even in so-called "Christian" nations since not all self-professed Christians have a biblical worldview. When pollsters ask Americans what they believe, only a small percentage give answers that really agree with what the Bible teaches. And most of the biggest names in academia, the media, politics, and entertainment—the influential people of this world—are not Christians. For example, 62 percent of philosophy professors are atheists.[1]

pantheon: *all the gods of a particular nation*

INTIMIDATION

Even if intellectual opposition doesn't come as a surprise, it's easy for Christians to be intimidated by the hostility they sense in the academic world. And the easiest way to avoid conflict is to just give the bully your lunch. When the most powerful force on the intellectual playground says religion doesn't belong there, some Christians hand over their baloney sandwich, apple, and juice box, and slink away from the slides and monkey bars where the bullies like to play.

COURTEOUS BULLIES

It's not that individual non-Christian scholars are all intellectual bullies; it's that most Western academics have accepted rules for their disciplines that exclude the influence of the Bible. Christian scholar Lesslie Newbigin, speaking at the University of Cambridge in England, told this story: "A Ph.D. student in this university recently wrote to me with the following problem: he had submitted the outline for his proposed dissertation. It had been accepted by his [academic] supervisor except for one chapter which he was told to remove, since it dealt with matters of faith, not of fact, and was therefore inadmissible. Faith is one thing, facts are something else."[2]

The student gave no indication that the supervisor was mean about it; Cambridge simply exists within a community that doesn't allow religion on certain parts of its playground. Western secular scholarship as an institution has therefore "bullied" Christianity, even if individual scholars do it courteously.

This climate of intimidation is one big reason why some Christians drift into thinking that the Christian life is only about spiritual things—such as Bible reading, prayer, helping those in need—and not about science, politics, and academics. It's easier to leave that territory to the secularist majority. And some Christians go a step further: they start seeing science, politics, and the intellect as part of a so-called **secular*** realm that should be kept separate from the sacred parts of life.

secular: *pertaining to the world and not religion, nonreligious*

Christians generally make this separation with some good motivations in their hearts. They do it in order to protect the sacred things they value. They think that by keeping their religion away from the playground where everybody else is, science and politics will play nice and let them keep their lunch.

Another big reason why some Christians leave the playground is that they see the moral corruption there. They feel that if they focus on spiritual things like Bible reading, prayer, and doing good to all people, they can avoid being contaminated by the moral mess of modern life. They see studying science or literature, engaging in politics, or writing for newspapers as dangerous. Secular activities, they feel, are best avoided because they are morally tainted by the influence of non-Christians. Such Christians divide the world in two not so much to protect their religion as to protect themselves.

But when you sort religion and science, or religion and politics, or religion and education into two separate compartments, you create some real problems. For one, you are guilty of applying an improper **dualism***—dividing in two what God has made one.

dualism: *dividing something into two opposing parts*

Some Christian worldview thinkers have used a two-story house as an illustration of this dualism. Dualists keep science, math, and everyday life in the lower story. For them, Bible reading, prayer, and the spiritual life go in the top floor, the upper story.

THE TWO-STORY VIEW IN THE SECULAR WEST

This two-story way of thinking about the world is popular not only with Christians. It is actually the dominant view of the secularized West in general. Simply put, secularists view post-Reformation (after 1520) Western European history as a bloody chronicle of religious wars. For example, the Protestants and Catholics who began the Thirty Years' War (1618–1648) both professed (as Abraham Lincoln would later put it about the American Civil War) to pray to the same God and read the same Bible. But that didn't stop them from slaughtering one another; it spurred them on.

intelligentsia: *the politically influential and powerful intellectuals in any given group*

The exhausted European intelligentsia* of the time began to look for a neutral way to solve conflicts before religion turned them into bloodbaths. When religion walks into the public square, everyone's temperature rises, and the guns and knives come out—or at least that's what Western elites thought. So, they concluded, it's better to just keep religion upstairs.

The two-story view places churchy and religious stuff on top and real-life stuff below. The implication is that real-life stuff can't be holy and that true Christians will spend as little time in the lower story as possible.

European intellectual René Descartes (reh-NAY day-KART) was one of these elites. In his quest for a neutral foundation for knowledge, he determined to doubt everything he couldn't know for certain, to dig down in his knowledge until he reached a bedrock level that no one could doubt or disagree with. His famous statement, "I think, therefore I am" (*cogito ergo sum*, sometimes called "the cogito") was the result. He was, in fact, a dedicated, churchgoing Roman Catholic. So it's all the more significant that he did not say, "God speaks, therefore I know." He started with himself: "*I* think."

Reason, he argued, could provide a neutral starting point for human knowledge. Subsequent Enlightenment philosophers believed that they could then build on that foundation and arrive at truth all humans could agree on. Religious disagreements could go on in the private world of the upper story, but religious wars—which happen in the public world of the lower story—could end.

aesthetics: *"a set of principles concerned with the nature and appreciation of beauty, esp. in art"* (New Oxford American Dictionary)

Secularists thus have their own **two-story view** of the world. The "lower story" is where most Western people put science, math, and the facts—stuff (they think) we can really know for sure. Everything else, stuff we can't really know, goes in the "upper story." That's where many people in our culture place religion, morals, and aesthetics*. It isn't just beauty (aesthetics) that's in the eye of the beholder; bioethics and Buddhism (morals and religion) have to go there too.

The two-story view of the secular West can be diagrammed like this:[3]

UPPER STORY

PRIVATE SPHERE	VALUES	NONRATIONAL
personal preferences	individual choice	noncognitive

LOWER STORY

PUBLIC SPHERE	FACTS	RATIONAL
scientific knowledge	binding on everyone	verifiable

This isn't all just theory. You've seen it. You know from experience that this is how most people in the West view the world. Suppose you are a senator in the Congress of the United States. You just know that "teens shouldn't have premarital sex because teen pregnancy is associated with lower high school graduation rates" is an acceptable argument to present in a debate in the Senate. Other senators may dispute the research you cite, but they won't dispute your strategy of citing it. But you also know that "God says sex before marriage is wrong" is *not* an acceptable argument in the Senate. Other senators won't dispute your Bible interpretation; they'll reject your argument simply because you cited the Bible or God. You know that as soon as you cite the Bible in any significant disagreement in the public square,* you'll be escorted up the stairs to the second story and told that you have to quit trying to impose your religion on the rational, scientifically verifiable facts downstairs in the living room. You're supposed to keep your religion private because it's not a public fact; it's just an unverifiable, unknowable personal preference.

public square: *a metaphor referring to all the many places (books, magazines, newspapers, the internet, city halls, courtrooms, Congress) where issues are debated publicly*

THINKING IT THROUGH 3.1

1. Summarize the two-story view.
2. Why do many Christians separate the "sacred" from the "secular"?
3. Why do many secularists separate the "sacred" from the "secular"?
4. How should Christians respond to bullying?
5. Provide two examples of two-story view thinking that you have observed. Include examples from both Christian and secular sources.

3.2 CRITIQUING THE TWO-STORY VIEW

The two-story view is wrong, but it isn't *all* wrong. There's something in it worth saving. To find out what it is, we'll have to look at two versions of the two-story view, the secular version and the Christian version.

THE SECULAR TWO-STORY VIEW

First, the secular. Every year on the first Thursday in February, American religion and politics get together for a prominent and well-attended event called the National Prayer Breakfast.

Every president since Eisenhower has attended the prayer breakfast, and when Barack Obama got his turn to speak to the large crowd in 2012, he chose to speak about the upper and lower stories. He seemed, in fact, to take direct aim at the two-story view. "We can't leave our values at the door" when it comes to political debates, he said.

> If we leave our values at the door, we abandon much of the moral glue that has held our nation together for centuries, and allowed us to become somewhat more perfect a union. Frederick Douglass, Abraham Lincoln, Jane Addams, Martin Luther King Jr., Dorothy Day, Abraham Heschel—the majority of great reformers in American history did their work not just because it was sound policy, or they had done good analysis, or understood how to exercise good politics, but because their faith and their values dictated it, and called for bold action.[4]

nonpartisan: *not biased toward the ideology of one political party as opposed to another*

GDP: *Gross Domestic Product, a measure of the combined economic strength of a nation; the total value of the goods and services the nation produces in a year*

This statement is perceptive, both about American history and about politics in general. When Abraham Lincoln issued the Emancipation Proclamation, when he gave the immortal Gettysburg Address, and when he led his precious Union through a long and bloody war, he wasn't driven by nonpartisan* economic studies demonstrating that the GDP* would increase if slaves were freed. Lincoln said in his second inaugural address, as the Civil War still raged,

> Fondly do we hope, fervently do we pray, that this mighty scourge of war may speedily pass away. Yet, if God wills that it continue until all the wealth piled by the bondsman's two hundred and fifty years of unrequited toil shall be sunk, and until every drop of blood drawn with the lash shall be paid by another drawn with the sword, as was said three thousand years ago, so still it must be said "the judgments of the Lord are true and righteous altogether."[5]

orthodox: *faithful to Scripture*

Lincoln was clearly motivated not by economics but by his personal moral outrage, his belief in divine justice. And Lincoln, though not an orthodox* Christian himself, knew that this appeal would motivate the average Americans listening to him. No president in American history has spoken more freely and more eloquently about God than Lincoln.

But the president of the United States is not powerful enough to overturn the two-story view. And it's clear that President Obama did not really want the barrier between religion and politics to come down. The very week before he gave the address to the National Prayer Breakfast, the president left a lot of Christians' values outside the door when his administration insisted that Christian employers had to pay for their employees' abortions. The so-called HHS Mandate, later struck down by the courts, would have forced the Christian owners of Hobby Lobby, for example, to pay for abortifacient contraceptives* for their female employees—or pay a $1.3 million fine for every day they refused.

abortifacient contraceptives: *drugs which destroy the fetus after conception*

platform: *officially declared policy position of a political party. Both the Republican Party and the Democratic Party have platforms.*

President Obama was the leader of the Democratic Party. Listen carefully to the wording in the official Democratic Party platform* on abortion:

> The Democratic Party strongly and unequivocally supports *Roe v. Wade* and a woman's right to make decisions regarding her pregnancy, including a safe and legal abortion. . . . Abortion is an intensely personal decision between a woman, her family, her doctor, and her clergy; there is no place for politicians or government to get in the way.[6]

The Democratic Party puts abortion squarely in the upper story. It is precisely because abortion is an "intensely personal" decision that government, they say, is not supposed to stand in a woman's way. Religion (notice the mention of "clergy") can play a role in advising an individual woman if she goes upstairs and asks for its advice, the platform says. But because abortion is so personal, religion is not allowed to come downstairs and outlaw abortions for all American women.

Democrats don't feel the same way about other murderous violations of human dignity. The Democrats are not opposed to using the power of government (or the influence of religion) to stamp out human trafficking.* A few paragraphs away from the abortion statement, they (rightly) call human trafficking "an affront to our fundamental values."[7]

human trafficking: *the sale of human beings as either domestic or sexual slaves*

So why are some values (such as opposition to abortion) supposed to stay private while others (such as opposition to slavery) are allowed to guide public policy? What makes Abraham Lincoln's values good and Hobby Lobby's bad?

The Democratic Party platform, it seems, is smuggling values from the upstairs to the downstairs through a laundry chute. And, to be fair, the Republicans do this too. Many American politicians talk as if they are guided solely by the facts and that their religion and personal values are not causing them to be biased. Their two-story view of reality leads them to *try* to keep religion and other private values upstairs—but without success. They can't do it. Their upper-story values still shape their lower-story policies.

The simple fact is that you can't live without values. Your values—your principles, what you think is important and worth protecting and promoting—guide all your decisions. You can try to shove all your values into the upper story, but they will always sneak downstairs. The Democratic Party is not making a neutral, valueless, fact-based decision on abortion. It simply values something else (perhaps sexual freedom or human autonomy?) over the lives of unborn children.

So it's commendable for President Obama to praise moral reformers like Martin Luther King Jr. It was right, too, for John the Baptist to shout downstairs, "King Herod, you can't have your brother Philip's wife!" (Matt. 14:3–4). It was a private sin *and* a public injustice for King Ahab to use his political power to steal Naboth's vineyard (1 Kings 21)—and it was right for God's prophet Elijah to say so.

JUDGMENTAL JUSTICE

Harvard professor Michael Sandel writes in his book *Justice: What's the Right Thing to Do?* about how your values always impact your decisions:

> Justice is inescapably judgmental. Whether we're arguing about . . . surrogate motherhood or same-sex marriage, affirmative action or military service, [the size of] CEO pay or the right [of a disabled golfer] to use a golf cart, questions of justice are bound up with competing notions of honor and virtue, pride and recognition. *Justice is not only about the right way to distribute things. It is also about the right way to value things.*[8]

"The right way to value things" stands at the very heart of the Christian religion. What am I supposed to value or to love most? Jesus answers this very directly: I'm supposed to love God most, then God's image-bearers (Matt. 22:34–40). Without God standing at the appropriate place on my value scale, I won't know how to value other things. Justice is inescapably judgmental because we all make judgments every day based on what we value.

But inviting us all to bring our values into politics forces us to answer this insistent question: whose values are going to win? Values have a way of clashing, and clashing hard.

THE RELIGIOUS TWO-STORY VIEW
Protecting the Faithful

That clash is what created the two-story view in the first place. When value systems clash, people can get hurt. Lunches can get stolen. Recognizing the danger, some Christians want to put significant distance between themselves and the rest of the world. They have created a religious version of the two-story view.

For example, if the study of literature is corrosive to good morals (kids may see obscenities or read about drug addiction), perhaps Christians should read only Christian books. If science attacks the existence of God, perhaps it is best to leave science to the atheists. These Christians would prefer as much as possible to live in the upper story. They might have to descend on Mondays to go to work, but they do it only as a necessary evil—to provide money for their families and to support missionaries.

Some Christians even see themselves as second-class citizens of the kingdom of God because they have to spend so much time in that lower story—because, in other words, they don't work in "full-time Christian ministry." One Christian school even made this view one of its stated goals: "To encourage each student to plan on full-time Christian ministry unless God clearly leads otherwise." For this group, staying in the upper story is the ideal.

But this view has its own dangers. Every Christian will have some view of science, politics, and journalism. You can't help it. If you don't work hard to construct a Christian view, you will probably absorb the default view of society around you—namely some form of modern secularism. If you try to do the impossible and stay in the upper story all the time, wrong ideas about the world will still get in through the air vents. And your own sinful flesh will be in the upper story with you, don't forget. These Christians want to protect themselves from the world, but the two-story view actually lets worldliness sneak in unnoticed.

Protecting the Faith

Another religious version of the two-story view attempts to protect the Christian faith itself, not just individual Christians. Prominent Christian worldview writer Nancy Pearcey tells the story of one Christian teacher who "strode to the front of the classroom, where he drew a heart on one side of the blackboard and a brain on the other." He told the class that "the heart is what we use for religion, while the brain is what we use for science."[9]

This teacher, it appears, was trying to protect religion from the power of modern science by putting religion and science out of each other's reach. But if secularists cannot live in the world without smuggling their values down into the lower story, then Christians certainly can't do it either. And shouldn't.

If God's Word speaks to all of life, the Christian is not free to ignore or be silent about what God says concerning science, mathematics, literature, ethics, and everything else in His world.

THE OTHER DITCH

If you haven't picked up on it by now, this book on biblical worldview takes a pretty negative view of the two-story mentality. And yet there's another ditch, too—on the other side of the road. If the two-story view cuts in two what God joined together, it's also possible to mix up things God keeps distinct.

Here's an illustration. In the movie *The Incredibles*, the super-fast-running boy Dash makes an insightful comment (especially for a ten-year-old) when he complains to his mom about not being allowed to use his super powers:

> **Dash**: But Dad always said our powers were nothing to be ashamed of, our powers made us special.
>
> **Mom**: Everyone's special, Dash.
>
> **Dash**: [muttering] Which is another way of saying no one is.[10]

It is possible to treat everything as sacred until nothing is, but some things in this world *are* more sacred than others. Extra sacred.

Think of Sunday. God, who doesn't need rest, took a whole day off after creating the world, Genesis tells us. Why would He bother? In fact, why bother creating the heavens and the earth in six days instead of one nanosecond?

He did this not for Himself but for us, to set up a weekly rhythm for our lives. He explains this in one of the Ten Commandments: "Remember the Sabbath day, to keep it holy," He said to the Israelites, "for in six days the Lord made heaven and earth, the sea, and all that is in them, and rested on the seventh day. Therefore the Lord blessed the Sabbath day and made it holy" (Exod. 20:8, 11).

Monday is important. You've got to obey God on Mondays. Thursdays, too, require twenty-four hours of love and obedience to God. And don't forget Saturdays—Christians don't get days off from Christianity; all our work and study is therefore "sacred," set apart from the way we would act if we weren't believers. But one day a week is still supposed to be special, set apart from the other days of the week. On that day you get to rest and focus on the Lord. You get to fellowship in a special way with God's people when the church, Christ's body, gathers together.

THE SABBATH AND SUNDAY

The Jews celebrate the sabbath on Saturday, as God instructed in the Old Testament. The way the sabbath became Sunday for Christians is a longer story, but it basically boils down to four reasons:

- **Event**—The resurrection occurred on "the first day of the week" (Matt 28:1).
- **Example**—The early church met on "the first day of the week" (Acts 20:7).
- **Precept**—Paul commanded the Corinthians to gather and give "on the first day of the week" (1 Cor 16:2).
- **Designation**—John refers to "the Lord's day" as if it's something all Christians would recognize (Rev 1:10).

Admittedly, these verses stop short of giving an explicit command to move the sabbath to a different day. But Christians throughout the history of the church have met on Sundays.

And just like one day is more important than the others, distinct from them, so the spiritual life is more important than other good and necessary things.

Just ask Martha. The Gospel of Luke tells her story:

> Jesus entered a village. And a woman named Martha welcomed him into her house. And she had a sister called Mary, who sat at the Lord's feet and listened to his teaching. But Martha was distracted with much serving. And she went up to him and said, "Lord, do you not care that my sister has left me to serve alone? Tell her then to help me." But the Lord answered her, "Martha, Martha, you are anxious and troubled about many things, but one thing is necessary. Mary has chosen the good portion, which will not be taken away from her." (Luke 10:38–42)

There *is* a difference between washing dishes and sitting at the feet of Jesus. If these two activities ever truly come into conflict, it's clear that Jesus should take priority—just like He did in Mary's situation. You need a prayer room to retreat to. You need a sanctuary in this fallen world, a place to sit at Christ's feet while the dishes soak in the sink. You need a safe place where you go to recharge for the constant battles you face in a fallen world and to learn what God expects of you out there.

But the dishes do need to get washed. And though you can't take dishes into your prayer closet with you, the neat thing about prayer is that you can take it to the kitchen. The spiritual life gets to have special focus on Sundays and during your devotions, but the spiritual life is supposed to fill and cover your work life and your education life and your dating life and your sports life too.

As one great theologian put it, that prayer room

> remains the center, the heart, the hearth, out of which all [the Christian's] thought and action proceeds and from which it receives inspiration and warmth. There, in fellowship with God, he is strengthened for his labor and girds himself for the battle. But that hidden life of fellowship with God is not the whole of life. The prayer room is the inner chamber, but not the whole dwelling in which he lives and moves. The spiritual life does not exclude domestic and civic, social and political life, the life of art and scholarship.[11]

The dishes won't wash themselves, political crises won't solve themselves, and important books won't write themselves. But if you're going to do those "secular" things as a faithful Christian, that's all the more reason to protect the "sacred" things: going to church, praying, reading the Bible, evangelizing, maintaining a real and personal faith. Don't fall into the ditch on the other side of the road.

PURITY IS IMPORTANT

And we can't forget that the Fall has happened. Because of the Fall, some Christians in some situations simply cannot pursue certain vocations because it would damage them spiritually or diminish the light they are supposed to shine on the world. The ancient church father Tertullian pointed out, for example, that in his day it was pretty much impossible for a Christian to be a sculptor. There is nothing inherently wrong with sculpture, of course—God commanded sculptures to be made in His own temple (Exod. 25:18–20). And sculpture, like any art form, is a way of expressing the creativity given to us by God the Creator. But in Tertullian's day it was difficult or impossible to make a living as a sculptor if you refused to make idols.

It is also becoming more difficult in the Western world for Christians to have some jobs that seem totally innocent, like baking or photography. Why? Because if you refuse to provide a four-layer cake or take pictures for a same-sex wedding, you may be sued and lose your business. Such lawsuits are already being filed.

Or consider this true story: a gifted ballet teacher with an extremely successful (and lucrative) ballet school became a Christian. As she began to grow in her love for Christ and her desire to obey His word, conflicts began to erupt. It wasn't with her Christian husband; he had no objection to her running the school. It was with her students and her teaching partners.

SHOULD A CHRISTIAN BUSINESS TURN AWAY HOMOSEXUALS?

If you try to keep your business life and your spiritual life totally separate the way the two-story view would suggest, you will run into troubling questions. For example, if you are a Christian wedding cake baker or a Christian wedding photographer or a Christian screen-printer, what will you do if a same-sex couple or the organizers of a white supremacist rally try to hire you?

This is very different from owning a restaurant. There you can't check at the door to see if your customers are racists or homosexuals—or adulterers or gossips (and based on 1 Corinthians 5:10, you shouldn't). You should serve with kindness everyone who's willing to maintain public decorum (that's why many restaurants post signs saying, "Shirt and shoes required").

But if you are asked to print an Aryan Nation (racist) T-shirt or bake a wedding cake with two men on the top, you are being asked to directly and obviously support what God condemns—racism (Gen. 1:27) and homosexual acts (1 Cor. 6:9–10). Our society happens to condemn one sin and not the other, so you'll only get sued if you refuse to serve the wedding. What you can't do in such situations is remain neutral.

The conflict wasn't mainly about modesty, though that played a role. The Christian ballet teacher began to see that the real motivation for most of her ballet students was to glorify themselves, to make a name for themselves. So she began to make changes in the way she ran the school. She wanted to minimize this motivation.

The students weren't interested. They left. The non-Christian teachers couldn't understand what she was doing; they thought she'd gone crazy. One of them even sued (and lost).

In this fallen world, there are times when even good, God-honoring jobs aren't available to certain Christians because the fallen state of the culture puts those jobs off-limits, or at least makes them very difficult.

THINKING IT THROUGH 3.2

1. Why is it impossible for secularists to be consistent in keeping values out of the public square?
2. How does the two-story view fail to protect the faithful?
3. How does the two-story view fail to protect the faith?
4. The two-story view cuts in two what God joined together; give an example of mixing up things God intends to keep distinct.
5. What are you supposed to value or love most?

3.3 CREATION, FALL, REDEMPTION

The two-story view has some strengths. It tries to protect some things of real value. But it has some fatal flaws. We can see those flaws if we'll go back to the Christian worldview, the Christian story of Creation, Fall, Redemption.

CREATION

God created this world and therefore owns it, so the biggest flaw in the two-story view is this: the Bible just won't let us divide the world into things God owns and things He doesn't. The Bible makes big claims. It claims that the earth and all it contains are the Lord's (Ps. 24:1; 50:12; 89:11; Exod. 9:29; 19:5). God says to Job, "Who has first given to me, that I should repay him? Whatever is under the whole heaven is mine" (Job 41:11). And don't forget Paul's simple encouragement to the Corinthians: "Whatever you do, do all to the glory of God" (1 Cor. 10:31).

God owns everything He created, and it's possible to glorify Him (or not) with every decision we make. That has to include politics and scholarship, music and sports. So the two-story view tells a lie about the way the world is: it says there's a broad area of neutrality over which God is not King.

Some of the most famous and stirring words in theology come from theologian, pastor, teacher, journalist, and ultimately prime minister of the Netherlands (1901–1905) Abraham Kuyper:

> There is not a square inch in the whole domain of our human existence over which Christ, who is Sovereign over all, does not cry: "Mine!"[12]

Kuyper also said, "No single piece of our mental world is to be hermetically* sealed off from the rest." You can't put religion and science in separate ziplock bags.

hermetically: *sealed so tightly that air cannot get in*

FALL

But because the whole creation is in the same ziplock, it was all contaminated when Adam fell into sin. And that creates two more problems for the two-story view, particularly the religious version:

(1) It sometimes seems to forget that *sin* comes with us into the upper story. We won't ever get away from it until the day Christ finally gets it away from us.

(2) The Christian version of the two-story view also fails to recognize something about non-Christian worldviews. Those worldviews are opposed to Christianity in more than just upper-story things; they stand opposed to God's claims in the lower story as well. You won't escape conflict by heading to the lower story, as if it were neutral.

Journalism and education are fallen just as much as sex and speech are. Non-Christians don't want God ruling their newspapers or their high school curricula, but God isn't going to give up His claims on that territory. God speaks to every aspect of individual and cultural human life. We shouldn't get in the way of God's program but instead participate with it.

REDEMPTION

As one of today's greatest critics of the secular two-story view put it, "A religion deprived of the opportunity to transform the culture in its every detail is hardly a religion at all."[13] Christianity, biblical religion, does have a program for world transformation. It's called God's work of "redemption."

When Jesus Christ, God in flesh, died on the cross to satisfy God the Father's anger for your sins, He did it "to *redeem* us from all lawlessness" (Titus 2:14). Scripture says that Christians "are justified by [God's] grace as a gift, through the *redemption* that is in Christ Jesus" (Rom. 3:24). Jesus is the one who descended into the dirty slave market of sin where we were all in chains, and He's the one who paid the money to buy us out of slavery. That's what "redeeming" means.

If the Bible is the story of what God is doing to glorify Himself by redeeming His fallen creation, then this redeeming—the redeeming of fallen humans—is surely the culmination of that story. Christ's death on the cross for human sin, followed by His triumphant resurrection from the dead, is the most important redemption God accomplishes in Scripture.

But that's not the only redemption He'll ever accomplish. It's important to recognize that human souls aren't all that God redeems. The Christian story does *not* end with God redeeming humanity by pulling us out of our universe and taking us to live with Him as spirits in some nonphysical dimension called "heaven." The Christian story ends with Christians back in physical bodies living on the earth. These bodies and that earth will both be what the Bible calls "new." They won't decay and break because of sin like they do now. Eternity, according to the Bible, doesn't take place in heaven. God will one day redeem souls, bodies, *and the whole earth*.

All creation is waiting for this redemption, Paul says: "The creation waits with eager longing for the revealing of the sons of God" (Rom. 8:19).

But why? Why is it waiting for some future day? Why does creation care what happens in the future? Paul answers that it's because

DOESN'T THE BIBLE SAY THAT THE EARTH IS GOING TO BE "BURNED UP"?

Scripture says that "the heavenly bodies will be burned up and dissolved, and the earth and the works that are done on it will be exposed" (2 Pet. 3:10). But what does *exposed* mean? Some Bible interpreters have argued that what Peter meant was that the earth would be "burned up."

But God promised the people of Israel He would give them their land "for an everlasting possession" (Gen. 48:4). Peter himself spoke of "the restoration of all things"(Acts 3:21 NASB)—strange if all things are going to be annihilated. Peter does predict a future day in which God's fire will burn the earth, but it will be like the fire in 1 Peter 1:7—a fire that doesn't utterly destroy, but instead purifies (like melting gold to filter out impurities). And that purification will make way for restoration.

> the creation was subjected to futility, not willingly, but because of him who subjected it, in hope that the creation itself will be set free from its bondage to corruption. . . . For we know that *the whole creation has been groaning* together in the pains of childbirth until now. And not only the creation, but we ourselves . . . groan inwardly as we wait eagerly for adoption as sons, *the redemption* of our bodies. (Rom. 8:20–23)

This is a dense statement with a lot of truth packed into it. But simply notice what it says: The creation is awaiting redemption—not just humanity. The creation is waiting to be "set free."

The apostle John said, "I saw a *new heaven* and a *new earth*, for the first heaven and the first earth had passed away, and the sea was no more" (Rev. 21:1). And what John saw happening in that new earth is very interesting:

> And I saw the holy city, new Jerusalem, coming down out of heaven from God, prepared as a bride adorned for her husband. And I heard a loud voice from the throne saying, "Behold, the dwelling place of God is with man. . . ." And he who was seated on the throne said, "Behold, I am making all things new." (Rev. 21:3–5).

The Christian hope is not escape but resurrection (2 Cor. 4:14). God will dwell with us on this earth—that's why the new Jerusalem, God's dwelling place, is said to "come down out of heaven." At the end of the Bible's story, God restores the world to the way He originally created it to be.

One day, God is going to reestablish His rule over all creation (1 Cor. 15:28). And that's why no true Christian can view secularism, the main non-Christian form of the two-story view, as a good thing. Secularism tries to push God off the throne He established over His own creation. It tries to steal from God what He owns, like an art thief stealing a canvas directly from an artist's studio. And this particular thief has the gall to turn around and say to the Artist, "You didn't paint this! It just *is*."

Christians who live by the two-story view are subtly confirming the thesis* of secularism. That's because American secularists don't try to ban religion outright. Instead, they push it out to the margins of society. They say it is supposed to be private and to have no effect on government, the arts, and the life of the mind. And this is just what the two-story view does when Christians hold it; it keeps the Bible from having its proper influence on vast portions of their lives. But the truth of the Creation, Fall, Redemption story shows that we must not let this happen to us.

thesis: *the point someone wants to prove*

KEY CONNECTIONS

Now it's time to make two key connections to bring this chapter on the two-story view together.

(1) If God has a future plan for all creation, then there will be a time when everything in creation is set right. Paul told a group of believers tempted to give in to "gnostic" dualism, an ancient form of the two-story view, "In [Jesus Christ] all the fullness of God was pleased to dwell, and through him to reconcile to himself all things" (Col 1:19–20). And if "all things" in creation are going to be set right, there must be a right way to do those things. Let's pause and think about what "all things" includes. It's not just people, as we saw from Romans 8; it's also creation. But it's not just animals, or even trees and lakes and ozone layer composition. "All things" means everything God programmed into His original creation. And as we'll see in the next few units, that's a lot.

"All things" means institutions and academic disciplines like sports, cooking, advertising, biology, agriculture, sociology, medical science, high finance. The list could go on for a long time: political science, cinema, computer technology, economics, geology.[14]

Christians are not used to thinking of these things as being part of our future. But, biblically speaking, they are. One day, these things will all be done the right way, God's way. Because fallen people (including Christians) are now running all these fields, they are all damaged by sin in minor or major ways. But one day Christ will reconcile them all to God. God through Christ will retake all the territory occupied by the enemy. The earth is the Lord's.

(2) And now for the second key connection: if there's a right way to run these things in the future God will set up for us, there's a right way to run them *now*. Without a biblical worldview there's no way you'll know how your own career is supposed to be run. Will you be a politician? A farmer? A teacher? A biologist? A marketer? An artist? A writer? A mom? There are God-honoring ways to be these things and God-dishonoring ways. There are ways to be these things that honor the way God made the world, and there are ways that ignore it.

If a worldview is a head-heart system that tells a single overarching story about the world, the dualism of the two-story view just can't work. We can't split life into the sacred things of the heart and the secular things of the mind. It is more than possible, it is our duty, to view all of life—upper and lower stories—from a biblical perspective.

And if a worldview includes practical action, it's possible to *live* all of life, to make every choice, in obedience to God. Religion must not be barred from reaching down to the lower story. Maybe that's why American evangelist Bob Jones Sr. said, "[For a Christian,] life is not divided into the secular and the sacred. . . . [To him] all ground is holy ground. Every bush is a burning bush. Every place is a temple [of worship]."[15]

THINKING IT THROUGH 3.3

1. How does the biblical worldview of creation correct the flawed two-story view?
2. How does the biblical worldview of the Fall correct the flawed two-story view?
3. What is biblical redemption?
4. How does the biblical worldview of redemption correct the flawed two-story view?
5. Explain in your own words the two key connections that were presented at the end of the chapter.

3 CHAPTER REVIEW

TERMS TO REMEMBER

secular
dualism
two-story view

Scripture Memory

Colossians 1:19–20

Making Connections

1. Give two reasons why many Christians separate life into a "sacred" realm and a "secular" realm.
2. Look at the chart on page 35. Where would secularists place the pro-life (anti-abortion) position on that chart? How about human trafficking?
3. Although Christians should abandon the distinction between the secular and the sacred, what distinctions should Christians maintain?
4. Rather than dichotomizing the world into the two-story view, what paradigm should Christians use to accurately live out a biblical worldview?

Developing Skills in Apologetics and Worldview

5. How should you respond to a secularist who wants you to keep your (biblical) values at home and out of the public square?
6. How can you guard against falling into the two-story view or the opposite ditch of no distinctions?

Examining Assumptions and Evidence

7. For what purpose did René Descartes doubt everything? Why was his conclusion about human reasoning flawed?
8. Explain why the secularist two-story view (diagrammed in the chart on page 35) is inaccurate.
9. Explain why the secularist two-story view can never be applied consistently.
10. What's your dream job? How would you be able to know whether you were doing that job in a God-honoring way?

Becoming a Creative Cultivator

11. Write a letter to the editor of your local newspaper about the place of faith in the public square.

2

CREATION

Chapter Four GOD THE CREATOR

In the beginning was the Word, and the Word was with God, and the Word was God. He was in the beginning with God. All things were made through him, and without him was not any thing made that was made.

Scripture Memory
John 1:1–3

Father, I desire that they also, whom you have given me, may be with me where I am, to see my glory that you have given me because you loved me before the foundation of the world.

John 17:24

4.1 GOD THE THREE IN ONE

The Christian story doesn't actually begin at the beginning.

It can't because one of the distinctive claims of the Bible is that there was a "time" before the beginning of our universe—and we can know about it. If "in the beginning, God created" (Gen. 1:1), then God must have existed before the beginning. Just like your parents had a life long before you were born, there was a time in which God existed with His own purposes, purposes that didn't necessarily have anything to do with us or our planet.

In fact, it's this time before time that will help us dig down to the true bedrock of a Christian worldview and even the real meaning of life. There couldn't be any overall meaning or purpose for our world if it came into being by accident. Big bangs don't have motivations any more than volcano eruptions do; they just happen. Only persons have purposes. And if you are going to have a Christian worldview, you need to know what motivated God to make this world in the first place.

> "WHEN YOU SAY, 'IT'S ALL CHAOS, MAN,' YOU'RE ALSO SAYING, 'YOU'RE POINTLESS.'"[1]
>
> —N. D. WILSON

LOVE AND MOTIVATION

Motivations—whether God's or yours—are interesting, complex things. For example, why did you get up this morning? Was it because your mom made you, or because you wanted to?

Either way or both ways, the operative motivation at your house this morning probably boiled down to one word: *school.* Your mom was motivated by school because if you don't graduate from high school the chances are higher that you will still be living in her basement, adding to her laundry piles, and eating her meatloaf at age thirty-six. Perhaps *you* were motivated by school for a related but different reason: because you're planning to head off to college, and high school is a stepping stone toward that goal.

But this analysis doesn't go far enough because going to college isn't an end in itself. You go to college for deeper reasons. Have you ever traced your motivations all the way to their root?

Why, in fact, do you want to go to college? So you can get a good job and make money—to provide for your future family? There's nothing necessarily wrong with that. Or maybe to train for service in Christ's kingdom? Nothing wrong with that either, of course.

But can we stop here? Is this what you live for? Future spouse and future kids? Future church ministry? Are these the things that motivate you? Maybe, but we're still not down to bedrock.

If you dig and dig to the very bottom of all your motivations, the Bible tells you what you'll find: love. It's ultimately what and whom you love (like God, like a future spouse and future kids—or, sadly, just yourself) that determines what you think and do. Motivations are built on loves. That's why Jesus Himself named (1) loving God with your whole heart and (2) loving others the way you love yourself as the two most important laws there are (Matt. 22:34–40). A Jewish expert in the law of God asked Jesus a question "to test him."

> "Teacher, which is the great commandment in the Law?" And [Christ] said to him, "You shall love the Lord your God with all your heart and with all your soul and with all your mind. This is the great and first commandment. And a second is like it: You shall love your neighbor as yourself. On these two commandments depend all the Law and the Prophets." (Matt. 22:36–40)

Every one of the rules in the Bible, Jesus says, depends on love. In other words, if you really love God with all your heart and love the people God has placed in your life as much as you love yourself, you will obey God's laws. Because that's all the laws are: a description of what life looks like when your loves are all in the right order. That's true today, too, even with mundane things like traffic laws. If you really love other people, you'll be a careful driver.

GOD IS LOVE

If love lies at the very center of what we are, it's not a coincidence that it lies at the center of who God is too. But we need to flip that order around. God doesn't love because we do; we love because God does and because we are made in His image. First John 4:8 says this with brevity ("Love is from God") and with beauty ("God is love").

And the centrality of love brings us to a very important worldview question, the most important and foundational question in the Christian worldview: ultimately, what or whom does God love? In other words, what are God's motivations built on? We can't ask God why He gets up in the morning or why He wants to go to college! We can't find out what motivates Him the same way we find out what motivates you, but we *can* listen to Him speak in Scripture.

And this is what He says:

> "Behold my servant, whom I uphold, my chosen, in whom my soul delights" (Isa. 42:1).

When God speaks about His "servant" in Isaiah 42, one of Isaiah's servant songs, He is speaking of Jesus more than seven hundred years before His birth.

And He also says:

> "This is my beloved Son, in whom I am well pleased" (Matt. 3:17).

And this is what His Son, Jesus Christ, says about Him:

> "The Father loves the Son" (John 3:35; 5:20).

Each of these three statements from the Bible says the same thing in a different way: God the Father loves God the Son. God's soul "delights" in His Son, Jesus. He loved Him before the first Christmas ever happened. And it's this love that gives us a window into what happened even before the beginning because, three decades after the first Christmas, Jesus prays this:

> "Father, . . . you loved me before the foundation of the world" (John 17:24).

> "BEFORE HE EVER CREATED, BEFORE HE EVER RULED THE WORLD, BEFORE ANYTHING ELSE, THIS GOD WAS A FATHER LOVING HIS SON."[2]
>
> —MICHAEL REEVES

This is what God was doing before He ever let there be light. His Son and Spirit were the delight of His heart before there were any other beings to love. And the love didn't go in only one direction. Jesus also said,

> "I do as the Father has commanded me, so that the world may know that *I love the Father*" (John 14:31).

There is little doubt that this love began before the world did.

THE INNER LOVE OF THE TRINITY

Digging deep into what the Bible says about God's loves brings us right into the middle of one of the most important doctrines of the Christian faith: the **Trinity**.

The doctrine is simple in a way but so profound that you'll never search it out completely. God is one and, in a different sense, God is three. The ancient Jews were taught to have no other gods before God, and they were told to say, "The Lord our God, the Lord is one" (Deut. 6:4). But when Jesus came, God revealed what He had hinted at in the Old Testament: there are three persons—Father, Son, and Spirit—in the one God. The Father is the director, the leader—the *father*. But this doesn't mean the Son is a second-place God, or the Spirit a third-place God. Since the earliest centuries of the Christian church, careful readers of the Bible have agreed that Scripture gives fully equal divinity to each of the three persons of the Trinity. Jesus, the Bible says, "is the radiance of the glory of God and the exact imprint of his nature" (Heb. 1:3; cf. Col. 2:9). John explains that "this was why the Jews were seeking all the more to kill [Jesus], because . . . he was even calling God his own Father, making himself equal with God" (John 5:18).

But why would God ask people to swallow such a difficult doctrine? Islam, in effect, makes *disbelief* in the Trinity one of its five doctrinal pillars. Most major splinter groups that have left Christianity—the Mormons and the Jehovah's Witnesses—have done so in part so they could avoid belief in the Trinity. It seems utterly irrational to them. Why hold on to this strange teaching?

Most importantly, Christians hold on to the doctrine of the Trinity because the Bible teaches it, and it's not up to us to teach logic to the owner of logic. But another big reason is actually *love*. Think about it: if God were one person, completely alone, there could not have been any love before He created other beings (whether angels, humans, or dogs). Love, then, couldn't be essential to God. Love could only be something else He created, a later add-on. Before creation, it wouldn't have been true to say that "God *is* love."

But the doctrine of the Trinity indicates that love existed before the world did—among the three persons: Father, Son, and Spirit. As one theologian put it, "When the love between . . . persons is happy, healthy and secure, they rejoice to share it. Just so it is with God. . . . Being perfectly loving, from all eternity the Father and the Son have delighted to share their love and joy with and through the Spirit."[3]

Christians have worked for a long time to understand the Bible's talk about the Trinity and the love inside it. We're past the limit of human capacities here. We have enough trouble understanding ourselves; what human could fully comprehend his or her Creator? Every illustration of the Trinity is a feeble attempt to describe a truth so big it can't fit in our minds, like one housecat trying to explain to another the literary themes of their owner's favorite novel. (See sidebar.)

But there's something here you do have to get: the love and joy and happiness of God is totally full. God is not and has never been lonely. Whatever motivated Him to create the world, it wasn't that He lacked something. He had in Himself—in the love and fellowship of the three persons—an infinite amount of everything He could ever need.

A PICTURE WORTH A THOUSAND WORDS?

It's impossible to accurately illustrate the Trinity. There's nothing exactly like the Creator in the world He created. An egg—with its yolk, white, and shell—can't illustrate Him, and neither can a shamrock with its three leaves. That's because God has no separable parts. The states of water—solid, liquid, gas—can't illustrate Him either because the same molecules of water can't be in all three states at once. Saying that God takes different forms at different times—Father sometimes, Son other times, Spirit at yet other times—is an ancient heresy called modalism. For centuries, all Christians have confessed the words of the Athanasian Creed: "We worship one God in Trinity, and Trinity in Unity."[4]

THINKING IT THROUGH 4.1

1. What is your ultimate motivation for everything in life?
2. What central biblical commands reveal that this is indeed the overarching motivation for all of life? What is the connection between God's law and your motivation for existence?
3. What is the ultimate motivation that caused God to create the world? Was His motivation to create the world due to anything that He lacked?
4. Why is the doctrine of the Trinity a necessary foundation for explaining God's ultimate motivation?
5. Why can't the evolutionary worldview truly justify any ultimate meaning and purpose in life? What is the necessary outcome of lacking ultimate meaning and purpose in life?

4.2 GOD THE SPRING

Just as human love is an echo of divine love, humans have goals because God does. In the last section we asked, "What does God love?" In this one we ask a similar but related question: "What does God aim at?" Since the Father loves the Son, who loves the Spirit, who loves them both—what goals grow out of this Trinitarian love?

GOD'S FINAL PURPOSE

The Bible answers this pretty directly. What is the end of all history, the overriding purpose the **triune*** God aims at in all He does? Put simply, it is His own **glory**—the display of His own amazing love, holiness, power, justice, and all the other things that make God God. When the apostle Paul described the culmination of the Bible's story, he described it this way:

triune: *three ("tri-") in one ("-une").*

> Then comes the end, when [Christ] delivers the kingdom to God the Father after destroying every rule and every authority and power. . . . When all things are subjected to him, then the Son himself will also be subjected to him who put all things in subjection under him, that God may be all in all. (1 Cor. 15:24–28)

"That God may be all in all." God's own uncontested rule and subsequent glory make up the goal He has aimed at in all His works throughout all time.

Paul says the same thing another way in his famous letter to the Christians in Rome. After finishing a massive section of intense theology about God's wise and gracious plan for the world, Romans 9–11, Paul just stops and marvels at the plan of God, quoting the biblical prophet Isaiah along the way:

> Oh, the depth of the riches and wisdom and knowledge of God! How unsearchable are his judgments and how inscrutable his ways! "For who has known the mind of the Lord, or who has been his counselor?" "Or who has given a gift to him that he might be repaid?" For from him and through him and to him are all things. To him be glory forever. Amen. (Rom. 11:33–36)

GOD'S GOAL: GOD'S GLORY

It's important to understand that these are not isolated verses. This goal—God's goal to display His own glory—is a pattern throughout the Bible. Have you ever noticed Bible statements like these? What motivates God in these passages?

- "The Lord will not forsake his people, for his great name's sake" (1 Sam. 12:22).
- "Our fathers, when they were in Egypt, did not . . . remember the abundance of your steadfast love, but rebelled by the sea, at the Red Sea. Yet he saved them for his name's sake, that he might make known his mighty power" (Ps. 106:7–8).
- "Bring my sons from afar and my daughters from the end of the earth, everyone who is called by my name, whom I created for my glory" (Isa. 43:6–7).
- "For my name's sake I defer my anger, for the sake of my praise I restrain it for you. . . . For my own sake, for my own sake, I do it, for how should my name be profaned? My glory I will not give to another" (Isa. 48:9, 11).
- "Father, the hour has come; glorify your Son that the Son may glorify you" (John 17:1).

We could list many, many more scriptural quotations that all say the same thing: when God makes a choice, He is motivated by His own glory, the honor of His own name, the display of His great power, the extending of His rule. God told Pharaoh, the king of Egypt who enslaved Abraham's family, "For this very purpose I have raised you up, that I might show my power in you, and that my name might be proclaimed in all the earth" (Rom. 9:17). God's goal in all He does is God's glory.

Glory and Love

The only way you can know God is for Him to reveal Himself to you. He has; the Bible says He's done it inside you by writing His laws in your conscience (Rom. 2:14–15). He has done it outside you through His creation, which shouts His glory all day (Rom. 1:20–21; Ps. 19:1–4). But conscience and creation can tell you only so much. You need words. And you have them. You've read a lot of them just now—words, of course, from the Bible.

And now you need to do an important piece of theological thinking with those words from the Bible, some thinking that you may never have been called on to do before. To have a right view of God, you need to notice an apparent problem with the two sets of Bible passages you've just read—the passages about God's love and the passages about God's goal, His own glory. The apparent problem is that these two groups of Bible statements don't seem, at first glance, to fit very well together. "God is love" and "God seeks His own glory in all He does"—how could both be true?

If it bothers you that God seeks His own glory above all else, it's probably because people you know who seek their own glory are offensively proud, arrogant, and self-absorbed. What's more, they're wrong. They aren't the exalted beings they think they are.

But God is. The reason it's wrong for humans to seek their own glory is that they're humans—fallen, finite humans. Boxer Muhammad Ali was famous for shouting, "I am the greatest!"[5] Of course, his greatness faded. But God truly is the greatest, in every category and for all time. God is right to be focused on His own glory because He is not one of us. He is infinitely wiser, more powerful, and more righteous than any human could possibly be. To show others His preeminent glory is just to tell the truth about the way things are. If He loved and valued anything else more, He would be lying. Even if He loved you more than He loves His own glory, He would be an idolater—and you would be His idol.

We are offended by arrogant, selfish people because their self-love comes out in the way they act. They're hard to be around; they don't give; they don't love. But this kind of twisted self-love is not what we see in God. We know that in part because God Himself came to live among us in the person of Jesus Christ. Was Jesus selfish, arrogant, and hard to get along with? No, God's love for Himself translated into a love for us that sent Jesus to a cruel death and the ultimate sacrifice. And yet the Bible says that God sent His Son to die for our sins precisely for "the praise of His glorious grace" (Eph. 1:3–6).

The End for Which God Created the World

Now we're ready to ask again the questions we've been raising here and there throughout this chapter: Why did God create the world? Why is there something rather than nothing?

Search online for that second question and you'll find out that it's a very old one. The online *Stanford Encyclopedia of Philosophy* carefully lists the answers philosophers have given over time, and there's a lot of disagreement among them. The author of this encyclopedia's article about "Nothingness" even raises the Bible's answer as a major possibility:

> The Genesis creation story suggests that God made everything without relying [on] any antecedent ingredients. The story also suggests that God had a reason to create. If this account could be corroborated we would have an explanation of why there are some concrete things.[6]

JONATHAN EDWARDS ON GOD'S GOAL IN CREATION

Early American pastor, theologian, and evangelist Jonathan Edwards dedicated close attention to this question: Why did God create the world? He answered it in a richly scriptural and carefully logical book called *A Dissertation Concerning the End for Which God Created the World*. He wrote, "It appears that all that is ever spoken of in the Scripture as an ultimate end of God's works is included in that one phrase, the glory of God. . . . In the creature's knowing, esteeming, loving, rejoicing in, and praising God, the glory of God is both exhibited and acknowledged; his fullness is received and returned. . . . The refulgence shines upon and into the creature, and is reflected back to the luminary. The beams of glory come from God, are something of God, and are refunded back again to their original. So that the whole is of God, and in God, and to God; and he is the beginning, and the middle, and the end."[7]

Jonathan Edwards
(1703–1758)

But the author dismisses the Bible's view. He says it would mean that "the existence of God necessitates the existence of the Earth."[8] In other words, he thinks the Bible is saying God had to create the world. This is no answer, he thinks.

But does the Bible really say He *had to*?

If God had been lonely or unhappy—if there had been no gloriously joyful Trinity living in perfect unity with one another eternally—then maybe it would make sense to see our world as something God had to make. Without us, who would He have to talk to? To love? Maybe creating the world all those years ago was His last attempt at finally making Himself happy.

But God isn't unhappy. He isn't lonely. That's us, not Him. We're the ones who, because of sin, are often unhappy. We're the ones who can't find ultimate contentment even in the best things in this earthly life, even in falling in love. Many marriages end in unhappiness even if they don't end in divorce. And even the best Christian marriages do not provide the perfect love we were born to want.

"WORTHY ARE YOU, OUR LORD AND GOD, TO RECEIVE GLORY AND HONOR AND POWER, FOR YOU CREATED ALL THINGS, AND BY YOUR WILL THEY EXISTED AND WERE CREATED."

—REVELATION 4:11

But God doesn't need more love. He doesn't need more education. He doesn't need anything. You can't give Him something that doesn't come from Him already (Rom. 11:35–36). At the foundation of the Christian worldview is a self-sufficient, joyful, triune God.

So why *did* God create the world? If He doesn't need it, why make it? The Christian answer puts God's desire to share His own glory together with the inner love of the Trinity.

Theologian Michael Reeves points out in his book on the Trinity that "while the Father loves the Son and the Son loves the Father, there is a very definite shape to their relationship. Overall, the Father is the lover, the Son is the beloved."[9] The Bible does mention the Son's love for the Father, but far more often it talks about the Father's love for His Son. The flow of love in the Trinity starts with the Father.

And this matters because the wellspring of love that starts with the Father flows through the Son and onto us. "As the Father has loved me, so have I loved you," Jesus said (John 15:9). Just like the Father loves the Son, the Son loves the church.

God created the world for the same reason a spring keeps bubbling out water: it's God's nature to overflow. The mutual love of the Trinity has a tendency to spill over. It isn't lack but abundance that makes God, the spring, pour out His love on creatures He creates. There is something rather than nothing because it is the very nature of God to pour out His love on—and display His wondrous glory to—others.

Westminster Confession of Faith: *a widely used summary of Christian doctrine written by English theologians in the seventeenth century*

The classic Westminster Confession of Faith* says that the "chief end of man," humanity's ultimate purpose, is "to glorify God and enjoy him forever."[10] But again, these are not two competing goals. *One absolutely essential part of glorifying God is, in fact, enjoying Him forever.*

Because that's what you do with a spring. You drink. The strongest way to recommend the purity and refreshment of a spring is just to drink and drink and drink till others start to see how valuable a treasure you've found.

And in this case the treasure finds you. Because that's His loving way. Jesus is the source of living water (John 4:10), and He gives it away freely to the thirsty (Isa. 55:1–5).

THINKING IT THROUGH 4.2

1. Why doesn't God need the universe?
2. How can God's ultimate motivation and ultimate goal fit together in harmony?
3. Why is neither the existence of God nor the achievement of His ultimate goal contingent on the existence of the world?
4. What should be the chief goal of all humans that provides ultimate meaning for their existence? What is the only way that humans can achieve this goal?
5. Why is a spring an appropriate illustration for describing the achievement of God's ultimate goal?

4.3 GOD THE UNRIVALED, YET GOD WITH US

How do you get to know an orange? Tasting it is a good start. But there are lots of other ways. You could slice it thin and put it under a microscope. You could take infrared photographs. You could dissolve it in acid and see what compounds it contains. You have lots of options; you're in control.

But that's not how you get to know a person. For you to get to know people, they have to be willing. They have to decide what they want to reveal to you and when. And you will probably have to open yourself up, too, at least a bit, if you expect them to open up. They probably won't get under a microscope, and it wouldn't help you get to know them better if they did because personal knowledge doesn't come primarily through scientific tools.

Some people treat God like a fruit. They're in control; they decide how to investigate Him. They let God know what He's allowed to be like and when. They might even insist that He meet them through microscopes, or they won't believe He exists.

But if God is a person—and a kind of person far greater than we can imagine, a tri-personal person, a person in whose image you are made—you're not in control of how you get to know Him. He is. You meet Him on His own loving terms. He decides what to tell you, and you have to open yourself up to receive it.

It sounds arrogant to most people when Christians claim to know God personally. But He came and met us; what else can we say?

THE BLIND MEN AND THE ELEPHANT

People who find Christians arrogant sometimes use the blind men and the elephant story to explain their viewpoint. It goes like this: some blind men encounter an elephant. Each of them, feeling a different part of the elephant, perceives the elephant differently.

One blind man, holding the elephant's tail, insists that the elephant is a rope. Another, touching the feet, insists that the elephant is a thick tree. Another, touching the elephant's side, is certain the others are wrong: the elephant is a stout, tar-papered building.

Americans and Western Europeans often tell this story as a rebuke to anyone who claims to know the truth about God—like Christians. All religions have truth, they say, just different parts of it. They urge Christians to admit that, as limited human beings, we have only a partial view of God. Other religions know things about Him that we don't know.

But there's something ironic here: how do those who tell the story know that all world religions are blind unless they themselves can see? How can they know that those religions are seeing only part of the elephant unless they are standing back and looking at the whole pachyderm? They are offended by Christians' claim to be right about God while other religions are wrong. But that's just what they're doing.

And *what if the elephant talks*? What if he says to the blind men, "I'm an elephant. That's not a fan; it's my ear." Will we think the men humble if they ignore him and keep on arguing?

It's true that people are limited. Worse, we're fallen. God's prophet Isaiah therefore urged his hearers centuries ago, "Stop regarding man in whose nostrils is breath, for of what account is he?" (Isa. 2:22). People can be wrong about God. But God has spoken. And no matter how arrogant it sounds to other people, we can't deny the truth of what our Creator has said.

GOD'S RELATIONSHIP TO THE UNIVERSE

The major religions of the world couldn't possibly be blind men all offering their partial "view" of the same God. That's because world religions have mutually exclusive views of God. They disagree so fundamentally about who God is that if one of them is right, the others must be wrong.

The major views of how God relates to His creation can be boiled down to five: (1) **materialism**, (2) **pantheism**, (3) **dualism**, (4) **deism**, and (5) **biblical theism**.[11]

Materialism

Materialism isn't exactly a view of God's relationship to His creation; materialists argue that there is no God, and thus there's nothing that can be called "creation." That's why it's the one view of the five that most people wouldn't call religious. For materialists, the universe is all there is. The classic expression of this view doesn't come from a philosopher but from a TV series, the famous documentary *Cosmos*

by scientist Carl Sagan. Released in 1980, the series has been viewed by half a billion people around the world.

The very first words in *Cosmos* are spoken confidently by Sagan: "The cosmos* is all that is or ever was or ever will be."[12] That's materialism. Sagan proceeds in the thirteen-part series to display the wonders of science and of the universe—and they surely are wondrous. But *Cosmos* is like a documentary about *Hamlet* that fails to mention Shakespeare. There is no Shakespeare; the play is all there ever was.

cosmos: *a synonym for* universe *that emphasizes the orderliness and coherence of what exists*

Though this kind of atheism seems to be the very opposite of religion, religious overtones are far from absent in the statements of materialists. Sagan died in 1996, but his wife Ann Druyan has championed his causes since then. And in her introduction to a re-release of *Cosmos*, she said this: "*Cosmos* is both a history of the scientific enterprise and an attempt to convey the soaring spiritual high of its central revelation: our oneness with the universe."[13] "Soaring spiritual high . . . revelation . . . oneness"—these are words that Druyan used precisely for their religious resonances.

Sagan, Druyan, and other materialists mean to inspire people with their view of existence. Sagan also said in that same first episode of *Cosmos*, "The cosmos is . . . within us. We're made of star-stuff. We are a way for the cosmos to know itself." In other words, human consciousness is the only instance we know of in which the atoms bumping around our universe have ever chanced upon a mirror. Sagan wants to convince his hearers that our self-awareness and our consciousness allow us to play an exciting role in a cosmic drama.

THE NEW *COSMOS*

When a new version of the *Cosmos* documentary was made in 2014, host Neil deGrasse Tyson—a charismatic astrophysicist like his mentor Carl Sagan—expressed a hope in science that sounds religious, just like Sagan did. Science often takes over the role of religion for materialists. Tyson said, "Science is an enterprise that should be cherished as an activity of the free human mind, because it transforms who we are, how we live—and it gives us an understanding of our place in the universe."[14]

But if pure empirical science, the kind that by ideology or by implication admits the existence of nothing but nature, gives us any understanding of our place in the universe, it's a deterministic place that can by no means transform how we live—because we don't have free human minds. We have the pieces of star-stuff the universe gave us by accident.

But it's difficult to see how materialism can really be inspiring because materialists are forced to conclude that humans not only have no souls, but no desires, beliefs, or goals. And where's the drama in finding out that you're the product of an unbending line of cause and effect stretching back as far as scientists can see? In this view, choices are illusions. Right and wrong, freedom and equality—these are just labels we use because using them confers evolutionary advantages on our species. Behind it all is nothing but matter and chance.

Materialism has been around—over and over again—throughout human history,[15] and it has never successfully answered its challengers. It turns out that being made of star-stuff isn't quite as noble as Sagan believed.

Pantheism

Pantheism argues that we're all made of god-stuff instead of star-stuff. There is no "God" in pantheism—we are all part of "god." The god-stuff that humans are made of is also what animals are made of. And rocks. And comets and the stars, the whole universe. In other words, god is everything, and everything is god. That god isn't a person and, really, neither are we—at least in the way Western people (due to the influence of the Bible) are used to thinking of persons. We are not individuals but inseparable parts of a universal whole. A prominent pantheist website explains,

> Pantheists see their personal religion as a system of reverent behavior toward the Earth rather than subscription to a particular creed. Because Pantheists

anthropomorphic: *human-like; such as a cartoon bird given hands and a human voice*

anthropocentrism: *a humanity-centered perspective*

identify God with Nature rather than an anthropomorphic* being, Pantheists oppose the arrogant world-view of anthropocentrism.*[16]

Pantheism purposefully downgrades God from a person to a thing—the universe. And it demotes man from ruler of creation to just another speck of stardust; they just call the stardust divine.

Dualism

There are multiple kinds of dualism. We talked about one kind of dualism in the last chapter: secularist dualism that says that even if there is a God, there's no reliable way of sorting out what's true about Him from what's false. This kind of dualism puts all the unknowable supernatural stuff in the "upper story" and lets people visit that upper story as long as they promise not to bring anything downstairs.

In another kind of dualism, God and the universe have always existed, but on parallel tracks that may or may not ever meet—depending on the particular view (since there are many species of dualism besides the one pictured in the diagram). Dualists think God and matter (the universe) make up the two major forces in existence.

People who have taken this view throughout history have tended to see these forces in opposition to each other. The goal of life, for this kind of dualist, is to escape the evil shackles of the material world and join the rational, eternal, harmonious, spiritual world in which God lives. Salvation becomes a way for the soul (the one part of humans that is not material) to escape from the world of flesh and blood into the ethereal* world of divine perfection. For dualists, the body itself is evil.

ethereal: *out of this world; heavenly; immaterial*

Since the early church, some Christians have felt attracted to this kind of dualism, but it isn't Christian. On the very first page of Scripture it is clear that God existed before His creation and that He views that creation as "very good."

Deism

Deism accepts that there is a God but maintains that He hasn't spoken to us. He is there, but He's silent. We're left to discern truth about him from nature. Deism, however, has no simple definition and no organization to speak of. There are no self-consciously deist institutions, whether schools, publishing houses, lobbying groups, or think tanks.* Deists have a website (deism.com) but no physical headquarters.

Nonetheless, you might be surprised to know that one of America's most prominent sociologists has said that deism is "the de facto dominant religion among contemporary U.S. teenagers."[17] That sociologist, Christian Smith, conducted a massive survey of American thirteen-to-seventeen-year-olds about their religion, and he concluded that their views are best summarized by the label **moralistic therapeutic deism**, or MTD. This is how Smith summarizes the "creed" of MTD:[18]

think tank: *a group of scholars who hold a particular political or religious viewpoint and conduct intensive research to promote it via academic papers, newspaper articles, books, and so forth*

1. A God exists who created and orders the world and watches over human life on earth.
2. God wants people to be good, nice, and fair to each other, as taught in the Bible and by most world religions.
3. The central goal of life is to be happy and to feel good about oneself.
4. God does not need to be particularly involved in one's life except when God is needed to resolve a problem.
5. Good people go to heaven when they die.

Point 2 is the *moralistic* part. Point 3 is the *therapeutic* part. Point 4 is the deism. But Points 1 and 5 are (sort of) taken from Christianity. Deism is parasitic; it takes a faith like Christianity and strips out the stuff that's offensive to human reason—or whatever passes for "human reason" at the time. Deism is to Christianity what a barbecue is to a snowman after sixty seconds. There's something left, but it's barely recognizable.

This category of deism is where we'd probably have to place MTD's cousin, American **civil religion**, a concept first named by sociologist Robert Bellah in 1967.[19] When US presidents say to disaster or accident victims, "Our thoughts and prayers are with you," when they put their hands on Bibles and solemnly swear oaths, when they end speeches with "God bless America," when they imply that Muslims and Christians worship the same deity—that's American civil religion. Its high priests are presidents. "God" in this civil religion is never defined, and he's mainly called in (as with MTD) to solve problems and benignly bless what we were all planning to do anyway. The god of American civil religion has been cut down to the size Americans like. As Voltaire reportedly said, "Ever since God made man in his own image, man has been trying to return the compliment."[20]

Biblical Theism

Our world is full of ideas about God. He's either nonexistent (materialism), or he's everything (pantheism). He's either at war with the universe (dualism)—or he doesn't really care about it much and just expects us not to mess up the furniture while He does His own thing (deism).

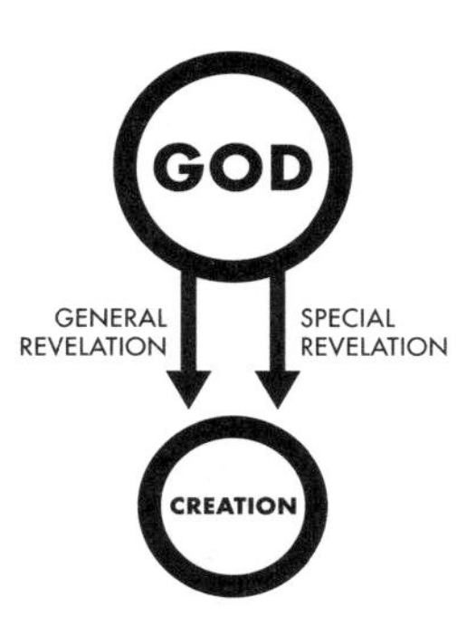

It's interesting how many of the views above are undercut by the Bible's opening statements. The very first words of Genesis reveal a personal God who stands above His creation but is deeply involved in it. And the rest of the Bible reveals, as Paul put it, "one God and Father of all, who is over all and through all and in all" (Eph. 4:6). If He's in all and through all, there's no room for materialism or deism. If He's over all, there's no pantheism.

God is distinct from His creation; He's not mixed up in it. He is what theologians call **transcendent**;* He transcends the limitations of time and space that apply throughout the universe He created. Wise potters don't get stuck in their pots (Isa. 64:8). God truly rules as King over His creation, even if there remains some yet-to-be-conquered territory (1 Cor. 15:25–26).

transcendent: *so far above as to be in a different category*

And God has no rivals in that exalted position. "I am God, and there is no other," He told Isaiah (46:9). God isn't in a fight with the universe, and even His conflict with Satan is one He could win in an instant if it served His purposes. One day, it will (Rev. 20:1–4).

But God isn't just transcendent; He is also what theologians call **immanent**.* He is deeply and lovingly interested in His creation, guiding its affairs from His sovereign throne. "In his hand is the life of every living thing and the breath of all mankind," Job says (Job 12:10). Jesus told us that not a sparrow (or even a human hair) falls without God's knowledge and consent (Matt. 10:29–30; Luke 12:6–7).

immanent: *personally present, accessible*

God once made the greatest ruler on earth eat grass for seven years. And when God mercifully restored Nebuchadnezzar to his exalted—but still earthly—dominion, he was compelled to confess that

> [God] does according to his will among the host of heaven
> and among the inhabitants of the earth;
> and none can stay his hand
> or say to him, "What have you done?" (Dan. 4:35)

The Bible displays both God's transcendence and His immanence:

> I am God, and there is none like me,
> declaring the end from the beginning
> and from ancient times things not yet done,
> saying, "My counsel shall stand,
> and I will accomplish all my purpose." (Isa. 46:9–10)

GOD WHO NEEDS NOTHING

Seth MacFarlane, the somewhat infamous comedy writer who created the raunchy TV show *Family Guy*, was executive producer of the new *Cosmos* documentary released in 2014. MacFarlane is an ardent materialist.

On September 11, 2001, MacFarlane was scheduled to fly on the American Airlines jet that crashed into the World Trade Center. NPR interviewer Terri Gross said to MacFarlane, "You were late. Your travel agent gave you the wrong time, so you missed being on that catastrophic flight. Do you ever think of the rest of your life as being this kind of gift? . . . It could have all ended for you that day."[21]

MacFarlane replied, "One of my favorite quotes by Carl Sagan is that we are—as a species and as a culture—we are significance junkies. We love attaching significance to everything, even when there is really no significance and something is just a coincidence."

MacFarlane told the interviewer that the near-death experience hadn't changed him at all. "I'm living the same way . . . as I was in 1999."

In a materialist's world, there is no significance, no overall purpose. All the things that happen to us are coincidences, and so are we.

But the Bible tells us what we all already know in our hearts at some level (Rom. 2:14–15): when God created this universe out of nothing, He did so with an end goal in mind. He was working to glorify Himself. But His act of creation wasn't selfish. It was an overflow of Trinitarian love, an overflow that God has poured into your own soul if you have submitted yourself to His rule. Christian apologist C. S. Lewis wrote, "God who needs nothing, loves into existence wholly superfluous creatures in order that He may love and perfect them."[22]

THINKING IT THROUGH 4.3

1. How does God relate to the universe according to materialism?
2. How does God relate to the universe according to pantheism?
3. How does God relate to the universe according to dualism?
4. How does God relate to the universe according to deism?
5. How does biblical theism characterize God's relationship to the universe, offering a corrective to all of the above false worldviews?
6. How could you refute someone who says the analogy of the blind men and the elephant shows that there's no possibility of accurate knowledge about the reality and truth of God?

4 CHAPTER REVIEW

TERMS TO REMEMBER

Trinity
triune
glory
materialism
pantheism
dualism
deism
biblical theism
moralistic therapeutic deism (MTD)
civil religion
transcendent
immanent

Scripture Memory

John 1:1–3; John 17:24

Making Connections

1. According to Scripture, what determines everything you think and do?
2. Why did God create the world—especially humans? What are some common incorrect reasons? Why are those reasons unbiblical?
3. According to the Westminster Confession, what is the main purpose of man? Explain how the two parts of the answer ought to work together.
4. How does Ephesians 4:6 demonstrate that God is both immanent and transcendent?

Developing Skills in Apologetics and Worldview

5. When you are evangelizing, some people may express the view that God's laws are burdensome obstacles that prevent them from having fun or a good life. What response would you give to this charge?
6. If you were witnessing to pantheists, what biblical truth about God would you want to impress on them (in contrast to their own concept of "god")? What would be some helpful Scripture passages?

Examining Assumptions and Evidence

7. Why does "God is love" (1 John 4:8) demand the doctrine of the Trinity?
8. How do God's love and glory work together?
9. Why is materialism a religious view?
10. Why is the analogy of the blind men and the elephant false?

Becoming a Creative Cultivator

11. Construct a philosophy of life—a statement that encapsulates your desired way of life. Then write a plan of action for your college years—a statement that enumerates how you are going to practically go about living out that philosophy.

Chapter Five MAN AND HIS MANDATE

Then God said, "Let us make man in our image, after our likeness. And let them have dominion over the fish of the sea and over the birds of the heavens and over the livestock and over all the earth and over every creeping thing that creeps on the earth."
So God created man in his own image,
in the image of God he created him;
male and female he created them.
And God blessed them. And God said to them, "Be fruitful and multiply and fill the earth and subdue it, and have dominion over the fish of the sea and over the birds of the heavens and over every living thing that moves on the earth."

Scripture Memory
Genesis 1:26–28

5.1 MIRRORS OF GOD

Star Trek is America's top sci-fi franchise: 726 episodes in five TV series—plus twelve films—over fifty years (so far). Many of the episodes focus on moral questions, and these are often generated by the Starfleet "prime directive." This directive is a form of intergalactic multiculturalism;* Starfleet officers are not allowed to interfere with the cultures of other planets, especially primitive ones.[1] But nearly every time the prime directive comes up in the show, it does so because the principle is in conflict with some other value Starfleet officers hold dear. Usually that value is human or humanoid* life.

In one episode, an alien scientist offers advanced medical knowledge to a Starfleet doctor to help save a crewmember whose life is threatened by an ugly parasite. The starship's crew members slowly discover that the scientist gathered this information through deadly experiments on living subjects, people from a planet his species had subjugated.* The Starfleet doctor argues firmly that it is immoral to use this knowledge. The alien points out in reply that "half the medical knowledge acquired on Earth came through experiments on lower animals!"

multiculturalism: *the idea that all cultures are not just different and valuable but equal in every respect; no culture is allowed to judge another*

humanoid: *in science fiction, an alien with human-like features (two arms and two legs, ability to walk upright, to speak, etc.)*

subjugate: *to violently bring someone else under your control*

PEOPLE FOR THE ETHICAL TREATMENT OF ALGAE?

People for the Ethical Treatment of Animals (PETA) proclaims its creed at the top of its webpage: "Animals are not ours to eat, wear, experiment on, use for entertainment, or abuse in any other way."[2] No Christian should ever abuse an animal, of course. The Bible says clearly, "Whoever is righteous has regard for the life of his beast" (Prov. 12:10). But God just as clearly gave humans the right to eat animals when He told Noah, "Every moving thing that lives shall be food for you" (Gen. 9:3).

But, given their evolutionary worldview, why should PETA supporters care more about animals than about insects or algae? Brian May (one of the few world-famous rock guitarists who also holds a PhD in astrophysics) was probably more consistent with evolutionary ethics when he said, "Human beings have no right to consider themselves any more special than any of our fellow survivors on the planet. And as far as being the dominant species, there is no question that bacteria, not us, are way out in front—in their numbers, in the number of environments they inhabit and even in total mass."[3]

"But not people!" the Starfleet doctor shouts angrily.

"It's convenient to draw a line between higher and lower species, isn't it?" replies the alien scientist.

The Starfleet doctor can only observe that the scientist is "barbaric."[4] The camera cuts to another scene. No reason is given in this episode, or in the whole *Star Trek* universe, for drawing a line of moral difference between animals and people. In fact, one episode (though admittedly not a well-regarded one) suggests that future evolution will turn people back into animals.[5]

SELF-PORTRAITS OF GOD

The Bible gives a reason to distinguish animals from people. It's on the very first page.

> Then God said, "Let us make man in our image, after our likeness. And let them have dominion over the fish of the sea and over the birds of the heavens and over the livestock and over all the earth and over every creeping thing that creeps on the earth."
>
> So God created man in his own image,
> in the image of God he created him;
> male and female he created them. . . .
>
> And God said to them, "Be fruitful and multiply and fill the earth and **subdue** it, and have **dominion** over the fish of the sea and over the birds of the heavens and over every living thing that moves on the earth" (Gen. 1:26–28).

When modern Western man chose a label for himself, it was *homo sapiens*, "wise man"—a thinking being.[6] That label certainly captures part of the truth. But the Bible's label is more satisfying, more complete: "image of God." When God took the dust of the ground and blew His living breath into it (Gen. 2:7), He made something unique in this universe. He made a kind of self-portrait.

That's what it means to be made in God's image, in God's likeness: we're images. *Image* and *likeness* are synonyms; the Bible doesn't draw any significant distinctions between the two terms. Both simply point to similarities between God and humans that no other creatures share, ways that we reflect God. But what similarities? What likenesses exist between man and the God he images?

At the very least, the image of God must include the abilities humans need in order to carry out the jobs assigned to them in the same verses that describe their position as image-bearers (Gen. 1:26–28). In order to fill the earth, subdue it, and have dominion over it, people need to have some of the capacities that God has: self-consciousness, rationality,* language, emotions, and the ability to form relationships with others. Without those capabilities, the work of dominion couldn't get done.

THE TRINITY IN GENESIS 1

Who do the *us* and the *our* in "Let us make man in our image" refer to? God can't be speaking to angels because the Bible never says that humans are made in the image of angels or that angels worked with God to create the world. Christians through the centuries have often seen an indication of the Trinity here, and John 1:3 supports this interpretation of Genesis 1:26 by noting that Jesus was the agent of creation. Also, Colossians 1:15 says that Christ Himself is the **image of God**. And, of course, the role of the Spirit in creation is mentioned in Genesis 1:2: "The Spirit of God was hovering over the face of the waters." The whole Trinity has been active in creation ever since; perhaps the phrase "our image" is part of a conversation inside the Trinity.

Animals have survival instincts, and they can respond in primitive ways to other creatures—dogs come when you call their names; they bark warnings to each other. But no one has ever caught a couple of them curled up in front of a fire conversing about the relative merits of rabbit and squirrel meat. Beavers haven't figured out how to use concrete in dam construction. Ancient gazelles never painted pictures of

rationality: *the capacity to think and reason logically*

humans on cave walls.[7] Human capacities so far outstrip those of animals that people are in a different category of being than animals are. We're image-bearers.

But there's more to the image than human abilities. The New Testament suggests that man's moral nature—and not just his personal capacities—is part of the image. Every human has a conscience, a heart that loves, and a desire to worship someone or something. That's why Christians are told to "put off" immorality and idolatry and instead "put on the new self, which is being renewed in knowledge after the image of its creator" (Col. 3:10). True Christians experience a process of renewal toward the image of God.

The capacities that come with the image are deeply damaged by sin (Eph. 4:17–18), but the image is never totally lost, even in an Alzheimer's sufferer or a comatose patient. The image can, however, be "marred" because of the moral responsibilities tied to it. It can be defaced, like a vandalized portrait on a wall. Your forefather Adam's sins—and your sins—are darts thrown at God's self-portrait.

That's why Aslan told one prince of Narnia, "You come of the Lord Adam and the Lady Eve. . . . And that is both honour enough to erect the head of the poorest beggar, and shame enough to bow the shoulders of the greatest emperor on earth."[8]

HUMAN VALUE

Animals have value. Jesus said that not a single sparrow is forgotten by God. But He must have had something of a twinkle in His eye when He added to His disciples, "You are of more value than many sparrows" (Luke 12:6–7). In contrast, the *Star Trek* universe has no God to give humanoids more value than birds or even crabgrass. Famous scientist Stephen Hawking said,

> The human race is just a chemical scum on a moderate-sized planet, orbiting around a very average star in the outer suburb of one among a hundred billion galaxies. We are so insignificant that I can't believe the whole universe exists for our benefit. That would be like saying that you would disappear if I closed my eyes.[9]

The materialist worldview (matter is all there is) wants self-consciousness and personhood to be things that dawned on humanity gradually as evolution ran its erratic course. They aren't willing to receive their humanity as a gift from someone else.[10]

But just as all love comes ultimately as a gift from God, so does all value and worth. Whatever God loves is valuable; God doesn't love worthless things. And the Trinitarian God's love flows to *you* in a special way because He has made you more valuable than any other part of His creation. He has made you in His own image. If you're unsure of your place in the world (join the club—a lot of teens feel that way), don't base your self-worth on being athletic, likable, or smart. You'll only be wracked with doubts whenever anyone comes along who exceeds you—and someone will. Instead, the image of God should be the foundation for your self-worth. Just rest your confidence in your Creator; your value is secure with Him.

MRI of a man (left) and a dog (right)—are dogs people too?

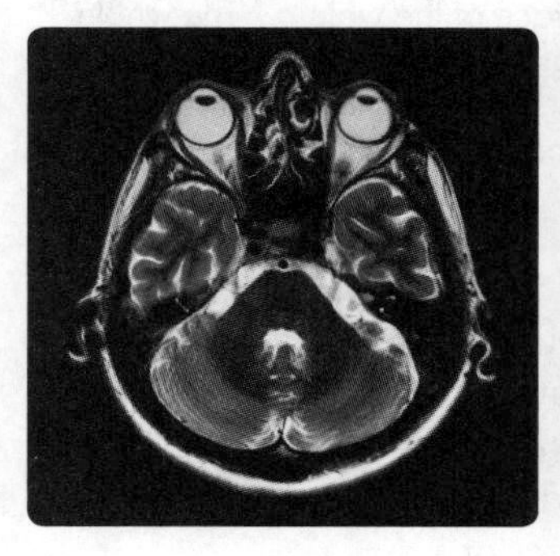

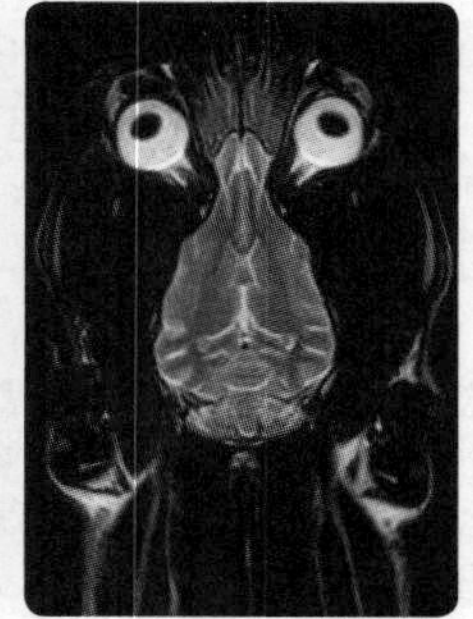

Apart from the biblical concept of the image of God, our perception of human value will be flawed. You get neuroscientists proclaiming, as one did after analyzing a series of canine MRIs, that "dogs are people, too."[11]

You hear NPR science journalist Robert Krulwich saying, "We're not different from other creatures, we're just more than other creatures."[12]

And you end up with the MTD we talked about in Chapter 4. Remember moralistic therapeutic deism—that watered-down form of Christianity in which God exists to make me happy and nice? Sociologist Christian Smith argues that MTD is the predominant religious belief of American teenagers today. One of the biggest truths that this view ignores is the status of humanity as being made in the image of God.

When MTD looks at the human self, it doesn't see a divine image-bearer, someone who gets his or her selfhood as a gift from above. It sees the self as the source, the originator, of all value and meaning. As fallen image-bearers, we're tempted to think that something is important and has value simply because we like it. Even when our parents are citing Bible verses and cautioning us to avoid certain friends or choices, we decide to follow our hearts. Smith writes that for adherents of MTD

> subjective, personal experience is the touchstone of all that is authentic, right, and true. . . . Right and wrong are determined not by external moralities derived from religious teachings, natural law, [or] cultural tradition. . . . Rather, clearly unaware that feeling itself is profoundly socially formed, individual subjective feeling establishes for individuals what is good and bad, right and wrong, just and unjust.[13]

People think their deism liberates them from all the rules of a religion or the commands of a god, but in reality their feelings about what is right and wrong are "profoundly socially formed." They exchange the glory of their Creator for the latest opinion polls. And public opinion offers no secure underpinning for the value of human life. Just ask the 44 million babies who are killed by their parents each year around the world.[14] Many people are appalled by the slaughter, but apparently they are too few to put an end to it.[15]

Ignoring Genesis 1:26–28 creates a vacuum, and what typically rushes into it is the concept of "self-esteem." Secularism has to find some way to increase human value without getting it from God. So a popular talk-show host's website offers articles with descriptions like this: "She spent years looking for validation in all the wrong places—until the day she discovered it was hers to give all along."[16] And many Americans dedicate their entire social-media presence to sharing platitudes* such as this one: "If you're still looking for that one person who will change your life, take a look in the mirror."[17]

platitude: *empty, inane, clichéd advice*

Without a God to give them value and purpose, people are stuck creating their own. Despair is the result because we were designed to be dependent on our Creator.

And without a God to forgive—and pay for—their sins, people can never make up for any personal value they feel they've lost. The cross, in fact, shows how much God values His image-bearers; though we are undeserving of salvation because of our sin, Christ didn't die for utterly worthless beings but for His image-bearers (Rom. 8:32). Now that our vital connection to God is widely denied, it just can't be accidental that depression is so common in modern Western society and that suicide is one of the top ten causes of death in the richest nation on earth.[18] And, on the flip side, now that our dependence on God is widely denied, it's no accident that many people think of themselves more highly than they ought to think (Rom. 12:3). They worship creatures—namely themselves—rather than the Creator.

We are made in God's image. There's no other lasting means of finding self-worth and no other way to be truly humble.

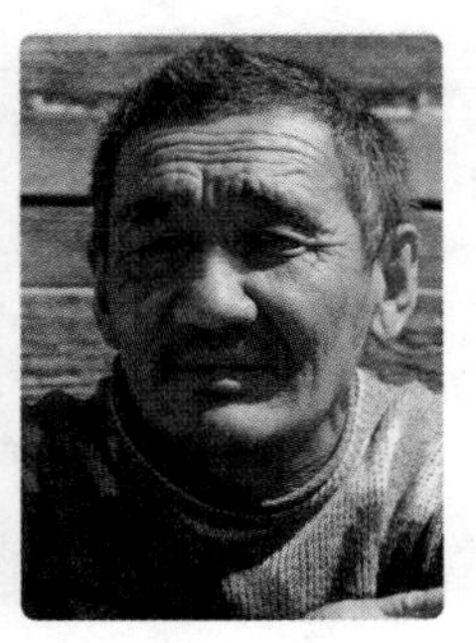

We all bear the divine image.

HUMAN OBLIGATION

And without the concept of the image of God, there's no firm foundation for the worth of others. If the world is built on the principle of "survival of the fittest," then some people are surely expendable. But the Bible poses love for your neighbor as the second most important commandment (after love for God; Matt 22:34–40) precisely because you aren't the only image-bearer in existence. Your sister's one too. The cranky people next door are too. And so are homeless people. Russians and Inuits and Kazaks and Tanzanians are as well. We're all portraits of God. We all bear the divine image. We didn't lose it in the fall of Adam. We know this because Genesis and James base moral commands on the image: you must not kill (Gen. 9:6) or curse (James 3:9) fellow humans because they are just as much God's image-bearers as you are.

Human rights (such as the right not to be forced to marry against your will) and social justice (such as the fight against South African apartheid and other forms of racism) must be firmly based on the image of God, or they will not be strong and lasting. They will come and go with public opinion. Remember the 44 million babies?

The secular metanarrative can't give humans their rights. It doesn't recognize who humans truly are, so how can we trust what it says about what we truly deserve? Personhood is a divine gift, and until we see it that way, we're just lucky animals.

THINKING IT THROUGH 5.1

1. What is the basis for human value in the evolutionary model of the world? What is the result of operating according to this model?
2. According to the biblical model, what is the transcendent and absolute basis for the value of every human regardless of that person's abilities, contribution, likability, and so on?
3. Why has the self-esteem movement developed? Why is it unbiblical? Why will it end in despair?
4. Where do "human rights" come from? What is the ultimate reason we should love our neighbors?
5. How does the image of God relate to what He said in Genesis 1:28–30?

5.2 MAN AND WOMAN GIVEN A TASK

THE CREATION MANDATE

If you miss the first five minutes of a long movie, you may never catch up. You'll be spending the whole film whispering to your fellow movie-watchers, "Now who was that guy?" The things that happen at the beginning of a complicated story—the characters who are introduced, the conflicts that begin—are essential for understanding that story. And the Bible is no exception.

Genesis 1 introduces a character: man. It describes this character: man made in the image of God. And it gives this character a job: fill the earth, subdue it, and have dominion over it. So there are two major theological ideas in Genesis 1:26–28 that you simply must grasp if you are to understand the rest of the story of the Bible: (1) humans are image-bearers of God, and (2) humans are rulers over God's creation.

That second theological idea is called the **Creation Mandate**. It goes like this:

> God said to them, "Be fruitful and multiply and fill the earth and subdue it, and have dominion over the fish of the sea and over the birds of the heavens and over every living thing that moves on the earth." (Gen. 1:28)

These are foundational divine commands for all humanity, and they have never been taken away.

MANDATE PART 1: FILL

There are two parts to the Creation Mandate in Genesis 1:28. The first is, "Be fruitful and multiply and fill the earth." In other words, mushroom and move. Have babies and settle new territory. This first part of the mandate itself divides into three imperatives:

- The command to "be fruitful" is, in one sense, a command to be like God. God creates; humans procreate. Animals do this instinctually (they received this blessing, too, in Genesis 1:22), but men and women are privileged to do it purposefully. And enjoyably—sex was not invented by Satan. (As C. S. Lewis pointed out in *The Screwtape Letters*, no pleasures were.)
- The command and ability to "multiply" were given to the animals also (Gen. 1:22), but animals aren't very good at math. No dingo in Australia knows whether the dingo population has risen or fallen in the previous century. But humans can count; we can both enjoy and obey this command to increase in number.
- And mankind can navigate. We can know whether or not we are spreading out to "fill the earth." This third imperative seems to be the logical result—and the divinely intended purpose—of the other two. The earth is a big place, and a varied place. None of us knows quite what the world was like before sin and before the Flood, but we have no reason to believe that the planet was somehow smaller. Filling it would take Adam and his descendants a long time. But that was God's command.

And it still is. God's basic intent for mankind is still to increase in number and fill up the good planet He gave us. It is true that after the Fall, some men and women are called to singleness (1 Cor. 7:17, 32–35), and some couples are incapable of having children (Gen. 29:31). God also stops short of specifying a required number of children for a married woman. Nonetheless, to be what sociologists call a "DINK" ("Double Income, No Kids"; a husband and wife who refuse to have children) is

WHAT TO EXPECT WHEN NO ONE'S EXPECTING

Thomas Malthus (1766–1834) was perhaps the first major modern demographer to raise the fear of overpopulation. Similar fears impacted American culture in a big way with the 1968 release of Stanford professor Paul Ehrlich's influential book *The Population Bomb*, which predicted that "in the 1970s hundreds of millions of people will starve to death" if world population wasn't kept in check. But Jonathan V. Last, author of the 2013 book *What to Expect When No One's Expecting*, argues that the population bomb never exploded and that Ehrlich's book was "one of the most spectacularly foolish books ever published."[19] Ehrlich managed to raise the alarm about overpopulation at the precise moment when birthrates plummeted worldwide. In the United States, this drop coincided with the wide availability of the birth control pill.[20] Worldwide, babies are now being born at just above "replacement rate," the rate necessary to hold populations steady. But many developed nations—notably Japan, Germany, South Korea, Greece, and Italy—have extremely low birthrates, lower even than China, which has a legally enforced one-child policy.[21] They're so low that, unless things change dramatically, those countries will decrease drastically in population, with economic and social consequences that are hard to predict.[22]

to live contrary to God's command—and His blessing, as we'll see. God has told His image-bearers to spread out over the planet He gave us. This command means something for your future *and* for your present: prepare now to be a good spouse and parent someday. It is probably what you're called to, even if it seems far away at the moment.

MANDATE PART 2: SUBDUE

Many people in the West are so worried about population growth that they're willing to nix the first half of the Creation Mandate. Influential American scientist Nina Fedoroff told BBC news, for example, "There are probably already too many people on the planet."[23] But in the same interview she inadvertently appealed to the Bible's answer to that apparent problem: the second half of the Creation Mandate. "We're going to need a lot of inventiveness about how we use water and grow crops," she said. Filling the earth and having dominion over it work in tandem.

Not all the earth is well suited for human habitation (scientists still don't know how human life holds on in northern Minnesota). And that's where the second part of the Creation Mandate comes in: "Subdue [the earth] and have dominion . . . over every living thing that moves on the earth."

> "FULFILLING THE CREATION MANDATE INVOLVES PRESSING GOD'S WORLD TOWARD ITS IDEAL AND MAXIMIZING THE WORLD'S USEFULNESS."[24]
>
> —BRYAN SMITH

Some Bible readers assume this just means that humans have authority over animals—we can domesticate oxen for farm work and keep cats as pets (cats only *think* they have dominion). And that's part of the truth. But note two other things the passage says: we're supposed to have dominion over "the birds of the air" and, according to 1:26, over "all the earth."

Dominion over the birds of the air? How are humans supposed to do that? Fly?

Why not? The possibility has always existed, even if it took a few millennia till the Wright brothers figured it out. And flying is no harder than subduing and having dominion over "all the earth." Humans still aren't masters of the ocean depths, for example. There are marine species we know very little about. Who will our Wright brothers of deep-sea exploration be? Rich resources are still hidden all over the globe, untapped by its designated kings and queens. We have a lot of work to do because subduing means "to bring out the potential of everything in the earth so that it will be of service to human beings as they bring glory to God."[25] To subdue the earth is to press God's world toward its ideal and to maximize its usefulness for mankind. That ideal won't fully come until Christ brings it in a cataclysmic judgment, but we're still called to press toward it.

It's important to clarify here that the command to subdue isn't a license to exploit or destroy. A glorious national park like Yosemite is not a waste of space, and a fetid dump is not a "subdued" piece of ground. When Italian authorities failed to create new waste-management facilities several years ago in Naples, the streets of that iconic Italian city literally filled up with garbage.[26] That's not subduing. One of the solutions city officials found was to send 200,000 tons of trash to the Netherlands, where advanced treatment facilities recycle or incinerate all garbage rather than putting it in landfills. That's subduing.

Yosemite National Park is not a waste of space, and a fetid dump is not a "subdued" piece of ground.

But subduing and having dominion go far beyond the negative work of taking out the trash; they mean developing the world positively. Genesis 2 tells us that God put Adam in the Garden of Eden "to work it and keep it." That's the model. *Develop* the world—"work it." And *preserve* the world—"keep it." It may start with you stepping outside today and mowing your lawn. It may culminate some day with you working as a civil engineer on a city planning commission to create a beautiful, functional urban space for your family and your neighbors.

Paradise for Adam and Eve was joyous but very busy. They were blessed to go fill and rule a big planet. Said one writer, "Eden certainly is not a paradise in which man passes his time in idyllic and uninterrupted bliss with absolutely no demands on his daily schedule."[27] And Adam and Eve had to do this work while an enemy, the serpent, worked to destroy them.

TEEN DOMINION

Dominion is for teens, not just adults. However, it may not seem like that's true right now. That's because most of your dominion work is preparation. Faithfulness in today's seemingly insignificant tasks is the only way you'll ever achieve the advanced kinds of dominion that become possible as you mature.

It may not be scientific, exactly, but famous writer Malcolm Gladwell's "ten-thousand-hour" principle carries some real wisdom.[28] He has observed that true mastery of anything—from piano performance to engine repair—takes about ten thousand hours of practice. That's four hours a day, six days a week, for eight years.

Some five-year-olds know exactly what vocation taking "dominion" will mean for them and get their ten thousand hours in by age ten, and they're playing circles around other pianists or point guards their age. Or, like fifteen-year-old Flynn McGarry, they're cooking incredible gourmet meals and charging $160 a plate for them—and then getting profiled on the national news.[29]

But Flynn had to work fifteen-hour days at age twelve to accomplish this feat. And he still has a lot to learn. Flynn is a creative chef who has pushed the culinary arts to a higher level, but he made national news precisely because he's an exception. It usually takes many more years for someone to achieve what Flynn has.

And that's OK. God doesn't gift everyone to be a phenom. If you're not sure how to take dominion, you can start by subduing your locker, your homework, and your daily chores. Then you'll have some space to grow into the role God has called you to fill.

Dominion is an exciting task that blossoms into all the major vocations you can think of—forestry, scholarship, politics, graphic design, business. And God has never taken His Creation Mandate away. Your dad and mom are probably obeying it right now, and so are you as you prepare for whatever calling God has on your life.

A BLESSING IN DISGUISE

The divine command to fill the earth may seem like a burden to people who don't want to sacrifice time and income opportunities to bring children into the world. The command to subdue the earth may seem arrogant to people who believe humans are just successful primates. But there's something left out of the Creation Mandate that might help change their view. Three little words that come before the commands to fill, subdue, and have dominion. Those words are, "God blessed them." God gave us the glorious tasks of the Creation Mandate as a *blessing*.

Think of it like this: when you say, "Have a great day! Do well on your test!" you are, in a grammatical sense, issuing commands. God did the same in the Creation Mandate. *Fill* and *subdue* are both imperative verbs. But when you say, "Have a great day!" you don't really mean it as a command to be obeyed but as a wish, a blessing to be enjoyed.

This blessing, a blessing all mankind receives, explains why people who don't even believe in God end up living out His Creation Mandate anyway. Some people who care nothing for their Creator still develop incredible skills in astrophysics, architecture, athletics, and the arts. Everyone is an image-bearer blessed with the ability to rule over God's world. The things mankind can do with the raw materials of our planet are utterly astounding, from the ancient pyramids to genome sequencing, from Herod's temple to today's computers. God blessed His image-bearers to be exceptional subduers, powerful kings and queens. You're called to do eternally enriching and satisfying work.

Because we are fallen, however, so is the way we exercise dominion. Astrophysical calculations are sometimes mistaken; architectural choices are sometimes ugly; athletics can become an idol; art can be blasphemous. Some odd and bitter person could say to you, "I refuse to have a nice day no matter what you say!" In fact, there are many people who live against the grain of God's blessings. They pointedly refuse to marry or bear children. They throw all their potential for productive work into a hole and do nothing to preserve and develop God's creation.

THINKING IT THROUGH 5.2

1. What two major theological ideas are introduced in Genesis 1:26–28, foundational for the rest of the Bible's metanarrative?
2. Identify and explain the two parts of the Creation Mandate.
3. How do fallen humans rebel against both parts of the Creation Mandate?
4. In what way is the Creation Mandate a blessing?
5. How can you, at the present time, get involved in exercising dominion over the earth?

5.3 MAN AND WOMAN CREATING AND CULTIVATING

The food you eat is one of the most obvious results of human dominion. In ancient times, most people ate whatever was in season, ate it all season, and maybe even ate it without seasoning.[30] But the incredibly varied food on your table today has probably traveled from multiple climates and time zones. And it comes from multiple sources: you eat meat or cheese from kinds of animals that had to be domesticated by enterprising farmers many centuries ago. Those farmers also had to figure out that oxen could pull plows, but lions couldn't. And have you ever stopped to think that even the plants you eat—wheat, lettuce, bananas—had to be "subdued" by people? Noah didn't step off the ark into a cultivated orchard. Humanity has had to discover which plants could be grown on purpose and which among those were worth growing. In fact, one of the reasons certain cultures have developed further than others may be that they happened to find themselves in parts of the world where crop yields allowed many people to leave farming behind and form cities.[31]

ALL FOOD AS ETHNIC FOOD

People in cities still need to eat, of course. Cities, therefore, are impossible without the amazing work of dominion we call the "grocery store." Think of the store where your own family shops. Think of all the foods it contains. You've probably even got a whole aisle full of exotic foods; the sign over it reads, "Ethnic Food." There you'll see mysterious cans and jars with Arabic and Hindi labels, food with unfamiliar tastes and origins.

There's another lesson about dominion in that aisle—because why aren't the other aisles at the store called "Ethnic Food"? Don't the foods in those aisles come from a particular culture? Or are they just normal?[32] Believe it: to many of the people in this world, American hot dogs and peanut butter are not normal. They are just as ethnic (and perhaps just as inedible) as super-spicy Thai curry is to you. All food is ethnic. Most of it comes from a different ***ethnos*** than yours—a different people-group or nation.

The point of connecting dominion to the ethnic foods in your local store is this—the work of subduing and having dominion is done in groups.[33] And we call these groups "cultures." A **culture**, as we touched on briefly at the end of Chapter 1, is what a particular group of people make of the world. Those people tend to live near each other and, typically, speak the same language. They tend to share broad agreement about how to make something of this world—in two senses. (1) They take the raw materials of the world and make the same kinds of food, the same kinds of clothes, the same kinds of tools and art and music. (2) They also tend to see the world in the same way. What they make of it—in the sense of processing it or understanding it—looks similar across the culture. Remember that one of the three components of every worldview is action. Culture is a worldview in action within a group.

THE CREATION MANDATE AND CULTURE

Culture is good. It's part of God's design. It's one of the seeds in God's creation that He intended to grow into great trees. You can see this at the end of the Bible's story, as we've already noted. There we're told that "the glory and honor of the nations" is brought into the new Jerusalem (Rev. 21:26). The Bible doesn't spell out what that means in detail, but the glory and honor of nations (like Egypt and Assyria, which Isaiah 19 says will be in the new earth) would have to include cultural products—just like the glory and honor of the French today would have to include their cuisine.

Various future nations might bring beautiful clothing, profound novels, or spicy curry into the new earth. (Hot dogs won't make it; there will be no death.) The last two chapters of Revelation speak of "nations" and "kings" as ongoing realities. Men and women "from every tribe and language and people and nation" will praise God at the end of time (Rev. 5:9). The point is that the nations don't go away in the eternal state, and nations always have cultures.

But it's not just the end of the Bible's story that reveals the value God places on culture. It's also the beginning. As the Garden of Eden is the seed of future cities, so the Creation Mandate is the seed that blossoms into multiple cultures. As soon as you start trying to live out the blessing of the Creation Mandate, you will start creating culture. The Creation Mandate is a command to create and cultivate our world: it's a command to build culture.

Imagine you are one of Adam's grandsons. As you grow up, your grandfather tells you about God's original blessing encouraging you to fill, subdue, and have dominion. The enormity of the project only adds to your excitement. There are precious secrets out there ready for you to find, like music and metallurgy* (whose discoverers are mentioned in Genesis 4:21–22). So along with your brothers and sisters and aunts and uncles, you work. You move some distance from your parents, subdue a plot of ground, and wrench as much bread out of it as you can by the sweat of your brow (Gen. 3:19).

metallurgy: *the study of metals and the technology for extracting them from ore to be made into useful objects*

You start to find real success after you manage to divert a nearby brook to irrigate your fields. You start to produce surplus grain—grain that your relatives across the ridge, who have no brook, are willing to barter for (they've got metal). But you can't get the grain to them without a cart, and you can't cart it to them without a bridge over that brook. So you work together with your relatives to build what you all need to facilitate trade.

A city begins to develop as more subsistence farmers adopt your irrigation practices and have food surpluses. A form of currency is invented and achieves widespread use. You gain enough of it to establish yourself within the city, and soon you become a leader there. The conflicts among various clans have to be adjudicated*, and someone has to pay for and manage the upkeep of roads and bridges the whole community uses—so a government is formed.

adjudicated: *judged, resolved, decided, arbitrated*

"Thousands of years after Genesis was written, we can see in a way its first readers could never have imagined just how much capacity . . . human image bearers had to fill the earth—just how much power was ultimately available to them, coiled in the physical elements' chemical and nuclear bonds, and emerging from the incredible complexity of the human mind and the fecundity [fruitfulness] of human culture." [34]

—ANDY CROUCH

This is all happening twenty valleys away too. And eighty. Over time whole nations develop, with their own foods, their own customs, their own architectural and artistic styles, their own folk songs, their own distinct clothing and pottery—their own

THE CREATION MANDATE AND THE GREAT COMMISSION

Aren't Christians left on earth for the sole purpose of evangelizing non-Christians? Wasn't that Christ's **Great Commission** to His disciples? And doesn't that supersede (replace) the Creation Mandate? The simple answer to all those questions is "No." Look at what Jesus actually said. He said, "Go . . . and make disciples of all nations, baptizing them . . . teaching them to observe all that I have commanded you" (Matt. 28:18–20). The good news about Jesus' death for human sin and resurrection to life isn't the only message Jesus commands His followers to share with the world. We're supposed to "make disciples," to teach people to do everything He's said—and He said that "not an iota, not a dot, will pass" from the Old Testament until all is fulfilled (Matt. 5:18). And that includes the Creation Mandate. Jesus didn't replace Genesis 1:28. Of course, if we help people build bridges and wells but fail to give them the gospel, we're disobedient to the Great Commission. People's relationships with God are vastly more important than what they eat for dinner, though both are important. One of the reasons Jesus gave the Great Commission was to free people to obey the Creation Mandate. The two are not enemies; they are laws given by the same King.

cultures. "Culture," says author Andy Crouch, is "the name for our relentless, restless human effort to take the world as it's given to us and make something else."[35] Different groups of people make different "something elses," but all humans make culture.

THE HORIZONS OF THE POSSIBLE

Crouch probes the Bible's teaching on culture with real insight, and his first chapter in *Culture Making* he entitled "The Horizons of the Possible." That's because culture, he points out, has a powerful effect on what any human being can do in obedience to the Creation Mandate. The culture you were born into makes some things possible and other things impossible, or nearly so.

It's now possible, for example, to have a blog—a personal internet page where you write regular entries for all to read. In the whole history of the world, blogs were impossible until about the year 2000. Now anyone can publish blog posts, attract a following, sell advertising, and maybe even write full-time. Blogs have changed Western culture, introducing some amazing possibilities that didn't exist when your parents were born.

We're used to thinking about what new cultural products—especially those we call "technology"—make possible, but we rarely stop to ask what they make impossible or difficult. But new features of culture always take away as well as give. Blogging, for example, makes it more difficult to squelch rumors. And it's impossible now for major media outlets to command the following they used to have. Newspapers and network TV used to be the only significant sources for major breaking news. Now there are millions of sources, some high quality and many not.

Or take porn. It used to take real effort to find it. Now, thanks to technology, it takes effort not to. Or take phones. Cellphones, especially, make it difficult to live and work without interruption. They make it difficult to escape other people's demands and have quiet, undistracted time with God or a good book. They make it difficult to make firm plans with friends—friends know they can always text you and tell you they're running thirty minutes behind, so you'll need to wait for them. Cellphones bring many benefits and can be used wisely for God's glory, but they show that not all aspects of culture in this fallen world are good. "The bad part of culture" is, in fact, an accurate definition of that bad thing the New Testament calls "the world" (1 John 2:15–17).[36] We sinners can always find a way to twist good things for sinful purposes.

CULTIVATING AND CREATING

It's precisely because of the power of culture—for bad or good—that Christians should pay attention to it. And as one helpful author said, "The way to change culture is to make more of it."[37] Yes, in this fallen world, change must often include getting rid of some element of a particular culture. But generally it needs to be replaced with something else. So one key way to change the culture of your school is to add something that wasn't there before. Maybe just genuine love for the uncool. Or maybe tangible cultural "goods" like a new school logo, or a bake sale, or a charity bike race.

You might even create a new "institution" which can attempt to do more lasting good, like making that bake sale and bike race annual events. Think what personal growth and what unity could take place in your school if you cooperated to reach goals of fundraising, evangelism, or community service. That could change the culture of interactions in the lunchroom pretty fast. Your creativity, one of the most Godlike things about you, has power to improve your cultural world.

But you need to be careful not to become arrogant and impatient. The things God put within your power to do are important, but modest. Think again of how God described Adam's job: He put Adam in the Garden of Eden "to work it and keep it" (Gen. 2:15). *Develop* it and *preserve* it. Create and cultivate. And that's still your job with whatever aspect of this world God hands you. You can't develop if you don't preserve. There's simply no way you could start over, for example, with music. It's too late. You've already inherited a musical tradition—a tonal scale, a notational system, a collection of instruments, a huge number of brilliant compositions for orchestra, choir, string quartet, and so on. Your job is to preserve whatever is true and good and beautiful in the tradition of whichever academic or cultural discipline God calls you to, and then work to develop it.

And why would you want to start over with Western music when the existing structures provide so much room for rich development? Some of the most beautiful and innovative music today may actually be that of such composers as Arvo Pärt of Estonia and John Tavener of England, artists who have purposefully reached deep into musical tradition to write pieces of astonishingly fresh contemporary power.

Every scale you play in music practice—on an instrument you didn't invent, using a scale that not all cultures use—is one step toward preserving a particular tradition of music. Your teacher is handing it to you, as it was handed to her. Only if you preserve this tradition can you add to it.

The opposite of preserving and developing can be seen in composers such as John Cage, who wrote the (in)famous *4'33"*, usually called "Four Minutes Thirty-Three Seconds of Silence." Cage also wrote "aleatoric" (or chance-driven) music that sounds like a cacophony of random sounds with no identifiable melody or structure. Cage was purposefully turning the Western musical tradition backwards and blasting it to bits.[38] He was eliminating music's good and beautiful development. He was, therefore, going against the grain of the Creation Mandate.[39]

Far from limiting one's freedom, it's actually structure and order that provide space for creativity to flourish—in music, in sports, in business, in medicine, in woodworking, in homemaking, in automotive engineering, in whatever dominion work you find yourself called to do. Creativity is possible because of who we are—God's image-bearers—and because of the structured world God gave us to subdue.[40]

DOMINION AND CULTURE

Humans have a nature given by God and a mandate from the same source. Take away Genesis 1, and we don't know who we are. Without Genesis, men and women have no ultimate identity. We don't know if we're accidental groupings of carbon atoms who only think we can think. We have no firm, ultimate foundation for human rights and social justice. We also have no purpose, no job to do, and no way to know whether our lives were spent well or wasted. We don't know if culture is good or bad. We don't even know if we're allowed to eat hot dogs.

But armed with God's original marching orders for mankind, you can know your place in the world. You don't have to know that your toddler will one day work for the woman who finds a cure for cancer. You just need to stay faithful filling the earth and teach the little image-bearers God gives you. You don't have to know that your job teaching autistic kids to communicate is going to result in important progress for the whole profession or that your thirty-seventh student will become a powerful Christian evangelist. You just need to take dominion over your little sector of the world and to put all the gifts of an image-bearer into that daily work.

Found your life on the foundational chapter of Scripture, Genesis 1. There you will find out who you are by finding out who you're imaging. You'll find your place in God's universe. You'll find your prime directive.

THINKING IT THROUGH 5.3

1. Explain how the formation of a cultural identity occurs.
2. As soon as you start trying to live out the blessing of the Creation Mandate, what will you find yourself doing?
3. How does the Great Commission enable people to better carry out the Creation Mandate?
4. Explain how Christians ought to involve themselves in a culture that is a mixture of both good and bad elements.
5. Name three ways your own culture affects the "horizons of the possible" for you.

5 CHAPTER REVIEW

TERMS TO REMEMBER

subdue/dominion
image of God
Creation Mandate
ethnos
culture
Great Commission

Scripture Memory

Genesis 1:26–28

Making Connections

1. What likenesses exist between humans and the God they image?
2. Rather than being based on survival of the fittest, what must human rights, social justice, and the worth of others be based on?
3. If you are to understand the rest of the story of the Bible, what two major theological ideas from Genesis 1:26–28 must you understand?
4. What necessarily results from groups of people carrying out the commands of the Creation Mandate?

Developing Skills in Apologetics and Worldview

5. How does the Christian worldview support human value in a world in which human life is often expendable—whether in school shootings or terrorist acts?
6. If your school is filled with cliques, how could you contribute to positive change in a way that honors all God's image-bearers?

Examining Assumptions and Evidence

7. Why do people cease to value others appropriately when the image of God is eliminated from their thinking?
8. Why can't you be liberated by simply following your own heart and being true to yourself? Why does the self-esteem movement fail to solve your need for confidence, value, and fulfillment?
9. Explain from Scripture why the Creation Mandate can also be called the Creation Blessing.
10. Why shouldn't the task of the Great Commission be viewed as a contradiction, replacement, or competitor with the task of the Creation Mandate?

Becoming a Creative Cultivator

11. Create a log that identifies and describes cultural activities you may already be involved in that positively contribute to the well-being of others. List one more cultural activity you could do that would make positive contributions to your school, church, home, or community.

Chapter Six EVERYTHING GOD MADE WAS VERY GOOD

The Lord by wisdom founded the earth; by understanding he established the heavens.

Scripture Memory
Proverbs 3:19

6.1 AND GOD SAW THAT IT WAS GOOD

If you've ever created something you've been justifiably proud of (not sinfully proud of, but proud in that elusive *good* sense), you know that there's no other feeling quite like it. To sit back and look at a design you created or a speech you delivered or a project you completed or a car you fixed or a garden you planned or a meal you crafted, and to know *I made something good*—there's a particular kind of satisfaction there you just don't get anywhere else. To exercise your creative powers and make something new and useful and beautiful and true, for yourself and your neighbor, is to be like God as only an image-bearer can be. When you wake up the next morning, the first thing you want to do is go look at your creation.

VERY GOOD

After the first five days of the creation week, God looked at the work He'd done up to that point, and "God saw that it was good" (Gen. 1:21). Light (day 1), sky (day 2), land and plants (day 3), sun, moon, and stars (day 4), and birds and fish (day 5)—all good. And then on the sixth day, after sculpting His self-portrait, God is extra pleased. "God saw everything that he had made, and behold, it was very good" (1:31).

Nothing in God's original creation was out of place; nothing was lacking. When God pronounced His creation "very good," it was truly good, morally good. Brand new in all the best ways. (There was one respect in which God's world wasn't like new, of course. He did create it with the appearance of age. There's no other way to create a grown tree, elephant, or man.)

There was only one exception to the creation's goodness, one thing in all of God's creation that, as He Himself said, was "not good," and that was that the man was alone (Gen. 2:18). But we shouldn't think this loneliness was an oversight on God's part, a mistake. Creating woman was something God intended to do all along. In any case, God fixed this one "problem" in creation very quickly and gave Adam a wife. God started us with a clean and beautiful slate. He made this world very good. The Fall didn't make a messy world worse; the Fall twisted a perfect world.

VERY VALUABLE

"God does not make junk," says one theologian, "and we dishonor the Creator if we take a negative view of the work of his hands when he himself takes such a positive view." God valued His creation so much that "he refused to scrap it when mankind spoiled it, but determined instead, at the cost of his Son's life, to make it new and good again." Not only does God not make junk, but "he does not junk what he has made."[1]

This is so true that even after the Fall of Adam, when the whole world was plunged into "bondage to corruption" (Rom. 8:21), the apostle Paul could give the following counsel to the young pastor Timothy:

> Everything created by God is good, and nothing is to be rejected if it is received with thanksgiving, for it is made holy by the word of God and prayer. (1 Tim. 4:4–5)

That doesn't mean that everything humans do with what God created is good. In fact, the goodness of God's creation often gets twisted and obscured in this fallen world. But it's still there; it never goes away. "Everything created by God *is* good," Paul said—not "*was* good." Like an inflatable beach ball shoved below the surface of a pool, you can suppress the goodness of creation for a while, but it always struggles to the surface. When Paul gave that counsel to Timothy, he was talking specifically about food. Like other things God created as good, food can be used for evil purposes: gluttons make food a god, and so sometimes (in a different way) do foodies.* Humans and human cultures can twist God's good gifts in evil ways, but those gifts are still good. Poppy seeds can be used to make deadly, addictive heroin—or killer lemon muffins.

foodie: *someone with a special interest in food; a gourmet, an epicure*

WHOSE FAULT IS EVIL?

Pointing out that all created things were originally good seems so simple and obvious. But it's crucial to mention it anyway because people are always trying to pin the blame for the world's problems on something other than their own insurrection.* And their chosen whipping boy* is generally something God made. Ultimately, then, they're blaming God.

insurrection: *organized rebellion against a rightful authority*

whipping boy: *an innocent party who bears the punishment for someone else's sin*

Let's look at three things God created that people sometimes blame for the problems in our world: the body, authority, and emotions.

Blaming the Body

Some people blame the body. A student at a Christian university once came to see his theology professor complaining that multiple health problems were making it difficult for him to study, and he wanted help discovering the spiritual source of those problems.

When the professor probed a little, it didn't take long to find out that the guy was consuming lots of junk food, getting little rest, and getting no exercise. The learned Bible scholar suggested to the young man that he needed a good diet, sufficient sleep, and regular physical activity.

The student was a little miffed; he was expecting a more theological answer. Anyway, he told his teacher, someday he'd get rid of his body when he died, so why bother taking care of it now?[2]

> ***"WE ARE NOT MERELY PASSENGERS RIDING AROUND IN SKIN-TIGHT RACECARS; WE ARE OUR BODIES. THEY EMBODY US."***[3]
>
> —FREDERICA MATHEWES-GREENE

The body isn't really you; it's just a skin-and-bone cage the real you is stuck in temporarily—that's the view assumed by a lot of people, even some Christians. And some people go one step further. They start saying that the cage itself is evil. The ancient Gnostics actually hated the body; they felt that "the divine spark of the human soul must be freed from the material constraints of the world in order to attain salvation and unity" with God.[4]

You could possibly come away from the New Testament with the mistaken idea that the body is evil—Paul does warn over and over again about the evil power of the "flesh." He even asks in Romans, after complaining bitterly about his sinfulness, "Who will deliver me from this body of death?" (7:24).

But Paul's answer is Christ—*and Christ has a body*. The teaching of the Bible is not that when we reach heaven we'll leave our bodies forever behind. The Christian hope is that "the dead will be raised imperishable" and that "this mortal body [will] put on immortality" (1 Cor. 15:52–53). Christ does not deliver us from our sinful bodies into a foggy world of floating spirits; He gives us our bodies back, just like He got His back—renewed, restored, transformed, perfect. When Paul speaks of "the flesh," he's talking about the sinful part of us, not our physical bodies. The human body is good. The Son of God Himself has one. You can't blame the problems in the world on the fact that people have bodies. Our bodies are deeply affected by the Fall, but they're not evil; they were created good and still are.

Blaming Authority

Sometimes authority and power get blamed for the world's predicament.* American culture, in particular, is suspicious of authority. Because of extreme individualism, says one Christian sociologist, there is "widespread American distrust of the government and other institutions of authority." This distrust, he says, is "incessantly depicted in television and movies, particularly those aimed at youth."[5] And this distrust has only increased with time.

predicament: *a difficult and unpleasant situation*

So, for example, the postwar-era Superman of the 1950s famously fought for "truth, justice, and the American way!"[6] But now, after the anti-authoritarian 1960s, it would be impossible for Superman to utter that phrase without a snicker coming from somewhere. The 1978 version of Lois Lane, for example, wisecracked after Superman used the phrase, "You're going to end up fighting every elected official in this country!" One of the most popular (and hyperviolent) action series of the 2000s, the Bourne trilogy, followed the odyssey of a CIA agent who discovers that his own government has betrayed him since his earliest days in their employ. This isn't to say that anti-authoritarian cynicism was nonexistent before the sixties, or that blind patriotism (*"My country can do no wrong"*) doesn't exist today. Humanity swings from one error to another. It's just to say that there's an overall antiauthoritarian tendency in US culture that you won't necessarily see in other cultures. (In fact, in some cultures, authority is revered to an unhealthy degree.)

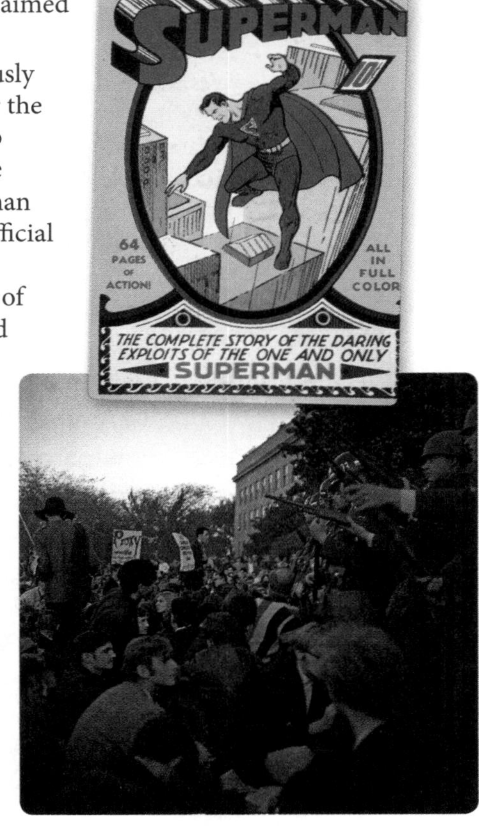

The Superman of the 1950s fought for "truth, justice, and the American way." But after the anti-authoritarian 1960s, no one can say that phrase without a snicker coming from somewhere.

But God put man and woman in authority over creation—and over their children (Gen. 1:28; Exod. 20:12). Think of the power mothers and fathers have over their kids. They could do any number of cruel things to them, especially when they're small, without anyone knowing (tragically, some parents do—this is a reason why authority itself gets a bad rap). If "absolute power corrupts absolutely," then why do the great majority of parents not treat their little kids with cruelty? Why, instead, do they sacrifice so much—like sleep, money, and time?

Because love turns authority into what it was created to be—a powerful force for good. As one author put it, "Love transfigures power. Absolute love transfigures absolute power. And power transfigured by love is the power that made and saves the world."[7] Authority is a good thing God created. Paul goes as far as to say, "There is no authority except from God, and those that exist have been instituted by God" (Rom. 13:1). You can't pin the blame for human problems on something God made *good*. If you do, you're blaming God.

Blaming Emotion

Another thing God made that sometimes gets blamed for all the trouble we're in is emotions. But God didn't just make emotions; He has them. The big differences between God's emotions and the human emotions patterned after them are that (1) no one can make God feel something He doesn't want to feel[8] and (2) God's emotions aren't tied up with a physical body like ours are. But even given these differences, we can see God's emotions everywhere in Scripture. He loves (John 3:16; 1 John 4:8), He hates (Ps. 5:5; Rom. 9:13), He's angry (Ps. 7:11), He's sad (Gen. 6:6). It's impossible to imagine a *person* who doesn't have any feelings whatsoever. We are all portraits of God, after all.

And yet feelings are very commonly blamed for the troubles in our world. Hans Rosling, a prominent Swedish doctor and professor of international health, told *The Economist* magazine, for example,

> We can eradicate poverty, we can solve the energy and the climate issues but we have to make the right investments. . . . I know a good world is possible *if we leave emotion aside and just work analytically.*[9]

Dr. Rosling's snubbing of emotion is not an isolated instance in the Enlightened West. It's not uncommon for Western people—especially in discussions believed to be within the realm of science—to talk as if emotion is flawed and unreliable while reason is not. But as one former employee of an abortion clinic has found out (see sidebar below), your gut reaction might be right and your careful rationalizations may be wrong.[10] Reason and emotion are both fundamentally good, and yet both are twisted by the Fall.

Interestingly enough, *The Economist* saw a contradiction in Dr. Rosling's negative view of emotions. The article noted,

> [Dr. Rosling's] ability to set aside his own emotions remains to be demonstrated. Like Florence Nightingale before him, what gives his work its persuasive force is not just rock-solid data . . . but his personal passion and enthusiasm.[10]

EMOTION CAN LEAD TO TRUTH

Abby Johnson says she always had a strong desire to help needy women. This desire led her to Planned Parenthood, the nation's largest abortion provider. But her life was radically changed one day when she was brought in to assist with an abortion procedure. Her website says that she "watched in horror as a 13-week baby fought [for], and ultimately lost, its life at the hand of the abortionist."[11]

This emotional experience led to "the full realization of what abortion was." She became "desperate and confused"—and soon, thankfully, she left Planned Parenthood and dedicated her life to the pro-life cause.[12]

The Bible provides the lenses necessary to see clearly what happened to Abby: her God-given conscience was violated (Rom. 2:14–15), and her emotional horror was the sign. Whatever her reasons for defending abortion in the past, it became clear to her that those were rationalizations obscuring the truth. Her God-given emotion actually led her back to the light.

Earthly authority and emotions were created, and created good, by God Himself. If either of them were evil, we would have no Dr. Roslings. He is, in fact, a scientific *authority* driven by a deep *passion* to improve the world, to maximize its usefulness for mankind. Authority and emotion are fundamentally good creations of God. No one should blame the good things God made for the mess we're all in.

HUMAN RELIGIOUS MUTINY

Other worldviews have blamed rationality or other good things God created. "All of these have been scapegoats,"* says worldview thinker Al Wolters, "that have drawn attention away from the real root of the trouble, human religious mutiny* against the Creator and his laws for the world."[13]

scapegoat: *an innocent party who takes the blame for some sin*

mutiny: *rebellion against one's rightful authority*

That Creator, it's true, gave Adam and Eve a creation that was undeveloped. Man was given the job to "subdue" it to better suit his needs (the Creation Mandate). In this sense, much of the good of creation was potential, not yet actual. But on that glorious sixth creation day "when the morning stars sang together and all the sons of God shouted for joy" (Job 38:7), when the world stood like an unopened present for God's second son, there was nothing deficient about the creation. When God handed the earth to Adam, it was everything a perfect Creator wanted it to be.

THINKING IT THROUGH 6.1

1. How did God assess His own creative work when He finished? What does this imply?
2. After the Fall, does God's creation become inherently evil? Why or why not?
3. Why do people tend to blame things such as the body, authority, or emotions for the world's problems?
4. Why aren't the body, authority, and emotions to blame for the world's problems? What is to blame?
5. Why might some people blame money, for example, as the source of evil in the world? What is wrong with such blame?

6.2 LAWS OF NATURE AND CREATIONAL NORMS

"Did God make the moon, kids?"

All the boys and girls in the Sunday school class shout "YES!" holding out the vowel for as long as they can.

"How do you know?" says the teacher, who usually teaches the high school class. The kids don't have any idea, but they've been in church long enough to catch on that the answer to most questions is either "Jesus" or "the Bible." Hailey quickly raises her kindergarten-sized hand and opts for the latter. "Right!" says the teacher. "The Bible says it right here in Genesis 1—God made the 'lesser light to rule the night.'"

"Did God make Saturn, kids?" Not all of them have heard of Saturn, so the chorus of yeses is not quite as loud this time. "How do you know?" asks the teacher. Hailey, who is very bright, figures she'll go for "the Bible" again. "Right!" says the teacher. "Genesis 1 says that God made the 'lights in the expanse of the heavens,' and that would have to include the planet Saturn."

"Did God make gravity, kids?" A few of the kids think she said "gravy," so they murmur, a little tentatively, "Nooo." (*Moms* make gravy, obviously.) Only Hailey says, "YES," but she's just going on her years of Sunday school instinct. The rest of the kids are quiet. "Right, Hailey!" says the teacher. "Genesis doesn't just tell us the things God made, but it tells us the jobs those things are supposed to do—like the sun ruling the day and the moon ruling the night. And those things are impossible without what we've come to call gravity. So God made gravity."

The kids are getting fidgety. But the teacher isn't picking up the cues. "Did God make marriage?" A feeble "yes" comes from Hailey, her instincts faltering. "Yes, God made marriage," the teacher says, "because God called humans to do jobs just like the sun and moon. He told them to fill the earth—and marriage is the first step God intends for that filling to be done."

The bored boys in the back are starting to poke one another, but the teacher goes on. "Did God make government?" Silence. The kids are lost. This is not a question for the five-year-old class.

LAWS OF NATURE

Saturn and the moon are obviously God's creations. Gravity is, too, once you understand how Saturn and the moon operate. Gravity is a "law of nature." Even the naughty boys in Sunday school know this. Or at least they find out when, in the deep devotion to Superman common to boys their age, they don a red cape and attempt to fly off the top of the living room couch. Every Superman-wannabe wearing a cast is testimony to the simple fact that gravity is an utterly unbreakable law.

Thus says the Lord, who gives the sun for light by day and the fixed order of the moon and the stars for light by night, who stirs up the sea so that its waves roar— the Lord of hosts is his name: "If this fixed order departs from before me, declares the Lord, then shall the offspring of Israel cease from being a nation before me forever."

—JEREMIAH 31:35–36

But try as you might, you will never find a Bible verse teaching little kids to obey the law of gravity. The Bible never says we can't fly faster than a speeding bullet or leap tall buildings in a single bound.

Even so, it's right to use the word *laws* when talking about the laws of gravity, of motion, or of thermodynamics—all the "constants" described by the tools of science. It's right to use the word *laws* because, like all laws, they are issued by a lawgiver. We don't know those scientific laws like God knows them; since we don't have any Scripture that tells us exactly how they operate, our understanding will always be limited, subject to revision. But we do know that God's speech continually upholds the order we see around us. The apostle Peter points out not only that "the earth was formed . . . by the word of God" but that "by the same word the heavens and earth that now exist are . . . being kept" (2 Pet. 3:5–7). And Paul says that in Christ "all things hold together" (Col. 1:17). God through Christ actively commands the universe to act the way it does, all day every day. God's law ordains and upholds the orbits of planets and the orbits of electrons. God wouldn't have to do anything, exactly, to destroy the universe. He could merely relax His hands and let it fall.

Nothing (and nobody) disobeys the **laws of nature**. Soccer balls always come back down no matter how hard you kick them into the air. Water always boils at the same temperature at a given height above sea level. Animals always follow their instincts (even though, as we'll see in Unit 3 on the fall of mankind, animals have been damaged by human sin). Seasons always come and go (Gen. 8:22). God upholds all these laws of nature by His personal word. These laws are so certain that the King of the Universe Himself swears by them (Jer. 31:35–36).

CREATIONAL NORMS

So God didn't just make stuff, physical objects. He also made the laws that govern those objects without fail. Including human beings. And yet both experience and (more importantly) Scripture demonstrate that the laws of nature aren't the only divine laws governing humans.

There are other divine laws that, unlike gravity, are indeed breakable. At least by humans. We are God's responsible creatures. We can make choices, and quite often (after Adam's Fall) we have all chosen to break the laws God gives us freedom to break.

God's word governs creation in two different ways, then, and it will be helpful for us to add a label for the laws we are responsible to follow. We'll use the term ***creational norms*** because these norms have been present since creation. A truly Christian worldview recognizes that God put all the stuff He made into a *created order*. He made creational norms—divine laws that govern the way human individuals and cultures operate. There are right and wrong ways to fulfill your God-given earthly task, no matter what it is.

Marriage Norms

Marriage is a good example of a creational norm. Because it was instituted at creation (Gen. 2:24) and built into the way the world works, it's no surprise that marriage is an extremely important institution in virtually all human cultures.[14] But those cultures sometimes forget that marriage wasn't created by people. That's why Supreme Court justices can't reinvent it. No one can—at least not without turning marriage into something that no longer deserves the title. The way God made marriage is the standard by which all future marriages must be judged.

Jesus used this very argument when some Pharisees asked Him about divorce. They asked, "Is it lawful to divorce one's wife for any cause?" Jesus answered,

> Have you not read that he who created them from the beginning made them male and female, and said, "Therefore a man shall leave his father and his mother and hold fast to his wife, and the two shall become one flesh"? So they are no longer two but one flesh. What therefore God has joined together, let not man separate. (Matt. 19:4–6)

Jesus' words form the foundation of the scriptural argument against not just divorce but polygamy, same-sex marriage, and all other sexual sin. Humans can't create "same-sex marriage" any more than they can make "four-sided triangles" or "dry water." *One man and one woman become one for life*—that's the pattern.

Note, however, that you don't discover this norm of creation from Genesis alone. Other portions of Scripture have rich things to say about what God created marriage to be. In fact, God kept the preeminent truth about marriage as something of a secret (with hints) for thousands of years. Paul reveals that secret in his letter to the Ephesians, namely that marriage is a picture of Christ's relationship to His church (Eph. 5:31–33). This relationship is a "creational" truth because it has always been true, ever since the foundation of the world (cf. 1 Cor. 11:8–9). But it was only revealed after Christ's incarnation.* We know about creational norms from more than just Genesis.

incarnation: *Christ's taking on flesh to become human as well as divine*

Farming Norms

And we know about more than just marriage. There are other creational norms. Look, for example, at what the prophet Isaiah has to say about farming:

> Does [the farmer] who plows for sowing plow continually?
> Does he continually open and harrow his ground?
> When he has leveled its surface,
> does he not scatter dill, sow cumin,
> and put in wheat in rows
> and barley in its proper place,
> and emmer as the border?
> *For he is rightly instructed;*
> *his God teaches him.*
>
> Dill is not threshed with a threshing sledge,
> nor is a cart wheel rolled over cumin,
> but dill is beaten out with a stick,
> and cumin with a rod.
> Does one crush grain for bread?
> No, he does not thresh it forever;
> when he drives his cart wheel over it
> with his horses, he does not crush it.
> *This also comes from the Lord of hosts;*
> *he is wonderful in counsel*
> *and excellent in wisdom.* (Isa. 28:24–29)

God teaches farmers how to do their job. But the Bible doesn't have an appendix listing wheat and barley cultivation practices. It doesn't include diagrams for crop-rotation or black-and-yellow stickers saying "WARNING: Do not use threshing sledges on dill." What Isaiah is saying is that a farmer who pays careful attention to the way his seeds and soil work together is actually listening to the voice of God. He'll only know it's God's voice, of course, if he reads his Bible. But once he does, he's discovering creational norms through his work that were put there by the Creator. God built certain "best practices" into the world of farming, and He'll teach them to people who are patient enough to listen.

Economic Norms

The Bible upholds the right of private property—otherwise many laws in the Pentateuch (including "thou shalt not steal") would make no sense. Scripture also teaches accountability for one's economic decisions—see the book of Proverbs, where the field of the lazy man gets overgrown with weeds (Prov. 24:30–34; cf. 1 Tim. 5:8). Both private property and economic accountability are cornerstones of Western capitalism. But the Bible stops short of specifying which economic system is best. Nonetheless, with the light of Scripture shining on God's world, we can discover truth—even economic truth. There are economic creational norms.

As the twentieth century unfolded, it was not at all clear which of the two major economic systems would prevail. For example, North Korea became a nation in the mid-1940s when the forces of democratic capitalism* and the forces of Marxist socialism* in Russia and China divvied up the Korean peninsula. Russia and China fought the United States to a stalemate over North Korea shortly thereafter (1953). Russia soon became the first nation to launch a satellite into space (1957) and, more importantly, the first to put a human up there (1961).

democratic capitalism: *an economic system in which the free market determines the value of goods, and people elect their own leaders*

Marxist socialism: *an economic system in which government planners determine the value of goods, and leaders are not elected*

But today there's only one nation's flag on the moon.[15] By the time it got there (1969), the seeds of the USSR's destruction were already beginning to germinate. The economic and political system of the old Soviet Union finally disintegrated as the century drew to a close (1991). The Cold War ended not with a bang but a whimper.

What did the world discover about economics in the last hundred or so years? Simply put, the lesson learned was that capitalism—though distinctly imperfect itself—is a better economic system than socialism.[16] And if the world needed any more proof, the fact that Chinese communism has successfully adopted capitalism should be sufficient. So did the world discover truth? Did it find some creational norms? No one should presume that any economic system is unaffected by the Fall. Capitalism often has significant downsides: people start to think that their greed is normal and even beneficial, the desires of the market drive art and leisure even when those desires are immoral, and so on. But one thing appears clear at the moment: no economic system in the history of the world has ever delivered so much poverty-ending wealth, so much subdue-the-earth opportunity, even so much physical height and health as capitalism. North Korean defectors say that one of the most eloquent arguments for capitalism was the standard of living they glimpsed (illegally) on South Korean television. In light of almost a century of socialism's disastrous and murderous failures, it's difficult to believe that Marxism fits within the creational norms set up by the Creator of economics. Capitalism can be improved upon,[17] but socialism is not the solution. It violates too many creational norms.

Capitalism and socialism are both affected by the Fall. But a simple look at their results suggests that the former fits better with creational norms than the latter.

DISCOVERING CREATIONAL NORMS

Discovering creational norms is like spelunking.* Spelunkers normally have powerful headlights on their helmets. Without them they'll almost certainly die, so they've got to pay some attention to the functionality of their lights. But they do that when they're on the surface. When they're actually in the cave, they don't spend time looking at their lights; instead they use the light to see the "path" in front of them, to light up their surroundings.[18]

spelunking: *cave exploring*

Likewise, the psalmist wrote, "Your word is a lamp to my feet and a light to my path" (Ps. 119:105). You've got to pay some attention to your light; learn it well. But the Bible will do you little good if you never take its truths out into the real world and let them light up your surroundings. You will never find the right path unless you pay close attention to those surroundings—using the light of God's Word. This is how you gain what the book of Proverbs calls wisdom.

Wise people put light and the world together to figure out the creational norms around them. And when a wise person discovers those norms, he or she is submissive to them. It's hard work to discover, like the farmer in Isaiah 28, the creational norms related to your calling. But it's not as if the Bible is unnecessary for you to be a good farmer. The Bible is a lamp illuminating whatever you're looking at—marriage, farming, economics, government, journalism, or education.

THINKING IT THROUGH 6.2

1. What is the label we use for God's governance over the fixed order and operation of the physical objects He created?
2. What is the label we use for God's governance over the roles and responsibilities of humans carrying out their social tasks of filling and subduing the earth?
3. What are some possible examples of God's design for marriage, farming, and economics?
4. How are creational norms discovered?
5. What are some undesirable results of working contrary to God's design in marriage, farming, and economics?

6.3 THE WAY THINGS ARE SUPPOSED TO BE

Was Nolan Ryan the best baseball pitcher ever? Check his stats against other pitchers' stats. That's the standard. Did you get an A+ on your last exam? Check your answers against the answer key. That's the standard. Did we put that oil filter on the motorcycle correctly? Check what you did against the owner's manual. That's the standard.

If there are no standards, there can be no evaluation, no judgment. Not all judgments are as easy to make as those about pitchers, exams, and oil filters. But all judgment is pointless without a standard to judge by. Without a standard, it's meaningless to call something right or wrong, good or bad.

Followers of the Abrahamic religions (Christianity, Judaism, and Islam) all look to specific holy books for their standards, especially moral ones. So they have a definite idea of where their standards come from. But atheists and other people who claim no specific religion—and this is a growing group in the West[19]—also have standards. Everyone does because standards are part of a person's worldview.

A great many people in the West, however, are fuzzy on what their standards are, especially their ultimate standard. They have a vague notion that everything they believe has been scientifically proven and that their particular beliefs are normal and unobjectionable; but that's as far as they go in acknowledging their own standards.

Occasionally, however, a thinker will step out into the public square and speak with perfect clarity as to the source of his or her standards. Feminist philosopher Linda Hirshman is one such thinker. In an interview on Beliefnet, Hirshman measured stay-at-home moms against her standards and found homemakers to be off base:

> Just because you choose to stay at home doesn't make it right; . . . you have to examine the decision for its worthiness up against some kind of standard other than what St. Paul told the Ephesians.[20]

Hirshman won't allow us to use the Bible as our standard—no Paul at all. The interviewer, naturally, asked her what standard she would offer instead: "You're asking what makes for a good life for women. How do you define 'good life'?" To Hirshman's credit, she was ready with an answer. She listed three replacement standards:

1. According to Plato and Aristotle, you've got to use your full human capacity.
2. According to Enlightenment thinkers, you've got to be independent, morally autonomous.

3. According to general human experience during European industrialization, you've got to do more good than harm.[21]

Hirshman called this set of standards "secular western goodness." And she told Beliefnet,

> I applied those standards to the decision [by women] to stay home and tend children and the household, and I found that they were, in fact, lacking. These women are not using their full human capacity. They are not independent, and they are not doing more social good than harm.[22]

Of course, Hirshman's standard hides the important questions about what counts as good and what counts as harm. And why pick Plato over Paul? Why, indeed, listen to Linda Hirshman? What gives any human being the right to define the good life (or morality) for any other? By what standard can we say that Hirshman is right and stay-at-home moms are wrong? It's her word against Mom's. She said, she said.

We need access to moral standards that transcend human disagreements, or all we'll ever be able to do is shout at each other louder (or shoot each other). Humans are all stuck on the same level, low to the ground; we need someone sitting above the fray to tell us who's right.

THE CHRISTIAN STANDARD

Every person raised in Sunday school knows that it's God's Word that provides the Christian standard. But the Bible is a big book full of all kinds of stories, and most of them contain a good deal of human sin—in what way can a bunch of stories and letters and prophecies and poems provide us a standard?

We need to be more specific. What is it in the Bible that reveals the standard by which we judge what we see in our world? The answer is rich and complex, but an important way you can summarize it is this: "Creation." The way God created the world is the standard by which we judge the way things in the world ought to be.

The Heavens Declare

The point of this chapter about laws of nature and creational norms is to show that God communicates truth outside of Scripture as well as through it. You can understand the truth outside the Bible only if you understand and obey and love the truth inside it. But if God's creation is fundamentally good, then it too must contain truth.

Just listen to David in Psalm 19. He talks about two ways God communicates truth to us. The first is nature:

> The heavens declare the glory of God,
> and the sky above proclaims his handiwork.
> Day to day pours out speech,
> and night to night reveals knowledge.
> There is no speech, nor are there words,
> whose voice is not heard.
> Their voice goes out through all the earth,
> and their words to the end of the world. (Ps. 19:1–4)

Nature is telling us something, but without audible voices and human words. Nature is telling us about the "glory of God" and "his handiwork."

In the second part of the psalm, David turns to the other major way God tells us truth: His written Word.

The law of the Lord is perfect,
reviving the soul;
the testimony of the Lord is sure,
making wise the simple. (Ps. 19:7)

We perceive God's moral law by reading the Bible. We perceive the laws of nature and creational norms by careful observation of His creation through the lens of the Bible's moral laws. All of God's laws reveal God's glory (Ps. 19:1, 7). Although only the Bible laws are written down—and that's very important to remember—the other laws are no less real. And they're no less good. If creation is fundamentally good, then creational norms are fundamentally good too. They lead toward fruitfulness and success in this created world.

In fact, the whole system of laws that God gave Israel through Moses can be seen as an application of creational norms to their situation. What did it look like in the Ancient Near East to follow creational norms? Read the Mosaic law, and you'll see. This is why Paul can say that the Mosaic law "is holy and righteous and good" (Rom 7:12).

Violating Creational Norms

When you violate a law of nature, your "punishment" comes quickly. You jump off the couch like Superman; you fall to the floor. You were never really flying.

But what happens when you don't care to follow creational norms for human behavior and society? When you violate a creational norm, it's like you're pushing hard against a powerful metal spring. You can push it down, but it's going to take a great deal of effort, and at any moment the coil may spring back into its original shape. That's why some worldview thinkers have pointed out that humanity is "coming perilously close to the point where the earth itself will impose certain norms on us."[23] They point to the example of industrial wastes:

> It is creationally unlawful to put chemical wastes into an ecosystem when they cannot be assimilated. If we persist in breaking such a law, eventually the ecosystem will break down completely and we will lose the resource essential to life. . . . Creation is law-bound.[24]

So you can't run your state like a dump. You can't run a family like an army, and you can't run an army like a family. You can't run a church or a school like a business. The basic elements of human culture fit into structures God has already set up. He has norms and expectations for them. If you violate those norms, eventually you'll face consequences.

So it's not quite accurate to say that you can't break the divine law of gravity, but you can break the creational norm of marriage. You can't break either divine law without consequences; it's just

RUNNING A COUNTRY LIKE AN ARMY

What happens when you don't choose to follow creational norms? Ask North Korea. The leadership of North Korea runs that nation like an army instead of like a nation. Almost four out of every ten people in North Korea are either in the military or in the reserve, and they keep a million-man standing army. (The United States has a million military personnel too—but the US population is six times bigger than North Korea's.)

In part by running his country like an army, "Dear Leader" Kim Jong Il ended up starving millions of his people to death in the late 1990s. One North Korean pediatrician who escaped the famine stumbled into the courtyard of a Chinese home and couldn't understand why there was a bowl of rice with meat in it just sitting on the ground. Suddenly she realized that it was a food dish for the family pet. It hit her that dogs in China ate better than doctors in North Korea. The size of the military budget was not the only reason for this mass starvation, but it was a significant contributing factor.[25]

The Bible never says in so many words that it's wrong to have a huge army and buy expensive missiles when your people are starving to death. God hasn't chosen to reveal all His creational norms explicitly. It can take hard work to discover them, but that doesn't mean they aren't there. God has provided direction—standards, criteria, principles—for how to run nations, schools, families, and businesses. To discover them is part of the blessing and task of the Creation Mandate.

that the consequences come immediately when you attempt to break a law of nature, but they may be delayed for a long while in the case of a creational norm.

Objections to Creational Norms: Baptizing Political Platforms

There are a few objections to the idea of creational norms that we should consider. The first has to do with political arrogance. People sometimes talk as if they've discovered the way God's world really is when all they're really doing is "baptizing" the positions of their particular political party—trying to borrow God's authority for their own ideas.

It is dangerous to join a political team and then go in search of all the creational norms (and Bible verses) you can twist to fit that team's views. Bumper stickers will tell you that God is in favor of or against all sorts of political positions and parties. Liberals and conservatives both do this: "Jesus would raise the minimum wage." "Guns are a God-given right."

A lot of people have it backwards; they're more concerned about getting God on their side than they are about lining up with His. They haven't worked hard to discern what God really wants—or whether He might possibly allow liberty on a given issue.

The existence of creational norms provides confidence that there is truth to discover in the world of politics and economics—and in every major field of human endeavor. God made this world. God made it *very good*. And whatever vocation you end up in—politics included—it will be a large part of your task to discover that goodness.

So some parties may indeed line up more closely with biblical views than others (issues such as abortion and same-sex marriage come to mind). But limited, fallen human beings should be very humble and careful in their search for norms outside of Scripture.

GOD REVEALED

There are basically two ways God reveals truth to humans today: the Bible and creation. Theologians call the Bible **special revelation**, and they call truth in creation **general revelation**. The classic Scripture demonstrating the difference is Psalm 19, which starts out by saying that "the heavens declare the glory of God" (general revelation) and ends by praising God's Word: "The law of the Lord is perfect, reviving the soul; the testimony of the Lord is sure, making wise the simple" (19:7). God's Word and God's world are both revelations of God. But there's a key difference, as David's song shows. The heavens do declare the glory of God, but "there is no speech, nor are there words" (19:3).

Objections to Creational Norms: Justifying Ethnic Prejudice

Another objection to the idea of creational norms comes from the way they have been used to justify ethnic prejudice. During South African apartheid,* there were plenty of Christian Afrikaners* who argued forcefully that since God created the races to be separate, they should stay that way. US Christians have often used the same argument.[26]

But in both nations, the idea that the races (whatever a "race" is—the modern concept of race as a distinct set of physical characteristics cannot be found in the Bible[27]) should remain separate often obscured what was really going on: oppression.

And that oppression tended to be used to further justify racial segregation. When a particular people group is oppressed—whether blacks in America and South Africa or Dalits in India—they lack the educational opportunities to improve themselves, and their oppressors begin to feel that they are racially superior to their lower-class neighbors.

apartheid: *"apartness," the policy of racial segregation that governed South Africa 1948–91*

Afrikaner: *a white resident of South Africa, descended from Dutch settlers of the seventeenth century*

The idea of creational norms should never make us conclude that *the way things are now is natural and good.* This world is so deeply fallen that we need the light of Scripture—telling us that all people are created in God's own image, for example—to help us discern when what seems "normal" to us (note the *norm* in that word) should not. The present state of the cosmos is *ab*normal, after all.

CFR

God made this world good, and both the stuff in it and the rules governing it are good too. The way God made this world is the standard by which we judge the way things ought to be.

This doesn't mean, however, ditching our clothes, razing our cities, and living in gardens like Adam and Eve. The Fall has happened since then, of course, and that has changed things drastically. But even if you set aside the Fall, the Bible shows that God didn't create the world static or stuck. He created it with a plan for what it would become—filled, subdued, and dominated—developed toward its ideal. And this isn't true only of visible, physical things like mountains and insects. In those six days of creation, norms for human culture were created too. When we create, we create within structures that God set up.

So boil anything in this world down to its basic elements, and you can say "CFR" about it. It was *created* good, but the *fall* has damaged it—and it only Christ's powerful *redemption* can restore it. This is true of marriage and economics and farming and ethnicity; it's also true of music, art, business, banking, communication, and all the things you're studying in school: history, science, math, and language.

Either the Creator is King over society and culture, or He is not. Either God has set up expectations for how farming and education are supposed to work, or you can just do what feels right and hope for the best. As one theologian put it, if God is not sovereign over every part of life, "we are then freed from trying to discern God's will in these places as well as any responsibility for following it."[28]

Humans can look forward to the day when Christ will truly rule over all aspects of human culture, conforming them to His will. We can't bring that day about. But we must not think to ourselves, "Why polish the brass on our sinking ship?" Christ cares about our ship, and we are blessed and called by the Creation Mandate to polish it for His glory. He will pull it out of the waves one day.

It's the work of a lifetime to see the created good in your vocation, to detect the sinful twisting that has marred it, and to work to push it in some small way back toward the biblical-creational standard. But if you use "secular western goodness" as your standard, creation will push back. It won't work. Use instead the light of God's Word shining on your path.

THINKING IT THROUGH 6.3

1. Why are standards necessary for all judgment?
2. What kinds of laws are given to us through special revelation? What kinds of laws are given to us through general revelation?
3. How might the consequences of violating a natural law and a creational norm differ?
4. How can you spot a false claim to a creational norm?
5. Think of a relative or someone else you know who lives in a nursing home. Does that person's life measure up to the standards of "secular Western goodness"?

TERMS TO REMEMBER

laws of nature
creational norms
special revelation
general revelation

Scripture Memory

Proverbs 3:19

Making Connections

1. List three aspects of God's good creation that are commonly blamed for the problems of the world.
2. What governs the operation of the physical universe? What governs the way human individuals and cultures ought to operate?
3. In order to evaluate or make judgment calls about anything in the world, what must you use?
4. What two forms of revelation should guide a Christian's judgment calls? Should one form take priority over the other?

Developing Skills in Apologetics and Worldview

5. How should you respond if someone who's complaining about the problems in the world proposes the solution of just doing away with all authority structures?
6. How should you respond when a well-meaning Christian blames emotion as the root of all sin?

Examining Assumptions and Evidence

7. Why should God's creation still be considered essentially good even in spite of the pervasive negative effects of the Fall?
8. Why should you heed the laws of nature even though the Bible doesn't directly command you to?
9. Evaluate the following argument: "Spotted hyenas are polygamous (males have multiple mates), so polygamy is natural and good."
10. Did God make government? Why or why not?

Becoming a Creative Cultivator

11. Pick one of the academic disciplines or cultural domains featured as a unit in this textbook: gender, marriage, and family; government; science; history; or culture and the arts. Make list of what you think might be some creational norms for that discipline or domain.

3

FALL

Chapter Seven **FAR AS THE CURSE IS FOUND**

Chapter Eight **COMMON GRACE, THE WORLD, AND YOU**

Chapter Nine **STRUCTURE AND DIRECTION**

Chapter Seven FAR AS THE CURSE IS FOUND

The creation waits with eager longing for the revealing of the sons of God. For the creation was subjected to futility, not willingly, but because of him who subjected it in hope that the creation itself will be set free from its bondage to corruption.

Scripture Memory
Romans 8:19–21

7.1 THE PERSONAL EFFECTS OF THE FALL

You probably have lots of dos and don'ts to keep track of—as a citizen of your nation, as a student in your school, and as a child in your family. Adam and Eve's "do" list was fairly short: fill the earth, subdue it, have dominion over it, and start by working and keeping the garden—the Creation Mandate. And yet inside that to-do list is a nearly infinite number of possibilities. Adam and Eve could do pretty much whatever they wished—because their wishes were aligned with God's.

Adam and Eve's "don't" list, by contrast, was just one item long:

> Of the tree of the knowledge of good and evil you shall not eat, for in the day that you eat of it you shall surely die. (Gen. 2:17)

WHAT BEFELL ADAM AND EVE?

The perfect man and woman, with perfect loves, perfect bodies, and perfect minds were very unlikely to disobey their one "don't." But for reasons we cannot fully know (because God hasn't revealed them), God allowed a malevolent force to enter His creation. And as that serpent approached Eve with the first temptation in the history of our planet, he knew he had to overcome God's threat that Eve would die. His chosen strategy is one he hasn't ever tired of using: he questioned the authority and truthfulness of God's word, and at the same time, God's goodness:

> He said to the woman, "Did God actually say, 'You shall not eat of any tree in the garden'?" (3:1)

That wasn't what God had said, of course. Even Satan's question twists God's speech. God said His image-bearers could freely enjoy the riches of every tree—every tree except one. But the serpent successfully wrested Eve's eyes away from that vast gift and got her to focus on the one thing she couldn't have. That's what all covetousness is, including yours.

> God said, "You shall not eat of the fruit of the tree that is in the midst of the garden, neither shall you touch it, lest you die." (3:3)

The crafty serpent saw an opening in Eve's words. He became bold; he contradicted God directly and then snuck in a half-truth.

> The serpent said to the woman, "You will not surely die. For God knows that when you eat of it your eyes will be opened, and you will be like God, knowing good and evil." (3:4–5)

Satan suggested again, without ever saying so, that God was not good, that God was withholding some pleasure from Eve—a life better than the one she had. Satan tricked Eve into seeking a good thing, but seeking it in an evil way. The serpent knew his prey: it was precisely because Eve was made in the image of God that she viewed being like God as a tempting prospect. Satan didn't create evil desires; he twisted good ones.

> When the woman saw that the tree was good for food, and that it was a delight to the eyes, and that the tree was to be desired to make one wise, she took of its fruit and ate, and she also gave some to her husband who was with her, and he ate. (3:6)

Genesis 2 makes it clear that God had made trees for just the reasons Eve was attracted to this one. The text says that He made "every tree that is pleasant to the sight and good for food" (2:9). So food is good. As is delight. As is being wise like God. Eve's sin began, as all sins do, when good things were bent the wrong way. God's good creations were used against Him. God's creatures tried to make themselves *equal to* Him instead of merely *like* Him.

"Sin is irrational. Why would anyone turn from the beauty and joy of covenant life with God and embrace its opposite? Or why would anyone think he could succeed in opposing God's omnipotent power?" [1]

—JOHN FRAME

WHAT CONSEQUENCES DID THE FALL HAVE FOR EVERY PERSON?

By the third chapter of the Bible, God's highest creation has already plunged into sin. A sin that happened embarrassingly fast would now take millennia to undo. But this epic, world-shattering Fall was so stupid. Like all of our sins, the pleasure was so miniscule compared to the subsequent pain. Adam and Eve ate, but as a result they felt empty rather than full.

Naked

The serpent, of course, had wrapped the truth around a lie. Yes, God knew that when Adam and Eve ate from the tree their eyes would be opened. But what they got when that forbidden juice hit their tongues was not a better life. What they experienced was something only humans can experience, and only because of sin: the shame of nakedness.

> Then the eyes of both were opened, and they knew that they were naked. And they sewed fig leaves together and made themselves loincloths. (Gen. 3:7)

It's a little awkward to say so, but you know this is true: to go without clothes around other people takes real trust. You trust a doctor when absolutely necessary, but only for a few minutes. You will likely one day trust a spouse because in a marriage two become one. And even in both of those trusting situations, you're never unaware that you're exposed. (Nobody ever forgets to put on clothes before going out.) The relationship Adam and Eve shared with each other and with their Creator must have been deeply rich and trusting if Adam and Eve never even realized they were without clothes. And now, with one act of defiance, that trust is shattered. The beautiful life they were given is gone.

Even the wickedest people on earth have not forgotten that they are naked. That barrier between humans and God, created by sin, remains. From Genesis 3 onward the Bible speaks of all people, all Adam's race, as being "dead in . . . trespasses and sins" and "by nature children of wrath" (Eph. 2:1, 3).

That is the sense in which Adam and Eve "died" on that dark day when man fell. Death is the loss of life. Since man is complex in his being—a spirit being and a physical being—the judgment of death is complex as well. Adam's inner man died immediately when he sinned; he was separated from God, the only source of spiritual life. But his outer man didn't die till he was 930 (Gen. 5:5).

WHY WEAR CLOTHES?

Why wear clothes? Why not just live according to God's original intention for Adam and Eve—and save a lot of money and time in the process? One theologian answers succinctly: "Being clothed is God's will for a witness to our fall. Taking your clothes off does not put you back into pre-Fall paradise; it puts you into post-Fall shame. That's God's will. It's why modesty is a crucial post-Fall virtue."[2]

The Bible says that "women should adorn themselves in respectable apparel, with modesty and self-control" (1 Tim. 2:9). And modesty is a concern for both men and women (Prov. 7:10; 1 Cor. 12:23). But the Bible never defines modesty. We are left to our scripturally informed judgment. Perhaps it would help to think of your clothing as a message to those who see you. That message is partly cultural. There are some situations in some cultures in which a certain clothing item means, "I wish to dress respectfully and appropriately for my setting; I do not wish to draw undue attention to myself." But there are other cultures where, no matter the situation, that same piece of cloth means, "I don't care what you think, I'm going to show off my body." Just as the same sounds can mean very different things in different languages (*gift* means "poison" in German), the same clothing can carry different cultural messages.

But clothing is not just cultural. There's intrinsic meaning in clothes too. So there are no cultures in which near nudity means, "I wish to demonstrate modesty and respect." Many men and women actually ought to feel the shame of Adam and Eve because of what they're wearing (or failing to wear) in public.[3] Looking with lust and arousing it are both sins (Matt. 5:27–30).

Jesus restores both kinds of life, spiritual and physical. He said, "Whoever believes in me, though he die, yet shall he live, and everyone who lives and believes in me shall never die" (John 11:25–26; cf. 2 Cor. 4:16). But just as Adam's physical death didn't occur till long after his spiritual death, perfect physical life will be restored (to believers) long after they get spiritual life. Until then, we face the effects of the Fall in our always-dying bodies.

Loving and Thinking

Adam's Fall flipped the world upside down. He was supposed to submit to God just as his wife submitted to him (Eph. 5:22), and as animals submitted to them both (Gen. 1:28). Instead an animal led Eve, who led Adam—who blamed God.

When Adam and Eve heard God coming, they did something image-bearers had never done before: they hid. When God found them, Adam explained, "I was afraid, because I was naked, and I hid myself." God replied, "Who told you that you were naked? Have you eaten of the tree of which I commanded you not to eat?" Watch how quickly Adam learns, serpent-like, to twist the truth: "The woman whom you gave to be with me, she gave me fruit of the tree, and I ate" (Gen. 3:10–12).

We're starting to see that the Fall has effects. Like a lie that requires a cover-up lie or like pollution that permeates an entire reservoir, sin spreads immediately through God's best creation. Adam's reasoning has been damaged: it is supremely irrational to make excuses to a God who sees all—and then to blame Him for the trouble you caused! The powers of logic given only to image-bearers have been damaged. The apostle Paul explains that, after the Fall of Adam, people are naturally "darkened in their understanding, alienated from the life of God because of the ignorance that is in them" (Eph. 4:18). *Understanding* and *ignorance*—these are words that focus on a person's mind or his thinking. Sin has twisted mankind's reasoning powers.

But it hasn't removed them. Adam actually uses exquisite logic in the three statements he makes to God. All three are true, and yet he manages to weave them together into a lie. He's not just listing off what happened; he's giving three reasons for the Fall. "First, there's *you*, God—you gave me this woman. Second, there's *she*—she gave me this fruit. (Then, last and certainly least, there's *me*—I ate.)" He admits to his role in the sin only after he condemns his Maker and his mate. The two beings Adam is supposed to love most, God and Eve, he throws under the bus.

So it isn't just his mind that's damaged. After Paul describes how Adam's heirs are all naturally "darkened in their understanding," he says quite clearly that their darkness is "due to their hardness of heart" (Eph. 4:18). Adam, deep in his heart, strayed from his purpose of loving God and neighbor, and he subsequently twisted his picture of reality to fit his wayward loves. This pattern still exists today: what you love drives what you think.

Those in the Flesh Cannot Please God

The Fall of man—mind and heart and spirit and body—is why people today go so wrong, both Hitler-wrong and *you*-wrong. Just as Adam hid from God's sight, people hide God from their own sight. People suppress their knowledge of God—knowledge that God says He gave them (Rom. 1:18–19). They have "exchanged the truth about God for a lie and worshiped and served the creature rather than the Creator" (1:25). Their thinking minds and worshiping hearts are twisted in wrong directions. "No one does good, not even one" (3:12). They do irrational, self-harming things. "No one seeks for God" (3:11).

> "THE IDEA THAT DESIRE EQUALS LICENSE COMES FACTORY-LOADED IN ALL OF US."[4]
>
> —JEFFREY KLUGER

In his book about **original sin**,* writer Alan Jacobs notes that "whatever the situation might have been for Adam and Eve, for us the devil on our shoulder is only truly dangerous because of the devil that's already inside us."[5] That's why, Jacobs says, a devil and an angel hovering over each shoulder of a cartoon character are usually pictured as miniature versions of that same character. There is good in every person because God's image is still resident in every person; but evil has touched every aspect of every man, woman, and child. God destroyed the world in Noah's day when He saw that "the wickedness of man was great in the earth, and that every intention of the thoughts of his heart was only evil continually" (Gen. 6:5). Even after He cleanses the earth with the Flood, He says, "The intention of man's heart is evil from his youth" (8:21). Nothing has changed.

original sin: *the theological term designating the fact that all humans are guilty sinners at their conception because of Adam's first sin*

The Bible teaches that the effects of the Fall are pervasive. They touch every aspect of every person. Your feeling, your willing, and your thinking are all damaged. But the Bible does not teach that all people are as bad as they could possibly be. Instead it says, "Those who are in the flesh cannot please God" (Rom. 8:8). And by "in the flesh" he means people who do not have spiritual life from God. Some non-Christians are incredibly generous and gracious; some are Hitlers. But the same spiritual death and ultimate rebellion runs through each group. No amount of good deeds can overturn the fact that, deep in their hearts, people are at war with God and not at peace with Him (Col. 1:21). Even if they do good, they refuse to do it for the only right reason there is: love for the loveliest Being in the universe.

A TWISTED FALL

Mormon theology teaches that eating the forbidden fruit was not actually a sin, just a "transgression." But it was a good thing, a necessary transgression, Mormonism believes. Mormons say that the command to "fill the earth" couldn't be obeyed until Adam and Eve ate of the tree. They were immortal and couldn't bear children until they became mortal by eating of the tree. And in the Mormon view, Adam ate the fruit of the tree only to show faithfulness to his wife—if she was going to be cast out of the garden, he wanted to be with her. Read Genesis 3 for yourself and decide. Does the Mormon version of the story fit the biblical account? And does the Bible authorize modern Mormon prophets (or anyone else) to add details to the story?[6]

Freedom and Slavery

As Frodo Baggins stands over the fires of Mount Doom at the climax of *The Lord of the Rings*, having reached the end of his quest to destroy the evil ring, he does the unthinkable. Instead of throwing the ring into the fire, Frodo puts it on and vanishes. But it's not clear whose decision it was, Frodo's or the ring's. Even Frodo avoids saying that it was his choice; he says only, "I do not choose now to do what I came to do. . . . The Ring is mine!"[7] In both book and film, Frodo speaks with a voice not quite his own—but yet his own. Tolkien doesn't tell us exactly what's going on inside the hobbit, but he does provide a picture of the power of sin that every Christian can recognize (Rom. 7:15–20).

Frodo's uncle, Bilbo, felt that power too. When Gandalf the wizard asks Bilbo about the ring, Bilbo snaps, "It is mine, I tell you. My own. My precious. Yes, my precious."

"It has got far too much hold on you," Gandalf warns Bilbo. "Let it go! And then you can go yourself, and be free."

"I'll do as I choose and go as I please," Bilbo replies obstinately.

But Bilbo's choosing and his pleasing are not free. While he still has the ring, Bilbo is in bondage, unaware that true freedom is not the liberty to do what you want, but the liberty to want what you should. Tolkien brilliantly pictures the tendency of sin to promise freedom and deliver slavery. That's the legacy of Adam's Fall—the enslavement of mankind. "Everyone who practices sin is a slave to sin," Jesus said (John 8:34). And no one in this sin-cursed world is exempt.

Thank God that God sent a second Adam, a sinless one, to set the captives free (1 Cor. 15:47).

THINKING IT THROUGH 7.1

1. Why does it seem unlikely that Adam and Eve would have disobeyed God if Satan hadn't been there to tempt them?
2. What did Satan's deceptive questions imply about God's word and character?
3. Describe the effects of the Fall on the whole person: the body, the affections, and the mind.
4. What does sin always promise? What is always its result instead?
5. Why aren't people as bad as they could possibly be? Why can't their good works compensate for their fallenness?

7.2 THE COSMIC EFFECTS OF THE FALL

It may surprise you to know that there were no twins born in the whole United States of America (including Puerto Rico and other U.S. territories) between 1987 and 2013. To giant pandas, that is.

On July 25, 2013, beautiful panda mother Lun Lun gave birth to cuddly twin boy bears Mei Lun and Mei Huan at the Atlanta Zoo, and the whole world said a collective, "Awww!" When the two tiny, wiggly, pink pandas were presented to the public, Mommy and little ones looked like try-outs for a cutest greeting card competition. A live, 24-hour-a-day PandaCam allowed panda enthusiasts from around the world to monitor the adorableness in real time.

Mei Lun and Mei Huan

But Lun Lun's keepers at the zoo knew that, for public relations purposes, they needed to handle this situation carefully. They prepared to rotate the babies, giving only one at a time to Lun Lun. Her public image—and that of all pandas—was at stake. That's because panda mothers typically keep twins alive only long enough to know if their chosen baby is healthy. Then they let the other baby die.[8]

If Lun Lun did that with either Mei Lun or Mei Huan, it would be bad for zoo business. Small children would be confused—"Mommy, why doesn't she feed that one?" Hallmark wouldn't come calling anymore.

But if Lun Lun had let one baby panda die, it would not have been unique—not among pandas, and not among mothers. Mother guinea hens walk so fast that they purposely leave some of their cute little chicks behind, weeding out the weak. Great black eagle moms regularly feed only one eaglet.[9]

> *"Are God and Nature then at strife,*
> *That Nature lends such evil dreams?*
> *So careful of the type she seems,*
> *So careless of the single life;*
>
> *That I, considering everywhere*
> *Her secret meaning in her deeds,*
> *And finding that of fifty seeds*
> *She often brings but one to bear."*[10]
>
> —ALFRED, LORD TENNYSON

THE HEART OF THE CREATION-EVOLUTION DEBATE

The conflict between creation and evolution may seem like it's all about radiometric dating, fossils, starlight, shale layers, and DNA analysis. It may seem like an epic war of science versus religion, reason versus faith. But it's really about dead panda babies. The real heart of the creation-evolution debate is a question: is the world the way it's supposed to be? In other words, is the present state of the cosmos normal or abnormal?[11] Are pandas supposed to let their babies die? *Are humans?* (About 20 percent of pregnant women had their unborn babies killed in a recent year.[12]) Are pain and death and terrible evil supposed to exist in this world?

The secular, materialistic, evolutionary worldview can't say anything is "supposed" to be. It just is. Material universes formed by random chance can't *suppose*. So when Alfred, Lord Tennyson, famously described nature as "red in tooth and claw"[13] in

1844, it was a description of evolution that both evolution's critics and its believers have adopted. Atheist Richard Dawkins is one adopter of the phrase: "I think 'nature red in tooth and claw' sums up our modern understanding of natural selection admirably."[14] Evolutionists think the phrase accurately describes the way things just are: species kill each other off in the never-ending struggle toward survival of the fittest. "The secrets of evolution are time and death," said Carl Sagan, "time for the slow accumulations of favorable mutations, and death to make room for new species."[15]

But creationists (or at least Christian ones) use the "red in tooth and claw" phrase as a criticism: death is abnormal. *This is not the way things are supposed to be*. Death wasn't in God's "very good" creation. Paul says clearly, "Sin came into the world through one man, and death through sin" (Rom. 5:12). If there had been no sin, there would be no death. And Paul says "one man" is responsible. That man, of course, was Adam. And yet his sin didn't affect just himself.

Rep. Adam

The US Congress is divided into two houses—the Senate and the House of Representatives. Representatives of what? Of *you* (if you live in the United States). They represent the voters who put them into office in whatever district they hail from. If the congresswoman from the 12th district of California votes "no" on H.R. 253, then it's as if everyone in that district voted against that particular bill.

But there are most definitely people in the 12th district of California who would have voted *for* that bill. And there were children and others in the district who were unable to vote but who are nonetheless affected by the decision. There are, in fact, animals and rivers and trees that are affected by votes in faraway Washington, DC, that they know nothing about. Not everyone can vote on every bill, so that's the way the American governmental system works.

And it's basically the way God's system works too. God appointed one representative for the entire human race. When that representative voted against God in the Garden of Eden, God treated that vote as if we all voted. Adam voted for the "de-Godding" of God. That audacious act was recorded on the books as the vote of the whole of humanity.

But Adam wasn't just the representative for the human race. He was also the ruler of creation; his sin was a terrible distortion of the Creation Mandate. So when Adam sinned, it was like he jumped into a hole with all of creation tied to his waist by a rope—including animals, rivers, and trees. When its God-appointed ruler fell into sin, *all of creation* was plunged into the same pit. The Fall, in other words, had "cosmic effects"—it touched the whole cosmos, the whole created order.

Two major passages of Scripture, both essential to a biblical worldview, describe these cosmic effects: Genesis 3 and Romans 8.

IS THE FALL FAIR?

Is it fair that we face so many perverse effects from Adam's long-ago sin? Theologian John Frame offers several responses:

1. We all sin just like Adam did. There are no innocent human beings.
2. If you had been in the garden, are you certain you would have done better than Adam did?
3. Humans are always tied to one another. There is no such thing as a true loner. Parents, for example, don't just pass on eye shape and hair color to their kids; they pass on moral character.
4. If treating Adam as our representative is unfair, so is treating Christ as our new representative.

At some point we have to simply trust that God is good even if He doesn't seek to exhaustively prove it to us. And yet—what other proof is needed besides Christ's self-sacrificial death for us? Adam jumped into a pit with a rope tied to him, and he pulled us all in. But the rope tying believers to Christ is stronger than the one tying them to Adam.[16]

Genesis 3 on the Cosmic Effects of the Fall

God knows all. So His questions to Adam and Eve as they hide from His face ("Where are you?" "What have you done?") are not requests for information; they're opportunities for Adam and Eve to repent.[17] (He doesn't give such an opportunity to the serpent because Satan is beyond redemption.) But Adam and Eve don't express sorrow for their sin, and God is ready with consequences—but not just bad ones. It is so typical of our gracious God that He doesn't even tell Adam and Eve what their punishments are until He has already promised to save them—eventually—from those punishments. Listen to what He says to the serpent:

> I will put enmity
> between you and the woman,
> and between your seed and her seed;
> He shall bruise you on the head,
> and you shall bruise him on the heel. (Gen. 3:15, NASB)

We'll discuss this statement in much greater detail in the unit about redemption, but you need to know that this seed who will bruise the serpent's head is none other than Jesus Christ. A bruised heel hurts, but a bruised head can be fatal. God is promising that a redeemer will come and beat Satan.

Then God turns to Eve:

> "I will surely multiply your pain in childbearing; in pain you shall bring forth children. Your desire shall be for your husband, and he shall rule over you." (Gen. 3:16)

Now one of Eve's most important roles—bringing new image-bearers into the earth to fill it—will involve multiplied pain. And her most important role, helping and complementing* Adam (Gen. 2:20), will be damaged too. The verb used in the phrase "shall rule over you" appears to mean that Adam will dominate Eve harshly (cf. Gen. 4:7). Bible scholar Derek Kidner says, "'To love and to cherish' becomes 'To desire and to dominate.' While even pagan marriage can rise far above this, the pull of sin is always towards it."[18]

complement: *to add to something in order to complete or perfect it*

It's when God turns to Adam that sin's cosmic effects become most clear:

> "Because you have listened to the voice of your wife and have eaten of the tree . . . , cursed is the ground because of you; in pain you shall eat of it all the days of your life; thorns and thistles it shall bring forth for you; and you shall eat the plants of the field. By the sweat of your face you shall eat bread, till you return to the ground, for out of it you were taken; for you are dust, and to dust you shall return." (Gen. 3:17–19)

God was to rule over man, but man rebelled. Man was to rule over the ground; now it will rebel against him.[19] Work ("the sweat of your face") is not itself a punishment because God gave Adam work to do before the Fall. But the very blessings of the Creation Mandate are now cursed: Adam's work of dominion will now be frustrating; thorns and thistles will constantly fight to thwart Adam's labors. The ground will still be fruitful, but it will also be cursed—good but fallen. And at the end of years—centuries—of often frustrating work, Adam will return as ashes to ashes, dust to dust.

Romans 8 on the Cosmic Effects of the Fall

The ground—including your own lawn—is still cursed today. Work—including your schoolwork—is still good but often frustrating. Childbearing is still painful, even dangerous.[20] Adam's terrible vote many centuries ago still counts, all around the world. The Christian hope is that one day God will put everything right.

But we're not the only ones hoping. "The creation waits with eager longing for the revealing of the sons of God," Paul says in Romans 8:19. That revealing is going to take place in the age to come, not in this time (8:18). There is a future glory that God intends to bring to His children. The important thing to note here is that the whole creation, not just people, is waiting eagerly for this day. The animals and rivers and trees are craning their necks, longing to be transformed into glory along with God's children—longing to escape the curse.

Paul explains that curse: "The creation was subjected to futility, not willingly, but because of him who subjected it, in hope that the creation itself will be set free from its bondage to corruption" (8:20–21). After Adam sinned, God subjected all of creation to "futility," to a frustrating inability to achieve its intended purposes. The thorns God sent as a judgment are always getting in the way. But He sent this judgment in a context of "hope"—the promise of Genesis 3 that one day the seed of the woman would bruise the head of God's enemy. It would be strange for creation to "hope . . . [to] be set free" if it's all going to be annihilated one day, as some Christians assume. No, when God's people are finally delivered from the effects of sin and gloriously transformed, creation will be too.

Humans are major characters in the drama of Creation, Fall, Redemption. Nature is our stage. But that doesn't make nature irrelevant. The nonhuman creation was deeply affected by the Fall too, and it will remain part of the drama God has written for all eternity. When the main characters are redeemed and restored (Rom. 8:19), so will the stage . . . lions and lambs, birds and beetles, rivers and trees, panda moms and panda babies. "The whole creation has been groaning," Paul says (8:22). Creation is stuck in the same hole Adam got us all into.

THINKING IT THROUGH 7.2

1. Which two chapters of Scripture are most important for the Christian doctrine of the Fall?
2. Since Adam was the representative of the human race, why does the rest of creation also have to suffer?
3. List each punishment and relate it to the corresponding task given in the Creation Mandate.
4. Is creation going to be completely annihilated one day? Why or why not?
5. Why isn't it unfair that we have to suffer the consequences of Adam's sin?

Somalia became a "failed state" in 1991 as societal institutions completely broke down.

7.3 THE CULTURAL EFFECTS OF THE FALL

Somalia, situated on the Horn of Africa, has often been called a "failed state." In 1991, the institutions that normally provide governmental, educational, and other services in a smoothly functioning nation simply broke down as civil war engulfed the land. Warlords took over, fighting each other for territory.

One of the first Western Christians to spend significant time in Somalia after war broke out was a missionary in nearby Kenya. He goes by the pseudonym Nik Ripken because he still serves Christ's kingdom in dangerous places around the world.

Nik started making regular trips into Somalia as the situation there became more and more desperate. Dead bodies littered the roads, and it often fell to him to have to choose which towns got food and water and which didn't. One time he found out that the people he had just given food to the day before were being raped and tortured by the people of another village who felt they deserved the food more.[21] It was emotionally devastating work, but Nik plowed forward with the love of Christ and the help of his godly wife back in Kenya.

Nik longed to tell people about Christ, but he knew that to do so was to risk not only his own life but theirs as well. Islamists in Somalia had driven out nearly all Somali Christians. On one special day, Nik was able to meet in a top-secret location with the four—*four*—Somali Christians known to be left in the country. They had precious Christian communion together.

Days later all four were dead, killed in a coordinated attack at separate locations around the (former) capital city, Mogadishu.[22]

Once, Nik entered a hut in a village and discovered three dead bodies—including those of a girl with her brush still in her hair and a grandmother still appearing to stir a pot. Nik and his team fell silent until one of his Somali staffers said with anguish, "You know, Dr. Nik, they used to call Somaliland a third-world country. But now we are a pre-world country."[23]

FALLEN CULTURE

Culture, intended by God as a blessing (a result of the Creation Mandate), can be twisted so far that it breaks. Government can fall apart. Education can just stop. Business and journalism and the arts can grind to a halt. Whole nations can effectively cease to be. Cultural institutions and laws and customs that took centuries to build can fall in a day. Developed and developing nations can regress to "pre-world" status.

utopia: *an imagined world in which everything is perfect*

But collapse usually takes longer than that; it's generally preceded by decay. And why do such failures happen anyway? Why haven't humans achieved utopia*? Because the Fall has touched everything God created. If, as the previous unit argued, God created family, sexuality, and all the institutions of society, then those things have been affected by Adam's Fall just like people have.

- Marriage: Consider that the out-of-wedlock birthrate among low-income American whites is 50%. Among the upper classes, that number is about 7%. Marriage as an institution is dying in the former group (and generally healthy in the latter).[24] Societies have always had to balance individual freedom to leave a difficult marriage with the responsibility parents owe to their children.[25] But now so little legal pressure is placed on parents to stay married (divorce is, legally speaking, quite easy) that America as a whole is undermining its most important institution.
- The family: Western families are under sometimes intense strain. The institutions and structures of society which used to support and protect them—church, school, even divorce laws—have been weakened. The important role parents are told to play in the spiritual formation of their children (Deut. 6:6–9) has been endangered by many cultural pressures.
- The arts: An occasional blasphemous piece of art makes the news (like the infamous painting of Jesus' mother dotted with elephant dung[26]), and pornographic art goes back at least to the time of Pompeii, where it was preserved by a volcanic eruption a mere fifty years after Jesus' resurrection. Blasphemy and pornography are obvious twistings of art. But so are kitsch* and schlock*; in other words, art unworthy of the name (though porn is obviously more morally degraded than a sentimental painting). Some music is evil, but some is just dumb—the musical equivalent of chocolate cheese in a can. The arts are fallen in numerous ways.

kitsch: *excessively sentimental art, considered to be done in poor taste*

schlock: *cheap junk*

- Education: Academia is deeply damaged by the Fall. The more educated you are, the more humble you (should) become about what you don't know. There are a lot of smart people out there. But that doesn't change the fact that most of Western academia ignores the reality of God completely. "God" is only an object of historical study, if that. What happens when you build a whole discipline on a godless foundation? Much of this book is dedicated to answering that question.

Culture is what we make of the good creation. When we are twisted, we create a twisted culture. So everywhere you look in human culture you will see not just individuals but cultural products and institutions that are distorted, abnormal, sick, dysfunctional, corrupted, and vain. They have all been twisted by the Fall. Stable marriages, loving families, well-cared-for environments, beautiful art, and insightful academic study are still visible. But evil has entwined itself like invasive vines around the good, weakening it and in some cases even obscuring it from public view.

Genesis 4

We don't have to guess that culture is affected by the Fall. It shows up right away in the Bible's story. From the Fall in Genesis 3 come its effects in Genesis 4. Cain murders Abel, an example of the Fall's effect on individual humans (Gen. 4:1–16). And immediately after that, the most fundamental human institution takes a significant turn away from the pattern God gave when Lamech, one of Cain's descendants, marries two wives (4:19). The Bible text doesn't comment on this twisting of marriage; it just reports it. But this polygamy* is obviously a significant deviation from the one-man, one-woman pattern of Genesis 2:22–24.

polygamy: *a marriage including more than just one man and one woman (typically "polygyny," a man having more than one wife)*

Sons born of this polygamous marriage, we are told, became the "fathers" of "those who dwell in tents and have livestock" (Jabal), "those who play the lyre and pipe" (Jubal), and those who forge "all instruments of bronze and iron" (Tubal-cain; 4:20–22). These descendants of Cain are living out the creation blessing. They are taking dominion. Music and metallurgy are complex skills; these were not intellectually deficient cavemen.

But what were these early men and women making with their newfound cultural skills? We don't fully know, but the text hints that it wasn't all good. The passage includes the first post-Fall poem. And what is it about? It's a boast from Lamech (the husband with two wives) about how he took murderous vengeance:

> Adah and Zillah, hear my voice;
> you wives of Lamech, listen to what I say:
> I have killed a man for wounding me,
> a young man for striking me.
> If Cain's revenge is sevenfold,
> then Lamech's is seventy-sevenfold. (Gen. 4:23–24)

Add the right beat, and it sounds just like the violent gangsta rap of right now. As with a lot of other poetry and music throughout history, a sinful man was using artistic power in the service of sin.

Fallen Culture and You

There are no safe places where you can get away from the effects of the Fall. You can't join a local civic chorus or orchestra and escape it; sin will be there. You can't play in a softball league or take gymnastics lessons or join a book club or even help in a ministry to the homeless without running into the twisting power of the Fall. And not just in the people, but in the very structures of the groups, the shared expectations and practices that define them—because of the fallen human affection and thinking that pervade them.

Sports, like all created things, are fundamentally good, but the culture of a sports team (or a whole sport!) may be excessively macho—even among girls. A sort of competition will go on among the players in which each is trying to out-crass the others. If you don't participate, you'll be seen as opposed to the team. A ministry to the homeless may be willfully blind to the harm it's doing by handing out food to certain people whose real need is job training and counseling.[27] All the structures of the organization may actually be set up to make well-off people feel good about helping the poor rather than being set up to actually help those in need.[28]

"THINGS FALL APART"

The Bible lays the blame for seemingly small, individual sins squarely at the feet of Adam and Eve. And the sins of big cultural institutions—the recording industry, university education, radio and television broadcasting—trace their roots back to Adam and Eve too. The effect of the Fall on cultures is why the Bible warns about the sinful power of the **world**, and not just of individuals in it (Rom. 12:1–2; 1 John 2:15–17).

The "world" in the Bible is "the totality of unredeemed life dominated by sin outside of Christ,"[29] says one theologian. Another simply defines the world as "the bad part of culture."[30] And after a chapter like this in which we've seen how far the effects of the Fall have traveled, it's apparent why God would use such an expansive word as *world*.

As the British poet William Butler Yeats wrote:

> Things fall apart, the center cannot hold;
> Mere anarchy is loosed upon the world.[31]

That's the way of our fallen planet, both the people and the cultures they inhabit. Without the gracious restraining hand of God, we would have all been like Somalia and become like Mogadishu (Isa. 1:9).

Missionary Nik Ripken's experiences in Somalia drove him to ask whether Christianity was capable of surviving in places of great persecution. When he began traveling to interview Christians who had been through terrible abuse for their faith—the former USSR, China, and places he didn't even dare name in his book—Nik discovered that the power of Christ's resurrection was able to give amazing life even in the deadliest of circumstances.[32]

This amazing spiritual life is one of the ways God shows His determination not to let the world crumble. He uses His children—you?—as lights shining in the darkness, as salt giving people a taste of the age to come.

THINKING IT THROUGH 7.3

1. Why does the Bible use the terms *world* and *worldly* to refer to fallen cultural expressions?
2. Can fallen humans make unfallen things?
3. Genesis 3 recounts the Fall and its consequences. What particular effects of the Fall does Genesis 4 exemplify?
4. Are fallen cultural expressions found only in certain segments of culture? Why or why not?
5. Give three examples of cultural institutions or products discussed in the chapter, noting at least one way the Fall has affected each example

7 CHAPTER REVIEW

TERMS TO REMEMBER

original sin
world

Scripture Memory

Romans 8:19–21

Making Connections

1. What details in Genesis 3 attest to the full extent of the Fall's effects on individuals: their relationship with God, their affections, their wills, their intellects, and their physical bodies?
2. Relate the curses God pronounced on the man and the woman in Genesis 3 to their corresponding elements in the Creation Mandate.
3. Describe how each of the following examples of a cultural institution has been touched by the Fall: marriage, family, the arts, education.
4. What cultural endeavors are noted in Genesis 4? How were those cultural institutions already suffering under the effects of the Fall?

Developing Skills in Apologetics and Worldview

5. If an unbeliever complains that it's unfair for all of us to have to suffer the consequences of sin because of Adam's representation, how would you respond?
6. Suppose a believer thinks all earthly things are temporary and irrelevant in the light of eternity. What if he said to you, "Why polish the brass on a sinking ship?" How would you respond?

Examining Assumptions and Evidence

7. Since every part of every person is touched by the Fall, can there be any social institutions, disciplines of study, or fields of work untouched by the Fall? Why or why not?
8. Since no aspects of individual humans remain untouched by the Fall, can there be any goodness manifested in the above-mentioned categories? Explain why or why not.
9. Provide one example of fallenness in popular culture and one example of fallenness in high culture.
10. Why is *worldliness* a fitting term to describe the bad part of culture?

Becoming a Creative Cultivator

11. What's one way you could align your wishes with God's and try to push back against the Fall by creatively cultivating something in line with the creation blessing of Genesis 1:26–28?

Chapter Eight COMMON GRACE, THE WORLD, AND YOU

Beloved, I urge you as sojourners and exiles to abstain from the passions of the flesh, which wage war against your soul. Keep your conduct among the Gentiles honorable, so that when they speak against you as evildoers, they may see your good deeds and glorify God on the day of visitation.

Scripture Memory
1 Peter 2:11–12

The fear of the Lord is the beginning of knowledge; fools despise wisdom and instruction.

Proverbs 1:7

8.1 COMMON GRACE

A group of sailors decides to push their good captain off the boat, take the cargo, and sell it in a distant port. The subsequent journey proves difficult until a leader arises to establish some order. He succeeds, and remarkably so. Soon the mutineers are the most courteous, hard-working, efficient crew on the high seas. They go out of their way to rescue the victims of damaged vessels. They obey all the maritime codes for international waters. They scrub up their ship, invent new uniforms for themselves—and politely neglect to talk about their origins as a group.

"How dare you question our morality!" the leader might say. "Anyone can see that we are honest men!"

> "FALLEN MAN IS NOT SIMPLY AN IMPERFECT CREATURE WHO NEEDS IMPROVEMENT; HE IS A REBEL WHO MUST LAY DOWN HIS ARMS."[1]
>
> —C. S. LEWIS

To which there is one appropriate response: *But you're all pirates!* Nothing they do—short of seeking forgiveness for their fundamental sin—can change that fact.

Our world is chock full of pirates, steering this beautiful planet away from its intended port. Stealing the good gifts of God and using them as weapons against Him—quite often while wearing a nice smile.

People can be outwardly very moral, but if their hearts are fundamentally oriented away from God, God cannot be pleased with them, or He Himself would be unjust.

GOD'S COMMON GRACE

Yet God loves even rebels, made as they are in His own image. He loves His enemies just as Jesus told us to love ours:

> Love your enemies . . . so that you may be sons of your Father who is in heaven. For he makes his sun rise on the evil and on the good, and sends rain on the just and on the unjust. (Matt 5:44–45)

This favor of God, given even to people who hate Him, is meant to be a sign pointing them back to their Creator. And His patience (1 Pet. 3:20) and

THE MOST OFFENSIVE VERSE IN THE BIBLE

C. S. Lewis observed that even a professing Christian may "at bottom . . . still believe he has run up a very favourable credit-balance in [God's] ledger by allowing himself to be converted."[2]

So perhaps the most offensive line in the Bible is one we looked at briefly in the previous chapter: "Those who are in the flesh cannot please God" (Rom. 8:8). At the end of the day—at the end of all days—none of the things unbelievers do will truly and finally please their Creator.

No cancer research, no business integrity, no suffering on behalf of the innocent—nothing will ultimately please God if it's done "in the flesh." Giving all your goods to feed the poor, even giving up your body to be burned for your ideals—it will all profit you nothing unless, at the center of your heart, there burns a love for the one true God (1 Cor. 13:1–3).

If you have no love for God, that love is precisely what the Bible promises God will give you if you accept the terms of the New Covenant instituted by Jesus: repent and believe the gospel. Turn from your sins, believe that Jesus died for those sins and rose again to give you new life, and you'll get a new heart that loves God as it should (Deut. 30:6; Jer. 31:31–33).

forbearance (Acts 17:30) with sinners is meant to do the same (2 Pet. 3:9). Paul told a group of pagans in the city of Lystra:

> In past generations [God] allowed all the nations to walk in their own ways. Yet he did not leave himself without witness, for he did good by giving you rains from heaven and fruitful seasons, satisfying your hearts with food and gladness. (Acts 14:16–17)

God makes good food grow even in the ground He cursed (Gen. 3:17), and He does this as a "witness" to His own goodness.

So there are people who, all the while they are receiving God's gifts, refuse to see them as the signs they are. They worship all sorts of things other than God and degrade* themselves in the process (Rom. 1:24–25). They don't deserve God's favor. No human ever does. But God still gives it to them.

degrade: *to dishonor and disgrace through sin*

What do we call God's favor, given even to people who deserve His judgment? "Grace." And yet, not all grace is saving grace because not all sinners are saved. When that divine favor is spread all around the world, given commonly even to unbelievers, we call it **common grace**.

Common grace, rightly defined, is an important component of a truly biblical worldview because it explains how fallen people who hate God can produce so much truth, beauty, and goodness for the rest of us to enjoy. Beautiful music, well-executed art, thoughtful films, smoothly operating cities, wise public policy, amazing medical advances—God's enemies regularly produce them all by God's common grace.

Restraining Sin

Common grace explains why the people the Bible calls "the wicked" aren't as evil as they could be: God's common grace restrains them from committing all the sin they would otherwise commit. Our good God pours His goodness on and through people made in His image, even if they are encamped with the rebel army. Consider some biblical examples:

- God stopped the tower-builders in ancient Babel from accomplishing their sinful purpose (Gen. 11:6–8).

- God kept the unbelieving King Abimelech from committing adultery with Abraham's wife: "Yes, I know that you have done this in the integrity of your heart, and it was I who kept you from sinning against me. Therefore I did not let you touch her" (Gen. 20:6).
- God even put limits on the wickedness of Satan. He could do nothing to Job without God's permission. "The Lord said to Satan, 'Behold, all that he has is in your hand. Only against him do not stretch out your hand'" (Job 1:12; cf. 2:6). And Satan did exactly what God permitted, no more.[3]

Promoting Good

God, by His common grace, doesn't just restrain evil; He promotes good. Did you notice how God referred to the "integrity" of Abimelech? God is even willing to call some of the actions of His enemies "good."

But wait a minute—where did these enemies get this "good"? Does Satan have a little "good" to hand out to his children along with the "evil" he's so well known for? The Bible says that sin is like a disease—"The heart is deceitful above all things, and desperately sick" (Jer. 17:9). How could people desperately sick with sin ever manage to do something that isn't itself infected?

If there is good in anyone at any time, that goodness has to come, ultimately speaking, from God. This is why God can look on sinful people and see His goodness reflected in them.

- This is true even of King Ahab, one of the Bible's biggest scoundrels. On the one hand, Scripture says, "There was none who sold himself to do what was evil in the sight of the Lord like Ahab" (1 Kings 21:25). But a mere four verses later—after a divine rebuke—Ahab (temporarily) humbles himself and God notices: "Because [Ahab] has humbled himself before me, I will not bring the disaster in his days; but in his son's days" (21:29).
- Jesus said to one audience, "If you then, who are evil, know how to give good gifts to your children, how much more will your Father who is in heaven give good things to those who ask him!" (Matt. 7:11). In other words, "evil" people can still give "good" gifts.
- "If you do good to those who do good to you, what benefit is that to you? For even sinners do the same." (Luke 6:33) Jesus was saying that "sinners" can "do good."

A non-Christian can humble himself, give good gifts, and do good to others. Some unbelievers killed Jews in the Holocaust; others risked their lives to save them. But even the most self-sacrificial actions are not "pleasing" to God in any ultimate sense—*because they're still the actions of pirates* (1 Cor. 13:3). Nonetheless, these actions are still better than pride and selfishness. In that sense, they are "good." Not everything God's enemies do is completely wicked. They are still capable of goodness, even great goodness. God, who is the definition of good, says so.[4]

TOTAL DEPRAVITY

An important theological term points to the pervasiveness of sin in people—**total depravity**. *Depravity* means moral corruption. But *total depravity* doesn't mean that people are as bad as they could be. Because of common grace they're not that bad. *Total* only means that moral corruption has touched every part of every person (e.g., there's no part—like the intellect, say—that has escaped the effects of the Fall).

CULTURE AND COMMON GRACE

Now we arrive at the point of this section: what is true of individuals is true of the cultures they form and are formed by. Your favorite meal at your local restaurant was probably designed, cooked, and served by non-Christians—as a result of millennia of cultural traditions formed, mostly, by God's enemies. Some of the most beautiful music known to man was composed by wicked people who hated God. Even your favorite bedtime story as a kid was probably written, illustrated, published, shipped, stocked, and sold by people with no love for God at all, no desire to please Him whatsoever.

A few Christian families choose not to listen to any music or view any art by non-Christians. But this choice overrules God's verdict: He said that these people, made in His good image and given the blessing of His Creation Mandate, can do genuine good. Even groups of wicked people, working together, can produce real good along with their evil. Buildings, bridges, books; cars, companies, cookery—all these prove that lost people can make truth, goodness, and beauty.

The key here is to recognize the ultimate source of that truth, that goodness, and that beauty. And there's only one possible answer. All truth is God's; all goodness is His; all beauty is too. If we refuse a gift from God because of its faulty wrapping paper, we are insulting Him.

What does the beauty of India's Taj Mahal, built by a Muslim emperor in the 1600s, say about God's common grace?

THINKING IT THROUGH 8.1

1. Why can't those who are in the flesh, rather than in Christ, ever please God—regardless of all the good things they do?
2. Define common grace.
3. Identify several reasons God provides common grace to rebels.
4. Why is common grace an important component of understanding culture from a biblical view?
5. Do cultures show common grace, or just individuals? How do you know?

8.2 THE WORLD

One of the most exciting stories in the book of Acts occurred during the apostle Paul's ministry in the city of Ephesus. Paul was busy turning the world upside down, and some of the idolaters who were shaken up in the process decided to launch a protest—a protest that quickly turned into a riot.

Most of the people in the huge crowd of rioters didn't know why they were rioting; they were just caught up in shouting, "Great is Artemis of the Ephesians!" (Acts 19:28, 32). Paul saw the ruckus as a great opportunity to evangelize the whole city; the local Christians knew that was a bad idea and wouldn't let him go into the amphitheater. Ignorant riots can easily turn deadly—and two of Paul's friends were in fact dragged into the brawl by the mob.

What finally stopped the crowd from hurting or killing someone? Common grace. These rioters were restrained from violence by the threat of greater violence—from a government that, as Paul said elsewhere, God had set up (Rom. 13:1–7). The town clerk managed to quiet the crowd and then sent them home by warning them that they might be charged with rioting. In some places in the world, the government itself is a mob, but this was one place where the mere existence of the government probably stopped a mob from murder.

COMMON GRACE THROUGH CULTURE

Cultures throughout history have existed at least in part for the purpose of restraining people from antisocial impulses. Cultures develop traditions, laws, and institutions in order to put pressure on people to serve whatever that culture believes to be the common good. Cultures, then, can be tools of God's common grace to restrain sin. Cultures also tend to bind generations together; older people take seriously their role of handing off beliefs and practices and stories to the young.[5] And it is in this way that a culture is preserved.

Beliefs and practices and stories can be false, of course—and yet they can still restrain sin. By God's common grace, even governments dedicated to the worship of false gods (like Rome was in Paul's day) still scare mobs away from sin.

But culture is fallen, and at different periods in different places, that fallenness may be especially obvious. The common grace in a culture may be nearly overwhelmed by a tide of sin. Think of today's Western **popular culture**, the mainstream culture of music, movies, and celebrities. It's impossible to avoid that culture if you live in the Western world; it's everywhere (1 Cor. 5:9–10). "More than any other cultural expression, [pop culture] reaches, embraces, enthralls, and influences the largest portion of the American public," says one Christian culture watcher.[6]

In *All God's Children and Blue Suede Shoes: Christians and Popular Culture*, Ken Myers writes that "popular culture . . . is a part of the created order, part of the earth that is the Lord's, and thus something capable of bringing innocent pleasure to believers."[7] Who doesn't like a great story, told with humor and insight through an entertaining movie? Christians are allowed to enjoy the good gifts of popular culture. Pleasure wasn't invented by the devil. "But," Myers says, "not everything that is permissible is constructive."[8] Myers says it's not necessarily the wicked content of the movies and top-forty hits that concerns him (although they are surely problematic); it's the whole mood that pop culture encourages. What does American popular culture value? It values what's now. It values pleasure, immediate gratification, the latest fad. It values what's young and new; older people are seen as tired or hokey, not wise.

Young people may indeed know things their grandparents don't, but what do you call a whole culture that assumes the superiority of youth wisdom as a kind of law? It's hard to even call it a culture because there's no way it can be passed on. Opinions from people who appear to be over thirty-five are automatically discounted. So Myers warns that dealing with pop culture can sometimes be as challenging for Christians today as confronting persecution and martyrdom was for first-century believers. Getting thrown to the lions is certainly not something anyone would want to face, Myers says, but at least it was a direct threat that was easily perceived. The danger in our era is that Christian character is eroded, ordinary enjoyments are ruined, and life itself is cheapened by the subtle influence of popular culture without our even being aware of it. [9] How can professing Christians—who are supposed to see culture as a good but fallen gift—live holy lives in a world like this?

Worldliness

A lot of them don't. They give in. They're worldly. There are many people who claim Christ's name who nonetheless refuse to take seriously the important biblical truth that the Fall has touched every aspect of human culture, just as it has touched every human. The "world"—the bad part of culture[10]—goes far beyond pop culture; **high culture** (like operas and fine art) and **folk culture** (like bluegrass and Mongolian throat singing) are touched by sin too. But opera and bluegrass stars don't typically make the evening news or the racy gossip magazines in grocery store checkout lines. Pop culture, precisely because it's everywhere, is perhaps uniquely effective in its effort to influence people toward the values of the world.

The "world" is like poison that has seeped into a pond. Fish aren't aware that they're swimming in water any more than humans stay conscious that they're breathing air. It takes deliberate effort not to be affected by something once it successfully passes itself off as a natural part of your environment. And the world's assumptions do seem so normal, so inevitable.

You may be used to thinking about individual sins like lying, cheating, and stealing. But **worldliness** is group sin. As one theologian aptly puts it, "Sin is not only personal but also interpersonal and even suprapersonal."[11] He means, of course, that sin goes beyond the merely human level: Satan is called "the god of this world" (2 Cor. 4:4). So, the theologian continues, "Sin is more than the sum of what sinners do. Sin acquires the form of a spirit—the spirit of darkness, the spirit of an age, the spirit of a company or nation."[12] Worldliness in Botswana or Kyrgyzstan can look different from worldliness in Bali or Karachi. Different cultures (and different eras) have different ways of expressing hostility and rebellion to God.

But they all do it. The world puts a constant pressure on all people. Including you. And that's why Paul's main comment about worldliness uses an image something like clay forced into a mold: "Do not *be conformed* to this world" (Rom. 12:2). To *be conformed* is to be passive, to let the world shape you with

CHIC VS. KITSCH

Many people are skeptical about the distinction between high culture and folk culture. To call opera and poetry "high" and bluegrass and romance novels "folk" (or worse, "low") sounds like elitist sneering. And in our postmodern world, people believe there are no real standards for beauty anyway—it's just different strokes for different folks. Some people like Shakespeare; some people like World Wrestling Smackdown.

But Christians know that because God created an ordered world, standards for beauty do exist—even if they are difficult to apply with perfect confidence. High and folk are proper distinctions to make. Christians, who are called to press God's world toward its ideal, ought to take part in the fine arts and to rise as high in them as God's gifting will allow.

But this doesn't mean folk culture should be shunned; folk music and art, regional novels, and other forms of "low" culture are appropriate in some settings (such as a state fair) where high culture isn't. Even pop culture carries some benefits for Christians. Pop culture can provide humor, relaxation, and entertainment—and these things weren't invented in hell. But those values are probably not enough to justify the amount of time and money many Christians spend on such things.

whatever force it exerts. Paul commands that you let another force mold you, a godly force: "Be transformed by the renewal of your mind" (12:2).

If you have come to think that your church or your parents don't see enough good in the surrounding culture, if you're constantly chafing under their expectations about your entertainment or clothing, then you need to take what Paul says in Romans 12:1–2 very seriously. Because he follows up his command not to be conformed to the world with a very practical promise: if you'll be transformed by the renewal of your mind, you will be able to "discern what is the will of God, what is good and acceptable and perfect" (Rom 12:1–2). Does that sound attractive to you? Do you want to do what is good, acceptable to God, perfect in His sight? Then start by admitting that your mind might need some renewing.

Do you have a category called "worldliness" in your own personal thinking as a Christian? Not just your parents' thinking or your church's thinking (though these are extremely valuable). Have you ever decided—on your own—not to do, watch, say, read, invest in, follow, or like something because you knew it was "worldly"? When was the last time you resisted the pressure of the world to press you into its mold?

"I rarely meet the young Christian who needs to be exhorted to engage their culture," says one American Christian writer. "They seem to consume what everybody consumes, and are in general agreement with the zeitgeist* that a steady stream of entertainment is the Fifth Freedom that our forefathers fought for."[13] Another leading Christian thinker said something similar:

zeitgeist: *typical attitude or outlook of a particular generation*

> When I am among evangelical Christians, I find that they seem to be more avidly consuming the latest offerings of commercial culture . . . than many of my non-Christian neighbors. They are content to be just like their fellow Americans, or perhaps, driven by a lingering sense of shame at their uncool forebears,* just slightly more like their fellow Americans than everyone else.[14]

forebears: *ancestors*

There are magnets so powerful they can lift semi-trucks, but they can't lift a twig. If you were perfect, you'd be like that twig. The magnetic pull of sin wouldn't affect you. But you're fallen. It's not a mark of holiness that you can "handle" worldliness and sin in your entertainment without being affected. It's a mark of blindness; you *are* being affected.

One more piece of advice on worldliness: don't make the mistake of believing that music and dress and other cultural "artifacts" (tangible goods produced by a culture) are meaningless. One of the authors of this book, as a small boy, once wandered around the first-grade lunchroom with his middle finger up, insisting, "It doesn't *mean* anything. It's not different from any other finger." Needless to say, his teacher (Miss Ferguson) kindly asked him to refrain from making that particular obscene gesture. Putting up your middle finger does mean something, at least in Western culture. You can walk around insisting that it means nothing—or that it means what *you* say it means, not what everyone else *thinks* it means. But your classmates will just stare at you (and then go tell Miss Ferguson). Yes, your heart is more important than your haircut. But your haircut, your hemline, and even your hand gestures are "texts"—messages you send to the world about what's inside your heart. (And if music, dress, and movies are meaningless, why do people care about them so much?) The heart is where worldliness begins, but it always shows up on the outside.

Asceticism

Worldliness is a huge problem because cultures are fallen. But don't forget that every culture, by God's common grace, still retains some good. Some people *do* forget that. Ascetics* are such people.

ascetic: *person who practices extreme self-denial, giving up even normal everyday pleasures*

There are comparatively few true ascetics in the Western world—and there's no one today quite like the ancient monk Simon Stylites, who lived on a tiny platform atop a pillar for thirty-seven years! But there are plenty of people who are missing some of the true good in human culture, high and folk.

If you view God as an ascetic, you're going to be confused (at best) when you find out that there's a lot of good in culture that you were missing. More than one Christian has come close to losing his faith because he grew up assuming that non-Christians couldn't produce truth, goodness, or beauty—only to find all three when he actually looked.[15] Instead, you need to expect to see good in your culture. And you need to see that goodness as a gift from a good God, an example of His common grace. "This is my Father's world," the old Christian hymn says, and "He shines in all that's fair." Ascetics miss this truth.

It is worth spending time and effort developing your ability to appreciate the finer things of culture—refined classical music, poetry, literature, high art, and architecture. One of the values of a good liberal arts education in high school and college is that it introduces you to good things in your cultural tradition that you never would have discovered on your own.

Pilgrims and Ambassadors

The Bible offers two metaphors that might help you as you try to avoid the two ditches of **asceticism** on the one hand and worldliness on the other: Christians are both pilgrims and ambassadors.

Every Christian, the Bible says, is a pilgrim. John Bunyan titled his world-famous allegory *Pilgrim's Progress* because every Christian is on a sacred journey. We're traveling through a place that's not really ours in order to get to the day when the whole place really *will* be ours. This is our Father's world, but for right now "the whole world lies in the power of the evil one" (1 John 5:19). And that's why we don't belong. We're pilgrims, sojourners, exiles (1 Pet. 2:11).

Exiles from other nations move to the United States on a regular basis, and they're usually easy to spot—because they never quite lose the accent of their native tongue. And that's just what you want as a Christian pilgrim. If you fit in just fine with the world around you, the world ruled by Satan, either you're not a pilgrim in the first place or you've forgotten that you don't belong.

That's sort of like an ambassador—which is another metaphor the Bible uses (2 Cor. 5:20)—who goes to a foreign country to represent the interests of his nation. Yes, an ambassador needs to learn the local language, or he'll do little good. But you don't want him becoming so totally assimilated into the culture that he forgets what he's there for.

As the US Secretary of State represents his nation's interests abroad, so a Christian needs to represent the interests of Christ wherever he lives.

THE SOJOURNER IN PSALM 119

Psalm 119 is the longest chapter in the Bible—176 verses, almost every one of which mentions the Word of God in some way. But the Word is not the only theme in the psalm. Another major emphasis is sojourning. The psalmist says, "I am a sojourner on the earth" (119:19), and "Your statutes have been my songs in the house of my sojourning (119:54).

And the theme pops up over and over throughout the psalm. The psalmist, because of his love for the Word of God, doesn't quite belong. He prays, "Take away from me scorn and contempt" (119:22), and he prays for "an answer for him who taunts me" (119:42).

One really remarkable thing about this scorning and taunting is that the psalmist presumably lived in Israel. He was a sojourner, a stranger, a pilgrim, an exile—even within the land God had promised and among God's chosen people. Someone with a truly biblical worldview and a heart of love for the Lord and his neighbor will never be at home and at rest until God puts all things under Christ's feet.

DARKNESS AND LIGHT

There is darkness, and there is light. We must never confuse the two. There is sin, and there is grace. We must never confuse the two. But for now, darkness and light as well as sin and grace are found in the church and in the world. In the end, only Christ will be able to separate the wheat from the weeds, the good from the evil. God invites you to enjoy all His good gifts; because of common grace, there is a way to make holy use of human culture. But because of the Fall, you dare not participate in any aspect of culture (pop, high, or folk) uncritically. God warns us about the dangers that pervade culture after the Fall. A life well lived is one that stays constantly aware of the tension between common grace and the Fall; a Christian life well lived seeks to "test everything [and] hold fast what is good" (1 Thess. 5:21).

THINKING IT THROUGH 8.2

1. Why is all culture—pop, folk, and high—in need of critique? What makes popular culture in particular an effective vehicle for worldliness?
2. Explain what worldliness is and what you must do to discern it in real life.
3. How would you describe an ascetic? What's wrong with the ascetic view of the world?
4. Explain how Christians must behave as pilgrims (sojourners) and ambassadors in this world.
5. How would you describe folk, high, and pop culture? What are some illegitimate and legitimate reasons for rejecting some forms of each of these kinds of culture?

8.3 AFFECTION DRIVES COGNITION

Identical-twin studies are a fascinating branch of psychology, especially when those twins have been separated at birth. Watching them grow up helps researchers figure out the roles nature and nurture play in forming our personalities and habits. Some psychologists who specialize in studying twins have actually concluded that "identical twins raised apart are as similar in personality as are identical twins raised together."[16] Other psychologists think that nature and nurture have a roughly equal effect on shaping a person.

No matter who's right, the issue raises a fascinating question: why do two people (like twins, perhaps) respond differently to the same information? Two people listen to the same sermon about the resurrection of Jesus Christ. One believes, the other scoffs. It has always been this way. It was this way among the people of Athens when Paul visited their city:

> When they heard of the resurrection of the dead, some mocked. But others said, "We will hear you again about this." So Paul went out from their midst. But some men joined him and believed. (Acts 17:32–34)

But why only some? They all heard the same words. It's hard to believe that anyone could be a better evangelist than the apostle Paul himself. Why did some in his audience believe and not others?

PROVERBS 1:7 AND THE FEAR OF GOD

The key verse[20] of the book of Proverbs provides insight into why people respond differently to the truth. Solomon said, in the very first chapter of the book, "The fear of the Lord is the beginning of knowledge" (Prov. 1:7).

Notice the two key words in this key verse: fear and knowledge. *Knowledge* is a **cognitive** word. It refers to your mental processes, your thinking, your "cognition." But fear isn't essentially a cognitive thing. It's a heart thing. Fear does involve your mind—babies don't fear hot stoves because they don't realize, cognitively, that extreme heat brings pain. But *fear* is a more emotional word than *knowledge*; it's related to your "affections," the bent or inclination or direction of your inner being. This verse says that the "affective" thing comes before the "cognitive" one. The fearing comes before the knowing.

But it's not fear in general that Solomon encourages you to have; it's fear of one specific object: the Lord, the God of the Bible. If you look at how the Bible uses the phrase "the **fear of the Lord**," you start to get a picture of what it means. It means a trembling awe and respect before a vastly more powerful, perfectly holy, and utterly good Being. This is not a cowardly fear, like a soldier running away from a battle. This is a holy fear, one actually filled with love. The prophet Isaiah even predicted that the Messiah Himself—the Son of God—would "delight . . . in the fear of the Lord" (Isa. 11:3).

The whole thesis of Proverbs is that you're not going to be able to understand the world the way it really is till you're right with God, till your inner person is inclined toward God in the right ways. First fear, then knowledge. One way to summarize this is to say, "Affection drives cognition." What you love determines what you think and what you know.

The smartest kids in the class don't necessarily get the highest grades—or learn the most. It's the students who love history or science who do the best at them. Affection drives cognition.

BORN THIS WAY

Pop music isn't generally meant to be taken seriously, but pop star Lady Gaga tried to preach a serious message in her worldwide hit "Born This Way."

> No matter gay, straight or bi,
> Lesbian, transgendered life,
> I'm on the right track, baby.
> I was born to survive.
>
> . . . .
>
> I'm beautiful in my way,
> 'Cause God makes no mistakes.
> I'm on the right track, baby.
> I was born this way.[17]

Gaga herself believes some things are evil—"prejudice" and "judgment," for example.[18] So how does she know that moral judgment is evil but homosexuality is blessed by God? (And isn't that a moral judgment?) The only way we can know what is creational and good versus fallen and evil is to let our Creator tell us.

And He says that "I was born this way" is never a valid excuse for sin. Because of Adam's Fall, we were all born in sin (Ps. 51:5). "If I am so bad that I can't delight in what is good, that is no reason God can't command me to love the good," wrote one theologian. "If I am so corrupt that I can't enjoy what is infinitely beautiful, that does not make me less guilty for disobeying the command to delight in God (Ps. 37:4). It makes me more guilty."[19]

THE FEAR OF THE LORD

Biblical scholar Bruce Waltke says that "fear of the Lord . . . involves both rational and nonrational aspects at the same time"—head and heart. It's rational because it can be memorized and taught (Ps. 34:11). But "'fear of the Lord' also entails a nonrational aspect," Waltke adds, "an emotional response of fear, love, and trust."[21]

A particular teenage guy might write very poor analyses of the literature texts he's assigned in class, but when he wants his dad's car keys on Saturday, he brings to bear his full powers of analysis, evaluation, and argument creation. His desires fire up his mental powers. Affection drives cognition.

When a guy's heart is turned toward a girl (perhaps one he has failed to notice in the previous twelve years as her classmate), his mental energies all become dedicated to thinking of creative ways to be near her and to please her and to win her affections. If he does win them, that girl's brain will be working on the same tasks as his. Affection drives cognition.

WHY SCIENTISTS ARE NERVOUS ABOUT THE BIG BANG

cosmology: *the scientific field dedicated to explaining the origin of the universe*

Affection doesn't always drive cognition in good directions. *Time* magazine interviewed scientist and popular author Brian Clegg after he wrote a book about various theories of how the universe began. He said scientists generally speak about the big bang as if it were a settled result of modern science. Clegg says it's not; it's a speculative cosmological* theory.[22]

The *Time* interviewer asked Clegg to mention the theory's major flaws, and Clegg responded that scientists have expected to find aftershocks from the big bang, changes in gravity rippling outward from the center of the explosion. Clegg pointed out that a great deal of cash has been expended in looking for those waves, and so far nothing has been found.

And then Clegg asked a simple question: why did the big bang happen in the first place? "There is no sensible answer . . . unless you move over into the religious side and say, 'Well, it began because God began it.' That's why quite a lot of scientists are nervous about the Big Bang."[23] They don't want a Someone outside the system telling the system to get going, Clegg said.

The interviewer said that he was troubled by Clegg's assertions that scientists won't question the big bang because that would unsettle their careers. Clegg replied that science is a club, a "social network" like any other: "In the end, there is almost a fashion in science—ideas that are in, ideas that are out."[24]

Affection drives cognition.

ROMANS 1 AND THE TRUTH OF GOD

"The fear of the Lord is the beginning of knowledge" is not the only verse in Scripture demonstrating that affection drives cognition. Think of this key passage in Paul's letter to the Roman Christians:

> The wrath of God is revealed from heaven against all ungodliness and unrighteousness of men, who by their unrighteousness suppress the truth. For what can be known about God is plain to them, because God has shown it to them. For his invisible attributes, namely, his eternal power and divine nature, have been clearly perceived, ever since the creation of the world, in the things that have been made. So they are without excuse. (Rom. 1:18–20)

What does it mean to "suppress the truth"? If someone doesn't want to admit to himself that his actions (getting drunk, say) have caused a tragedy, he may compress that truth into a dark corner in his heart. He lets himself believe that the fatal car accident he caused was really the fault of poor brakes in his truck. He never lets the truth out in the air long enough for it to be confessed. He starts living his life as if a lie were true, and any time the truth tries to get out he shoves it back into its tiny corner.

Follow Paul's logic: God is angry because wicked people He created suppress the truth. But the truth about God isn't just in our hearts (though it is there—God put it there, as Paul will later show). The truth is all around us. It's plain, evident, obvious. God has shown it to us. Truths about God that are invisible become visible in His creation. You can't see God's "eternal power," for example. But you can see its effects in every intricately designed flower on the planet. You can't see His divine nature (His "Godness") directly, but you can see it reflected in every human face around you. It is, indeed, "the things that have been made" by God that bear His stamp and point to Him. Some plastic toys say "Made in China" on the bottom. Stamped all over our globe, from the tropics to the ice caps, is another label: "Made by God."

The beautiful things "that have been made" point to God's "eternal power and divine nature" (Rom. 1:2–21).

So what? So truth-suppressers have no excuse. How can Amazonian tribal people who've never heard of Jesus be blamed for failing to become Christians? Well, it's true that they don't bear the same amount of blame as someone raised in church who denies the Christian faith. But from their earliest lies as children they—like every person on the globe—have suppressed the truth that is evident all around them.

> "CREATION AS A WHOLE GIVES 'VISIBILITY' TO THE INVISIBLE GOD."[25]
>
> —SINCLAIR FERGUSON

Every one of God's human creatures knows, at some level, that God exists and that He's eternally powerful. It takes a wicked act of willful suppression to become ignorant of God. Everyone—everyone—knows his Creator. That's why one Christian apologist* can say that any atheist has two basic beliefs:

apologist: *someone who defends his viewpoint from attacks (from Latin* apologia, *a defense)*

(1) God doesn't exist, and
(2) I hate Him.[26]

IGNORANT OF WHAT YOU CAN'T NOT KNOW

What does it do to people when they suppress and deny what they can't not know? Their thinking gets twisted, darkened. That's why Paul told the Ephesian Christians,

> You must no longer walk as the Gentiles* do, in the futility of their minds. They are darkened in their understanding, alienated from the life of God because of the ignorance that is in them, due to their hardness of heart. (Eph. 4:17–18)

Gentiles: *non-Jews, but in this context "non-Christians"*

The Bible does not teach that non-Christians are stupid or uneducated. A non-Christian intellectual can be like a sharp, well-honed buzz saw—but one often sawing in the wrong direction. The Bible does not say that the one thousand Steves of Project Steve or the countless other college professors, mechanical engineers, biomedical researchers, artists, and writers in the non-Christian world are stupid.

And you are a Christian, if you are one, not because you are extra smart. In fact, God tends to choose "what is foolish in the world to shame the wise" (1 Cor. 1:27). You are a Christian because the hard heart you used to have has been replaced by the soft heart God gives to all His children (Jer. 31:31–34; Ezek. 36:25–26). And non-Christians see the world the way they do and know what they know "due to their hardness of heart."

These passages of the Bible are pointing to one of the key ingredients of a person's worldview: what we called earlier the "head-heart system." In these passages, the head-heart system appears to be the reason why your reasoning works the way it does. This is why people with the same intelligence, similar experience, and apparently equal amounts of common grace nonetheless disagree on basic issues of human existence. Thinking (head) and loving (heart) are tied closely together. You think what you think because you love what you love. Affection drives cognition.

THINKING IT THROUGH 8.3

1. What's the problem with trying to excuse sin by claiming you were just born that way?
2. Define the fear of the Lord.
3. Why is the fear of the Lord crucial for correct knowledge?
4. What does it mean to suppress the truth, and what is the result of suppressing the truth?
5. Explain how non-Christians can be both intelligent and foolishly ignorant at the same time.

8 CHAPTER REVIEW

TERMS TO REMEMBER

common grace
total depravity
popular culture
high culture
folk culture
worldliness
asceticism
cognition
fear of the Lord

Scripture Memory

1 Peter 2:11–12; Proverbs 1:7

Making Connections

1. What are the two overarching benefits of common grace?
2. Identify the two responses to culture Christians must avoid.
3. Where does worldliness begin, and how does it manifest itself?
4. What ultimately determines the way people interpret the evidence they see?

Developing Skills in Apologetics and Worldview

5. Respond to the following claim: Christians ought to reject any cultural product created by an unbeliever and accept any cultural product created by a believer.
6. Evaluate the viewpoint that music is amoral or neutral.

Examining Assumptions and Evidence

7. Why can't you evaluate a person's goodness by outward morality alone?
8. Why are non-Christians "darkened in their understanding, alienated from the life of God" (Eph. 4:18)?
9. Why can't you excuse your sin by claiming, "I was born that way?"
10. If many non-Christians are intelligent (and they are), then why do they embrace falsehoods?

Becoming a Creative Cultivator

11. Keep a journal for one week, daily noting all your observations of both common grace and worldliness.

Chapter Nine STRUCTURE AND DIRECTION

And try to discern what is pleasing to the Lord. Take no part in the unfruitful works of darkness, but instead expose them.

Scripture Memory
Ephesians 5:10–11

9.1 UNDERSTANDING STRUCTURE AND DIRECTION

C. S. Lewis was one of the most influential apologists for the Christian faith in the last century, and part of his genius was that he used a variety of literary genres to advance Christian ideas, from children's literature to a science fiction trilogy. The second book in his sci-fi series, *Perelandra*, tells a creation story very similar to that of the Bible, but this one's not about Earth but about Venus. The Great Lord and Great Lady—the first two members of the human-like race God has placed on Venus, which they call Perelandra—have lost each other on the sea-covered planet's floating, shifting islands. And just as God told Adam and Eve not to eat of one tree, God has told the Lord and Lady of Venus that they must not sleep on the "fixed lands," the only "terra firma" in that world.

Satan arrives to tempt the Perelandran woman to break that simple command. While Earth's Eve seems to have taken only moments to fall into sin, Venus's first mother outlasts many mind-bending conversations with the devil.

Satan in Lewis's story focuses much of his energy on twisting the woman's love for God. He tries to get her to believe that living independent of her Creator is actually the best way to please Him. But she implicitly trusts and deeply loves her Creator, who is as real to her as the air and water—so what Satan says generally sounds ridiculous to her.

God sends her a helper, an English professor from Earth named Ransom. As a Christian, he attempts to explain to the unfallen woman just what breaking God's commands will do to her race and her planet. He knows from bitter earthly experience.

The lady is perplexed, and Ransom has a difficult task: How do you explain the seriousness of sin to someone who has never seen anyone disobey the Creator? Words like *sin* and *bad* and *wrong* mean nothing to the Great Lady. She has never seen such a thing. So he chooses *bent*. He describes those who disobey God as "bent ones," beings who have twisted, distorted, or perverted the good God put in them.[1]

Ultimately, Perelandra's first inhabitants do not disobey their Creator, and Satan is banished. A new world is born without sin, and God's creatures are free to flourish according to His perfect design. They aren't "bent."

BENDING THINGS BACK INTO THEIR PROPER SHAPE

Lewis's story about Venus is very different from what happened on Earth, of course. Our Great Lady gave in—and so did her husband. God actually permitted the sin within Satan to slink into our world without marring it; but as soon as God's appointed rulers sinned, they plunged the earth into ruin. "The earth and its condition is and remains a human responsibility," says one author. "[So] Satan can wreak havoc on the good earth only by first controlling mankind."[2] Every bit of perversion, sickness, and evil in this world can be blamed on the sin of the race God made to rule it. We have bent our world pretty badly.

But by God's common grace—and His amazing grace, special* grace—all humans are capable of the opposite kind of bending. They're capable (*only* by the grace of God, the fountain of all goodness) of bending things back into their proper shape. What else do you call it when a school with terrible discipline problems gets cleaned up? Or when a rotten law—like the racist Jim Crow laws in the American South—gets scrubbed from the books? Or when society as a whole starts to praise exercise and condemn smoking? Or when slaves get freed, musical traditions become more beautiful, and technology progresses? Situations can and do improve in this world. They go from being bent to being less bent. And as we saw in the common grace chapter, that bending back pleases God.

special grace: *the grace of God given to regenerate fallen sinners; the grace that makes people Christians (1 Pet. 1:3).*

Everything in this world is moving in one of two directions: it's either bending or getting bent back. Christians are called to join the bending-back operation that God is already engaged in. Of course, God is the only one powerful enough to bend the whole world back into shape, but that shouldn't stop us from doing hard de-bending work ourselves. (God is the only one who can completely sanctify us, but that doesn't stop us from pressing toward holiness till He does so.)

"Try to discern what is pleasing to the Lord," Paul said to the Ephesian Christians (Eph. 5:10). In any given situation, look for the things that are going in the right direction, the things that please God. But be careful; Paul adds, "Take no part in the unfruitful works of darkness, but instead expose them" (5:11). In other words, if you see "bent ones" bending God's creation away from God's purposes, expose the bad bending. Point it out to the world.

Biblical worldview thinker Al Wolters uses two labels to help Christians do this discerning of good and evil—**structure** and **direction**. "Direction" is the bending, whether bad bending or good bending. "Structure" is the way things are supposed to be before they get bent, the way things are supposed to be when they get bent back. Think of a flexible, springy metal pole sticking out of the ground. "Structure" is when the pole is perfectly straight. "Direction" is when the pole is getting bent, whether the bending is going away from its original structure or back toward it. "Structure" is good because God created everything good. "Direction" can be good or bad.

DIRECTION: GOOD

Bending it back toward its intended order

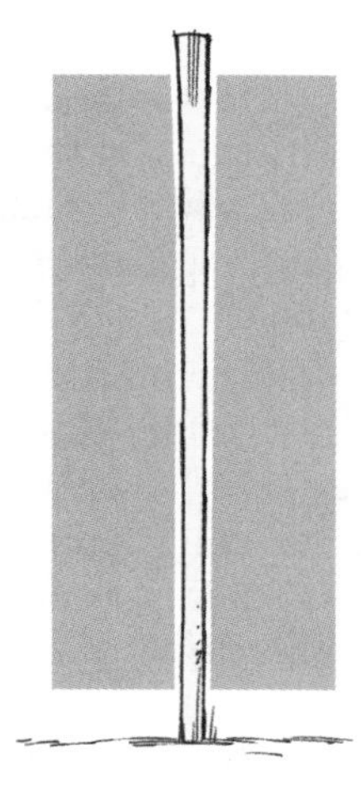

STRUCTURE

God's created order

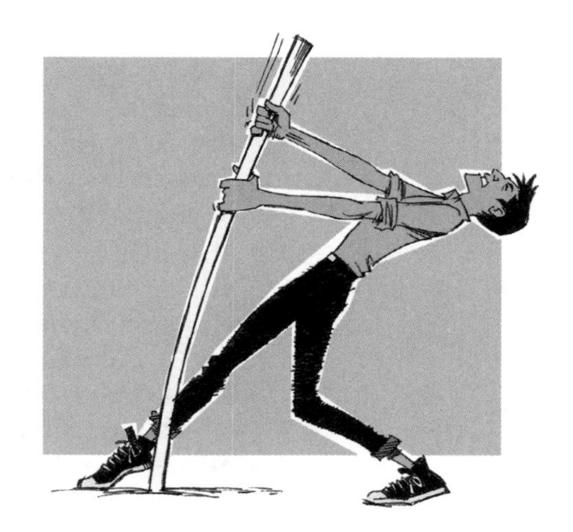

DIRECTION: BAD

Bending it toward fallen human nature

Metal poles can get bent in any direction—just like sin can twist God's good creation in numerous ways. There are political extremists on the left and the right; both sides have bent the pole of God's created structure, just in different directions. (And that doesn't mean political moderates are right, either—they have their own ways of bending the pole.)

Let's develop this pole metaphor just a bit further: no matter how much you bend a metal pole, if it is firmly anchored in the ground—in concrete, say—it's going to stay connected. Likewise, fallen humanity can bend creation only so far. Homosexuals will never be able to produce children on their own. Polluting factories will ultimately not get away with pumping endless chemicals into the water supply. Drug addicts and drunks will not be able to get their highs and still drive safely on their side of the road. Non-Christians are stuck in the world God gave us all, not in the one they want. That metal pole resists being pulled, and sometimes springs back into place. God's created structures endure all the abuse they receive.

Straight Structure

Of course, you can only know a pole is bent if you have some idea of what it looked like when it was straight. And that's why the Creation-Fall-Redemption metanarrative of Scripture is so important. It tells us that every created thing was originally good, and it gives us guidance as to what that good looked like (what we've called "creational norms"). This guidance is something that other prominent worldviews out there fail to give. Here are just two examples:

- Classic secularists (see Unit 6 about government) steadfastly refuse to describe what the ideal world would look like (what the pole looks like when it isn't bent). They point out that different cultures and religions disagree over the shape of the perfect world, and if you try to claim that your view is right, someone else will just come along and offer a different opinion. Then you'll have a fight on your hands. Better not to talk about the pole.
- In philosophical materialism, matter is all that exists. Who can say which states of matter are "good" and which are "bad"? They're just there. They're just obeying physical laws; they're not guided by any intelligence. Birthday parties happen, genocide happens. The big bang giveth, and the big bang taketh away.

But the Bible gives us the power to make moral judgments—in part because it tells us that the world has a structure, and a good one. It isn't just churchy, religious stuff that can be good (that's the way other religions tend to view the world).[3] No, the New Testament says that "everything created by God is good" (1 Tim. 4:4). Mere stuff can be good. Not neutral. Good.

By itself, no created thing is sinful. It's only when moral agents such as humans pick up creation and use it that it can get bent in bad directions. But God's people can pick up creation and use it for holy purposes too. In other words, they can "sanctify" it. Every God-created thing in this world can be "sanctified" by God's children, 1 Timothy 4:4–5 says. And this book has worked hard to show that good creational norms govern not just physical things but also institutions and disciplines such as marriage, government, academic research, and the arts. These nonphysical things can all be bent, but they can all be bent back too.

Direction Detection

You have to know about something's structure before you can discern its direction. But make no mistake: every created thing has a direction. C. S. Lewis said, "There is no neutral ground in the universe: every square inch, every split second, is claimed by God and counterclaimed by Satan."[4] There is a spiritual battle going on *in* this world—and it's going on *for* the world. The creation is what each side is trying to win, with mankind as the ultimate prize. Satan is trying to destroy the creation; God is trying (and will, in His time, succeed) to restore it to the way He intended it to be.

Because of this tug-of-war over creation, you must not assume that anything in creation is amoral or neutral. Music and sports, cartoons and novels—they're all going somewhere, and sometimes two somewheres at once. Your local soccer league may be headed in a good direction: it may be increasing the players' skills while recognizing that family and church take precedence over sports. Meanwhile, the high school football culture may be headed in a bad direction: football may become a community god, and the players may goad each other into being arrogant and obnoxious. Your local downtown area may be headed in good and bad directions, revitalizing run-down buildings but enabling (and subtly encouraging) drunkenness on the weekends.

So when we say that every created thing in this world—even marriage, government, and the arts—can be sanctified, we don't mean that Christians should necessarily try to sanctify every particular expression of those things in their cultures. Some institutions or cultural systems are so bent that they are best abandoned for now. Drama and theater, for example, had become so corrupt in seventeenth-century England that the Puritans were probably right to put an end to them while they held political power. At the same time, students at Christian liberal arts colleges today can benefit from Shakespeare's insight into human nature by producing his plays. It would not be right for conservative Christians to abandon drama entirely. Different circumstances call for different applications of the same unchanging biblical truths. Wisdom is needed, and discernment.

BABIES IN THE BATHWATER

This chapter is dedicated to helping you discern what's created and what's fallen in the world around you. You know the cliché: Don't throw the baby out with the bathwater. Anywhere there are babies (created structure), there's bathwater (fallen direction). Let's learn to distinguish the two. In the next unit, we'll focus on saving the babies; in this chapter we're just going to spot them out there bobbing in the water.

THINKING IT THROUGH 9.1

1. What do the terms *structure* and *direction* mean?
2. Explain the illustration the textbook uses to picture how the concept of structure and direction works.
3. Why is it necessary to define structure? What should determine the definition of structure?
4. Why can't there be any neutral ground in the universe?
5. Even though Christians are to make sanctified use of God-created things (general categories), should they try to sanctify every particular human use of creation? Why or why not?

9.2 SEX IN A FALLEN WORLD

Structure and direction are abstract concepts, and often the best way to understand difficult ideas is to see them worked out in real life. So let's get real practical. How do the labels "structure" and "direction" help us discern the good and evil in real-life situations?

Remember, in this chapter we're focusing on discerning fallen direction. The other direction—the redemptive direction—will have to come up soon, but it will take a back seat till we can explore it more fully in the next unit (Unit 4—Redemption).

In this section we'll discuss the fallen direction of a topic that can't and shouldn't be avoided: sex.

THE SITUATION WE'RE IN

What is sex like in our world? When you look out on the moral landscape of Western sexual life, what do you see?

Asking "what is sex like?" is akin to asking "what are people like?" Sex—like the people who engage in it—is different all over the place. But there are certain observable international trends. One of them is "hooking up," or sex without relationship and without commitment. It's not as if this has never existed before, but it has appeared only recently as part of the national conversation in America.

Washington Post reporter Laura Sessions Stepp wrote a book called *Unhooked: How Young Women Pursue Sex, Delay Love and Lose at Both*. She followed the lives of nine young women, ages sixteen to twenty-one, as they navigated the hookup culture in their high schools and colleges. This culture has developed, Stepp says, in place of the dating culture of earlier American generations. After Stepp befriended these girls, she interviewed them about how they had "hooked up" with varying degrees of eagerness. As a middle-aged feminist, Stepp wrote her book in part to help other young women who are hurt and confused by their own sexual choices.

Not all young women who read Stepp's work were appreciative. One challenged her in an online discussion of her book on the *Post* website: "Do you think that in your book you are making a judgment that hooking up is wrong? . . . As long as people are [practicing safe sex,] then why should they be judged for the choices they make?" Another young woman wrote, "I started hooking up because I felt it was healthier to have [my] physical needs met."[5]

This is the current worldly perspective on sex in the West: sex is not a moral issue at all. It's just a bodily function, like scrubbing dead skin cells off your hands with the right kind of soap. People think the only relevant moral issue is consent. Did the participants agree? Then no one else can say a word.

To people shaped by this view of sex, the Christian perspective sounds repressive—as if Christianity views sex itself negatively. And numbers of ex-Christians claim this is precisely the message they got while they were in church: "Sex is bad. It's a duty for married couples and necessary for the propagation of the species, but it's basically dirty."

CONSENT AND ABUSE

The University of California system has instituted a "yes means yes" policy for sexual activity among its students. This means that any sexual act is permissible as long as both partners explicitly say "yes" to it. Anything else can be called rape if one partner so chooses.[6]

Consent is a moral issue when it comes to sex. Rape and other forms of sexual abuse are horrific things, and one of their worst elements is the violation of human choice that they force on victims.

But consent is not the only relevant moral issue in a sexual act because people can consent to things that are wrong and self-destructive. Secularism reduces people to their physical impulses; the Bible sees people as embodied souls. Damage done to someone's body is a terrible thing, and so is damage done to someone's spirit, his or her "inner being" (Eph. 3:16). And illicit sex, consensual or not, inflicts precisely that kind of internal damage.

On any number of ex-Christian websites, people testify that they have been liberated from the Christian view and now see sex as simply a pleasurable, healthy exercise. One convert to atheism—sadly, the daughter of a Christian leader—wrote,

> For a long time I couldn't have sex with my boyfriend (of over a year by this point) without crippling guilt. I had anxiety that I was going to Hell. I felt like I was standing upon glass, and, though I knew it was safe, every time I glanced down I saw death.[7]

"Christianity," such people often say, "guilted me into thinking that sex was bad, but I discovered when I tried it that I had been lied to. I just had to get past my inhibitions." To a culture that views sexual freedom as the highest good and sexual pleasure as the very definition of pleasure, Christianity's view of sex sounds downright sacrilegious.

THE STRUCTURE OF SEX

As you stand on the part of life's timeline before marriage, you're going to have to take someone else's word for what the best way forward is. You (hopefully) don't know from personal experience which sexual choices will bring you pain and which will bring you present and eternal joy.

So trust what the Creator of sex says: the world has everything backwards when it comes to sex (1 Pet. 4:3). The ultimately biblical concepts of structure and direction can help us get it straight. What's structural about sex, and how is it being bent in fallen directions?

The structure is clear in Scripture: God created sex, so sex is good. ("Sex is bad" is not the Christian view.) Sex's structure is revealed in many places in the Bible, but it can be boiled down to this—Enjoy sexual intercourse often—within the covenant bonds of exclusive, one-on-one, heterosexual marriage. (See Exod. 20:14; 1 Cor. 7:1–6.)

Paul is very clear that married couples should engage in sexual intercourse regularly (1 Cor. 7:4–5). And one of the reasons he says so is that sex has incredible spiritual power: it unites people. Sex is structured to unite a man and a woman on a deep level, and that created purpose doesn't go away even when the man is an adulterer and the woman is a prostitute. Paul said, "He who is joined to a prostitute becomes one body with her" (1 Cor. 6:16), and then to prove this point Paul quoted the Genesis 2:24 principle: "They shall become one flesh." The created structure of sex can't be avoided; it's present even in a wicked place like a brothel.

> ***"Prostitution does not eliminate the goodness of human sexuality; political tyranny cannot wipe out the divinely ordained character of the state."***[8]
>
> —AL WOLTERS

Paul doesn't focus on the joy of sex, but other parts of the Bible do. God's main answer to worldly perspectives on sex is the promise of enjoyment. In fact, there's an entire book of the Bible dedicated to painting the "structure" of sex in beautiful colors. You may have been told that this Bible book isn't about sex at all, but about something "spiritual" (sex *is* spiritual, of course). But there's no way around it: God devotes a whole book of the Bible to sex. That book is Song of Solomon (or Song of Songs). And it doesn't take a clinical approach to sexuality, like an instruction manual; it's celebratory. The point is to praise profoundly, with intense poetry, the enjoyment God gives to married men and women so that you're enticed to follow God's plan. Why work at engaging in sex rightly? Because, when practiced according to its created structure, there is no joy quite like it.

Of course, we shouldn't forget the first purpose God gives in Scripture for sex: procreation. Part of the joy of sex is the privilege of being used by God to bring into existence more image-bearers. Bearing children after the Fall is painful; and that same Fall has poisoned male-female relations, making sex difficult for many couples. But the potential to bring children into the world and the joyful power of sex to unite a married couple are both precious values that need to be protected.

SEX IN ITS FALLEN DIRECTION

If sex had no created structure, you could do whatever you wanted and, if you played your hormones right, you'd get away with it. Sex couldn't be bent in wrong directions if there were no structure to bend. But when the author of *Unhooked* was told by a reader of her book not to judge the hookup culture, she replied wisely, "There are no condoms for the heart. Girls shouldn't fool themselves into thinking that just because they're enjoying a physical experience, they won't feel something afterward. Example: the number of girls who check their cell phones the day after a hookup, wondering why he hasn't called or messaged them."[9]

Sex—as part of its created nature—unites people, even if they say they don't care and don't want it to. And men can't escape that created structure any more than women can. Solomon asked this question about adulterers many centuries ago: "Can a man carry fire next to his chest and his clothes not be burned?" (Prov. 6:27). If Solomon were writing today, he might say, "Can you keep porn on your phone and never experience any negative consequences? Can you play the field for ten years with no adverse effects on your eventual marriage?" A man who uses a woman solely for her body is denying that she bears God's image. He's insulting her Maker. He's violating the most beautiful earthly picture of Christ's relationship to His church (Eph. 5:31–32). He's twisting a structure God made. Make no mistake: it's not just girls who face negative consequences for engaging in extramarital sex.

Sex, of course, gets twisted in a lot more ways than those mentioned here. Sexual abuse of minors, for example, is a horrendous sin with lasting consequences (Luke 17:1–2). The Bible says that "it is shameful even to speak of the things" that wicked

SATISFACTION, SEXUAL SINS, AND SINGLENESS

You're living in a unique time in world history. The internal pressure to give in to sexual immorality is just as intense as ever, but Satan now has more powerful and invasive weapons than he's ever had before. The internet is a great tool for many good purposes, but it's also the most efficient spreader of sexual immorality ever invented. You may be addicted to online porn—or trapped by a hundred other kinds of sexual sin, from graphic romance novels to sexting.

Get help. It's not too late for you. You're not meant to fight your battles alone. Seek out a trusted parent, pastor, or teacher. God, by His grace and the power of the Holy Spirit, can make sexual sin a thing of your past (1 Cor. 6:9–11). "The blood of Jesus. . . . cleanses us from all sin" (John 1:7).

There are many illicit sexual pleasures available to the singles in Western society. If you're a Christian, you must deny yourself—but not merely for the sake of denial. You must set before yourself a grand and holy motivation: one day God will very likely give you the pure sexual satisfaction found only in a spouse. The need for self-denial and the battle against lust won't end when your wedding day arrives.

But you will enter a very different phase. God's advice to singles of marriageable age is pretty blunt: "Because of the temptation to sexual immorality, each man should have his own wife and each woman her own husband. . . . For it is better to marry than to burn with passion" (1 Cor. 7:2, 9). God's normal answer to sexual temptation is a husband or a wife.

DIRECTION: BAD
hookup culture

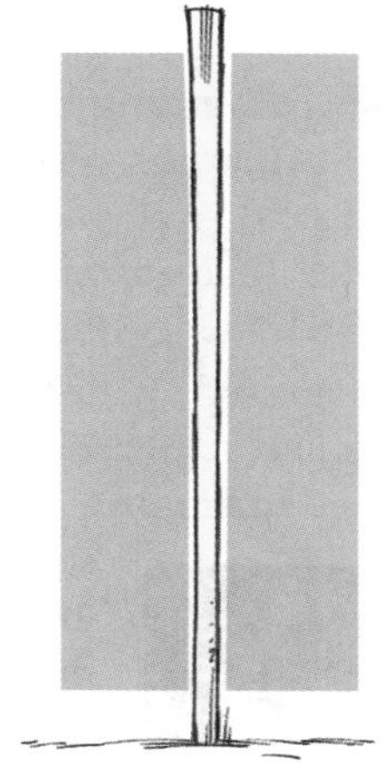

STRUCTURE
within the covenant bonds of exclusive, one-on-one, heterosexual marriage

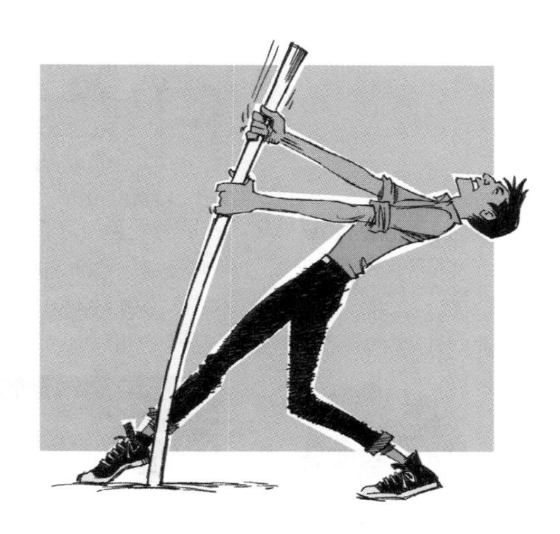

DIRECTION: BAD
forbidding marriage

people do "in secret" (Eph. 5:12). Because sex is such a powerful experience, people have dedicated immense energy to inventing ways to bend it away from God's structure.

And it's possible to bend sex in something other than a libertine* direction. Paul warned about those who "forbid marriage," and it was partly in response to them that he said, "Everything created by God is good, and nothing is to be rejected if it is received with thanksgiving" (1 Tim. 4:4). Some religious groups today have the reputation, at least, of being prudish.* Whether this is fair or not, the Victorian era is often thought to be one in which respectable people were much more eager to talk about death than about sex. (In our era, of course, it's just the opposite.) Perhaps some people do need to be exposed to Song of Songs and to verses such as Proverbs 5:18–19, where God tells husbands to be "intoxicated" with the love—and the bodies—of their wives. If people do exist who deny that sex ought to be pleasurable, that's what they need to hear. But there seem to be very few of them left in America.

libertine: *totally disregarding moral rules*

prudish: *excessively wary of any discussion of sexual topics*

THINKING IT THROUGH 9.2

1. What does the hookup culture insist you can do without? What's problematic with this viewpoint?
2. Why isn't it legitimate to claim that the Bible opposes sex? Why do some unbelievers say that the biblical position is repressive?
3. For what purposes did God design sexual relations?
4. According to 1 Timothy 4:1–3, what sexual deviation was being promoted by those who had departed from the faith?
5. Why is the created structure for marriage the only appropriate means for fulfilling God's purposes for sex?

9.3 OTHER STRUCTURES BENT IN BAD DIRECTIONS

Have you ever seen a caricature? It's a picture of someone with purposefully distorted features. A large nose becomes a huge nose; a spacious forehead becomes a football-field-sized one. Presidents and other public leaders probably get caricatured more often than anyone else. A good caricaturist manages to hold on to enough reality that the leader is still instantly recognizable.

A good caricature exaggerates certain features but leaves enough reality to make the figure recognizable.

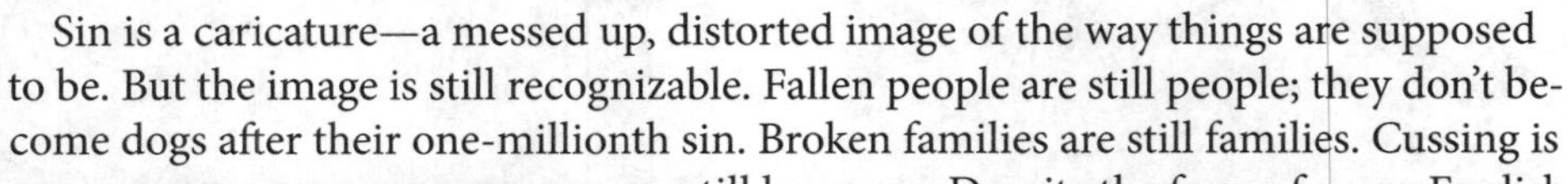

Sin is a caricature—a messed up, distorted image of the way things are supposed to be. But the image is still recognizable. Fallen people are still people; they don't become dogs after their one-millionth sin. Broken families are still families. Cussing is still language. Despite the fears of many English grammarians over the centuries, all the grammatical faults (and the cussing) of the masses have never succeeded in killing the capacity for linguistic communication. Sin has distorted every created thing to some degree, but never so much that the created order itself breaks down.

The previous section examined one created thing—sex—that people have twisted in sinful directions. But fallen sex, as we saw, is still sex. Sex still does the deep uniting of people that God created it to do. The created order never breaks down.

This section looks at several more examples of fallen direction twisting the created structure: materialism, technology, and language.

MISGUIDED MATERIALISM

Throughout most of this book, ***materialism*** is used to name the philosophical position that matter is all that exists. That's sense 1 for the word in most dictionaries. But listen to sense 2: "the tendency to treat material possessions and physical comfort as more important or desirable than spiritual values; a way of life based on material interests."[10] One clever person has called this "affluenza."[11] If matter really is all that exists, then you might as well get all the matter you can—especially the green paper matter with pictures of presidents on it. Have your best life now. He who dies with the most toys wins.

EPICUREANISM AND MATERIALISM

Most major ideas out there are not new. Materialism—the idea that matter is all there is—is a philosophy that can be traced back at least to Epicurus, a Greek philosopher who died almost three hundred years before Jesus was born. Epicurus stressed that pleasure was the only thing we know to be good. He doubted the existence of the gods and recommended that people not engage in crime not because it was wrong but because they might get caught—and might worry about getting caught, diminishing their pleasure. Ironically, *materialism* today often means trying to amass a lot of stuff since this world is all we get. But Epicurus took his philosophy of materialism in the opposite direction: the more stuff you have, the more worries you create. So live simply.

Materialism is, quite obviously, not a Christian point of view. Jesus said, "Do not lay up for yourselves treasures on earth, where moth and rust destroy and where thieves break in and steal, but lay up for yourselves treasures in heaven" (Matt. 6:19–20).

So what possible created good could lie at the heart of materialism? Matter. Stuff is intrinsically good because God made it. It's part of the structure of creation. That doesn't mean you should get as much as you can; that would be bending the acquisition of stuff in a fallen direction. God tells us to give some stuff away to the church and to poor people, and He warns us that stuff can be used for fallen purposes.

But God put us into a material world, and you're going to have to gather some of those materials if you hope to do God's will. "Everything created by God is good, and nothing is to be rejected if it is received with thanksgiving" (1 Tim. 4:4). Paul later tells the rich not to "set their hopes on the uncertainty of riches, but on God, who richly provides us with everything to enjoy" (1 Tim. 6:17). God gives us stuff, and He gives it to us for our enjoyment. But when we set our hopes on and organize our lives around that stuff, we're guilty of materialism. Materialism twists something good in an evil direction.

TWISTED TECHNOLOGY

Technology is a broad term for the tools humans develop to aid them in the work of dominion. If you're a Christian, you probably believe that materialism is wrong, but you may assume—at least in practice—that technology is all good.

And it is, at heart. God structured the world to require tools. We aren't Inspector Gadgets with built-in magnifying glasses, drills, and earth movers hiding in our hats. We need to invent and construct tools to help us do our work.

We don't usually think of all our tools—hammers, tape measures—as "technology," just those tools that have microchips in them. Tech gadgets are so useful. How can such amazing tools as these be twisted in fallen directions?

Simply put, when technology gets bent, we become the tools of our tools. Our tools become our gods, and we become their devoted servants. And that goes beyond the obvious things, like people who cannot stop texting even when they're driving. Technological tools, for all their power for good, also have the power to shape their users in negative ways they don't see.

It goes beyond the obvious fact that television, movies, and the internet are efficient spreaders of wicked content. No, technology itself has power regardless of what's on the screen, and tools themselves carry messages. Every piece of technology implies something about the way the world ought to be, and every piece of technology both gives and takes away. It makes some things easier and some things more difficult.

Let's take television as an example. TV is a well-accepted technology, one that is being transformed by the internet age but by no means destroyed. TV assumes that people need constant access to entertainment, and it makes nonstop diversion possible. It also makes it possible to tell certain rich stories that don't fit well in books or movies. At one time TV made possible a fairly united American culture: everybody watched the same shows because there were only three or four channels to watch across the nation.

But think of what the medium of television itself leads viewers to expect: entertainment or diversion. Like Twinkies, this isn't so bad taken in small doses. But some people leave the TV on all day (and eat Twinkies the whole time). American kids watch as much as thirty-five hours of television a week—the same number of hours French people are legally permitted to work.[12] What does that many weekly hours of diversion do to people—especially kids? [13]

A technology like television is very difficult to resist, no matter what it is you're watching. Humans were created by God to enjoy entertainment. That's part of our structure in this created order. But TV can easily bend that structure—actually, bloat it—into something monstrous.

CORRUPTED COMMUNICATION

Language is actually not a creation of God, or not exactly. But it's not a creation of humans either. Language may in fact be part of God's essence; the three persons of the Trinity appear to have used language before the creation of the world (Gen. 1:26). And even today they use it among themselves (John 16:13–15). When God made the first image-bearers, they were invited to share the divine privilege of language.

> *"Language is wonderful and mysterious. It is so because it is a gift of God to us. It reflects and reveals him."* [14]
>
> —VERN POYTHRESS

Individual human languages, however, do appear to be subsequent creations of God. English, Chinese, Urdu, and all other languages can trace their roots to Babel (Gen. 11). And what amazing creations they are! Do you realize that almost every sentence you speak, if it's long enough, is a brand new creation in the history of the world? No one has ever said exactly those words—and yet people understand you perfectly. The capacity for language is clearly hard-wired into human babies; animals can communicate (anyone with a dog or a cat knows this), but they don't have language. The complex rules of syntax that you grasped as a toddler are far beyond them.[15]

The created structure of human communication is evident all throughout the Bible. Words exist, most fundamentally, for the love of God and neighbor. And they have great power to accomplish these purposes. Words can praise God, sing to God, describe God, and pray to God. They can edify, encourage, and instruct people. Words don't just transmit information; they do things. They change our world.[16]

That's the structure of human communication. But what does language look like when twisted in fallen directions? Let's look at just two cases—too much language and bad language.

Too Much Language

On April 1 one year, National Public Radio posted a link to an article on its Facebook page with a big headline: "Why Doesn't America Read Anymore?" Only there was no article, just a short explanation that the whole post was an April Fool's joke. But the commenters weighed in anyway, ignoring the "article" and posting their thoughts after having read only the headline. One Facebook commenter blamed "I-Pads and smart Phones." Another complained, "People don't have the attention span or the patience to read."[17] They didn't get the joke.

The internet has made it possible to be slow to hear and quick to speak on a global scale. Quick speech is not all bad; Twitter and other social media have given a voice to oppressed people in nations run by tyrannical governments. But they've also given a voice to "trolls," people who troll around the internet looking for people to verbally abuse and conversations to ruin. And most significantly, the internet has provided a platform for so many voices that no one could possibly keep up with it all. For all the good it does, the internet has become something of a worldwide shouting match.

"Be not rash with your mouth," Solomon advised, "nor let your heart be hasty to utter a word before God, for God is in heaven and you are on earth. Therefore let your words be few" (Eccles. 5:2). James says Christians should be "quick to hear, slow to speak" (James 1:19). These verses reveal one way the amazing gift of language gets twisted in our fallen world. People use too much of it in the presence of others. They talk too much. The created structure of language is built on love for God and others. When you talk too much, you twist that purpose to your own ends.

Bad Language

Why are cuss words bad? Have you ever wondered that? Mom's "because I said so" is a sufficient answer for six-year-olds, but not for you. Try applying the concepts of structure and direction here. Bad words are bad, generally speaking, because they take some of the most personal and sacred things in the universe and twist them in the wrong direction, out of the structures they belong to.

Religious terms used for cursing—names and words such as *God*, *Christ*, *damn*, and *hell*—take some of the most powerful realities in all human existence and wrench them out of place. The existence of damnation is one of the most terrible realities we know; and the love and authority of Jesus Christ make up the most glorious reality we know. These words belong in serious and reverent places. Cuss words throw these realities in the dirt. Their power is still present, even in the dirt, but it's twisted. People want that power; that's why these words are used by so many—even atheists who deny that Christ condemns anyone to hell.

It's similar for words that describe sexual and excretory functions. Sex has intrinsic power, and using sexual words as curses twists that power out of the only place it belongs, the marriage bed. Song of Solomon does speak literally of sexual matters (e.g., 1:13)—but only to a point. Beyond that, it resorts to figurative language (2:3–4).[18] The most graphic sexual imagery in the Bible is reserved for intense divine denunciations of Israel's sins. (See Ezek. 16.)

"Modern thinking typically supposes," writes Christian thinker Ron Horton, "that the goodness of nature justifies the flaunting of nature and . . . that the impulse for concealment implies shame." This is a wrong idea, Horton says. "The divine view combines high respect and secrecy."[19] There are times to talk about sexual and excretory functions. There's a structure to human communication that creates safe spaces for each kind of talk. But those spaces are private. Far from shaming those things, it gives them the kind of respect and privacy they deserve (1 Cor. 12:23–24).

Right Language

Human communication, including language, gets twisted all day long all over the world. About the only people who don't misuse their tongues are infants—though some of them get so angry that you sense they would curse if they could. But let's make a simple CFR point: language is still a good thing, despite the twisting. "No human being can tame the tongue" (James 3:8); it's true, but taking a lifelong vow of silence is not the solution to twisted speech. Your goal in language isn't merely negative—to avoid talking too much or saying the wrong thing. It should be positive—using the right words to bless God and your neighbor.

STRUCTURE STICKS AROUND

The existence of corrupt politicians doesn't eliminate the goodness of government. The existence of hatred doesn't eliminate the goodness of emotion. (In fact, it's our moral duty to hate certain things in a fallen world. David wrote in Psalm 139:21, "Do I not hate those who hate you, O Lord?") Everywhere you turn in your daily experience you will see created structures skewed in fallen directions. You will see good creations of God twisted, bent, bloated, and shrunken into caricatures of what God intended. But the Fall isn't the end of the story. Rest assured that God can untwist, unbend, unbloat, and unshrink His creation.

And He will. Read on.

THINKING IT THROUGH 9.3

1. Why would it be wrong (and impossible) to reject the use and enjoyment of all material goods?
2. At what point does a good tool become twisted in a fallen direction?
3. Identify the purpose and describe the power of communication.
4. What are two major ways in which communication can be twisted in a fallen direction?
5. Why shouldn't religious words and bodily functions be used as curses?

9 CHAPTER REVIEW

TERMS TO REMEMBER

structure
direction
materialism
technology

Scripture Memory

Ephesians 5:10-11

Making Connections

1. When humans bend God's good creation in a wrong direction, what should be the twofold response of Christians?
2. What's the only moral stipulation demanded by secularists for sexual relations? Why isn't this sufficient?
3. Does the Bible teach that sex is good or bad? Explain your answer.
4. How does consumeristic materialism follow from philosophical materialism?

Developing Skills in Apologetics and Worldview

5. How should you respond to someone who says that the way God made one particular marriage—Adam and Eve's—doesn't rule out the possibility that other arrangements (polygamous, homosexual, etc.) might be acceptable to Him?
6. If you were Miss (or Mr.) Ferguson, what would you say to the first-grader with his middle finger up?

Examining Assumptions and Evidence

7. Is there any created thing that is not being bent either toward or away from God's design?
8. Why is there a limit on how long and how far humans can bend God's creation in a wrong direction?
9. Why is God's structure for sex the only righteous means of sexual expression?
10. Why is technology good? Why is it so powerful?

Becoming a Creative Cultivator

11. In one or two paragraphs, briefly evaluate an additional created structure using the paradigm of structure and direction. (Topic ideas: art, literature, music, hunting, automotive design, journalism, engineering, or biology.)

REDEMPTION

Chapter Ten **AN EVERLASTING KINGDOM**

Chapter Eleven **REDEEMED FOR GOOD WORKS**

Chapter Twelve **THE MISSION OF THE CHURCH AND YOUR VOCATION**

A
Ω

Chapter Ten **AN EVERLASTING KINGDOM**

And I will put enmity between you and the woman, and between your seed and her Seed; He shall bruise your head, and you shall bruise his heel.

Scripture Memory
Genesis 3:15 NKJV

10.1 THE HISTORY OF REDEMPTION IN THE OLD TESTAMENT

Readers love to be swept up in epic stories. Science fiction writer Isaac Asimov's famous Foundation trilogy, for example, covers a thousand years and the fate of millions of planets. *The Lord of the Rings* is pretty epic by itself, but author J. R. R. Tolkien gave it a backstory going back centuries (which true fans can read in *The Silmarillion*), and he even invented languages for it. The *Star Wars* saga claims to be an epic that happened "a long time ago in a galaxy far, far away."

There is no story more epic than the one you personally are playing a role in right now, the great story that engulfs all stories—the story of what God is doing to glorify Himself by redeeming His fallen creation.

This big story of Scripture—the metanarrative of the Christian worldview—contains many highs and lows. God created us in His own image and honored us with the task of ruling His world—that's a height. But we have rebelled against His goodness—and there's nothing else as low as that. God's image within us is now twisted, and our calling to have dominion has been frustrated.

But this is not the end of the story. The Bible not only tells us what we have done to ourselves and our world; it also tells us the remedy for our predicament. The actual events of Creation and the Fall take up just a few pages of the Bible (though they remain important to all the pages that follow). But the Bible takes its time telling the history of **Redemption**. It begins in Genesis 3 and doesn't end until Revelation 22.

The Bible's heavy emphasis on Redemption presents us with a significant challenge that you may have already noticed: it's not easy to figure out the main point of a story that lasts many hundreds and hundreds of pages and covers thousands of years of history. But the purpose of this chapter is to identify that main point. We need to learn what Redemption is all about, and then we need to examine its implications for how we understand the world.

We can't tell you the whole epic story—that's what the Bible is for. But we can go over the high points to show how that epic story flows through the whole of Scripture.

THE SEED OF THE WOMAN

"In the beginning, God created the heavens and the earth" (Gen. 1:1) He gave man and woman, His highest creations, a unique status and a unique job—they were made in His image, and they were to fill and rule the earth for His glory.

One marvelous proof of God's grace is that the same passage that records the Fall of those image-bearers into sin also records the beginning of Redemption. While God is speaking a curse on the Serpent (Satan, according to Rev. 12:9), He gives a whisper of hope to the human race. In Genesis 3:15, God tells the Serpent that he is cursed to fight a long war he cannot win. A seed given to the woman will oppose Satan and frustrate his plans. There will be times when it appears that the Serpent is winning the war, but his victories will prove to be nothing more than bruises on the heel of the woman's seed. In the end, the seed of the woman will leave the head of the Serpent crushed.

Genesis 3:15 is the thesis statement for the whole Bible. It expresses in just a few poetic lines the whole history of Redemption. It's a verse thick with meaning. And it is possible to uncover this meaning, but you have to look at the rest of biblical history to do so. That is, after all, how a thesis works. But before we work through what Genesis 3:15 leads to, we need to consider where Genesis 3:15 came from.

Before the Fall, God had stated that man was to rule over the world while still under God's greater rule over him. But now man has sinned. So God promises to send another man into this broken world: the seed of the woman. This man will do what the first man was supposed to do: he will subdue and have dominion. And in order to do that, he has to crush the enemy's head. The dominion God commands humans to take in Genesis 1:28 will not be set aside. It will be restored—by a man, the seed of the woman.

But who is this Seed, and how will he subdue and have dominion? Those are the questions that the rest of the story answers. The authors of the Old Testament begin to answer them by unfolding a series of covenants.

SEED AND OFFSPRING

Some translations of the Bible use the word *seed* in passages such as Genesis 3:15. Some use the word *offspring*. Both terms have the advantage of being either singular or plural. You can say, "Hey, give me the last sunflower seed!"—that's singular. Or you can say, "I planted sunflower seed in my garden this year." That's plural because you're not talking about just one seed. Hopefully you planted more than one!

The Hebrew word for *seed* can refer to one seed (singular) or to a whole pile of seed (plural).

The same is true of the word *offspring*. It can be singular or plural. Your parents probably don't use that word to describe you unless they're trying to be a little funny. But if you're an only child, they can tell someone, "This is our offspring." Or if you're one of several children, they can say, "These are our offspring." Same word, but one use is singular, and the other is plural.

To make things even more interesting, *seed* and *offspring* can refer to an immediate descendant or a much later one—or a large group of later descendants. So think of your great-great-great-grandfather. You are his seed. So are lots of your cousins and aunts and uncles and people you've never met. And so was each of his children. The word *seed* is flexible.

All this is important because God used an ambiguous word—one that could mean either singular or plural, soon or much later—on purpose. There are good reasons for that choice, but you'll have to keep reading to find out what they are.

The Noahic Covenant

By Genesis 6, serious problems are already evident in God's good creation. "The sons of God" (perhaps a reference to the seed of the woman) intermarry with the "daughters of men" (perhaps a reference to the seed of the Serpent). In time the two lines become impossible to distinguish. Eventually, mankind is so wicked that God sends a Flood that destroys the whole world. Only Noah and those on the ark that God commands him to build are saved. Even after this drastic (but righteous) punishment the basic problem still persists because "the intention of man's heart" remains "evil from his youth" (Gen. 8:21). As one early American theologian noted, "If [God] was to drown them as often as they deserved it, one deluge must follow another continually."[2]

"THE SCOPE OF REDEMPTION IS AS GREAT AS THAT OF THE FALL; IT EMBRACES CREATION AS A WHOLE."[1]

—ALBERT WOLTERS

Instead of continuing to rain down punishment on the earth, God makes a covenant with Noah, with his seed, with all the creatures on the earth, and with the earth itself. God promises to not further curse the earth, to preserve regular seasons, and to never again destroy the earth with a flood. In the course of the covenant, God reaffirms that fallen man still bears His image and that in spite of the effects of the Fall, mankind is still to carry out the Creation Mandate (Gen. 9:1–7).

The Noahic Covenant promises to make the earth a stable place while God works out His plan for redeeming mankind. But how can God withhold due punishment from people who never cease being wicked? In Genesis, God institutes the covenant in response to Noah's sacrifice (Gen. 8:20–22). And this has always been God's way: sin must be paid for by blood.

The Abrahamic Covenant

The next stage in God's plan to redeem the world occurs centuries later—God operates on a time scale we can't use, one beyond the individual human lifetime. God reveals Himself to an unknown idolater in the city of Ur (Josh. 24:2–3), a man named Abram ("exalted father"). God graciously calls him away from all that he has known, changes his name to Abraham ("father of a multitude"), and makes three solemn promises to him (Gen. 12:1–3).

- First, God promises to give him a "seed"—offspring, people. From the body of Abraham will come a great and mighty nation.
- Second, He promises to give Abraham a land where this seed will live and thrive.
- Third, He promises to bless all the families of the earth through Abraham and his seed.

Seed, land, and blessing: God's epic story of Redemption now begins to take shape. God had told Adam and Eve to fill the earth—now Abraham's seed would "be fruitful and multiply" in fulfillment of that promise. God had told Adam and Eve to take dominion—now Abraham's seed would have a land over which they could rule. And these blessings are not for Abraham's seed alone—now every family of the earth will be blessed. It is through Abraham that the "seed of the woman" promised in Genesis 3 will come. But throughout the coming epic story, many threats will arise to these three promises.

The Mosaic Covenant

In obedience to God, Abraham's family moves to the land of Canaan. When famine later threatens to wipe out that family (putting at risk the seed promise), they move to Egypt under the leadership of Jacob, Abraham's grandson. There they remain for the next four centuries. During these years the family grows to become a nation—but a nation of slaves under cruel Egyptian pharaohs.

God raises up Moses to lead this new nation back to the land God promised to Abraham. As a motley group of slaves, they have managed to hold on to some of their traditions (Gen. 32:32), but they need to be molded into a true nation to fulfill God's promise to Abraham.

So the Hebrews have an appointment with their God at Mount Sinai. Here God makes another covenant, the Mosaic Covenant. Unlike the Abrahamic Covenant, this one includes a major condition: if the people of Israel will agree to live by God's laws, He will make them a kingdom of priests. They will stand above all the nations of the earth in glory and privilege. They will also serve the nations of the earth as a priest does, by showing the world how to approach God in an acceptable way.

The Israelites accept God's condition. They promise to obey God's rules so that they can become His kingdom of priests.

God is slowly working out His plan to redeem the world. The Mosaic Covenant clarifies the Abrahamic Covenant by telling us more about the land promise and the universal blessing promise. It tells Israel how to live in the land of Canaan, turning it into a place where godly dominion replaces the sinful dominion of the Canaanites. It also tells us how God will bring a blessing to all nations. Israel will spread God's blessing to other nations by serving as the priest nation. God has called these people to Canaan not so that He can save only them, but so that He can use them to bring the whole world back to Himself.

But the "seed" in the promise to Abraham (and to Adam and Eve) is still left unclear. Is the seed one or many? Like any good author, God leaves some questions to be answered in later chapters of the epic.

The Davidic Covenant

God gives the land of Canaan to the people of Israel as He promised. But they repeatedly sin and rebel against His law. He punishes them but never abandons them.

In time He raises up a king for them, David the son of Jesse. David is the greatest king the nation will ever have—precisely because he loves the Lord his God with all his might. He has left us some of the richest poetry in our Bibles, the Psalms. And in the middle of his reign, God makes a covenant with David.

In the Davidic Covenant, God promises that David's dynasty will last forever. God's actual wording is especially significant:

> I will set up your seed after you, who will come from your body, and I will establish his kingdom. . . . I will be his Father, and he shall be My son. . . . Your kingdom shall be established forever. (2 Sam. 7:12–16, NKJV)

David also wrote psalms exploring and elaborating the marvelous promise God had given him (see Pss. 2, 22, 45, 89, and 110). The Seed of David, says Psalms, will "rule in the midst of his enemies" (Ps. 110) and then "make the ends of the earth his possession" (Ps. 2).

We're getting more clarity on the seed promise: the seed of the woman—the seed promised to Abraham—will be, specifically, David's seed. David will have a great and mighty descendant who will defeat the enemies of God's people and rule forever. It seems that this seed will be a single person. But He will be a person like no one the world has ever known. He will be divine as well. God Himself, somehow, will be His Father. This **Seed** will be the Son of God.

A psalm by David's famously wise son, Solomon, reveals that this Seed will not rule over only Israel; He will rule over the entire world (Ps. 72:8), and his rule will enforce justice that will be a blessing to all nations (Ps. 72:1–4, 17).

A PRAYER FOR THE FUTURE KING

Psalm 72 is a Messianic psalm written by Solomon, and here's what he prays for the future King in that psalm:

> "Give the king your justice, O God, and your righteousness to the royal son! May he judge your people with righteousness, and your poor with justice! Let the mountains bear prosperity for the people, and the hills, in righteousness! May he defend the cause of the poor of the people, give deliverance to the children of the needy, and crush the oppressor!" (Psalm 72:1–4)
>
> "May he have dominion from sea to sea, and from the River to the ends of the earth!" (Psalm 72:8)
>
> "May his name endure forever, his fame continue as long as the sun! May people be blessed in him, all nations call him blessed!" (Psalm 72:17)

Jesus is the only king who could ever be God's answer to these prayers.

Exile

David's reign is a bright spot in a long story of Israelite sin and failure. Thirty-two of the Jewish people's forty-two kings were bad, and the other ten all had plenty of faults. Readers of Kings and Chronicles may be excused for wanting to tear out their hair as they watch these kings and their people fall into idolatry over and over.

God's mercy lasts for many human lifetimes, but God did promise back at Mount Sinai that violations of the covenant would bring terrible judgment. In the end God sends the Babylonians to take His people captive—including the descendants of King David. And this isn't a random judgment: it targets precisely God's promises to Abraham and David about the land.

It even leads many people to call those divine promises into question. Aren't the people supposed to have the land "forever"? The Abrahamic Covenant promised a seed, a land, and a blessing for all the world. But now the land is gone, the seed is in exile, and the hope of a universal blessing seems all but impossible. Small nations just don't recover from mass captivity. (Where are the Hittites* today?)

Hittites: *an ancient people who lived in the Promised Land before the Israelites did*

The New Covenant

But even in judgment, God remembers mercy. It was to Jewish exiles in a faraway city that God gave the prophet Jeremiah a special message:

> Days are coming, declares the Lord, when I will restore the fortunes of my people, Israel and Judah, says the Lord, and I will bring them back to the land that I gave to their fathers, and they shall take possession of it. (Jer. 30:3)

And then came these even more precious and tantalizing words:

> I will make a new covenant with the house of Israel and with the house of Judah, not like the covenant I made with their fathers. (Jer. 31:31)

The Mosaic Covenant required God's people to obey God's laws. But their history demonstrates over and over again that this obedience was something they simply could not maintain. The fall of Adam had infected his descendants too deeply. Even with perfect laws and God on their side in battle, the Israelites were lacking something essential. Jeremiah revealed what that essential thing was:

> This is the covenant that I will make with the house of Israel after those days, declares the Lord: I will put my law within them, and I will write it on their hearts. And I will be their God, and they shall be my people. And no longer shall each one teach his neighbor and each his brother, saying, "Know the Lord," for they shall all know me, from the least of them to the greatest, declares the Lord. For I will forgive their iniquity, and I will remember their sin no more. (Jer. 31:31–34)

The people needed new hearts. They needed God to redeem not just their surroundings or their government but their innermost beings.

The New Covenant makes obedience not the condition of the covenant (as it was with the Mosaic Covenant) but the certain result. In the New Covenant, people don't obey God in order to be His people; they become His people, and they therefore obey Him.

God's people in the New Covenant need never fear His anger or His judgment. Their guilt is removed forever: "I will forgive their iniquity."

But how? How can this New Covenant ever take place? God's people are in exile at this point in the Bible's story. And more importantly, how could a just God forgive the sins of His people, let alone all the Gentiles? Being a just judge, He couldn't just let them all off the hook. A judge has to follow the law, even and especially if He made the law.

The Direction of The Epic

The covenants of Scripture all point toward the future because if God is going to keep them all—and He is—He has some glorious work left to do. Abraham is going to get a land, and not just any land but a very particular one: the land of Canaan. And David's Son needs to sit on a throne in that land. God can't utterly destroy this world and still keep His promises. In fact, the biblical covenants suggest that God doesn't plan to replace this world but to restore it.

THINKING IT THROUGH 10.1

1. Why was the Noahic Covenant necessary?
2. What three promises did God give to Abraham? How do those promises relate to the Creation Mandate?
3. What makes the Mosaic Covenant distinct from the other covenants?
4. What is the promise of the Davidic Covenant?
5. What does the New Covenant provide that none of the other covenants could provide?

10.2 THE COMING OF THE KINGDOM

It is hard to keep track of everything that a big book like the Bible is saying. The promises and stories and genealogies and poems and laws and songs and proper names come at you so fast that it's almost impossible to put them together in any sensible way—until you see them all as part of an epic story. Seeing all the little stories like Jonah and Noah and Joseph as part of one big story—what God is doing to glorify Himself by redeeming His fallen creation—is absolutely key to understanding the Bible.

This chapter on Redemption is not just repeating stories you already know; it's trying to put them together into that one big story so you can hold on to them. It's easier to catch a hundred M&M's if someone tosses you a bag containing that many than if he throws them at you a handful at a time. If you've been following the big story, you may (and should) find yourself curious about how it's going to turn out, even if you think you already know the answer!

THE GOOD NEWS IN THE NEW TESTAMENT

Repeatedly, the Old Testament tells us what God will one day do to fulfill the grand, sweeping promise of Genesis 3:15: the Seed of the woman will crush the head of the Serpent. When we turn the last page of the Old Testament to begin the New, we pass from the age of promise to the age of fulfillment. We meet the Seed.

Jesus of Nazareth

The New Testament opens with the account of an extraordinary birth. Before this birth, an angel appears to the baby's mother, Mary, and announces: "You will conceive in your womb and bear a son, and you shall call his name Jesus." The angel goes on to explain the greatness of His mission: "The Lord God will give to him the throne of his father David, and he will reign over the house of Jacob forever, and of his kingdom there will be no end" (Luke 1:31–33).

Mary is perplexed when she hears this news. She's not married. How could she have the child that would fulfill these promises? The angel explains that the Holy Spirit will cause her to conceive. She will indeed be the mother, but the boy will have no human father: "The child to be born will be called holy—the Son of God" (Luke 1:35).

This human child, David's descendant, will nonetheless be a Son of God. As a man, He fulfills the seed promise of Genesis 3:15. He is the seed of a real-life descendant of Eve. And as God's own Son, He fulfills the promise that David's great descendant would also be the Son of God (2 Sam. 7:14).

And Jesus is something else God promised to David: a king. The King. The very first thing Jesus announces, and the very center of His message, is "The time is fulfilled, and the kingdom of God is at hand; repent and believe in the gospel" (Mark 1:15). The turning point of world history has come, and He is it.

The Kingdom

All through the Old Testament, God had been promising the coming of a **kingdom**. One day a dominion—a rule—would come to earth, crushing the Serpent, saving God's people, defeating the enemies of God, and exalting God's people to rule and reign forever. Now at last the kingdom has drawn near.

The kingdom has drawn near because the King has arrived. This is the most important point made by the four Gospels. When Jesus teaches the crowds, they are amazed that He speaks with kingly authority. When He calms a storm, He rebukes the wind and the waves with a kingly voice, and immediately all is still. Creation itself knows that it's in the presence of the King.

Even the kingdom of Satan knew that the King had come. "What have you to do with us, Jesus of Nazareth?" said a demon to Jesus. "I know who you are—the Holy One of God!" (Mark 1:24). And when the King commanded those demons to get out, they obeyed. "If it is by the Spirit of God that I cast out demons," Jesus said, "then the kingdom of God has come upon you" (Matt. 12:28).

Death and Resurrection

Jesus could have cut a straight path to full kingship. He could have put everything under His feet two thousand years ago. He could have ended all opportunity for salvation and brought only judgment to the world.

But that was not His plan. He was seeking worshipers for the Father (John 4:23), so He came not to bring judgment but to bring salvation. In the verse right after the most famous verse in the Bible, Jesus explains, "God did not send his Son into the world to condemn the world, but in order that the world might be saved through him" (John 3:17).

That salvation required a price. For the kingdom to come fully, the King had to suffer. This, too, is something that the Old Testament had predicted. Psalm 22 revealed that the King would be forsaken by God (Ps. 22:1) and that the enemies of God would pierce His hands and His feet (22:16). And Isaiah 53 explained why: "He was pierced for our transgressions; he was crushed for our iniquities . . . and with his wounds we are healed" (Isa. 53:5). There could be no kingdom without kingdom citizens. And in this world of sin, there can be no kingdom citizens without forgiveness. How can a just and holy God forgive people who have rebelled against His rule? There is only one answer: the sacrifice of the one perfect man, the Son of God.

If we think through the history of Redemption, we realize that this sacrifice—the death of the innocent to pay the penalty due the guilty—was God's plan from the beginning. The original promise was not simply that the Seed of the woman would conquer, but that the Seed would suffer. "You shall bruise his heel" was just as much a part of the prophecy as "he shall bruise your head." In fact, the bruising of the Seed's heel was the only way to bruise the Serpent's head. Only by Christ atoning for man's sin could creation be released from God's curse. Man was guilty of the same crime against God that Satan was. Man and his world could not be healed without atonement. There could be no kingdom without the cross.

But even the cross is not the end of the story. Jesus didn't come simply to die. He came to subdue and have dominion. So when He had completed His atoning work, God raised Him from the dead, and in doing so invested Him with the full authority of the great King. When Jesus speaks to His disciples after the resurrection, He speaks not as a prince, someone about to take rule, but as a newly crowned King: "All authority in heaven and on earth has been given to me" (Matt. 28:18).

And when the apostles proclaim the gospel, they proclaim the authority of the conquering King. Peter tells the Jews on Pentecost, "Let all the house of Israel therefore know for certain that God has made him both Lord and Christ, this Jesus whom you crucified" (Acts 2:36). When Peter proclaims the gospel to the Gentiles, he tells them, "[Jesus] is Lord of all" (Acts 10:36). And when John introduces his readers to the glorified Christ, he calls Him "the ruler of kings on earth" (Rev. 1:5). Jesus isn't waiting to be crowned. He is now King of all.

SPREADING THE GOSPEL OF THE KINGDOM

Much of the New Testament is devoted to telling how Jesus spread this good news "to the end of the earth" through His apostles.

The Acts of the Apostles

The preaching of the apostles in the book of Acts announced to all people that the kingdom of God had finally come. Christ, the apostles proclaimed, was the King and future Judge (Acts 10:42). The book describes Paul's ministry this way: "From morning till evening he expounded to them, testifying to the kingdom of God and trying to convince them about Jesus both from the Law of Moses and from the Prophets" (Acts 28:23).

To enjoy the benefits of the kingdom, according to the apostles' preaching, people had to repent and believe in Christ. These believers will escape the coming judgment of God, and they will rule and reign with Jesus forever.

The New Testament Epistles

Paul and other apostles continued presenting this message in the letters they wrote to various early Christians around the Roman world.

In letters (or epistles) such as Romans and 1 Peter, the apostles explain the significance of the great events in the history of Redemption. Paul in particular seeks to explain why Gentiles and Jews belong together in the church as brothers and sisters.

It's important to understand that Paul saw the gospel he preached as consistent not only with Jesus' message but with the Old Testament—including the seed promise of Genesis 3:15. Paul explained that when God promised to give Abraham a Seed, He was speaking specifically of Christ, not of a whole host of Jewish descendants: "Now to Abraham and his Seed were the promises made. He does not say, 'And to seeds,' as of many, but as of one, 'And to your Seed,' who is Christ." (Gal. 3:16, NKJV).

Paul neatly answers the question of who the Seed is: it's Jesus. The Seed, then, is singular, not plural.

But wait: all true believers are included in this Seed because they are considered to be "in Christ":

> There is neither Jew nor Greek, there is neither slave nor free, there is neither male nor female; for you are all one in Christ Jesus. And if you are Christ's, then you are Abraham's seed, and heirs according to the promise. (Gal. 3:28–29, NKJV)

Paul explains, then, how sometimes the seed seems to be one person, Christ, but at other times, it seems to be a whole company of people, all of the saved. The Seed who crushes the Serpent in God's promise to Adam and Eve seems to be singular (Gen. 3:15), and so does the Seed who sits on the throne in God's promise to David (2 Sam. 7:12–16). But the seed that fills the land of Canaan (Gen. 12:7) and rules the world (Dan. 7:27) includes all the people of God.

Paul didn't invent a new religion called Christianity (and neither did Jesus). The New Testament sends hundreds of anchors back into the Old Testament. It claims over and over to be the continuation of the story begun in the Garden of Eden. And it ends with a future look at the new earth.

THE END OF THE STORY

The Book of Revelation

The book of Revelation describes the events leading up to the restoration of the earth. The apostle John is given a vision of God's throne in heaven. He sees God on His throne holding a scroll filled with the judgments that God has determined to pour out on a world of unbelief and sin. But the scroll is sealed, and no one is found worthy to take the scroll and break open its seals.

Until Jesus steps in. "Worthy are you to take the scroll," the elders in heaven say to Jesus, "for you were slain, and by your blood you ransomed people for God from every tribe and language and people and nation" (Rev. 5:9). Jesus has brought the blessing God promised Abraham to every family on earth, and Revelation tells of the time when He will fully cleanse the earth from sin, destroying all the works of the Serpent (1 John 3:8).

The rest of the book of Revelation tells how God completes this work. Jesus takes the scroll, opens its seals, and judges the earth—purging it of all who have refused to repent. Satan himself, "that ancient serpent . . . the deceiver of the whole world" (Rev. 12:8), is driven from the earth and cast into the lake of fire—along with all who have followed him. Then the earth becomes what it was meant to be from the beginning: the kingdom of God, ruled by His Christ, the second Adam. "The kingdom of the world has become the kingdom of our Lord and of his Christ, and he shall reign forever and ever" (Rev. 11:15).

JESUS SAVES AND JUDGES

The twenty-four elders praise Jesus in Revelation 5:9, "Worthy are you to take the scroll and to open its seals [judgments], for you were slain, and by your blood you ransomed people for God from every tribe and language and people and nation." So . . . Jesus is worthy to judge because He saved? What's the logic here?

The idea is that Jesus is judging in a "restorative" way. He's not just obliterating an enemy planet; He's judging the world in order to purge it, and ultimately to restore it. In order for Him to restore it, He has to provide atonement for it. He can judge because He saved mankind.

The People of God

Jesus' judgment of the earth is something the martyred saints in heaven beg for:

> O Sovereign Lord, holy and true, how long before you will judge and avenge our blood on those who dwell on the earth? (Rev. 6:10)

From the very first murder in history, the blood of godly people has called out for God's vengeance. God's children are part of the seed of the woman, and they have suffered repeated bruisings from the Serpent and his seed. And yet they—we!—have been promised eternal triumph because we are in Christ. "If you are Christ's, then you are Abraham's seed, and heirs according to the promise" (Gal. 3:29, NKJV).

The story of Redemption ends with a promise of what will become of Christ's people: "And night will be no more. They will need no light of lamp or sun, for the Lord God will be their light, and they will reign forever and ever" (Rev. 22:5).

"They will reign." The story of the Bible begins with a divine command for men and women to take dominion over the earth. We failed in that task, but the Son of Man has received the kingdom on our behalf. In Him, all the saints of the Most High have subdued the earth and will enjoy an eternal dominion.

THINKING IT THROUGH 10.2

1. What larger mission did Jesus come to fulfill, and what qualified Him to fulfill it?
2. Why did Jesus proclaim that the kingdom had drawn near? How did He demonstrate that the kingdom had drawn near?
3. How did the death and resurrection of Jesus fit in with the larger mission that He had come to fulfill?
4. What future promise does the story of Redemption give to God's people? How does that promise relate to the original Creation Mandate?
5. How is the message of the gospel connected to Jesus' larger mission?

10.3 RESTORING GOD'S GOOD CREATION

When you get a hole in the knee of your pants, you have several options. You can patch it, but that will look funny. You can pay to have it rewoven, but that's very expensive. Restoring something broken is often more costly, in fact, than just replacing it outright. But restoration is precisely what God has in store for His broken creation.

One of the main lessons to learn from the history of Redemption is that God is sparing no expense, not even the cost of the lifeblood of His Son, to restore His good creation. And it isn't just people that God plans to redeem. He has committed Himself to giving His people a particular land—in fact, to restoring the entire globe. All of God's creation will get restored, including our cultural life.

So the general picture of eternity that many people in America have is all wrong. When they think of heaven, they envision the apostle Peter standing at a gate, lots of dead people with wings sitting around on clouds strumming harps—a picture of, well, holy boredom. Eternal cloud-based harp-strumming isn't most people's idea of a desirable life.

Nothing in this popular image, however, can be found in the Bible. We have little scriptural description of heaven at all, perhaps because that's not where believers will spend eternity anyway. Heaven is a temporary stopover. Eternity will take place on the new earth (Rev. 21:1–22:5). And on that new earth, Christians will not be airy angels with nonphysical spirit bodies. On the new earth, you will get your body back—completely restored.

God does not plan to replace the created order with something entirely different, turning us all into beings from another dimension or something, like the kinds of crazy forms of life you encounter in science fiction stories. Redemption means "restoration," not "replacement."

Let's say that again: Redemption means "restoration," not "replacement." The new earth will be what this earth was always meant to be, not something entirely different.

The earth is like a four-year-old boy who contracts a serious disease. The disease saps his strength and deforms his limbs. But he still grows in many of the ways healthy boys do. His parents would be rightly insulted if a doctor said, "This boy is dying; we suggest you get a new boy." The parents love the boy they have, disease and all. But when he's twelve, doctors find a cure, and he begins the process of healing. The boy makes it to age twenty and by then no longer has any trace of that disease. He becomes what he was created to be—a healthy man.[3]

The earth has been progressing toward the purpose God intended for it despite the disease of human sin. And when sin is removed from the planet, the planet can be fully healed—restored to be what it was created to be. Not just people but environments, nations, cultures, academic disciplines—everything will be restored to its original purpose.

RESURRECTION

Popular symbolism and imagery about heaven have found their way into the church, so this idea of restoration may come as a surprise to you. And you shouldn't take a textbook's word for it. Let the Bible say it instead.

For example, Jesus repeatedly told His followers that after His death, He would be raised to life (Luke 9:22; 24:7). And when Jesus showed Himself to His disciples after His suffering, He proved that His physical life had been restored, not replaced. "Put your finger here," He told Thomas, showing him the wounds He received on the cross. "And put out your hand, and place it in my side. Do not disbelieve, but believe" (John 20:27). Jesus did not simply come back to life. He was restored to the same body He had lived in previously. And accepting this as true is essential to believing the gospel message.

The Bible teaches that what Jesus experienced is what every believer will experience. Paul says that the believers' resurrection bodies will be like Jesus' body: "We shall . . . bear the image of the man of heaven [Jesus]" (1 Cor. 15:49).

And this isn't a minor subpoint tucked away in the appendix in a thick theology book. Paul says that this hope of resurrection is central to the whole Christian belief system. He tells the Corinthians that "if the dead are not raised," then "your faith is futile and you are still in your sins" (1 Cor. 15:16–17).

The Christian hope is not the ultimate weight-loss program—getting rid of our bodies completely. No, the Bible promises the "redemption of our bodies" (Rom. 8:23). We will be restored to the physical life we were designed for: free from illness, weakness, and any possibility of death or deterioration. As it was with Jesus, so it will be with us. We will live a glorious existence in our bodies. Just as Jesus left behind an empty tomb, so will every believer leave behind an empty grave.

THE KINGDOM OF GOD

Redemption does not put us on clouds forever. It puts our feet firmly on earthly ground.

The order that God intended for the universe was that humans should rule over the world, with God ruling over all. That's the point of the Creation Mandate (Gen. 1:28). That order, of course, was disrupted when we fell into sin. But God did not abandon this order. In Genesis 3:15, He revealed His plan to restore the human race to its original calling.

> ***"HE WILL MAKE ALL THINGS NEW RATHER THAN MAKING ALL NEW THINGS."[4]***
>
> —BRUCE RILEY ASHFORD

If you prefer eternal cloud-sitting, the Bible's vision of eternal human rule over the earth may seem unattractive. But the Bible says in its last two chapters (Rev. 21–22) that the center of the new earth will be a city, the new Jerusalem. And what goes on in cities? All kinds of things have to happen to make a city run, and redeemed people will be running that city and its society. They'll be making human culture.

In some ways, this work will be very different from what has been known throughout the history of civilization. It will be different from Cain's city, a city built after he had strayed "from the presence of the Lord" (Gen. 4:16). And it will be very different from all of the Babylons in world history, cities renowned for their pride (Gen. 11:4), their cruelty (Jer. 50:15–16), their oppression and immorality (Ezek. 16:44–58), and their ill-gotten wealth (Rev. 18:6–8). In New Jerusalem, all of city life will be lived according to God's standards and expectations (Rev. 21:27)—according to creational norms.

But viewed from another perspective, New Jerusalem will look familiar. It will bear some resemblance to all of the great cultures—even the final Babylon. Just as the merchants of the earth carried on a prosperous trade in Babylon (Rev. 18:11–13), so the kings of the earth will trade with New Jerusalem (Rev. 21:24–26). Just as Babylon was a place of great wealth (Rev. 17:4–6) and was famous for its prominent situation (Rev. 17:9), so New Jerusalem will be wealthy beyond imagination (Rev. 21:18–21) and will be situated in a place of marvelous prominence (Rev. 21:15–17).

How will this trade be managed? Who will put this wealth to proper use? How will this prominence be maintained? This, we may infer, is the task of the redeemed—the ones who are called to reign forever on the earth (Rev. 22:5). Some will work in farming, some in architecture, some in the making of tools and musical instruments, some in engineering, some in government.

Viewed from a biblical worldview, none of this is surprising. This city is the final restoration of the Creation Mandate in Genesis 1:28. It is the restoration of the order God intended for the world from the very beginning.

IMPLICATIONS

God hasn't abandoned any aspect of human life, and neither should we. Marriage and family life shouldn't be avoided but should be restored to God's original intent. Scientific endeavors should not be abandoned as hopelessly secular; they should instead be engaged in from a Christian perspective so that God's glory may once again be declared in them. Politics ought not to be deemed forbidden for Christians but should be viewed as a legitimate place for Christian efforts of renewal. And the whole world of culture and the arts shouldn't be left to unbelievers but should be taken up by believers as a place for Christian witness.

It's true that many Christians have endeavored to live out Redemption in these areas in ways that are ineffective or, worse, in ways that compromise Christian belief and practice. But the failure of others doesn't mean that these areas should be abandoned. (Many Christians have compromised their beliefs in their attempts at evangelism or have proved ineffective in their attempts at foreign missions. But we don't give up on evangelism and missions.) The kingdom of God, the life and ministry of Jesus—the whole history of Redemption—tell us that seeking to live for Redemption in these areas is part of God's plan. Our duty is to figure out how to do this well, guided by biblical wisdom. And that's what the rest of this unit is about.

THINKING IT THROUGH 10.3

1. What does Redemption mean? What doesn't it mean?
2. How does the Christian hope of resurrection impact the overall Christian understanding of Redemption?
3. What will be at the center of the new earth and what activity will be taking place there?
4. Whether evangelizing or seeking to live redemptively, what must Christians always be wary of doing, according to the text?
5. Why shouldn't Christians abandon culture and its institutions?

10 CHAPTER REVIEW

TERMS TO REMEMBER

Redemption
Seed
kingdom

Scripture Memory

Acts 2:42

Making Connections

1. Compare and contrast the New Covenant people of God and the Old Covenant people of God.
2. List the six tasks involved in the mission of the institutional church. What are the two key passages that define the mission of the church?
3. What biblical command is the basis for determining what kind of work is legitimate?
4. What biblical commands form the basis of how believers should go about doing their work?

Developing Skills in Apologetics and Worldview

5. What guidelines should a local church establish in order to make sure that its work in its local community supports the primary tasks of its mission?
6. What guidelines should a person establish in order to make sure that work does not become an idol?

Examining Assumptions and Evidence

7. Why is church membership necessary for believers?
8. Why is it dangerous to view the church as completely synonymous with the kingdom?
9. Why is it important to understand that everyone working a legitimate job works in service to God?
10. When Christians do their work, are they actually causing the world to progress toward final redemption? Explain why or why not.

Becoming a Creative Cultivator

11. What is one thing you think your church could do to reach out to the community?

Chapter Eleven REDEEMED FOR GOOD WORKS

You are the light of the world. A city set on a hill cannot be hidden. Nor do people light a lamp and put it under a basket, but on a stand, and it gives light to all in the house. In the same way, let your light shine before others, so that they may see your good works and give glory to your Father who is in heaven.

Scripture Memory
Matthew 5:14–16

11.1 OUR PLACE IN GOD'S STORY

The author of *The Lord of the Rings*, J. R. R. Tolkien, once commented that stories like his, at their best, serve as "a far-off gleam or echo of evangelium [the gospel] in the real world."[1] Tolkien succeeded in echoing the gospel in his own story, and his trilogy is the number-two best-selling work of fiction in history.

One conversation in Tolkien's epic tale illuminates his comment. The main characters, Frodo and Sam, sit on the slope of Mount Doom contemplating their story. Sam speaks:

> We shouldn't be here at all, if we'd known more about it before we started. But I suppose it's often that way. The brave things in the old tales and songs, Mr. Frodo: adventures, as I used to call them. I used to think that they were things the wonderful folk of the stories went out and looked for, because they wanted them, because they were exciting and life was a bit dull, a kind of a sport, as you might say. But that's not the way of it with the tales that really mattered, or the ones that stay in the mind. Folk seem to have been just landed in them, usually—their paths were laid that way, as you put it. . . . I wonder what sort of a tale we've fallen into?[2]

Frodo admits he doesn't know but isn't bothered by that because "that's the way of a real tale. Take any one that you're fond of. You may know, or guess, what kind of a tale it is, happy-ending or sad-ending, but the people in it don't know. And you don't want them to."[3]

Sam agrees and starts recounting what happened to some other individuals in the story: "But that's a long tale, of course, and goes on past the happiness and into grief and beyond it. . . . Why, to think of it, we're in the same tale still! It's going on. Don't the great tales never end?"[4]

Frodo replies, "No, they never end as tales . . . but the people in them come, and go when their part's ended."[5]

Theodrama

"The tales that really matter" never end. That's truer of the metanarrative told by the Bible than it is of any other story. That's why enduring human tales like Tolkien's can point to the gospel. We can say of the people who played their parts in God's tale, from Adam to Ruth to Paul, that their "paths were laid that way" by a divine storyteller.

And when all their adventures and ours are over, we will begin—in the words of Tolkien's friend C. S. Lewis, the words Lewis used to draw his own famous tales about Narnia to a close—"Chapter One of the Great Story which no one on earth has read: which goes on forever: in which every chapter is better than the one before."[6]

SALVATION AND JUDGMENT

If you have a heart Jesus Christ has made new, that new heart thrills to hear that the big story isn't over. The story just can't be over—there are too many people who are suffering and too many who are rebelling. Many of God's image-bearers are doing both. If Jesus Christ rose from the dead and ascended to heaven to be crowned King and Lord of all, why are there any sufferers or rebels left in His dominions?

Part of the answer lies in Jesus' final words to His disciples: "You will be my witnesses in Jerusalem and in all Judea and Samaria, and to the end of the earth" (Acts 1:8). Jesus is not content to have a kingdom with only a few citizens in it. He wants His Father's house to be full (Luke 14:15–24). And He has chosen to accomplish this mission by sending His followers into all the earth. Empowered by His Holy Spirit, they are to go everywhere announcing the good news that the King has come and has triumphed over sin, suffering, and death.

"The Son of Man came to seek and to save the lost," Jesus said of Himself (Luke 19:10). "Lost"—that's you. That's every person in every family on earth. Jesus came to find and rescue us. Is there any truth more precious?

And yet countless lost people refuse the King and His salvation. They—we—twist God's good gifts in wicked directions. Think of your good brain. Who or what are its incredible powers serving?

It's hard for us humans to feel the weight of sin because we're not God. Sin is the "de-Godding of God."[7] And sin "offends God not only because it assaults God directly, as in impiety or blasphemy, but also because it assaults what God has made."[8] Sin must and will stop, or God isn't God.

So Jesus didn't tell His apostles to preach only salvation. He told them to preach coming judgment. Said the apostle Peter, "He commanded us to preach to the people and to testify that he is the one appointed by God to be judge of the living and the dead" (Acts 10:42).

amnesty: *the act of pardoning a group of people or setting prisoners free*

The King has ascended His throne. He is ruling, and He's a merciful monarch. But the opportunity for amnesty* will one day end. The King will eventually turn from salvation to judgment.

Christian Reconstruction?

The story of Scripture tells how we failed to rule over God's world and how Jesus restores us to that rule. A cursory reading of this story may leave a person with the impression that Christians are called to rule the world right now. They're obligated to seek the top spots in media companies and the most influential positions in government. From these positions they are to exert a cultural domination that drives out sin and corruption while bringing in godliness and virtue.

But there's a problem with that kind of thinking—it's foreign to the New Testament. Jesus didn't try to climb the corporate ladder or take over the Roman emperor's palace. Likewise, the early church didn't try to co-opt the positions of power in first-century society. It is true that by the end of the story (Rev. 22), sin and corruption are driven out of God's world. But forcing sin out is not the church's role in God's story—or even Jesus' part while He walked the earth. He didn't try to use the power of cultural domination to bring about redemption, nor should the church.

To some, these observations seem to contradict the whole idea of the kingdom of God. If that kingdom has come, why doesn't the New Testament present Jesus as a King with real power—the power to stop evil and overcome God's enemies? Why does it present the church as a persecuted community? Answering these questions requires us to take another look at how the Bible presents the coming of the kingdom of God.

CHRISTIAN RECONSTRUCTIONISTS

Christian Reconstructionism teaches that the moral and civil aspects of the Mosaic law are the standard of righteousness that should be incorporated into the law codes of all nations. Christian Reconstructionists are typically postmillennialists, and they advocate using democratic means to reconstruct US society according to God's law.

In the vision God gave Daniel about the rise and fall of the great kingdoms of the earth, each is presented as a vicious beast that comes to prominence and then fades (Dan. 7).

THE KINGDOM OF GOD: *ALREADY* AND *NOT YET*

The Old Testament is rich with prophecies concerning the coming of the Messiah—and with Him the coming of the kingdom of God. These prophecies make it clear that the Messiah's coming will be good news for some and bad news for others.

In the vision God gave Daniel about the rise and fall of the great kingdoms of the earth, each is presented as a vicious beast that comes to prominence and then fades (Dan. 7). When the last kingdom rises, Daniel sees "one like a son of man" coming "with the clouds of heaven" (7:13). He then sees Him approach "the Ancient of Days," from whom this Son of Man receives an everlasting kingdom, and with the power of this kingdom He saves His people and defeats God's enemies. For the "saints of the Most High," this is very good news because it means that they will be delivered from oppression and be allowed to "possess the kingdom forever" (7:18). But for those who oppose God's working in the world, it's the worst news imaginable. They will be "consumed and destroyed to the end" (7:26).

Some of those prophecies have been fulfilled already in Jesus. But many, especially the ones promising the destruction of God's enemies, have not yet been fulfilled. There is at the same time an *already* and a *not yet* in the rule of Jesus.

Already

The very first recorded sermon of Jesus was based on Isaiah 61. Standing in the synagogue of His hometown of Nazareth, He read,

> The Spirit of the Lord God is upon me, because the Lord has anointed me to bring good news to the poor; he has sent me to bind up the brokenhearted, to proclaim liberty to the captives, and the opening of the prison to those who are bound; to proclaim the year of the Lord's favor. (Isa. 61:1–2)

After reading the passage, Jesus sat down to teach and began by saying, "Today this Scripture has been fulfilled in your hearing" (Luke 4:21). Isaiah 61 wasn't just an important prophecy that He cared deeply about. Any scribe or Pharisee could have said that. Jesus claimed that He had been sent by God to *fulfill* Isaiah 61. He said that the promises of Messianic blessing in that prophecy were about *Him*. The poor, the brokenhearted, the captives—Jesus said that He had brought them good news. It was *already*; they needed to wait no longer.

Other statements of Jesus also stress the *already*. Throughout His preaching He said things like this: "The kingdom of God has come upon you" (Matt. 12:28). And the very title Jesus used for Himself, "the Son of Man," was a connection back to Daniel 7 and the vision of the Ancient of Days handing Him an everlasting kingdom. Every time Jesus called Himself by that phrase, He was making a claim: He was the ruler of that kingdom.

As the "Son of Man," Jesus had incredible kingly power: "The Son of Man has authority on earth to forgive sins," Jesus said (Matt. 9:6). And "all authority in heaven and on earth has been given to me" (Matt. 28:18).

Not Yet

But Jesus knew that His kingdom had not yet conquered all its enemies. In front of the Sanhedrin right before His crucifixion, He made a promise: "You will see the Son of Man seated at the right hand of Power and coming on the clouds of heaven" (Matt. 26:64). "You *will* see," in other words. The kingdom is not all here yet. It couldn't be—because many things the Old Testament prophets promised about the kingdom hadn't (and still haven't) come to pass.

The Old Testament predicted a kingdom of salvation, and that had already come in Jesus. But it also promised a kingdom bringing judgment—and that has not yet occurred. This fact confused some people, especially John the Baptist. It made John question whether or not Jesus was even the Messiah. He had introduced Jesus to the world as the one who would pour out the Holy Spirit on some and the fire of God's wrath on others (Matt. 3:11–12). But now John was in jail, imprisoned by an immoral but powerful king. So John sent messengers to Jesus to ask Him, "Are you the one who is to come, or shall we look for another?" (Matt. 11:3).

In Jesus' answer to John the Baptist, we find an important clarification: "Go and tell John what you hear and see: the blind receive their sight and the lame walk, lepers are cleansed and the deaf hear, and the dead are raised up, and the poor have good news preached to them. And blessed is the one who is not offended by me" (Matt. 11:4–6). With these words Jesus reminded John that His kingdom is what the Old Testament predicted. Jesus did not fail to do what He had come to do—all the things He said He would do in His first sermon.

Jesus did something very interesting in that sermon in Nazareth. He very clearly stopped His quotation before the end of the sentence. And what did He purposefully leave out? The prophecy says that the Messiah will come to proclaim not just salvation but also "the day of vengeance of our God" (Isa. 61:2). Jesus had brought God's kingdom to this world, but only in salvation and not yet in judgment and wrath on God's enemies.

Once you understand that the kingdom has *already* come in salvation but has *not yet* come in judgment, some of Jesus' most important parables begin to make much better sense. Jesus, for example, compares His kingdom not to a mighty warrior crushing his enemies but to a farmer scattering seed (Matt. 13:3–9). Most of the ground, in fact, rejects the seed, and in those places no crop is produced. But some

ground receives it, and in those places a great harvest is reaped. Jesus later explains that the seed is the good news that the kingdom of God has come and that the different soils are the different people who hear the good news (13:18–23). Some receive the news and are transformed. But most reject it. What happens to those who reject it? Nothing—for now. The farmer in the parable doesn't try to obliterate the bad soil. He just lets it lie there.

The wheat and the tares are allowed to grow together until the end of the age.

And think about the next parable Jesus told. He compares the kingdom to a field where both wheat and weeds are planted (Matt. 13:24–30). The wheat are the people of God; the weeds are God's enemies. The point of the story is that both are allowed to grow together until "the end of the age" (13:37–43). Only in the final judgment will the weeds be dealt with.

LIVING IN THE GAP

One of the great mysteries that Jesus' preaching explained was that the Old Testament prophecies speak of the kingdom in general terms, and in those general terms it seems that the kingdom of God and of His Messiah comes all at once—salvation and judgment in one great "Day of the Lord." But when Jesus begins teaching the crowds, He explains that the kingdom comes in two phases. First comes salvation—the forgiveness of sins, the gift of the Holy Spirit, reconciliation with God, and new life in Jesus Christ. Then, after a certain period of time has elapsed, there's judgment—the full destruction of God's enemies, the cleansing fire of God's wrath on the earth.

Christians today are called to live in the gap between kingdom salvation and kingdom judgment, between the *already* and the *not yet*. We're privileged to experience the blessings of God's salvation, and some divine wrath for sin does fall in this age (Rom. 1:18), but we must wait with patience for the full vindication that will come at the final judgment. So we're blessed now to see sinners repent and receive God's gift of forgiveness. We are also blessed to play a role in the advancement of Jesus' saving work around the world as the Holy Spirit empowers our prayers and our labors. But since now is not the time for judgment, our time is not the time for reigning. Now is not the time for us to seek cultural domination. Now is not the time for "winning."

THINKING IT THROUGH 11.1

1. How can we know that we aren't living after the time of God's completion of the big story of Scripture?
2. Even though Jesus has been crowned King, what mission has Jesus given to the church?
3. What is Christian Reconstructionism?
4. What part of the Old Testament Messianic kingdom promises did Jesus already begin to fulfill, and what part has He not yet begun to fulfill?
5. What is it about the church's place between salvation and judgment that makes Christian Reconstructionism incorrect?

11.2 WITNESS AND GOOD WORKS

In 2009, Manuel was a pastor in Colombia, in a region controlled by the Revolutionary Armed Forces of Colombia (FARC), a rebel group. FARC had closed many other churches in the area, but Manuel had spent eight years pastoring there despite the threats. One day when FARC guerillas made an appointment to meet Pastor Manuel, he thought they might actually be going to give him authorization to hold church services as he had asked.

Instead, they shot Pastor Manuel five times. One of the ringleaders who was inside the house with the pastor's family yelled, "Make sure that dog stays dead." The men shot the pastor again.

Pastor Manuel's wife cleaned his bloody face and dragged his body underneath a tree. In spite of her tears, she got her Bible and began to give the gospel to everyone who came by. Her ten-year-old son told her, "Mom, don't worry. Dad died for Christ, and now he is with Christ."[9]

For most American Christians, this story feels a million miles away. It almost sounds made up—would a ten-year-old really say such a thing? Could a brand-new widow possibly do what Manuel's wife did? But believe it: violent persecution is a daily reality for many believers around the world. And there are modern-day Christian martyrs.

FARC rebels have been heavy-handed in their treatment of fellow Colombians, including Christians.

Their stories ought to make you feel keenly a sense of violated justice, of righteous anger. John tells in Revelation how he saw in heaven "the souls of those who had been slain for the word of God and for the witness they had borne." And this is what they cried out to God: "O Sovereign Lord, holy and true, how long before you will judge and avenge our blood on those who dwell on the earth?" (Rev. 6:9–10).

John says, "They were each . . . told to rest a little longer, until the number of their fellow servants and their brothers should be complete, who were to be killed as they themselves had been" (Rev. 6:11).

SUFFERING FOR DOING GOOD

Jack (not his real name), a strong Christian, had risen through the ranks at his business over twenty years to become a high-ranking executive. The company was generating over $20 billion in annual revenue and had more than a hundred thousand employees worldwide. One day in a boardroom full of other executives, a new company policy was announced. "We are planning to provide marital benefits to same-sex couples. Does anyone have any objections?"[6a]

"I do," Jack said, and he asked for time to put together his thoughts. In a later meeting he explained the biblical viewpoint on homosexuality, starting with these words: "I believe I am the worst sinner in this room." People listened respectfully. A few Christians told him privately that they were glad for what he did. One non-Christian said, "Diversity goes both ways." And Jack later got a promotion.

But not everyone was pleased. Jack was (and is) a faithful and winsome witness who has worked hard on the skill of asking people questions about their spiritual lives and then sharing the gospel with them. Jack's message—that Jesus is the only way to God (John 14:6)—ran right into the strong push for "diversity" at his company.

A canny political operator saw this as an opportunity to get rid of Jack. One day Jack was called into a meeting and summarily fired. His evangelism and his opposition to homosexuality were the stated reasons. Diversity went only one way in that room.

Jack has bills to pay like anyone else. He said, "I don't dare claim to be in the same category as people that have died for Christ . . . [but] when you take a person's livelihood away, and they've got four children, you are taking away their life in some senses of the term."

But then Jack said, "It was one of the greatest moments of my life. . . . I walked away from millions of dollars of income, and basically it was so clear to me at that moment that what really mattered [to me] was being right with God."[10]

SUFFERING

During this time between salvation and judgment, Christians are not to expect cultural triumph and a life of health, wealth, and prosperity. We're supposed to expect suffering. Early in Paul's missionary work, he told new converts in Lystra and Iconium, "We must through much tribulation enter into the kingdom of God" (Acts 14:22, KJV). Later, just before the end of his second missionary journey, Paul explained to believers in Rome that now "we suffer with [Christ] in order that we may also be glorified with him" (Rom. 8:17). And just before he was martyred, Paul told Timothy, "If we endure, we will also reign with him" (2 Tim. 2:12). Throughout his ministry, Paul taught that before we enter the triumph of the kingdom brought about by judgment, we must endure the suffering of the kingdom brought about by salvation.

Suffering is the unavoidable result of living in a world where the kingdom of Satan overlaps the kingdom of God. When salvation is proclaimed in Jerusalem, Ephesus, Rome, New York, Los Angeles, and Beijing, many people repent and enter God's kingdom. They enter the kingdom of forgiveness and holiness, but they also leave behind the kingdom of sin and darkness (Col. 1:13). And Satan will not accept their desertion without a fight.

This is the reason that all through its history, the church has suffered persecution. Think about Paul's experiences in the book of Acts. When the apostle came to Ephesus, he preached and persuaded people "about the kingdom of God" (Acts 19:8). A large number of people—both Jews and Greeks—believed and became part of the church in that city. But as the kingdom of salvation grew, so did the anger and hatred in the other kingdom.

Of course, the members of this other kingdom didn't think that they belonged to Satan or that they were fighting to recapture power for the king of hell. Satan prefers to keep people in the dark about such things. But it's clear from Acts 19 that many in

Ephesus wanted to stop what the church was doing. Here's how Demetrius, an idol-maker, spoke to his fellow Ephesians about Paul and the church:

> This Paul has persuaded and turned away a great many people, saying that gods made with hands are not gods. And there is danger not only that this trade of ours may come into disrepute but also that the temple of the great goddess Artemis may be counted as nothing, and that she may even be deposed from her magnificence, she whom all Asia and the world worship. (Acts 19:26–27)

The growth of God's kingdom directly threatened Demetrius's income. If Paul continued to persuade people to repent and believe the gospel, Demetrius might have to find a new career. But it also threatened his cultural pride. If Paul continued to see success, the pinnacle of Ephesian culture—the temple of Artemis—might become an object of scorn. So Demetrius was willing to do whatever it took to stop the growth of the church.

This was an early version of the very same culture war that exists in America today. And the "good guys" didn't win. God's judgment didn't fall on Demetrius because Jesus' authority is extended in this world to advance salvation, not to bring judgment. So Paul was left vulnerable. He was proclaiming a gospel that robbed Satan of his subjects. And when Satan fought back, divine judgment didn't strike Satan down. To be sure, Jesus didn't abandon Paul. He protected him and got him safely out of Ephesus (Acts 19:35–41). But it was Paul who had to leave the city, not Demetrius. And a few years later, when Paul's race had been run, history tells us, he was martyred for the kingdom of God.

We, too, are called to live vulnerable lives. We believe a gospel that the world finds offensive. When an alcoholic turns to Christ, he offends the pride of his old drinking buddies. When a concerned Christian writes an article about the evils of sexualized entertainment, those who provide that entertainment will do what it takes to protect their income. When government officials find that the preaching of the gospel makes them look corrupt, they will likely come down hard on the preacher instead of the corruption. And it may be that in the short term, evil seems to triumph. That's because Jesus now exercises His royal power to save, not to judge. So now is not the time for winning. Now is not the time for reigning.

Lives of Witness

When Jesus stood before Pilate, the governor asked if He was indeed a king. Jesus told him, "For this purpose I was born and for this purpose I have come into the world—*to bear witness* to the truth" (John 18:37). In His earthly ministry, Jesus was called to the task not of crushing His enemies but of testifying to the truth, the truth about Himself.

Witnessing is the task of Jesus' followers too. The book of Acts opens with Christ telling His disciples, "You will receive power when the Holy Spirit has come upon you, and you will be my witnesses . . . to the end of the earth" (Acts 1:8). In the story that follows, we learn that they are to bear witness to the fact that Jesus is exalted to God's right hand (5:31), that Jesus will one day judge the world (10:42-43), that people must repent and believe (20:21), that God is gracious to sinners (20:24), and that the kingdom of God has come (28:23). In other words, they testify to the kingdom salvation that has *already* come and to the kingdom judgment that has *not yet* come.

A significant portion of the church's witness in Acts was verbal. Paul spent countless hours preaching, discussing, debating, and explaining (Acts 19:9). Witnessing in the New Testament is never less than verbal. But it is often more. Our witness includes how we live. The church testifies to the kingship of Jesus by turning away from idolatry and sexual immorality (15:29; 16:4; 17:6–7). It bears witness to the kingdom of God when its members work hard at their jobs and then give generously to others (20:33–35). It testifies to Christ's triumph over sin and death as husbands love their wives, children obey their parents, and masters treat their servants with fairness and respect (Eph. 5:25–6:9). For the Christian, all of life is witness because, according to the gospel of the kingdom, Jesus has been made Lord of everything. As Paul taught the Ephesians, Jesus has been exalted "far above all rule and authority and power and dominion . . . not only in this age but also in the one to come" (Eph. 1:21).

This whole-life witness isn't all that different from what people everywhere do all the time. In every culture, people bear witness to some grand narrative by the way they live. People engage in predictable patterns of behavior based on the dominant story of their culture. For some cultures that story is about Zeus battling Hades; for others it's about species evolving in difficult environments. These stories guide and shape how people rear their children, pursue their education, view marriage, and seek justice in society. All people everywhere orient their lives by what they believe the world's grand narrative to be.

The difference with the church, of course, is that God has revealed to it the true grand narrative. Through the gospel we learn that Jesus has fulfilled the dominion that the first Adam failed to fulfill. He is exalted far above His enemies, and He now directs His followers, the church, to bear witness to this triumph in every part of life. We are to shine our light so people glorify God (Matt. 5:16–17).

The challenge for the church today is that it's hard to live out a grand narrative that people all around us don't believe. So believers are tempted to testify to God's story for just one day a week—and by default to embrace the story of their culture for the rest of the time. But this approach to life leaves the church ineffective and confused. Jesus is Lord not just of worship but also of marriage, of art, of business, of politics, of education. So believers must learn to engage in these aspects of their lives guided by God's narrative and not by the world's.

Lives of Good Works

The American culture war turns a lot of Christians into whiners. When non-Christians see something like *The American Patriot's Bible* sitting on the shelf in a bookstore (see sidebar), they get one clear message from Christians: "This is *our* country, and you're stealing it from us!"

And whining isn't the only sin Christians commit; sometimes Christians themselves become Machiavellian* political agents—they use underhanded tactics to defeat their political opponents, and they excuse themselves by pointing to their righteous goals. One Christian political leader reportedly walked around a gathering collecting sign-ups for her newsletter and then turned around and used those signatures on a petition.

WORDS OF JESUS IN RED, WHITE, AND BLUE?

The American Patriot's Bible is a copy of the full text of the Bible (New King James Version) interspersed with pictures of George Washington, Frederick Douglass, Abraham Lincoln, Ronald Reagan, and other famous Americans. There are sidebars praising America's Christian heritage and urging Americans to return to their roots. The overall message is that the United States is, by all rights, a Christian nation and not a secular one.[11]

Whining and underhanded political tactics are both terrible witnesses to the kingdom. The New Testament letters were written to Christians living in a pagan society but never recommend whining or cheating. Instead one of them says,

Machiavellian: *scheming, deceptive, unscrupulous*

> Keep your conduct among the Gentiles [non-Christians] honorable, so that when they speak against you as evildoers, they may see your good deeds and glorify God on the day of visitation. (1 Pet. 2:12)

Peter, who lived in a culture both hostile to Christianity and ignorant of it—a dangerous combination now growing quickly in America too—repeatedly tells his readers that doing good works is one of their most important forms of witness:

> For this is the will of God, that by doing good you should put to silence the ignorance of foolish people. (1 Pet. 2:15)

There's a famous verse in 1 Peter that Christian-worldview proponents like to point to. It instructs believers to always be "prepared to make a defense to anyone who asks you for a reason for the hope that is in you" (1 Pet. 3:15). But you need to realize this isn't a call to pick a fight. The verse goes on to call Christians to provide their defenses "with gentleness and respect." And in context, the reason non-Christians might even ask Christians about the reasons for their hope is precisely that those Christians are "zealous for what is good" even when they "suffer for righteousness' sake" (1 Pet. 3:13–14).

This emphasis on good works is found all throughout the New Testament. Paul said to the Ephesians that "we are . . . created in Christ Jesus for good works" (Eph. 2:10). We have been remade through the saving work of Jesus Christ so that now we can give ourselves to the lifelong pursuit of good works.

And Jesus Himself, in His foundational Sermon on the Mount, explains that Christians are supposed to be like light: "Let your light shine before others, so that they may see your good works and give glory to your Father who is in heaven" (Matt. 5:16).

Jesus' sermon describes what those good works are supposed to look like. When faced with the temptation to be angry and bitter, the person pursuing good works seeks forgiveness and reconciliation. When faced with the temptation to lust, the follower of Jesus does whatever it takes to have victory over that sin. When faced with the temptation to abandon his marriage obligations, the kingdom citizen chooses instead to stay true to his vows. When faced with the temptation to ignore the plight of the poor, the believer chooses to be generous. When faced with the temptation to hate those who hate him, the Christian chooses to love and to prove that love by praying for his enemies and seeking to do them good.

The follower of Jesus does all of these things because this is how he would want others to treat him if the tables were turned—and this is how he shows that Jesus Christ is worthy of trust and obedience no matter what. By living this kind of life, he bears eloquent testimony to the fact that God's appointed King has come, has triumphed, and now offers salvation to all. If He hadn't triumphed over sin, could anyone live in this world as His kingdom citizens now live?

THE HEALTH, WEALTH, AND PROSPERITY GOSPEL

Some television preachers talk about God as if He's aching to get you a new car, if only you'd have a little more faith (and if only you'd donate a little seed money to that preacher's "ministry"). God is certainly permitted to provide new cars for His children. Every car owned by a Christian is, in a real sense, a gift from God. And God cares about our needs, even for transportation. But making sure we have sufficient stuff is not the top item on God's agenda for His children. What we need is "holiness without which no one will see the Lord" (Heb. 12:14). And a new car isn't going to get us to that destination. Like all things worth having, holiness is going to take some suffering. Promises of health, wealth, and prosperity are not a gospel because they're not truly good news.

THINKING IT THROUGH 11.2

1. Instead of cultural triumph, what must Christians expect to experience during the time between salvation and judgment? Why?
2. What caused the cultural conflict described in Acts 19, and why didn't Paul win?
3. According to the book of Acts, what specifically must believers verbally bear witness to when giving the gospel?
4. Explain one reason why witnessing must be more than verbal.
5. What, ideally, should impel unbelievers to ask Christians about the reasons for their hope in Christ?

11.3 PUSHING IN THE RIGHT DIRECTION

Teenagers should know what it's like to be placed between the *already* and the *not yet*. You're already capable of doing a lot of things (such as driving, working, or perhaps even getting married), but some of them may be things that your life circumstances don't allow you to do. There can be a lot of tension between the abilities you already have and the opportunities that have not yet come your way. Part of your calling right now is to wisely navigate this time of tension.

And that's the calling of all Christians, no matter their age, in between Christ's salvation and His judgment. How can you wisely navigate this time of tension when Christ really rules but hasn't yet brought all things "under his feet" (Ps. 8:6)?

The concepts of structure and direction should be a help to you in this. Everything has a God-given, created structure, and everything is pushed at least a little bit in the wrong direction by the Fall. Everything is moving either in a fallen direction or back in a redemptive direction.

If you really take hold of these biblical concepts, they'll liberate you from a misleading but common question. In a consumer culture overflowing with options for how you can spend your money, your time, and your life, it's tempting to ask yourself merely, "Is this thing good or bad?" But understanding structure and direction allows you to ask a wiser and more helpful question: "What is structural about this thing, and what is directional?" Once you answer that, you can ask the more practical question, "What's the proper redemptive response for me?"

In Chapter 9, we talked about the structure and direction of sex, matter, technology, and language. Given the way those things are viewed and used in our fallen world, what's the proper redemptive response for you? How can you witness to the power of Christ's salvation and live a life of good works in each of these areas?

SEX

First consider human sexuality. Right now in the United States of America, four out of ten children are born to unmarried mothers. Among some subgroups in society the number climbs as high as seven out of ten.[12] This doesn't necessarily mean that these kids' dads are absent, but it does mean that their dads have chosen not to make (and their moms have chosen not to insist on) the only public promise of family stability in existence: a wedding.

One of the most important tools of countercultural witness Christians have right now—and one of the most important defenses of the Christian faith—ought to be our loving, stable families. Sex binds a man and a woman together, but that bond is not an end in itself. Ideally, sex binds the husband and wife for a further reason: a stable bond is what their children need in order to thrive. The Bible doesn't promise every Christian sexual satisfaction in a perfect marriage. But it sets up guidelines and creates a (church) community in which loving, strong marriages can grow.

Do you want this? Do you really? It will take participation in that community, it will take intense effort, it will take suffering—ultimately, it will take divine grace—for you to survive the sexual onslaught of Western culture and to create a beautiful family. If you are as fallen as the Bible says you are, it matters what music courses through your earbuds. It matters what the cheerleaders wear and what the guys let each other say about the cheerleaders. It matters what internet filter you have—guys and girls.

One of your goals should be to become the kind of person whose marriage makes other people say, "Their light has so shined before others that we have seen their good works and give glory to their Father who is in heaven." Never underestimate the power that your own inconspicuous family has as a light in darkness.

What does a life of witness and good works look like when it comes to stuff?

MATTER

Materialism—not the philosophical kind, but the shopping-mall and storage-unit kind—is another powerful force in Western culture that is pushing people in sinful directions. Plenty of people seem to live by the bumper-sticker motto, "He who dies with the most toys wins."

What does a life of good works, a life of witness, look like when it comes to "matter," to stuff? What is the proper redemptive response for a Christian living in a culture of consumerism?

One of the most countercultural things you could do would be to give up your "rights" as a Western consumer and start being generous with your money and your time. Generally speaking, you can always make more money if you're willing to work more hours. And sometimes you may need to do just that. But a Christian can be salt in his or her neighborhood and shine like a light in his or her workplace by opting out of overtime pay and sales bonuses and dedicating time instead to evangelism or orphan care or Meals on Wheels or a million other ways to give. Christians can afford to be generous because God won't forget so much as a cup of cold water given in Jesus' name (Matt. 10:42).

One of the things that should motivate Christians in their work is precisely the opportunity to earn income so they can turn around and give some of it away.

TECHNOLOGY

Many people, almost all of them adults, are raising alarms about the power of technology in society. Adult readers are complaining that technology distracts them and shortens their attention spans. Politicians are complaining that the internet has polarized public discourse. Moms are complaining that smartphones have ruined the family dinner hour. And tech has created problems in lots of other cultures around the world; there's a summer camp in China to help teens who are addicted to the internet.

Where are the teens who are concerned about the power of tech? It's so easy to go with the flow, to never question the way your culture deals with technology. You don't do right so that others will notice, but others *will* notice if you push back against the Fall's effects in the area of technology. Human beings can make it to age eighteen without owning the latest smartphone or having unrestricted internet access.

What could you do (or not do) with your cellphone in order to witness to the power of Christ's salvation? What do "good works" look like on the internet? The call of Christ to be salt and light may not be very dramatic. It may mean tossing your phone into your room before family dinners without being asked. It may mean looking for people to encourage online rather than people to bash. Christians are called to be salt, to be different. And we're called to be light, to be different for the purpose of displaying the truth.

LANGUAGE

Language is one of the most powerful tools God has given to humans—powerful enough, James says, to "[set] on fire the entire course of life" (James 3:6). James marvels about the tongue: "How great a forest is set ablaze by such a small fire!" (3:5).

The tongue can ruin in a moment a good reputation that took a lifetime to build. But not all forest fires are bad. Some clear out underbrush to make way for future growth. The tongue can also comfort in a moment a pain that's been building up for a lifetime.

A lot of English speakers, and not just Christians or even conservatives, think that English is disintegrating, that it's getting worse and worse as time goes on. That's highly debatable; in fact, people have been making similar complaints for hundreds of years, and somehow English hasn't died. The Fall has damaged our messages far more than it has damaged the medium of English itself. Writers can still use English to create powerful, beautiful, enduring prose. And they do, in the service of all kinds of messages and ideas. Shouldn't Christians, who have been given the task of teaching the nations everything Jesus commanded, care deeply about the power of their words? Paul warned us not to trust in the power of our own words, but he himself used eloquent speech and powerful rhetoric to deliver that very warning (1 Cor. 1:17). Christians have the gospel. We have something to say. We should care deeply about how to use language to glorify God and to testify to His truth.

STRUCTURE AND DIRECTION

Christian missionaries face structure-and-direction questions every day. They seek to live in solidarity with the culture where they minister because the gospel of Jesus Christ is for every culture. Christianity is not—as North Korean, Iranian, and Chinese government leaders like to say—a Western religion. It's a global one. Every culture has beauty and value all its own. And yet part of the missionary's job is to view the surrounding culture through biblical lenses. And, inevitably, some things will look dark. Parts of every culture are headed in the wrong direction and need to be resisted and pushed back toward God's structure.

This will always be the case until Christ comes in judgment. Till then, a Christian will never fully belong in this world even though God owns it and Christ rules it.

Paul's gospel message brought change to Ephesus, as we saw. Likewise, the Wesley brothers (John and Charles) and their gospel message brought great change to Britain. William Wilberforce was salt in the wounds of that same nation until it stopped the slave trade. John Calvin, with his extremely careful and attentive Bible teaching, brought reform to Geneva, Switzerland. And the Puritans founded all sorts of prominent Christian institutions in New England. All of these people, based on their Christian beliefs, brought about great change. And yet that change was always disappointing in some ways. Most of it didn't really last. And some of it ended up paving the way for new distortions to come along. That's just the nature of living in the gap between salvation and judgment.

We need the prayer Paul prayed for the Colossians. He prayed that those believers would be "filled with the knowledge of [God's] will in all spiritual wisdom and understanding, so as to walk in a manner worthy of the Lord, fully pleasing to him, bearing fruit in every good work and increasing in the knowledge of God" (Col. 1:9–10). We need that discernment in order to be salt, to be light, and even to suffer in this time between the times.

THINKING IT THROUGH 11.3

1. As a teen, what kinds of activities could hinder not only the stability of your future marriage but also your witness for Christ?
2. How could you be a countercultural witness with your material things?
3. How could you be a countercultural witness with your use of technology?
4. How could your use of language be a witness to the culture?
5. Why would instability in your marriage and family life make it more difficult to testify about your Christian faith?

11 CHAPTER REVIEW

TERMS TO REMEMBER

Christian Reconstructionism

Scripture Memory

Matthew 5:14–16

Making Connections

1. Since Jesus Christ rose from the dead and ascended to heaven to be crowned King and Lord of all, why are there any sufferers or rebels left in His dominion?
2. Should a verbal witness be replaced by a life of good works?
3. What are the four major areas mentioned in the chapter in which Christians can bear witness to their pagan culture by pressing things back toward God's created structure?
4. What is the proper redemptive response for a Christian living in a consumeristic culture?

Developing Skills in Apologetics and Worldview

5. How would you respond to someone who claims that the kingdom of God has not yet come at all in any form?
6. How would you respond to someone who claims that the kingdom of God has already fully come before Christ's Second Coming?

Examining Assumptions and Evidence

7. Compare and contrast Christian Reconstructionism with the two-story view that you learned about in Chapter 3. Which view is correct?
8. Why must Christians live vulnerable lives?
9. Is the story of Adam and Eve in Genesis 2:18–25 descriptive or prescriptive? What evidence within the passage can you point to for your answer?
10. Why are so many people concerned about the negative impact of technology on society?

Becoming a Creative Cultivator

11. List one piece of technology that you use. In what ways can that device be used for good? In what ways can it be used for bad? Write out a plan for combatting any temptation it may pose to you:
    - What specific problem can you identify and describe?
    - What makes this problem tempting?
    - How often and how long have you been struggling with the temptation?
    - How does this problem affect you and others?
    - What "fences" can you set up to keep you from the problem?

Chapter Twelve **THE MISSION OF THE CHURCH AND YOUR VOCATION**

And they devoted themselves to the apostles' teaching and the fellowship, to the breaking of bread and the prayers.

Scripture Memory
Acts 2:42

12.1 THE MISSION OF THE CHURCH

Epic stories have heroes—whether they are modern epics like *The Lord of the Rings* and *Star Wars* or ancient epics like *The Odyssey* and *The Aeneid.* The hero is the focus of the epic. He overcomes the odds, he succeeds in his quest, and he achieves great victory. Jesus, of course, plays that heroic role in the drama of Scripture, the story of redemption.

And yet it isn't wrong for a Christian, when he learns of this great story, to want to play a "heroic" role too. It's natural, even godly, to have the ambition to live out your portion of the story of redemption by doing something of significance for the kingdom of God.

Some believers think that to be a Christian hero a person has to be a "full-time Christian worker." In this view, the most important and heroic role a Christian can play is pastor (or pastor's wife), missionary, or Christian school teacher—a job in which you're doing "ministry" all day.

These are certainly important callings—and sometimes the people God calls to fill these roles are positively heroic. But to think that such people are the only ones who serve God in their work is to buy into the two-story view.

We want this book to help you think in a Christian way about every part of your life. The Christian life and God's plan of redemption aren't limited to the church, Christian education, and mission work. When you graduate and get a job, you should do that job, whatever it may be, in service to Christ as a Christian. This thought is liberating for many Christians. They come to realize that they're not second-class Christians in a slot below "full-time Christian workers." They can live lives of service to God in their jobs as well.

Sadly, important truths are often misused. Some people who have gotten excited about living as Christians in all of life have lost their excitement for the church. Others have decided that since Christians are to be involved as Christians in all of life, the church's mission includes not only evangelism and discipleship but also running food pantries, working to save endangered species, providing clean water in impoverished parts of the world, and much more. These are good, necessary, and excellent things for Christians to do—but are they the mission of the institution called the church?

The church has a vitally important mission. When Christians neglect the church and its mission, they damage God's work in the world. The same is true when Christians load the church down with other missions so that its true mission is lost in the clutter. On the other hand, the church is not all of life. God never intended it to be. Six days are for working, and God does not call most Christians to work for the church. Both church and the work that God calls Christians to do are important parts of God's plan of redemption.

WHAT THE CHURCH IS FOR

What is the church *for*? Why does the church exist in the first place? Can't people be saved without it? In order to know these things, we've got to look at how the church fits into God's plan of redemption. As we saw in Chapter 10, God works out His plan of redemption through a series of covenants. The final covenant in God's plan—the New Covenant—is the one that gives us the church.

The Mosaic Covenant that God made with Israel had a flaw. Actually, the problem was with the people in the covenant—they couldn't keep the requirements of the covenant. Though individual Israelites could be saved by calling on God in faith (Deut. 30:6; Rom. 10:9–10), the covenant couldn't ensure that the people of Israel would love and trust God. This, of course, didn't surprise God. He predicted it when He made the covenant (Deut. 30:1). God used the persistent failures of His people throughout the Old Testament, culminating in exile from their land, to show that some other covenant was needed.

The prophets Jeremiah and Ezekiel were given the exciting message that this New Covenant was in fact coming. Here are the words of God that Jeremiah recorded:

> Behold, the days are coming, declares the Lord, when I will make a new covenant with the house of Israel and the house of Judah, not like the covenant that I made with their fathers on the day when I took them by the hand to bring them out of the land of Egypt, my covenant that they broke. . . . For this is the covenant that I will make with the house of Israel after those days, declares the Lord: I will put my law within them, and I will write it on their hearts. And I will be their God, and they shall be my people. And no longer shall each one teach his neighbor and each his brother, saying, "Know the Lord," for they shall all know me, from the least of them to the greatest, declares the Lord. For I will forgive their iniquity, and I will remember their sin no more. (Jer. 31:31–34)

Under the Old Covenant, the Mosaic Covenant, some Israelites had to tell other Israelites, "Know the Lord!" because they didn't know Him. But Jeremiah says that everyone who is part of this New Covenant will know God.

Ezekiel helps clarify these promises by recording God's intent to actually change even the affections and desires of His New Covenant people—from the inside out:

> I will give you a new heart, and a new spirit I will put within you. And I will remove the heart of stone from your flesh and give you a heart of flesh. And I will put my Spirit within you, and cause you to walk in my statutes and be careful to obey my rules. (Ezek. 36:26–27)

Anyone who's familiar with the dismal failures of the Old Testament Israelites (and who knows his or her own sinful heart) should be glad to read such a wonderful New Covenant promise. The Old Testament story ends with Nehemiah literally tearing out the hair of the Jewish men who had returned from captivity only to commit the very same sins that got their grandparents exiled in the first place.

And we don't have to wonder whether the New Covenant is yet to come. Jesus launched it when He shed His blood on the cross. Presiding over the Last Supper on the night He was betrayed, Jesus said, "This cup that is poured out for you is the *new covenant* in my blood" (Luke 22:20).

And the New Testament (a title that simply means "New Covenant") shows that the promises of Jeremiah and Ezekiel have begun to be fulfilled. Jesus' sacrifice made it possible for God to remember the people's sin no more. And the Spirit's arrival on the day of Pentecost (Acts 2:4) meant that God Himself lived in every New Covenant believer.

The New Testament does reveal something that was only hinted at in the Old Testament, however. Though God originally promised the New Covenant to Israel

ORGANISM

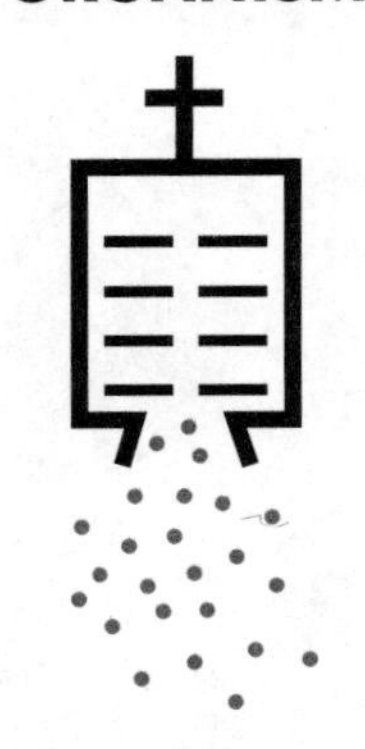

(Jer. 31:31), He poured out His Spirit on Gentiles as well as Jews (Acts 10:44–48). Gentiles, too, have God's law written on their hearts (2 Cor. 3:3). The New Covenant creates a new group of people, including both Jews and Gentiles, who get God's grace in a new way (Eph. 2:11–15).

That group is the church. The church is the New Covenant people of God. Under the Mosaic Covenant, the people of God formed a nation that included believers and unbelievers. But in the New Covenant, the people of God come from every nation, and every one of them, by definition, is a believer. As a result all true Christians can be said to be part of Christ's church (Eph. 2:8–15). But the church exists in specific locations (Acts 9:31; 11:22; 13:1; Rom. 16:1; 1 Cor. 1:2; Philem. 1:2). In these locations it has leaders (Acts 14:23; 20:17; Titus 1:5) and members (1 Cor. 5:4–5; 2 Thess. 3:14–15). Because of this, some theologians distinguish between the church as an *organism* and the church as an *institution*. As an organism, the church is the entire body with Christ as its head. But as an institution, the church gathers into local assemblies. This distinction will be important for understanding the mission of the church.

INSTITUTION

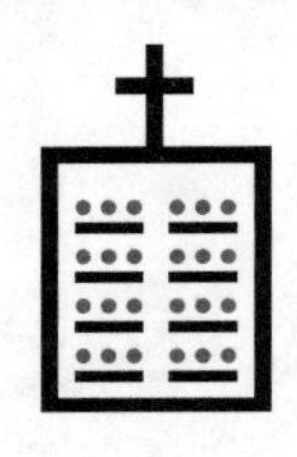

THE CHURCH AS THE KINGDOM OF GOD?

As you learned in Chapter 10, God made covenants with humans throughout biblical history for the purpose of establishing His kingdom on earth. At the heart of God's plan of redemption is the establishment of His kingdom, ruled by the perfect Man. But in Chapter 11, you also learned that Christians live in the gap between the coming of the kingdom in salvation and the coming of the kingdom in judgment. In this gap people are to prepare themselves for the coming of the kingdom in judgment by entering the kingdom by faith now (Luke 17:20–18:30). The church proclaims "good news about the kingdom of God" so that people can enter the kingdom by faith (Acts 8:12; 14:22; 19:8; 20:25; 28:31). It is for this reason that Jesus said, "On this rock I will build my church. . . . I will give you the keys of the kingdom of heaven" (Matt. 16:18–19).

Don't dismiss church as matter of routine weekly attendance. The church is a vital part of God's plan for establishing His kingdom and redeeming His world. The church is the outpost of God's kingdom in the present evil age. On the other hand, the church is not the fullness of that kingdom. The church's mission is not to conquer kingdoms by force and to ensure by force that Christendom encompasses the entire world. To say that the church *is* the kingdom is a dangerous and damaging idea. That misconception led the church of the Middle Ages to become a political and even military power.[1] Some of the popes in those days even had their own armies. When the church believes it is the kingdom, it begins to do what it ought not to do and neglects its true mission.

So what is the true mission of the church? For what purpose did God establish the church as an institution?

SHOULD EVERY CHRISTIAN JOIN A LOCAL CHURCH?

Some form of church membership is demanded by the New Testament. The logic of church membership is simple: both Jesus (Matt. 18:17) and Paul (1 Cor. 5:5) command Christians to excommunicate from the church any who refuse to repent of their sins (after making loving appeals to them, of course). You can't be kicked out of a group you're not part of in some recognizable way. Whether that means signing a form or publicly giving your salvation testimony and getting voted in, you need to join a church. If you're a Christian, you need—and should want—the pressure other Christians put on you to do right. You need to be "kickoutable." And you need encouragement; the members of a church are supposed to "stir up one another to love and good works" (Heb. 10:24).

THE INSTITUTIONAL CHURCH IN ACTION

Jesus tells us what the church's mission is in Matthew 28:18–20. The basis of that mission is His own kingly authority. Before Jesus presented the church's mission to the apostles, He declared, "All authority in heaven and on earth has been given to me" (Matt. 28:18). And then Jesus used the little word *therefore* to draw a conclusion from that authority:

> Go therefore and make disciples of all nations, baptizing them in the name of the Father and of the Son and of the Holy Spirit, teaching them to observe all that I have commanded you. (Matt. 28:19–20)

At the beginning of Acts, Luke records the first sermon preached after God established the church. The apostle Peter proclaimed that Jesus was the exalted King, seated at the right hand of the Father (Acts 2:33–36). Luke goes on to tell what the early church did. Those who submitted to Jesus as King engaged in four activities:

> They devoted themselves to the apostles' teaching and the fellowship, to the breaking of bread and the prayers. (Acts 2:42)

These passages from Matthew and Acts outline the primary activities the institutional church should be doing even today. It can all can be summed up in a single phrase: *making disciples* (i.e., mobilizing followers of Jesus). But there are six ways the institutional church is to do this: evangelizing, baptizing, teaching, fellowshiping, participating in the Lord's Supper, and praying.

Evangelizing

This mission is very different from that of Israel under the Old Covenant. The number of Israelites didn't grow as a result of Israelite missionaries going out to invite the Gentiles in; the nation grew from the inside, the way families do, by having children. Christians, heirs of God's command to "fill the earth," also have children, but those children don't automatically become part of the New Covenant. In order for the church to grow, evangelism has to happen—and Jesus told us to make it happen all over the globe.

From the earliest days of the church, as recorded in the book of Acts, citizens of God's kingdom have done just what Jesus told them to do: they have been witnesses to Him around the world (Acts 1:8). The apostle Paul asked the Ephesians to pray that He would be a bold witness (Eph. 6:19). Acts includes some pretty amazing stories that record God's answer to that prayer (Acts 16:25–30). And Paul was not alone. Christian evangelism was happening all over the ancient world, especially after God sent a wave of persecution that drove most of the original Christian church out of Jerusalem (Acts 8:1–2). This work of evangelism has continued throughout the history of the church. During some periods, this part of the mission has seemed to all but disappear. At other times, it has flamed up and burned brightly around the world.

Baptizing

Most people are on the broad road to destruction, Jesus said (Matt. 7:13–14). Most of God's image-bearers, because of the blindness brought on by the Fall, don't consider the good news to be all that good. They reject it and keep on skipping or trudging toward doom.

But some people do listen, and some do repent (Acts 17:34). When people turn from sin to Christ, Jesus commands them to take the very first step of discipleship—

baptism (Matt. 28:19). At Pentecost, baptism was the response of those who received the Word. When people were baptized, they were added to the church (Acts 2:41).

Baptism is a public means of confessing that a person is a follower of Christ (1 Pet. 3:21). It can become commonplace for American Christians, but in many parts of the world, publicly confessing Christ through baptism is a difficult and dangerous thing to do. Yet few things are of greater importance or bring greater joy than confessing to be a follower of the Savior.

Baptism is also a symbol that the new Christian is now united with Christ (cf. Rom. 6:4). It's through the believer's union with Christ that he receives Christ's righteousness. Baptism is also a symbol that the Christian has received the Spirit and is united to other believers in the body of Christ (1 Cor. 12:13). Baptism is the visible sign of the New Covenant.

Teaching

But baptism is only the beginning of discipleship. Teaching people to observe all that Jesus commanded is a huge job because He really said a lot! Christ's phrase "all that I have commanded you" includes the entire Bible. The Bible is a big and sometimes complicated book. So teaching is a key component of disciple-making.

The very first description we have of what the newly established church did after Pentecost shows that the believers took Jesus' words quite seriously: "They devoted themselves to the apostles' teaching" (Acts 2:42). That teaching is such an important part of the church's work that Christ marks out particular believers and gives them the necessary gifts to teach (Eph. 4:11). The ability to teach is a requirement for church leaders (1 Tim. 3:2).

And yet pastors and other church leaders are not supposed to be the only people who teach truth in your church. They teach so that *all* Christians can learn to "speak the truth in love" (Eph. 4:15) and even sing the truth to one another (Col. 3:16). Preaching and teaching the content and application of Scripture is the key means by which Christians are taught to be disciples of Christ, are guarded against false teaching, and are drawn together in unity with each other (Eph. 4:14–16).

Christians do lots of important things in their lives. This book talks about many of them. But nothing the Christian does will be done well if it is not informed by Jesus' teaching. For Christians to live like Christ in every other area of life, they need to know the teaching of Scripture. Listening to the preaching and teaching of God's Word is also an important act of worship. It's a way of showing that you recognize Jesus as your King and that you will obey all that He commands.

Fellowshiping

Church is not simply a school where people come to learn theology. Nor is it a motivational seminar that provides Christians with advice about issues that interest them. Teaching theology is an important part of the church's mission. Applying that teaching to everyday life is also important for the church. But the church is made up of people who have relationships with each other. This is why the earliest Christians "devoted themselves to . . . fellowship" (Acts 2:42).

Fellowship refers to the unity of believers. Christians hold Christian things in common with each other. Believers are truly one in Christ. They are united to Him as one body to its head. The teaching of apostolic doctrine has unified their view of the world. So teaching is an important part of fellowship, but it's not the totality.

The unity of fellowship works itself out in practical ways. Becoming a Christian in first-century Israel was a costly thing to do. It meant losing friends. Losing friends meant losing business partners and customers. It may have meant that many would experience real poverty. In the face of this, Christians provided material support for each other (Acts 2:44–45). Today when a church member loses a job, often others in the church help out with food and money. When a family member becomes very ill, other Christians are there to help. This kind of unity was so important to the early church that a group of godly leaders was selected to make sure that Christians in need were provided for by the church (Acts 6:1–6).

Participating in the Lord's Supper

Luke also says the earliest Christians devoted themselves to "the breaking of bread" (Acts 2:42). "The breaking of bread" in this context includes the Lord's Supper. The Lord's Supper is the eating of bread, which symbolizes the body of Christ that was broken on the cross, and the drinking of the fruit of the vine, which symbolizes the blood Jesus shed on the cross.

The Lord's Supper was frequently observed by the early Christians for several purposes. Jesus commanded that His followers observe the Lord's Supper in remembrance and in proclamation of His establishment of the New Covenant by the sacrifice of His body and His blood (1 Cor. 11:23–25). Frequent participation in the Lord's Supper should result in frequent personal examination and confession of sins (11:28). Partaking together of the Lord's Supper is another sign of believers' unity in Christ (10:16–17). On top of it all, by doing this act of worship, Christians look forward to the return of Christ (11:26). Regular observance of the Lord's Supper is one of the ways Christ intends for His church to remain focused on the central aspects of the Christian life.

Praying

Finally, the early Christians devoted themselves to prayer (Acts 2:42). Prayer in church can take many forms. Often the psalms and hymns that are sung by the church are praises and prayers to God. In many churches the pastor will lead the church in prayer. Sometimes believers gather in smaller groups to share prayer requests and to pray for each other. Paul often begins his letters with prayers for the churches he's writing to, which shows that Christians should pray for others beyond their local assembly.

Many times Christian prayers focus on the health needs of people Christians know. Health is an important thing to pray about, but it isn't the most important subject for prayer. A look at the prayers of Paul gives some insight into the kinds of prayers Christians should pray. First of all, Paul's prayers are full of thanksgiving. Paul is thankful that fellow Christians grow in faith and love. He's thankful that they persevere in persecution (2 Thess. 1:3–4). Second, Paul asks the church to pray for the salvation of people and for the opportunities that others will have to share the gospel (1 Tim. 2:1-3; Eph. 6:18–20). Third, Paul prays for Christians to become holy. He prays that God would count believers worthy of entering His kingdom. He prays that whatever desires these Christians have for doing good and for working out their faith in lives of good works will be fulfilled (2 Thess. 1:11–12). He prays that Christians will be "pure and blameless" as they await Christ's return (Phil. 1:10). Paul prays that Christians will overflow with love for each other (Phil. 1:9; 1 Thess. 3:12). Fourth, Paul prays that God will protect Christians so that they can live their lives as God intends (1 Tim. 2:2). Fifth, Paul recognizes that what he prays for can only be

WHAT ABOUT SINGING?

Singing is a major part of Christian worship. It's not listed alongside teaching and prayer as part of the church's mission because it's actually included in both. Many psalms and hymns are praises to God, and praise is a kind of prayer. Other songs are requests addressed to God. Finally, some psalms, hymns, and spiritual songs are opportunities for Christians to teach each other. This is why Paul writes that Christians should be "teaching and admonishing one another in all wisdom, singing psalms and hymns and spiritual songs" (Col. 3:16).

accomplished by the power of God (2 Thess. 1:11–12), so he prays that the Spirit will bring about what he's asking for (Col. 1:9–11; Eph. 3:16).

Prayer is difficult work, but imagine what would happen if God's people really devoted themselves to praying that God would fulfill whatever desires Christians have for doing good. For every other part of the Christian life to succeed, prayer is the essential foundation.

A GOSPEL THAT'S TOO SMALL?

Evangelism and discipleship are never-ending tasks. New people are always being born who will need to be evangelized and then discipled. The challenge is great; the task is vast. And yet some people think this biblical vision of the church's mission is too limited. If God's goal is to redeem and restore the entire created order, shouldn't the mission of the church be as broad as the mission of God? Christians who think this way wouldn't deny that the church's mission includes verbally preaching the gospel. They would simply say that the church's mission also includes creation care, the arts, care for the poor, political action against social injustice, and more.[2]

This discussion is not merely academic. You may soon have to choose a church for the first time in your life, and it matters a great deal what that church sees as its mission. Creation care, the arts, the poor, social justice—these are all good and important things. But a church that sees them as its mission is in danger of missing its real mission.

This is where the distinction between the **church as organism** and the **church as institution** becomes important. All Christians are part of the body of Christ. This body doesn't move in and out of existence every Sunday morning as the church gathers and scatters. The church as organism carries out all manner of good works in the name of Christ in a wide variety of vocations, as we'll see in the next section. But this is not the case with the church as institution. The institutional church focuses on the mission of making disciples through evangelism, baptism, teaching, fellowship, the Lord's Supper, and prayer.

This distinction between the organic church and the institutional church can be seen clearly in that the commands God gives to the institutional church and the organic church, though overlapping at points, are distinct. Two pastors who wrote a book about the mission of the church say:

> There are some commands given to the local church that the individual Christian just should not undertake to obey on his own. An individual Christian, for example, can't excommunicate another Christian; but the local church is commanded to do so in certain situations. Nor should an individual Christian take the Lord's Supper on his own; that's an activity the local church is to do "when you come together" (1 Cor. 11:17–18, 20, 33–34). In the same way, there are commands given to individual Christians that are clearly not meant for the local church as an organized group.[3]

Husbands, for example, are told to love their wives, and children are told to obey their parents. The church as a whole can't do those things.

God didn't give the church the gifts or the power to bring justice to the world. He ordained government for that purpose. Churches shouldn't have electric chairs, militias, or income tax forms. When the church tries to claim the authority of government, as it sometimes has in the past, bad things happen. Likewise, when the church as an institution seeks to provide solutions to intractable environmental issues or to resolve the problem of inner-city joblessness or to bring about the end of malaria—problems occur. There are other institutions that God has ordained to see to those tasks.

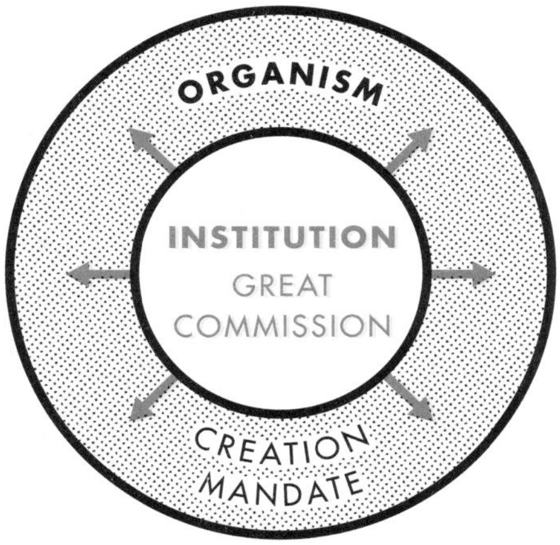

The church as institution and its mission to fulfill the Great Commission are central to how the church as organism participates in the Creation Mandate.

The institutional church, nonetheless, does have an important role to play in all of these areas. Prayer for righteous and just government should be a regular part of gathered church worship (1 Tim. 2:1–2). The church should preach against unjust and unrighteous laws. It should set a vision for what a righteous society would look like. The church also has a responsibility to disciple Christians to live biblically in the vocations God has called them to. And some believers are, in fact, called to government service, job-creation initiatives, or malaria prevention. They need to be taught by the institutional church how to be the organic church—how to do their work for love of God and neighbor in obedience to the Bible. Pastors ought to include in their sermons biblical counsel for engineers, lawyers, teachers, doctors, marketers, plumbers, and construction workers.

WHAT THE CHURCH CAN DO

Sometimes the church can do things outside its direct mission in order to further that mission. For instance, sometimes a church will establish a community outreach for the purpose of both evangelizing the lost and discipling its own members. A church may find that its members are evangelizing many people suffering from addictions. It may start an addiction ministry both to reach out to these people and to train its own people how to more effectively minister to those in need of help. Similarly, medical missions seeks to minister to people's health needs as a way of showing the love of Christ and gaining a hearing for the gospel, but the church is not given the mission of providing healthcare. Imagine the distraction from the church's real mission if local churches were also expected to manage all of the area hospitals. Yet medical missions is still a legitimate avenue for ministry.

Similarly, the church is not given the task of helping neighborhood children with their homework. That is, of course, an excellent thing for Christians to do, especially in communities where students struggle academically. A church may choose to participate in a public school tutoring program because it gives the opportunity both to help students academically and to present the gospel.

When churches consider such ministries, they need to ask the right question. The question is not whether this is a good thing to do. There are many good things that Christians should do that the church is not commissioned to do (such as running hospitals). The right question is: will this further the church's mission?

The Church's Unique Role

The church should focus on the mission God gave it rather than trying to add more job skills to its résumé. God has given to the church, and the church alone, the ministries of the Word and the ordinances (baptism and the Lord's Supper). It is through the church that week by week God's Word is proclaimed to His people. It is through the church that week by week Christians gather to praise, thank, and petition God together. It is through the church that Christians regularly commemorate the death of Christ and look forward to His return. It is through the church that week by week Christians share together their common fellowship in Christ. This is how they meet to encourage each other and to meet each other's needs. It is through the church that the kingdom of God has an outpost on earth. The wider world should be able to look at the church and be attracted to Christ.

With a comment the apostle Paul makes in one of his letters, God draws back the curtain to give us a glimpse of what He's doing through the church. Paul wrote to a small group of believers in the ancient city of Ephesus that it is "through the church" that "the manifold wisdom of God [is] made known to the rulers and authorities in the heavenly places" (Eph. 3:10). Very few people in Ephesus in the first century knew or cared what a small group of Christians was doing on some back street. But angels were watching. What God is doing in His church is something that heavenly beings look at and marvel. Through the church, God is accomplishing His eternal purposes.

Paul makes a beautiful statement of those purposes in that same letter to the Ephesian church:

> [God] put all things under [Christ's] feet and gave him as head over all things *to the church*, which is his body, the fullness of him who fills all in all. (Eph. 1:22–23)

Incredibly, God's work of putting the world under the rule of Christ is for the church's benefit. The church is the body of Christ, the King of Kings. This is an esteemed position.

THINKING IT THROUGH 12.1

1. What is it in Jeremiah 31 and Ezekiel 36 that makes the New Covenant church most different from the Old Covenant people of God, Israel?
2. What are the two different aspects of the church, and what is their significance?
3. What six tasks are included in the biblically defined mission of the local church?
4. List at least two reasons given in this chapter that church is not optional for Christians.
5. How might a neighborhood medical clinic further a church's mission? How might it possibly undermine that mission?

12.2 THE VOCATION OF THE CHRISTIAN

The institutional church has a limited, though very important, mission, but the organic church spreads out each week into the many institutions that exist in our world. The mission and calling of Christians as they work in the world is as broad as the creation itself.

In the Middle Ages the idea developed that certain Christians had a special **vocation**, or "calling," from God. People with vocations were priests, monks, and nuns. All other work was mere "secular" work, worldly work that was lower than that of those who had a "calling."

Many contemporary Christians know that the Protestant Reformation recovered and clarified the Bible's emphasis on justification by faith. But another very significant challenge the Reformers made against medieval Christianity was in this area of vocation. Martin Luther in particular argued that God calls people to work in many different areas. Every legitimate job is a vocation. All people can serve God in their work. This is a powerfully biblical idea, but even today the old medieval concept of two levels of spirituality in work has a stronghold.

The medieval concept of "secular" work being on a lower level than the "sacred" still influences the thinking of many.

THE GOODNESS OF WORK

Everything God created is good, and all legitimate jobs are, in a very real sense, created by God. So all legitimate jobs are good. A "legitimate job" is one that flows out of the Creation Mandate, God's command to fill the earth, subdue it, and have dominion over it. Some jobs are sinful and simply exist to help others sin. Those are jobs that have twisted the Creation Mandate.

This mandate is too big for one person to fulfill. And many of the skills needed in the work of the Creation Mandate are so specialized that, in order to do them well, you have to dedicate yourself to years of study. We need each other to get the job done; every vocation is a calling by God to obey a slice of the Creation Mandate.

It's true that the Fall complicated our work. Every vocation now involves elements of frustration, dreariness, and waste. But Genesis shows that God created a world that needed human work. God planted the Garden of Eden, and yet He "had not caused it to rain" (2:5). Yes, "a spring was going up from the land and was watering the whole face of the ground" (2:6, marginal reading). But this river that watered the garden (2:10), perhaps by flooding it as the Nile still does in upper Egypt every year, would only be beneficial to the kinds of plants that require farmers to cultivate them. That's the only way to make sense of Genesis 2:5, which says that "no bush of the field was yet in the land and no small plant of the field had yet sprung up—for . . . there was no man to work the ground." From the very beginning, God built a world that needed human work.

Not only is work rooted in the Creation Mandate and the nature of the creation itself, work is also a way of fulfilling the two great commandments. Good work can display love for God: "The gardener makes nothing, but rather gathers what God has

WORK OUTSIDE OF WORK

Christians aren't always paid for the work that God has called them to do. Some Christians might coach in a youth sports league for the opportunity to be a Christian mentor to some young people. Others might volunteer at a local school to help struggling students with homework. Another might volunteer at community events both to benefit the community and to build redemptive relationships with an eye toward sharing the gospel. This volunteer service doesn't bring a paycheck with it, but God calls some Christians to this work too.

made and shapes it into new and pleasing forms. The well-designed garden shows nature more clearly and beautifully than nature can show itself."[4] Work fulfills the command to love God with all of one's being because work, ideally, takes what God has created and uses the abilities that God has given to humans to show off the beauty of God's creation "more clearly and beautifully."

Good work also fulfills the second great commandment, "Love your neighbor as yourself."[5] Martin Luther pointed out in Reformation era Germany that when Christians pray, "Give us this day our daily bread," they are praying for the work of the baker, the work of the farmer, and the work of government in preventing war or fraud in the marketplace.[6] We all need bread, and when the farmer, baker, soldier, and police officer do their jobs, they are serving the rest of us. Ideally, that service should be done out of love.

DISTINCTIVELY CHRISTIAN WORK

Work that is done in obedience to God and out of love for God and neighbor is work that is pressing toward redemption. But Christians press toward redemption not only in how they do their work but in what they do. Work presses toward redemption when it is done in a distinctively Christian way, in a biblical way.

Not all Christians like this idea, however. Some argue that there really is nothing distinctively Christian about the vocations of carpenter, cashier, firefighter, plumber, landscaper, or goat breeder aside from the virtues of diligence, respect, and honesty that all people recognize as good. It's true that by common grace, and through attention to the creational norms governing these vocations, non-Christian people often do them just as well as or better than Christians.

Even in these very practical vocations, other things being equal, there will prove to be a difference between those who do their work out of love for God and neighbor and those who don't. But what if you expand the list of vocations to include research biologists, philosophers, historians, bioethicists, educators, and legislators? In these vocations the distinctions between the Christian perspective and non-Christian perspectives are often stark. A consistent, godly Christian philosopher simply could not do his work without sounding very different from his non-Christian colleagues at academic conferences. A Christian research bioethicist will have divine guidance in Scripture for his or her work on stem cells or cloning.

Christians are obligated to think about how being a Christian affects their work as scientists, teachers, elected officials, or artists. Much of the rest of this book is designed to help Christians in this way. When Christians attempt to do their work from a Christian perspective, they press that work in a redemptive direction, toward its created structure.

REDEEMING THE TIME

One of the reasons that the old medieval distinction between monks and miners, pastors and printers is still popular is that Christian service seems to have an eternal dimension. When you preach or evangelize, you are laying up treasure in heaven, aren't you? But secular work seems to fade. If you're a house painter, that fading is quite literal. And as Mr. Incredible once said, "No matter how many times you save the world, it always manages to get back in jeopardy again. Sometimes I just want it to stay saved! You know, for a little bit? I feel like the maid; I just cleaned up this mess! Can we keep it clean for . . . for ten minutes!"[7]

The only work worth doing, therefore—some Christians think—is the kind that gets people truly saved, like spiritually saved. Such Christians argue that only human souls will last forever, so work that focuses on souls is more important than other work. Working, in this view, is something of a necessary evil because we all have to eat in order to evangelize.

True Christians who love the Lord with all their hearts have often struggled over the issue we're discussing. Here's a point that may be helpful: remember that Christians don't actually redeem anything. They don't redeem people when they share the gospel. They don't redeem culture or science or education. They can press toward redemption or live in light of redemption in evangelism *and* in their "secular" work. But ultimately, redemption is brought about by Christ Himself.

There's one interesting exception. One verse in the Bible tells Christians to redeem something. Paul told the Ephesians that they should be "redeeming the time, because the days are evil" (Eph. 5:16, KJV). Paul had just been urging the Ephesians to "take no part in the unfruitful works of darkness, but instead expose them" (Eph. 5:11). And the conclusion he drew from the reality of darkness and the power of divine light was that believers should "redeem the time."

Like those first-century Christians, we live in a "present evil age" (Gal. 1:4). And precisely "because the days are evil," Paul says we should make the best use of these days that we can. Christians can redeem evil time by living righteously. They can redeem the time by walking wisely (Eph. 5:15). It's as if we can bring some part of the age to come into the present.

When Paul spells out what "redeeming the time" looks like in Ephesians 5, he doesn't focus on a bunch of holy, monkish, spiritual practices. Instead he makes a few comments about life in the church body but then devotes most of his letter to explaining how Christians ought to function in their normal everyday relationships. He talks about husbands, wives, children, *and workers* (Eph. 5:15–6:9).

Evangelism is quite obviously important to Paul, who was a missionary himself, but his examples of "redeeming the time" never mention it. Paul apparently saw no contradiction between the importance of work and the importance of evangelism. The two do not have to be in competition.

WORK AS JOYFUL VEXATION

As Christians, we do good work, we do hard work, not because it will bring in Christ's kingdom or establish some kind of permanent redemption in our corner of the world. All work is still frustrating and temporary. A Christian in government may spend a lifetime working hard to get righteous laws enacted only to see them swept away by injustice after the next election. A Christian businessman may see great success squandered by his heirs. Or a financial crisis or natural disaster may turn decades of hard work into dust.

Ecclesiastes is blunt about these fallen realities of life. Life in a fallen world is unsubstantial, transitory, and unsatisfying. "What has a man from all the toil and striving of heart with which he toils beneath the sun? For all his days are full of sorrow, and his work is a vexation" (Eccles. 2:22–23). Yet throughout Ecclesiastes, Solomon counsels the reader to find joy in this life—especially in work. "There is nothing better than that a man should rejoice in his work, for that is his lot" (3:22).

But many people make their work an idol. They look to it to bring them not just wealth but something they crave even more—prestige, power, or ultimate satisfaction. If that's what you want out of your career, your idol will most certainly let you down. Worse, instead of looking to God as your greatest source of satisfaction and security, you have replaced Him with something from His creation. But if you can simply accept the pleasure of a hard day's work as a gift from God, you'll be redeeming the time and bringing praise to God as the giver of the gift.

Whether God allows your work to help reshape your society in positive ways, or whether He allows your influence to shrink and your life to be threatened, you must be faithful—and keep an eye on the return of Christ to set things right.

THINKING IT THROUGH 12.2

1. What is the ultimate reason for engaging in any legitimate work?
2. What are the primary purposes that should orient how all legitimate work must be done?
3. In addition to the way Christians carry out their work, what should make their work truly distinctive?
4. What does Paul mean when he instructs Christians to "redeem the time"?
5. Why is work both joyful and full of vexation at the same time?

12 CHAPTER REVIEW

TERMS TO REMEMBER

church as institution
church as organism
vocation

Scripture Memory

Acts 2:42

Making Connections

1. Compare and contrast the New Covenant people of God and the Old Covenant people of God.
2. List the six tasks involved in the mission of the institutional church. What are the two key passages that define the mission of the church?
3. Pick a job—your father's job, your job, or your dream job—and explain how (or whether) it flows out of the Creation Mandate of Genesis 1:26–28.
4. Referring to that same job (question 3), explain what it would look like if the person doing it were truly motivated by love of God and neighbor. How might that make the job different than if the person were motivated solely by money?

Developing Skills in Apologetics and Worldview

5. What guidelines should a local church establish in order to make sure that its work in its local community supports the primary tasks of its mission?
6. What guidelines should a person establish in order to make sure that work does not become an idol?

Examining Assumptions and Evidence

7. Why is church membership necessary for believers?
8. Why is it dangerous to view the church as completely synonymous with the kingdom?
9. Why is it important to understand that everyone working a legitimate job works in service to God?
10. When Christians do their work, are they actually causing the world to progress toward final redemption? Explain why or why not.

Becoming a Creative Cultivator

11. What is one thing you think your church could do to reach out to the community?

5

GENDER

Chapter Thirteen THE MAN AND THE WOMAN IN CREATION

Then the Lord God said, "It is not good that the man should be alone; I will make him a helper fit for him."

Scripture Memory
Genesis 2:18

13.1 MARRIAGE AND FAMILY

Chris Milloy, a writer for the popular online magazine *Slate* (one of the top websites in the United States and Canada[1]), is angry at doctors for committing one simple sin: telling parents the gender of their children at birth.

> Why . . . must this person be a boy and that person be a girl? . . . As a newborn, your child's potential is limitless. The world is full of possibilities that every person deserves to be able to explore freely, receiving equal respect and human dignity while maximizing happiness through individual expression.[2]

Milloy feels strongly about this, apparently, for personal reasons: he now calls himself "Christin" and dresses and identifies as female. His opinions don't sound nearly as extreme to Western ears now as they did a very, very short time ago. Even if they haven't reached Milloy's conclusions, many Westerners share his presuppositions. Milloy has only taken his worldview to its logical end with regard to gender. And he urges others to follow:

> Infant gender assignment is a willful decision, and as a maturing society we need to judge whether it might be a wrong action. Why must we force this on kids at birth? . . . What could be the harm in letting a child wait to declare for themself who they are, once they're old enough?[3]

Activist Sarah Wright, writing for another prominent online source, the *New York Times*, takes a view of marriage much like Milloy's view of gender: she denies that it really exists.

> We believe the arbitrary nature of elevating some relationships above others is unethical, and we advocate for fairness and equality among all caretaking relationships.[4]

The institution of marriage, Wright thinks, should probably be discarded. Or society should at least be open to "more choices for more people"—three people, eight people, people of the same gender, people of any gender on the LGBTQ* continuum, people of genders yet to be invented. How about identical twins? Elderly siblings? The definition of marriage, in her worldview, becomes so large and inclusive as to be meaningless.

Gender-deniers and marriage-deniers aren't like Holocaust-deniers and moon-landing-deniers (such people do exist); they're like gravity-deniers. They're not lunatics; they're rebels.

But creation is stubbornly resistant to change, and all of us, Christians and non-Christians, have to live in it. Even smart people with graduate degrees who write in major news sources can't be gravity-deniers for long. God's creation has a way of bouncing back when people suppress it. And the Western world is in the act of suppressing one of the hardest truths in the world to deny: the God-created realities of gender, marriage, and family.

LGBTQ: *lesbian, gay, bisexual, transgender, queer*

GOD'S DESIGN FOR MARRIAGE

On the sixth day of creation, God created a man. And He didn't provide any other options for self-definition. "Man" was it. "Man" was his very name ("Adam" means "man"). God also created a woman. She didn't get to choose her sexual identity either. And her name, "Eve," given to her later by her husband, was chosen precisely because she is the "mother of all living" (Gen. 3:20). Gender is not arbitrary; it is a given—a God-given.

The same is true of the first marriage. God didn't bring Adam and Eve together as debate or tennis opponents. He brought them together to be "one" (Gen. 2:24), to be husband and wife.

The same God-givenness is true of the family: the very first thing God told Adam and Eve to do was to "be fruitful and multiply," to have kids. From the very beginning, gender, marriage, and family were central to God's design for creation. And it's safe to assume that He knows how they should work better than writers on popular news websites do.

A great number of those writers don't like what God has to say about the family because it puts limits on the freedom they demand. The apostle Paul describes the authority structure God instituted this way:

> The head of every man is Christ,
> the head of a wife is her husband,
> and the head of Christ is God [the Father]. (1 Cor. 11:3)

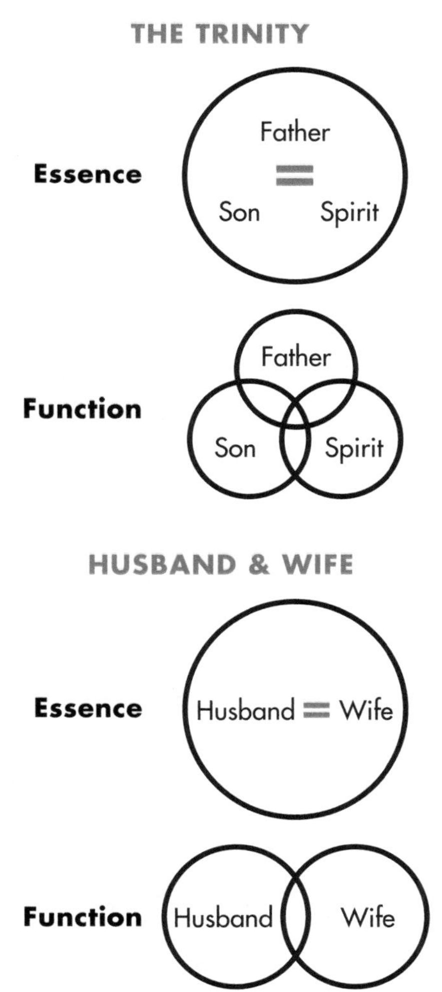

The authority structure in a marriage is like the one in the Trinity. (Have you seen enough examples now to understand why the Trinity is so fundamental to the Christian faith?) That's what *head* most naturally means in a context like this one: "authority."[5]

But note that the Father is not greater than the Son or more God-like somehow. The members of the Trinity—Father, Son, and Spirit—are all equal. They're equal in power, in wisdom, and in glory. So when Paul says that "the head of Christ is God," he's not denying their equality; he's speaking of the different roles they have in relationship to one another. Among the members of the Trinity, God the Father takes the lead, and Jesus obediently follows. Often during His earthly ministry Jesus insisted, "I have come . . . not to do my own will but the will of him who sent me" (John 6:38). No person of the Trinity is more important or necessary than another. But in their glorious work of creation (Col. 1:16) and redemption (John 3:16), they fulfill distinct roles. The Father, Son, and Spirit are all equal in essence, but each is unique in function.

And that's just the way it was with the first two created humans. From the earliest pages of Genesis we can discern this same kind of distinction between the husband and the wife: equal in essence, different in function. Neither is more important or better than the other; God has simply assigned them different roles in order to accomplish what is best for the good of the human race and for His own glory.

Husband and Wife: Equal in Essence

Saying that Adam and Eve were created equal isn't theological guesswork. The text of Genesis 1 demonstrates it. Adam and Eve were both created in God's image (Gen. 1:26). They were both created to rule, to "have dominion" (1:28). And they were both given the command to fill the earth (1:28). Neither could do it without the other.[6]

Sexual union was, to state the obvious, a good thing created by God—and, by inference, the first thing He tells the first couple to do: "Be fruitful and multiply" (1:28). Christians don't need to be embarrassed that one of the primary reasons marriage exists is the sexual union between husband and wife for the purpose of bearing children. Husbands and wives are supposed to become lovers (see the Song of Solomon) and then fathers and mothers, filling the earth with children who know and love God.

Husband and Wife: Unique in Function

The equality of husband and wife, of man and woman, is one biblical teaching that doesn't offend too many Western people. But Scripture's assigning of different functions to men and to women has become highly offensive, especially to many educated secular people.

Even some professing Christians, driven by extreme pressure from the world, deny that men and women were created to complement one another, to fill different roles. One popular Christian feminist blogger went so far as to call this idea a "false gospel."[7] The battle over Genesis is so fierce because it stands at the foundation of the Christian worldview. But Genesis is simple in its clarity: "Male and female he created them" (Gen. 1:27). God designed the man and the woman with specific distinctions, and not merely biological ones. From the beginning, for example, the woman was made to be a "helper" for the man (Gen. 2:18).

This section will take a closer look at the roles God prescribed for married men and women.

GENDER ROLES IN MARRIAGE

If biblical beliefs about gender roles are going to be offensive, then Christians ought to at least be certain they're getting those beliefs from the Bible and not just from *Leave It to Beaver* (a 1950s sitcom featuring what most people would call a traditional family). And Genesis is the place to start; the Bible says so. When Jesus was asked about divorce, He appealed directly to Genesis (Matt. 19:5–6). And Paul even tells us that there is theological significance in the simple fact, found in Genesis, that Adam was created first (1 Tim. 2:13). In other words, we're supposed to draw conclusions from Genesis about how to live our own lives as men and women.

The Role of the Man as Husband/Father

Take note of a few points from the most foundational chapters of Scripture: It was to Adam that God originally gave the authority to name the animals (Gen. 2:19–20). It was from Adam and for Adam that God created the woman (2:22). It was Adam who got to name his wife (2:23; 3:20). And, significantly, it was Adam who got in more trouble after the Fall. Not only does God give Adam forty-four words of judgment while his wife gets a mere thirteen (3:16–19), but God's rebuke to Adam starts with these words: "Because you have listened to the voice of your wife . . ." In other words, Adam hadn't just disobeyed; he had overturned the authority structure God set up.

He let his wife lead him. (This doesn't mean husbands shouldn't listen to their wives, of course.)

The apostle Paul reads Genesis the same way. To prove his statement that "the head of a wife is her husband" (1 Cor. 11:3), Paul offers this argument: "For man was not made from woman, but woman from man. Neither was man created for woman, but woman for man" (11:8–9). We must not miss the importance of this. In order to explain the roles of husband and wife during his own day in the middle of the first century AD, Paul appeals to the way God ordered His creation at the very beginning. Fatherly leadership was not a result of the Fall. God created the man to lead the family.

Husbands and fathers do have final authority (under God) within their homes (Eph. 5:22; 1 Pet. 3:1). But if you've never been an authority or a leader, you may have the wrong idea about leaders. You may think of them as bossing other people around, getting to do things the way they want. But leadership in a fallen world mostly means giving up time you'd rather spend on something else to help others. Men (especially husbands) should run *to* problems, not *away from* them. A biblically faithful man doesn't sit passively by while the family blows up. Neither does he abuse his authority or throw his weight around; the wife is an authority in the home too, just one arranged underneath her husband (Paul speaks of women "managing their households" in 1 Timothy 5:14). And on practically the first page, the Bible says a husband should "hold fast to his wife" (Gen. 2:24). That doesn't mean to keep a tight rein on her; it means he persists in showing her faithful love (Eph. 5:25, 28–31) and honor (1 Pet. 3:7). The man is also to be primarily responsible for providing for his children, both their physical needs (cf. 2 Cor. 12:14) and their spiritual nurturing (Heb. 12:6–11). He is not to "provoke them to anger" with ungracious sternness but to train them "in the discipline and instruction of the Lord" (Eph. 6:4). There is joy in fatherly leadership—both in spite of and because of the difficulty.

In short, as a husband and father, the man has the unique and primary role as loving leader, spiritual nurturer, protector, and provider.

LOVE IN THE TRINITY AND LOVE IN MARRIAGE

Michael Reeves writes,

> Therein lies the very goodness of the gospel: as the Father is the lover and the Son the beloved, so Christ becomes the lover and the church the beloved. That means that Christ loves the church first and foremost: his love is not a response, given only when the church loves him; his love comes first, and we only love him because he first loved us (1 Jn 4:19).
>
> That dynamic is also to be replicated in marriages, husbands being the heads of their wives, loving them as Christ the Head loves his bride, the church. He is the lover, she is the beloved. Like the church, then, wives are not left to earn the love of their husbands; they can enjoy it as something lavished on them freely, unconditionally and maximally. For eternity, the Father so loves the Son that he excites the Son's eternal love in response; Christ so loves the church that he excites our love in response; the husband so loves his wife that he excites her to love him back. Such is the spreading goodness that rolls out of the very being of this God. [8]

The Role of the Woman as Wife/Mother

Although both the man and the woman were created equal by God, the wife holds the unique position of being created for her husband (1 Cor. 11:9). God perceived that Adam's aloneness was "not good," and took the initiative to fashion the woman with whom he could share his life.[9] God created the woman to be a "helper fit for him" (Gen. 2:18, 20), a partner specifically designed by God for Adam's benefit, to share life with him and to fulfill God's will together.

WHAT SUBMISSION MEANS

"Wives, submit to your own husbands" is taken by secular women to be Exhibit A proving that the Bible is not just outdated but hateful. But maybe this attitude says more about secular men than about anything else.

The very passage in which Paul tells wives to submit also includes much longer instructions to husbands, leading off with, "Husbands, love your wives, as Christ loved the church and gave himself up for her" (Eph. 5:25). Yes, Scripture tells a wife to submit. And the true test of submission comes when a wife disagrees with her husband; that can be difficult to swallow in a culture that values autonomy (self-rule) so highly.

But the Bible also calls for a husband to love, honor, and cherish his wife as Christ does the church. Christianity encourages husbands through positive means (Christian fellowship, Bible teaching) and negative means (the threat of church discipline) to stay faithful to their wives and children.

Christianity isn't just a set of rules and principles; the Bible creates a community—the church—in which the truth is supposed to be lived out. If secular women had husbands who loved them like Christians are supposed to love, would they still consider submission such a dirty word?

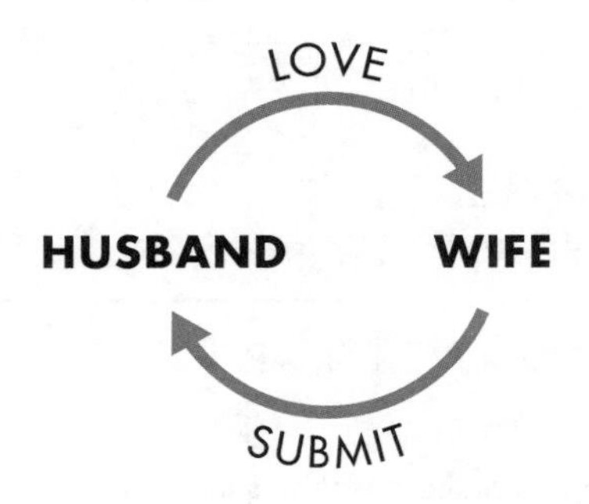

Just as the man as husband/father was created to be a loving leader, the woman as wife/mother was created to be a submissive partner, responsible to fulfill roles unique to her. As a "fit helper" for her husband, her function is to help him to fulfill the calling God has given him. Wives are instructed to "submit" to their husbands "as to the Lord" (Eph. 5:22; cf. 1 Pet. 3:1). In other words, it is the wife's role to place herself under her husband's authority; he is never told to make her submit. This is a fallen world, so no submission to any other human may be absolute. But that didn't stop Paul and Peter from telling wives to submit.

The woman has also been created by God with the special role of bearing children, a position of great honor (Gen. 3:20; Prov. 31:28). In fact, when Paul says that the woman will be "saved through childbearing" (1 Tim. 2:15), he's most likely referring to the fact that a woman shows her faith in God by fulfilling her God-ordained role, which significantly includes (but is not limited to) childbearing.[10] Furthermore, if giving birth to children is essential to God's command to rule over the earth, then the role of the woman is indispensable to God's divine plan.

But the wife's role does not mean she has second-class status. Her responsibilities are incredibly important. She is called by God to love her husband and her children (Titus 2:4), to manage the home (1 Tim. 5:14; Titus 2:5), and to participate in the spiritual nurture and discipline of her children (Prov. 1:8–9; 1 Tim. 5:10). The beautiful portrait of the wife and mother held as the crowning example in Proverbs 31:10–31 depicts a woman who honors and supports her husband (31:11–12) and who works sacrificially, wisely, and diligently to care for the daily needs of her family (31:13–27). She is praised and honored by her children and husband (31:28–29) and is referred to as one who "fears the Lord" (31:30) because she is honoring the role for which God created her.

In short, as a wife and mother, the woman has the unique and equally important role of submissive partner, companion, child-bearer, and homemaker.

CREATIONAL NORMS

In this chapter we're talking about gender at Creation, not after the Fall or in Redemption. So we'll talk about objections and exceptions in Chapter 14 about the effects of the Fall on gender. What about the issues of divorce, child abuse, and marital conflict? Those things can only be called good or bad in relationship to a standard, and Genesis 1–2 sets the standard.

You can also see that standard in yourself, to a degree. Men and women simply are different, beyond (but including) mere anatomy. A culture that's reluctant to say so—like elite American culture—is pushing against creational norms.

THINKING IT THROUGH 13.1

1. What makes gender, marriage, and the family objective realities rather than arbitrary social constructs?
2. How do you know that men and women are equal in their created essence?
3. How do you know that men and women are given different roles?
4. Describe what the key functions are for a husband/father and for a wife/mother.
5. Why is it both rebellious and ultimately fruitless to try to redefine gender, marriage, and the family?

13.2 GOD'S DESIGN FOR FAMILY

An infamous phrase in the American culture war over abortion showed up in the *New York Times* when a Planned Parenthood activist told her personal abortion story. Amy Richards was in her early thirties; she had a boyfriend and lived in a walk-up apartment in New York City. And she found out she was having triplets.

"My immediate response was, I cannot have triplets," she wrote. "I would have to go on bed rest in March. I lecture at colleges, and my biggest months are March and April. I would have to give up my main income for the rest of the year."[11]

"My immediate response was, I cannot have triplets."

And to make matters worse, she thought, "I'll never leave my house because I'll have to care for these children. I'll have to start shopping only at Costco and buying big jars of mayonnaise."[12]

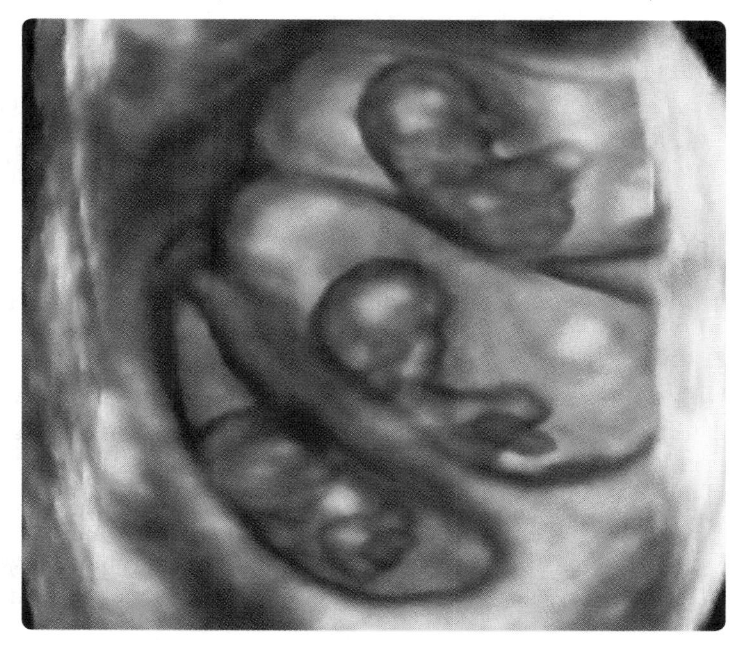

Costco mayonnaise. That's the infamous phrase. Amy Richards murdered two of her unborn children—stopping two heartbeats—in part because she didn't want to have to join the embarrassingly large families who often shop at warehouse stores like Costco.

So she glanced at her boyfriend and asked her doctor, "Is it possible to get rid of one of them? Or two of them?"[13]

Of course, it was possible; she was eight weeks along. Her boyfriend wondered aloud if they should keep the triplets, but Richards dismissed the idea. And two shots of potassium chloride later, she was carrying only one child.

If this were an isolated case, it would be tragic enough. But many educated Western people seem to have chosen to have fewer children for the same reason Richards used to justify her abortion—avoiding Costco and the other incoveniences and expenses of a large family. You may already know this from personal experience. Big families are considered odd. They get mocked. Parents with lots of kids hear snide remarks from strangers at the grocery store.

THE GIFT OF CHILDREN

Before you can even get close to answering the question "How many children should I have?" you have to acknowledge that in the Bible children are, quite literally, a blessing and a gift. "God blessed them. And God said to them, 'Be fruitful and multiply and fill the earth and subdue it'" (Gen. 1:28). Throughout the Bible, the ability to bear children is a sign of God's favor (33:5, but compare 30:2; Deut. 28:4; Ps. 113:9).

Psalm 127:3–5 sums up the attitude that God's people had toward their children:

> Behold, children are a heritage from the Lord,
> the fruit of the womb a reward.
> Like arrows in the hand of a warrior
> are the children of one's youth.
> Blessed is the man
> who fills his quiver with them!
> He shall not be put to shame
> when he speaks with his enemies in the gate.

The Bible stops short of saying how many children count as "multiplying." And different married couples may have different-sized quivers—some can handle ten kids (financially, emotionally, physically), and some can't. So most Christians in America have not prohibited "family planning"—controlling when and how many children a couple has. But the biblical attitude toward children is still noticeably positive in a world in which that perspective isn't always appreciated.

THE ROLE OF CHILDREN

Genesis says that Adam "fathered a son in his own likeness, after his image, and named him Seth" (Gen. 5:3). Do you recognize that language from Genesis 1? It's there so we make no mistake: the image of God passes from generation to generation. Image-bearing didn't cease with Adam and Eve (cf. Gen. 9:6; Ps. 8:3–8). Neither did human dominion. Adam and Eve couldn't have filled the earth without being fruitful and multiplying, of course. The blessing and task of dominion passes to all children.

But children exercise dominion (as people in general do) under the authority of others—namely their parents, in most cases. "Honor your father and your mother, that your days may be long in the land that the Lord your God is giving you" (Exod. 20:12). Paul explicitly commands children to "obey" their parents (Col. 3:20), but note that the context indicates that this applies primarily to children in the home. There may possibly be times in the life of an adult child when he honors his parents without obeying them (Gen. 2:24), but the command to honor parents for both young and old is treated as so important in all of Scripture that those situations ought to be rare. Under Old Testament law, extreme violations of this command to honor one's parents could carry the death penalty (Exod. 21:15; Deut. 21:18–21; Prov. 20:20; 30:17). In the New Testament, not only is the command to honor and obey repeated

(Eph. 6:1–2), but disobedience to parents is listed as one of the extreme sins that marks the degradation of humanity (Rom. 1:30) and is a sign of unbelief (2 Tim. 3:2).

One of the marks of a godly person is his willingness to believe that God knew what He was talking about when He made honoring and obeying parents such a strong command. Yes, parents can be wrong. But when they're not clearly wrong, and when you (as a high school student in their home) have exhausted reasonable appeals, whatever they say is God's will for you. Just rest in the submissive role God has given you—life decisions won't always be so easy. If they don't like a particular boyfriend or girlfriend or television show or activity or college choice, God's word to you is "obey." Most parents won't micromanage you till you're thirty, but even if they do, they deserve your honor whenever biblically possible.

THE NURTURING OF CHILDREN

Before God's people entered the Promised Land, He gave them specific instructions regarding the nurturing of their children. First, they were to keep the words of God always before their children (see Gen. 18:19):

> These words that I command you today shall be on your heart. You shall teach them diligently to your children, and shall talk of them when you sit in your house, and when you walk by the way, and when you lie down, and when you rise. You shall bind them as a sign on your hand, and they shall be as frontlets between your eyes. You shall write them on the doorposts of your house and on your gates. (Deut. 6:6–9)

Second, they were to keep the works of God before their children:

> When your son asks you in time to come, "What is the meaning of the testimonies and the statutes and the rules that the Lord our God has commanded you?" then you shall say to your son, "We were Pharaoh's slaves in Egypt. And the Lord brought us out of Egypt with a mighty hand. And the Lord showed signs and wonders, great and grievous, against Egypt and against Pharaoh and all his household, before our eyes. And he brought us out from there, that he might bring us in and give us the land that he swore to give to our fathers. And the Lord commanded us to do all these statutes, to fear the Lord our God, for our good always, that he might preserve us alive, as we are this day. And it will be righteousness for us, if we are careful to do all this commandment before the Lord our God, as he has commanded us." (Deut. 6:20–25)

The future of the nation lay in the hands of these children, and God had two basic instructions for parents to protect that future: keep repeating what God had said and keep repeating what He had done. Israel ultimately failed to show forth God's glory in the land in part because they neglected to nurture their children (Ps. 78:5–11).

Today, Christian sons and daughters don't automatically follow the words and works of God out of love for Him any more than ancient Hebrew kids did. Children must be trained—ideally by parents who will nurture them "in the discipline and instruction of the Lord" (Eph. 6:4). God intended for the family to be a protected and loving environment where kids can learn the appropriate affections and skills necessary to love and follow God with their lives, to be a blessing to their families and to their society. The home is where parents encourage their children to develop talents, critical thinking skills, a strong work ethic, and ministry abilities that they will employ in the service of God and others. This includes preparation for their life's callings as husbands/fathers or wives/mothers. Parents are not rearing mere children but "future child-rearers" who will, by God's grace, repeat this whole process in their own families in the future. The home is also where parents both teach and model for children the right kind of love they should have for others, so that children learn to serve one another. Preeminently, the family is where children learn to love God.

EXTENDED FAMILY

Moses, the author of Genesis, draws an interesting theological conclusion from the story of Eve being given to Adam: "Therefore," he says, "a man shall leave his father and his mother and hold fast to his wife, and they shall become one flesh" (Gen. 2:24). So a man changes his relationship with his parents when he gets married; the husband and wife start their own family unit that is in a definite way separate from what has gone before.

This doesn't mean, however, that grandparents and great-grandparents are to be shut out. In Deuteronomy 4:9, God instructs His people to make His words and works known to both their children and their children's children (cf. 2 Tim 1:5). Grandparents (and aunts, uncles, and other extended family) do not share the father's immediate responsibility for his home, but they should not cease to be consistent spiritual examples and an encouragement to both parents and children.

Christians do bear some responsibility for their relatives, especially aging parents.

And though each family unit—father, mother, and children—is distinct, the Bible does call on children to care for aging parents who can no longer help themselves. Jesus had extremely harsh words for the Pharisees who were neglecting their responsibility to provide for their parents (Matt. 15:3–9). And Paul says, "If anyone does not provide for his relatives, and especially for members of his household, he has denied the faith and is worse than an unbeliever" (1 Tim. 5:8).

THINKING IT THROUGH 13.2

1. Why should married couples try to have children?
2. What does widespread disobedience to parents in a society indicate about that society?
3. What is the normal obligation of children in the home when their personal opinions are at odds with their parents' wishes?
4. What two things of God must parents keep before their children as they nurture them spiritually to be leaders for the next generation?
5. How should adult children treat their parents?

13.3 GENDER ROLES BEYOND THE NUCLEAR FAMILY

In the grand story of life as told by evolution, the strong dominate the weak, and males in particular are most successful when they produce as many offspring as possible with as many females as possible. Evolutionists can and do resist this reasoning when applied to humans, but it's difficult for them to justify why they do. The evolutionary metanarrative gives mankind no higher purpose than procreation, and if male domination leads to more kids, then mankind is achieving that purpose. Women who spend their key childbearing years climbing the corporate ladder instead of having babies are violating the purpose for which evolution has made them: gene transmission.

The Bible, of course, gives women and men a higher purpose than procreation—though it certainly makes procreation a high purpose. Men and women are both image-bearers, and are both called by God to exercise dominion for God's glory whether or not He grants them children, and whether or not they are married.

This chapter has argued that men and women live out their dominion with different God-given roles. But unless you've been raised in a cave with no Wi-Fi (and perhaps even then), you must be aware that not all Christians agree that men and women are given different roles. Two major positions are influential: (1) **complementarianism**, which sees the sexes as serving in complementary roles, and (2) **egalitarianism**, which sees every role in home, church, and society as equally open to women and men (see sidebar on next page for more information).

The previous section discussed gender roles in marriage and the family; this section will discuss gender roles in church and society.

GENDER ROLES IN THE CHURCH

We'll start with gender roles in the church, an issue which should be less controversial than gender roles in society because the Bible speaks more directly about the qualifications for church leadership than it does about those for societal leadership.

But controversy has only increased over time; the argument between complementarians and egalitarians on this issue has been worn into grooves, with both sides saying the same things for decades. We'll follow the argument with a point-counterpoint. Egalitarians will get the first word, complementarians the last.

The basic reasoning of the egalitarians, those who think pastoral roles should be open to women, is very simple. They say that all people of either gender should be allowed to "exercise their God-given gifts with equal authority and equal

CHRISTIANS IN CONFLICT

Christians, particularly American ones, disagree about gender roles. There are two major perspectives and two major organizations representing them: The Council for Biblical Manhood and Womanhood (CBMW) represents complementarianism, and Christians for Biblical Equality (CBE) represents egalitarianism.

CBMW believes that "distinctions in masculine and feminine roles are ordained by God as part of the created order."[15] In other words, God created the sexes to complement one another.

CBE believes "that the Bible, properly interpreted, teaches the fundamental equality of men and women of all ethnic groups, all economic classes, and all age groups" and "that women and men are equally created in God's image and given equal authority and stewardship in God's creation."[16] CBE argues that God gifts women to be pastors, leaders, and breadwinners just as He gifts men to fill these roles.

Labelling this second view as "egalitarian" implies that complementarians don't see men and women as equal, but the very first words in the CBMW doctrinal statement are, "Both Adam and Eve were created in God's image, equal before God as persons and distinct in their manhood and womanhood."[17] The real issues dividing the two groups are whether men and women can be considered equal while fulfilling different roles and (more importantly) whether the Bible in fact limits certain roles (particularly in church and family leadership) to men.

Which side do you fall on? If you want to earn the right to an opinion on the issue, studying the Scripture passages dealt with in this unit is the place to start.

responsibility in the church, the family, and society."[14] In other words, if a woman has the spiritual gifts, the speaking gifts, and the administrative gifts necessary for pastoring, where did she get those gifts? And if God gave her those gifts, doesn't He expect her to use them?

Egalitarians base much of their thinking on Galatians 3:28: "There is neither Jew nor Greek, there is neither slave nor free, there is no male and female, for you are all one in Christ Jesus." If there's no more male or female now that we're all one in Christ, they say, then what point is there in telling women not to teach in church?

But complementarians respond by pointing out that this isn't all Paul says about gender roles in church. He told Timothy, "I do not permit a woman to teach or to exercise authority over a man" (1 Tim. 2:12). He also said to the Corinthians, "The women should keep silent in the churches" (1 Cor. 14:34).

Since God inspired Paul's words, all Christians have a duty to read their Bibles in such a way that the two statements ("there is no male and female" and "I do not permit a woman to teach") fit together harmoniously—and both complementariness and egalitarians attempt to do so.

Egalitarians tend to harmonize the passages by arguing that Paul was speaking only to the very narrow situation faced by Timothy or the problems of the church in Corinth. They think Paul didn't mean to forbid all Christian women everywhere and at all times from taking leadership and teaching roles in church.[18] They propose various hypothetical situations in which there were a lot of boisterous women in Timothy's particular church who were perhaps even trying to teach doctrinal error. It's *those* women who were supposed to be quiet.[19] (Some egalitarians also attempt to invalidate the teachings of the Pastoral Epistles by denying that Paul wrote these books.)

Complementarians respond by noting what Paul argues in 1 Timothy, the most direct passage on the qualifications for pastoral leadership:

> Let a woman learn quietly with all submissiveness. I do not permit a woman to teach or to exercise authority over a man; rather, she is to remain quiet. For Adam was formed first, then Eve; and Adam was not deceived, but the woman was deceived and became a transgressor. (1 Tim. 2:11–14)

Complementarians point to the word *For*. They say there's a logic in Paul's words: "Women can't teach or lead men because Adam was formed first." That logic doesn't sound very specific to Ephesus, they say. It sounds universally applicable.

Egalitarians, in turn, respond that what Paul prohibited was women who took authority they weren't supposed to take—women who "usurped" or "seized" authority. Women who get authority in the appropriate way are acceptable.

Complementarians, at this point, tend to throw up their hands and say, "Isn't God allowed to tell men and women what to do in church, even if American culture hates it?" They point out that only men are invited to seek the office of pastor (1 Tim. 3:1–7; Titus 1:5–9); that Paul says pastors are supposed to be good fathers, faithful to their wives, having obedient children (1 Tim. 3:2, 4–5; Titus 1:6); that deacons must also be "the husband of one wife, managing their children and their own households well" (1 Tim. 3:12).

In response, egalitarians also tend to throw up their hands and say, "Does it make sense for God to give gifts to women that He won't let them use?" Egalitarians are, then, taking the argument back to the beginning of the groove. They complain that complementarians are wiping out the usefulness of half the church.

Complementarians have recognized that their whole message can't boil down to "No!"—a list of all the things women can't do in church. So they point out that the Bible honors women both young and old as examples of piety and good works as they serve others, rear their children, and keep their homes (1 Tim. 2:9–10, 15; 5:4–15; Titus 2:3–5). And they admit that God does gift women to be teachers. Paul specifically instructs older women "to *teach* what is good, and so train the young women to love their husbands and children, to be self-controlled, pure, working at home, kind, and submissive to their own husbands, that the word of God may not be reviled" (Titus 2:3–5). Christian women are free to teach children (just not men) and to share the gospel with anyone, man or woman, boy or girl. In the complementarian view, both men and women serve in unique and vital roles in the church, and young Christian men and women should learn to fulfill these roles also. Just like in the home, men take the lead in giving spiritual direction, in providing for the church, and in protecting the church against error.

GENDER ROLES IN SOCIETY

When *The Lion, the Witch and the Wardrobe*, written in 1950, was made into a movie half a century later, there was one line in the novel that was sure to get the ax. When Lucy Pevensie meets Father Christmas, he gives her a small cordial of magical healing medicine—and a small dagger. But he instructs her, "The dagger is to defend yourself at great need. For you . . . are not to be in the battle."[21]

"Why, sir?" Lucy asks. "I think—I don't know—but I think I could be brave enough."

"That is not the point," Father Christmas replies. "Battles are ugly when women fight."

Notice how gently C. S. Lewis, the author of the Narnia tales, states his point. He and Father Christmas don't question whether the little girl could be brave. Lucy is, in fact, the most "spiritually gifted" person in the series. She loves and trusts the lion Aslan—representing Jesus Christ—so much that she would surely rush into battle if Aslan commanded her to, but "that is not the point."

In the movie Lucy also says, "I think I could be brave enough." But Father Christmas's reply is subtly different: "I'm sure you could. [But] battles are ugly affairs."[22]

(And in the book, Father Christmas also tells Lucy's sister not to fight, while in the movie he leaves that possibility open to her. Neither girl ends up fighting, but "that is not the point.")

What happened in fifty years to make it impossible to say "Battles are ugly when women fight" in a major motion picture? The film's director, Andrew Adamson, told *USA Today*, "I had just come off two films that I hope are empowering for girls. I didn't want to turn that message around." Adamson said that he instead wanted to send a message that "applies to boys and girls equally."[23]

Western culture often seems to believe that the way to "empower" girls is to tell them women can be just like men. And let's remember, that's partly right: women are divine image-bearers just like men; they are given gifts by God just like men; they share equally in the glory of being human.

But they also have distinct glories, glories men don't have (and vice versa). "Nature itself," Paul says, teaches that a woman's "long hair . . . is her glory," to give just one example (1 Cor. 11:14–15). It is not empowering to erase the distinct glories God has given to women. And their role in society, as this section will argue, is one of those glories.

Mature Masculinity and Femininity

First, we must begin with an admission: the Bible simply doesn't say much about how women's roles in society differ from men's. Whether or not women are "allowed" to become CEOs of Fortune 500 companies—or senators, or heads of state—is probably not the right question to begin with. The complementarian view doesn't claim to have found ironclad scriptural rules about female gender roles outside home and church.

Instead complementarians make an inference: if God tasks men with ultimate (though not sole) authority in the home and in the church—and if He does so based, ultimately, on the order in which they were created—then shouldn't male leadership be the default in society, too? As Christian writer Marvin Olasky said, "God does not forbid women to be leaders in society . . . , but when that occurs it's usually because of the abdication of men. As in the situation of Deborah and Barak, there's a certain shame attached to it"[24] (Judg. 4:9).

Not all Bible-believing Christians find this reasoning persuasive. But there are other hints within Scripture that the inference is accurate.

One of the hints is that very story of Deborah. Egalitarians are eager to point to Deborah as an example of a God-approved female leader in Scripture. And she is that—sort of. The Bible never says a single negative thing about her. She was truly godly, and she did not sin in taking leadership. But her story appears in the book of Judges—and the whole point of that book is that God's people were getting the leaders they deserved because of their sin. There are many hints in the story that female leadership was an indictment* of the males for not stepping up to the plate. When the military leader Barak refused to meet the enemy without Deborah at his side, Deborah declared, "I will surely go with you. Nevertheless, the road on which you are going will not lead to your glory, for the Lord will sell Sisera into the hand of a woman" (Judg. 4:9; cf. Isa. 3:12).

indictment: *an expression of strong disapproval; serious criticism*

An egalitarian may immediately say, "But that was a very different culture!" And he or she would be right. But the complementarian case for gender roles in society is "cumulative"—it doesn't rely on one absolutely clear proof text. So think of another scriptural hint: if women are to be bearing children (1 Tim. 2:15) and "working at home" (Titus 2:5), when exactly are they going to climb the corporate ladder?

Of course, many women are called to singleness—or, though feeling called to marriage, they nonetheless haven't been asked to be in one. Complementarians stop short of saying that single women should not take leadership positions in society, because the Bible doesn't say that. Instead, the (complementarian) Council for Biblical Manhood and Womanhood prefers to speak of the characteristics of masculinity and femininity as "dispositions" or tendencies—not "rules." Listen to how CBMW defines maleness and femaleness:

> At the heart of mature masculinity is a sense of benevolent responsibility to lead, provide for and protect women in ways appropriate to a man's differing relationships.
>
> At the heart of mature femininity is a freeing disposition to affirm, receive and nurture strength and leadership from worthy men in ways appropriate to a woman's differing relationships.[25]

"What makes men men*, or women* women*, is intrinsically connected to the majesty of the God in our design. We each exist as we do in order to display that glory."*[26]

—JONATHAN PARNELL

Men and women have "differing relationships." No sound complementarian will ever claim that all women must submit to all men. There's room in definitions like these for fully feminine supervisors standing in authority over fully masculine employees. But these definitions, if in fact they reflect divine creational norms, show that in general men are to lead and women are to support that leadership. Some women can lead men while receiving and nurturing those men's own leadership capacities. But complementarians tend to doubt that such is the norm.

In most cultures the men take the lead in the workforce and government, and the women serve in supporting roles, caring for family and keeping the home. And the Bible, at the very least, doesn't question this tendency. This does not mean that women can never make contributions to what the men are doing; precisely the opposite. Wives are not "helpers" unless they make contributions. So we have wonderful New Testament examples such as Priscilla, a woman who takes a major role alongside her husband, Aquilla, in strengthening the early church, even helping to train one of its most effective early preachers (Acts 18:24–28). There were many women invested in the ministry of the first-century church (for example, Phoebe in Rom. 16; Lydia in Acts 16; Euodia and Syntyche in Phil. 4:2–3).

Your Role

When world-famous Olympian Bruce Jenner declared that he was a woman (changing his name to *Caitlyn*) and was featured in a photo shoot and on a *Vanity Fair* cover, he was loudly applauded all over American culture. There's a terrific amount of cultural pressure on Christians to drop the whole idea of gender, let alone any idea of gender-specific roles in church, home, and society. But God is the Creator; He has a right to tell us how to live our lives. And He loves us. When God says something as clear as "male and female he created them" (Gen. 1:27), we must listen. When He says, "Wives, submit to your own husbands" (Eph. 5:22), then an attack on gender roles in the home becomes an attack on the Bible, a denial of God's goodness, love, and wisdom as well as a challenge against His authority.

And as for Christians in the egalitarian/complementarian debate (which is pretty well all of us), the only thing we can do is keep going back to Scripture. We can't do what one blogger did when she said, "No one seems to know for sure what [1 Timothy 2:12] means, and frankly, I've just about given up on figuring out exactly what's going on with it."[27]

Are the Bible passages mentioned in this chapter so unclear that it's impossible to understand them? What do you think? You don't have the option of being noncommittal. You will likely choose a church and a mate in coming years. God's Word about gender roles needs to guide you as you make these life-altering choices.

Simply put, in most cases a man should expect to marry, become a father, and lead and protect his home. In most cases a woman should expect to marry and become a mother, supporting her husband's calling and caring for her home. Godly young men and women should pursue this course first. And if along the way God makes His will plain that someone is called to singleness instead, each should be willing to follow God's leading. At the very least, Christian men and women should willingly raise up the role of wife, mother, and homemaker as an honorable and important calling. That calling demands incredible creativity and may necessitate considerable education. It does not demean women. To demand absolute equality in the functional roles of the sexes is to deny men and women the special glories God gave them.

THINKING IT THROUGH 13.3

1. What do you think women's roles in society would look like if people lived out the evolutionary worldview with consistency?
2. Contrast the complementarian and egalitarian positions.
3. How do egalitarians attempt to harmonize Paul's instructions about male leadership roles in the home and church?
4. The Bible specifically mentions that a woman's long hair is her glory (1 Cor. 11:14–15). Can you list another feminine glory suggested by Scripture? How about a masculine one?
5. Explain the real issue that divides complementarians and egalitarians.

13 CHAPTER REVIEW

TERMS TO REMEMBER

complementarianism
egalitarianism

Scripture Memory

Genesis 2:18

Making Connections

1. Based on the realities of the Trinity and God's created order, how should and shouldn't *equality* be defined?
2. Was the father made the leader of his family before or after the Fall? Why is this significant?
3. Summarize the roles and responsibilities of parents and children in the family.
4. According to 1 Timothy 2:11–14, why is male leadership the norm in the church?

Developing Skills in Apologetics and Worldview

5. How should you respond to someone who presupposes that a woman's submission to her husband is outdated and oppressive?
6. How should you respond to someone who argues that denying women certain leadership roles in the church implies that women are not equal to men?

Examining Assumptions and Evidence

7. Why can't humans adjust and redefine gender norms?
8. Should parents expect their adult children to obey them? Why or why not?
9. Why are complementarians required to "make an inference" when it comes to gender roles in society?
10. What biblical support exists for generally expecting men to lead in society?

Becoming a Creative Cultivator

11. Suggest a specific family activity that can bring you, your siblings, and your parents together socially and spiritually.

Chapter Fourteen MARRIAGE TWISTED

To the woman he said, "I will surely multiply your pain in childbearing; in pain you shall bring forth children. Your desire shall be for your husband, and he shall rule over you." And to Adam he said, "Because you have listened to the voice of your wife and have eaten of the tree of which I commanded you, 'You shall not eat of it,' cursed is the ground because of you; in pain you shall eat of it all the days of your life."

Scripture Memory
Genesis 3:16–17

14.1 DYSFUNCTIONAL FAMILY RELATIONSHIPS

You probably don't remember American sitcom *Murphy Brown*. The show, about a successful female TV journalist, ended its run in 1998. And only the politics junkies among high schoolers are likely to recognize the name of Dan Quayle, who was vice president of the United States under George H. W. Bush (1989–93).

But the fact that Dan Quayle criticized Murphy Brown in one line of an otherwise forgotten political speech is something you do need to know. Quayle was discussing the absence of "mature responsible men" from the lives of too many American boys. And then he made this one-sentence observation:

> It doesn't help matters when prime-time TV has Murphy Brown—a character who supposedly epitomizes today's intelligent, highly paid, professional woman—mocking the importance of fathers by bearing a child alone and calling it just another "lifestyle choice."[1]

Quayle touched off a media firestorm. To this day he is mocked and derided for his comment.[2] The sitcom writers saw the controversy as an opportunity and managed to weave video of Quayle's speech into the show. The Murphy Brown character delivered this tart response to Quayle:

> Perhaps it's time for the vice president to expand his definition [of family] and recognize that, whether by choice or circumstance, families come in all shapes and sizes.[3]

In one sense, Ms. Brown was right. Not all single parents choose to be single parents, and families of two are indeed a different size than families of twenty.

But Brown was wrong overall. No one can expand—or contract—the very definition of *family* because the right concept of the family is something humanity discovers in the Bible and creation, not something it invents.[4]

For some people in Western culture, family has come to mean any grouping of people who love each other enough to share a relationship. Marriage and the family are no longer governed by the design of a Creator.

God's design for marriage and family was twisted mere moments after Adam and Eve ate the forbidden fruit: the very first casualty of the Fall was the openness Adam and Eve had enjoyed. "Then the eyes of both were opened, and they knew that they were naked" (Gen. 3:7). The Fall immediately began bending the first family out of shape even further when Adam blamed Eve (and ultimately God) for the sin he'd committed (Gen. 3:12). In the next chapter of Genesis, Cain murdered Abel. The world's very first family was dysfunctional.

This section will focus on how the Fall has twisted the family, including the intimacy and the roles of husbands and wives as well as the roles of parents and children.

TWISTED MARITAL INTIMACY

God, for our own good and His own glory, instructs us, "Let marriage be held in honor among all, and let the marriage bed be undefiled." And Scripture goes on to warn that "God will judge the sexually immoral and adulterous" (Heb. 13:4). "Among all" nations, "among all" cultures, "among all" people reading this book, marriage and the "marriage bed" (meaning sexual relations) should be "held in honor" (considered precious). The Bible allows only one man and one woman in that bed, and they are to be one for life.

But humans have invented many ways to twist the precious gift of sex:

- **Fornication** means sexual relations between unmarried partners. The Bible doesn't need to get into a lot of specifics;; it just condemns sexual immorality in very general terms.[5] Christians are supposed to "flee youthful passions" (2 Tim. 2:22) and "abstain from sexual immorality" (1 Thess. 4:3).
- **Adultery** is sexual relations between a married person and someone else outside the marriage. Over 90 percent of Americans actually agree, at least verbally, with biblical morality here, telling pollsters that adultery is wrong.[6] But remember Jesus' warning: adultery can be internal, not only external (Matt. 5:27–28).
- **Polygamy** violates the scriptural norm for marriage too.[7] God gave Adam only one wife (Matt. 19:5). The extreme troubles brought on by all of the prominent polygamous marriages in Scripture (Abraham, Jacob, David, Solomon) support the point: polygamy does not fit God's design for marriage. All the positive biblical instruction about marriage presents one man, one woman as the ideal (Prov. 12:4; 18:22; 19:14; Eph. 5:22–23).[8]

If people reject the creational norm,

then anything goes.

Child sexual abuse (and subsequent cover-up), date rape, incest, bestiality, prostitution, homosexuality, immodesty, porn—the list of twistings could go on and on. And all around the world, it does. Mankind has been pretty creative and energetic in its efforts to dishonor marriage and corrupt the precious gift of the marriage bed. And we've created books, movies, magazines, and internet sites to celebrate and promote every single corruption. All of these specific sins (and more) may be placed in the categories named in Hebrews 13:4—"sexual immorality" and "adultery." The Bible doesn't have to get very specific about which sexual acts are immoral; it's everything outside of the marriage bed.

Illicit sex is (often) pleasurable, maybe very pleasurable. The Bible doesn't deny that sin brings pleasure, but it's fleeting (Heb. 11:25). And you probably know at least some of the pain that the twisting of sex has caused people: addiction, guilt, broken relationships, disease. Poverty, too, is often one result of illicit sex, particularly when teenage pregnancy is involved.

One of the most moving stories in the New Testament is about a prostitute (Luke 7:36–50). Sexual sins can be forgiven and cleansed like all others. But the negative consequences of illicit sex display to the world that immorality runs counter to creational norms. It violates the way the world was made to work.

SINGLENESS AND CHILDLESSNESS

Singleness and childlessness are not sins. Yes, God blessed marriage and childbearing in the Creation Mandate, and they are encouraged and celebrated throughout Scripture as the normal life pattern for most believers. But there are godly people mentioned all through the Bible who were unmarried or childless. And, as the New Testament teaches, God actually calls and gifts some men and women for singleness (1 Cor. 7:7), freeing them to devote themselves more completely to the Lord (1 Cor. 7:32–34) and to accomplish a unique mission in His name. Paul purposefully gave up the privilege of marriage so that he could have greater flexibility in his mission to preach the gospel (1 Cor. 9:3–27). John the Baptist was also single for his special calling. And Jesus Himself, who referred to singleness as a gift (Matt. 19:11), remained single. By implication, since it is God who is the giver of children in the first place (Ps. 127:3; 139:13), childlessness may also be the will of God for married believers who share an exceptional calling.

TWISTED SPOUSAL ROLES

Statistically speaking, ten years from now, most readers of this book will be married. And it's sad to say so, but God promised long before you were born that the results of the Fall would put negative pressures on your marriage. "Your desire shall be for your husband," God told Eve in the Garden of Eden, "and he shall rule over you" (Gen. 3:16). In other words, "You will desire to rule over your husband, and he's going try to lord it over you instead." Common grace means not all marriages fall apart, but the gravity of the Fall pulls spouses into these behavior patterns: women will be tempted to rule their husbands, and men will be tempted to be domineering over their wives.

Adultery and porn are perhaps more obvious sins, but they tend to start with simpler, subtler ones like those God mentioned would come in Genesis 3:16. Sexual sins are outward signs of other sins that are present at the very core of the marriage relationship: a failure of the husband and the wife to live in harmony according to the unique roles God has assigned to them.

Twisted Husbands

Look around at the marriages you see. Those that aren't doing well tend to fall into the two categories God listed in Genesis 3: either the wife rules the (hen-pecked) husband or the husband is overbearing, angry, and bitter toward his wife. But the Bible is clear: "Husbands, love your wives, and do not be harsh with them," Paul says in Colossians 3:19.

Have you ever picked some large, juicy-looking blackberries from a bush by the side of the road? They can be extremely tasty. Or they can be spit-it-out-right-now bitter. And you can't tell just by looking at them. So it is with husbands. A man may look like he's fulfilling his role as leader, but his leadership has actually wrenched out all the sweetness of love and grace God calls for. Some husbands think biblical leadership means wives don't get to offer their opinion, rebuke their husband's sins, or make any decision—or income—whatsoever. That's foolish; God gives men their wives to help them. And wives are authorities within their families.

On the other hand, of course, you've got your La-Z-Boy, leave-me-alone husbands who don't step up and provide any leadership at all. Some men have actually lost their marriages because of their devotion to video games (many grown men do more gaming than high schoolers).[9] Biblically faithful men run to the problem, not away—whether it's a mouse, a toddler Armageddon, or an angry outburst for which a man needs to ask forgiveness of a quietly crying wife or child. Some husbands force their wives to take leadership in the family because they never find the energy to do so themselves. But husbands are called to take the lead in spiritual nurturing, protection, and provision for their wives and children. Husbands have to make the final call on controversial matters, yes, but husbands must also, like Adam, take final responsibility if things go wrong.

Twisted Wives

God gave wives the role of submissive partner, companion, childbearer, and homemaker—and these responsibilities can also be twisted through the Fall. For example, a wife can give in to the fallen urge to dominate her husband or even to live in rebellion against his authority (Gen. 3:16). And rebellion can take many forms, from outright resistance to her husband's leadership to subtle strategies of manipulation. Either form is a refusal on her part to trust in the divinely created order of marriage.

TWISTED FAMILIES

Families get twisted by the Fall too. The "nuclear family" is an accurate description of some homes because everybody's got a finger poised over the red button, just waiting to blow up at each other.

Sins of Parents Against Children

Sometimes it's the parents' fault. One of the main parenting instructions the New Testament gives is "Fathers, do not provoke your children to anger" (Eph. 6:4). Through the writings of author Charles Dickens people get a taste of the exasperation and bewilderment of a child whose caregivers mistreat him. Little Pip in *Great Expectations* is brought up being beaten for the slightest perceived infraction, and it's heart-wrenching to listen to the boy's confused reactions.

Sadly, child abuse didn't go away after Dickens wrote novels exposing it. And in a full 80 percent of child abuse cases, the parents are the abusers.[10] Physical and sexual abuse of children still occurs—even murder. That, of course, is what abortion is—mothers murdering their own children.

But the more common form of childhood exasperation comes from angry dads. Dads (like moms) may be impossible to please, sometimes insisting that their children follow petty rules. Some parents punish their kids severely, speak to them rudely, or make them fearful.[11]

SEXUAL ABUSE

There is one especially damaging sin that parents sometimes commit against their own children: sexual abuse. Children may not want to get their parents in trouble, but sexual abuse and physical abuse need to be reported both to church leadership and law enforcement. What an abuser does to one child may be repeated with younger siblings. And an abused child will have great difficulty finding healing if his or her abuser is never brought to justice. The best way to protect children is to expose the offender. And every teacher, principal, and pastor should be aware of relevant mandatory reporting laws for suspected child abuse and neglect.[12]

Sins of Children Against Parents

The Ten Commandments tell children very simply, "Honor your father and your mother" (Exod. 20:12). Most children seem to have this desire innately. And yet it's still a responsibility—and not just because kids get pretty much everything they have from their parents; they must honor them because it is the way God has designed the family to function.

But you're not a young child. You're a teen. Teenagers have brains, skills, talents, and ideas. In more and more ways, they tend to feel ready to take charge of their lives, but Western culture subtly encourages them not to do so, even though that may sound odd. The world wants teens to have freedom, not to be held back by their parents. But the kind of freedom Western culture encourages teens to have is not an adult freedom but a teenage one.

Teenager is a comparatively recent invention. The word first showed up in English in the 1940s.[13] Before that, a thirteen- to nineteen-year-old's place in society was based not as much on age as on his or her ability to function as an adult. Girls tended to marry at much younger ages. Young men would go to work when they were strong enough. Or if they learned their Latin and could pass a college entrance exam, they might go to college at fourteen—age didn't really matter. More recently, several factors in our society—including good things like the development of secondary education (high schools) and laws regulating the legal work age, and not-so-good things like the rise of the teen subculture of entertainment and fashion—have detained a lot of young people in a sort of holding pattern where they're not encouraged to mature or allowed to be "grown up." Instead they're expected to "live it up," consuming as much as they can the offerings of popular culture.

Patricia Hersch describes this social phenomenon in her book about teens, *A Tribe Apart*.

> Somewhere in the transition from twelve to thirteen, our nation's children slip into a netherworld of adolescence that too often becomes a self-fulfilling prophecy of estrangement. The individual child feels lost to a world of teens . . . notorious for what they do wrong, judged for their inadequacies, known by labels and statistics that frighten and put off adults.[14]

The trends, styles, language, and technology in our culture change so quickly that parents can appear hopelessly out of date to their teenage children because of seemingly outmoded ideals and traditions.

Teen culture is a departure from God's creational norms. While not all teens openly rebel against their parents, many are tempted to keep Mom and Dad ignorant of whatever they're up to.

Just because society considers teens as not quite adults, that doesn't exempt you from the command to children to honor their parents. Even if all of Western culture refuses to enforce this norm, God through His acts of providence will. The person who "mocks a father and scorns to obey a mother" (Prov. 30:17) is warned that he will come to a terrible end. Rebellion against parents leads to a life of dysfunction that ends in tragedy.

HOPE FOR WHOLENESS

Cultural pressure has never in history pushed people consistently toward holiness. God placed you into this culture in this part of history—your job is to live out your Christian life in the middle of these unique challenges and opportunities. Twisted sex, in various electronic forms at least, is easily available to you. And the sexual choices you are making right now may hurt your future marriage. On top of that, you've got to live as a fallen child of fallen parents and with fallen siblings.

Why not give up? Because your conscience and your Bible agree. Because sex has a created structure you will not be able to violate forever. Because God is in charge of you and your body. Because the reward is as great as the dangers are intense.

THINKING IT THROUGH 14.1

1. List at least three kinds of sin that according to the Bible are a corruption of God's design for intimacy.
2. List some scriptural reasons why it is wrong to look down on unmarried people.
3. What two types of husbands cause antagonistic relationships with their wives? What two types of wives cause antagonistic relationships with their husbands?
4. What do parents do to sidestep (and even abandon) their God-given responsibility? What do children/teens do to frustrate their parents' God-given responsibility?
5. How should and shouldn't the family be defined? Explain why.

14.2 HOMOSEXUALITY

Rosaria Champagne Butterfield was everything some Christians fear: a successfully tenured* university professor of queer theory,* a pro-homosexual activist, and a practicing lesbian. Rosaria, for her part, viewed conservative Christians through the haze of a massive cultural divide. They were to her an object of fascination, disgust, and academic study. She writes,

> The closest I ever got to Christians during these times were students who refused to read material in university classrooms on the grounds that "knowing Jesus" meant never needing to know anything else; people who sent me hate mail; or people who carried signs at gay pride marches that read "God Hates Fags."*[15]

tenured: *achieving a permanent job as professor; a mark of academic success*

queer theory: *the study of homosexuality*

fag: *a demeaning and offensive term for male homosexuals*

So when she wrote an op-ed piece attacking Christianity for the local newspaper and it yielded a stack of nasty letters from Christians and kudos from fellow liberals, Dr. Champagne was not surprised. She separated the letters neatly into boxes on opposite sides of her desk: fan mail and hate mail.

Except there was one letter that didn't fit. It was from a conservative Christian pastor in her town. It hovered between the boxes because it was a letter of disagreement—but not of hatred. It asked probing questions and invited further contact. It actually found its way into and out of her trash can more than once before Rosaria, intrigued, decided to meet its author.

After two years of friendship with this gracious pastor and his wife, Rosaria became what she calls an "unlikely convert" to the Christian faith. She is now everything that some homosexuals fear: a married homeschool mom who submits to her husband (a pastor) and lives to follow God's Word.

Because of her remarkable story and her obvious gifts as a thinker and communicator, Dr. Butterfield is in high demand as a speaker at churches, schools, and conferences around America. She's become a leading spokeswoman for the orthodox* Christian perspective on homosexuality.

orthodox: *the established, traditional, mainstream view*

LGBT: *lesbian, gay, bisexual, transgendered*

Rosaria provokes strong reactions. Nine pro-**LGBT*** students at the University of South Florida stood in front of her with their backs turned during her entire speech there.[16]

Then there was the large evangelical Christian college that invited her to speak in chapel. Around a hundred students (all of whom had previously signed a community covenant promising to abstain from "homosexual behavior and all other sexual relations outside the bounds of marriage between a man and woman"[17]) staged a demonstration regarding Rosaria's visit. They sat silently on the chapel steps and held signs saying things like "We're all loved by God" and "I'm gay and a beloved child of God."[18]

Rosaria Champagne Butterfield

THE "GAY CHRISTIAN" MOVEMENT

In 1988, almost 60 percent of Americans thought homosexuality itself should be illegal; the idea that homosexuals would be allowed to marry was, to say the least, unpopular. Less than a generation later, over 60 percent of Americans think homosexuality should be legal, and almost that many think gays and lesbians should be allowed to marry.[19] (Another relevant statistic is that only about 2.3 percent of Americans call themselves gay, lesbian, or bisexual.[20]) In 2015, the Supreme Court of the United States legalized gay marriage in all fifty states in a bitterly contested decision.

theological liberals: *professing Christians who deny that the Bible is completely trustworthy and tend to go wherever the culture does*

monogamous: *marrying and staying sexually faithful to only one partner*

The SCOTUS decision didn't surprise anyone; America's commitment to empty concepts of "liberty" and "equality"[21] made it all but inevitable. What's surprising is that the tidal wave of support for homosexuality in America has swept up so many Christians—and not just theological liberals.* A growing movement of "gay Christians" argues that the Bible is God's holy Word and that it has nothing negative to say about faithfully monogamous* homosexuals. They make some intellectually demanding arguments; they're not ignorant of Scripture. The pro-gay protestors at the Christian college drew their slogans straight from the "gay Christian" playbook.[22]

One of the signs read, "Rosaria's story is valid, mine is too." "Gay Christians" are happy enough for a person to come to Christ and leave a same-sex partner; they simply want the freedom to keep theirs. Rosaria met with these protestors privately and was not persuaded by their arguments. Nor were they persuaded by hers.[23] Should everyone just agree to disagree?

CFR and Homosexuality

This is a confusing time. That's why you need Bible study skills and a biblical worldview. You need Bible study skills because the "gay Christians" use sophisticated arguments about the meaning of New Testament Greek words, about Bible interpretation in general, and about the relationship of the two testaments in Scripture. This is not the place to enter those detailed arguments (see the sidebar on page 209 for recommended books).

This is the place, instead, to remember Creation, Fall, Redemption. If you don't see the Bible as the story of a good creation twisted by Adam's Fall and then restored to its purpose, you'll miss the most important argument in the whole homosexuality debate, which is this: the way God created the world is the standard by which we should judge the way things ought to be.

What is the created structure of marriage? It's what we saw in the previous chapter: a man and a woman (Gen. 1:27) being put together by God for life (Mark 10:9) so the wife can help her husband (Gen. 2:18), so the husband can love his wife (Eph. 5:25), and so the two of them can become one (Gen. 2:24) with the result that they multiply (Gen. 1:28). Homosexual relationships can never meet this standard.

Homosexuality is a worldview issue because to defend homosexual acts as acceptable to God is to deny that the design of our bodies implies anything about their purpose.[24] And that strikes at the heart of the Creation, Fall, Redemption worldview. Read your Bible and your body: homosexuality is a sinful twisting of sex.

At the same time, fallenness is not limited to unbelievers. It is to be expected that some of God's children will experience unwanted homosexual feelings. The Bible never promises that Christians will be immune to certain temptations. It also never says that homosexual desires are purposefully chosen or that therapy (or heterosexual marriage) will "cure" anyone of same-sex desires. The Bible does promise, however, that true Christians will grow in holiness. And it demands full repentance from all sexual immorality (1 Cor. 6:9–10).

The "gay Christian" movement regularly points out that Jesus never said anything about homosexuality.[25] But He didn't have to mention it explicitly to condemn it. What He did was appeal to the way God created the world (as did Paul in Romans 1:26–27). When asked about divorce, Jesus showed that he considered God's original design for human sexuality to be authoritative: "Have you not read that he who created them from the beginning made them male and female?" (Matt. 19:4).

Jesus puts His divine finger on the real issue: "Have you not read?" Multiple times Jesus held the Jews of His day responsible for how they read Scripture, and He will hold us responsible too (Matt. 12:3, 5; 22:31). And this is what Paul says: "Do not be deceived: neither the sexually immoral, nor idolaters, nor adulterers, nor men who practice homosexuality . . . will inherit the kingdom of God" (1 Cor. 6:9–10). And "The law is . . . laid down . . . for the lawless and disobedient, for the ungodly and sinners, for . . . men who practice homosexuality, enslavers, liars, perjurers, and whatever else is contrary to sound doctrine" (1 Tim. 1:9–10).

DID JESUS AND PAUL KNOW ABOUT SEXUAL ORIENTATION?

One of the arguments of the "gay Christian" movement that has proven very useful for them is that the apostle Paul simply didn't know about homosexual orientation—and therefore never considered the possibility of faithful, monogamous gay unions.[26] What Paul condemned (they say) was homosexual relations that exploited other people, like men sexually abusing boys. It takes some familiarity with ancient Greek literature to answer this argument, and here's the answer of one of the world's major New Testament scholars:

> When I read the accounts from the early Roman empire of the practice of homosexuality, then it seems to me they knew just as much about it as we do. In particular . . . they knew a great deal about what people today would regard as longer-term, reasonably stable relations between two people of the same gender. This is not a modern invention, it's already there in Plato.[27]

We should not act as if the modern concept of sexual orientation (invented in the nineteenth century[28]) is a stable reality to which the Bible needs to adjust. The Bible is the reality to which our concepts need to adjust. Our Creator has the right to tell us what to do with our bodies.

The real effect of the "gay Christian" movement's arguments is to cast doubt on whether or not God is capable of communicating moral expectations clearly through His Word. One prominent "gay Christian" leader, who left his wife for a male partner, just shrugs his shoulders when he reads the passages where Paul most clearly condemns homosexuality. "Greek scholars don't know exactly what [Paul] means," he claims.[29]

The work of biblical scholars is extremely valuable, but scholars have worldviews just like the rest of us—worldviews that can cause them to misread the scriptural text.[30] Listen to the honest admission of Luke Timothy Johnson, a liberal New Testament scholar:

> I think it important to state clearly that we do, in fact, reject the straightforward commands of Scripture, and appeal instead to another authority when we

> declare that same-sex unions can be holy and good. And what exactly is that authority? We appeal explicitly to the weight of our own experience and the experience thousands of others have witnessed to, which tells us that to claim our own sexual orientation is in fact to accept the way in which God has created us. By so doing, we explicitly reject as well the premises of the scriptural statements condemning homosexuality—namely, that it is . . . a symptom of human corruption, and disobedience to God's created order.[31]

What's the point of having a divinely revealed book if it isn't allowed to tell us we're wrong? Jesus Christ, the Judge of all the earth, will be justified in saying to the "gay Christians" on judgment day, "Have you not read . . . ?"

WHO'S "HUNG UP"?

One Christian public intellectual was being interviewed by a secular journalist. The first question was about homosexuality. So was the second. Then the third question was, "Why is it that we're talking about homosexuality?" The Christian thinker replied, "Because you called me and asked the questions!"[32] It is possible to harp on an issue. Is it excessive to spend a whole section of this textbook on homosexuality? Are we targeting homosexuals for special hatred just by talking so much about homosexuality?

No. The secular world is insistently bringing it up. And Christians need to have biblical answers ready, or what good is our Bible and our Christianity? Christians have begun, here and there in America, to pay fines for refusing to bake cakes or take photos for gay weddings. One case, *Elaine Photography v. Willock*, went all the way to the U.S. Supreme Court.[33] The Christians lost. That's one reason to study what Scripture has to say about homosexual acts. You may be called upon to pay a price for your view, and you'll want to be sure you're really standing on the Bible and not just your own gut reaction to gay sex.

> ***"Many of the advocates of unqualified acceptance of homosexuality . . . seem to be operating with a simplistic [theology] that assumes whatever is must be good: they have a theology of creation but no theology of sin and redemption."***[34]
>
> —RICHARD B. HAYS

But fighting the culture war or convincing "gay Christians" they're wrong should not be your primary reason to study this issue. Investigate what Scripture says so you can walk alongside fellow Christians at your school or in your church who experience this particularly difficult temptation. In doing so, you'll learn something about the power of your own sin and the power of Christ's salvation. Many, many practicing homosexuals testify that they did not choose their sexual desires—in fact, they were desperate to get rid of them. Some looked to psychological therapies, and some went "straight" but eventually gave in to their homosexual desires again.[35] But Christ can redeem someone from even the strongest sinful desires, gay or straight, or He is not

RECOMMENDED BOOKS ABOUT SAME-SEX ATTRACTION

What does the Bible teach about homosexuality? You're going to have to face that all-important question; you won't be able to escape it. And you need to dig deeper than this textbook does. Here are four recommendations.

Secret Thoughts of an Unlikely Convert by Rosaria Champagne Butterfield is a thoughtful autobiographical account of one lesbian's conversion to orthodox Christian faith. Butterfield is willing to praise the homosexual community for its virtues (particularly the hospitality she learned there) and criticize the sins of her own Christian community (including homophobia). But she gives solidly biblical answers to questions about homosexuality.

What Does the Bible Really Teach About Homosexuality? by Kevin DeYoung covers the Bible's teaching on homosexuality positively; then it answers common objections against the traditional view—such as "The Bible hardly ever mentions homosexuality" and "The God I worship is a God of love."

Is God Anti-Gay? is a short book by a British pastor who himself has experienced unwanted same-sex attraction. Sam Allberry writes with grace and biblical intelligence.

Compassion Without Compromise: How the Gospel Frees Us to Love Our Gay Friends Without Losing the Truth by Adam Barr and Ron Citlau focuses on the Christian's goal: love for God, faithfulness to His Word, and love for all God's fallen image-bearers.

God in flesh. It may take a lifetime, but He can do it. And He doesn't leave anyone to face temptation alone. Christians have His Holy Spirit, we have His Word, we have prayer, and we have the church, including both fellow Christians and pastors (Heb. 10:24). Heterosexual marriage may, in God's providence, eventually be God's provision for a Christian struggling against unwanted same-sex attraction. And yet celibacy is also a legitimate option (1 Cor. 7:8, 17).

The fight against sin isn't easy for anyone; Christians aren't guaranteed easy lives or freedom from sinful desires (in this life). But "God is faithful" to His children, "and he will not let you be tempted beyond your ability" (1 Cor. 10:13). He'll give grace.

Rosaria Champagne Butterfield always asks to meet with the protestors who show up at her talks on homosexuality. "And even if I don't have people demonstrating, after a chapel message or an open lecture, I make sure that students know what coffee shop I'll be at, and for how many hours, and I've never been alone."[36] There are sound, biblical answers to whatever questions you may have about homosexuality, and there are Christians willing to provide them in a loving and personal way.

THINKING IT THROUGH 14.2

1. What makes the "gay Christians'" rejection of the biblical worldview even more perplexing than other homosexuals' rejection of it?
2. What should be the standard by which we judge the way things ought to be in this world?
3. What is the created structure of marriage?
4. Why shouldn't it be surprising that even Christians face homosexual temptations?
5. How should Christians respond to homosexual temptation?

14.3 COHABITATION AND DIVORCE

"The relations between men and women have changed more in the past thirty years than they did in the previous three thousand,"[37] says marriage researcher Stephanie Coontz.

> Until the late eighteenth century, most societies around the world saw marriage as far too vital an economic and political institution to be left entirely to the free choice of the two individuals involved, especially if they were going to base their decision on something as unreasoning and transitory as love.[38]

Romantic love is, biblically speaking, supposed to be part of marriage (again, see Song of Solomon). But marriages based solely on love are indeed problematic. Coontz has observed that the very feature which makes marriage-for-love so attractive has "an inherent tendency to undermine the stability of marriage as an institution."[39] That is, if a marriage is formed and based solely on romantic love, then once that love dies so does the marriage. If that idea doesn't sound so bad to you, you're not thinking like the dependent child you (probably) are. Marriages produce children, and divorces hurt children.

The prevalence of the love-based marriage has also contributed to another cultural trend: **cohabitation**. More than 50 percent of America's engaged couples live together before the wedding. And that percentage doesn't include couples who live together without ever getting married at all.[40] Living together before marriage is now the most typical path to marriage in the United States.[41]

A recent study showed, however, that 60 percent of first premarital cohabitations do not result in marriage after three years.[42] And for cohabiting couples who do marry, that particular path into marriage doesn't seem to have helped Americans avoid finding the pathway out of marriage a few years later. Divorce rates rose in the twentieth century to staggering heights, and they appear to have decreased now only because fewer people are actually getting married.[43] "This is the generation so afraid of divorce that it is also afraid of marriage," according to two family researchers.[44]

About half of young people ages fifteen to nineteen claim to be sexually active,[45] and around 70 percent of all high school seniors agree that it is a good idea to live together before marriage.[46] Cohabitation and divorce are far more likely to affect you—and tempt you—than homosexuality is. Let a biblical worldview shape the way you look at these sins before your choices make it difficult for you to listen to God's instruction.

SHACKING UP

There never was a golden age in which all the people in any nation followed God's ways and hated evil. Public morals always go up and down. Cultures trade new sins for old ones. There was a time, for example, when a US president could get away with racism but not adultery; now it's the opposite (it would be best if he could get away with neither, of course).

So there was a time in American society, a time your grandparents probably remember, when cohabitation was frowned upon. As a PBS special about the twentieth century pointed out, "Cohabitation was almost impossible in the United States prior to the 1960s. Laws prevented unmarried couples from registering in hotels, and it was very difficult for an unmarried couple to obtain a home mortgage." Only a tiny percentage of Americans cohabited in 1960. But in the forty years after that, "cohabitation moved from disreputable and difficult to normal and convenient."[47]

Cultural pressure wasn't the only factor. Before the birth control pill came along in America in the 1960s, those having sex risked pregnancy. But the pill joined other cultural forces in the "sexual revolution" to twist the sexual morality of American culture (and that of most other developed nations).[48]

Worldview and Cohabitation

The Bible condemns cohabitation when it condemns fornication, and perhaps little more needs to be said. But cohabitation, like homosexuality, still provides a good opportunity to use the lenses provided by Creation, Fall, Redemption. We are led to ask again, "What was the original marriage like?" There was no preacher around to conduct that first marriage, no flower girl, no ring bearer, and no photographer. But the essential elements of a true marriage were there: a covenant and a (hetero)sexual union.

Friends make covenants—Jonathan and David did (1 Sam. 18:3). But without sexual union, it's not marriage.

Unmarried people form sexual unions—that's what cohabiting is. But without a covenant, it's not a marriage.

Couples become truly "married" only when they vow before a witnessing community to join together in a covenant bond—and to remain faithful to one another, sexually and in every other way. They also agree to "sanctions"—negative consequences if they violate their vows.

There's something about romantic love that inspires promises of eternal devotion. But when a fourteen-year-old boyfriend whispers "I'll love you forever" in the ear of his thirteen-year-old girlfriend, that's not a covenant. It's sweet nothings (emphasis on the nothings) because he almost certainly can't (and won't) keep such a promise.

But when that young man and young woman, with a few more years of maturity, stand tall at a church altar "before God and these witnesses" and solemnly promise "till death do us part"—then, and only then, do they have a covenant. Some cultures use rings to symbolize this union; others use an exchange of pigs. The symbols can differ, but the covenant and the sexual union both have to be there for a relationship to be called a marriage.

When a couple takes covenant vows and enters a sexual union, they're aligning themselves with God's intent for creation. They're choosing to participate in an institution created at the foundation of the world.[49] In contrast, cohabitation removes one of the essential elements of marriage, thereby dishonoring the marriage bed (Heb. 13:4).

One secular defender of cohabitation disagrees: "If you wait until marriage to have sex, you're taking an enormous risk. What if you're not compatible? Or what if you regret not having shopped around?"[50] Cohabitation is an attempt people make to avoid risk. They are demanding that God not put them through any pain that, to them, seems unnecessary. So they test the waters.

BISEXUALITY AND MARRIAGE

The most persuasive pro-LGBT argument in the Western world may well be what leading Supreme Court lawyer Ted Olson has said: "Allowing people of the same sex to marry the person that they love . . . does no damage to heterosexual marriage."[51]

But think about what it means for the institution of marriage when public opinion affirms the morality of the LGBT movement. Think, in particular, about the *B* in that abbreviation. If we're celebrating the sexual identity of bisexuals, we're inviting them and encouraging them to have multiple sexual partners. The presence of bisexual neighbors may do no direct harm to the heterosexual marriages in adjacent homes, but cultural expectations at a broader level do exert a pressure on marriage.

If the major symbolic powers in a culture—the president,[52] the Supreme Court, entertainers, experts—all acknowledge bisexuality as a distinct sexual identity, what reason can they give to limit marriage to two people? Heterosexual monogamy just becomes one more sexual identity on the menu. Adults are encouraged to express themselves sexually even if it gives unstable lives to their children.

But cohabiting brings its own terrible risks. It produces insecurity in both partners, especially the woman, who may waste her best opportunity to bear children (it's harder for women to conceive as they get older). Men may leave the "union" at the time they're most needed, namely when children come along, and when it's most difficult for a woman to find another mate. Cohabitation may steal from someone his or her only chance to share the joy of raising children to adulthood with one special person. Cohabiting is not a shortcut to a happy marriage; it's a short-circuit.

GLOBAL ATTITUDES TOWARD DIVORCE

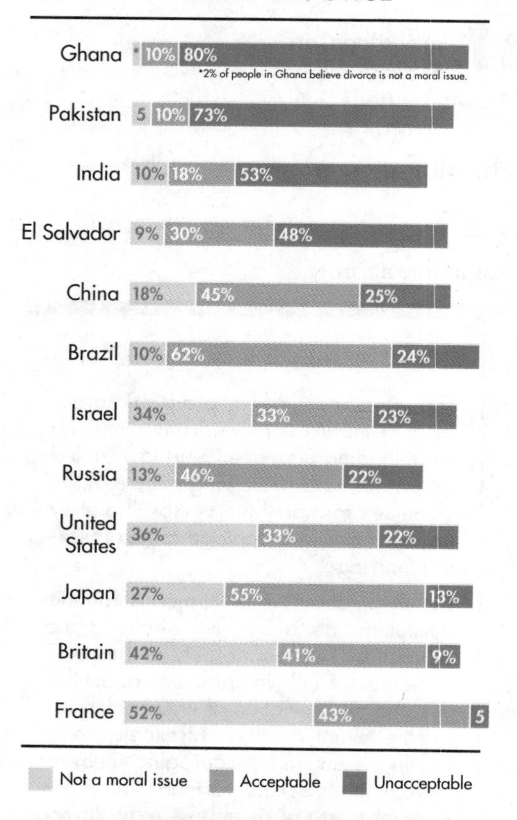

SPLITTING UP

Cohabitation is union without the safety net of a lifelong, public pledge of faithfulness. Divorce, on the other hand, breaks that union, rips apart that safety net, and violates that pledge. Divorce is one of the ultimate twistings of marital roles, the very opposite of God's original instruction that a man should "hold fast" to his wife (Gen. 2:24; cf. Matt. 19:3–5; Mal. 2:16).

The rate of American marriages ending in divorce grew to an unprecedented high in the twentieth century. In 1900 the divorce rate was only 7 percent, but by 1940 the percentage had almost tripled. In 1965 the rate reached 25 percent and in 1970 jumped to 35 percent. The numbers continued to climb. In only five more years, the divorce rate stood at 49 percent! This dramatic increase was due in large part to the **no-fault divorce** laws states began to adopt starting in 1969, eliminating the legal requirement to prove one partner's wrongdoing in order to obtain a divorce.[53] In the 1970s, the divorce rate continued to climb, and recent research shows that it "increased substantially after 1990 and is now at an all-time high."[54] One opportunistic jeweler even tried to cash in on the brevity of marriages by offering wedding rings for rent.[55]

In a fallen world, marriages will always be far from perfect. Sometimes they will break apart. God in Scripture recognizes this reality. When marriages break apart, people get hurt. Women and children especially are put at risk—financially and in many other ways.

NO-FAULT DIVORCE

A no-fault divorce is one in which you get a judge to end your marriage for nothing more than alleged "incompatibility." In the United States, says one writer, "you can come home from work and tell your spouse the marriage is over and he or she can do nothing but cry, and fight for the best financial payout possible. Try doing that with Verizon. Or while under contract to buy a home. Or with your gym membership. You'll get laughed at."[56] Eight in ten divorces in America are one-sided—the other spouse doesn't want the divorce.[57]

Feminists fought for the freedom to leave their marriages in the 1960s and '70s. Prominent feminists such as Betty Friedan, author of *The Feminine Mystique*, were ecstatic when no-fault divorce swept America. But decades later, they've noticed that it tends to hurt rather than help women.[58] Women are left financially vulnerable and without support in the exhausting and difficult job of raising children alone.

God Himself set up legal structures in Israel to handle divorce. It can't be wrong for modern governments to do the same. But for the sake of all the people who are harmed by divorce, laws should put pressure on people to uphold their vows rather than making it easy to abandon them.

HITCHING UP . . . AGAIN

Faithful Christians who don't deserve it may end up in the ranks of the divorced. No serious interpreters of Scripture are saying that such people—the "innocent parties" in a divorce—are sinning merely by finding themselves in that category. (Of course, there isn't always an innocent party in a divorce; sometimes both stubbornly refuse to forgive.) The real question, and one that genuine Christians admittedly disagree about, is whether or not remarriage after divorce is ever permitted.

Getting into all the details about the Bible's teaching on divorce is something you should certainly do (see sidebar for a recommended resource). You need to study the issue and come to a conclusion before you get married, or even before you meet your future spouse.

> STUDYING DIVORCE AND REMARRIAGE
>
> One excellent resource on the issues raised in this unit is a book by Andreas Köstenberger and David W. Jones called *God, Marriage, and Family: Rebuilding the Biblical Foundation* (Wheaton: Crossway, 2010). The chapter in the book on divorce and remarriage provides a concise summary of Christian viewpoints on the question.

Worldview and Divorce

But this is a book on biblical worldview. So focusing on the insight on divorce provided by a Creation, Fall, Redemption perspective, there are two points to make:

First, marriage was created to be an unbreakable bond. When the Pharisees challenged Jesus about His view of divorce, He explained to them, "Because of your hardness of heart Moses allowed you to divorce your wives, but from the beginning it was not so" (Matt. 19:8). Jesus appealed to Genesis—to creation—to undermine divorce. He began by saying,

> Have you not read that he who created them from the beginning made them male and female, and said, "Therefore a man shall leave his father and his mother and hold fast to his wife, and the two shall become one flesh"? So they are no longer two but one flesh. What therefore God has joined together, let not man separate. (Matt. 19:4–6)

God made marriage, and God makes marriages. No one has the authority to terminate a marriage, not even the two people in it. If there had been no Fall, there would be no divorces.

Second, marriage is a picture of an even deeper reality, the relationship between Christ and His church (Eph. 5:32). One day, when Christ redeems the world, He will fully purify His bride and marry her for all eternity (Eph. 5:25–27). Divorce, even divorce among non-Christians, shatters this precious picture (as does a homosexual relationship or cohabitation). It tells a lie about Christ's undying love for His people.

When husbands and wives cheat on each other, they are also damaging the picture God created. That's why throughout the Bible marital infidelity (adultery) is consistently used as a picture of spiritual infidelity, as in Ezekiel 16 and many other passages.

FORGIVENESS FOR THE FALLEN

The point of having a biblical view of divorce, cohabitation, and homosexuality—and all other twistings of the purposes of sex and marriage—is not to cause anyone to be discouraged or to despair. Some teachers teaching this material are divorced. Some students reading it have had premarital sex. No sin places someone beyond the reach of God's grace.

You can't know now all God's reasons for bringing this topic to your attention right now. But you can trust that the God who created marriage knows best how to set up yours.

THINKING IT THROUGH 14.3

1. Why do marriages based solely on romantic love often disintegrate? Why doesn't cohabitation solve this problem?
2. What are the two essential elements in marriage?
3. Should a nation have laws allowing for divorce? What should those laws promote?
4. What did God originally create marriage to picture?
5. What cultural factors may play a role in the rise of cohabitation?

14.4 GENDER ROLES IN A FALLEN WORLD

In 2012, a high-ranking member of the Obama administration, Anne Marie Slaughter, decided to quit her job for "family reasons." Such resignations happen all the time, and "family reasons" is usually a euphemism* indicating that someone was fired. But this case was different: Slaughter was a mother, and when she said she was quitting for family reasons, she meant it. She explained in a much-discussed article in *The Atlantic* that "juggling high-level government work with the needs of two teenage boys was not possible."[59] Slaughter admits that women of her generation were taught the "feminist credo" that they could "have it all"—marriage, children, and career. But constant shuttling between New Jersey (she taught at Princeton) and Washington, D.C., just wasn't working for her family even though her husband had agreed to take over parenting duties so she could further her career.

euphemism: *an indirect or vague expression used in place of one that is considered offensive*

Slaughter is a highly educated, thoughtful, dedicated, and articulate woman, whose expertise is in high demand. She's an academic. She's a card-carrying member of the American elite. She wrote her *Atlantic* article both to defend her choice to leave her government job (many feminists criticized her for it) and to push society to adjust its expectations so that other working moms would not be forced to make the decision she did.

The American dream is that you can be anything you want to be. And Western individualist societies do provide a level of freedom for their citizens that is certainly not available to many other people in the world. But social expectations do and will play a role in what you—man or woman—can become. Those expectations will arise out of the major worldviews represented in a society. Will women be expected, in general, to be the primary caregivers for children? Will men be expected, in general, to be the primary breadwinners for their families? These are inescapably worldview-ish issues. Your view of where the concepts of "male" and "female" came from will necessarily determine your answers to these pressing questions.

And thanks to the Fall, people are very confused about such questions at the moment. (The comments in response to Slaughter's article online demonstrated this quite clearly.) The landmark book about complementarianism observes that

> confusion over the meaning of sexual personhood today is epidemic. The consequence of this confusion is not a free and happy harmony among gender-free persons relating on the basis of abstract competencies. The consequence rather is more divorce, more homosexuality, more sexual abuse, more promiscuity, more social awkwardness, and more emotional distress and suicide that come with the loss of God-given identity.[60]

Without the Bible, it's anyone's best guess what society should look like. People can make gender roles into whatever they can get other people to agree to. (That's precisely what they've been doing, of course.) But with the Bible, any effort to build a society must be based on a certain foundation. And man and woman, equally created in God's image but called to different roles, are part of that foundation. Complementarity is meant by God to be a building block of human society.

There's a certain amount of flexibility in a complementarian approach. If a man is paralyzed and can't work, the Bible does not forbid his wife from becoming the family breadwinner. And the Bible contains few strict rules—mainly general principles—when it comes to men's and women's roles in society (their roles in family and church are more precisely delineated).

But a culture intent on pushing past even flexible boundaries will experience some resistance from the creation. Mrs. Slaughter's teenage sons needed their mom; they were created that way. The foundations of society will crumble if people ignore the creational norms of gender.

WHERE OUR SOCIETY IS HEADED

Of course, the Fall has twisted the gender roles God gave us, so there are cultures in which women are stifled and left uneducated and men are allowed (or even encouraged) to be overbearing or distant. But the created order is still visible everywhere you go even though sin has damaged it deeply.

Western individualist societies seem to be twisting the created order of gender roles in a new direction. There are women of course, who get stifled (simply because they're women) in America, and there are men who are harsh and violent toward their wives. Those sins are old. But leading Westerners are also pushing something relatively new—or at least rare—in world history: the idea that all differences between men and women are mere social constructs, false ideas built by society. In this view, men's and women's respective body parts may have some obvious differences, but all roles and identities for men and women in society (and in the family) are interchangeable. Proponents of this view say there's no good reason for women to do more housework than men or to stay home with the kids. There's no good reason why women generally grow their hair longer than men or why some sports or pastimes are more associated with men than women.

Our society doesn't yet know what to do with people who bend previously accepted categories of gender. Wellesley College, an all-women's school in Massachusetts (founded in a day when, sadly, women were not generally allowed to go to college), now has a few dozen students who were born female but no longer identify as women. A small number of them identify instead as men; the rest simply reject the idea of gender or want to position themselves somewhere in between "male" and "female."[61] What do you do when a "trans man" wins Wellesley's hoop-rolling contest, an annual tradition begun in 1895? Do you check for testosterone injections?

Even the liberal students of an elite institution such as Wellesley weren't sure what to do when that happened in 2013. A number of them sheepishly told a journalist that they went to a women's college to be in a place full of and led by, well, women. Letting some of those women become men seemed wrong somehow—but they didn't want to give their names after expressing that opinion. They feared being shouted down with cries of "discrimination."

lesbian: *"Their women exchanged natural relations for those that are contrary to nature" (Rom 1:26).*

gay: *"The men likewise gave up natural relations with women and were consumed with passion for one another, men committing shameless acts with men" (Rom 1:27).*

bisexual: *one who is sexually attracted to both men and women*

transgender: *self-identity that blurs gender lines*

transsexual: *a person who feels he or she belongs to the opposite sex*

queer: *homosexual [referring more to political views than sexual desires]*

questioning: *someone who questions traditional norms for gender and sexuality*

intersexual: *physically sexually ambiguous*

asexual: *a person without sexual desires*

pansexual: *someone who has given up all sexual and gender distinctions*

WHEN TO DISCRIMINATE AND WHEN NOT TO

Life is discrimination. You can't be a rational adult unless you choose pie and reject poison and, daily, choose the right path and discriminate against the wrong one. And you can't help discriminating against certain people—we don't hand out driver's licenses to the blind, no matter who cries discrimination.[62]

It would be wrong, of course, to refuse to give a voter registration card to a blind man because of his blindness. That's illegitimate discrimination because blindness is irrelevant to voting in presidential elections. But it is relevant to driving.

Someone's sex is irrelevant to his or her citizenship, to gasoline prices, to membership in an online computer-coding forum. But sex is relevant when it comes to admission into an all-girls school—or a marriage. An all-girls school with a few guys is no longer an all-girls school, and an all-girls relationship is not a marriage.

God made some women more athletic and some more delicate (Deut. 28:56–57). He gave some men artistic and academic gifts, and He gifted some of them to be middle linebackers and firefighters (Exod. 31:1–5). Christianity doesn't force every person into some ideal personality type. But there is a limit to allowable variation: men are men, and women are women. A society that allows people to bend gender past the breaking point will lose out on the unique values each sex provides.

WHAT WE'RE LOSING OUT ON

Years ago, before anyone thought gay marriage was coming to the United States but after homosexuality began to be portrayed widely on television, one of the authors of this book was a camp counselor at a Christian camp. He noticed two seventh-grade girls, both homeschooled, and both very sweet, godly, and feminine (as they are to this day as young adults), who were holding hands as all the campers took a hike down a nature trail. Soon other campers, who were not so sheltered, began to point and snicker. "Lesbians!" they whispered loudly. It was a slander, not true in the least.

But what if it were true? Still, no Christian should be hateful toward homosexuals. All the way down to seventh grade (and below!), Christian students should not bully "queers." In fact, name-calling is where bullying starts. And all the way up to the level

DO CHRISTIANS PROMOTE HATE?

Is opposition to homosexuality an act of hatred? Not all homosexuals think so. One gay activist wrote, "Just because someone doesn't support gay rights doesn't automatically make them a hateful bigot. I have immediate family members who . . . believe my sexual orientation is sinful, but I've honestly not once questioned their love for me. I understand that they have deeply held beliefs about morality, which they would argue are born out of love and concern for me, not hatred. I certainly want to challenge their thinking on this, but their unwavering agreement and support for my position is not a prerequisite for our relationship."[63] If you have gay relatives or friends, you should act in such a way that they would be able to write something like this about you. They need to know both that the Bible names their sexual desires as sinful and that you love them.

of church leadership, a truly Christlike pastor will not be nasty toward the transgendered. A godly person's heart will ache for the pain all confused people experience because of the Fall, and for all the hardship they cause themselves and their families.[64]

But Christians are not being bigoted or hateful to insist on distinctions between the sexes. We are trying to preserve something precious in the created order and to help people live in a way that is best for them.

Why does it matter to you if someone else wants to cross-dress? Because people hurt themselves when they violate creational norms. And when people "come out of the closet" and into a new sexual identity, says one writer, they "hustle a lot of good and natural feelings back in."[65] Public gender-bending and homosexuality make close male friendship, especially, very difficult. It's hard to have a Jonathan-and-David or Sherlock-and-Watson friendship when people are snickering at you behind your back.

When the BBC rebooted the Sherlock Holmes stories (yet again) in a series called *Sherlock*, confusion over Sherlock and Watson's sexuality became a running joke. On screen, the two men's close relationship and intense loyalty to one another just felt weird. Gay jokes were brought in to relieve the tension. This didn't happen in the 1930s screenplays of Sherlock Holmes. It didn't have to. Gay jokes didn't occur to anyone. That innocence is one thing society loses when gender lines are crossed.

Society also loses fathers who walk out on their children for gay lovers. Another thing that's lost is the very possibility that children can grow up without the burden and confusion—and possible temptation—of seeing men kiss men and women "marry" women. Society may also lose the very definition of marriage; if gender is only a social construct, there's no good reason to forbid homosexual marriage and no good reason to limit marriage to two people—or even two humans. Homosexual activists call this argument "scaremongering," but when asked what marriage is, they struggle to find an answer that doesn't open the definition so wide that it's meaningless.[66]

THE THREE WAVES OF FEMINISM

Western feminism has come in three widely recognized waves over the past two hundred years. The first wave (1840–1920) was largely a helpful revolution overturning unfair laws that kept women from things like voting, receiving equal pay for the same job, or pursuing the same level of education as men. So the result of the early feminist movement was generally to release women from an unbiblical application of male authority that was dominating them instead of recognizing their shared rule over God's creation.

But feminism did not stop there. In the second wave (1960–1990) feminists continued to fight for the things that they did in the first wave but centered their efforts largely on overturning the biblically legitimate authority of male leadership, which they argued was patriarchal and relegated women to second-class citizenship. This wave resulted in many societal changes—more women in the workforce, the rise of child-care centers, and laws giving women a right to abortion.

The third wave (1990–present) has aggressively attacked creational norms of gender and the whole idea of distinctions between maleness and femaleness.

MURPHY BROWN AND DAN QUAYLE

Popular entertainment both reflects and shapes American values. There is a progression from *I Love Lucy* and other 1950s sitcoms in which even husbands and wives slept in separate beds, through *The Brady Bunch* (1970s) in which two families blended after (apparent[67]) divorce, to *Ellen* (1990s) in which the title character came out as a lesbian, to *Modern Family* (2010s) in which a gay couple adopts a child.

Murphy Brown and Dan Quayle belong in that story. Remember them? Quayle criticized the TV character's decision to bear a child out of wedlock, and Brown (in her TV role) responded with indignation. But what did Quayle actually say?

> We cannot be embarrassed out of our belief that two parents, married to each other, are better in most cases for children than one. That honest work is better than handouts—or crime. That we are our brothers' keepers.[68]

Murphy Brown the TV character was offended that Quayle would prescribe what families should look like, but the real-life actress who played her responded somewhat differently. Years later Candice Bergen told the Television Critics Association, "His speech was a perfectly intelligent speech about fathers not being dispensable, and nobody agreed with that more than I did."[69]

THINKING IT THROUGH 14.4

1. What determines the answers to societies' questions about gender roles and responsibilities? What should determine the Christian's answers?
2. What new idea or view about gender is Western society pushing for?
3. What happens to a society that allows people to bend gender away from God's creational norms to the breaking point?
4. What is the goal of the current (third) wave of feminism?
5. What does society lose as a result of gender-bending?

14 CHAPTER REVIEW

TERMS TO REMEMBER

fornication
adultery
polygamy
LGBT
cohabitation
no-fault divorce

Scripture Memory

Genesis 3:16–17

Making Connections

1. What must govern the definition of marriage and family?
2. Which temptations are Christians immune to? Why?
3. What essential element does cohabitation remove from the union of a man and a woman?
4. How does gender-bending result in a loss of innocence?

Developing Skills in Apologetics and Worldview

5. How can you be as wise as a serpent and as innocent as a dove in expressing your opposition to homosexuality (Matt. 10:16)?
6. Is it illegitimate discrimination for a Christian restaurant owner to refuse to cater a banquet for the Ku Klux Klan (an overtly racist and violent group)? Is it illegitimate discrimination for a boy to refuse to wrestle a girl at a junior-high wrestling meet?

Examining Assumptions and Evidence

7. Why should polygamy be considered a violation of God's scriptural and creational norms for marriage?
8. Why must abuse be reported both to law enforcement and to spiritual leadership?
9. Why should homosexuality be considered a sinful twisting of sex, according to Genesis 1–2?
10. Why did God permit divorce in the Mosaic law?

Becoming a Creative Cultivator

11. Write three to six paragraphs to
    (a) describe teen culture,
    (b) evaluate any positives or negatives of teen culture, and
    (c) propose alternatives to teen culture (e.g., ways teens should strive to be mature, contributing members of their families).

Chapter Fifteen **MARRIAGE REDEEMED**

He who finds a wife finds a good thing and obtains favor from the Lord.

Scripture Memory
Proverbs 18:22

15.1 REDEEMING MARRIAGE

There's something about romantic love that leads two people swept up by it to promise to love each other forever.

Forever? Like, for eternity? Who could possibly be certain about being able to keep such a promise? Eternity is a long time. A lot of things could happen between now and forever, and they probably will.

The traditional English wedding vows are a bit more realistic, asking partners to promise love only "as long as you both shall live." Those vows are also more biblical because not only does the Bible give widows and widowers the right to remarry, but Jesus actually taught that marriages don't continue beyond the grave. "When [believers] rise from the dead, they neither marry nor are given in marriage, but are like angels in heaven" (Mark 12:25).

WE'LL BE LIKE ANGELS?

Christ's comment that believers will be "like angels in heaven" (Mark 12:25) seems to be one of the reasons people tend to envision eternity as full of winged people sitting on clouds strumming harps. The fact is, we know very little about what the angels do. The Bible doesn't have a lot to say about them. We know that humans are of an order higher than angels; we will "judge angels," Paul says (1 Cor. 6:3). And as you learned in Unit 4, we do know that humans in the new earth will have plenty of enjoyable and enriching work. We also know that eternity is not a long enough time to ever explore all the depths of an infinite God.

If you're tracking with the CFR argument of this textbook, this ought to raise a big question in your mind. If Christ's work of redemption restores the world to the way God created it to be, where in the world is marriage? Marriage was certainly there at creation. Why does it go away when we get to eternity?

The human race will be complete in the new earth, of course; the globe will be fully populated with the offspring of Adam and Eve. Human marriage won't be needed for procreation anymore.

But actually, the testimony of the Bible is that marriage will not, in fact, cease to exist. It will be fulfilled—in another marriage, the one between Christ and His people.

In the new earth, marriage will be redeemed. Revelation 19 speaks of "the marriage supper of the Lamb." The climax of the complete restoration of all things on the new earth is the coming of Christ to receive His bride. This bride includes all those who have put their faith in Him and have been cleansed from their sins by His death in their place (Rev. 19:7–8). Christ will openly and visibly unite in full fellowship with everyone He has made righteous—both Jews like Abraham and Gentiles like Augustine—and they will know indescribable joy with Him forever.

In short, we could say that there will be no more marriages on the new earth because the ultimate marriage between Christ and His bride will have already taken place.

THE GOAL OF CHRISTIAN MARRIAGE

It's this ultimate marriage of Christ and His bride in the book of Revelation that helps us make sense of the most important New Testament passage on marriage and family—Ephesians 5:22–6:4. Only by seeing marriage as part of the grand story of Creation, Fall, and Redemption can you understand your own future marriage, if the Lord gives you one. Marriage and family play key roles in God's plan to redeem the earth.

But to understand Paul's words to husbands and wives in Ephesians, you have to understand what Paul meant earlier in his letter where he says that, through the death of Christ, God has united two of the most incompatible people groups in human history—Jews and Gentiles—bringing them together into fellowship and actually "creating" one new family (Eph. 2:11–22).

Jews and Gentiles in Paul's day were not one. They were deeply divided. Jews in the New Testament era didn't even eat with Gentiles (Gal. 2:11–14).

But God used the death and resurrection of Christ to bring the human family back together again into fellowship, both with one another and with Himself—as if an old-time family feud between two sets of outlaws miraculously ended in peace with each other and with the government. Paul says that the purpose of this newly united family of believers is to grow in unity with one another as they grow in Christ (Eph. 4:1–16).

It's after all this important theological background information that Paul mentions the topic of marriage to the Ephesian believers. Even the unnoticed marriages of ordinary people living in that city in ancient Turkey were sending messages, Paul said, about the unity God plans to bring to the earth. Every marriage, then and now, is supposed to be a picture of intimate fellowship and union with Christ.

The Redeemed, Submissive Wife

Paul ties his instruction to wives—"Wives, submit to your own husbands"—directly to the great reality marriage is portraying. Submit, Paul says, because "the husband is the head of the wife even as Christ is the head of the church, his body, and is himself its Savior" (Eph. 5:22–23). Just as the church submits to Christ, wives are supposed to submit to their own husbands.

Wives are commanded to submit to their husbands (not to all men) in several other places in the New Testament (Col. 3:18; 1 Pet. 3:1; Titus 2:5). But those husbands are themselves commanded to submit to God (1 Cor. 11:3) and, to a lesser degree, to church leadership (1 Pet. 5:5) and even to other Christians, including their wives (Eph. 5:21). These other authorities and influences should help make sure that a wife's submission is given to a man worthy of such a gift. The Bible doesn't tell women (or men) to stick around if they are being beaten or otherwise abused.

Paul's summary word to wives at the end of his discussion about marriage in Ephesians is not about submission, per se, but about respect: "Let the wife see that she respects her husband" (Eph. 5:33). Many wives are afraid to submit to their husbands because they do not trust them, but there is redemptive power in a wife's respect and honor toward her husband. Husbands get better at husbanding when they sense their wives respect them. When a woman waits for her husband to get his act together before she'll give him respect, she loses an opportunity to bring healing to their marriage as a whole. A gracious, submissive wife can even be God's means of winning an unconverted husband to Christ:

NO JEWELRY? NO BRAIDS?

Newsweek magazine often publishes provocative attacks on Christian doctrine around Christmas and Easter. The job recently fell to journalist Kurt Eichenwald, who made this charge against the Bible (among many, many others): "[First] Timothy is one of the most virulently anti-woman books of the New Testament, something else that sets it apart from other letters by Paul. . . . It says women must dress modestly, can't embroider their hair, [and] can't wear pearls or gold."[1]

Eichenwald is one for four in those claims. Yes, Paul said women must dress modestly (1 Tim. 2:9). But careful readers will note that he didn't say women can't braid their hair or wear jewelry (and Paul isn't "anti-woman"). Paul said that women's real "adorning"—the things that display their personal glory to others—must not be merely external (see also 1 Pet. 3:3). "Modesty and self-control" (or "decency and propriety," as another translation puts it) ought to be a woman's true and ultimate adorning. Women with no earrings who have never cut their hair can nonetheless lack modesty and self-control. And women with jewelry and a contemporary hairstyle can have those godly qualities. Externals do matter, but the heart matters more. The outside reflects what's on the inside.

> Wives, be subject to your own husbands, so that even if some do not obey the word, they may be won without a word by the conduct of their wives, when they see your respectful and pure conduct. (1 Pet. 3:1–2)

Respectful, pure, gentle, quiet—these traditionally feminine qualities seem quaint to many in the twenty-first century. Women today are more apt to be told, "Let it go," "Be yourself," and "Follow your heart." Biblically informed femininity is still countercultural in much of the world. It means developing those graces and character traits needed in a submissive partner, companion, child-bearer, and homemaker. Girls should grow into women of grace and dignity, kindness and inner beauty, having compassion and tenderness, modesty and strength of conviction, and a strong sense of their own purpose as first surrendered to God and later, if God so leads, to a husband.

The Redeemed, Loving Husband

The main responsibilities of wives are to submit to and respect their husbands, but the main thing God repeatedly tells husbands to do is to love their wives (Eph. 5:25, 28, 33; Col. 3:19). And the standard for "how much" a husband is to love his wife is set immeasurably high: "as Christ loved the church and gave himself up for her" (Eph. 5:25). Jesus didn't have an escape plan. He gave His bride the last full measure of devotion.

The New Testament elsewhere fleshes out what manly love for one's wife looks like. Colossians 3:19 likewise tells husbands not to be "harsh" with their wives. And 1 Peter 3:7 instructs husbands, "Live with your wives in an understanding way, showing honor to the woman as the weaker vessel." A wife with a biblical worldview isn't offended by this verse, and a husband with such a worldview doesn't expect his wife to be one of the guys. He treats her with the loving care a "weaker vessel" requires. A loving husband pays attention to his wife's emotions, her stamina, and even her preference that all the doors be locked at night.

Biblical masculinity is simply the collection of attitudes and character traits that one would expect to see developing in a male, if indeed his role is to serve as loving leader, spiritual nurturer, protector, and provider. When he reaches manhood, he's going to be called on to shoulder the ultimate responsibility for family finances, for discipline of children, and possibly for spider assassination. So boys should grow into men who are strong, courageous, hard-working, able to take responsibility, able to lead, able to defend others, yet kind and gentle toward those they are called to protect. And to whatever extent a young boy does not manifest these qualities or value them, he must be nurtured and challenged in this direction. This is God's calling for him as a man.

A truly loving husband takes an unconditional delight in his wife and makes her feel safe. He's patient with multiple outfit changes on Sunday morning while the clock ticks. He does household chores without being asked. He has a flower budget. If a husband thinks, "I'll show her affection when she's worthy of it," he's got the cart before the horse. A woman will become worthy of affection when her husband showers her with it. Doing what you are supposed to do has a redemptive effect on your spouse. If you insist on waiting for your spouse to start the process of redemption, you may be waiting for a long time—maybe "until death do [you] part."

> "I HAVE YET TO MEET A WIFE WHO DIDN'T WANT TO FOLLOW A HUSBAND WHO WAS SACRIFICIALLY LOVING AND SERVING HER."[2]
>
> —DAVID PLATT

Love doesn't mean treating a wife as incapable or even protecting her completely from all harm (as if any human could do that). Christ in the New Testament led His church, His bride, into deep waters. Christians under Christ's care had their goods stolen and were mocked, reviled, and imprisoned (Heb. 10:34; 1 Pet. 3:9). But Christ asked them to do only those things that He Himself was willing to do. And all that they did was to their own honor and joy: they were carrying out the work of redemption on earth and felt privileged to play a part, even if it involved suffering. When the apostles were arrested and beaten, they "rejoic[ed] that they were counted worthy to suffer dishonor for the name" (Acts 5:41).

A loving husband will need to lead his wife through difficult times—every couple faces trials, especially if they have children. Read about pioneer men and women of the American West, such as Ma and Pa in *Little House on the Prairie*. These people were tough, and they went through terribly frightening and difficult times. And yet there is an irrepressible joy in the stories Laura Ingalls Wilder tells—these pioneers felt privileged to play a part in the expansion of the American frontier. In addition, Ma was a *woman* and one who saw it as her duty to bring up her little prairie girls with feminine civility. Pa was a *man* and one who treated his wife with tender care. He relied on her heavily for simple survival, but there were certain jobs he never asked her to do.

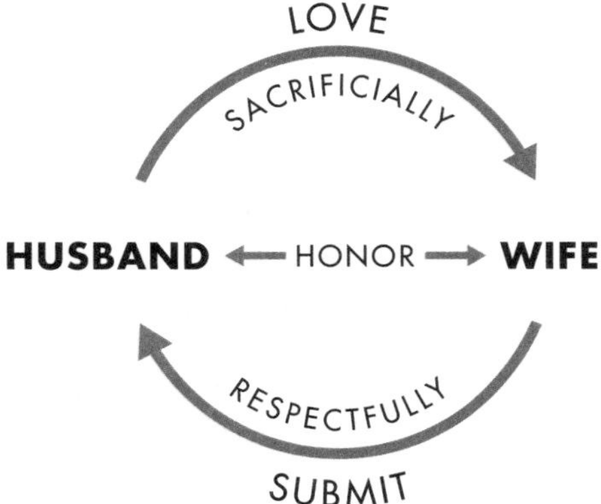

The Redeemed Marriage

The best way to redeem your own marriage is to learn to follow God's ways long before you reach the altar. But Christ is such a powerful Redeemer that He can restore failed or failing marriages. And He can restore immoral people to sexual purity. Slavery to sexual sin is one of the more common chains people

WHY RISK MARRIAGE?

Marriage involves risk in a fallen world. It's true, as one well-known Christian writer said, that "more pain is experienced in marriage and parenting than anywhere else in the world, [but] this is the cost of covenant-making and covenant-keeping love. It cost Jesus his life to be in that kind of relationship."[3]

And yet Jesus still did it. Why? Scripture tells us that He endured the cross "for the joy that was set before him" (Heb. 12:2). The writer of Hebrews doesn't say what joy it was, exactly, but surely Christ's future union with His bride was a massive part of it. Spouses and children will sometimes disappoint and fail you, but they can also bring you joys like no one else can. In order to get life's greatest joys you have to risk experiencing life's greatest pains.

are bound by. Christ can free them. Divorce, adultery, pornography, and guilt from all three—Christ died to destroy them.

In a book such as this we cannot address in detail all the issues that arise in a marriage relationship. But at the core of every marital problem is either a husband who is not loving his wife sacrificially, as Christ loved the church, or a wife who is not submitting respectfully to her husband, as the church is to submit to Christ. Often we find both. A harsh, unloving husband makes it difficult and even grueling for his wife to follow his leadership. Or a wife distrusts her husband or tries to take the authority in the marriage, making it strenuous for a husband to lead. When these root sins go unchecked, they lead to the symptoms others can see: neglect or despondency, loneliness, verbal or physical abuse, hunger for gratification outside of the marriage, and ultimately divorce.

The biblical solution to marital sins is the same as it is for all other sins: repentance and faith. A man must turn from his sin, confess it to his spouse, and seek cleansing and change from the Lord in faith. A woman must do the same. The changes a man undertakes must prompt him to love and lead his wife. The changes a woman makes must lead her to respect and submit to her husband. This may sound overly simplistic. And there is certainly more than this to learn and to do, but never less. The husband's love and the wife's submission are at the core of the New Testament teaching on marriage. These are the roles that make the marriage a reflection of the unity of Christ and His church, and therefore they represent the pathway of redemption apart from which no marriage can be restored.

THINKING IT THROUGH 15.1

1. Why is it more biblical for couples to vow to love each other as long as they both shall live rather than vowing to love each other for eternity?
2. How will marriage be fulfilled in the new earth?
3. What necessary character quality makes a wife's submission to her husband possible?
4. Why should the husband shoulder the ultimate responsibility for the family?
5. What is at the core of every marital problem? Explain why.

15.2 REDEEMING FAMILY

The *New York Times* asked teenagers to comment on a scientific study surveying attitudes about the family. "Joey" said that he thought the "normal family" doesn't exist since everybody does something different. In our culture no one can precisely define *family* anymore because people just take life as it comes. "There isn't anything wrong with that though," he said. "A lot of the times different is better."[4]

"Walker" agreed that the definition of *family* is hard to pin down, but he thinks the problem is that families don't spend much time together. Both parents (if they haven't split up) have jobs, and the kids are stuck at home alone or in daycare. Mealtime is no longer an occasion for togetherness. He concluded that *family* means "both parents and their children coming together and being with each other."[5]

Which vision of the family do you want, Joey's or Walker's? And more importantly, which vision is most similar to the one we see through biblical lenses? Do you want everybody (including your own future spouse) defining "family" the way that suits him or her, or do you want "both parents and their children coming together and being with each other"? Christ, through His redemptive power, offers you the latter vision.

FAMILY VALUE

Family is a good thing, something of great value. But it is not an ultimate thing. It is a means to an end. That end, that purpose, is that the glory and knowledge of the Creator would spread throughout the world. Families are the temporary means by which God is bringing about that larger purpose. Families are God's way of filling the earth with those who are in full fellowship with Him and with one another.

So when we order our marriages and order our families according to the principles God has set forth in Scripture, we are not obeying random, made-up rules. We are participating in redeeming something God has made for His glory, and we're doing it by fulfilling His original plan.

Since the Fall, God has been always about the business of bringing His true family back into fellowship with Him. There has always been a true **family of God** throughout history, comprised of all those who know God through faith. And ever since the first members of that family (Adam and Eve) were put out of the garden, God has been about the business of restoring that family to a place of peace with Him and with each other. The final meeting place of that restored fellowship is the new earth.

Adam and Eve's first two sons were Abel, who "did well," and Cain, who did not "do well" (see Gen. 4:4–7). And so it has always been ever since Eve picked fruit from the forbidden tree. Cain's family, Genesis shows, proved wicked (Gen. 4:23). His brother Seth's family, by contrast, was marked by people calling on the name of the Lord (Gen. 4:26).

By the time we reach Genesis 5, there are already two distinct people groups living on the earth: those who have rejected God and those who cling to God—the members of God's true family. God saves this true family by sparing Noah and his lineage in the Flood. After that, the Bible records a remarkable history of how God continued to preserve His family, particularly through Abraham and his descendants, the nation of Israel. God even referred to the nation of Israel as His family, often calling them His sons and daughters (e.g., Exod. 4:22; Isa. 43:6; Jer. 31:9; Hos. 1:10; 11:1).

But not all Israel was true Israel (Rom. 9:6–7). Being born as Abraham's seed didn't make you a member of God's true family. And on the flip side, God never intended for Israel to be His whole family. He made them, instead, a "light" to all the nations, calling all people to come back into fellowship with God and His family. One of God's first promises to Abraham was, "In you all the families of the earth shall be blessed" (Gen. 12:3).

Hidden in that last sentence is Jesus Himself. He was the Seed of Abraham, who blessed all the families of the earth by offering a way back to God. And Jesus made the "family of God" concept clear. One day, as he was teaching in a house, someone told Him, "Your mother and your brothers are outside, seeking you." Jesus paused and asked, "Who are my mother and my brothers?" Then, looking around the room at those who were listening, He said, "Here are my mother and my brothers! For whoever does the will of God, he is my brother and sister and mother" (Mark 3:31–35).

The church—which Jesus Christ brought about through His death and resurrection—is a visible expression of this same family. The church is "the household of God" (1 Tim. 3:15), and Christians are spiritual "brothers" and "sisters" to one another (cf. 1 Cor. 4:14–15; 1 Thess. 2:7, 11; 1 Tim. 5:1–2). The church is full of people who enjoy oneness with God because they have embraced God's Son, Jesus. The church is a "foretaste of glory divine," a big sign pointing to the day when the whole world will be reconciled to God.

> I do not write these things to make you ashamed, but to admonish you as my beloved children. For though you have countless guides in Christ, you do not have many fathers. For I became your father in Christ Jesus through the gospel. (1 Cor. 4:14–15)

> But we were gentle among you, like a nursing mother taking care of her own children. For you know how, like a father with his children, we exhorted each one of you. (1 Thess. 2:7, 11–12)

> Do not rebuke an older man but encourage him as you would a father, younger men as brothers, older women as mothers, younger women as sisters, in all purity. (1 Tim. 5:1–2)

What does all of this mean for us? It means that when the world looks at the church, it ought to see a family of people in fellowship with one another because they have been brought into fellowship with God through a common family member, the Lord Jesus. And just as the marriage union is a way to demonstrate that fellowship, the other relationships in the family prove it too. When parents fulfill their God-given role in the lives of their children, and children respond to their parents as God intended, it is a visible sign that God is indeed redeeming the world, reconciling the families of the earth to Himself one family member at a time, until all believers are united with God as one family on the new earth.

REDEEMED, OBEDIENT CHILDREN

Paul instructs children,

> Children, obey your parents in the Lord, for this is right. "Honor your father and mother" (this is the first commandment with a promise), "that it may go well with you and that you may live long in the land." (Eph. 6:1–3)

In the previous chapter, we noted how difficult it is for children—especially teen-agers—to obey their parents cheerfully, quickly, and completely. From birth, our natural tendency is not to get *under* authority but *around* it. And the struggle to obey often gets harder during the teen years.

To make matters worse, the trends, styles, language, and technology in our culture change so quickly that your parents can appear to you to be hopelessly out-of-date, with their outmoded ideals and traditions. You may not openly rebel against your parents, but increasingly you're tempted to keep them out of your business, trying to live a life of your own.

A word of encouragement: your ability to honor and obey your parents—or any authority—is really a matter of whether or not you're trusting God. God gave you the authorities you have (Rom. 13:1–7). You may wrestle with godly obedience, but you can trust that God has given you the parents He wanted you to have and the family and the experiences He wanted you to have. Even sinless Jesus had to "learn obedience" as He was growing up (Luke 2:51–52; Heb. 5:8).

And another encouragement: there's something redemptive about living in submission to your parents. Submissive teens receive better parenting—usually. By doing what they're supposed to do, they encourage and help their parents to do what they're supposed to do. But a rebellious teen can trigger a downward spiral of fallenness.

When you obey your parents, you are aligning yourself properly under God's authority, and you're declaring to the world that you can live in harmony with Him and with those He has placed in your life. You are playing a role in Christ's work to redeem the world back into fellowship with Him.

REDEEMED, NURTURING PARENTS

Paul also gives this instruction to parents:

> Fathers, do not provoke your children to anger, but bring them up in the discipline and instruction of the Lord. (Eph. 6:4)

In these brief words are the seeds for redeemed parenting: what to do and what not to do.

The Negative and the Positive

First, fathers in particular—and parents in general—are told what not to do: don't create strife in the home. Children begin their lives weak and vulnerable, under their parents' complete control, at their parents' mercy. Redeeming the parent-child relationship means eliminating all physical and emotional abuse. It means there's no cold authoritarianism under which children can never do anything quite right. Parents who are harsh with their kids create an atmosphere in which the marks of redemption are not able to flourish.

Second, however, parents are told what to do instead of provoking their kids. They must "bring them up," or train them. Applying the kind of discipline and instruction that's "of the Lord," they are to model their behavior on the way the Lord deals with His own children.

Discipline

In Ephesians 6:4, the word *discipline* includes both training and corporal punishment. "For the moment all discipline seems painful rather than pleasant," Hebrews 12:11 says, "but later it yields the peaceful fruit of righteousness to those who have been trained by it" (cf. Prov. 3:11–12). If discipline isn't painful, it's not the kind of godly discipline the Bible speaks of.[6]

Many countries around the world—forty-one by last count—ban spanking. Sweden was the first in 1979. There is now an organization called "Global Initiative to End All Corporal Punishment of Children."[7] And from a secular standpoint it's completely understandable. How else can secular governments be expected to react when so much violence against children occurs in their nations? But misuse of physical discipline isn't a good reason to eliminate its proper use. Biblical discipline requires different levels of response from parents, starting with teaching, then warning, then enforcing.[8] Proverbs is clear about that last level: "Whoever spares the rod hates his son, but he who loves him is diligent to discipline him" (Prov. 13:24). Discipline should not arise out of anger but out of love. Parents who love their children discipline them in wise and measured ways, as God instructs. And when they do, they redeem discipline.

Instruction

In Ephesians 6:4, the word *instruction* refers to the careful, consistent teaching that God directs parents to give to their children (Deut. 6:7–25; Ps. 78:5–8; Prov. 22:6). That is, parents are to keep before their children in all areas of life both what God says in His Word and what God has done for them. Parents may be tempted to neglect their responsibility to instruct by only disciplining their children for wrong behavior but never taking the time to offer positive instruction. Or their church may provide wonderful instruction for their children so that they do not feel the urgency of instructing in the home. But parents should take personally God's command to instruct their children because they're ministering to the world by preparing godly children who will enter the world, helping to fill the earth with the light and knowledge of God as we come nearer the final redemption.

NEUTRAL PARENTING?

Some parents today raise their kids without religion so as not to bias them toward one religion or another. They want to be religiously neutral and let their kids make their own decisions about religion. Of course, every child must make his own decision.

But parents can't really be neutral. If you raise your kids as if belief in God is optional, that in itself is a worldview, a religious perspective.

Instead you should try to follow the words of Deuteronomy 6: "These words that I command you today shall be on your heart. You shall teach them diligently to your children, and shall talk of them when you sit in your house, and when you walk by the way, and when you lie down, and when you rise." You can't make your kids believe, but you do have the privilege of pouring more influence into them than anyone else on the planet.

THE HEARTS OF THE FAMILIES

The very last promise of the very last book of the Old Testament is that God will, at the end of time, "turn the hearts of fathers to their children and the hearts of children to their fathers" (Mal. 4:5–6).

How can families know this blessing while we await the final redemption? Through repentance and faith. If the other people in your family won't repent and believe, seek God's grace and do it yourself anyway. Pray that the Lord would bring a taste of the new earth to your own family.

THINKING IT THROUGH 15.2

1. What is the ultimate goal of the earthly family?
2. How did Jesus define the true family of God?
3. What should motivate obedience of children to their parents?
4. What two major tasks are given to parents, and what is one major error parents are warned against?
5. Why is "neutral" parenting an impossibility?

15.3 REDEEMING GENDER ROLES

One Christian apologist tells the story of a boy named Ezekiel Bulver, who learns a useful but false lesson. He hears his parents arguing, and his mother says to his father, "Oh, you say that because you are a man."[9] Ezekiel is a very bright boy, and he realizes in a flash, "I don't have to refute anybody's arguments; all I have to do is show that my opponent's background or situation gave rise to his idea, and then I can dismiss it."

The apologist called this "Bulverism." And it's actually quite similar to "postmodernism." Postmodernism isn't really an ism, then. It's a destroyer of isms. It's an acid, a solvent that breaks down other people's claims.

Postmodernism (going back to Friedrich Nietzsche) sees arguments not as true or false but as power grabs. Suppose a tenured professor of literature says that the writings of Charles Dickens are classics and ought to be taught in class. Of course, he would say that; he wants to preserve the privilege of other white males like himself and Dickens. Or imagine that a head of state says that the threats to his nation are dire and he needs to declare martial law. Of course, he would say that; he wants to preserve his own power.

Professors and presidents do make power grabs. Postmodernism is right about that. And someone needs to "speak truth to power" by telling powerful people they're wrong and standing up for the little guy.

But postmodernism is such a powerful acid that it melts the bottle it's in. Maybe women in a society can tell men, "You just say that because you're men and want to hold on to your power!" But then who's to stop the men from telling the women, "You just say that because you're women and you want our power for yourselves!" Postmodernism leaves us with "might makes right."[10]

The only way weak victims can get strong oppressors to stop is to appeal to an authority above those oppressors—ultimately, God Himself. Not all truth claims are just claims or power grabs. All people, both victims and oppressors, both men and women, really are made in God's image and really do have an essential equality. It's a biblical worldview that restores all people—and both genders—to their proper places of dignity.

WOMEN IN THE NEW TESTAMENT

How would men and women function in the world if the Creation-Fall-Redemption story were not true? What if humans were not created by a loving God, if marriage and family were not ordained by His design, if the relationships we share in the home were merely the results of purposeless evolution? Nothing in this "big story" about the world could stop the strong from dominating the weak. When it came to gender roles, the physically stronger sex would probably dominate the other. Male-dominated cultures would be the normative mode, and women would always be subservient to men, treated as second-class citizens or worse.

But an authority far above men has told them not to exploit their physical strength: "Husbands, live with your wives in an understanding way, showing honor to the woman as the weaker vessel" (1 Pet. 3:7). The Bible recognizes the slighter physical frame God gave women and urges husbands not to take advantage of them, but to be sensitive to their needs and to treat them with the understanding and respect they deserve as fellow image-bearers.

This honor that the Bible gives to women is even more pronounced when we consider the typical male domination over women in the ancient cultures back when the Bible was written. The well-documented restrictions on women in the first century, for instance, show that they were subject to the same types of strictures we see today in most Muslim countries. Roman women were confined mainly to the home. Typically, women in Roman culture were poorly educated, and they were not given equal access to the benefits of Roman law.

Even in Jewish society, women were poorly educated, had little or no authority in decisions, were not considered reliable enough to testify in legal matters, were restricted in the activities of the temple and synagogues, could not go out unveiled or talk to strangers, and were mainly confined to the homes of their fathers or husbands with little or no say in the matter. (The Bible, specifically Proverbs 31, does not support all these restrictions.)

Christ redeems women by raising them to the height of honor they were originally given at creation. The attitudes Jesus and the New Testament apostles demonstrated toward women—and what they taught about women—were countercultural in key ways. "Jesus treated women with dignity and respect and he elevated them in a world where they were often mistreated."[11] Jesus was surrounded by female supporters (Luke 8:2–3) and was close friends with women (Luke 10:38–42; John 11:1–44). Jesus accepted sincere, emotional worship from women (Luke 7:36–50; Matt 26:6–13). He commended women (Mark 7:24–30; 12:41–44; Luke 10:42), spoke of women in His parables (e.g., Matt. 13:33; 24:41; 25:1–13; Luke 15:8–10; 18:1–8), and taught women as well as men (Mark 6:34; Luke 10:39). Women were the first to arrive at the empty tomb, becoming the first-ever witnesses of Jesus' resurrection (Matt. 27:57–28:10).

Jesus' conversation with a Samaritan woman (John 4:1–42) is a major event in John's Gospel—an occasion when Jesus was willing to break several social norms.[12] Jesus conversed with the woman personally in broad daylight, showed concern for her soul, answered her questions, and offered her salvation. This incident doesn't seem that striking to us today only because we don't understand how unusual it was for a Jewish male to show equal respect to a female, especially in public, especially to a divorced-five-times-and-currently-cohabiting Samaritan female (4:16–18). But the disciples understood; "they marveled that he was talking with a woman" (4:27).

The apostles later followed Jesus' lead in their attitude toward women. Women were greatly involved in the ministry of the early church.[13] Although men took the lead—as they were instructed to do by the apostles—women were cared for and commended in the New Testament, and they ministered alongside men, filling important roles. Women were present in the upper room (including Mary the mother of Jesus) when the Holy Spirit was given to the church (Acts 1:14). Lydia and a group of faithful women helped Paul to launch his ministry to Philippi (Acts 16:13–15). Priscilla worked alongside her husband to instruct Apollos in the way of God (Acts 18:26). A great number of the apostle Paul's coworkers were women.[14] For example, Paul spoke of two women in particular who "labored side by side with [him] in the gospel" (Phil. 4:1–3).

> ***"People in our culture have a great need to see role models of biblical manhood and womanhood that flesh out God's design for men and women."***[15]
>
> —ANDREAS AND MARGARET KÖSTENBERGER

When a woman lives redemptively, she rejoices in the design of God and attempts to develop herself in accordance with a woman's position as an image-bearer of God, a disciple of Christ, and usually, a helper to her husband. Sometimes girls get the impression that unless they're just like boys, they're missing out. That's simply not true. God has different plans for boys (in general) than for girls (in general). If you're a girl, don't try to be a boy. Run track if you want to—but not just because the boys are doing it. Take a computer programming course if you want to—but not because there are too few women in the tech field. The cultural push to get all professions to a fifty-fifty gender split implies that women can't have glory until they match men. That's clearly not biblical thinking.

As a girl, you don't merely want to think rightly about God and His design yourself. You want to help others to think rightly as well. This means taking a hard look at what you're communicating to others through your words, your clothes, and even your Instagram account. Living redemptively means looking at the way you act in a group of people and avoiding those behaviors that don't communicate femininity. It means looking at your career options and choosing to pursue something that won't get in the way of your following God's design for men and women at home and in the church. Since God hasn't given us specifics in these areas, we have to pray and use the wisdom God provides. Whatever we choose, our goal should be the same—to hold up the truth that God has revealed in the Bible.

A biblical worldview doesn't demean women or relegate them to second-class citizenship. Rather, Christ redeems women from domination and raises them to their original status of co-regents infused with dignity and treated with distinct honor.

MEN IN THE NEW TESTAMENT

But women are not the only gender whose roles are mentioned in the New Testament. The roles of men are also addressed and often in a way that instructs men how to manage their strength and position rather than abuse them. When Paul addresses the male leadership of Corinth, he says, "Be watchful, stand firm in the faith, act like men, be strong" (1 Cor. 16:13), recognizing the role of strong leadership and protection that men are to exercise in the church. But men in particular are also exhorted to be loving, faithful, pure (1 Tim. 4:12), patient, kind, peaceable, and gentle even when facing those who oppose the truth (2 Tim. 2:22–26)—virtues that are not always associated with the dominant male. When Paul recounts his ministry to the Thessalonian believers, he likens himself to both a nursing mother caring gently, lovingly, and sacrificially for her children (1 Thess. 2:7–9) and to a nurturing father, exhorting and encouraging those in his care (2:11–12). This analogy is significant; while Paul still delineates specific roles for men and women, he's willing to define his own ministry in terms that elevate and honor both roles, recognizing that fathers and mothers serve alongside each other as they minister to their children.

If you're a guy, you need to understand true manliness. When a man lives redemptively, he rejoices in the design of God and attempts to live in accordance with his position as an image-bearer of God and the leader of his family. He will try to develop the skills and character of a leader. It's your responsibility to take care of others, particularly women and children and those who are weaker than you. You have a responsibility to lead people in the right direction. And you're supposed to be known as a man who can work. By upper high school, *play* should phasing out of your vocabulary. You should be thinking of your chores, your schoolwork, and even your basketball team as work that God has called you to do right now. In your work you're developing skills that you'll need as God calls you to more and more responsibility.

You can promote the truth by the way you act and talk. One idea you have to fight against is the idea that there's no such thing as masculinity. Some people think that's just something people make up. But as one pastor pointed out, "The reason people can cross-dress is because clothing communicates masculinity and femininity."[16] Living redemptively means taking a look at what you wear and avoiding those things that don't clearly communicate masculinity. It also means evaluating what you say and the way you treat others by asking yourself, "Does this help others think rightly about God and His design for men and women?" That kind of thinking isn't simple, and it isn't always the same—when Paul wrote the New Testament epistles, he probably wasn't wearing blue jeans. But in every culture Christian men should embrace the symbols that communicate that they have adopted the role God designed for them.

Some theologians argue that redemption through Christ erases gender roles. After all, they say, Paul declares in Galatians 3:28, "There is neither Jew nor Greek, there is neither slave nor free, there is no male and female, for you are all one in Christ Jesus." But Paul is referring to the fact that there is complete equality when it comes to receiving Christ and being welcomed into the family of God. Oneness in Christ transcends all other human relationships because those who are in Him belong to Him equally.[17] This was revolutionary in the New Testament era. In the church, men no longer have special privilege of closeness to God, as the Jewish men had been given in the temple. Slaves and free persons worshiped in the Chris-

SIMPLE EXAMPLES OF BIBLICAL MASCULINITY

Scenario 1: During a well-attended Thanksgiving service at a local church, a number of people found themselves in a crowded overflow room watching the service on a closed-circuit TV. The church had prepared to recite Psalm 103 together as part of the service, but when the time came, the audio inexplicably went off. Someone had to "lead" the recitation of Psalm 103, and fast, or no one would know when to start. People looked around nervously for a few moments, not sure what to do. No formal church leadership was in the room. What does a true man do? He speaks out loud and clear: "Bless the Lord, O my soul, and all that is within me, bless his holy name." He doesn't lead so he can enjoy the spotlight for a moment—most people won't even know who spoke up. He does it to serve others, so they don't have to be embarrassed in an awkward situation.

Scenario 2: A young man likes a girl but isn't sure she likes him back. He could find a sneaky, non-risky way of making her reveal her feelings before he reveals his. But a truly masculine young man does not do this. He puts his neck out and leads. He risks being embarrassed and hurt so she doesn't have to. He makes the phone call (to the girl or maybe even her dad!) and he does the asking out. He pays for the hamburgers. He has an end goal in mind for the relationship; he isn't just playing around.

tian assembly alongside each other, and amazingly, so did even Jews and Gentiles—and men and women.

Nevertheless, the oneness that men and women share equally in Christ does not negate their God-given, unique roles. Nor does Paul ever suggest such a thing in his other writings; he only puts those roles in the context of redemption, which unites men and women to the Lord and to each other in new ways.

Therefore, in Christ both men and women should still pursue the God-given roles assigned to them from the beginning of creation. Salvation does not release men and women from their responsibility to fulfill God's design but rather energizes them to do so, leading them to redeem their roles to function in the way God originally intended. Various cultures, including church cultures, have struggled to maintain the proper biblical balance between the redeemed roles of men and women, sometimes allowing men to be abusive and uncaring with their power and authority and at other times encouraging women to throw off their God-given role in the name of equality. Nevertheless, by carefully following the instructions given in Scripture in light of the redemption that is in Christ, men and women can be examples of the kind of peace and harmony God is restoring on earth as they humbly take up the roles that God has assigned to each.

CULTURAL DIFFERENCES

Different cultures will have different ways of expressing the biblical principles that men and women are equal in essence but unique in function. A given cultural practice—like men opening doors for women—may not be strictly necessary. But a young man who wants to be masculine, as well as a young woman who wants to be feminine, will work to discover the culturally appropriate ways to show respect to one other as male and female beings. They won't try to break down the distinctions between men and women but will attempt to honor them because they know that men and women play special roles alongside each other in the redemption of the world.

THINKING IT THROUGH 15.3

1. What kind of justice are you left with if you follow Bulverism?
2. Provide two examples that demonstrate that Jesus exalted women's roles in His ministry.
3. Provide two examples that demonstrate that the early church exalted women's roles in ministry.
4. What virtues ought to define biblical male leadership in contrast to domineering male leadership?
5. How should you relate to the applications of gender norms made by your particular culture?

15 CHAPTER REVIEW

TERMS TO REMEMBER

family of God

Scripture Memory

Proverbs 18:22

Making Connections

1. In what one specific way will believers be like angels in their resurrected bodies?
2. According to Ephesians 5:21–32, what mystery is human marriage patterned after?
3. What should the parent-child relationship picture when parents and children fulfill their God-given roles?
4. According to 1 Peter 3:7, how should a godly husband treat his wife?

Developing Skills in Apologetics and Worldview

5. How should you respond to parents who may feel reluctant to raise you with bias toward their own Christian beliefs or ethical values?
6. How would you respond to someone who claims that Galatians 3:28 teaches that gender roles no longer exist?

Examining Assumptions and Evidence

7. When God restores the world, why will human marriage no longer be needed? Restate both reasons given in the chapter.
8. What underlying character quality is necessary for a wife to be submissive? What underlying character quality is necessary for a husband to be loving?
9. Why do submissive teens typically get better parenting?
10. How should salvation affect the ways husbands and wives live out creational norms about gender?

Becoming a Creative Cultivator

11. Different cultures have had different ways of showing respect and honor between the sexes. Evaluate several such recommendations from a recent book on etiquette and write a brief paragraph summarizing your evaluations.

GOVERNMENT

Chapter Sixteen **FOUNDATIONS OF GOVERNMENT**

When one rules justly over men, ruling in the fear of God, he dawns on them like the morning light, like the sun shining forth on a cloudless morning, like rain that makes grass to sprout from the earth.

Scripture Memory
2 Samuel 23:3*b*–4

16.1 WHAT GOOD IS GOVERNMENT?

The 1960s-era bumper sticker "Question Authority" appeared on millions of cars for a reason: it resonated deeply with US culture.[1] Individual autonomy—making your own rules—has come to be the American way. You know that American distrust in government runs deep when even the president of the United States himself says, "Government is not the solution to our problem; government is the problem."[2] When Ronald Reagan said that in his first inaugural address, he was complaining about his predecessor; he didn't mean government is inherently bad (he was a politician after all). But plenty of people today seem to think it is bad. Americans from all points on the political spectrum are deeply suspicious about the goodness of government—and about institutions in general.

Christians, too, may think of government as a necessary evil. They may assume that government exists only because of the Fall. After all, there were only two humans living in the pre-Fall world, and presumably they had no tax forms to fill out.

But Christians who view government through a biblical lens will see—as with so many other things we've discussed—that government was a good institution created by God, that it is now fallen, and that it will be redeemed. One of the most important themes in Scripture is, in fact, the "government" of God—what we generally call God's "kingdom." God has, of course, always ruled (no one has ever toppled Him from His heavenly throne, not Hitler, not Satan). So when the Bible talks about the **kingdom of God**, it's actually speaking of the rule of God *through a human that God appointed.*

God's original intent was that mankind would have godly dominion (a kingly word) over the earth, and God didn't give up this plan when Adam fell (Gen. 1:26–28; 9:1–7). Instead God appointed a different man to rule the earth, a son of David. He told King David, "Your house and your kingdom shall be made sure forever before me. Your throne shall be established forever" (2 Sam. 7:16).

KING JESUS

That son of David was, of course, Jesus. And it was the good news about His divine kingdom that made up Jesus' central message. He traveled all over Israel proclaiming "the good news of the kingdom of God" (Luke 4:43). His disciples did too. When Peter preached at Pentecost, he proclaimed that Jesus had been enthroned at the Father's right hand (Acts 2:30–36). When Paul preached from prison in Rome, his subject matter was the kingdom of God (Acts 28:31). And Revelation tells us that when Jesus returns to this earth, He will come as a judge and a conquering king (Rev. 19:15–16). He will "establish justice in the earth" (Isa. 42:4).

This King promises that He will set up his government on the earth. Isaiah 9:6 says of the Messiah that "the government shall be upon his shoulder"—He will carry the weight of authority. Jesus really will rule. Government is not a necessary evil but part of God's Creation Mandate.

God laid the foundation for government as He laid the foundation for the earth. Government, then, is not a patch put in place to manage the damage caused by the Fall. Government has been part of God's good and glorious plan from the beginning.

Interestingly, Jesus' kingship doesn't mean that humans no longer have any ruling to do. Psalm 8 speaks of fallen man as "crowned with glory and honor," and the passage says that God "put all things under his feet." That's king language. And Revelation 22:5 says that the redeemed will one day reign with Jesus over all the earth. All humans are blessed with the capacity to rule over God's creation, and one day some of us will.

THE RIGHT TO RULE

Human authority to rule benevolently over creation is clear. Birds, animals, and fish were placed under our dominion. But what about people? Does any human have a right to rule over another human? All people are made in God's image. Every one of us has been given dominion over the earth. So why do some people rule over others?

First, you must understand that equality and authority are not opposites. Within the Trinity, the Spirit submits to the Son, who submits to the Father (John 4:34; 14:24; 16:13). This order of authority within the Trinity doesn't mean the Son is less God than the Father. They are equal; they simply have different roles. Equality and authority can live peacefully together.

Hopefully, you already know this from experience because you see it in your parents. In a good marriage—like in the very first marriage—the husband and wife are equally image-bearers, but each plays a different role in the household. The father has final authority, but also final responsibility. The wife is his helper, as Eve was created to be (Gen. 2:18). Paul says that this fact established an order of authority between husband and wife (1 Tim. 2:12–13).

This order, this institution we call marriage, began in the Garden of Eden as part of God's command to be fruitful and multiply. Like all other institutions, marriage is a set of customs and laws that has endured in society. And some institutions, like marriage, have endured so long that they powerfully define the rules and roles for human behavior.[3] The institution of marriage provides rules and roles for husband, wife, and children.

Marriage is, of course, not the only institution in our world. As humans carried out the Creation Mandate, more institutions naturally developed. For instance, when Abel became a keeper of sheep he began to develop patterns of behavior for shepherds. If he hired others to work for him in keeping the sheep, then the roles of employer and employee—another structure of authority—would have been created. If Jubal not only invented the lyre and pipe but organized groups of musicians to play them together (Gen. 4:21), he would have created another institution with its own roles and structure of authority (somebody has to decide the tempo).

There were no employers and employees, conductors and players when only Adam and Eve existed. But by the end of Genesis 4 roles like these were developing as society grew in complexity. And out of this process of development government probably emerged.

Even if the world had remained unfallen, the increasing complexity of human life would have meant that institutions like government had to come. Imagine that two cities have developed along the Pishon River in the land of Havilah (Gen. 2:11). One of the cities wants to divert most of the Pishon for irrigation. The other city, downstream, wants the water level to remain high enough for its ships carrying bdellium and onyx stone up and down the river to trade with other cities. Each of the two cities is pursuing good goals: subduing the earth, taking dominion. But they have to figure out a way to work together in this endeavor. The two cities might send representatives who can meet with each other to work out a mutually agreeable solution. The Creation Mandate doesn't explicitly give humans the authority to rule other humans, but for the mandate to be carried out, authority structures such as those in the family and in government would need to emerge.

In order for humanity to maximize the use of God's world (including conflicting claims over water resources as in the picture), human government must develop.

Even in a world with no sin, people would need government. Government is not a necessary evil but a natural outgrowth of the Creation Mandate. Of course, since the Fall occurred so early in human history, the earliest statements about government in Scripture occur as the Creation Mandate is applied to a fallen world, not a perfect one (Gen. 9:1–7).

INVENTED VERSUS INSTITUTED

The Bible never tells us anything about the first human governments. The family groupings in Genesis—and the nations that arose from them—suggest that human government emerged from the family. Perhaps a patriarch began ruling over his growing clan. Or perhaps leaders were selected according to ability as Moses later did after the Israelites' Exodus from Egypt (Exod. 18:21–22). The latter may be more likely since government is fundamentally different from family.

God has not told us how government came about or what exactly it should look like. So God's people have some liberty when it comes to the forms of government they participate in. Christians should not think that only democracies or only monarchies are approved by God. Israel itself existed under various forms of government that God Himself set up. Israel was first led by Moses and the elders of their tribes; later it was led by the elders alone; later by judges (who were primarily military leaders, not judicial officials) and then kings.

But Scripture is clear about one thing—government is God's creation, not a mere human invention. Peter says, "Be subject for the Lord's sake to every institution ordained for people" (1 Pet. 2:13, ESV marginal reading). Somebody had to do the instituting of the institution we call government; this verse shows that it was God. Peter is saying that government is a creation of God for humans that they must submit to. And in Romans, Paul says that the individual rulers who are in power "have been instituted by God" (Rom. 13:1). God's purpose for rulers is that they be servants for our good (Rom. 13:4, 6).

TWISTED POWER

Governments have power from the Highest Power. But governments are made up of fallen people who twist that power in various ways. Many governments have twisted that power so far that they use it to kill the people God intends them to serve. Many more twist that power just enough to shake some money into their own pockets. No wonder so many people (Americans included) have an anti-institutional and anti-governmental bias.

THINKING IT THROUGH 16.1

1. How do you know that government is more than just a patch put in place to manage the damage caused by the Fall?
2. Is the authority of one human over another a consequence of the Fall? Why or why not?
3. Why must authority structures emerge as humans begin to carry out the Creation Mandate?
4. List two Bible verses that declare that government was ordained and instituted by God.
5. Why do many Christians believe that government is a necessary evil?

16.2 WHY DO WE NEED GOVERNMENT ANYWAY?

In Dickens's *Great Expectations*, the narrator Pip observes that "in the little world in which children have their existence . . . , there is nothing so finely perceived and so finely felt as injustice."[4] There is nothing more frequently on the lips of kids than "That's not fair!" When you were a kid and someone treated you unjustly—whether they took your turn on the swing or swiped the slightly bigger piece of orange—your little heart cried out for justice.

And as you've grown up and learned about how viciously unjust people in this world can be, your now bigger heart has cried out for justice too. The dozens of Holocaust museums around the world are dedicated to telling searing stories of injustice—Jewish children hanged and gassed, old rabbis beaten, women treated like animals. And the museums tell these stories precisely so that we feel deep in our consciences that what we're seeing is terribly wrong.

Assuming you are not the one guilty of creating the injustice, there are three basic ways to achieve justice in this sin-cursed world:

Justice Option 1: Achieve justice yourself by taking revenge. There have been at least thirteen movies in eight languages titled *Revenge*[5] because, let's face it, this option feels so right. Revenge is such a powerful and common human emotion because injustice bothers us all so much that we want to do something about it right away. But in our angry hands, such a reaction often creates more injustice.

Justice Option 2: Let God bring about justice. This is the very direct, very specific advice of the Bible. God takes complete ownership of all revenge: "Vengeance is *mine*," He says. "*I* will repay" (Rom. 12:19). God is a just, all-powerful King who will one day judge the world. We are commanded to leave justice in His hands.

Justice Option 3: Let God do it *through government*. Paul explains carefully in his letter to the Romans that every legitimate ruler "is the servant of God, an avenger who carries out God's wrath on the wrongdoer" (Rom. 13:4). Injustice makes God angry too. And though some injustices will not be made right until the whole world is, some will be corrected in this life by God's tool, government.

Options 2 and 3, then, are not in conflict. Or at least they need not be. (Romans 13:4 comes right after Romans 12:19, after all.) Correcting injustice is something humans care about because we are made in the image of a God who also cares about injustice. And promoting justice turns out to be the most important function of government.

JUSTICE: GOVERNMENT'S PARAMOUNT PURPOSE

In the first chapter of Deuteronomy, Moses tells the people of Israel as they stand at the border of the Promised Land how they have grown into a nation in need of a government. The first thing that Moses charges these leaders in Israel to do is to "judge righteously" (1:16). In other words, "do justice" (Mic. 6:8). Moses then specifies one characteristic of justice: judges are not to show any favoritism toward the rich and powerful (Deut. 1:17).

God made Solomon king precisely so that he could "execute justice" (1 Kings 10:9), and Solomon praises justice highly as one of the very purposes for having a king: "By justice a king builds up the land, but he who exacts gifts tears it down" (Prov. 29:4); "If a king faithfully judges the poor, his throne will be established forever" (Prov. 29:14).

Martin Luther King Jr. (1929–1968) called for justice to "roll down like waters."

Three Hebrew prophets—Jeremiah, Isaiah, and Amos—rebuked Jewish rulers for failing to live up to Solomon's standard. And those prophets still speak today through their words in Scripture. Martin Luther King Jr. used a beautiful line from Amos in his famous "I Have a Dream" speech: "Let justice roll down like waters, and righteousness like a mighty stream!" (Amos 5:24).

King was right to use those words on the National Mall in Washington, D.C., because this ideal of the just ruler is not only for Israel; it's for today's rulers too. Psalm 72 speaks of how the Messiah will treat the "poor with justice," saving "the lives of the needy" from "oppression and violence" (72:1–3, 12–14). Psalm 82 says that God judges all rulers (82:1). He condemns them with a biting question: "How long will you judge unjustly and show partiality to the wicked" (82:2). Gentile kings will also be judged for their injustices (Amos 1). God expects all kings to rule justly..

Whose Justice?

It's good that one of the purposes of the US Constitution, set out in the preamble, is to "establish justice." The major biblical purpose of government is indeed to build a solid foundation for justice.

But whose justice? People don't always agree on what counts as justice. Harvard professor Michael Sandel has noted that the deep disagreements in our society over what is true and good have pressed many people to search for neutral, nonjudgmental definitions of justice. One of the most popular and enduring attempts to find such a definition is utilitarianism.[6]

Utilitarian Justice?

Utilitarianism, a philosophy developed by philosophers Jeremy Bentham and John Stuart Mill, is based on the seemingly simple, unobjectionable principle of "utility." It teaches that whatever brings the greatest happiness to the greatest number of people (and avoids the greatest amount of pain) is good. It's moral. It's just.

And utilitarianism does sometimes deliver justice. Most economic policies in America are defended via utilitarianism. Politicians argue that a particular tax cut will help millions of people get jobs while costing the wealthy only a tiny tax increase. That's maximizing utility.

But Sandel tells the story of four British sailors stuck on a raft way out in the ocean; three of them decided to eat the cabin boy, seventeen, in order to keep themselves alive. One unmarried young orphan gets zero happiness, but the others all get to keep their lives; their kids get to keep their fathers.[7] That's maximizing utility too.

ANOTHER PROBLEM WITH UTILITARIANISM

If the goal of utilitarianism is "maximizing utility," or bringing the greatest happiness to the greatest number of people, who could possibly have enough wisdom to know what would do that? Are all of your individual decisions successful in bringing you the joy and pleasure you desire? Probably not. Then who can be trusted to know what choices and policies will bring the greatest happiness to your whole nation, or to all mankind?

There is an answer: God. Our Creator knows best how to make us happy. He Himself is a happy God. But utilitarians don't generally consult Him. They want to define happiness their own way.

So most teenage cabin boys in drifting lifeboats object to utilitarianism for reasons that should now be obvious. The same goes for ancient Christians who got thrown to lions in Rome. Sandel says,

> Yes, the Christian suffers excruciating pain as the lion mauls and devours him. But think of the collective ecstasy of the cheering spectators packing the Coliseum. If enough Romans derive enough pleasure from the violent spectacle, are there any grounds on which a utilitarian can condemn it?[8]

Or if framing an innocent person would prevent a violent, deadly riot—doesn't it become the utilitarian's duty to frame that person?[9]

People know in their God-given consciences (Rom. 2:14–15) that framing innocents, tossing Christians to lions, and eating cabin boys can't be right. We all know, then, that utilitarianism is wrong—at least if it tries to portray itself as a complete explanation of morality.[10]

Most people, at least sometimes, assume that certain actions *really are* right and others *really are* wrong—whether they appear to "maximize utility" or not. But that assumption only forces us back to the question of *whose justice*: Which actions are right? Whose idea of justice is the correct one?

Neutral Justice?

Non-Christian philosophers have worked hard to come up with neutral definitions of justice, morality, human rights, and the good life that everyone can agree on. But as following any discussion on the internet will quickly show you, it's harder to find agreement than it is to find your car keys when you're running late.

If people can't even agree on what marriage is, how can they agree on who should be allowed to marry? If they can't agree on what a person is, how can they agree about abortion or euthanasia? People in this fallen world will always disagree over what's moral and just, over what's best for a nation, a state, or a school district. The battle over justice never stops; it's going on everywhere all the time. Who can possibly sort out these disagreements?

Justice Founded on the Image of God and His Word

Only someone with a God's-eye view can sort them out. And there's only one Someone like that. He has told us what we need to know about justice, morality, and the good life: the Bible teaches that justice is what God does. Morality is defined by God's own character. And the good life is the transformation of God's fallen image-bearers into the image of God's Son for His glory (Rom. 8:29; Phil. 1:10–11).

The Christian vision of justice grows out of that image of God because *the value people have as God's image-bearers places certain obligations on us*. Our neighbors, because they're made in God's image, have a right to be treated in certain ways.[11]

Old Testament laws provide some good examples:

- Because people bear God's image, they have a right to life—murder is always an injustice (Gen. 9:6).
- God's image-bearers also have the right not to be enslaved because that steals a person's life. The Old Testament gave the same punishment to all who engaged in human trafficking (whether enslaving, transporting, or purchasing slaves) as it did to murderers (Exod. 21:16; Deut. 24:7).
- Because women bear God's image just as men do,they have the right not to be objectified or raped (Exod. 22:16–17). (A society that allows lewdness and pornography all over its entertainment media is violating this obligation.)
- Because image-bearers who cultivate God's world create value by their work, they have a right to be paid for that work (Lev. 19:13; Jer. 22:13–17). By prohibiting stealing in the Ten Commandments, God grants people the right to own their property (Exod. 20:15, 17).
- People have the right to keep their good name (Exod. 23:1).
- Vulnerable people have a right to fair treatment from those who are better off (Exod. 22:21–27; 23:6–9).

The Bible provides a stable foundation for justice—and a high bar for rulers to measure up to. Perfect justice has never existed on earth since the Fall; even sinless Jesus was nailed to a wooden beam. But when He was, He was purchasing justice for the whole world. One day, when He comes as King, we'll have it.

THINKING IT THROUGH 16.2

1. From childhood, what major need do all people yearn for because of the fallen actions of others toward them?
2. How can that yearning be satisfied biblically?

3. What philosophy teaches that whatever brings the greatest happiness to the greatest number of people (and avoids the greatest amount of pain) is good? Why is this philosophy wrong?
4. How does the Bible promise that this yearning will be satisfied?
5. Throughout Scripture, when God addresses the task of government, what is His chief concern that government carry out?

16.3 WHAT SHOULD GOVERNMENT DO AND HOW?

The Great Famine in China (1958–61) killed an estimated 45 million Chinese, a death toll roughly equivalent to the number of civilians who died worldwide as a result World War II.[12] The Chinese government long referred to this deadly time as "Three Years of Natural Disasters." Drought did play a role, but the bigger truth is that Chairman Mao Zedong's Great Leap Forward program took away the private property of farmers, gave them unwise mandates about how to farm, mismanaged and stole their crop yields, and then blamed the resulting famine on the farmers—millions of whom then died of starvation. Mao may not have pulled a trigger or ordered a bombing run, but he (along with his government) still ended up being one of the worst butchers in history.[13] Uneducated Chinese farmers, with no political representation and no free press to put pressure on the government, were completely at Mao's mercy.

To be killed in a war by an unjust enemy is bad enough; to be killed in peacetime by your own government is certainly worse. How did things go so wrong? We can't know unless we know what things look like when they go right. And how will we know that? The Bible gives us God's view of the duties of government.

Mao Zedong
(1893–1976)

Mao's "Great Leap Forward" yielded a great famine; governmental injustice claimed the lives of millions of Chinese.

JUSTICE AND THE DUTIES OF GOVERNMENT

Government is ordained by God to provide justice for the governed—justice based on their rights as image-bearers. This justice, according to Scripture, includes duties regarding defense, morality, and the poor.

Defense

Ensuring the defense of the nation is one of the ways that a government ensures justice—since wars almost always create injustices. God gave government the power of the sword, according to Romans 13. And if another nation threatens a people, their government has the right and responsibility from God to defend them. Throughout the Bible, and especially in the Old Testament, God expects those of His people who have any power to oppose injustice and oppression, to protect the weak.

Police protection against criminal activity is another way the government ensures justice. So is a judicial system that upholds the rule of law—no bribes or favoritism. And, of course, such a system depends on lawmakers to pass just laws.

Morality

Most people in the West would agree that a government is responsible to defend its people, but they do not always agree about a second responsibility of government: promoting morality and discouraging its opposite. But promoting a particular vision of morality is impossible to avoid because justice always requires moral judgments. As one writer put it, "Laws represent . . . the moral aspirations of a given society."[14]

That's obvious when we're talking about laws against murder and theft. It's obvious when we talk about laws against racism. In the civil rights era, America woke up to (at least some of) its moral obligations to African Americans, a group it had first enslaved and then relegated to second-class citizenship. Civil rights laws helped teach America that racism was wrong not just in formal, legal ways, but in personal ones.

But the right and moral way is not always so easy to see. It can't be found in popular slogans, even slogans as respected as ones about "freedom" or "equality." We must always ask, "Equality in what respect? Freedom to do what?" The great politician Edmund Burke said, "The effect of liberty to individuals is, that they may do what they please: we ought to see what it will please them to do, before we risk congratulations, which may soon be turned into complaints."[15]

Liberty means nothing without some moral vision of what you're free from—and free for. A great number of Americans who clamor "Liberty!" and "Equality!" when they want gays to be able to marry are silent when Christian businessmen wish to have the liberty to refrain from funding abortions in their employee healthcare plans. Freedom and equality aren't usually what either side in a big debate is really after; they're both after a particular kind of society.

And it will always be this way because God's image-bearers are moral creatures. We seem to have a drive to shape the world with our moral visions. God, in fact, despite being all too aware of the evil that rulers are capable of, says He has sent rulers "to punish those who do evil and to praise those who do good" (1 Pet. 2:14; cf. Rom. 13:3). Even modern secular societies will never escape the moral purpose of government, no matter how often they insist that they are worldview-neutral. As Solomon says, "Righteousness exalts a nation, but sin is a reproach to any people" (Prov. 14:34).

So Christians ought to advocate for truly moral laws—such as laws restricting divorce (Matt. 19:1–12), pornography (Matt. 5:27–30), child abuse (Eph. 6:4; Mark 9:42), prostitution (1 Cor. 6:18), and abortion (Exod. 20:13). And we ought to promote family unity (Gen. 2:24), hard work (2 Thess. 3:10), and ethical business dealings (Prov. 11:1).

Politics is the art of the possible, as Otto von Bismarck said.[16] Even the laws God wrote for His chosen people allowed for the ugly reality of divorce; God hated it but regulated it. God knew that hardened sinners would leave their spouses no matter what the law said, so He regulated divorce to constrain it and minimize its negative impact (particularly on women and children) in Israelite society. And Christians may have little power in society to do any legal advocating for anything. The first Christian to enter India could probably do no more than pray and evangelize in the face of the terrible practice of widow-burning called *suttee*. And even when Queen Victoria of England outlawed it in all India in 1861, Christians were a distinct minority in that land. They most definitely imposed their morality on the majority, but surely they did right.

There are plenty of Christians in America today. Surely it is right for us to try to protect the unborn, for example, from the injustice of being slaughtered. We will never succeed in banishing all sin from the world, but that is no excuse for doing nothing about it till Christ returns.

Poverty

Reasons. The government also has duties concerning the poor, and the Bible offers rich wisdom for this issue. Scripture gives several reasons why people are poor.

(1) Sometimes a disaster—such as a famine or a death in the family—plunges people into poverty (Ruth 1:1–5; Job 1:13–19).

(2) Other times people are poor because they're lazy (Prov. 14:23; 24:30–31) or unwise in the way they use their money (21:17).

(3) Finally, some people are poor because they are oppressed by corrupt governments or selfish employers (cf. Amos 5:11).

Responses. These different causes for poverty demand different responses.

(1) If a disaster comes, governments may need to join nongovernmental organizations such as the Red Cross to send help when people in far-flung places need it, which is *right now*. "Relief*" is what you do when tsunamis or hurricanes or sieges have suddenly displaced thousands of people, cutting off their supply of food, water, and jobs.

relief: *aid given to help people affected by wars, disasters, and so on*

(2) But not all people with inadequate food need relief. The lazy poor should not receive a handout. Paul told the church in Thessalonica, "If anyone is not willing to work, let him not eat" (2 Thess. 3:10). These poor should be told to work and be given help to find jobs since the Bible presents work as the appropriate way of getting income (Prov. 10:4; 12:27; 22:29). A government that gives money to a man on the street is not necessarily being kind; it's actually being unjust—to him and to taxpayers—if he can work for himself. It's paying for him to continue in his sin without as many consequences. And it's paying him with money taken from other people's taxes. That's unjust.

(3) It's not always possible to know quickly, however, whether someone is poor through laziness or because of oppression. So the Old Testament made provision for all poor people. God encouraged individuals to be generous, of course, but He designed a role for government too. Individuals were required by law to leave the corners of their fields unharvested so that the poor could, through their own hard work and not through a handout, get some food (Lev. 23:22). And on a government level, Israelite towns levied a 10 percent tax every three years for those in need (Deut. 14:28–29). People with unpayable debts were also given a legal way to pay off those debts through their labor (Deut. 15:12–15).

Christians today are not bound by these Mosaic laws, but we are wise to use them as guidelines for our own situations—just as Gentile nations in Moses' day were supposed to do (Deut.

LIMITS ON ENSURING JUSTICE

Not every sin is a crime. The difference between the two is not always easy to see. Some actions may be wrong but don't fall within the jurisdiction of the governmental sphere of authority; they fall under another sphere's authority. A brother may act unjustly toward his sister, but typically this is handled by the parents not the sheriff. However, if an aspect of that sin calls for penal justice (domestic abuse, for instance), then, in addition to the other authority's response, the government should also be called in to address the issue.

For example, God Himself permitted the ancient Israelites to divorce, Jesus explained, because of their "hardness of heart" (Matt. 19:8). A government that makes no provision whatsoever for divorce, such as the Philippines, can't keep it from happening—some men there just leave their wives without signing any papers. Laws are needed to contain the damage.

Christians in governmental positions must strain toward the ideal while being fully aware how far short the possible will always fall until the world's true King fully reigns.

4:6). The one earthly government that God has so far set up played a limited but definite role in taxing to help the needy. But the most significant thing God's system did for the poor was to safeguard opportunities for them to work to provide for themselves without being exploited.

THE MODES AND MOTIVES OF GOVERNING

How can we best structure government to deliver justice? We have to wisely use our experience viewed through a biblical lens in our attempt to formulate the best kind of governmental structures. The ancient Greek philosopher Aristotle offered a helpful outline naming six forms of government. He considered three of them good and three bad, based on the motivations of those who ruled.[17] Over the centuries Christian thinkers have refined Aristotle's ideas (as reflected in the chart) to make them consistent with biblical principles.

FORMS OF GOVERNMENT	MOTIVATIONS OF RULERS: THE COMMON GOOD	MOTIVATIONS OF RULERS: SELF-INTEREST
RULE BY ONE	**monarchy**	**tyranny**
RULE BY A FEW	**aristocracy**	**oligarchy**
RULE BY THE MANY	**commonwealth**	**pure democracy**

Rule by One

Monarchy is a familiar example of rule by one. This form of government has the advantage of decisive leadership. A truly powerful king doesn't have to wait to act until groups with different opinions can agree about what to do. And a virtuous monarch is able to set the moral tone for the nation.

On the other hand, a ruler can be a tyrant or a dictator who's treated like a god (or a powerful president who's seen as being above the law). Since he doesn't have to wait for Republicans and Democrats to agree, he can do evil without anyone standing in the way.

Rule by a Few

Aristocracy: *commonly viewed as people of inherited wealth; here it means merely the wise citizens*

Aristocracy is rule by a select group of wise citizens. An aristocracy can be a great way to run a country because it can tap into the collective wisdom of the wise and virtuous, which is likely to be superior to the wisdom of a single monarch. And a small group may find it easier to come to agreement than a whole society will. Sometimes decisions do need to be made fast, and putting things to a national vote takes too much time.

But small groups of elites can also be as wicked, immoral, and tyrannical as any dictator.

Rule by the Many

Commonwealth is rule by the many for the good of all. It has the advantage of gaining widespread support for its policies. It also may benefit from gathering wisdom from many sources. But it can be terribly inefficient.

What's worse is when all have the right to vote and they vote for the immediate gratification of their own selfish desires. A majority can be worse than a tyrant in its treatment of a minority it doesn't like. What if the majority of people in a given nation think that those with mental disabilities should be put to death (as happened in Germany under Nazi rule)?' should be replaced with "What if the majority of people in a given nation think that those with mental disabilities should be sterilized (as happened in America in the 1920s)? One of the most powerful arguments against rule by the many is demonstrated by certain comments about news articles or blogs you read on the internet—you know, the ones that make you wonder, even if they agree with you, "Are these people legally allowed to vote?"

Mixed Reviews: Which Form Is Best?

Many thinkers over the centuries have concluded that a good system will try to mix the three basic forms of government in a way that limits their defects and promotes their virtues. For instance, the American founders gave the United States a single president who could be active and decisive in executing the laws of the land and providing for the defense of the nation. They also brought in the commonwealth approach through the election of legislators to the House of Representatives. But many of the founders deeply distrusted pure democracy. They believed that the mass of people needed wise and virtuous leaders to guide them. For this reason the president is not selected by direct vote but through the Electoral College. Senators also were originally chosen by state legislatures, and Supreme Court justices were (and still are) appointed by the president with the consent of the Senate. This is a kind of aristocracy, though not one of birth but (hopefully) one of wisdom and virtue.

Is this mixed form of government a good idea when viewed through a Christian worldview? Basically, yes, it is; this framework tries to take human fallenness and finiteness into account.

- It acknowledges the truth that people are **fallen** and cannot be trusted to act unselfishly unless there are checks and balances. Absolute power corrupts absolutely. If you somehow find a benevolent dictator, chances are that his son will not be so benevolent (like Rehoboam in 1 Kings 12:12–14).
- Also, a government structure that draws insight from people in all walks of life recognizes that humans are **finite**. We need each other's perspectives and knowledge. We need intellectuals, and we need factory workers; all classes of people have been called to dominion over God's world. And humans will always be finite—heaven won't make us gods. So we will always need each other's wisdom, even in the new earth.

SPHERES OF AUTHORITY

Ronald Reagan may have been right when he said in 1981 that the US government was creating more problems than it was solving. And the "Question Authority" slogan isn't necessarily bad if you add two little words: "*Sometimes* question *an* authority." Human authorities are far from perfect; at times they need to be questioned. But to question authority in general is to dishonor the great Authority who has invested His authority in all other authorities. God instituted government. It is a good thing we all need.

Nonetheless, government is not the only institution that God has granted authority to. That's why this unit on government comes after the one on marriage, family, and gender roles. Fathers have authority whether a government says they do or not. Likewise, God has given genuine authority to the church and its leaders, even if a government says that no churches are allowed.

Government, family, and church are parallel authorities. Ideally, they would never need to reach into each other's realms. Churches shouldn't be setting speed limits on interstates, and governments shouldn't be telling churches who they can and cannot hire to pastor them. God seems to have set limits on the authorities He instituted. To give just a few more examples, most people would sense that something is wrong if the state took children to court for not eating their vegetables or if the government fined an employee of a local business for being perpetually late to work.

Every authority has its proper sphere. Children who break family rules should be disciplined by parents; employees who fail to meet company expectations should be dealt with by their managers; and congregations who hire pastors shouldn't have to check with a government official first.

totalitarianism: *a form of government in which the totality of life comes under the government's control or oversight*

When a government tries to reach into spheres where it doesn't belong, we have totalitarianism.* When that happens, the other institutions of society tend to wither rather than flourish.

And yet, among these various institutions, the state has a unique role. God established government to exercise authority and prevent injustice in other spheres. If a father fails to feed or clothe his children or if a business defrauds its customers, the state should intervene. However, the role of the state is not to operate within or take over the tasks of the many other institutions that exist.

THE FUTURE OF GOVERNMENT

Government is not a necessary evil; it is a good institution ordained by God to ensure justice. And government will always be with us. When our true King comes, we'll still have government. Jesus told His disciples that they would one day "sit on twelve thrones, judging the twelve tribes of Israel" (Matt. 19:28). Evidently, Christ's rule won't be so absolute that no other rulers will be needed. He will rule through lower-level rulers.

> For to us a child is born, to us a son is given; and the government shall be upon his shoulder, and his name shall be called Wonderful Counselor, Mighty God, Everlasting Father, Prince of Peace. Of the increase of his government and of peace there will be no end, on the throne of David and over his kingdom, to establish it and to uphold it with justice and with righteousness from this time forth and forevermore. The zeal of the Lord of hosts will do this. (Isa. 9:6–7)

THINKING IT THROUGH 16.3

1. Identify three major duties of a just government.
2. Explain why a just government ought to carry out each of the three major duties.
3. What are the three basic forms of government? Identify the ways in which each one can be good or bad.
4. Which system of government is best suited to uphold justice and why?
5. How should the sphere of governmental authority function alongside other spheres of authority such as the family and church?

16 CHAPTER REVIEW

TERMS TO REMEMBER

kingdom of God
utilitarianism
monarchy
aristocracy
commonwealth
tyranny
oligarchy
pure democracy

Scripture Memory

2 Samuel 23:3–4

Making Connections

1. Tell a brief story of how you think government would have emerged in an unfallen world.
2. Why do humans care so much about correcting injustice?
3. What's wrong with a utilitarian view of justice?
4. Explain the limited role of government in society. How can you know when government has overstepped its bounds?

Developing Skills in Apologetics and Worldview

5. If someone tries to argue that government would not be needed in an unfallen world, how would you respond?
6. If someone tries to argue that Christians shouldn't try to legislate anyone's morality, how would you respond?

Examining Assumptions and Evidence

7. What role does the image of God in man play in our understanding of justice?
8. Are Justice Options 2 and 3 (page 242) contradictory? Why or why not?
9. Is there only one biblically legitimate governmental structure? What factors should good government seek to balance?
10. Why shouldn't every sin be criminalized by the laws of a government?

Becoming a Creative Cultivator

11. Choose one of the following issues: abortion, same-sex marriage, legalizing marijuana, aid for the poor, or racism. Write a one-page plan for how a Christian should discuss this topic in the public square. What challenges should you anticipate? How will you respond effectively?

Chapter Seventeen **POLITICAL PERSPECTIVES**

God takes His stand in His own congregation; He judges in the midst of the rulers. How long will you judge unjustly and show partiality to the wicked? Vindicate the weak and fatherless; do justice to the afflicted and destitute. Rescue the weak and needy; deliver them out of the hand of the wicked

Scripture Memory
Psalm 82:1–4 (NASB)

17.0 IDOLATROUS IDEOLOGIES

Polite society in America tends to avoid discussion of two topics: religion and politics. (And this unit is about both of them.) But why? Why frown on talking about two things everybody has to deal with in some way or other?

It's because long experience has taught people that conversations about these two topics tend to either go nowhere or get heated quickly. Or both.

And why is that? Because to be perfectly right about either one requires a God's-eye view. And if you have that—or think you do—there's going to come a point where debate with your opponents can't go on because you've reached a bedrock level of disagreement. That's true of religion, and it's true of politics.

On the religious side. People simply can't know by themselves why we are all here, what has gone wrong with our world, and how to fix it. That's why they look to their worldview, which is based ultimately on faith.

On the political side. The world is too complex for any human (given all our limitations) to perfectly predict which political policies will be successful. That's why people look to their political ideology,* which is also ultimately based on faith.

A **political ideology** is sort of like a worldview. One political scientist suggests that it has three parts: "(1) a critique of existing society, (2) a vision of a better future, and (3) a strategy for getting from here to there." And she points out something very key: "All three are usually informed by an underlying concept of human nature."[1]

Political ideologies, then, are actually theological because concepts of human nature are theological. So political ideologies are religious—even if their proponents don't think they are. And Christian political theorists have pointed out that these ideologies tend to be false theologies in two ways. First, when they name the great evil in the world, it's almost always something other than human sin. It's some part of God's good created order. On the flip side, when they name the great savior that will come and rescue humanity, it's almost always something other than God. In this chapter we will look at popular political ideologies and consider some real-life examples of these errors.

> *"For all the apparent conflict among [political] ideologies, all are subspecies of the larger category of idolatry."*[2]
>
> —DAVID KOYZIS

Even though political ideologies all have problems, Christians shouldn't expect any ideology to be wrong on every point. All the prevalent political ideologies have correctly grasped one or more creational norms. In addition, the good things in

ideology: *a set of beliefs that serve as the basis for a system of thought* creation that these ideologies look to for salvation from the problems of life really exist—they're just insufficient to save.

Every political ideology can see corruption, oppression, and other problems in human government. But Christians cannot simply adopt the view of one of the popular political ideologies because these ideas have been warped by the Fall and are rival worldviews to the biblical one.[3] In this chapter we will examine four of the most prominent political ideologies: liberalism, democracy, socialism, and conservatism. These are not the only ideologies out there, but they are the most influential in the Western world.

17.1 LIBERALISM

In the United States, people are used to thinking of politics as divided between liberal and conservative. And in general, Democrats are liberal; Republicans are conservative. This is helpful as far as it goes, but America isn't the only country with liberals and conservatives, and **liberalism** existed long before the donkey and the elephant of US political cartoons.[4]

Liberty gets a statue in America, but not an agreed-upon definition. What are people free "from," and what are they free "for"?

LIBERALISM DELINEATED

Liberalism historically has been used to describe political ideologies that make liberty (from *liber*, Latin for "free") their fundamental value. And if you know anything about American Republicans and Democrats, you'll see immediately that both are liberal in that classical sense. The two parties agree that liberty is good—just not on what liberty is and what people should be free from and free for. Republicans are more likely to be classical liberals—people who are trying to conserve the ideals of limited government especially as promoted by the Democratic-Republicans in the early days of the United States. Democrats are more likely to be progressive liberals, those who think that government should be expanded to ensure that people gain greater liberties (often meaning sexual freedoms in particular).[5]

Classical Liberals

The roots of classical liberalism are found in John Locke and Adam Smith. Locke taught that humans have basic natural rights to life, liberty, and property. Locke and others from his time saw the state* as the greatest threat to these rights. Therefore they developed a political theory that protected the freedoms of the individual and limited the power of the state.

Classical liberals were not opposed to the state. They thought the state had some important functions—but limited ones. The state was supposed to protect people's rights and property. But it only existed, in Locke's view, by the consent of the people being governed by it. If a government started trampling people's rights instead of protecting them, the people had a right to rebel.

---

state: *a nation and its government; or in other contexts, one of the fifty political divisions that make up the United States of America*

Classical liberals believed that all men were created equal, but that in everyday life people don't live equally. In a free society, some people are going to become wealthy through a combination of hard work, wisdom, and social advantages. Others are going to become poor, whether through unchosen difficulties such as physical injury or through personal failures such as laziness and foolishness.

Progressive Liberals

Inequality is precisely what resulted from the industrial revolution. Wealth came to some, and with it came power. At the turn of the twentieth century, many began to think that the wealthy (and their big businesses), not the state, were the greatest threat to liberty.

People who found themselves trapped in dangerous, low-wage, long-hour jobs didn't seem to be free in the fullest sense of the term. This led to a new form of liberalism, called progressivism. The progressives thought that government regulation could be used to ensure freedom for those who were not wealthy or powerful. Large businesses would be broken up by trustbusters to give smaller businesses a better chance. Regulations about wages and worker safety would provide benefits that the workers desired but did not have the power to achieve. Progressive liberals also developed the welfare state—food stamps, low-income housing ("the projects"), and so on. They thought that government needed to take an active role in providing people enough money to have freedom of opportunity.

Liberty is the key idea here—but as Christianity's power in the West faded and ideological secularism grew, the concept of liberty among progressives expanded. By the 1960s, progressives began to insist that people should have the freedom to decide what the good life is. To say that there's a "common good" that people should agree on violates the liberty of individuals. All moral judgments of others are suspect. This kind of liberalism wanted to open up liberty for sex outside marriage and (therefore) for abortion. They wanted freedom for easy divorce, recreational drugs, and uncensored entertainment.[6]

Progressives have in many ways won the cultural battle for freedom in these areas. But whether they care to admit it or not, they have run into a divine wall. God sometimes gives people over to the sins they desire (Rom. 1:24). These freedoms go against God's created order, and so freedoms have become slaveries. Sex outside marriage has led to family breakdown and subsequent poverty, particularly within already vulnerable communities. Use of recreational drugs (including alcohol) has also wreaked havoc in countless lives and in the society as a whole.

Progressives have an answer, however: use government to take away the consequences of people's negative choices. Put a big financial pillow at rock bottom so it's not so hard for people. Government then gets bigger to the point of being difficult to contain.[7]

Libertarians

welfare state: a state in which the government takes responsibility for aspects of citizen's financial security and health

This expansion of the scope of government by the welfare state* provoked a response, at least in America. In the decades after World War II, libertarianism was born. Libertarians are similar in many ways to classical liberals, but libertarians want to see an even more minimal role for government—or no role at all.[8] Libertarian writer Murray Rothbard holds that even the police, the military, and the courts should be owned by private companies, not run by government and funded by tax dollars. Each individual should pay for whatever amount of service he desires.[9] Others see some role for government. Libertarian David Boaz says, "Individuals have the right to do whatever they want to, so long as they respect the equal rights of others. The role of government is to protect individual rights from foreign aggressors and from neighbors who murder, rape, rob, assault, or defraud us."[10] For the libertarian there is no "society." There are simply individuals who have entered into agreements with other individuals. The libertarian holds that all these agreements should be free; none should be forced by the government.

Libertarians tend to agree with progressives about moral freedom. Rothbard argues for the freedom "to engage in such 'victimless crimes' as pornography, sexual deviation, and prostitution."[11] But unlike progressive liberalism, libertarians insist that people must live with the consequences of their choices.

Liberalism has a long history of development. It comes in many forms, and the older forms don't necessarily go away when the newer forms emerge. This means that several varieties of liberalism exist today, and they're not all compatible. But there is a common denominator; they all hold to the core value of liberty.

LIBERALISM EVALUATED

When you evaluate a political ideology, you must remember that it is "informed by an underlying concept of human nature."[12] At the heart of each form of liberalism is an emphasis on liberty as the great good which must be defended. For liberalism this liberty, or self-rule, is often overemphasized and out of balance with other norms that God built into the created order.

Classical Liberalism

Classical liberals (and libertarians) place a high value on the free market.* And, in fact, there seems to be something structurally right about giving businesses the freedom to excel, about allowing competition to drive innovation, and about creating a situation in which people must strive to better themselves and the world around them. The greatest force for reducing poverty around the world has been the free-market system.

free market: *a market in which the government does not interfere in the competition between private companies*

But everything is fallen, including the market. Some classical liberals speak as if whatever the market does or drives must be right. Nineteenth-century classical liberals objected to safety regulations and child labor laws. Though classical liberals today accept such laws, some will argue that they were unnecessary. They think the market would have moved away from child labor on its own. Similarly, the classical liberal is not likely to grant that people can be paid unfair wages in a free market system. The market determines what is fair. But the Bible is clear that powerful people do oppress the poor by not paying them a fair wage (Deut. 24:14; Prov. 3:27; 29:7; Jer. 22:13–17; Mal. 3:5). The government has a mandate from God to ensure justice, even if classical liberals (and libertarians) call it "meddling." It is therefore right for the government to insist on safe working conditions and to prohibit businesses from employing young children at low wages while depriving them of the opportunity to get an education.

Another danger classical liberals (and libertarians) face is reducing everything to markets. Instead of talking about inculcating morals, some speak of creating the right incentives for desired behavior. So parents provide financial incentives for their children to earn good grades, or churches are organized to market their religion to consumers. When everything is seen as a market, moral considerations get sidelined.[13]

Progressive Liberalism

Progressive liberalism must be severely criticized for often working to free people from creational norms. Most recently these freedoms have centered on freedom from sexual norms. At the foundation of God's plan for the world is mankind made in the image of God, male and female, with the commission to "be fruitful and multiply" (Gen. 1:28). So it should be no surprise that those who want freedom from creational norms want freedom from gender roles, freedom from sexual morality, freedom to choose one's own gender, and more. The Creation Mandate also teaches that work is good, yet many progressive poverty programs reward people for not working. The Bible places such a high value on work that Paul actually says that people who can work but don't shouldn't get to eat (2 Thess. 3:10).

Life in God's world doesn't work when people try to live apart from God's laws. It's like fish trying to be free from water or people trying to be free from oxygen. So progressives appeal to government to mitigate the consequences their freedoms bring. But this only distorts the purpose of government. Government's primary purpose is to ensure justice. But a government that aids the effort to seek freedom from creational norms will be bound to perpetuate injustice. In addition, God has designed the world to work with multiple institutions, each with its own structures. God designed the family to nurture and raise children, and businesses to buy and sell products, and the state to ensure justice. If the state attempts to run a business, oversee worship in a church, or manage how families raise their children, it will likely carry out those functions poorly.

This is not to say that progressives are wrong about everything. The Old Testament law demanded safe working conditions (Exod. 21:29), provided a basic safety net for the poor from tax revenues (Deut. 14:28–29), and established laws that required individuals to provide for the poor (Lev. 19:9–10; Deut. 24:21). Individuals provided the aid, but the law required them to do so.[14] Laws like these ensure justice as God defines it. They stand in contrast to attempts to live contrary to creational norms.

Libertarianism

Libertarianism is wrong because it grabs on to the creational norm of individual accountability and turns it into an idol: individual autonomy. Individual accountability means that people have to live with the consequences of their choices. Their laziness does not obligate others to ensure that the lazy have all the comforts of life. But individual autonomy asserts that the government should never force anyone to do anything. Most libertarians wouldn't get rid of the government altogether, but they would give it the sole role of protecting individual autonomy.

The Bible teaches, however, that individuals are meant to be part of communities. Sinners will be held accountable as individuals (Ezek. 18:4), and people are saved as individuals (Rom. 10:12–13). And yet God places individuals in groups that are meant to work together—in the family (Gen. 2:18, 24), in nations (Gen 12:2; Rom. 13:1–7), and in the church (Eph. 4:16, 25). It is good for us to be accountable to others and obedient to our God-given authorities, even and especially when they contradict us.

Look at the places in the world where people are free to do what is right in their own eyes without government intrusion, such as Somalia. People there are not truly free. They're caught among the gears of a country grinding to a halt. Of course, this is an extreme example, and most libertarians would want a basic government to maintain order. But it does confirm the observation of the early American theologian

Isaac Backus: "It is so far from being necessary for any man to give up any part of his real liberty in order to submit to government, that all nations have found it necessary to submit to some government in order to enjoy any liberty and security at all."[15]

Government is not a necessary evil; it is a God-established (though fallen) good.

LIBERTY TO EXCESS

Liberalism overemphasizes liberty. It looks to freedom as a savior from many problems. But liberals easily get carried away with cries for liberty while not stopping to ask themselves, "Liberty to do what?" Liberty, like justice, must be based on moral judgments. Will those moral judgments be shaped by individual desires or by Scripture?

THINKING IT THROUGH 17.0 AND 17.1

1. What is an ideology? List the three parts of a political ideology.
2. Why are all political ideologies religious?
3. How is the term *liberalism* used in political science? How is the term used differently in American politics?
4. What key problem is common to all three kinds of liberalism?
5. Create a chart showing the three kinds of liberalism and identifying any biblical or unbiblical concerns, values, and approaches.

17.2 DEMOCRACY

For many Americans, **democracy**—like liberty and equality—has achieved the status of an unquestionable good. Rule "of the people, by the people, and for the people" is right up there with "God helps those who help themselves" among the sayings most likely to be mistaken for Bible verses.

But democracy needs the CFR treatment like everything else does: what's creational about it, what's fallen, and how do we push what's fallen back toward creational norms?

HISTORICAL PERSPECTIVES ON DEMOCRACY

Judging by the root words underlying *democracy*, you would think it simply means "people power" (Greek, *demos* = people, *kratia* = power). But democracy isn't a simple idea. It tends to include the right of all citizens to vote for their leaders, freedom of speech, and freedom of the press.[16] Most Americans, Christians included, believe that democracy is the best form of government. US foreign policy frequently pushes for or defends democratic elections in other nations—Americans tend to trust that democracy will work because they assume people will vote according to their own best interests.

But not all Christians throughout history have felt this way. As democratic

The gathering of democratically elected representatives in one room is a powerful symbol of democracy for Americans.

ideas developed at the end of the medieval period, many Christians remained suspicious and concerned about democracy.[17] Early American theologian John Cotton (1585–1652) said, "I do not conceive that ever God did ordain [democracy] as a fit government either for church or commonwealth. If the people be governors, who shall be governed?"[18]

Cotton had good reasons for his concerns. The biggest champions of democracy were often Enlightenment thinkers who were very critical of biblical Christianity.[19] Like Cotton, many Christians worried that democracy placed too much emphasis on human freedom and not enough on righteousness. Democracy, they feared, would allow fallen people to define "the vision of the good" that society was supposed to aim for.[20] Christians also wondered if the people determined the laws that govern morality, what would keep a society from moral self-destruction.[21]

American Christians began to favor democracy, however, around the time of the War for Independence.[22] But even then the embrace of democracy was not total. Some early Americans, both Christians and others, did not trust the people to rule. They worried that the majority could become tyrants just as much as kings could. For this reason, the American constitutional system was a system of representative government that placed checks and balances on the people as well as on the elected officials.[23]

In God's providence, Christian morality was strong enough throughout most of nineteenth-century American culture to keep democracy from eroding public morals.[24] Democracy even gained moral authority as the champion of the rights of slaves and laborers in the 1800s and as the opponent of totalitarianism in the 1900s. When both Christianity and democracy saw a common enemy in godless communism, the link between Christianity and democracy was practically cemented.

EVALUATING DEMOCRACY

Democracy, does have a basis in God's creational design (as do the other political ideologies we're looking at in this unit—liberalism, socialism, and conservatism). Most obviously, God created all people as image-bearers who are given the responsibility of ruling over the world (Gen. 1:26–28). Since all people are fundamentally equal and are given divine authority to rule the world, it seems appropriate for all citizens to have a say in the political process.

Christians can also rejoice in democracy because it gives them a voice. Christians in a democracy are actually invited, along with all other groups, to shape the culture and governance of their nations. This is a solemn opportunity which should not be wasted. Also, along with democracy there usually comes a measure of religious tolerance and respect for the individual conscience. This tolerance gives Christians the space to live out their faith privately and publicly.

C. S. Lewis saw "two opposite reasons" for supporting democracy: "You may think all men so good that they deserve a share in the government of the commonwealth, and so wise that the commonwealth needs their advice. . . . On the other hand, you may believe fallen men to be so wicked that not one of them can be trusted with any irresponsible power over his fellows."[25] You can easily hear both justifications for democracy in the evening news. Lewis firmly adopted the second point of view.

But democracy commits the same kind of error other political ideologies do. It tends to find the source of evil in the world in a part of God's good creation order. Democracy tends to see authority itself as the source of evil—and equality as the solution. As they say in Australia, "Cut down the tall poppy." In other words, don't let one person rise above anyone else. This is understandable given how people throughout history have abused their authority. But authority is a part of God's good created order, so opposition to authority leads to evils of its own. For instance, disrespect for the creeds and confessions of orthodox Christianity led to a proliferation of unorthodox religions in the United States in the 1800s. Unitarianism, Mormonism, Jehovah's Witnesses, Christian Science, and many other sects could flourish because Americans thought that everyone could choose whatever understanding of the Bible was right in his own eyes.

Another evil that can result from democracy is that its push for equality and resistance to authority can act as acid that dissolves a society's values. People who point the way toward higher values—higher art, higher aspirations—are mocked and shouted down. They're "elitists" who "put on airs." Lewis warns, "When equality is treated . . . as an ideal we begin to breed that stunted and envious sort of mind that hates all superiority. That mind is the special disease of democracy, as cruelty and servility are the special diseases of privileged societies."[26]

Sexual morality has also been a casualty of the acidic work of democracy. In the past, Western morality was deeply formed by (though not perfectly consistent with) a biblical worldview. So Westerners frowned on sexual activity outside of marriage. It is true that those who struggle with immorality—especially women—didn't always get the compassion, help, or forgiveness Jesus would have shown them. You can't blame a child for being born out of wedlock. But today democracy has joined other factors to reverse this situation. Our culture is in a rush to affirm immorality, whether heterosexual or homosexual. "Judge not lest ye be judged" has been twisted by democracy into a rejection of all moral judgments.

JUDGE NOT?

When Jesus said, "Judge not, that you be not judged" in the Sermon on the Mount (Matt. 7:1), did He mean that no one is allowed to make a moral judgment about anyone else's behavior? No, He not only makes such judgments Himself throughout that sermon, but He encourages others to make them. He called some people "hypocrites" (Matt. 6:16), and He told His followers, "First take the log out of your own eye, and then you will see clearly to take the speck out of your brother's eye" (Matt. 7:5). Jesus' point was that you are to be willing to be judged by the same standard you use in judging other people. In other words, don't be hypocritical.

When Saddam Hussein's Iraq fell to US forces in 2003, many Americans naively believed that kicking out the dictator and setting up fair elections would solve Iraq's problems in short order. President George W. Bush expressed the sentiments of many Americans in his second inaugural address: "It is the policy of the United States to seek and support the growth of democratic movements and institutions in every nation and culture, with the ultimate goal of ending tyranny in our world."[27]

But what actually happened in Iraq was that the majority Iraqi religious group (a version of Islam called Shia) used democracy to dominate the minority religious group (a version of Islam called Sunni). The result has been a lot of bloodshed. Democracy was not a salvation for the people of Iraq. Similarly, democracy in Gaza brought the terrorist group Hamas to power. Some analysts have wondered if Afghanistan would have achieved greater stability under a king than it has under a democracy.[28] The success of democracy is dependent on the values of a nation. Without Christian morality, a democratic structure will not itself produce justice. Yet democracy's egalitarianism can be an acid that eats away at the Christian concept of authority.

THINKING IT THROUGH 17.2

1. What do the root words that make up the term *democracy* mean?
2. What kinds of freedoms does democracy often allow?
3. Why were some early Americans concerned about a purely democratic system?
4. Why have American Christians typically favored their democratic system?
5. How can a democratic system go wrong?

17.3 SOCIALISM

Socialism is generally viewed negatively in the United States by both conservatives and liberals (though not necessarily by progressive liberals). But the basic idea of **socialism** may seem pretty attractive to many readers of this textbook: the whole society—and not just the elite—should share in that society's wealth. In many forms, the entire country should own the factories and industries which earn money for the nation. Instead of enriching a select few with obscene wealth, the profits of oil companies and mattress factories and farms and automobile assembly plants should go to everyone, even and especially the workers who keep them running. There are different socialist systems employing different ideas about the roles of government, the market, and economic planning. But all of them view eliminating economic inequality as fundamental to creating a **utopia**.*

utopia: *an ideal society*

EXPERIMENTS IN SOCIALISM

Socialistic ideas existed in various forms all the way back to Plato, but attempts to actually practice socialism began in the late 1700s and early 1800s.[29] The oppression of the poor by wealthy landowners led some to propose an end to private property and an end to money. Instead, they believed that all people should share in common the benefits of their work by having necessities distributed to all as they need them.

This drawing shows how Owen envisioned his utopian community.

Robert Owen (1771–1858)

New Harmony

An early socialist experiment in the United States was led by an enterprising and idealistic British factory owner named Robert Owen, who had already improved working conditions for workers at his mill in Scotland. Under his watchful and benevolent eye, his mill had gone from a filthy place staffed by equally filthy people (in every respect) to a model of efficiency and good manners. Owen basically invented daycare for small children. He reduced work hours from fourteen a day to eight, and children under ten were not allowed to work at all but were sent to school.

Owen decided he could do more good by setting up an entire community in America according to socialist principles. All that was needed was proper social conditioning, Owen felt, and a harmonious society would develop. In his Indiana town of New Harmony, he abolished private property and money, and he called for the sharing of all things in common.

But the people of New Harmony, although they had come there at Owen's invitation, balked. Owen's system for distributing the common goods was complex and inefficient, and the people set up a black market. Too many of the people were idle anyway, and not all the kinds of workers needed to make the community work were interested in joining Owen's experiment. The community split and eventually failed.

Karl Marx

Karl Marx
(1818–1883)

Karl Marx scorned the failure of "utopian socialists" like Owen. He believed that socialism would arise through class warfare that would break out into revolution. Marx believed that the upper-class employers (the bourgeoisie) that hired the workers and owned the factories (the means of production) were in a fatal conflict with lower-class workers (the proletariat). Marx believed that conflict would arise between workers and owners because the capitalist system* is inherently unjust.

Capitalist manufacturers of locomotives, for example, always charge more for their train engines than they cost to produce, so Marx thought they were unjustly taking profits they didn't work for. Marx didn't think managing or investing in a business counted as real work at all.[30] Therefore, he said, managers and investors should not share in the profits created by the workers. Marx thought that economic crashes would get worse and worse. He predicted that as more workers became unemployed or recognized the failures of capitalism, they would rise up in revolt. The revolution would eventually culminate in socialism.

But the bottom-up revolution never came. Some socialists responded by forcing a revolution from the top down—that was Vladimir Lenin's approach. Others, those we now call "social democrats," have argued that instead of pushing for a revolution, socialists should work democratically to continue to help workers by promoting the redistribution of wealth or government ownership of certain businesses.

capitalist system: *a system in which businesses are privately owned and operated for profit*

EVALUATION OF SOCIALISM

Like other political ideologies, socialism has grasped some significant truths.[31] It emphasizes the equality of all people. Christians, because of their belief in the image of God in man, agree. Socialism perceives that those with wealth often use it to oppress others. The Bible, again, agrees that such actions are unjust and wrong. Many passages in Scripture condemn the oppression of the weak by the powerful. Socialists also perceive that humans live in communities, and the Bible supports certain kinds of communal ownership. Families and churches are good examples.

But at its core, socialism calls evil something that God calls good: the right to private property. Socialists sometimes go so far as to say that "property is theft." In pure socialism, all land is owned by everyone. All businesses are shared too.

Many of the laws God gave Israel through Moses protected property rights (Exod. 21:33–33:14). Would the eighth commandment—"You shall not steal" (Exod. 20:15)—make any sense if God didn't recognize the value of private property? The early church in Jerusalem did voluntarily share its goods, but even in that sharing, the apostle Peter affirmed that it was the right of all the Christians to keep their property if they wanted to (Acts 5:4). No authority, in the government or the church, was forcing them to give it away.

So socialists run up against God's law—and therefore against creational norms—when they reject private property. And whenever humans do that, things fall apart. Here's what happens with socialism. The goal of socialists is to arrange society so everyone owns everything. But "everyone" is too nebulous a group to run a business or to manage land. So a particular institution—the state—has to step in and run businesses and manage lands. Where does that leave the vast majority of the citizens? They end up working for the government, often in abject poverty. There is a great irony here. Socialism has roots in the democratic ideal of equality, but state-enforced socialism tends to become very undemocratic. Another irony is that property ownership under socialism really just moves from the hands of common people to the hands of the elites. Socialism emerged in part out of concern for the plight the poor and oppressed. That's a good concern. But it ends up making people even poorer by taking away from them one of the few things of value that they own—their land.

You shouldn't demonize the good things in God's creation (such as private property) or idolize them (such as equality). When you do, the inconsistences and tensions in your ideology mess up your society. Very few people flee from capitalist nations to strictly socialist countries such as Cuba and Venezuela.

THINKING IT THROUGH 17.3

1. What is socialism's basic idea?
2. What is a utopia? According to socialism, what must be overcome in order to achieve that utopia?
3. Who tried a socialist system in America, and why did it fail?
4. Who believed that the only way to achieve a utopian restructuring of society was through class warfare?
5. What legitimate concerns does socialism have? What is fundamentally wrong with socialism?

17.4 CONSERVATISM

Conservatism usually refers to belief in the value of traditional practices, values, and institutions in politics and society. American conservatives typically value hard work, honesty, individualism, freedom, and the traditional family—precisely because that's what American culture used to stand for. Conservatives in other nations value their own culture's language, values, and social hierarchies. **Conservatism**, then, isn't really one easily identifiable set of views. It's relative to the situation.

CONSERVATISM IN THE ABSTRACT

An intelligent observer looks for the substance behind the labels people like to wear. If someone says he's a "liberal," you'd better find out what he wants to be free from and to be free for (and whether or not your freedom is any concern of his). Someone else might claim to be a "conservative," but a conservative in Saudi Arabia is likely to be conserving something very different from what a conservative in Japan wants to conserve. A Russian conservative in the 1990s would have wished for a restoration of the Soviet system while American conservatives of the same time period were rejoicing in its collapse. The label *conservative* means nothing until you know what the person wants to conserve.

It ought to be fairly obvious to Christians that conservatism in the abstract has the capacity to go very wrong. What if the cultural tradition it's trying to conserve is a wicked one? Sometimes evil gets so woven into a cultural tradition that violence is the only way to get rid of it. For instance, the antebellum American South had many noble qualities worth preserving, but it took the horrendous bloodshed of the Civil War to deal with the terrible sin the entire Southern economy was based on. Race-based chattel slavery might have eventually withered away without the war, but that would have been no consolation to the slaves who would have been parted from their wives, denied education, and not given the freedom befitting image-bearers of God until another century had passed.

There's another reason conservatism by itself can go wrong. The Creation Mandate calls for growth and change. God intended for Adam and Eve and their descendants to move forward in the work He had given them—build, change, and grow.[32] When Jubal invented musical instruments (Gen. 4:21), it would have been wrong for Adam to say, "Our culture doesn't do that."

THREE STRANDS OF AMERICAN CONSERVATISM

American conservatism exists in three strands: traditional conservatism, laissez-faire conservatism, and neoconservatism.[33]

Traditional Conservatism

Edmund Burke (1729–1797)

William F. Buckley (1925–2008)

In America, *conservative* probably most often refers to a loosely organized movement often traced back through twentieth-century American public intellectual William F. Buckley to eighteenth-century British statesman Edmund Burke. Buckley and Burke and other traditional conservatives shared a reverence for exactly that: tradition. They felt that tradition preserved the wisdom of the ages, and that's what they were trying to conserve in the face of progressive liberals who were working hard to undermine and jettison that wisdom. One of the most valuable elements of the tradition has been the Christian idea of **natural law**.* Traditional conservatives

---

natural law: *the moral structure that God has revealed to humans in creation and which is discerned through reason and experience (equivalent to what this book labels* norms*)* believe that there is a created order and that society will collapse if it violates that order. That order includes social hierarchies; it is good for some segments of society to set high moral and cultural standards that other segments of society can aspire to. Lastly, traditional conservatives approve of many of the benefits of the free-market system, but they aren't afraid to critique the morality of players in the market.

Laissez-Faire Conservatism

laissez faire: *the philosophy that people should be allowed to do as they please; a "hands-off" approach to something*

Because a conservative is defined by what he or she is trying to conserve, the **laissez-faire*** conservative is something of an irony because he's trying to conserve liberalism—either classical liberalism or libertarianism. It's a bit confusing, but laissez-faire conservatives are a recognizable group. And they *are* conservatives in one sense: they're trying to preserve the mutual toleration practiced at America's founding. Laissez-faire conservatives may or may not believe in natural law, but they do believe in freedom. In contrast to traditional conservatives who want the government to ensure justice on moral issues, laissez-faire conservatives tend to think that the free market will rein in people's vices—or even turn them into public goods. They often get impatient with the traditional conservative view when it appears to them that moral issues are getting in the way of good politics. However, some religious Americans seek to combine traditional moral values with classical liberal economics.

Neoconservatism

Neoconservatives were at first Democrats who supported Franklin Roosevelt's New Deal as morally necessary to help the poor and the civil rights legislation as morally necessary to protect the rights of black Americans. However, the next generation of neoconservatives became skeptical about the effectiveness of Lyndon Johnson's welfare vision (the Great Society). Neoconservatives were also concerned about the moral decay and lawlessness of the counterculture of the 1960s and 1970s. Defenses of Marxist dictatorships by the New Left struck them as naive and morally problematic.

Over time, neoconservatives transitioned from the Democratic Party to the Republican Party. They found themselves able to work with conservatives in a number of areas while retaining some distinctiveness. For instance, rather than blocking social welfare legislation, they were more inclined to offer alternative reforms that they thought would be more effective.

When evangelical Christians became more politically involved, they found allies more readily among neoconservatives than among laissez-faire conservatives. Though most neoconservatives were not evangelical Christians, they were rooted in the classical philosophical tradition and concerned about moral issues.

internationalism: *a political ideal that seeks to overcome nationalism by uniting people above the bonds of loyalty they feel to their individual countries*

In foreign policy, neoconservatives reject isolationism as impractical for a large nation with global interests. They are also nationalists and are suspicious of internationalism.* They believe that America should take an active role opposing oppressive regimes and in promoting democracy around the world.

EVALUATING THE THREE STRANDS

American conservatism is a complex phenomenon that is made even more complicated because most American conservatives don't fit neatly into one category or another. They may have been influenced by ideas from all three strands.

The strengths and weaknesses of the laissez-faire approach and certain aspects of neoconservatism have already been evaluated in the sections on liberalism and democracy, but traditional conservatism deserves closer attention. In the United States, this group has been highly influenced by Christianity. The conservative understanding of natural law is similar to this book's teaching about creational norms: God built the world to work in a certain way, and when in the name of freedom people go against these norms, consequences for society follow.

The traditional conservative also recognizes that humans are inclined to do wrong. In biblical terms, humans are sinners. The Christian and the conservative both know that this sin will infect whatever utopia people can come up with. It is for this reason that conservatives prefer small changes worked out over a long period of time rather than changes that are massive and potentially disruptive. This is also why conservatives favor reforms on the local or state level. If something goes wrong, as surely it will, the effects will be limited. Whatever goes right can spread gradually to other places. For instance, conservatives champion charter schools and private schools rather than across-the-board reforms imposed by the federal Department of Education. The leadership at some private and charter schools may make poor decisions. Those decisions, however, only affect a small portion of the population. Successes, on the other hand can spread naturally to other schools. But nationwide reform has to get everything right for everyone across the nation, or the consequences will be wide-ranging and difficult to fix.

"MEN OF INTEMPERATE MINDS CANNOT BE FREE. THEIR PASSIONS FORGE THEIR FETTERS."[34]

—EDMUND BURKE

Not all forms of conservatism are good. It depends on what they're conserving, and that has to be measured by Scripture. There has emerged in the United States a kind of conservatism that has been influenced by Scripture, and it does provide a good model for Christian political activity. But even traditional conservatism must beware of turning tradition into an idol and making change of any sort the great evil. God intends for His world to develop, and that means change. Furthermore, the past is a mixed bag of good and evil. Traditional conservatives sometimes appeal to Western culture as if it were an infallible standard, but Scripture—the only infallible standard—is what's needed in order for anyone to accurately judge what should be preserved and what should be relegated to the ash heap of history.

POLITICS AND YOUR FUTURE

Social media is a platform for promoting various causes. For some people, the hot-button issue is eating organic. For others, it's running or Christianity. But for many, it's politics.

If you read the comments on political posts, you know they often get excessively nasty. People don't write as if others are mistaken; they write as if their opponents are Satan's spawn. Few people, it seems, recognize that other people's political opinions tend to form a consistent pattern. Most of the American political opinions you are likely to encounter are described by the ideologies in this chapter. If you can see that truth with clarity, you will be able to add some light to discussions sadly lacking in both clarity and light.

And if you can also see that no government or political system will be perfect until Christ reigns from the new Jerusalem, you can contribute even more light. Every major political system has something good to offer, but each one is also twisted in some way. Perhaps it will be your calling to serve your community, your state, or your nation as a politician. Getting a broad and clear understanding of politics now will help you greatly as you pursue that calling. Whatever your calling, that understanding will help you to press for a government that preserves creational norms, especially as they are revealed in Scripture.

THINKING IT THROUGH 17.4

1. What is conservatism?
2. Why is conservatism, as a general idea, sometimes good and sometimes bad?
3. Define the term *laissez faire*.
4. Describe the beliefs and values of the three kinds of conservatism by comparing and contrasting them.
5. Some conservatives have advocated "fusionism," an attempt to unite the three strands of American conservatism. Is a fusion of these three strands possible? Explain why or why not.

17 CHAPTER REVIEW

TERMS TO REMEMBER

ideology
political ideology
liberalism
state
welfare state
free market
democracy
socialism
utopia
conservatism
natural law
laissez-faire

Scripture Memory

Psalm 82:1–4

Making Connections

1. What makes every political ideology religious?
2. Identify both the great evil and the great savior in liberalism, democracy, socialism, and conservatism.
3. Explain the difference between individual accountability and individual autonomy.
4. What are the strengths of traditional conservatism? What are its weaknesses?

Developing Skills in Apologetics and Worldview

5. How should you respond to someone who argues that socialism is the political system that is most compassionate, fair, and consistent with biblical values?
6. How should you respond to a neoconservative who argues that spreading democracy and free elections around the world is an important way of making the world a better place?

Examining Assumptions and Evidence

7. What turns a political ideology into an idolatrous false theology?
8. Why do Christians tend to favor limited democracy?
9. Why did Marx think that managers and investors were acting unjustly by not returning all profits to the workers?
10. Why is a laissez-faire approach incompatible with biblical Christianity?

Becoming a Creative Cultivator

11. Choose a political topic that is currently under debate (e.g., immigration reform, renewable energy, legalization of recreational drugs, etc.). Explain your position on the issue and identify which political ideology it most closely aligns with (or explain how it combines the concerns and values of several ideologies). Defend your position from the accusation that it violates creational norms or that it elevates a creational norm as the savior.

Chapter Eighteen **THE GOAL OF GOVERNMENT**

The kingdom of the world has become the kingdom of our Lord and of his Christ, and he shall reign forever and ever.

Scripture Memory
Revelation 11:15*b*

18.1 THE COMING KING

It happens every four years in America: Christian leaders take to their blogs on Election Day to remind a flustered Christian community that no matter who wins, God won't be unseated from His throne. He won't be surprised. God is still the supreme Ruler; Christ is still the King of Kings. God can't lose an election.

But a lot of Christians do seem to forget this most ultimate reality of their faith. They betray their lack of confidence in God's control when they go to school and work the day after the election utterly despondent, angry, and disbelieving because their candidate lost.

They also betray their failure to trust in a sovereign and all-wise God when their side wins and they are elated, certain that the future will be brighter because their candidate triumphed. When then-Senator Barack Obama ran for election as president of the United States, a striking popular poster pictured him above four block letters: HOPE. Many Americans placed a great deal of hope in President Obama, as others placed hope in a long line of politicians before him. But no politician ever quite lives up to the hype—and yet people get swept away by it every election season, all over the world.

Christians need not be pessimists; world leaders can do true good. George Washington, Winston Churchill, and others are revered for good reason. But read a biography of any great man or woman of political history—Queen Victoria, Caesar, even King David of ancient Judah—and you'll see a distinctly imperfect person. The Fall doesn't skip over heads of state. No mere human is a safe place for all your hopes. There's only one Messiah. "In him will the Gentiles hope" (Rom. 15:12).

THE REIGN OF CHRIST IN THE PRESENT AND THE FUTURE

The title "Messiah" was first used in Scripture by an obscure Israelite woman during a period when God's people had no king and everyone did what was right in his own eyes. It was Hannah, the mother of Samuel. How did this (probably) uneducated but (obviously) godly woman, living over a thousand years before Christ, know that "the Lord will judge the ends of the earth; he will give strength to his king and exalt the horn of his anointed" (1 Sam. 2:10)? She was seeing with the eyes of a prophet. And what did she see? The word translated "anointed" is the Hebrew word *Messiah*—Hannah saw Jesus.

Two Comings of One King

What did she see Jesus doing? Repeatedly throughout her prayer (much like a famous prayer many years later from another young mother, Mary of Nazareth), Hannah saw this king, this Messiah, bringing justice to the world. She saw Him putting down the arrogant and powerful and raising up the humble and oppressed. The Old Testament consistently predicts a king and Messiah who "will reign in righteousness, and . . . justice" (Isa. 32:1).

This promised justice is why John the Baptist urged people to repent in preparation for the Messiah's

People commonly put a great deal of hope in political leaders, but fallen humans are not a safe place for hope.

coming. The coming of the Messiah's kingdom wasn't good news for anyone opposed to His rule. For the unrighteous and the unjust, the coming of the Messiah meant judgment.

But something unexpected happened when the King actually came. Jesus taught that He was splitting His kingly work into two comings to earth. The first coming would bring mercy and salvation. He was holding off judgment till the second time He would come. Jesus left a lot of wrongs unrighted when He ascended to heaven nearly two thousand years ago. His miracles and healings were signs of what His coming kingdom would be like, but only signs. Jesus left a lot of sick people unhealed and a lot of dead people unraised when He returned to heaven. (And those He did heal and raise eventually all died.) Jesus did not then—and has not yet—put all wrongs right in this world.

Jesus could have judged the world as its rightful King at that time, but instead the climax of Jesus' first coming was His laying His life down under the judgment of God for all mankind's sin. But Jesus was, of course, not defeated. The cross was His greatest triumph. It enabled Him to "seek and to save the lost" (Luke 19:10) because it opened the only entrance into heaven with the only key in existence: blood sacrifice.

But you already read all about this in Unit 4. Why are we reviewing it here? Because we can't understand our present unless we understand our future. Jesus will one day come in judgment and will "put all things under his feet" (Eph. 1:22; cf. 1 Cor. 15:25–28). But even in this age, Jesus said, "All authority in heaven and on earth has been given me" (Matt. 28:18).

All Authority

It's important to notice what Jesus as the Messianic king does and does not command His disciples to do after He stakes this claim to universal authority. He doesn't tell them to take over the government of Israel and shake off the shackles of Rome. He doesn't tell them to seize power and to impose justice on the world. Instead He tells them to go throughout the world making disciples of the King—people who will do all that He commands in every area of their lives.

Psalm 110 is the psalm Jesus quoted most often in His earthly ministry. It begins with God the Father saying to the Messiah, "Sit at my right hand, until I make your enemies your footstool" (110:1). Jesus is on that throne now (Acts 2:32–36), but He's got enemies. The psalm says that, for now, the Messiah must "rule in the midst of" those enemies (110:2). So Christians, even though they're citizens of the kingdom of

YOUR KINGDOM COME

When Jesus taught His disciples to pray "Your kingdom come" (Matt. 6:10) in the Model Prayer, what did He mean? There seem to be basically two options: He meant either something future or something present. Either that kingdom will come someday, or it's already here.

Or both. The kingdom of God is simply God's rule through Jesus Christ. And is that rule here? Yes, in Psalm 110 the Father tells Christ to "rule in the midst of [His] enemies," and that's happening right now. And yet that rule is not complete; He's still got enemies.

"Your kingdom come" is a prayer that Christ's rule would spread even now, broader and deeper. It's also a prayer that Christ's rule would become complete. When you pray that phrase, you're asking that Christ's rule would extend to more people and that it would go more deeply into the people (like you?) who are already under Christ's rule. We should also pray that Christ will achieve the ultimate triumph over all His enemies.

an all-powerful King, are often persecuted and even killed by lesser kings. It is also for this reason that powerful people still act unjustly. But Christ's kingdom will not be defeated. His kingdom, like yeast permeating dough, is always spreading (Matt. 13:33).

Christ rules, and Psalm 110 says that He will one day "shatter kings" and "execute judgment among the nations" in "the day of his wrath" (110:5–6). The king-shattering and other judgments are His job, not ours. We have other work to do.

None of this means that Christians are to abandon government and focus only on evangelism. The first thing we must do is pray for our rulers (1 Tim. 2:1–4). But we also get to promote true justice and the claims of the true King within government—while remembering that only Christ has the authority to advance His kingdom by violent force (John 18:36).

THINKING IT THROUGH 18.1

1. How does the Old Testament describe the reign of the Messiah?
2. Why has injustice continued to be a problem in the world even after Jesus came as the Messiah?
3. What are the roles and responsibilities of believers as citizens of Christ's kingdom and as citizens of nations within this world?
4. Based on Scripture, explain how believers can trust in Christ's sovereign judgment and also express joy or sorrow in response to righteous or wicked rulers (Pss. 42:9; 43:1–2; Prov. 11:10; 14:34; 21:1; Eccles. 3:16–17; 4:1–3; 5:8–9; 7:14).

18.2 CHURCH AND STATE

Most Americans assume that there's supposed to be a "wall of separation between church and state," but after that the details get murky. Where is the wall supposed to be exactly? And how high? Low enough to talk over, or high enough to create a prison for one side or the other?

Biblically speaking, the church and the state have to have some sort of relationship because both government and the Christian religion claim similar roles in society. One writer observes that both the church and the state are

> about governing people. Both lay down rules for doing so. Both regard these rules as expressing moral values, the way things ought and ought not to be. Both insist that these normative rules are authoritatively binding on people. Moreover, any religion is a comprehensive worldview which necessarily includes the political, social, and all the other dimensions of human life.[1]

How can two institutions that make such sweeping claims possibly get along?

State over Church

STATE
CHURCH

At some points in history, the state has claimed authority over the church. Roman emperor Constantine set this precedent by convening church councils—and thereby claiming the authority to do so.

This view—often called **Constantinianism**—misunderstands the nature of Christ's present reign. The kings of the earth are required to pay homage to the Messiah and to obey His word (Ps. 2:8–12). Kings (and presidents and prime ministers) are appointed by God (Rom. 13:1), but their failure to submit to Him doesn't automatically remove them from power (Dan. 2:21–23). Nor does their appointment by God give them authority over the church or its doctrine. Instead Christ, the Head of the church, appoints evangelists as well as pastors and teachers over that church (Eph. 4:11).

Church over State

CHURCH
STATE

The medieval Roman Catholic Church flipped the state-over-church position on its head, claiming a church-over-state view instead. If the pope is Christ's representative on earth (Christ's "vicar"), then of course the pope has authority over any other human leader. The Roman Church recognized that the state had its own rightful sphere in which it functioned, but when Charlemagne was crowned Holy Roman Emperor in 800, it was the pope who did the crowning—implying that he had authority over the emperor. Four hundred years later, another pope put all of England under an interdict* when the English king didn't like the pope's appointment of an English archbishop. And it was the English king who had to give in in the end. Also, the Inquisition carried out by the Roman Church punished heretics with the sword of the state.

interdict: *a restriction imposed by the pope barring a nation from participating in the sacraments*

But simply put, nowhere in Scripture is the church given the power of the sword or legal authority over the civil government.

Civil Religion

America has never, since its forming as a nation, had either a state-over-church or a church-over-state system. One alternative we have had is **civil religion**, "the appropriation of religion by politics for its own purposes."[2] People in public pray to and praise god (with a lower-case *g*), a god they never bother to describe in any detail. Does this god have a son, Jesus? Does this god send anyone to hell or express preferences about sexual ethics? If politicians answered these questions, the god they refer to wouldn't unite the nation anymore. Protestants, Muslims, Catholics, and Jews can all sing "God Bless America" only if everyone glosses over sticky theological questions.

Civil religion grew out of a compromise between the "theistic rationalism" of many American founders and the traditional Protestant Christianity practiced by much of the American populace.[3] Leaders such as Thomas Jefferson believed in god, in the moral teachings of certain parts of the Bible, and perhaps even in some final judgment. But they felt it was against reason to believe in the deity of Christ, the Trinity, and salvation by grace through faith in the death and resurrection of Christ.[4]

Because the civil religion of the United States is so closely tied to Christianity, it is sometimes difficult for Christians to discern the differences between the two. A Christian can pledge allegiance to "one nation under God" while standing next to someone who means something very different by the phrase.

This places American Christians in an awkward spot. While we don't want to see God's name, prayer, or the Ten Commandments banished from public life, civil religion twists all of these things into something in service of a god-puppet telling us what we want to hear. American Christians shouldn't render homage to the god of American civil religion any more than the early Christians could offer incense to the supposedly divine Roman emperor.

In the end, civil religion has proved to be a step toward secularism. When largely Protestant nineteenth-century America searched for a common denominator of belief, what resulted was a generically Christian civil religion. But as the United States became more religiously diverse, the number of cultural values all Americans could agree on shrank considerably. Opposition to divisive and controversial religions in public life became opposition to religion in public life, period.[5]

CHRISTIANS AND AMERICAN CIVIL RELIGION

Christians need discernment to spot civil religion since in America it often makes use of Christian rhetoric and symbols. Civil religion was in play when Americans progressively moved from speaking of "Protestant morality" to "Christian virtues" (which included Roman Catholics) to "Judeo-Christian" values (Jewish and Christian) to the values of the "Abrahamic faiths" (meant to include Islam). When you separate the morality of several religions from the doctrines of those religions and then put that morality in service of the nation, you've got civil religion.

Civil religion also links piety and patriotism, and it promotes a manifest divine destiny for the nation. Some people speak of those who die in service of the nation as if they're therefore guaranteed a place in heaven. When representatives from multiple religions are gathered together to pray in the face of a national tragedy as if they are all praying to the god of the nation, this is civil religion.

While Christianity has influenced American civil religion, civil religion has also influenced American Christianity. When US Christians are suspicious of theology and creeds in favor of a practical religion, they are being influenced by civil religion. When they think the style of worship in church doesn't matter to God (but matters a lot in how to attract people to the church), they are being influenced by civil religion. These are major breaks from Christian orthodoxy and alignments to rational religion that have widely infected American evangelicalism.

Excluding Religion from the State

STATE

Western nations have over time developed a proposed solution to the shattering of political-religious unity: secularism, yet another version of church-state relations.[6] During the process of secularization, the wall of separation between church and state becomes an ever-tightening circular wall, with the church inside and the state outside. People can go in and out pretty freely as long as they leave their religion inside.

The story of secularism's rise has already been told in Chapter 3 on the two-story view. A brief recap: The Reformation shattered the religious unity of Europe. A growing cultural and intellectual force began to collect behind the idea that banishing religion from public life would restore unity and keep the peace. If religious reasoning could be excluded from politics, law, education, or anything that a society does together, then religious conflicts would cease. Religious people could still attend their places of worship, and they could talk about their religions among themselves, but only among themselves. Why is it so hard to talk about your faith to non-Christians today? Because the force of secularism is strong in America—and even stronger in many other Western nations.

Secularists assume that they shut religion up for its own good; they think their "neutral" viewpoint is the only way to keep the peace. But secularism doesn't really resolve societal conflict. It just adds a new competitor to the list of groups seeking political power—a competitor that thinks it's a referee. That referee has handed out a simple rulebook to the other players in the game. (When those players ask, "Who made you the ref?" they are politely ignored.) The rule is that no religious or metaphysical* assumptions are allowed in the public square.

metaphysical: *related to unseen realities*

For example, a few years ago the Supreme Court of the United States considered two important cases on euthanasia* and refused to legalize doctor-assisted suicide. Six prominent philosophers filed an official legal brief with the court—"The Philosopher's Brief," it was called. One of the authors, New York University professor Ronald Dworkin, wrote,

euthanasia: *killing a person who is terminally ill to prevent further suffering*

> Denying [doctor-assisted suicide] to terminally ill patients who are in agonizing pain or otherwise doomed to an existence they regard as intolerable could only be justified on the basis of a religious or ethical conviction about the value or meaning of life itself. Our Constitution forbids government to impose such convictions on its citizens.[7]

In other words, the only justifications for stopping someone from committing suicide are private "convictions" that ought never to show their faces in public. Only neutral, secular reasons are allowed out in the sun.

Legal scholar Steven D. Smith wrote a book on secularism in which he demonstrates that Dworkin and other secularist referees can't abide by their own rules.[8] Dworkin—and numerous US judges writing legal opinions on euthanasia—defended euthanasia only for terminally ill patients, not healthy young people. But if we allow a terminally ill eighty-three-year-old to end her physical pain with a doctor's help, why would we not let an otherwise healthy twenty-three-year-old end her emotional pain the same way? Smith showed that Dworkin and the judges kept arguing that there's a "normal life span" that shouldn't be violated. Dworkin said it was a "cosmic shame" for healthy young people to take their own lives.[9]

"Men being all the workmanship of one omnipotent, and infinitely wise maker . . . are his property, . . . made to last during his, not one another's pleasure."[10]

—JOHN LOCKE

But this is a religious and ethical assumption! Why should the fact that most people live to seventy or eighty force me to stay alive that long if I don't want to? How does Dworkin know what the cosmos thinks? And why should the cosmos care if I don't want to live in it anymore? Nature can teach us how to live our lives only if nature has a Creator. Secularism denies that we can know what this Creator says—but then it smuggles in religious assumptions anyway. It has to. You can't have a society with no ethical commitments.

When secularists exclude religious conceptions from even being considered in public discussion, they are being just as coercive* as the religious groups they view as intolerant. Harvard professor and moral philosopher Michael Sandel summarizes the problem:

coercive: *compelling someone to do something by use of force or intimidation*

> Asking democratic citizens to leave their moral and religious convictions behind when they enter the public realm may seem a way of ensuring toleration and mutual respect. In practice, however, the opposite can be true. Deciding important public questions while pretending to a neutrality that cannot be achieved is a recipe for backlash and resentment.[11]

Church Influencing the State

CHURCH

STATE

If Christians were allowed to bring their moral and religious convictions into the public realm, what would that look like?

We saved the best model of church-state relations for last, one in which the church influences the state. "All authority in heaven and on earth has been given" to the Messianic King (Matt. 28:18). But what should be clear by now is that Christ has not delegated all of His authority to any one sphere of human life. God has authorized fathers to rule their families as fathers. He has authorized congregations and their leadership to exercise rule in their churches. He has authorized kings and presidents, parliaments and congresses to rule over nations. He has not authorized the state to rule over the doctrines and practices of the church or the church to begin parenting the children of its members or the church to impose policy decisions on the government. God has created different institutional spheres, each with its own authority under Him.

And yet God has called for all of these authorities to submit to the authority of His Messianic King (Ps. 2:8–10). This means that the church has the responsibility to speak about all of life, including governmental life, just as the Bible speaks to all of life. The biblical prophets applied Scripture to the rulers of their day. When the secular ruler Herod took his brother's wife, John the Baptist told him it was "not lawful" for him to have her (Matt. 14:4). According to whose law? Not Roman law, but God's law. When King Jehoiakim cheated workers of their wages so that he could have a magnificent palace built, God sent Jeremiah to confront his wickedness (Jer. 22:13–23). Micah denounced the unjust rulers of Judah (Mic. 3:1–3).

All legislation is related in some way to moral issues. Someone's moral view will be legislated. It is therefore appropriate for churches to speak to the moral issues raised by legislation. This does not mean that churches are to craft public policy—they aren't. That responsibility lies beyond the church's authority. However, as they carry out their ministry of preaching the Word, it is right for churches to apply that Word to all of life. If politicians become Christians—or if young Christians are called to political work—how will the church disciple them? It is right for churches to disciple Christians who hold public office not only about aspects of personal character but also about the content of their political and governmental work.

Historically, Christians have spoken out against governmental injustice in significant ways. Churches and mission agencies spoke out against US president Andrew Jackson's removal of Indians from their own lands.[12] Many Christians—with British parliamentarian William Wilberforce as the leading example—spoke out against the international slave trade.

THINKING IT THROUGH 18.2

1. Why shouldn't the state be allowed to rule over the church or the church over the state?
2. Define *civil religion* in your own words.
3. What motivated Western secularism to exclude religion from the operations of the state?
4. Can secularism eliminate all religious assumptions from debates in the public square? Why or why not?
5. How should the church relate to the state?

18.3 CHRISTIAN POLITICAL PRUDENCE

A Christian business owner commented on an online news article about the First Lady of the United States. He wrote, "Get this trash out of Washington! I may have to respect her husband, but she was never elected to anything."[13]

What do you think of that comment? Is it right? He means that Romans 13 tells him to honor the governing authorities. The First Lady isn't an authority, so he doesn't have to honor her.

But he didn't read his Bible carefully. Paul actually said, "Pay to all what is owed to them: taxes to whom taxes are owed, revenue to whom revenue is owed, respect to whom respect is owed, honor to whom honor is owed" (Rom. 13:7). Average citizens don't owe the First Lady obedience, but they surely owe her respect.

So it isn't right to make such comments. But is it effective? Well, sort of. If your goal is to debase national political discourse, degrade public trust in national institutions, and make your political opponents feel justified in dismissing your concerns—then it's effective. But if your goal is to lead a peaceful and quiet life, godly and dignified in every way (1 Tim. 2:2), then it's simply wrong to call the First Lady "trash" online.

People who see the world through CFR lenses will choose not to demonize their opponents because they know that every politician, every politician's wife, every voter, and every voter's wife is created and fallen. As dissident Soviet intellectual Alexander Solzhenitsyn famously said, "The line separating good and evil passes not through states, nor between classes, nor between political parties either—but right through every human heart."[14]

What does Christian politics—politics that recognizes that line between good and evil—look like? Truly Christian politics presses for God's will to be done, but in a prudent way backed by prayer. And Christian politics is full of Christian virtues such as humility, respect, and boldness.

PRAYING FOR ALL PEOPLE

Christians in first-century Rome didn't have much if any political power—especially the many Christian slaves. Even today, not all Christians live in countries where their participation in government is allowed. No matter what their situation, however, Christians can do two things: pray for all people and press for God's will to be done.

Praying is something that all Christians may do under any form of government at any time in history. Paul makes prayer for those in authority a duty for all Christians.

> I urge that supplications, prayers, intercessions, and thanksgivings be made for all people, for kings and all who are in high positions, that we may lead a peaceful and quiet life, godly and dignified in every way. (1 Tim. 2:1–2)

Pray for all people, but specifically for governmental authorities. And why? In order that we might lead peaceful lives. When rulers rule well, that's what we get—peace.

And hopefully we get even more. We are to pray that government would permit us to live lives that are also "godly." One Christian goal for government is that it would allow Christians to practice their faith "in every way," in every area of life. Persecuted Christians around the world don't have this freedom. We ought to pray that God, through their governments, would give it to them—and that Christians in Western nations would get to keep their existing religious freedoms. There's no guarantee that this will happen. We should pray.

We should pray, for example, that Christian businesses such as Hobby Lobby and Elane Photography would be free to do their work in accordance with their Christian principles. Hobby Lobby is a massive multibillion dollar corporation owned by Christians. Elane Photography (which was mentioned in Chapter 14) is a mom-and-pop small business, also owned by Christians. Both have come under legal pressure because the owners have tried to run their businesses consistently with their Christian values. Hobby Lobby faced a court case because it would not provide abortifacient contraceptives* to employees (employees who are already paid nearly double the minimum wage, along with generous health insurance). Elane Photography faced a court case because the owners, a married couple, refused to do the photography for a homosexual wedding. (They were willing to serve homosexual customers but felt that supporting a same-sex marriage ceremony was not compatible with their beliefs.)

abortifacient contraceptive: *a means of birth control that causes an abortion*

A society that won't allow Christian businesspeople to do business in a Christian way is not a society at peace or a society in which people—including businesspeople—can live "godly" lives "in every way." So we should pray for change.

PRESSING FOR GOD'S WILL TO BE DONE

Prayer is the most powerful thing Christians can do because God is the most powerful force in human politics. "The king's heart is a stream of water in the hand of the Lord; he turns it wherever he will" (Prov. 21:1). But when we pray, God isn't required to operate directly, as it were—changing individual politicians' minds or sending hurricanes to block certain legislators from participating in important votes. God can do that if He wants to, of course, but more often His pattern seems to be to use "means." That's us. We can be instruments in God's hands. While we pray, we can vote, we can protest, we can organize, we can write, we can debate—and most readers of this book can (one day) run for office. Under our great King, Christians have a responsibility to press for the King's laws to be obeyed in every nation.

Theonomy

The idea of "pressing for the King's laws to be obeyed" makes many people, including Christians, uncomfortable. They object that it will lead to **theocracy** (God-rule) or **theonomy** ("God's law"). So some careful distinctions need to be made. Theonomists believe that the Old Testament law as a whole, including penalties like stoning, is still in force today unless the New Testament has explicitly stated otherwise. Theonomists want Gentile nations to use the Old Testament to establish their laws.[15] Leading theonomist Greg Bahnsen has written, "We must recognize the continuing obligation of civil magistrates to obey and enforce the relevant laws of the Old Testament, including the penal sanctions specified by the just Judge of all the earth."[16]

But theonomists have made a grave mistake: not even Christians, much less the unsaved, are bound by the Mosaic law today as their covenant. The Mosaic law has been replaced by the New Covenant (see "Free from the Law" on page 77; cf. Rom. 7:4–6; 1 Cor. 9:21; 2 Cor. 3:3). It is therefore wrong to seek to impose the Mosaic Covenant with its penalties on Gentile nations. Theonomists are also too optimistic about Christians' ability to transform the world. The New Testament promises suffering and persecution for God's people in the present age (cf. 2 Tim. 3:12).

Even though theonomists have made some significant errors, we shouldn't overreact. Christians should not be afraid to say publicly what the Bible says about public matters.

Pluralism

Other Christians feel uncomfortable appealing to the Bible in matters of public policy because they think there's no point. Most people in the public square don't believe the Bible is God's Word, and if we appeal to it, they'll immediately cry foul: "You're trying to impose your religious beliefs on us!"

Influential legal theorist John Rawls (one of the authors of the "Philosopher's Brief" quoted above) argued that in a pluralist society (one containing multiple belief systems), everybody should leave "comprehensive doctrines" out of public discussion. He said that people should make their arguments on reasonable, nonreligious grounds. In other words, you can't say, "We should limit divorce because God disapproves of it in Scripture." You must say instead, "We should limit divorce because it has a statistically negative impact on high school test scores, teen pregnancy rates, and future economic outcomes." Those are "secular" reasons.

But Rawls's view fails. First, as this book has pointed out repeatedly, there is no neutral moral ground where we can all live in peace. Everybody has a worldview, a viewpoint. To tell Christians that they can't bring up the biblical one is to stack the deck against us before we get to say a word.

Second, everybody knows that Scripture is the Christian's ultimate authority. So when Christians try to argue against abortion or same-sex marriage in a secular way, other people will see through the attempt. They'll call us out for trying to smuggle our Christian beliefs into the debate, and they'll criticize us for hypocritically pretending to be secular. That's precisely what has happened with the intelligent design (ID) movement.* Not all ID proponents are even Christians, but their whole effort is still seen by secularists as a way to sneak biblical creationism into public schools.

intelligent design: *the view that evolution could not have produced the orderliness and complexity of the universe, indicating that there was an intelligent cause*

It would be much better for Christians—as graciously and carefully as they can—to mount arguments against secularism, appealing to Scripture as their final authority. When little boys want to identify as female at their public school, using the girls' restrooms and joining girls' sports teams (this is happening),[17] we can say, "God made us male and female, and the way God created the world is the standard by which we judge the way things ought to be."

Christians don't have to tear down the entire established order to root out secularism. Secularists, by God's common grace, are right about a great number of things. And Christians should not attempt to persecute (or exile, or stone) secularists; that's not how Christ's kingdom advances in this age. We should work for the good of secularists—even Muslims and other non-Christians of all sorts. Our love for those neighbors

FREE FROM THE LAW?

In 1 Corinthians 9:20, Paul indicates that as a Christian he was not under the Mosaic law. Hebrews 8:13 teaches that the New Covenant made the old Mosaic Covenant "obsolete" and "ready to vanish away."

But neither Paul nor the author of Hebrews (if he was someone other than Paul) is teaching that the Christian is free from all law. Paul hastens on to say that he wasn't "outside the law of God, but under the law of Christ" (1 Cor. 9:21). And the New Covenant in Hebrews quotes God's promise, "I will put my laws into their minds, and write them on their hearts" (Heb. 8:10).

The Mosaic law was a particular application of God's law to a specific people in a particular culture at a particular time in a particular stage in redemptive history. This means that we should expect strong similarities between God's expectations then and now as well as some differences. For instance, laws against murder and adultery are rooted in God's eternal will. Murder does not become acceptable under the New Covenant. But modern governments that seek to conform their laws to God's laws do not need to set up cities of refuge, nor do modern penal codes need to prescribe stoning for adultery (cf. Lev. 20:10; Deut. 22:23–24). Instead the Mosaic law serves, in part, as an example of how to apply God's law to people who live in many different cultures and at different times in God's plan of redemption. It is still a source of guidance even though Christians are under a different covenant.

will make our efforts at political renewal harder to criticize.

Preserve the Good, Reform the Evil

Christ is King, but for now He does His work in a fallen world. Government and citizenry alike are full of sinners. A perfect utopia, therefore, simply won't happen in this age. Christians are right, then, to be skeptical about revolutions that promise utopia, as the French Revolution did. Those revolutionaries had lofty goals for the new society that they wanted to create, but their push for change degenerated into a reign of terror.

A little bit at a time. Because of sin, some "solutions" only make problems worse. Wise Christians will want assurances that a proposed solution will really be a net positive in the end. Small changes worked out over a period of time are often best. And, generally speaking, reforms are most effective when tried first on a local level before being rolled out on a large scale. If something goes wrong, as surely it will, the impact will be limited. Whatever goes right can spread gradually to other places.

This means that a Christian political program will have two prongs. It will seek to preserve what's good while seeking to reform what's evil. Christians should recognize "that no existing social, political or economic arrangement is ever completely without redeeming features."[20] The reason for this is clear: cultures are built by God's image-bearers working with God's good creation. Even in a fallen world, good remains in every culture. These are the features that the Christian wishes to conserve and protect from revolutionary policies that may sweep away the good with the bad. Since cultures extend in time as well as place, Christians value the insights of tradition, realizing that tradition contains a great deal of wisdom and practical life experience.

And yet the people of earlier generations were no less prone to sin and error than people in our times. While appreciating tradition, Christians recognize that the past was not uniformly better than the present. The Creation Mandate implies that humans will always be working to improve creation and culture; Christians also need to press for the righting of injustices. This is one of the purposes of government.

Slavery as an example. The tiny New Testament book of Philemon provides a key example of preserving the good and reforming the evil. In it, the apostle Paul counsels a Christian slave-owner, Philemon, on what to do with his runaway slave, Onesi-

WHY CAN'T WE JUST GET ALONG?

As religious (and irreligious) diversity within nations increases, standards of morality are no longer shared. "Culture wars" are the result, battles that haven't yet resulted in the shedding of blood.[18] Why can't people agree to disagree? Where is the tolerance that Americans, at least, used to practice with one another?

Tolerance itself has become a battleground in America. Theologian D. A. Carson argues that a new definition of tolerance is overtaking the old one. Under the old regime, Protestants, Catholics, Jews, and rationalists all accepted the rights of their neighbors to hold their beliefs—even though they firmly believed that their neighbors were wrong and they were right. Under the new tolerance one may no longer hold firmly to his own beliefs or morality; he must concede that all beliefs or morality are potentially true. To say someone is wrong is intolerant. Of course, this view cannot be lived out consistently. Usually the morality of the powerful ends up being smuggled in.[19]

For the Christian, tolerance cannot be an ultimate value. In the end Christ will tolerate no false belief or immorality. But at present Christians walk a fine line. On the one hand, the Christian has no confidence that rulers are going to embrace true religion, so tolerance is a good that enables Christians to live and worship around the world. Christians can champion religious freedom because without it many Christians would not be free to live and worship God as they should.

On the other hand, Christians recognize that the gospel is something that must be received, not enforced. It is impossible to force someone to have faith. This is another reason to champion freedom of religion. And yet, certain religious practices cannot be tolerated. It is good to not tolerate the burning of widows, polygamy, human sacrifice, or conversion by the sword even though all these have been claimed as religious practices by various religions. Even tolerance is judgmental. In making these judgments, Christians have no obedient option except to articulate God's viewpoint.

mus. Onesimus had become a Christian during his flight, and he had connected with Paul in Rome. Paul loves Onesimus as a son and wishes for him to be able to stay. But he still sends him back to his master. Some people look at this fact—along with New Testament instructions that tell slaves not to be too concerned about their status as slaves (1 Cor. 7:21) and to obey even cruel masters (1 Pet. 2:18)—and they wonder if the New Testament supports slavery.

It doesn't. This becomes clearer when you realize that the Old Testament permitted only certain types of servitude in Israel. No one was to be made a slave against his own will. Israelites who became slaves typically did so to work off debts. But they could be held only for six years, and in the seventh the master was not only to free them but was also to provide for them generously, so they could set up an independent life again (Deut. 15:12–14). Only if the slave requested it—perhaps because he valued the financial security of working for a good master—could he be someone's slave for life. In contrast, kidnapping someone or buying, selling, or possessing such a stolen person was a capital crime in Israel (Exod. 21:16). The Bible cannot be used to justify the kind of slavery that existed in the United States, a kind of slavery that began with man-stealing and continued as a permanent, race-based institution.

Turning back to the New Testament, many Bible interpreters have recognized that Paul sowed the seeds of slavery's demise in his dealings with Philemon and Onesimus. Paul instructed Philemon to receive Onesimus back not merely as a slave, but as a brother (Philem. 1:16). Paul forbade Christian masters to intimidate or threaten their slaves (Eph. 6:9)—which makes beating absolutely out of the question. Further, masters are told to remember that they are slaves to their heavenly Master; earthly masters don't have a status higher than their slaves in the eyes of God:

> Masters, . . . stop your threatening, knowing that he who is both their Master and yours is in heaven, and that there is no partiality with him. (Eph. 6:9)

Advising a slave revolt in the first century would have been unwise. It would have made conditions for the slaves worse, not better. Thus the New Testament preserves the good (a stable, functioning social order) and begins to reform the evil (slavery). Furthermore, planting the seeds of slavery's demise actually worked. It led to the virtual elimination of slavery in medieval Europe—though sinners, being sinners, found other means of oppression. And when slavery was revived among Europeans during the Enlightenment, Christian arguments again played a large role in this second demise.

FOUR CHRISTIAN POLITICAL VIRTUES

After the Supreme Court legalized elective abortion in 1973, Christians began to organize politically to end abortion . . . or at least limit it. But the defeat-versus-limit question has caused consternation for some Christians: "How can you compromise with baby-killers?" The answer is that baby steps aren't necessarily compromise. Compromise happens when you give up the long-term goal for a short-term gain, or when you assume that the end justifies the means. The long-term goal of the pro-life movement—ending all abortion—can be achieved slowly. In fact, the movement has seen remarkable success in restricting abortion. If the pro-life movement had taken an all-or-nothing approach, many people would not be alive today. Instead, pro-lifers have worked assiduously and creatively to come up with legal ways to protect unborn children. Some laws call for abortion doctors to have admitting privileges at local hospitals. Others require parental consent or a waiting period. And some prohibit abortion after "viability," the point at which babies can possibly survive outside the womb (twenty-two weeks). Some pro-life legal efforts have been unsuccessful, but overall progress on the issue in America has been undeniable.

Prudence

Prudence means understanding your situation, seeing what good can be accomplished in it, knowing what options are both morally legitimate and likely successful—and then pursuing the wisest goal in the wisest way. Prudence is a key virtue for Christians involved in politics (Prov. 8:12–16). The Bible does not provide specific revelation about how to frame laws, manage campaigns, or even who to vote for in a presidential election. But the Bible was written to help Christians live wisely in every aspect of their lives. Prudence is knowing the best way to get from here to wherever you ought to be.

For example, Christians and radical feminists fundamentally disagree about the structure of the family and the roles of men and women in society. But they both see pornography as degrading, and both oppose domestic abuse of women. A politically prudent Christian can reach across the aisle and cooperate with someone who wants the same biblical things even if their motivations are ultimately different.

Boldness, Humility, and Respect

Of course, some fundamental disagreements will always remain. Cooperation is sometimes impossible. On these matters the Christian should state the Christian position boldly, but not brashly. Repeatedly, Scripture urges Christians to engage their opponents humbly and respectfully. As the apostle Paul told one pastor,

> Remind [Christians] to be submissive to rulers and authorities, to be obedient, to be ready for every good work, to speak evil of no one, to avoid quarreling, to be gentle, and to show perfect courtesy toward all people. For we ourselves were once foolish, disobedient, led astray, slaves to various passions and pleasures, passing our days in malice and envy, hated by others and hating one another. (Titus 3:1–3)

If Christians participated in political life with these virtues, they would stand out in a positive way. Sadly, too often Christians speak with the same harshness, quarrelsomeness, and sometimes even untruthfulness about their political opponents as the lost world does. Even under a ruler such as Nero, who had starkly unchristian policies, Peter says to "honor the emperor" (1 Pet. 2:17).

THE RIGHT TO REVOLT?

What if a government gets to be so bad that people begin to talk about revolution? Should Christians join in? Should they lead the effort?

Opinions on Revolution

Christians have historically disagreed over this matter.[21] Martin Luther said no. Christians have a duty to disobey the government only when it requires them to disobey God. They should pray and speak out against injustice, but they should not revolt. Luther gave four reasons for this position. First, rulers are accountable to God, and God will judge those rulers who are disobedient. Second, rebellions rarely bring the benefits that people want. Luther says, "For insurrection lacks discernment; it generally harms the innocent more than the guilty." Third, God has explicitly forbidden rebellion in Scripture (Deut. 32:3–5; Rom. 12:19). Fourth, when Christians rebel, it undermines their gospel witness.[22] Luther concurred with church fathers such as Justin Martyr—and most of medieval Christendom—in this opinion.[23]

Reformer John Calvin agreed with Luther, but he was willing for lower-level officials to actively oppose a tyrant. And some of Calvin's followers took that a step further. They argued that rulers and their people were bound together by a covenant. A ruler who violated the covenant lost the right to rule, and political leaders under him could ensure that he left office.[24]

Enlightenment philosopher John Locke built on this idea in his discussion of a social contract and a right to rebellion.[25] A tyrant ceases to be a king, he argued—so rebellion against him ceases to be true rebellion.[26]

The problem with Locke's view is that the concept of a covenant or contract between the ruler and the people is not found in Scripture. Babylon and Rome didn't get their rule over Israel through a social contract; God gave it to them directly (Ezra 5:12). The Bible even recognizes the rule of kings who got it by immoral means (for example, Jehu in 2 Kings 9:14–37). Romans 13 could hardly be more direct:

> Let every person be subject to the governing authorities. For there is no authority except from God, and those that exist have been instituted by God. Therefore whoever resists the authorities resists what God has appointed, and those who resist will incur judgment. (Rom. 13:1–2)

When Israel started demanding a king, God warned them about what life under a king would be like. And He never made provisions for a coup d'état*(coo day TAH) (1 Sam. 8:11–17). Even David, who had been designated by God as the next king of Israel, would not fight against the reigning king because he was the Lord's anointed (1 Sam. 24:9–11).

coup d'état: *a sudden and usually violent attempt by a small group of people to overthrow the government*

History of Revolutions

Luther's concern that revolutions typically do more harm than good is borne out by modern history all over the globe. This does not mean Christians must submissively do whatever a government asks. Sometimes, Christians must obey divine authority rather than human authorities (Acts 5:29). In these cases, Christians must hope that God will deliver them, or they must simply suffer whatever punishment comes (Dan. 2:18; 6:22). Shadrach, Meshach, and Abednego got the balance just right:

> Our God whom we serve is able to deliver us from the burning fiery furnace, and he will deliver us out of your hand, O king. But if not, be it known to you, O king, that we will not serve your gods or worship the golden image that you have set up. (Dan. 3:17–18)

What would've happened in Nazi Germany if all the Christians—and there were many—had been Shadrachs, Meshachs, and Abednegos? What if they had spoken boldly against Hitler's tyranny? What if Christian businessmen had insisted on continuing to serve Jewish customers? What if Christian soldiers had refused to fight an unjust war? What if Christian owners of chemical plants had declined to supply Zyklon B for the gas chambers? There are ways to resist evil government apart from outright rebellion and insurrection.

"WHILE HISTORY DOES NOT EXACTLY REPEAT ITSELF, IT DOES TEND TO RHYME."[27]

—ED PANOSIAN

FINAL REDEMPTION

Right now our job as Christians is to press for prudent reforms that push the world in small ways toward what it will look like one day when Christ redeems it. Despite the frustrations and setbacks that will most certainly come, we must continue to work. As with every other cultural activity mentioned in this book, our belief in the future coming of Christ doesn't remove our responsibility to submit to Christ's rule now in every way we can, even in politics and government. But only Christ's coming can achieve final redemption.

In the dark days of the judges, Hannah sang a song that proclaimed the power of God to exalt the humble and to humiliate mighty oppressors. Realizing that only the Lord could do this, Hannah closed her song with an appeal for Yahweh to "give strength to his king and exalt the power of his anointed [Messiah]" (1 Sam. 2:10). Hannah's prayer comes at the beginning of the story of King David. And it's through David's descendant, the Messiah, that God promises to "shatter" the nations that oppose Him (Pss. 2, 110).

The prophet Isaiah predicted that this same Messiah—called "Mighty God"—would sit on the throne of David (Isa. 9:6–7). This Davidic king, the Bible says, will rule the world in righteousness (11:3–5; 16:3–5). But Christ will not abolish human government. The climactic verse of the climactic book of the Bible is, "The kingdom of the world has become the kingdom of our Lord and of his Christ, and he shall reign forever and ever" (Rev. 11:15).

The government of God on the renewed earth will be eternal. But interestingly, the government of God will work through the same human dominion God blessed mankind with in Genesis 1:26–28 (cf. Ps. 8:6; Heb. 2:5–10). Daniel prophesied that God's people would themselves have dominion in God's future kingdom (Dan. 7:18, 22, 27). And John says that under the Messiah, the saints "will reign forever and ever" (Rev. 22:5). The twelve disciples in particular, Jesus said, will "sit on twelve thrones, judging the twelve tribes of Israel" (Matt. 19:28).

Revelation 21:24 reveals that there will be "nations" and "kings" throughout all eternity. These kings will bring "the glory and the honor of the nations" into the new Jerusalem (21:26). Kings and their citizens will still have a role to play—as kings and as citizens—for all eternity. This is government redeemed.

THINKING IT THROUGH 18.3

1. What two tasks should Christians engage in regardless of their political situation?
2. What do the terms *theocracy* and *theonomy* mean? Summarize the political philosophy behind them, and explain why it's wrong.
3. Why shouldn't Christians refuse to appeal to the Bible in order to defend their political positions?
4. What should be the two prongs of a Christian political program?
5. What are four Christian political virtues? Choose one virtue and give an example of how it should affect Christian political discourse.

18 CHAPTER REVIEW

TERMS TO REMEMBER

Constantinianism
civil religion
theocracy
theonomy
prudence

Scripture Memory

Revelation 11:15*b*

Making Connections

1. List the five positions on church and state relations.
2. If Christ has assigned different realms of limited authority to the state and church, then how should the church relate to the state?
3. Why is praying the most powerful thing Christians can do in their political involvement?
4. Why can two Christians who have the same basic beliefs and values still disagree about what is a prudent political tactic or appropriate cooperation?

Developing Skills in Apologetics and Worldview

5. Explain whether or not you should participate or how you should participate in the following civil religious activities in the American public square: (a) saying the Pledge of A-llegiance, (b) observing a moment of silence, and (c) praying an interfaith prayer.
6. How should you express a biblical dissatisfaction with corrupt political policies or wicked rulers?

Examining Assumptions and Evidence

7. Why should Christians participate in government even though their task as citizens of Christ's kingdom is to spread the gospel?
8. Why is the secularist exclusion of biblical authority not a neutral position?
9. Differentiate the theonomist position from the position endorsed by this book.
10. How would you differentiate between rebellion and appropriate Christian resistance to wicked rulers?

Becoming a Creative Cultivator

11. Find a news article that opposes Christian moral values. Write a response that is characterized by the Christian virtues of prudence, humility, respect, and boldness. After it's reviewed by your teacher, you may want to submit it as a letter to the editor of the publication or website that published the news article.

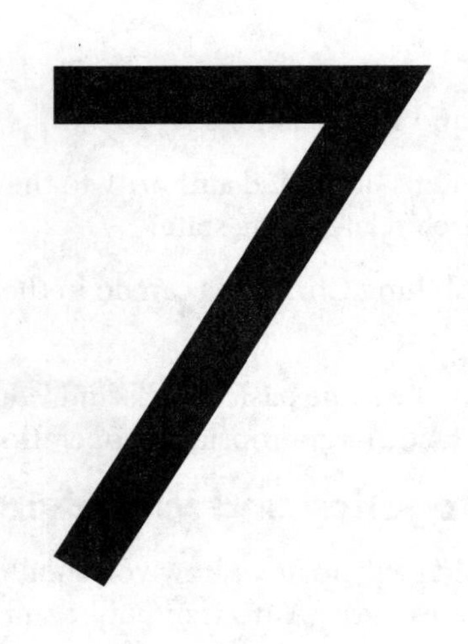

SCIENCE

$E=MC^2$
$E=MC^2$

Chapter Nineteen SCIENCE IS SOMETHING GOD CREATED HUMANS TO DO

Great are the works of the Lord, studied by all who delight in them.

Scripture Memory
Psalm 111:2

19.1 SCIENCE BELONGS TO CHRISTIANITY

Scientism is "excessive belief in the power of scientific knowledge and techniques."[1] That's kind of funny—the very definition of *scientism* is "belief," not "knowledge." And yet adherents of **scientism** commonly claim, "Faith is the great cop-out, the great excuse to evade the need to think and evaluate evidence."[2] But scientism is a faith, a worldview, like any religion.

Atheistic, materialistic scientism even has saints and martyrs, just like other belief systems. Watch the most recent incarnation of the *Cosmos* documentary, and you'll meet one: Giordano Bruno (c.1548–1600). As *Cosmos* presents it in a series of animations, Bruno was persecuted by cartoonishly wicked Christian clerics for daring to suggest that the universe might be infinite and that the stars might have their own planets. The way *Cosmos* tells it, Bruno was burned at the stake for his crimes against Christian dogma, becoming one of the first people to die for the one true science.[3]

Bruno and Galileo—as well as others—are often made to fit what science historian Lawrence Principe calls a "widespread myth," namely that "during the 16th and 17th centuries and during the Middle Ages, there was . . . a camp of 'scientists' struggling to break free of the repression of 'religionists.'" Principe calls stories like the one *Cosmos* tells about Bruno "folkloristic fabrications."[4]

Instead of "religion" and "science" being at war in the Renaissance period, Principe says, "the investigators of nature were themselves religious people,"[5] and many clergy members were among them. In fact, "theological motivations—the desire to read [divine] messages in the Book of Nature—provided the single greatest driving force for scientific inquiry throughout the entire early modern period."[6]

Principe shows in his book *The Scientific Revolution* that Christianity didn't hinder science; it propelled it. As well it should have—and still should—because science is something God created humans to do.

SCIENCE AS SOMETHING GOD CREATED HUMANS TO DO

You might be called by God Himself to study the "book of nature" by becoming a working chemist, botanist, geologist, or one of the countless other scientific callings. Don't let the myth of a necessary conflict between science and religion stop you from answering that call.

And don't let any other secularizing ideas about science stop you either. The only truly good reasons to be a scientist are, in fact, *Christian* reasons—and that doesn't mean merely using science as a witnessing tool (although you can and should do this). Your actual day-to-day work with chlorophyll, hydrofluorocarbons, computer models, and DNA sequencers ought to be motivated precisely by your Christianity.

Once there was a Christian chemist who worked at Milliken, a major textile manufacturing company, who put his head on his pillow every night wondering whether he was doing any good. Christ's kingdom wasn't expanding in any obvious ways because

Out of love for their lost neighbors, Christian chemists should strive to develop better carpet fibers.

of his work. All the carpet fibers he refined and all the pipe casings he developed didn't seem to have anything to do with Jesus Christ.[7] He began considering a job change—maybe he was called to full-time ministry?

But look at the public relations material on the Milliken website that describes the work of scientists at the company:

> Deep Science at Milliken combines the structure and order of the scientific method with immense curiosity and creativity. It penetrates the surface to get to the underlying physics and chemistry that constitute our world. Science extends our understanding of the fundamental nature of things, enabling us to benefit humanity by creating new technologies that are both more effective and friendlier to nature.[8]

This paragraph borrows and relies on multiple Christian ideas: (1) Only the Christian worldview guarantees that the scientist will find "structure" and "order" in creation. (2) Curiosity is an essential quality for obeying the Creation Mandate. (3) Creativity is part of our nature as God's image-bearers. (4) Science, though it doesn't actually get down to "the fundamental nature of things," surely does enable us to "benefit humanity" through technology. Science is a key way to love our neighbors as ourselves.

Lying hidden in his own company's promo materials are some hints to the Milliken chemist that his work *does* have everything to do with his faith. Science is a major tool helping us to obey the Creation Mandate. We are supposed to "fill the earth and subdue it." In fact, the only way we *can* fill it is by subduing it. Population growth is a good thing that nonetheless brings challenges: where will all these people get sufficient food, clean water, and adequate shelter? The chemists at Milliken get to focus on one important element of the shelter question: how can a growing population get affordable, durable, clean flooring for their homes and workplaces? Science—along with politics, economics, and other fields—helps provide good solutions to those problems.

Christianity is not a threat to science. Why would God threaten something He created us to do? Science is just the label we give to some of the most useful methods of subduing creation and ruling over it. Those methods didn't get invented in 1900—or 1600. They began, in seed form, in the Garden of Eden before the Fall.

> God blessed them. And God said to them, "Be fruitful and multiply and fill the earth and subdue it, and have dominion over the fish of the sea and over the birds of the heavens and over every living thing that moves on the earth." (Gen. 1:28)

Mankind cannot possibly take dominion over the wide array of created things—fish, birds, insects—without a set of skills we have come to call "scientific." Science is something God created humans to do.

THREE CHRISTIAN ASSUMPTIONS THAT MAKE SCIENCE POSSIBLE

Christianity isn't merely compatible with science; it is essential to it. The religion of the Bible is the foundation that makes science possible. Consider three assumptions, drawn straight from a biblical worldview, without which science would be impossible.

Assumption 1: Nature Is Orderly

The first assumption is that **nature is predictable, orderly, and governed by laws.** God said to Noah,

> While the earth remains, seedtime and harvest, cold and heat, summer and winter, day and night, shall not cease. (Gen. 8:22)

"There is superficial conflict but deep concord between science and theistic religion, but superficial concord and deep conflict between science and naturalism."[9]

—ALVIN PLANTINGA

He told Jeremiah that He had made a "covenant with day and night and the fixed order of heaven and earth" (Jer. 33:25).

There was a time in Western history—in that portion of the premodern era called the Middle Ages—when it was actually difficult being an unbeliever. It wasn't just that you were surrounded by people who believed in God or that social pressure was put on you to believe (though that was all true), it was that your whole thought world was structured by and in God. Other views seemed utterly implausible. The word *atheist* didn't even enter the English language until the late sixteenth century. God was a given.

It was, in fact, the order and rationality of Western civilization's God that became the major basis for modern science. As Lesslie Newbigin, a Christian thinker and missionary to India, put it,

> Historians of science have devoted much thought to the question why the marvelous intellectual powers of the Greeks, the Chinese, the Indians, and the Egyptians, in spite of their achievements in science and mathematics, did not give rise to the self-sustaining science which has dominated our [Western] culture for the past two hundred years.[10]

A big part of the answer seems to be this: Christianity provided assurance that the apparent contradictions of our experience can be resolved. If my body temperature is 98.6° F one day and 99.3° the next, there's a rational explanation to be found. So while Western alchemists, astrologers, and naturalists were poking around God's world and discovering its open secrets—while they were becoming what we today call "scientists"—other worldviews around the globe kept equally intelligent people in their armchairs. Why should someone who believes that "all that exists is emanation from primal being"[11] (Newbigin's description of Hindu philosophy) bother to perform experiments? Why should animists work to discover the properties of granite, when everybody knows that the granite spirit controls those properties at his whim?

It's Christianity that allows chemists at Milliken to do their work with the confidence that the processes they perform in a lab in 2019 will yield the same results when they hit the manufacturing floor in 2021.

The Roman Catholic Jesuit order produced numerous mathematicians, scientists, and educational institutions in the early modern era. Whatever their theological errors, they did have a sound motto: "To find God in all things." Science historian Lawrence Principe comments, "While Jesuits emphasized this incentive, it was not unique to them—it undergirded virtually the entire Scientific Revolution." [12]

One clarification is needed here: the Christian view of divine order in creation is not "uniformitarian." Christians do not believe that God set up the laws of the universe, wound it up, and let it go. (That's deism, remember.) God still rules over His own natural laws, and He can suspend them or stretch them if He desires. That's what we call a "miracle." Non-Christians may see the supernatural miracles in the Bible and conclude that Christianity does not teach an orderly universe. But the miracles are viewed in the Bible as remarkable happenings precisely because they are exceptions to the general rules of God's action in the world.

There are Christians who step into the deistic ditch, however. Says theologian Vern Poythress,

> Christians have sometimes adopted an unbiblical concept of God that moves him one step out of the way of our ordinary affairs. We ourselves may think of "scientific law" or "natural law" as a kind of cosmic mechanism or impersonal clockwork that runs the world most of the time, while God is on vacation. God comes and acts only rarely through miracle. But this is not biblical. "You cause the grass to grow for the livestock" (Ps. 104:14). "He gives snow like wool" (Ps. 147:16). Let us not forget it. If we ourselves recovered a robust doctrine of God's involvement in daily caring for his world in detail, we would find ourselves in a much better position to dialogue with atheist scientists who rely on that same care.[13]

God acts directly to sustain the order He created. This is the foundation on which every chemist at Milliken stands—and at least one of them should know it.

Assumption 2: Humans Are Capable

The second assumption drawn from Christianity and without which science could not exist is that **the human mind is capable of creatively describing the predictable natural order in useful ways** (Gen. 1:27). We're able to study our world and imagine future possibilities. There are some problems with wood floors—so we invent rugs, then carpets, then Scotchgard. There are some problems with our maternal survival rates—so we invent antiseptics and train obstetricians. There are some problems with our commute times and our fuel costs—so we invent superhighways and efficient vehicles.

Because we are made in God's image, we can approach nature the same way a mechanically minded kid approaches a lawnmower engine. He's thinking, "A human being like me designed this thing and put it together, so I should be able to take it apart, put it back together, and figure out how it works."

Likewise, cells and galaxies are complicated. But, ultimately, an Engineer with a mind like ours put them together. In principle, we should be able to figure out how they work. Human minds are patterned after the divine mind, so God's creations should be understandable and usable by the people made in His image.

From the atheistic viewpoint of scientism, whatever produced the universe is something totally different from us. It's an impersonal force or a huge bang. Imagine a lawnmower engine "built" by a tornado blowing stuff around a junkyard—it would be unreasonable to expect anyone to be able to understand how it works. Adding in the "deep time" that modern science relies on doesn't change that fact. Even a billion tornadoes blowing stuff around a billion junkyards for a billion years can't "design" anything.

Science relies on the predictability of the natural world, and yet it thrives on something unpredictable: human creativity. Alexander Fleming discovered the first antibiotic (penicillin) by accident while pursuing the somewhat odd task of making small paintings using microbes in petri dishes. Fleming noticed a fungus growing in one of his little pieces of petri-dish art that was killing bacteria. Other researchers had seen the same thing and thought nothing of it. But "Fleming's discovery of the effects of penicillin, the compound produced by the fungus, was a function of his eye for the rare, an artist's eye."[14] It was his God-given creativity that gave us penicillin, a life-saving drug without which you might never have been born. (The great-grandmother of the author of this chapter died of an infected tooth in 1935 because penicillin hadn't yet been introduced.)

Humans are capable of discovering new ways to use the predictability of the natural order.

Assumption 3: Humans Have a Right to Use Nature

The third (ultimately Christian) assumption without which science is not possible is that **human beings have the right and the responsibility to rearrange nature in order to meet their needs**.

What gives humans the right to capture or kill an animal, or to cut down a tree?

It's not *what* gives us the right, but *who*. God did. He gave humans dominion over the earth, even over animals that don't deserve to die. If this point seems obvious to you, it shouldn't. Not today, when people as prominent as England's Prince Phillip can say, "In the event that I am reincarnated, I would like to return as a deadly virus, in order to contribute something to solve overpopulation."[15] Many people are openly questioning whether or not humans have a right to change the environment or even to kill animals.

Humans do not have a right, of course, to destroy our planet or to commit cruelty against animals (Prov. 12:10). But if you're going to take a strictly rigorous approach to science, especially experimental biology, you will have to put bacteria and lab mice into positions they did not choose to be in. The relationship between humans and the rest of creation, even and especially living creation, is one the Bible calls "rule" or "dominion" both before the Fall (Gen. 1:28) and after it (Gen. 9:2–4). Anyone who's excited about science has to be able to justify that relationship. And unbelievers have to borrow from a Christian worldview to do so.

God said to Noah,

> The fear of you and the dread of you shall be upon every beast of the earth and upon every bird of the heavens, upon everything that creeps on the ground and all the fish of the sea. Into your hand they are delivered. Every moving thing that lives shall be food for you. And as I gave you the green plants, I give you everything. (Gen. 9:2–3)

The Bible clearly gives mankind the right to kill and eat animals. And beyond that, every living thing is "delivered" into our hands. This is a privilege and a responsibility.

Without a Christian worldview, the only authority we have over animals is the unstable position we get by being temporarily on top of the evolutionary heap.

NON-OVERLAPPING MAGISTERIA

Many educated people in Western society have accepted the idea that science and religion will stop bickering and get along only if each stays on its own side of the back seat. Scientist Stephen Jay Gould called this **NOMA**—Non-Overlapping Magisteria (see page 3). In other words, religion gets morality; science gets the physical world. What seems to be a tidy division really isn't, says physicist Paul Davies in a *New York Times* op-ed piece:

> Science has its own faith-based belief system. All science proceeds on the assumption that nature is ordered in a rational and intelligible way. You couldn't be a scientist if you thought the universe was a meaningless jumble of odds and ends haphazardly juxtaposed.[16]

Davies points out that physicists and astronomers who manage to look deeper into the atom or outer space "expect to encounter additional elegant mathematical order. And so far this faith has been justified."[17]

Davies, an atheist, says he has often asked other physicists why physical laws work the way they do. Some reply that it's not a matter of science, and others claim the reason is unknown. Davies finds that the most common response is, "There is no reason they are what they are—they just are." But as Davies says, that's faith![18]

Both science and religion have to believe that something exists beyond the cosmos—such as an inexplicable deity or an array of principles of physics that likewise cannot be explained. Davies doesn't believe that in the beginning, God created the heavens and the earth. But, he says, science cannot claim the "reasonable" high ground: "Until science comes up with a testable theory of the laws of the universe, its claim to be free of faith is manifestly bogus."[19]

It's easy to think that science is a secular field that Christians are trying to break into, perhaps so they can use some of the cultural power science has gained. And secularism is only too happy to tell this version of the story over and over. But it's simply not true. Science requires faith, in two senses: (1) science has to start with some kind of presupposition taken on faith, and (2) the present tradition of science didn't take off until Christian presuppositions allowed it to do so. The Bible reveals that science is a God-created good.

THINKING IT THROUGH 19.1

1. Define *scientism*.
2. Science is a God-established good because it is a tool that enables someone to do what?
3. When did scientific work begin?
4. Summarize the three Christian assumptions that justify scientific work.
5. Why can't science and faith be separated?

19.2 THE ULTIMATE PURPOSES FOR SCIENCE

Every American past a certain age remembers where he was when the Twin Towers in New York were struck by terrorists in jetliners on 9/11. Every American past *another* certain age remembers when man first set foot on the moon on July 20, 1969. Nowadays, space launches don't always make much news. Today's high school students did not experience 9/11, let alone the moon landing. So it may be hard for them to grasp how culturally momentous the Apollo 11 mission was—and not just for Americans. Half a billion people watching around the world felt that the human race itself had accomplished something.[20] That is, of course, why astronaut Neil Armstrong said as he set foot on the lunar surface, "That's one small step for a man, one giant leap for mankind."[21]

Armstrong composed those words not on the long trip to the moon but after his spacecraft had successfully landed. He wasn't sure he would make it, he said, and it seemed presumptuous to compose the words before that moment.

Armstrong wasn't alone among astronauts in being personally moved and humbled by the experience of space. Astronaut Gene Cernan later offered his reflections in a documentary on the moon landings:

> I felt that I was literally standing on a plateau somewhere out there in space, a plateau that science and technology had allowed me to get to. But now what I was seeing, and even more important, what I was feeling at that moment in time—science and technology had no answers for it, literally no answers. Because, there I was—and there you are, there you are, the earth: dynamic, overwhelming, and I felt that the world was just . . . There's too much purpose, too much logic. It was just too beautiful to have happened by accident. There has to be somebody bigger than you, and bigger than me. . . . There has to be a creator of the universe.[22]

Cernan got the message the apostle Paul says humans are supposed to get: "[God's] invisible attributes, namely, his eternal power and divine nature, have been clearly perceived, ever since the creation of the world, in the things that have been made" (Rom. 1:20).

A TOOL FOR DISCOVERING THE GLORY OF GOD

It took the airless clarity of space for Cernan to see one of the two major purposes of science, the glory of the Creator (we'll get to the other one in a moment). God's eternal power and His divinity—His "Godness"—are visible to the naked eye in the beauty of the stars. "The heavens declare the glory of God, and the sky above proclaims his handiwork" (Ps. 19:1).

That glory is also visible every day at the powerful Iguaçu Falls in Brazil, in the majestic Himalayan Mountains, in the stark beauty of the Canadian tundra, in the swaying palms of Hawaii. And God apparently enjoys creating beauty whether others will experience it or not. "There are beautiful things in this universe we have never seen and never will—sunsets on faraway planets and a thousand other splendors known only by their Creator—that have no apparent evangelistic purpose."[23] These beauties simply declare God's glories, even without a human audience (though angels may be watching!).

Zoom in on creation a bit closer, and God's glory is there too. When British evolutionary biologist and geneticist J. B. S. Haldane was asked what nature taught about its Creator, he came up with a mildly mocking response: "God has an inordinate

Iguaçu Falls

Himalayas

Canadian tundra

Hawaii

fondness for beetles."[24] His intent was to suggest that the four hundred thousand beetle species seem like overkill if God created the world. Couldn't God have been satisfied with, you know, ten different kinds of beetle? Haldane wanted to make the God hypothesis look ridiculous.

But what if Haldane was, strictly speaking, right? What if God does have an exuberant affection for His creation, so much so that He had to sort of make Himself stop after four hundred thousand beetle species? (This is true even though many of these species have developed providentially over time through speciation.) We know from Scripture that God created the world out of an overflow of the love and joy within the Trinity. Why shouldn't God lavish some of that love on beetles?

The tools of science are marvelous in their ability to reveal and describe the gloriously creative and unfathomably wise work of God. One study used scientific tools to examine the flight of various kinds of birds. Pigeons made tons of noise as they passed over the highly sensitive microphone; peregrine falcons made substantially less. Owls made almost none, barely a blip. The mice they prey on never hear them coming. Advanced optics and increasingly sensitive and accurate instruments allow us to look closer, listen harder, and even feel more keenly the truths God has placed into His creation. You can't help but marvel when you watch slow-motion footage of an owl in flight.[25] What a design!

There is no "evidence" for a godless, materialistic, evolutionary view of the universe. Make no mistake: the primary truth found in every created thing is the glory of God. It takes willful suppression to deny it (Rom. 1:18).

We live in a fallen world, of course, so science also reveals the insidious effects of human sin on the cosmos. But those effects can never fully cover up the glories. God's eternal power and divine nature are still visible in the creation, and they always have been.

Scientists who love their Creator can take special delight in that glory, and they ought to. One of the marks of a calling to science is the feeling of wonder and joy that even a sixth grader can get when doing a project for the science fair. But we should all have that delight in whatever aspect of the creation our calling leads us to explore. Our world is as beautiful as it is amazing. Science is a God-created good because nature is meant to be, among other things, a pathway straight to the Creator.

A TOOL FOR LOVING YOUR NEIGHBOR

The first major purpose of science fits together with the greatest commandment in the Bible: love the Lord your God with all your heart. But, of course, there's also a second greatest commandment: love your neighbor as yourself. And in the day-in-day-out, rinse-and-repeat process that a Milliken chemist goes through as he searches for the best carpet fiber recipe, his neighbor may be the easiest motivation for him to keep in mind. His neighbor needs flooring, and his neighbor just had a third child and a blown minivan transmission. The chemist can make soft, beautiful, affordable carpet fibers simply because he wants a paycheck, or he can make them for that new neighbor baby who's going to learn how to crawl on that carpet.

The command to love your neighbors is not a command to love them *more* than yourself, but *as much as* yourself (still an extremely difficult command to obey with any consistency). Wanting to earn money isn't necessarily bad, but it's a mark of good character when the neighbor baby motivates a chemist as much as his paycheck does. Many people find it more satisfying to do a significant job—a job that matters to other people—than to do a mindless job, even if it pays better.[26] Work can be absolutely mind-numbing and even dehumanizing, especially if all you're making is more junk for future yard sales.

Science and the technologies based on it are capable of meeting so many genuine human needs. "Love your neighbor as yourself" can carry you very far in scientific work, as it can in most vocations. The second major purpose of science, then, is making wise use of the world for the benefit of your neighbor.

For example, back in the 1950s, concern for the needs of others took the work of one female chemist into every home in America. Ruth R. Benerito was aware of a problem that her male colleagues probably didn't care as much about: the cotton clothing of the day required lots of ironing, a job which fell mostly to women. Dr. Benerito and her team developed the chemical processes for making cloth wrinkle-free. Her work also made clothing resistant to stains and fire. Not so incidentally, this development also revitalized the post-war cotton industry and saved countless American jobs.

Benerito was inducted into the National Inventors Hall of Fame for her work. Certainly she and the dozens of other scientists on that list had various motivations for their work. Perhaps they did their work just for money or prestige, but—at least the way their biographies tell it on the website—it's hard to come to that conclusion.

Mostly, according to the site, they were fascinated by the potential of their innovations and did their work to meet human needs.

This is the Creation Mandate of Genesis 1:28. This is subduing and having dominion. This is cellulose fibers saying like toddlers at naptime, "I don't want to lie down!" and chemists coming along and making them do it for the sake of homemakers everywhere. This is pressing God's world toward its ideal. This is maximizing the usefulness of the creation for the benefit of others. This is science.

HOW YOUR WORK CONNECTS TO GOD AND NEIGHBOR

Loving God and loving your neighbor are the ultimate purposes of every academic discipline and cultural domain, not just of science. The connection between your work (whatever it is) and God's glory is one you must be always exploring, and the connection between your work and the good of your neighbor must also be strong. The work of science generally makes those connections obvious. Science, rightly done, focuses relentlessly on God's creation, and it generally serves some useful purpose for mankind—or it wouldn't get funded. Science is a God-created good that points people to God's glory and makes wise use of the creation for the benefit of other people.

The vast majority of the work of day-to-day scientists, even the non-Christian ones (remember the 1,642 Steves who believe in evolution?), is good. The conflict between "religion" and "science" shouldn't blind us to this fact. But that conflict does matter because it lies at the very foundation of science. Did God make the stuff of creation or not? Is the world fallen, or is there some other explanation for the red teeth and claws we can see in nature? The way you answer these questions will make a difference in your view and practice of science. Your love for God and others must fuel your work, or else your science—no matter how much good it does—will be ultimately immoral.

> ***"Science is increasingly seen as a fully human activity, involving a variety of social, cultural, and religious factors that go beyond mere reason and the senses."***[27]
>
> —PETCHER AND MORRIS

THINKING IT THROUGH 19.2

1. How do the tools of science reveal God's glory?
2. What is one of the marks of a calling to scientific work named in this section?
3. How do the tools of science enable humans to love and serve their neighbors?
4. What are the ultimate purposes for every academic discipline and cultural endeavor?

19.3 CREATIONAL NORMS FOR SCIENCE

The story of the Bible runs from a garden to a city. And there are no cities without science. Even the earliest cities, those showing up in Genesis 4, had to use the basic sciences to build dwellings and appropriate water sources (and sewage systems). No modern city could possibly survive without science. Take just that one essential element of a city: plentiful fresh water. Geologists may find the water. Engineers pump the water across the city. Chemists purify the water. Botanists test the water. Entomologists examine the city reservoir for mosquito larvae. Ichthyolo-

Proto-Indo-European: *the hypothetical language that gave rise to one of the largest language families in our world*

gists study the fish in the reservoir for bloodstream contaminants. (And, of course, astrophysicists *drink* the water and linguists tell us where the word *water* comes from in Proto-Indo-European.* What would the modern city be without *them*?)

As with government and other aspects of human culture, science is not an accident. If the Fall had never happened, science would still have developed. It would have developed differently—and sooner. There would be no conflict between faith and science. But the human race wouldn't have gone on living in gardens forever.

Science is part of the created structure of the cosmos, and it is governed by creational norms—laws God built into His creation. Bend those created structures in the wrong direction, and your science may break. This chapter will suggest five creational norms governing science.

Determining what these creational norms are is not as straightforward as determining the norms for marriage and family life. In that realm, the Bible lays out explicitly what many of the norms are. Science, however, is more like farming (in fact, farming uses the tools of science extensively). The Bible doesn't give instructions for farming, but God has designed a world in which crops grow well under certain conditions and not under others. When the farmer learns how best to grow his crops, it's because "God teaches him" (Isa. 28:26).

The Bible explanation for this is that wisdom was the first of God's creations. Wisdom personified says, "The Lord created me at the beginning of his work, the first of his acts of old. Ages ago I was set up, at the first, before the beginning of the earth" (Prov. 8:22–23, ESV margin). This means that wisdom is closely linked to the creation event. In the verses that follow, Wisdom claims that she existed before the world began, and that she observed God as He ordered His world. The point is that God created wisdom to be built into His world. Those who find wisdom find out how to live in the world.

"WISDOM IS . . . THE FIRST PRINCIPLE OF THE WORLD AND THE PATTERN BY WHICH IT WAS CREATED."[28]

—DUANE GARRETT

God doesn't teach only Christian farmers. And Christians aren't the only ones who do good scientific work. So believers can learn a great deal from the science of non-Christians. And yet, "The fear of the Lord is the beginning of knowledge" (Prov. 1:7) as well as "the beginning of wisdom" (9:10). Wisdom is God's creation, and it is *God* who teaches, through the general revelation of His creation. Those who reject God are going to miss some of the basics for how life works. Thus, science done by Christians should always be similar to and yet different from science done by those who deny their Creator.

FIVE CREATIONAL NORMS FOR SCIENCE

The creational norms for science can be summarized in five principles.

Norm 1: Organized Empirical Study

The first creational norm governing science arises out of the regularity and predictability of God's rule over the created order (Gen. 8:22). The norm is this: humans need to perform organized **empirical** study of the created order in order to find ways to maximize its usefulness. *Empirical* just means "using the five senses." Empirical truths are those things you can know by observation or experience. But science goes beyond common-sense experience by using technological tools that have demonstrated their usefulness over time and by demanding "organized" study.

Any kid can perform the experiment of touching the inside of the refrigerator and then touching the back of it and discovering that one is cold and the other is hot. But it takes a thermometer—a technological tool—to determine the precise difference in temperature. It takes a microscope to see microbes. It takes litmus paper to determine pH. Tools help humans gather information through physical experience.

And science takes things a step further by insisting on "organized" study. It isn't enough for that Milliken chemist to show that a certain carpet fiber holds its color even after exposure to ultraviolet light. He will have to test it rigorously at different temperatures and for different time periods—anything he can think of that may be relevant (remember that creativity is a necessary part of science).

Things you take completely for granted reveal astonishing hidden layers of complexity when you subject them to the light of empirical investigation. Language, for example, is something (almost) every human uses all day every day. But how many language users have any idea about how the Great Vowel Shift affected the pronunciation and spelling of modern English? How many of them understand the actual source of the grammar rules they learn about in English class? Organized, empirical study (sometimes using tools such as spreadsheets, digital recorders, etc.) has proven itself to be the most useful way to answer many specific questions about language.

Norm 2: Model Making

Modern scientists, along with modern Western culture in general, tend to see science as a record of more or less unbroken progress, hindered here and there by religious or economic interests. This is a powerful myth because the current pace of technological and scientific change is obvious to nearly everyone in the world.

But scientists must not fall into the trap of talking as if their ways of viewing atoms and electrons and quantum mechanics are the best and most ultimate descriptions of reality. It is God's Word that defines reality at its most ultimate level. It is that Word that gives order to the creation. We need to step back and admit some of the limitations on our knowledge.

As Thomas Kuhn argues in *The Structure of Scientific Revolutions*, science proceeds through a series of "paradigm shifts," revolutionary changes from model to model. But any claim to have arrived at the final "truth," the bedrock reality, the world "as it truly is in itself," is premature because a new model may be right around the corner. Even a very good model cannot be a complete and perfect representation of the truth. There will always be unanswered questions. "To be accepted as a paradigm, a theory must seem better than its competitors," Kuhn said, "but it need not, and in fact never does, explain all the facts with which it can be confronted."[29]

Kuhn says that models tend to build up "anomalies" over time—inconsistencies, like those that ultimately overturned the Ptolemaic model of the solar system. That geocentric model actually explained some important observations in a very satisfactory way. It explained why the earth seems, to anyone standing on it, to be immovable. It explained why the sun rises and sets. It's a great deal easier, for most human purposes, to say, "What a beautiful sunrise" than to say "The morning appearance of the sun as my location on the earth rotated to reveal it was gorgeous!"

Over time, however, anomalies were found in the geocentric model. Thinkers had to invent more and more complexities to explain away the facts that didn't fit and keep the model working. For example, it would be one thing for the sun to orbit around the earth, but as astronomers began to realize how far away the stars are, they began to see how impossible it was for the stars to be orbiting the earth too.

When Copernicus came along with a new model, the heliocentric model, it was not immediately accepted with open arms. But after Kepler modified it, thinkers began to see how many things it explained well. The heliocentric model became the new paradigm—the new set of assumptions governing astronomers in their work.

However—and this may seem odd at first—the heliocentric model doesn't explain everything. From our perspective on earth, we do revolve around the sun. But what about from the perspective of the Milky Way Galaxy? From that vantage point, both sun and earth are moving. And what about from a standpoint outside the Milky Way? Our whole galaxy is moving. Which vantage point is the "correct" or "ultimate" one?[30] Does the current scientific model explain *all* of the physical forces operating on the earth, from that ultimate vantage point?

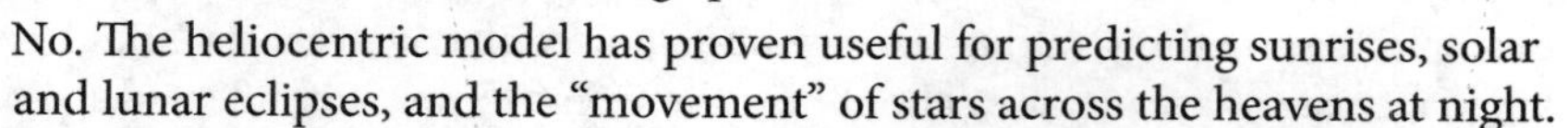

No. The heliocentric model has proven useful for predicting sunrises, solar and lunar eclipses, and the "movement" of stars across the heavens at night. Usefulness, not Truth with a capital *T*, is what we look for in models. The earth really does orbit around the sun, but it would be arrogant of us to think that the heliocentric model is a complete explanation or that this model will never be tweaked. Think of how foolish previous generations of scientists look because of some of their confident predictions. Models change. They go through paradigm shifts. Even the scientific laws we make use of every day are not laws in the same sense that the Ten Commandments are. They're models. They're explanations of the data. Only what God says counts as a universal law.

Solomon noted that humans "cannot find out what God has done from the beginning to the end" (Eccles. 3:11). Not "all the work of God" is comprehensible to us. "Even though a wise man claims to know, he cannot find it out" (8:17). God is the one with the ultimate viewpoint. He's got the whole world in His hands, and He knows all the stars by name. We don't.

So the second creational norm governing science is that science is about "modeling" the natural order. You can never see everything at the same time; there will always be more things outside your view than in it, and humans have no "ultimate" vantage point to stand on. Good science uses models as summaries or packages of the data. These models set the rules and pose the questions that guide scientific inquiry, but they are subject to change.[31]

Norm 3: Communication

In 1982, Buckminster Fuller wrote a book in which he estimated that the sum total of human knowledge doubled between 1500 and 1750. It doubled again, he said, by the beginning of the twentieth century.[32] Today, thanks to computers and the internet, human knowledge is said to be doubling every year or two.[33]

But this deluge of technical data and scientific information isn't worth very much if people don't know about it and can't access it. The work of science, in every scientific field, relies on the work of communication. That's why scholars in various fields have conferences and publish journals; that's why they help make documentaries and why they write books for the general public.

"Of making many books there is no end, and much study is a weariness of the flesh," Solomon said (Eccles. 12:12). It's true that some scholarly articles dig into topics that are so obscure that (1) only three people on earth can understand the article and (2) even they won't read it because it's so boring. And there is such a profusion of writing in the world that hardly anyone can keep up with all the writing in his or her field. There are few Renaissance men (or *polymaths**) left, people who have wide mastery over multiple academic disciplines. Instead, most people develop specialties. Instead of studying bugs, they study beetles. Instead of studying beetles in general, they study bombardier beetles.

polymath: *someone who has in-depth knowledge of a variety of subject areas or disciplines*

"Much study is a weariness" (Eccles. 12:12), but how much is too much? The Bible praises Solomon himself for being a scholar—a kind of early scientist—a careful student of nature in multiple fields:

> God gave Solomon wisdom and understanding beyond measure, and breadth of mind like the sand on the seashore, so that Solomon's wisdom surpassed the wisdom of all the people of the east and all the wisdom of Egypt. . . . He spoke of trees, from the cedar that is in Lebanon to the hyssop that grows out of the wall. He spoke also of beasts, and of birds, and of reptiles, and of fish. (1 Kings 4:29–33)

That's dendrology, zoology, ornithology, herpetology, and ichthyology, respectively. And though it isn't the main point of the passage, note that Solomon "spoke" about his knowledge to others. Ideally, human scholarship in any given field should be like a big team, with people building on and checking each other's work. (Checking academic work is called "peer review," and though it's not failsafe, it's a necessary part of the work of science.) It's certainly possible to write boring, pointless papers, but it isn't possible to run out of useful things to say for other people's benefit.

And if the good of your neighbor is your motivation in publishing—rather than self-promotion or increased grant money—you'll also be more likely to do ethically and morally upright work.

Norm 4: Standardization

In order for a scientist in Botswana or a student in the Andean mountains of Bolivia to benefit from the work of a roboticist in Korea, they have to speak the same scientific language. A unit of mass in one place has to be equivalent to a unit of mass in the other, as much as is humanly possible. That's why there's a literal cylinder of platinum and iridium sitting in a vault in Paris that defines what a kilogram is for the rest of the world. It's the standard.[34] There is also an international prototype meter, but that standard has been replaced. Now the meter is the length of the path travelled by light in vacuum during a time interval of 1/299,792,458 of a second.[35]

What havoc would it wreak on the global economy if the standard for the inch was, say, the length of the current queen of England's thumb? You'd have to make new rulers every time there was a new ruler (think about that for a second). Scientific measurement would be greatly complicated, not to mention housing construction. You've inherited a system of standards that was by no means easy to establish—how do you make *absolutely* sure that a metal rod in America is *exactly* the same length as one in France? And how would you like to make up Latin names for every creature in existence?

For human beings to make use of each other's work in the subduing of the earth, they have to follow the fourth creational norm for science: standardization. This isn't to say that the current standard always deserves its place—the meter is, ultimately, an arbitrary measure. More useful systems of measurement could possibly be invented. But the existence of a standard is itself a necessary part of science.

The use of international standards is, in part, a humble recognition that the Creation Mandate is given to all mankind, not just wealthy nations—and not just scientists. We humans need each other—everyone, in every field—to carry out the work of subduing and having dominion.

Norm 5: No Truth Without Goodness and Beauty

In the final unit of this book, Culture and the Arts, we'll talk a great deal about truth, goodness, and beauty. We'll argue that these three realities are most themselves when they are together. But that's not just true of the arts; it's also true of every domain of human culture, including science.

Science must stay within moral and ethical boundaries. The pursuit of "truth" becomes a lie if it takes a shortcut past goodness. If stem-cell research kills human beings—even tiny, unicellular human beings—it's not worth doing. The serpent was right: Adam and Eve managed to learn some new things they never could have known except by tasting the forbidden fruit. But how much better our world would be if we didn't know those terrible things!

On the positive side: sustainable forestry is a marriage of truth, goodness, and beauty. Totally denuded hillsides, covered in stumps, are ugly. And they're generally useless for any practical purpose. It isn't *good* to use up a resource like trees when it's more than possible to just plant more. Scientific truth isn't worth having at all costs. Some moral costs are too high.

WHAT IS SCIENCE?

No authoritative definition of science exists because there's only one person who knows what science truly ought to be—and He hasn't told us what science is. At least, He hasn't told us in so many words. The Bible contains no "definition" of science. Nonetheless, the elements of this chapter build up to a definition something like this:

> **Science** is the collection of observations, explanations, and models produced through an organized study of nature for the purpose of enabling people to exercise good and wise dominion over God's world for the glory of God and the good of mankind.[36]

Non-Christians have grabbed the cultural mantle of the "scientist." But it belongs to Christians. Science is a biblical calling. Science is a God-created good.

THINKING IT THROUGH 19.3

1. Since the creational norms for science are not explicitly stated in Scripture, what is needed to discover the pattern (the norms) by which the world was created?
2. Because the created order operates with regularity and predictability, which norm governs scientific study?
3. Because of the limitations on human knowledge, which norm governs scientific study?
4. Why is communication an important norm for science?
5. Why is standardization an important norm for science?

19 CHAPTER REVIEW

TERMS TO REMEMBER

scientism
NOMA
empirical
science

Scripture Memory

Psalm 111:2

Making Connections

1. What general tool provides the necessary skills for exercising expert dominion over a wide variety of created things?
2. Give the reference for a Bible verse in which God assures humanity that the earth will remain orderly until the end of time.
3. What are the two main purposes for science (and any other academic discipline or cultural endeavor)?
4. Science is not the best source for understanding the ultimate reality of this world. What is?

Developing Skills in Apologetics and Biblical Worldview

5. How should you respond to someone who challenges the human right to make use of natural resources at all?
6. How should you respond to someone who justifies a scientific endeavor because it will provide answers even though it ignores the sanctity of human life?

Examining Assumptions and Evidence

7. Why is it historically misguided to say that Christianity is at threat to science?
8. What divinely ordained reality, named in this chapter, makes organized empirical study possible?
9. Why can't science provide humans with absolute truth?
10. Why are communication and standardization necessary for scientific work?

Creative Cultivation

11. Suppose you're a member of a team of scientists and engineers that has been assigned the goal of developing a more efficient way to irrigate fields so as to minimize waste through evaporation and runoff. Briefly describe how creational norms would influence the different aspects of your work.

Chapter Twenty **FALLEN SCIENCE**

They exchanged the truth about God for a lie and worshiped and served the creature rather than the Creator, who is blessed forever! Amen.

Scripture Memory
Romans 1:25

20.1 SCIENCE IS FALLEN

A fascinating book titled *Yesterday's Tomorrows: Past Visions of the American Future* is full of pictures of what people once envisioned the future would be like. The things people in 1950 thought we'd have by now are sometimes silly: flying cars, hose-washable indoor furniture, robotic servants. Those dreams often tell us more about the people who had them than they do about us. But people in the past sometimes predicted the future pretty well: computers in your pocket, videophones, online shopping.

One thing that strikes any reader of *Yesterday's Tomorrows* is the sheer optimism of American culture. Americans shot for the moon, and they made it. Not only did they make it, but they did it at a time when even the vision of the computers of the future (as seen, for example, in the original *Star Trek*) was primitive. The moon landing was an incredible accomplishment, perhaps the crowning achievement on the huge list of US scientific and technological successes.

No one alive in America can ignore those successes. They take us—and go with us—everywhere. A Frenchman actually coined the phrase, but it is a very American thing to say: "Every day, in every way, I am becoming better and better."[1]

Americans are, by constitution, not as interested in thinking about the dark side of their scientific and cultural advances. The announcer on pharmaceutical commercials rhapsodizes about the drug's benefits, but he races through the side effects in a muted voice. We like to trumpet our success in curing childhood diseases, but we may fail to mention that geriatric* diseases (such as Alzheimer's and Parkinson's) are on the rise.[2]

Virtually all scientific advances have unintended consequences. We need to train ourselves to ask not only what science and technology give, but what they take away. Technological advances have given us cars with multiple computers and dozens of sensors to prevent and diagnose failures. Whereas cars of a previous generation started to falter when the odometer hit 40,000 miles, now they often don't begin having trouble until 150,000. But there's a downside even to this technological success: cars are now so complicated that they experience bizarre failures that are expensive to fix; most people can't fix their own cars anymore. Scientific and technological gains generally come with some kind of loss, a loss that often goes unnoticed.

The wealth of information at our fingertips still hasn't overcome the downsides of scientific progress. It's like the imaginary animal in the Dr. Dolittle stories, the "pushmi-pullyu."[3] It was a rare two-headed llama, with one head on each end. (This allowed the pushmi-pullyu to eat and talk at the same time without being rude, a valuable skill.) But both heads couldn't walk "forward" at the same time. There is something stopping us from the leap forward we may have expected science to provide.

geriatric: *related to older people or the aging process*

SCIENCE AND THE FALL

From a biblical worldview perspective, we don't have to guess what that hindrance is. We know what's frustrating our science and technology, and it's not Murphy's Law. It's the Fall of man.

> And to Adam [God] said, "Because you have listened to the voice of your wife and have eaten of the tree of which I commanded you, 'You shall not eat of it,' cursed is the ground because of you; in pain you shall eat of it all the days of your life; thorns and thistles it shall bring forth for you; and you shall eat the plants of the field. By the sweat of your face you shall eat bread, till you return to the ground, for out of it you were taken; for you are dust, and to dust you shall return." (Gen. 3:17–19)

After the Fall, all work is at least a little bit frustrating. Farmers can never get rid of all pests and weeds. Editors can never eliminate all typos. Teachers can never produce perfect SAT scores among their students. Piano recitals, plays, and concerts never go exactly right. Moms never have perfect kids (despite what their Facebook profiles portray). Instant riches aren't really . . . instant.

The price of a loaf of bread around the world is the same it has always been: sweat. And in the end, all your hard work doesn't win the battle against the decay of creation. All the bread you eat can't fend off death, the final curse.

That curse affects science in particular in at least six major ways:

1. Science Is Frustrated

The work of science has become frustrating; "thorns and thistles" of all sorts continually get stuck in the gears. Science carries risks and side effects; it encounters speed bumps.

Untold money has been poured into cancer research, but a cure is still highly elusive. Countless other human problems are crying out for solutions. Science in a fallen world doesn't fully deliver on its promise. Science will never sweep us into "the next phase of human evolution," let alone into heaven on earth.

2. Science Is Diverted

A second problem with science in a fallen world is that false and even idolatrous ideas can lead science astray, distracting us from more fruitful scientific work. Adam and Eve didn't know about electrons, and even in an unfallen world it likely would have taken time for the human race to progress toward organized, empirical study of such tiny things. And they wouldn't have accomplished a moon landing the first year.

But an unfallen human race would have avoided certain scientific dead ends. They never would have gotten sidetracked into thinking that one must appease the barley god in order to guarantee a good harvest. They might have tested many ultimately erroneous hypotheses, but the barley god would never have played a role. And unfallen people would not have dabbled in the occult or superstition (Deut. 18:10) by, for example, using divining rods ("dowsing") to locate underground water sources. Bad religious ideas can mislead science.

Bill Nye, a pro-evolution scientist and television personality, has made precisely this complaint about creationists:

> If you want to deny evolution and live in your world that's completely inconsistent with everything we live in the universe, that's fine. But don't make your kids do it, because we need them. We need scientifically literate voters and taxpayers for the future. We need engineers that can build stuff, solve problems.[4]

If Nye were right about evolution, then he would probably be largely right about the negative effects of creationism on science. But since he's wrong, the tables are turned: belief in evolution is what's negatively impacting science, not belief in biblical creationism. Wrong models of the origin of the world can't help but have an impact on someone's scientific work (and on whether someone goes into science in the first place). Evolutionists can do good scientific work by God's common grace, and creationists sometimes do bad work because of their own fallenness. But, other things being equal, the CFR perspective will help rather than hinder good science.

3. Science Has to Study a Fallen World

mitigate: *lessen or reduce*

The work of science is often dedicated to mitigating* the effects of the Fall. If there had been no Fall, there would be no need for cancer research or for sleep studies for apnea patients. Presumably, no one would ever have heard of seismology, and there would be no need for Doppler radar to spot tornadoes. This is another sense in which science is diverted from its original intent. Science is very useful in a fallen world, but just think what it could have done—and will do—in an unfallen world.

4. Science Is Mistrusted

People in the general public who hear about science on the news and read about it on the web or in magazines have been affected by the Fall too. Prejudice may keep such people from acknowledging the value of scientific work. Certain ideas may be so far ahead of their time that it will take two generations before people accept them. In other words, the Fall leads some people to resist the truth or usefulness of a certain scientific model.

When an Ebola outbreak struck West Africa, cutting a deadly path through villages and cities alike, many Westerners clucked to themselves: "If those primitive people would just trust the doctors and accept their preventive measures, they'd save their own lives." Western people often look down on cultures that distrust Western medical science.

But America and Europe have strong pockets of that same distrust, and it isn't limited to hyper-conservatives. Those who call themselves "very liberal" have the highest distrust of genetically modified organisms (GMOs) such as corn and soybeans,[5] and "anti-vaxxers" (people who believe that childhood immunizations are responsible for autism and other maladies) are found at similar rates among liberals and conservatives.[6]

How can someone "know" that childhood vaccines cause autism or that GMOs are dangerous? God hasn't ruled on either matter in Scripture, so it would seem there's only one way to know: organized, empirical study. A nonscientist who has never done or even read such a study would need to have a pretty strong reason for distrusting them.

5. Science Is Exalted

Distrust of science does not seem, however, to be a big problem among educated Western people. Rather, the primary problem is an exaggerated faith in science. People commonly hand science a scepter and a crown that don't belong to it and then ask it to do a job it can't do. Science has become almost a religion in its own right. True science has been largely replaced by "scientism," the belief that the scientific method is the only way to truly know anything. In this view, things that can't be measured can't be truly known.

"We come to know what is real," says prominent atheist and Oxford biologist Richard Dawkins, "in one of three ways."

> We can detect it directly, using our five senses; or indirectly, using our senses aided by special instruments such as telescopes and microscopes; or even more indirectly, by creating models of what might be real and then testing those models to see whether they successfully predict things that we can see (or hear, etc.), with or without the aid of instruments. Ultimately, it always comes back to our senses, one way or another.[7]

People commonly hand science a scepter and crown that don't belong to it and then ask it to do a job it can't do.

Science is something God created humans to do. But not when defined this way. This is science exalted to a status above its Creator. It's a complete reversal of the emphasis of the Bible. "The fear of the Lord"—of a God you cannot see—"is the beginning of knowledge" (Prov. 1:7). Scientism says that seeing is believing. The Bible says that believing is seeing.

> By faith we understand that the universe was created by the word of God, so that what is seen was not made out of things that are visible. . . . And without faith it is impossible to please him, for whoever would draw near to God must believe that he exists and that he rewards those who seek him. (Heb. 11:3, 6)

6. Scientists Are Fallen

Non-Christian intellectual and novelist Kurt Vonnegut once spoke to the graduating class at the Massachusetts Institute of Technology (MIT), a prominent American university. He knew that sitting before him was

> a full house of young people who could do what the magician Merlin could only pretend to do in the Court of King Arthur, in Camelot. They could turn loose or rein in enormous forces (invisible as often as not) in the service or disservice of this or that enterprise.[8]

"In order to survive and even prosper," he told the budding graduates,

> most of you will have to make somebody else's technological dreams come true. . . . My brother got his doctorate [from MIT] in 1938, I think. If he had gone to work in Germany after that, he would have been helping to make Hitler's dreams come true. If he had gone to work in Italy, he would have been helping to make Mussolini's dreams come true. . . . He went to work for a bottle manufacturer in Butler, Pennsylvania, instead. It can make quite a difference not just to you but to humanity: the sort of boss you choose, whose dreams you help come true.[9]

Vonnegut gave an A+ to the scientists and engineers who built Hitler's concentration camps. "They surely solved all the problems set for them."[10] Obviously, excellent scientific work can be given as a service to a violent and even murderous ideology.

But scientists don't just serve fallen people; they *are* fallen people. Ernst Haeckel, a nineteenth-century Darwinist, produced a famous series of drawings of the embryos of various vertebrates. He attempted to validate evolutionary theory by showing that "ontogeny recapitulates phylogeny"—in other words, that embryos go through stages resembling the evolution of their ancestors. But Haeckel deliberately misrepresented certain embryonic lines in order to overstate the similarities; in other words, he lied through his drawings. Haeckel's work has now been discredited, but his illustrations are still used in some secular science textbooks.

It's impossible to say whether scientists are any more or less ethical than people in other professions. And Christians themselves are not free from all temptation to stretch the truth. But this fact must be kept in mind: scientists are fallen.

FRUSTRATED, DIVERTED, MISTRUSTED, EXALTED, AND FALLEN

The tools of science are pointed at a cursed world and put in the hands of fallen people, who create technologies used by other sinners. Add in human limitations—we're not omniscient—and there's a lot of room for error in science.

But God blessed us at creation to fill the earth, subdue it, and have dominion over it. The Fall frustrates that blessing but doesn't remove it. And one day, of course, it will be fully restored.

THINKING IT THROUGH 20.1

1. Why won't science ever be the ultimate savior of humankind?
2. What distracts science from fruitful work?
3. What kind of work must science focus on because the world is fallen?
4. What two extremes represent wrong responses to scientific work?
5. Why must scientists carefully choose the boss for whom they work?

20.2 SCIENTISM: SCIENCE EXALTED

Christians aren't the only people who've noticed how scientism has risen to the status of a new Western religion. One recent book, written largely by non-Christians, is entitled *Scientism: The New Orthodoxy*.

What are the doctrines of this new faith? We can't answer that till we establish the big story (the metanarrative, remember?) out of which those doctrines arise.

> ***"It is a tenet of scientism that only certifiably scientific knowledge counts as real knowledge. All else is mere opinion or nonsense."*** [11]
>
> —RICHARD N. WILLIAMS

Scientism's story is substantially the same as the story of scientific naturalism (or metaphysical naturalism), the idea that matter is all that exists. So once upon a spacetime,* BANG! This particular cycle of existence began. A long, long time later, a few motley planets scattered around the cosmos were in temperate zones around their stars, and life was able to form. An unbelievably long series of minor genetic changes in that life killed most of it off but left enough of it to make us. As the first and only beings with consciousness and language, we can take charge of our environment, and we therefore have a responsibility to do so. Science is the only reliable tool we have for understanding ourselves and our world. One day in the distant future, this cycle of

spacetime: *a mathematical model in physics, combining time and space into a single continuum* the universe will run down and all energy will dissipate. Then, maybe, it will all begin again.

This is the big story of scientism, which generates its own creed: "I believe that matter is all there is, undirected evolution got us here, and only religious bigotry and time stand in science's way as it speeds up the process of human development."

Scientism has done a fairly good job of catechizing* people with its creed. Make any kind of controversial comment on a public news website—maybe something like "Jesus died for our sins and rose again three days later"—and other people will, understandably, respond with variations of "Prove it!" But what do they mean by "prove it"? What, in their minds, counts as proof?

If you respond with some variation of "God said so in the Bible," you'll soon find out how much influence scientism has. You'll very often hear, "That doesn't count as proof! Show me the science!"

One Christian was engaged in just such a discussion with a friendly atheist about the moral status of homosexuality. The Christian objected, on moral grounds, to homosexual acts. The atheist got right to the scientistic point: "By all measurables, children raised by homosexual parents have the same potential as children raised by heterosexual parents. . . . There are no demonstrable effects [from living in a gay household]."[13]

The atheist simply could not see the scientism hidden in his word *demonstrable*. He couldn't even conceive of a way to "demonstrate" something that wasn't a scientific way. Throughout the conversation, he kept coming back to that scientism: "I would [have] to see some research showing two same-sex couples kissing to be psychologically damaging to someone."[14]

Organized empirical study is useful in moral debates (and how children fare in gay households is relevant to that debate[15]). But science isn't ultimate. There are truths—facts—that the scientific method can't see but God can. If Christians implicitly agree to let science be the final court of appeal for truth, they have let their Bibles slip from their hands. They have given science an authority God never gave it. They have exalted science to the status of an idol.

WORSHIPING THE CREATION RATHER THAN THE CREATOR

Steven Pinker, a prominent atheist and a Harvard psychology professor, is the chair of the *American Heritage Dictionary* usage panel. Pinker has said that "the worldview that guides the moral and spiritual values of an educated person today is the worldview given to us by science."[16] And he's right.

But that's wrong. God has given this world natural laws that make science possible. It's idolatrous to believe in these

A FULL DEFINITION OF SCIENTIFIC NATURALISM

Scientific naturalism is "a worldview which holds that there is nothing but natural elements, principles, and relations of the kind studied by the natural sciences, i.e., those required to understand our physical environment by mathematical modelling."[12] This view can also be called "physicalism," which is distinguished from "materialism" by including spacetime, dark matter, and forces and physical energies in its category of "all that exists."

catechizing: *giving formal religious instruction in the dogma of a particular religious group*

THE RELIGION OF REASON, THE CREED OF SCIENCE

Well-known nineteenth-century orator and agnostic Robert Ingersoll actually wrote a "creed of science":

> Superstition is not religion. Belief without evidence is not religion. Faith without facts is not religion. What is religion? To love justice, to long for the right, to love mercy, to pity the suffering, to assist the weak, to forget wrongs and remember benefits—to love the truth, to be sincere, to utter honest words, to love liberty, to wage relentless war against slavery in all its forms, to love wife and child and friend, to make a happy home, to love the beautiful; in art, in nature, to cultivate the mind, to be familiar with the mighty thoughts that genius has expressed, the noble deeds of all the world, to cultivate courage and cheerfulness, to make others happy, to fill life with the splendor of generous acts, the warmth of loving words, to discard error, to destroy prejudice, to receive new truths with gladness, to cultivate hope, to see the calm beyond the storm, the dawn beyond the night, to do the best that can be done and then to be resigned—this is the religion of reason, the creed of science.[17]

laws and yet not believe in the Lawgiver they come from. It's idolatrous to believe in a "cosmos"—an ordered realm—in the first place without believing in the God who gave it order. Humans have always been worshiping created things rather than the creator (Rom. 1:18–31). For most of human history, it was the sun or the moon or the Nile or the eagle that people worshiped; now it's often the cosmos as a whole.

Atheist Richard Dawkins defines biology as "the study of complicated things that give the appearance of having been designed for a purpose."[18] That little word *appearance* is a direct denial of what God says everyone can see if they have the hearts to look (Rom. 1:20). Scientism is an alternate belief system, a radically different worldview.

Christian philosopher Alvin Plantinga comments that scientific naturalism (or scientism)

> plays many of the same roles as a religion. In particular, it gives answers to the great human questions: Is there such a person as God? How should we live? Can we look forward to life after death? What is our place in the universe? How are we related to other creatures? Naturalism gives answers here: there is no God, and it makes no sense to hope for life after death. As to our place in the grand scheme of things, we human beings are just another animal with a peculiar way of making a living.[19]

Science is something God created humans to do, but scientism is an idolatrous twisting of that good gift.

MISSA CHARLES DARWIN

The term *mass* can refer not only to a Roman Catholic ritual but also to an ancient musical form used by both Protestants and Catholics. Bach's *B-Minor Mass*, for example, is a cultural treasure. The classic mass form features multiple movements: *Kyrie* ("Lord"), *Gloria* ("Glory"), *Credo* ("I believe"), and *Agnus Dei* ("the Lamb of God"). The lyrics, in Latin, are taken either from the Bible or (in the case of the *Credo*) from a biblically rich ancient Christian creed.

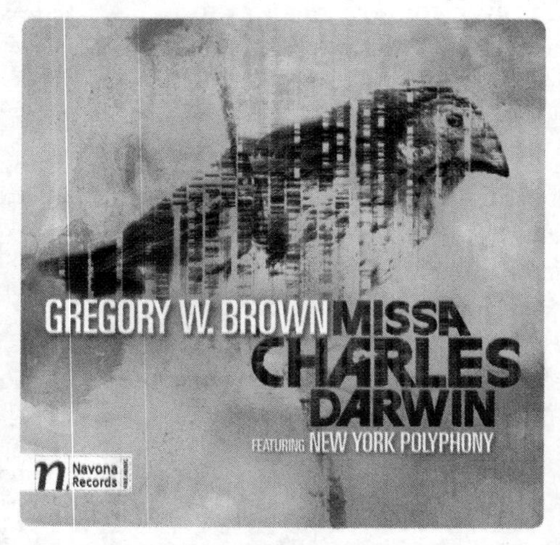

Scientism now has its own mass, the *Missa Charles Darwin* (*missa* is Latin for "mass"). The piece was written by composer Gregory W. Brown for the very capable men's group New York Polyphony. "Unlike traditional Mass settings, however, the sacred texts have been replaced with excerpts from *On the Origin of Species*, *The Descent of Man*, and Darwin's extant correspondence."[20] Brown said the texts "represent a modern secular approach to explaining how we've come to be as a species."[21]

Scientism shows up clearly in the Alleluia movement: "It is those who know little and not those who know much who so positively assert that this or that problem will never be solved by science."[22] The mass celebrates "one general law, leading to the advancement of all organic beings namely, multiply, vary, let the strongest live and the weakest die."[23]

GIVE THEM ONE FREE MIRACLE

Scientism and naturalism aren't exactly the same thing. Scientism focuses on how you know anything and says *it's through the scientific method*. Naturalism focuses on the nature of the universe and teaches that there is no supernatural. But the two views tend to go together in the modern West. Both clubs have a sign on the door: No gods allowed. No divine revelation. No miracles . . . except one.

The big bang is allowed into the clubhouse through the backdoor. Countercultural intellectual Terrence McKenna was a sharp critic of scientific naturalism; he observed that it requires what he called a **singularity**, an unrepeatable, unexplainable event. "In order to kickstart the . . . engine," McKenna said, "you have to go outside the system."[24] In other words, said McKenna, "Science is saying, 'Give us one free miracle and we'll explain the rest.'"[25] McKenna, a non-Christian, observed that

> the dominant and virtually unchallenged myth of our origin is either that God created us in seven days along with all the rest of creation or that the universe was born out of nothingness in a single moment for no reason. These are the two choices on the menu.[26]

McKenna described the myth of scientific naturalism this way:

> Give me the first ten-to-twelve nanoseconds, and if I can do smoke and mirrors in that, then the rest will proceed quite in an orderly fashion. Now that's orthodoxy.[27]

Naturalism clearly crosses over into the realm of religion, as McKenna argues. It requires faith. It isn't pure empirical science. Even naturalism needs a miracle.

THE MYTH OF NATURALISM

Naturalism has proven over the centuries to be a powerful myth. Lucretius, a Roman philosopher who died half a century before Christ was born, wrote an epic philosophical poem called *On the Nature of Things* in which he argued for a naturalistic view. Centuries later, scientific naturalism has proven to be a **myth** in both senses of that term:

> **myth** 1. A widely held but false belief or idea: *he wants to dispel the myth that sea kayaking is too risky*. 2. A traditional story, especially one concerning the early history of a people or explaining some natural or social phenomenon, and typically involving supernatural beings or events: *the heroes of Greek myth*.[28]

Naturalism is appealing as a traditional story because it quite literally puts us humans at the top of the heap. We're the most advanced beings we know. And that gives us a power and an authority to make the world into whatever we want it to be.

Naturalism doesn't allow any supernatural beings into the clubhouse, only natural ones. But the dictionary says it can still count as a myth since supernatural *beings* are only typically part of the definition. The myth of naturalism gets along fine with just one supernatural *event*, the big bang.

SCIENTIFIC NATURALISM AND THE TWO-STORY VIEW

Genuine Christians are sometimes influenced by naturalism. One of the authors of this textbook was on a flight to deliver a paper on presuppositions and worldview at an academic conference. He wound up sitting next to a bubbly high school science teacher who had a double-major degree in science from Duke University. She had enrolled in Duke as a young-earth creationist but left professing to believe in evolution as well as the Bible. As they discussed the possibility of squaring the Bible with evolutionary theory, the author asked, "What role does the Fall of man play in your scientific work?"

"None," she replied.

"Why not?"

"Because you can't prove it."

MIND AND COSMOS

Thomas Nagel, well-known atheistic philosopher and New York University professor, dropped something of a bomb on scientism in his book *Mind and Cosmos: Why the Materialist Neo-Darwinian Conception of Nature Is Almost Certainly False.* He argued that non-material aspects of life such as consciousness, reason, morality, and experience—are really real even though not material. Nagel was attacked by prominent defenders of scientism such as Steven Pinker, who tweeted about "the shoddy reasoning of a once-great thinker."[29]

Philosopher Alva Noë of the University of California (partially) defended Nagel from such attackers: "He is questioning a certain kind of orthodoxy, and they are responding in the way the orthodox respond."[30] Noë said in a piece on NPR, "One reason we may feel inclined to react in this way is that we don't want philosophers washing science's dirty laundry in public in a way that runs the risk of allowing anti-naturalistic religious dogmatism to get a foothold."[31]

The author replied, "Who determines what counts as proof?"

Tension shot up between seats 9A and 9B. The science teacher felt the challenge of that question. She blushed a little—and changed the subject.

This young woman would never deny that God exists. She's not a naturalist in that sense. But scientism had successfully pushed her into a two-story universe where significant things God has said can't be "proven."

If you leave God out of your scientific work, you're giving in to the pressure of naturalism. It's also a form of idolatry because it turns something other than God into an absolute.

Even other non-Christian thinkers have concluded, as Terrence McKenna did, that "we are blinding ourselves to the intentionality present in our world."[32] Thomas Nagel, an atheistic philosopher, has also famously searched for what he calls a "mind," which he thinks may be responsible for creation.

It has been God's intent all through history that people "should seek God, and perhaps feel their way toward him and find him" (Acts 17:27), as Paul said to a group of Greek philosophers. He continued,

> Yet [God] is actually not far from each one of us, for "In him we live and move and have our being"; as even some of your own poets have said, "For we are indeed his offspring." Being then God's offspring, we ought not to think that the divine being is like gold or silver or stone, an image formed by the art and imagination of man. The times of ignorance God overlooked, but now he commands all people everywhere to repent, because he has fixed a day on which he will judge the world in righteousness by a man whom he has appointed; and of this he has given assurance to all by raising him from the dead. (Acts 17:28–31)

In their search for something absolute, for a miracle to explain our existence, scientific naturalism has stumbled into truth: the universe is not a closed system of merely physical causes. But we must not make gold or silver or stone—or dark matter or the big bang—into a god. In the beginning, it was God who created the heavens and the earth.

THINKING IT THROUGH 20.2

1. What's the only kind of knowledge that counts as proof if a person presupposes the worldview of scientism? Explain why.
2. How does scientific naturalism define "good"?
3. What's the one miracle that scientism can't escape? Why must it be taken by faith?
4. Why do many people find the naturalistic worldview appealing?
5. Where was the scientific naturalism in the Duke University graduate's comments on the plane (pages 309–10)?

20.3 SCIENTISM: A FAULTY WAY OF LIVING

Intelligent Life magazine asked seven prominent writers for their take on the questions, "What's the point? Does life have meaning?" Author and *New Yorker* reporter Elizabeth Kolbert responded:

> Most of us would . . . prefer to believe our lives have a higher purpose than those of *E coli* [bacteria]. The very capacity to aspire—to truth and beauty, fame and fortune, intimacy and immortality—is one of the characteristics that sets modern humans apart from other species.[33]

But Kolbert thinks it's wrong for us to impose the way we think on nature itself, to try to make the world fit our ideas of it. As Darwin put it, "Endless forms most beautiful and most wonderful" have evolved.[34] Kolbert emphasizes that they've done it without our help and will go on evolving when we're no longer here.

"Perhaps the wisest thing we could try to do is to make peace with pointlessness,"[35] Kolbert said. She agrees with Darwin that the point of our lives is to pass on our DNA. Since that plan went along fine for billions of years before the human species ever appeared, Kolbert says, nature can hardly be expected to change its methodology merely because some people today don't consider it meaningful.

THE MEANING WE CREATE

Scientific naturalism is the major worldview alternative to Christianity among thoughtful Western people. Do you find its vision satisfying? Are you prepared to make peace with pointlessness?

Prominent atheistic cosmologist* Lawrence Krauss thinks you should do both: "The two lessons I want to give people is that, you're more insignificant than you ever thought, and the future is miserable. And those two things should make you happy, not sad."[36]

cosmologist: *a scientist who focuses on the origins of the cosmos*

Why would anyone want to make peace—and even be happy—with such a worldview? What could possibly make such a bleak vision of the world attractive? Listen carefully to Krauss as he answers that objection:

> We should rejoice [that] this remarkable accident that led to our existence and that . . . consciousness evolved on a random planet in the middle of a random galaxy in the middle of nowhere. Four billion years into that time, consciousness evolved. . . . It's amazing, and the meaning in our lives is the meaning we create, and we should enjoy it and make the most of our brief moment in the sun.[37]

That's precisely it. If there is no God, the meaning of our lives is up to us. We rule ourselves. To many people, this is a liberating thought. Well-known atheist Thomas Nagel himself noted that the "scientific world view . . . owes some of the passion displayed by its adherents precisely to the fact that it is thought to liberate us from religion."[38]

Materialism's story can't be right.

NATURALISTIC MORALITY

"Aha!" some Christians will say. "Atheism and scientism lead directly to immorality, and all atheists (and maybe even all scientists) are wicked!" That's exactly what atheists (and some scientists) think Christians say about them. But it isn't the Christian view. By God's common grace, atheists can be nice uncles, faithful taxpayers, and successful scientists (Matt. 5:46–47).

> "I DON'T BELIEVE IN GOD, BUT I MISS HIM."[39]
>
> —JULIAN BARNES

A biblical worldview doesn't demonize atheists; its challenge to atheism and scientific naturalism is more subtle than that. We're not saying atheists can't have morals; the Bible, in fact, says they do. What we're saying is that they can't explain their morality in a satisfying way.

Popular astrophysicist Neil DeGrasse Tyson nonetheless insists, "Science . . . transforms who we are [and] how we live—and it gives us an understanding of our place in the universe."[40] And atheistic Harvard professor Steven Pinker says that science "illuminates . . . the deepest questions about who we are, where we came from, and how we define the meaning and purpose of our lives" and goes on to declare that "the moral worldview of any scientifically literate person . . . requires a radical break from religious conceptions of meaning and value."[41]

But there is a fundamental problem here. Science, in the naturalistic view, can only describe what *is*. It has no authority to tell us what *ought to be*. Science can observe, "People typically behave like this." It cannot command, based on purely scientific grounds, "People ought to behave like that."

THE IS-OUGHT PROBLEM

British philosopher David Hume—although a materialist and religious skeptic himself—noticed that in a naturalistic worldview, there is an unbridgeable gap between what *is* and what *ought to be*. This has become known as the "is-ought problem" or the "**naturalistic fallacy**."

For example, it undoubtedly *is* that some eagle chicks kill their younger siblings.[42] *Ought* they to stop? Or *ought* human siblings to follow their example?

Those who use the tools of science can tell us (at least to a degree) what *is*, but they can't tell us what *ought to be* unless they smuggle in assumptions from somewhere outside science.

IF HUMANS WERE REALLY JUST ROBOTS

Skeptical humanist writer Kurt Vonnegut wrote an experimental novel in which the main character, Dwayne Hoover, is told that "everybody on Earth [is] a robot, with one exception—Dwayne Hoover." When Dwayne finds out that he lives in a mechanistic universe, his morality goes haywire. He explains his wife's suicide to himself (she drank Drano) by saying, "She was [just] that kind of machine!" He violently attacks two women because "he honestly believed that they were unfeeling machines." Dwayne says, "I used to think the electric chair was a shame. I used to think war was a shame—and automobile accidents and cancer." But not after finding out that other people are entirely physical: "Why should I care what happens to machines?"[43]

Atheistic philosopher John Gray, former professor at Oxford and visiting professor at Harvard and Yale, has demonstrated the disconnect between atheism and morality with a simple point: there have been many atheisms, and they have been associated with many different moralities. Why assume that the current crop of influential atheists (many of them scientists) have picked the right one?

> The racial theories promoted by atheists in the past have been consigned to the memory hole—and today's most influential atheists would no more endorse racist biology than they would be seen following the guidance of an astrologer. But they have not renounced the conviction that human values must be based in science; now it is liberal values which receive that accolade.*[44]

accolade: *praise*

The idea modern atheists seem to have is that "liberal values can be scientifically validated and are therefore humanly universal." But Gray asks,

> How could any increase in scientific knowledge validate values such as human equality and personal autonomy? The source of these values is not science. . . . It's not that atheists can't be moral. . . . The question is which morality an atheist should serve.[45]

What Gray says of atheism is true of scientific naturalism as well. And therein lies the trouble. As Gray says, you can't get a "universal morality" that isn't "borrowed from theism." The whole idea that man is making some kind of moral progress toward an evolutionary goal is actually "a hollowed-out version" of the Christian story.[46]

The big story of scientism doesn't portray human beings as moral agents struggling for a more just future society. It turns us into very complex "rocks" that do what our electrons and protons tell us to do. Rocks fall when dropped; people feed babies, help little old ladies across the street, and lie and murder. Whatever spreads our genes is "good." Scientific naturalism turns morality into "evolved herd survival instinct (nonbinding, of course, and as easy for us to outgrow as our feathers were)."[48]

"More than anything else, our unbelievers seek relief from the panic that grips them when they realise their values are rejected by much of humankind. What today's freethinkers want is freedom from doubt, and the prevailing version of atheism is well suited to give it to them."[47]

—JOHN GRAY

So scientific naturalism leads directly to **determinism** or **fatalism**—the idea that human freedom is an illusion, that we don't have "wills" at all, that we just do what we were programmed by evolution to do. As we observed in the very first chapter of this textbook, a person who believes that will tend to think,

> It doesn't make sense to call anything in this world "right" or "wrong" if we are all random atom collections. What does it matter if I hate my sister or I ate all your candy? Or if I love porn? So what? That's just what protoplasm does at this elevation above sea level.[49]

All Thunder Comes from On High

In one sense, we ought to be grateful that today's leading atheists are so dedicated to a moral vision. That vision isn't *completely* wrong. The work they do for the poor and even to fund scientific labors no doubt does a lot of genuine good. Some of the most prominent atheists, such as the late Christopher Hitchens, have sounded like old-time barnstorming tent-revivalists as they preach with holy passion against the moral evils of the day.

We should be grateful for their inconsistency because the truly consistent atheist would be more like the most influential atheist of the nineteenth century, Friedrich Nietzsche (1844–1900). He was an existentialist and **nihilist*** who believed in a "will to power" that crushes anyone in its way. Or they'd be more like Elizabeth, a twenty-two-year-old college student with a major tanning-salon habit. "If I get skin cancer, I'll deal with it then," she told a reporter. "I can't think about that now. I'm going to die of something."[50] *That* kind of morality is consistent with atheism.

nihilist: *a person who believes life is pointless and that moral values have no basis*

TAKE ME TO A CHURCH WITH NO ABSOLUTES

"Take Me to Church," a pop song by Irish musician Hozier, became a viral global hit, reaching the number-one slot in twelve countries and the top ten in twenty-one others.[51] In it Hozier complains about the Christian church's restrictive view of sex. By contrast, he sings, "My church offers no absolutes—/She tells me 'worship in the bedroom.'/The only heaven I'll be sent to/Is when I'm alone with you."[52] The worldview Hozier offers, at least within the limits of his song (and public comments he's made about it[53]), is only-sex-is-real-ism. There are no absolutes in his church (um, *absolutely* no absolutes?) except this one: sex feels good.

This may be great for Hozier—he gets what he wants out of his idol. But is it great for the woman he worships? In a "church" with no absolutes, how long will his worship last? Will he stick around when a more attractive idol presents herself? And what about any children Hozier's worship produces? Sexual freedom sounds like a good deal to a lot of adults, but few people stop to ask kids whose dads have left their families what they think about it.

Consistent atheism doesn't produce moral crusades. When an atheist does thunder about some injustice in the world, he stands "in the boots of forefathers who knew that all thunder comes from on high."[54]

MORAL ABSOLUTES

Richard Dawkins, perhaps the leading public atheist in the English-speaking world, has actually admitted that absolute right and wrong are hard to derive from scientific naturalism, or as Steven Pinker puts it, "Scientific facts do not by themselves dictate values."[55] But, with a quick sleight of hand, Dawkins turns this admission into a defense of his view: "It is pretty hard to defend absolutist morals on grounds other than religious ones."[56] Dawkins' trick is in that word *absolutist*. He knows his readership: people don't want to give anyone else, even and especially God, "absolute" rule over their choices.

But if morality isn't absolute, what is it? It's relative and debatable. It's whatever people more or less agree to. And if you find yourself a Jew in 1940s Germany or an African slave in nineteeth-century America, you'll just have to wait till the opinion polls go your way, if they ever do. That's why atheist John Gray says, "Anyone who wants their values secured by something beyond the capricious human world had better join an old-fashioned religion."[57]

Christianity offers "conversion"—a total remaking of someone's life that will give him freedom from sin. Atheistic scientism also promises that a conversion to unbelief will remake someone—and free him from "sin" by changing the definition.

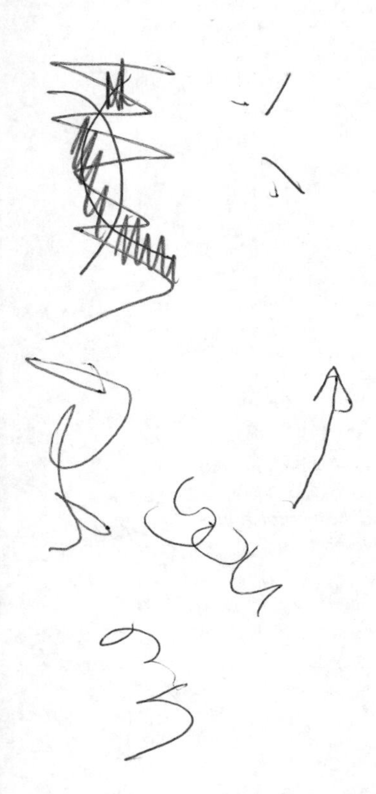

THINKING IT THROUGH 20.3

1. Although atheists have morals, why can't they use science to justify their morality?
2. How morality operate in scientific naturalism?
3. What is a nihilist?
4. Why is it dangerous to deny absolute morality?
5. Who determines the meaning of life according to the scientistic worldview? Why must that approach be doomed to failure?

20.4 SCIENTISM: A FAULTY WAY OF KNOWING

John Nash, a brilliant mathematician who received a PhD from Princeton in 1950, wrote his dissertation on what's now called game theory, an extremely complex field. In 1994, Nash won the Nobel Prize for mathematics. But in between those two events, he was insane. Diagnosed as a schizophrenic, he heard voices and believed that people from outer space were attacking his work.[58] He emerged into sanity again after a decades-long period of madness, and his reflections on that experience are very interesting:

> People are always selling the idea that people who have mental illness are suffering. But it's really not so simple. I think mental illness or madness can be an escape also. . . . If things are not so good, you maybe want to imagine something better. In madness, I thought I was the most important person of the world and people like the Pope would be just like enemies, who would try to put me down in some way.[59]

Madness can be a refuge from the truth. In one sense, that can actually work pretty well for people. And who has the right to tell a John Nash, "Snap out of it and live in the real world!"—if the world he's created for himself gives him more pleasure than the mad, mad world the rest of us live in?

(Although Nash acknowledges that he chose mental shutdown as an escape, not all mental dysfunction is a choice. Dementia, blunt trauma injuries, fetal alcohol influences, infections, and many other truly physical problems can wreak havoc with brain function. Whether the dysfunction is chosen or not, the suffering is real, and it calls for compassionate understanding and care.)

WHAT A FOOL KNOWS

It's the fool who "says in his heart, 'There is no God'" (Psalm 14:1). The God-denier lives in an irrational world of his own foolish creation. And it can actually work pretty well for him—from one perspective (Ps. 37:35; 73:3–9). That world gives him more pleasure (at least temporarily) than the one that actually exists, the one that God made.

But God says that the very beginning of knowledge is fear of the Lord (Prov. 1:7), and we've given some attention to that claim in previous units. If scientism—scientific naturalism—says in its heart, "There is no God," then we can expect that it will not merely be a faulty way to live (the topic of the previous section) but a faulty way to *know*. Even in his madness, John Nash knew a great deal. He knew there was a pope; he continued to speak English and to eat and drink; still resident in his brain was a wealth of mathematical skill. But very few people would be satisfied with Nash's method of knowing.

Even in its madness, scientism knows a great deal. But Christians should not be satisfied with its method of knowing.

SCIENTISM AND KNOWLEDGE

Proponents of scientism make their view of knowledge perfectly clear. As Steven Pinker says, religion is *out*:

> Most of the traditional causes of belief—faith, revelation, dogma,* authority . . . —are generators of error and should be dismissed as sources of knowledge.[60]

dogma: *a truth claim made by a religious authority*

As Richard N. Williams says (in a critique of scientism), the scientific method is *in*:

> Only certifiably scientific knowledge counts as real knowledge. All else is mere opinion or nonsense. Scientific knowledge is defined in terms of the method by which it is obtained. . . . There is a certifiable and specifiable method (or manageable set of methods) that counts as scientific.[61]

Scientism even attempts to exert control over academic disciplines that haven't generally been regarded as scientific. Scholars and teachers in the humanities—literature, art, music, philosophy, and so forth—are now feeling the pressure to use scientific methods in their own disciplines.[62]

But is the scientific method the only genuinely reliable path to knowledge in all fields of human life? No, and two arguments we've seen before are effective against this scientistic idea: (1) empiricism can't prove empiricism, and (2) there are no uninterpreted facts.

1. Empiricism Can't Prove Empiricism

The scientific method is a form of the philosophical view called **empiricism**. "Empiricists claim that sense experience is the ultimate source of all our concepts and knowledge."[63] They may use instruments such as microscopes or telescopes to amplify their ability to see, or decibel counters to amplify their ability to hear, but "ultimately, it always comes back to our senses, one way or another." [64]

Presumably, proponents of scientism would insist that you can "know" that our senses are the only reliable way to get truth. But how can you prove through empirical methods that empirical methods are the only reliable way to know? That is a presupposition you must take on faith. In fact, it's circular reasoning.

What authority do Richard Dawkins and Steven Pinker have to tell anyone that "faith," "revelation," and "authority" are bad ways to know and empiricism is a good way to know? It just so happens that they both participated in a roundtable broadcast addressing that question.[65] Everyone in the discussion appeared to agree that if religious people would just get some education and listen to scientific authorities instead of religious ones, such people would be a great deal better off.

But the host of the show, card-carrying liberal Chris Hayes, pushed back. He said that he didn't have time to read up on all of the science in every field and that even if he did he would still be taking the word of the scientists who did the studies he was reading. He doesn't have time to repeat all their experiments, even if he knew how.

peer-reviewed: *evaluated by experts in the field before being published*

cognoscenti: *the smart people; those "in the know"*

> I consider myself a pretty educated person. . . . I read peer-reviewed* studies. . . .[But] if I am honest with myself I am still at a fundamental level relying on trust to a certain degree, and there's no way of getting around that. And to pretend that "Oh, what we the enlightened cognoscenti* do is so different from what [religious conservatives] are doing who just trust authority" I think is really self-delusional.[66]

Dawkins agreed partially with what Hayes was saying:

> Nobody can read up all the scientific literature. The best scientist in the world can't keep up with science outside his or her own field. And so there really is a matter of trust.[67]

But Dawkins insisted that

> science has earned the right to trust, because you know that when people are challenged in science they can produce the evidence. They can say, "Look, here's [a study by] Brown and McAllister [in] 2008 showing so and so. You can actually cite chapter and verse.[68]

CLAIMS AND TOOLS

A debate was held at George Washington University between two teams of academics regarding the proposition: "Liberals are stifling intellectual diversity on [university] campus[es]."[69] Interestingly enough, all four debaters considered themselves liberals, and yet the "pro" side won the debate. They persuaded twice as many of the previously "undecided" people in the audience as the "con" side did.

The con side fell back on a form of scientism for their defense, saying, "A college professor should not tell you what to think. He or she should give you the tools to think for yourself."[70] This may initially sound good (and there's some truth in it since college does give you intellectual tools). But ultimately, it's a way of claiming neutrality: "Hey, I'm not making any claims about what's true! I'm just giving you the neutral tools and procedures to help you come to the right conclusion on your own." This is a standard strategy of scientism; it ignores the fact that even intellectual tools are not neutral in a fallen world.

In other words, we should trust scientific evidence because of all the scientific evidence for trusting scientific evidence. Dawkins (and Pinker, who said much the same) are using circular reasoning. They are using empiricism to prove empiricism.[71]

A biblical worldview does *not* lead to a radical skepticism which refuses to trust all the work of unbelieving scientists. The great majority of the work of today's scientists, no matter their religious views, is valuable. But the worldview foundation of your knowledge matters. If you're called on to either trust God or trust your own eyes—and those are truly your only two options—the biblical position is clear: "We walk by faith, not by sight" (2 Cor. 5:7) because "the fear of the Lord is the beginning of knowledge" (Prov. 1:7).

The irony here is that scientism can't respond by saying, "We walk by sight, not by faith." They, too, must exercise faith: they must believe that the five senses are the only reliable way to know.

2. There Are No Brute Facts

Much of Unit 1 was dedicated to making the second argument against scientism's preferred way of knowing. That argument is simply that there are no uninterpreted facts. Everyone sees all scientific evidence through the worldview lenses he's wearing. It's not a simple and obvious process to move from the facts on the ground to a theory in your head. People wearing different lenses will come up with different theories.

"How the Elephant Got His Trunk"

Did you ever hear Rudyard Kipling's *Just So Stories* as a kid? They're fanciful tales written to explain "How the Camel Got His Hump," "How the Leopard Got His Spots," and other things all well-rounded children need to know. In one of the stories, "How the Elephant Got His Trunk," we discover that a young elephant was too curious and stuck his stubby nose into the mouth of a crocodile. The croc snapped his mouth shut and began a tug-of-war that ended up stretching the elephant's nose into the length it now has.

Once children accept the idea that silly events in the distant past explain features of our world today, the possibilities are endless: they can come up with hypotheses for why bananas are yellow (an unfortunate incident involving highlighters), where red hair comes from (a guy who accidentally swallowed fire), and why all children have to go to bed earlier than they want to (because of the monsters under the bed, of course).

The problem with these stories is that they're "unfalsifiable." There is no evidence for them except the power of the overall worldview that generates them. So it's fruitless to argue with a child who accepts that worldview. If you try, he'll just go away thinking, "What more proof does that grown-up need? Highlighters and bananas are clearly the same color!"

Evolutionary theory comes up with plenty of "**just-so stories**" about the world, and particularly about characteristics of human society. Name any major feature of human existence, and educated people will make guesses as to how evolution brought it to us.

Take religion, for example. One of the leading secular moral philosophers of our day, Jonathan Haidt of New York University, attempted to explain the existence of religion from an evolutionary perspective in his book *The Righteous Mind: Why Good People Are Divided by Politics and Religion*. Haidt knows that the standard evolutionary answer is that humans, like other animals, are "hypersensitive to agency."[72] Our brains are trained to detect the difference between movement caused by wind or water and movement caused by an "agent"—a being that can move under its own power and that may therefore pose a threat (or an opportunity). Atheists such as Richard Dawkins argue that humans, because of this capacity, started seeing supernatural agency behind purely natural events. Religion, in other words, was one huge evolutionary mistake.

But Haidt offers a somewhat more positive assessment of religion. In his view, religion is a group-level adaptation. Morality inside a group helps the whole group be more successful. Other things being equal, the group of human animals with the more successful moral rules will beat the one with a worse morality. In other words, survival of the fittest doesn't just work on an individual level, but at a group level.[73]

But this is a just-so story. Where, exactly, is the evidence for it? And what kind of evidence could ever be found for it? The story is unfalsifiable; it draws all of its persuasiveness from the power of evolutionary theory, not from the observed evidence. Only if evolution is true does it make any sense. So Haidt can't turn around and logically claim that the existence of religion is evidence that evolution occurred.

TRUE MYTH

Before C. S. Lewis became a Christian, he was an ardent believer in the myth of scientific naturalism. But, he says, "Long before I believed Theology to be true I had already decided that the popular scientific picture at any rate was false."[74]

> The picture so often painted of Christians huddling together on an ever narrower strip of beach while the incoming tide of "Science" mounts higher and higher corresponds to nothing in my own experience. That grand myth [of evolutionary progress] . . . is not for me a hostile novelty breaking in on my traditional beliefs. On the contrary, that cosmology is what I started from. Deepening distrust and final abandonment of it long preceded my conversion to Christianity.[75]

C.S. LEWIS'S OBJECTION TO SCIENTISM

Lewis mentions another major objection to scientific naturalism—what he calls its "absolutely central inconsistency." This objection may be a little more difficult to understand than the two already presented in this chapter, but it's a strong argument.

He explained that science claims to rely on inferring things based on observations. If the inference is invalid, the whole structure collapses. Lewis questions whether we can be certain that matter in the farthest reaches of the universe behaves according to the principles a scientist observes in his laboratory on earth. If not, or as Lewis puts it, "unless Reason is absolute,"[76] then "all is in ruins." But those who promote this worldview want us to believe that reason is nothing more than the accidental result of unthinking matter in its current phase of perpetual and pointless evolving. What's contradictory about this is that we are expected to accept this proposition but simultaneously reject the very basis of it.

Lewis concluded,

> The difficulty is to me a fatal one; and the fact that when you put it to many scientists, far from having an answer, they seem not even to understand what the difficulty is, assures me that I have not found a mare's nest* but detected a radical disease in their whole mode of thought from the very beginning. The man who has once understood the situation is compelled henceforth to regard the scientific cosmology as being, in principle, a myth; though no doubt a great many true particulars have been worked into it.[77]

Modern-day writer Francis Beckwith offers an illustration supporting the same point Lewis made. The materialist can only defend his viewpoint by drawing inferences based on reasons. To do that, he has to be able to act as a rational agent—to think. Materialism teaches, however, that thinking is something the brain does entirely in a physical sense; it functions according to the laws of physics and chemistry the same way other bodily organs do and is also affected by natural selection. If thinking is a "nonrational" process, then the results of our reasoning, including the ideas that materialism grows out of, are not trustworthy.

Beckwith illustrates the problem this way:

> If while I'm playing Scrabble, the letters randomly spell "materialism is true," should I change my belief and embrace materialism? Of course not, for this collection of letters is the result of nonrational forces or chance. But if the brain's "reasoning" is like the random string of Scrabble letters, then its apparent [results]—including the claim that materialism is true—are arrived at in no more rational a fashion than the phrase "materialism is true" on the Scrabble board.[78]

mare's nest: *a fraud, illusion, deliberate hoax*

It's like John Nash, the mathematician who went insane. He only crawled out of madness and back to sanity when he began arguing with the voices in his head. He explained, "I began rejecting them and deciding not to listen." Nash observed that "to some extent, sanity is a form of conformity."[79] He meant that "sanity" in any given culture means going with the flow of what people around you believe about the world.

But what if they're all fallen people who believe foolish things? Even well-educated people actually believe that we all got here from nowhere and evolved from nothing—and they think science proves it. ("That's orthodoxy," says Terrence McKenna.) If you believed that spoiled meat spontaneously generated maggots, they would laugh at you. But they can say "life created itself" with a straight face. Going with that flow is what's crazy. It suppresses the truth evident all around us (Rom. 1:17–32).

Lewis was converted when his friend J. R. R. Tolkien, author of *The Lord of the Rings*, urged him to see Christianity as a "**true myth**."[80] Lewis began to realize that the Bible told a powerful story that explained the world (another meaning of the word *myth*, see second definition on page 309), and he began to believe that it all really and truly happened. Jesus really lived a sinless life. He really died and rose again.

Christianity doesn't ask you to deny the evidence in front of your face, but it does demand that you interpret that evidence through the lens provided by God in Scripture. As one theologian has said, "Any decision to distrust God's words is a decision to trust someone else's."[81]

THINKING IT THROUGH 20.4

1. Provide two arguments against the view that the scientific method is the only genuinely reliable path to knowledge in all fields of human life.
2. If people don't have the time and expertise to confirm every scientific experiment for themselves, then what must they rely on for their knowledge?
3. Why is it impossible for believers of scientism to deny that they walk by faith?
4. What is a just-so story?
5. According to C. S. Lewis and Francis Beckwith, why is rationality incompatible with the worldview of scientism?

20 CHAPTER REVIEW

TERMS TO REMEMBER

singularity
myth
naturalistic fallacy
determinism/fatalism
nihilist
empiricism
just-so stories
true myth

Scripture Memory

Romans 1:25

Making Connections

1. List six ways that science has been affected by the Fall.
2. In scientism's worldview, what is the only kind of knowledge that counts as proof?
3. In scientism's worldview, where does meaning in life come from?
4. In scientism's worldview, why should we trust scientific evidence?

Developing Skills in Apologetics and Worldview

5. How can you go about proving a moral claim (such as that human trafficking is harmful) without using the tools of empirical science?
6. How can you prove that scientism can't justify any moral claims?

Examining Assumptions and Evidence

7. How do wrong worldview models impact the work of science?
8. Is scientism consistently naturalistic? Why or why not?
9. Why is it dangerous to make up your own meaning and morality?
10. Why can't rationality be justified in scientism's worldview?

Becoming a Creative Cultivator

11. Find one current event that exemplifies at least one of the six ways that science has been affected by the Fall. Identify the way in which the Fall has affected science, and explain how it could be corrected with a biblical worldview approach.

Chapter Twenty-One

READING GENESIS AND DOING SCIENCE

And God saw everything that he had made, and behold, it was very good. And there was evening and there was morning, the sixth day.

Scripture Memory
Genesis 1:31

21.1 READING GENESIS 1–3 AS FOUNDATIONAL TO A BIBLICAL WORLDVIEW

One of the meanest things today's secular press can call someone is a "fundamentalist." Even the normally gracious *New York Times* columnist David Brooks, for example, complained in one of his regular pieces about "the stupidity of the fundamentalists."

> Fundamentalists are people who take everything literally. . . . They are incapable of seeing that while their religion may be worthy of the deepest reverence, it is also true that most religions are kind of weird.[1]

Brooks's columns are actually often friendly to religion[2] (Brooks is a non-observant Jew*[3]). But in this comment about fundamentalists, he's taking the classic liberal line: "Hey, religion is useful for making people nice, but when religious people start *actually believing* that Jesus walked on water or rose from the dead, that's just weird." Brooks isn't talking only about religious weirdos in a cult compound somewhere; his comments are critical of all serious Christians (though he has "fundamentalists" of all religions in mind).

TAKING EVERYTHING LITERALLY

We need to look closely at the leading example of weirdness that Brooks points to, the idea that so-called fundamentalists "take everything literally." There are two major ways you could take this comment. Either he means that fundamentalists take themselves and their world too seriously, or he means that strong religious believers are tone-deaf to literary devices such as metaphor, allegory, and hyperbole. Perhaps he has both ideas in mind.

In any case, Brooks is saying that he knows the standard by which religion and religious reading ought to be judged. He knows which religions count as "too serious," and he knows which interpretations (of the Bible, the Qur'an, the Vedas, etc.) count as "too literal."

And either way, conservative Christians probably don't measure up to Brooks's standards. Conservative Christians believe that countless people around the globe are on what Jesus called the broad way to destruction, and that after their deaths it will be too late for them to find the narrow way that leads to life (Matt. 7:13). Such a worldview tends to make you joyful about God's grace in your life and serious about the fate of others—ten times the New Testament calls on Christians to be "sober."

But let's take up the other possible charge, that conservative Christians are "**literalists**" (i.e., they take the Bible too literally). Most people who make that accusation mean that, according to their worldview, Red Seas don't literally part, big fish don't literally swallow prophets for three days and spit them out, and messiahs don't literally get resurrected.

---

non-observant Jew: *an ethnically Jewish person who does not engage in the religious practices of Judaism*

And most important, universes don't literally get created in six days. The real focus of the common charge that Christians take the Bible too literally is just one passage of Scripture: Genesis 1. In fact, the cultural pressure on Western Christians to abandon a straightforward reading of Genesis 1 is immense. If you don't drop it, you might get called a "fundamentalist" in the *New York Times*.

But Genesis 1 is fundamental to biblical Christianity. If you give it up or change it, you give up (or change) the foundation Creation-Fall-Redemption provides for the entire Christian worldview. Christianity stands or falls with Genesis 1. You can't have your cake and let scientific naturalism eat it too.

LITERAL OR FIGURATIVE?

The Bible uses countless metaphors; metaphor is a natural feature of every human language. No one could communicate without it. Here's a metaphor you know: "Time is money." Think of all the ways that metaphor shows up in English:

You're *wasting* my time.
This gadget will *save* you hours.
How do you *spend* your time these days?
That flat tire *cost* me an hour.
I've *invested* a lot of time in her.
You need to *budget* your time.
Is that *worth your while*?
He's living on *borrowed* time.[4]

These metaphors are so common that we don't even think of them as figures of speech.[5] People are well practiced at metaphor, in other words. So no one is confused when Jesus says, "I am the door" (John 10:7ff.), or when the author of Hebrews says, "Our God is a consuming fire" (Heb. 12:29). No serious Christian takes *everything* in the Bible literally—if seeing Jesus as a literal door and God as a literal fire is what "literally" means.

REDEEMING SCIENCE

If you're a Christian, you're called to be an agent of redemption, to push the (apparent) conflict between science and religion back into harmony. As part of that calling, you'll have to come to grips with Genesis 1. But the debate over the origins of the universe is so complex, what can you do? Where can you start? We suggest two things:

(1) Recognize the role one's worldview plays in the debate.

(2) Focus on the truly significant theological issues in the area of **origins**,* namely the questions of (a) whether Adam and Eve ever existed and (b) whether there was death before the Fall.

origins: *the study of the beginnings of the universe and human life*

1. Recognizing the role worldview plays in the debate

There's one traditional, straightforward way of reading Genesis 1; there's one totally opposite view—scientific naturalism—in which Genesis 1 is a fairy tale and the big bang is our mother; and there are multiple views in between, all trying to bridge the gap in some way. Some think God guided evolution, others that He got it started and then went on a long vacation.

Christian biologist Gerald Rau has written a helpful book titled *Mapping the Origins Debate*, in which he lays out as objectively as possible the various views on how the cosmos (and life, and species, and humans) came to be. People from all over the spectrum have praised the book; they think Rau was fair to their positions, while recognizing that such a complex issue is hard to summarize. Even the strongly naturalistic National Center for Science Education (the organization that sponsored the "Project Steve" mentioned in Chapter 1) was willing to say that the book "offers a semi-fair analysis of different viewpoints."[6]

Rau begins his book, as we began this unit, by talking about what science and the scientific method are. He argues that every major view of the origins of life and the universe has the same "facts," the same "evidence," to explain. The major models of how we all got here are different for one reason: "Each [model] flows logically from its philosophical underpinnings."[7] Rau stresses that

> each model rests on and is inextricably connected with particular philosophical presuppositions. Apart from that, it is nonsense. Thus, when passing judgment on a particular model, we are usually not judging its logical consistency or ability to explain the evidence as much as its philosophical or religious roots.[8]

As Rau maps out the various models, he notes that the spectrum of major views lines up with "the degree of interaction between the supernatural and natural worlds."[9] The various views can be summarized this way:[10]

NATURALISTIC EVOLUTION	UNDIRECTED EVOLUTION	PLANNED EVOLUTION	DIRECTED EVOLUTION	OLD-EARTH CREATION	YOUNG-EARTH CREATION
There is no supernatural interaction with the natural world because there is no supernatural.	Deism: God started the creation but then let it go its own way.	Deism with a twist: God perfectly laid out the path for evolution in advance but has not been involved since.	God has been actively intervening in the process of evolution from the beginning, but through natural processes.	God jump-started major portions of the evolutionary tree at different times throughout history.	God created the entire planet and all life in it within the last 7,500 years in basically the form we see today.

Do you see how God's involvement in His creation increases as you move from left to right in the chart? This observation alone doesn't solve the debate: God can create worlds and run them any way He wants to. But if Rau is right that the various positions all arise out of prior philosophical commitments, the debate becomes a bit simpler. We can focus on the philosophy (or theology) and save the evidence for later. Someone who believes in a deistic God simply won't come to the conclusion that the evidence is in favor of young-earth creationism—or naturalism—until he gives up his deism. Someone who believes that God reigns sovereignly over every detail in His creation naturally will not be interested in the deistic positions on the chart.

World-famous scientist Stephen Hawking is known for his work on black holes and for his best-selling book, *A Brief History of Time*. He's also known for working through the incredible adversity of Lou Gehrig's disease (ALS). He is director of research at the Centre for Theoretical Cosmology at the University of Cambridge in England. He told the *New Scientist* in an interview,

> Science is increasingly answering questions that used to be the province of religion. The one remaining area that religion can still lay a claim to is the origin of the universe, but even here science is making progress and should soon provide a definitive answer to how the universe began.[11]

LIMITS OF HUMAN REASON

In the final paragraph of *A Brief History of Time*, Hawking describes what the goal of scientific naturalism is:

> If we do discover a complete theory [of the universe and its origins], it should in time be understandable in broad principle by everyone, not just a few scientists. Then we shall all, philosophers, scientists, and just ordinary people, be able to take part in the discussion of the question of why it is that we and the universe exist. If we find the answer to that, it would be the ultimate triumph of human reason—for then we would know the mind of God.[12]

Contrast this with Paul's striking statement on knowledge: "'For who has understood the mind of the Lord so as to instruct him?' But we have the mind of Christ" (1 Cor. 2:16).

Stephen Hawking is clearly a person of faith. Everybody is. At the bottom of every model of the earth's origins is a bedrock of belief or trust in some authority.

Just because faith plays a key role in determining your position on the origin of the cosmos doesn't mean any model is OK as long as you really believe it. But the foundational role faith plays in every model cannot be denied either. One key way of living redemptively when it comes to science is helping other people see the role their worldview—their faith—plays in the model they adopt.

THINKING IT THROUGH 21.1A

1. What specific origins position is foundational to biblical Christianity's metanarrative of Creation, Fall, and Redemption?

2–4. Summarize what differentiates the following positions from one another:

- Naturalistic Evolution versus Undirected Evolution
- Undirected Evolution versus Planned Evolution
- Planned Evolution versus Directed Evolution versus Old-Earth Creation

5. In what way do the major views on creation and evolution correspond to views about the supernatural?

2. Focusing on the truly significant theological and exegetical issues

So which authority do you trust? Which proposed bedrock should your faith rest on? Every serious Christian alive will give the same ultimate answer: you trust God. And God has revealed facts about the origin of the universe in the Bible—specifically (but not only) in Genesis 1.

But interpretations of Scripture themselves arise out of theological presuppositions. Rau says about his chart,

> Each of the six models of origins presented here is intimately wedded to a certain theological interpretation of scripture, so the model and the theology rise or fall together. Since we each have a faith commitment to a certain theology, we also have a faith commitment to a corresponding model. To change our model we also need to change our theology and admit that what we believed is incorrect. This is something few are willing to do, so the conflict continues.[13]

Here are the different views that the major models take on Genesis:

NATURALISTIC EVOLUTION	UNDIRECTED EVOLUTION	PLANNED EVOLUTION	DIRECTED EVOLUTION	OLD-EARTH CREATION	YOUNG-EARTH CREATION
Genesis 1–3 is ancient myth; there is no God.	Genesis 1–3 is ancient myth; there is a God, however.	Genesis 1–3 provides some general theological truths, but Adam and Eve weren't real individuals.	Adam and Eve were real individuals linked to previous ancestors by evolution.	The days of Genesis 1 were not literal twenty-four-hour days. Adam and Eve came from a pre-existing race of hominids but were the first humans.	The days of Genesis 1 were literal twenty-four-hour days; Adam and Eve were created from the dust of the ground.

Some disagreements Christians have over the interpretation of Scripture aren't very serious because not every statement in the Bible is equally important. That might sound odd, even sacrilegious. But Jesus Himself said:

> Woe to you, scribes and Pharisees, hypocrites! For you tithe mint and dill and cumin, and have neglected the weightier matters of the law: justice and mercy and faithfulness. These you ought to have done, without neglecting the others. (Matt. 23:23–24)

In other words, the Jews were supposed to give God a tenth of everything, even tiny spices. But pursuing justice, mercy, and faithfulness is more important than counting anise seeds. They weigh more.

How much do you think the creation of man and woman weighs? Is that issue more like counting seeds or more like doing justice and mercy?

We really ought to let the Bible answer that question. We've already argued that Scripture's entire story rests on the creation account in Genesis 1. Now let's discuss some of the evidence, searching out what parts of the creation narrative are most important in the rest of Scripture.

historicity: *historical authenticity; having actually existed or happened in the past*

The two most important elements of Genesis 1, as seen throughout the Bible, are the historicity* of Adam (whether or not he really existed) and the question of death before the Fall. And these two points, as we'll see, are closely related.

The Historicity of Adam

You can't believe in the evolution of humans from earlier, ape-like creatures without turning the Adam story in Genesis 1 into some kind of metaphor (at best). If Adam is the product of evolution, then God didn't take him from the dust of the ground and breathe life into his nostrils. That's all just symbolic. And if Eve is the product of evolution, she wasn't made from Adam's side to be his helper. So maybe "Adam" and "Eve" were just two hominids* to whom God decided to give the gifts of moral conscience and language, or maybe their story is entirely symbolic because the ancient Israelites couldn't understand the big bang. If you reject a straightforward reading of Genesis 1, Adam and Eve can be whatever the latest evolutionary models want them to be.

hominid: *member of a primate family in the evolutionary taxonomy that includes the human species as well as orangutans, gorillas, and chimpanzees*

But Adam and Eve's story is very difficult to read as metaphor or symbolism. For one thing, Adam is given a lifespan that sounds just like those of the other people in Genesis. "All the days that Adam lived were 930 years, and he died" (Gen. 5:5). If Moses (the author of Genesis) intended for Adam to be a mere symbol, that's an odd detail to include. It would be like a stranger at an airport coming up to you and saying, "Excuse me, I'm Sterling Ryznich, and this is my poodle, Sarah, whose mother died last Wednesday. Can you tell me the time?" Why is he giving you all this information? It isn't relevant if his sole purpose is finding out the time.[14] Likewise, if Adam and Eve are mere symbols, why mention Adam's lifespan or Eve's little comments when Cain and Seth were born (Gen. 4:1, 25)?

Granted, Adam's lifespan is nothing like we see today. But it was nothing like what Moses saw, either, and he still faithfully recorded it. In Genesis, lifespans after the Flood are much shorter than lifespans before it.

genealogy: *a record of a person's ancestors*

Several genealogies* in the Old and New Testaments also list Adam, and none of them includes a footnote saying that he didn't really exist. He's treated just like the other people in the family tree of King David and King Jesus (1 Chron. 1–9; Luke 3:38). If Adam didn't really exist as a historical person, did Abraham? Or Joseph? Or anybody else in Genesis? Where does the metaphor stop and the history begin?

Perhaps even more important, theologically speaking, both Jesus and Paul assume that Adam really existed and that he was created before Eve. As we discussed in Unit 5, Jesus based His whole argument about marriage on the fact that Adam and Eve were "created . . . male and female" and "joined together" by God (Matt. 19:4, 6). Paul makes several points from the fact that "Adam was formed first, then Eve" (1 Tim. 2:13; cf. 1 Cor. 11:9).

Paul also makes an even more significant theological point from the story of Adam, a point about Fall and Redemption. One theologian explained that point very well:

> Paul draws an important analogy [in Romans 5 and 1 Corinthians 15] between Adam and Jesus. Just as the first Adam introduced *sin and death* to all humanity through his disobedience in the garden of Eden (eating the forbidden fruit), now Jesus, the second Adam . . . , introduces *life* through his *obedience*. . . . For Paul's analogy to have any force, it seems that both Adam and Jesus must be actual historical figures. . . . A historical Adam has been the dominant Christian view for two thousand years.[15]

LOOKING FOR EVE?

If you search an online Bible for *Eve*, you'll get just four hits. Her name appears twice in the Old Testament and twice in the New. But one app allows you to search for "Person: Eve" and pick up all the references to her in Scripture, even if she's just called "Adam's wife" or "the woman." You'll find more than eighty references to her that way.

The theologian who wrote that paragraph is Peter Enns, writing in a book called *The Evolution of Adam*. Enns was dismissed in 2005 from the biblically orthodox seminary he taught at because he began to doubt (and later did deny) what he had said in the above quotation. Enns himself laid out the options as he saw them:

1. Accept evolution and reject Christianity. [Enns, to his credit, did not wish to do this.]
2. Accept Paul's view of Adam as binding and reject evolution. [Enns, to his discredit, did not wish to do this either.]
3. Reconcile evolution and Christianity by positing a first human pair (or group) at some point in the evolutionary process. [Back to Enns's credit, he just couldn't make this option work with what the Bible says.]
4. Rethink Genesis and Paul.[16]

RETHINKING GENESIS

Among conservative theologians who profess to believe in the truth of Scripture, John Walton has probably done the most ingenious job of making Genesis fit modern evolutionary theory.

Walton views the passage literally—sort of. In his view it is an account of the origin of the world, but it is not a scientific account—nor one that should be harmonized with science. Instead it is an ancient account full of ancient symbolism. He is confident that *create* means "give function to" or "make useful." In other words, God took the physical stuff already in existence and gave it new functions. Walton says that the seven days of creation reveal what the function of the creation is. Ancient temples were dedicated in seven-day ceremonies. The function of the seven days in Genesis 1 is to take the already existing creation and give it the function of a cosmic temple for God.[17]

But careful readers have raised serious questions about Walton's approach. (1) Other Hebrew scholars doubt Walton's claim that *create* means "give function to." They point to numerous instances in which the Hebrew word is not being used to grant functions and other contexts in which material creation is in view.[18] (2) Walton himself is forced to admit that the dedications of ancient temples were not always seven days in length.[19] The Israelite tabernacle, for instance, was dedicated in a single day (Exod. 40). (3) For Walton's view to be true, he has to be sure that he is correctly interpreting the cultural background information that he insists must shape the interpretation of Genesis 1. But other scholars, who are equally expert in this material, do not always share Walton's interpretation of the evidence.[20]

cosmology: *a theory or model of how the physical universe began and how it works*

The final option is what Enns went for, and this is how he did it: he said, "The fact that Paul considered Adam to be the progenitor of the human race does not mean that we need to find some way to maintain his view."[21] Enns said we have to "leave room for the ancient writers [of Scripture] to reflect and even incorporate their ancient, mistaken cosmologies* into their scriptural reflections."[22]

In other words, the apostle Paul was simply wrong.

People like Enns commonly laugh at ignorant "fundamentalists" (there's that word again) who, they say, need to stop reading so "literalistically." But in doing so, they're laughing at Jesus and Paul too.

The best answer to any argument that says Paul (let alone Jesus) was wrong is the question that Augustine of Hippo asked many centuries ago (see sidebar): if you reject one thing the Bible says, what's to stop you from rejecting everything? Either the Bible carries God's authority, or it doesn't. Jesus and Paul say Adam was a historical figure. Jesus, in this age, permits you to disagree. But those who want to live redemptively and bring healing to the world must trust the authority of their Creator. A rock-solid faith in God's Word is one of the best gifts you can give to the world.

PICKING AND CHOOSING FROM SCRIPTURE

Augustine (AD 354–430), who lived in the North African city of Hippo, wrote the following to Faustus, a bishop in the Manichaean religion that Augustine himself once followed. The founder of Manichaeism believed that Jesus' revelation was incomplete.

> It is one thing to reject the books [of the Bible] themselves, and to profess no regard for their authority, as the Pagans reject our Scriptures, and the Jews the New Testament . . . ; and it is another thing to say, "This holy man wrote only the truth, and this is his epistle, but some verses are his, and some are not." And then, when you are asked for a proof, instead of referring to more correct or more ancient manuscripts, or to a greater number, or to the original text, your reply is, "This verse is his, because it makes for me; and this is not his, because it is against me." Are you, then, the rule of truth? Can nothing be true that is against you?[23]

Death Before the Fall

The second truly significant theological issue in the origins debate also has to do with Adam, though not with his creation but with his fall. Just as Paul's writings are one of the key reasons Christians are not free to believe that Adam and Eve are mere symbols or metaphors, Paul provides strong theological reasons to believe that a man named Adam truly fell, bringing evil and death into the world. Paul wrote in his rich letter to the Roman Christians,

> Sin came into the world through one man, and death through sin, and so death spread to all men. . . . Death reigned from Adam to Moses, even over those whose sinning was not like the transgression of Adam. (Rom. 5:12–14)

Death came into the world "through sin," beginning with Adam. So how could death have happened for millions of years before that, as in the evolutionary view?

Paul says that death came into the world through the sin of Adam. Some readers say that Paul meant only human death, not animal death. (Even animal death makes some of the six models on Gerald Rau's chart impossible—which ones?) But think about Genesis 3. Clearly, the animal creation was affected by Adam's fall. And a few pages after Romans 5, in Romans 8, Paul details how it was affected. Read carefully, with CFR in mind:

> The creation was subjected to futility, not willingly, but because of him who subjected it, in hope that the creation itself will be set free from its bondage to corruption and obtain the freedom of the glory of the children of God. For we know that the whole creation has been groaning together in the pains of

childbirth until now. And not only the creation, but we ourselves, who have the firstfruits of the Spirit, groan inwardly as we wait eagerly for adoption as sons, the redemption of our bodies. (Romans 8:20–23)

The creation, Paul says, has been "subjected to futility" and is in "bondage to corruption." It's "groaning . . . in the pains of childbirth." And that, to state the obvious, is bad. And yet if evolutionary models of the origin of animal and human life are accurate, this death, futility, corruption, groaning, and pain had been going on for millions of years before Adam and Eve came along.

> *"Why must God the Son become incarnate, live our life, die our death, and be raised for our justification? Scripture's answer is clear: We need a redeemer because Adam as the first man and covenantal head of the human race brought sin, death, and destruction into this world, and it is only by the last Adam, our Lord Jesus Christ, that it can be paid for and reversed."*[24]
>
> —STEPHEN WELLUM

So here's the key question: Could God possibly have called such a world "good," as He does in Genesis 1? Could God have looked at millions of years of dead panda babies and said with satisfaction, "This is very good"? And think about the layers of fossils, every one of them representing the drowning, disease, or dismemberment of an animal. Think about your own dog getting his throat punctured by a wolf and his legs ripped off, his intestines exposed. Think about your grandma, her body eaten away from the inside out with cancer. *Is this good?*

All theories of evolution—all of them—say that death is necessary, if not exactly good. Death at least brings progress. Evolution is time and death, time and death.

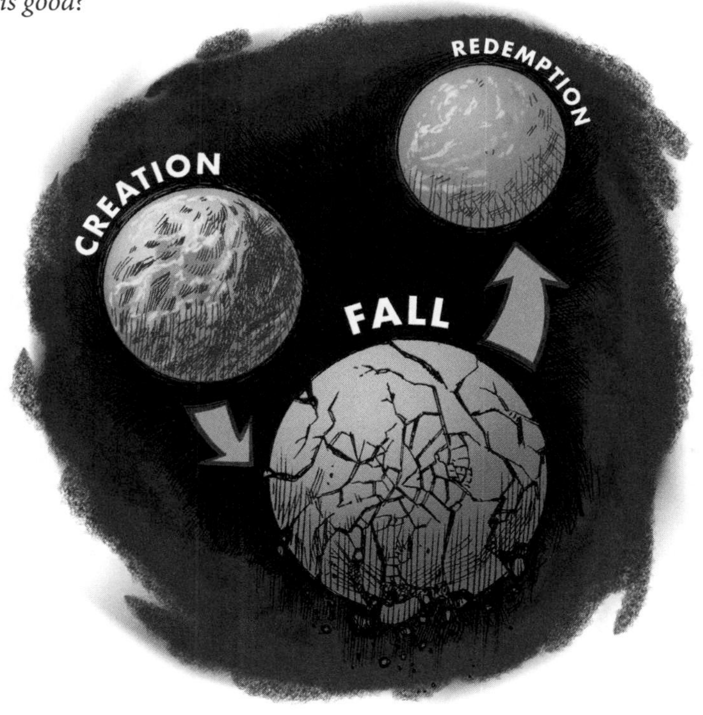

Paul, in contrast, says that death came into this world through sin. Paul, under the inspiration of the Holy Spirit, says that the creation itself is waiting, groaning for death to end.

Christians who believe in evolution do have explanations for how God could call the world "very good" in Genesis 1. They say, for example, that God called the world "good," not perfect; they say that sin brought spiritual death to humans, but physical death was already present. [25]

They can say this, but by doing so they create further problems. The impulse to put the Bible together with evolution has always been defended by saying that if

Christians ignore scientific consensus, Christianity and the Bible will be discredited. But evolution isn't the only challenge to a biblical worldview. One of the other major challenges is the question of how an all-good, all-powerful God could create a world with so much death and suffering. Bible-believing Christians have always had a solid scriptural answer: death and suffering came through the Fall of Adam. But theistic evolutionists can't say that; for them, death has always been around. They avoid the error of atheism by disagreeing with much of modern biology and geology, but they have created another problem: blaming God and not humans for suffering and death.

Christians ought to know in their consciences and from their Bibles that death doesn't belong here. Christians should also know that death will one day be "swallowed up in victory" by the work of Jesus Christ (1 Cor. 15:54).

WHAT DAVID BROOKS REALLY MEANT

When David Brooks of the *New York Times* criticized "fundamentalists" for "tak[ing] everything literally," what he really meant was something like this:

> You ought to read the Bible according to a standard other than itself—namely my standard. My worldview standard says that doing justice, loving mercy, and walking humbly are good. So take Micah 6:8 literally. But my worldview standard says that God didn't create the world in six twenty-four-hour days, so don't take Genesis 1 literally.

But if you read the Bible according to the standards the Bible sets for itself—if you let the whole Bible speak—Adam has to be a historical figure; he has to be the person who brought sin and death (for animals and humans) into the world. We have a question of authority: who gets to determine which parts of the Bible we're allowed to believe? Remember, the decision not to trust God's words is always a decision to trust someone else's. And without Creation as the Bible presents it, Fall and Redemption aren't resting on any foundation.

Before Charles Darwin persuaded educated Western people that their great-great-grandparents were primates, no one ever read Genesis 1 to say that Adam was a metaphor for human moral consciousness. They read it to mean that God created Adam, breathing life into dirt.. You're dirt too. The Bible compares us all, in fact, to clay on a potter's wheel (Rom. 9:21). And when the Potter talks, it's a good idea to listen hard—even if other pieces of clay are contradicting everything He says.

THINKING IT THROUGH 21.1B

1. If Adam and Eve are actually the products of evolution, why must their creation in Genesis 1 be reinterpreted as a metaphor?
2. Why is it problematic to reinterpret Adam and Eve's creation as a metaphor?
3. Why must a biblical Christian reject the view that Paul was mistaken about Adam being a historical person?
4. Could God call a world full of painful animal death "very good"? Why or why not?

21.2 CHRISTIANS IN THE SCIENCES

No one is in charge of science. Not the top scientist in the biology department at Harvard or Cambridge or MIT. Not a science czar at the United Nations. Not the author of a book on the *New York Times* list of science bestsellers. No one person sets the "rules" for how science is practiced. And no one person can change the rules. They are agreed upon, more or less, by the scientific community. And that community itself has fuzzy boundaries. Who counts as a "scientist"? It depends, to a degree, on which scientist you ask. For all the vaunted objectivity of science, scientists manage to have some pretty heated arguments and even to trade personal insults. "John Christy has made a scientific career out of being wrong," said one prominent scientist about a Christian climatologist (in private e-mails that went public in 2009). "He's not even a third-rate scientist." [26] Why the mockery and the put-downs if science is all about objective data? The reality is that "science is like any other social network. It's a lot easier to go along with the crowd." [27]

And the crowd has made its expectations pretty clear. "No supernatural beings allowed" is right at the top of the list. Second place may go to "The universe is basically the way it has always been." As evolutionary materialist Bill Nye put it to Christian creationist Ken Ham in a public debate viewed by millions, "Natural laws that applied in the past apply now." [28]

Like Ham, many scientists believe that a supernatural being created the world, and that this world is most emphatically *not* the way it's supposed to be—it's fallen. How can such people hope to make it in the world of science?

Sometimes they don't make it, as Chapter 11 in the Redemption unit pointed out. In this age, God promises His people suffering along with whatever victories He chooses to give. It's hard to work, let alone to rise to a place of influence, in a scientific profession that says you don't count as a scientist. It's harder in some fields than in others, depending on how far away from creational norms those fields have been bent. Besides that, Paul informs us,

> We do not wrestle against flesh and blood, but against the rulers, against the authorities, against the cosmic powers over this present darkness, against the spiritual forces of evil in the heavenly places. (Eph. 6:12)

Faithful Christians in Western science will run into opposition of one kind or another. And when they do, they need to push back—nicely.

PUSHING BACK NICELY

That pushback, in fact, needs to be not just nice but full of genuine love—love for God, for one's neighbor, and for the creation. A Christian full of that love and gifted by God to be a scientist can do truly great things. And those great things will be even more effective than pointing out the Christian origins of science. If scientifically trained and gifted Christians let their lights so shine before others that those others save money—or increase the safety of their kids, or experience healing, or benefit from one of the countless other gifts good science and technology can bring—it will be hard to argue that Christianity is antiscience. If you have scientific gifts, use them to serve your neighbor, and see what good will come. Christians should be known more for their good works in science, for positive things, than for saying "no" to the reigning scientific consensus about evolution or naturalism.

Many, many conservative Christian scientists around the world are doing precisely this kind of good scientific work in a wide range of scientific fields. The mere existence of every one of these believing scientists is pushing back nicely against the opposition Christianity faces from much of the scientific community. Here are just a few examples.

John Baumgardner

John Baumgardner, a creationist with a PhD in geophysics and space physics from the University of California at Los Angeles, developed a computer model called "Terra" that predicts how the earth's crust might react under certain conditions. He used Terra to make a model for how Noah's flood may have occurred, and the program is so robust that it is used by geophysicists all over the world. *U.S. News & World Report* called Baumgardner "the world's pre-eminent expert in the design of computer models for geophysical convection, the process by which the Earth creates volcanoes, earthquakes, and the movement of the continental plates."[29]

MRI: *(magnetic resonance imaging) a device that produces an image of internal organs*

Raymond V. Damadian

Raymond V. Damadian is a good example of a scientist who has pushed back. He developed the science behind the MRI* and built an operational prototype. And he's a committed young-earth creationist.

Danny Faulkner and Ron Samec

Ron Samec and Danny Faulkner are astronomers who have written and contributed to many scientific papers with titles such as "Photometric Study of the Solar Type Pre-Contact Binary, V2421 Cygni."[30] They have done a good deal of work on binary star systems, pairs of stars which orbit around a common center—work which helps us understand the physical forces operating in our universe.

Steve Figard

Steve Figard is a conservative Christian, a young-earth creationist with a PhD in biochemistry from Florida State University. He has made numerous contributions to his field, especially in cancer research. He developed "five immunoassays related to cancer (free and total PSA, CEA, AFP and CA19-9)."[31] In layman's terms, he developed tests that can detect the presence of cancer. Figard directs the Cancer Research Lab at Bob Jones University.

John Hartnett

John Hartnett is an expert in the design of atomic clocks. He has numerous professional publications. His creation research has focused on the development of a creationist cosmology, one using a modified metric tensor coupled with Einstein's general theory of relativity.[32]

Mark Horstemeyer

Mark Horstemeyer is the chairman of computational solid mechanics at the Center for Advanced Vehicular Systems (CAVS) and a professor of mechanical engineering at Mississippi State University. He has numerous professional publications and is an expert in the computational modeling of physical materials. He has been an editor for the *Proceedings of the International Conference on Creationism*, which has been very influential in the push to develop rigorous models of science based on Scripture. [33]

D. Russell Humphreys

Humphreys worked for Sandia National Laboratories from 1979 to 2001. His research for Sandia ranged from nuclear physics to superconductors. Later on at the Institute for Creation Research, he worked on the RATE project—Radioisotopes and the Age of The Earth—which challenged evolutionists by proving the presence of helium in zircon crystals, where the evolutionary model predicts no helium. Humphreys has also contributed many papers to peer-reviewed creationist journals. He is on the board of directors of the Creation Research Society, the oldest creationist organization in the United States. He has developed a creationary model for planetary magnetic fields and has made pioneering efforts in creation-based cosmologies. [34]

PEER-REVIEWED CREATIONIST JOURNALS

Peer review is the system whereby articles submitted for publication in scholarly journals are subject to blind review by other experts (blind in that those reviewers aren't told the names of the authors whose papers they're evaluating). There are currently three peer-reviewed creationist publications:

- *Creation Research Society Quarterly*
- *Journal of Creation*
- *Answers Research Journal*

Georgia Purdom

Georgia Purdom received a PhD in molecular genetics from Ohio State University in 2000; she has worked for Answers in Genesis and has led the Microbe Forum, a group researching the role of microbes in the world before and after the Fall.

Joel Salatin

In the science of sustainable local farming practices, Joel Salatin is a recognized leader. He calls himself a "Christian libertarian environmentalist capitalist lunatic farmer" (and he should add "punchy writer" to the list—the man can write, and he's the author of multiple books and articles). One journalist said of Salatin, "He's not going back to the old model. . . . He is just looking totally afresh at how to maximize production in an integrated system on a holistic farm. He's just totally innovative." [35] Salatin is out speaking a hundred days a year, promoting his farming methods. He says, "What we aspire to is to have the best food available." [36]

John Sanford

Sanford was a professor at Cornell University for more than twenty-five years. His research focused on plant genetics. While a professor, he invented the "gene gun" and contributed to developing better crops. He published a book, *Genetic Entropy and the Mystery of the Genome*, that extends Haldane's dilemma into modern terms. His book clearly demonstrates that the human genome cannot be millions of years old based on mutation rates. [37]

Jonathan Sarfati

Jonathan Sarfati is an intellectually gifted individual. He doesn't know how he does it, exactly, but he is able to play as many as twelve games of chess at once while blindfolded. And he can win (his record is eleven victories and no losses at a chess club in his home country of New Zealand). Sarfati's doctoral work was in chemistry, focusing on spectroscopy. He has worked with Creation Ministries International and has edited the peer-reviewed *Journal of Creation.*

Andrew Snelling

Andrew Snelling's doctorate is in geology, and he's one of the relatively few scientists in the world permitted to take rock samples out of the Grand Canyon. He has written or contributed to nearly three hundred articles in various publications, many of them seeking to popularize the work of creation science.

Kurt Wise

baraminology: *a discipline in creation biology studying the "created" (Hebrew:* bara*) "kinds" (Hebrew:* min*) and forming a taxonomy*

Kurt Wise received an MA and a PhD in paleontology from Harvard University; his credentials are undeniable. Even evolutionist and atheist Richard Dawkins said that Wise "may well be creationism's most highly qualified and most intelligent scientist."[38] Years ago when he came to a personal point of crisis over the conflict between creation and evolution, he explicitly chose to believe the Bible's account of human origins. Wise has devoted much time to the discipline of baraminology.*

REMEMBERING THE FALL

These scientists would be the first to tell you that they are far from the only Christians in science—and that they're far from perfect, far from omniscient. Accepting the Bible's authority doesn't automatically make them right about all their scientific claims, any more than it ensures you get an A+ on all your calculus quizzes. These scientists struggle against the effects of the Fall in their own work—and in their own hearts—in countless ways. (And inclusion in this list doesn't mean they agreed to be on it or that BJU Press perfectly agrees with all of them.)

But Bill Nye can relax. He wanted "scientifically literate voters and taxpayers for the future," and "engineers that can build stuff, solve problems."[39] He was worried that creationism would keep that from happening. God forbid. Rather, it's the first chapter of Genesis that calls on us to press God's world toward its ideal and maximize its usefulness. Creationists can be—and many *should* be—scientists.

REMEMBERING COMMON GRACE

No one on the list above would deny that non-Christians can do valuable work, even morally good work, in science. When Jewish physician Jonas Salk developed the polio vaccine, saving and improving the lives of countless children, he was pushing back the effects of the Fall. He was restoring a little slice of the lives of these people to the way those lives were supposed to be. Legs that would have been crooked are now strong and straight. That's good.

And, of course, the list of non-Christians who have made significant and beneficial scientific advances (not all advances are beneficial) is much longer than the list of Christians. That fact is a reason for humility and hard work, not for admitting defeat.

The History of Science

Let's go back to the history of science for a moment. The typical story told by scientism is that science and religion have been at war since the time of the Greeks. Oxford professor and historian of science Peter Harrison says,

> The history of science, on one very common understanding, has three distinct stages. Science is said to have had its origins in Greek antiquity when philosophers first broke away from the myths of their forebears and sought rational explanations for natural phenomena. Science subsequently suffered a setback with the advent of Christianity, going into significant decline in the Middle Ages. But it then emerged triumphant with the scientific revolution of the seventeenth century when it finally broke away from religion and set out on its progressive path to the present.[40]

But Harrison doesn't buy it. The idea that mankind used to believe in myths but has moved on to rationality is "difficult to sustain," he says. The Greek tradition of medicine, for example, began with Hippocrates, the source of the Hippocratic oath (which, historically, Western doctors have taken at the beginning of their medical careers). But this ancient "scientific" tradition coexisted perfectly well with the religious cult of Asclepius, the Greek god of healing. In fact, the Hippocratic oath begins with references to two Greek gods: "I swear by Apollo the physician, and Asclepius the surgeon."[41]

Scientists today, despite their claims to be concerned with "just the facts," still mix reason and myth (remember the "just-so stories"?). The myths scientists believe in today don't seem like myths to them because so many people accept them. But a lot of people believed in Asclepius too. (To this day, we use the word *hygiene*, which comes from Hygiea, Asclepius's daughter, goddess of cleanliness.) Every piece of knowledge has always come with faith attached—for everybody, not just for Christians.

Doing Science Yourself

This historical argument should give Christians gifted in science added confidence that they do belong in the scientific world. But if Christians aren't actually *doing* science, the argument is probably worthless. Christianity is not merely compatible with science but generates it—so if it's your calling, go do some science. Push back nicely against the reigning view that science must be naturalistic. Subdue the earth, and take dominion over it.

Maybe you could be like Michael, a high school student (using BJU Press materials) who made it into *Popular Science*'s list of top teenage scientists and inventors. Michael saw human needs and worked on solving them. First, he noticed his own need: he was always forgetting to turn out the lights and getting in trouble for it. So at age ten he invented a contraption that would turn them off automatically using light and motion sensors. By age sixteen he had moved on to other people's needs, inventing a nasal spray that can stave off dangerous diabetic attacks and save lives.[42]

If you're gifted in science—which is almost the same as saying, "If you love science"—then you may be called to that hard work. And you'll need to do it according to the creational norms for science laid out in Chapter 19.

A SOMEWHAT HYPOTHETICAL QUESTION

Consider this imaginary scenario. You go to an academic conference full of scientists. You present a historical paper describing how different cultures over time have defined what counts as "knowledge." You take questions. Up pops a hand. The top biology professor from MIT asks: "So what do *you* think counts as knowledge?"

If you were to answer that question with, "I think the fear of the Lord is the beginning of knowledge," you would get a written invitation not to come to next year's conference. You broke the rules of the discipline.

So what *do* you say? What do you think?

You'll need to learn to do organized empirical study and then to build a model that explains the resulting data. You'll need to work to communicate your findings, work according to standards (and adjust existing ones if they need to be adjusted), and work according to norms of goodness and beauty.

Christians who believe the Bible—Adam, Jesus, Paul, all of it—need to set new expectations for funding and research in the sciences. We need more research projects run on creationist presuppositions. We aren't going to solve all difficulties for the creationist viewpoint right away, such as the question of how stars can be millions of light-years away in a galaxy that's only six thousand years old, but creationists are working on it. Secular science takes lots of time and money to get to answers, with a huge number of dead ends along the way. (In fact, one secular scholar wrote a widely read article titled, "Why Most Published Research Findings Are False."[43]) Creation science needs time—and even false starts—too.

Good science from Christians is one of the best apologetics for the Christian faith right now—if indeed creationist scientific models make more successful predictions than evolutionary models. Christianity is ready to tackle the work of science.

THINKING IT THROUGH 21.2

1. Other than just defending the biblical view of origins, what else should Christians who are scientists be doing?
2. Summarize at least three important scientific contributions that demonstrate that creationists are not antiscience.
3. Does the fact that someone is a Christian make him a good scientist or that someone is a non-Christian make him a bad scientist? Explain why or why not.
4. Summarize the creational norms necessary for meeting a particular human need (i.e., for *doing* the work of science).
5. What does the coexistence of Hippocratic medicine with the worship of Asclepius in ancient Greece tell us about the relationship of religion and science?

21 CHAPTER REVIEW

TERMS TO REMEMBER

literalists
origins

Scripture Memory

Genesis 1:31

Making Connections

1. What underlying worldview presupposition will determine where somebody will land on the spectrum of origins views and which model they will resort to in order to explain Genesis?
2. What are two major biblical truths that are often undermined when Genesis 1 is reinterpreted rather than read according to its straightforward meaning?
3. Who sets the rules for how science should be done? Might some of those rules be erroneous?
4. What could perhaps be a more effective way to witness to the truth and substance of the Christian worldview than mere debates over origins?

Developing Skills in Apologetics and Worldview

5. How should you respond to someone who claims that people's view of origins isn't important as long as they believe the gospel?
6. How should you respond to someone who claims that a belief in creationism will negatively affect the work of technological advancement?

Examining Assumptions and Evidence

7. Differentiate a literalist interpretation of "Our God is a consuming fire" (Heb. 12:29) from a straightforward interpretation of that statement.
8. If Christians believe that Genesis is mistaken about origins, how does that necessarily affect their interpretation of the rest of Scripture?
9. Why are the theological truths of humankind's fallenness and God's common grace vital to understanding the quality of scientific work done by both believers and unbelievers?
10. Answer the question in the sidebar on page 336.

Becoming a Creative Cultivator

11. Identify a physical need in your classroom. Hypothesize a technological tool that might solve the problem.

8

HISTORY

Chapter Twenty-Two **FOUNDATIONS FOR HISTORY**

[God] made from one man every nation of mankind to live on all the face of the earth, having determined allotted periods and the boundaries of their dwelling place, that they should seek God, and perhaps feel their way toward him and find him. Yet he is actually not far from each one of us.

Scripture Memory
Acts 17:26–27

22.1 HISTORY BEGAN

"In the beginning, God created" (Gen. 1:1). A Christian philosophy of history is founded on this creation.

> All things were made through him, and without him was not any thing made that was made. (John 1:3)

Only God is eternal. Everything else, at some point in time, began.

Without the creations of that first chapter, we couldn't have "history" in any meaningful sense. It's not just that God in Genesis 1 provides a model for history by giving us a chronologically ordered list of what happened on seven successive days. It's that in Genesis we meet time divisions in the first place. God set the order in the heavenly bodies "for signs and seasons, and for days and years" (Gen. 1:14). God built the march and measurement of time into His creation in the beginning.

The early theologian Augustine, under pressure from the reigning worldviews of his day, thought it was unworthy of God to take a whole week to create the world. He theorized that God actually created the world instantly and that the seven days of Genesis are only an analogy.[1] But the Bible goes out of its way to specify that God used "days," days with a "morning and evening" like our own days. Humans are often impatient with God's timing (2 Pet. 3:4), but since the beginning God has worked out His will through history.

Creation took time; and so does redemption. God could have sent Jesus Christ immediately to die for the sins of Adam and Eve. But He didn't. He allowed a great deal of time to pass—a great deal of history to transpire—while the Fall worked out its effects all over the planet.

God let sin have increasing reign for a thousand years before He wiped out almost all life on the planet with a flood. But even then, Christ's redemption was still far off in the future. God chose to work out His redemptive purposes through all the many generations of history in one particular family, Abraham's family—until the ultimate coming of Abraham's seed, Jesus Christ. And now for over two thousand years God has unfolded in history the spread of His church over the world.

It should be no surprise, then, that much of the Bible is straight history. Genesis is entirely history, as is the first half of Exodus. Even the Mosaic laws in Exodus, Leviticus, and Deuteronomy are delivered not in a mere list but as part of a long story.

Some of the earliest Old Testament prophets were also historians of a sort, recording God's view of Israel's history from the time of Joshua through the Babylonian exile in the books of Joshua, Judges, Samuel, and Kings. The final book of the Hebrew Bible is Chronicles, a history that spans from Adam to the end of the exile.

THE FLOW OF BIBLICAL HISTORY

Understanding Scripture requires keen historical awareness, something not all readers of the Bible have. You may have heard some people complain that Christians pick and choose which Bible verses they'll follow. They condemn homosexuality, for example, but not eating shrimp—even though Leviticus prohibits both.

The Bible's awareness of history is vital to answering this complaint. The Mosaic law was a historical covenant in force between the time of the Exodus and the time of Christ. Certain laws in the Mosaic Covenant reflect God's moral expectations for all time. For instance, God's condemnation of homosexual desires and actions is rooted in the creation order (Gen. 2:22–24), stated in the Old Testament law (Lev. 20:13), and reaffirmed in the New Testament (Rom. 1:26–27; 1 Cor. 6:9; cf. Matt. 19:4). Other laws in the Mosaic Covenant served as pictures or object lessons for the people. They were valid while the covenant was in force, but not afterward. Jesus "declared all foods clean" (Mark 7:19). Thus, Christians, who are under the New Covenant, not the Mosaic Covenant, do not have to observe food laws (Heb. 8:6–13; Acts 10:15). All of the Bible is beneficial for the Christian, but not all of it is directly applicable. To know which parts are and which are not requires historical awareness.

Historical awareness is important for understanding other biblical doctrines as well. Paul argues very specifically that Abraham was justified by faith before he was ever circumcised, as Jewish law later demanded (Rom. 4:9–12). Paul makes this historical argument to demonstrate that circumcision cannot be a requirement for justification.

God could have written a logically organized systematic theology book with an appendix full of precise, unchanging behavior rules. He could have handed the book to Adam and provided translations for new language groups as they developed. But He didn't.

"I can only answer the question, 'What am I to do?' if I can answer the prior question, 'Of what story do I find myself a part?"[2]

—ALASDAIR MACINTYRE

He unfolded both His creative work and His redemptive work historically, and then gave us a Bible narrating and explaining that work. And that Bible tells us that He didn't create all humans at once (as He may have done in the case of angels) and place them in the new Jerusalem. Instead God began with two individuals in a garden and told them to fill and develop the world. When humans reproduce, they don't bear other adults but children who have a lot of growing and developing to do.

And God brought His people through a period of childlike development too. The Bible itself says that the Old Testament law treated God's people like children; the law was like a "guardian" that we no longer need (Gal. 3:24–25). In the Old Testament, God took His eternal law and applied it in specific ways to Israel's life in the Middle East. The prophets declared precisely what God's will was for the people. But in the New Testament, the apostles reason with God's people and work through lengthy explanations about how God's eternal law should be applied to various situations (e.g., 1 Cor. 8:1–9:27). Why the change? Part of the answer is that God's people had matured. In the Old Testament, they were "children" who needed God to apply His law to their specific situation. In the New Testament era, they're full-grown sons who can look back at the general statements of God's will in the Old and New Testaments, at God's specific Old Testament applications, and can reason through to the right application in their time and place.[3] The point is that God designed even the way His people relate to His law to go through a process of development.

The social structures and institutions that define the horizons of the possible for various cultures—the things that fill history textbooks—have also gone through a process of development in God's providence. In Eden, nations, governments, schools, businesses, trade associations, banks, airlines, internet standards consortiums, and a host of other institutions did not exist. These institutions developed over the course of history.

THE PROGRESS OF DIVINE REDEMPTION

Once again, why would God design a world that works by development over time? The Bible does not address this question directly. However, looking at Scripture gives us some clues. The progress of redemption reveals things about God's power, wisdom, and glory that would not have been put on display otherwise. Israel's system of sacrifices, for example, provides us with a richer understanding of Christ's death. Similarly, Christ didn't immediately come as the perfect Prophet, Priest, and King. Instead, God raised up prophets (Moses, Elijah), priests (Aaron, Eleazar), and kings (David, Solomon) so that their successes and failures could provide a background for understanding the significance of Christ's roles.

It's one thing to say, "Sin is bad." It's another thing to make readers feel the injustice and irrationality of sin by putting it on display in the history of the Israelite nation. Likewise, "grace is undeserved favor" is a nice thing to say, but grace is seen to be more glorious when the path to the cross and the resurrection of Christ unfolds over time.

The development of cultures also allows the glory of God to be displayed through the skills of His image-bearers. A world in which humans produce the pyramids, Aristotle's writings, Bach's music, and the Saturn V rocket needs history to develop. One generation builds on the insights and skills of those that preceded it.

THINKING IT THROUGH 22.1

1. What is a Christian philosophy of history founded on? Explain why.
2. Why does God design redemption to unfold through a historical process?
3. Why would God design a world that develops over time?
4. What does a developing history allow humans to accomplish?
5. Propose an alternative to the seemingly arbitrary application of the Old Testament law by Christians today.

22.2 WHY STUDY HISTORY?

It's good to study history for three worldview reasons: (1) History helps us understand the ways and works of God. (2) History teaches life lessons—as atheist philosopher George Santayana said, "Those who cannot remember the past are condemned to repeat it."[4] Since all knowledge comes with historical background, the opposite of history is amnesia. (3) History provides a sense of cultural identity. That's why schools around the world teach students the histories of their respective nations.

UNDERSTANDING THE WAYS AND WORKS OF GOD

The historical narratives of Scripture are given primarily so that God's people can understand His ways and His works. God has at various points in history acted to further His plan of redemption. But these acts of redemption require interpretation, something provided, in part, by the historical books of Scripture.[5] Christians believe that not only the historical records in Scripture but also those interpretations are inspired by God. The Bible both tells us historical things only God could know—like what day man was created on—and explains the significance of those things. Even the order in which Adam and Eve were created was significant, for example, though we wouldn't have known what it meant if God hadn't told us (1 Tim. 2:12–13).

God offers explanations of the foundational acts of redemption. For instance, we know from Scripture what no Roman centurion on Golgotha could have known, and that no scientific measurement, then or now, could ever determine: that a despised and rejected man dying on a cross was bearing the weight of the world's sins on His shoulders.

Though the foundational acts of redemption that need divine explanation have been accomplished, that doesn't mean God is now inactive. He is still actively working out His plan of redemption in the world. He has told us that this is one of His purposes He will accomplish (Gal. 4:4). So Christian historians are called to connect those purposes (as revealed in Scripture) with the events they study. They are also justified in drawing conclusions about what God may be doing in the world.

You just read a statement that's very controversial, even among Christians. Did you see it? The issue is this: can a Christian historian really discern God's purposes in history? At a specific level, he'd better be careful. Speaking for God is not something anyone should take lightly. But failing to speak for Him isn't either.

When the historian sees the gospel spread, he can look to Scripture and see this as one of God's stated purposes in human history. He can look at the ways God prepared people to receive the gospel or historical events and ideas that led people to turn to the gospel. He can suggest that God moved in history in those ways to further His gospel purposes. Of course, even when the gospel faces setbacks, God is still working out His will in the world. In those situations, the historian should turn to what the Bible says about the suffering that His people can expect.

The Merneptah Stele, created in Egypt about 1,200 years before Christ, has the first mention of "Israel" in written sources outside the Bible.

Obviously, the Christian historian who undertakes such study must be humble because he doesn't have the insight into the significance of events that the biblical historians had as recipients of divine revelation. But he does understand something that non-Christian historians refuse to acknowledge: the broad sweep of God's purpose for history.

LEARNING LESSONS FOR LIFE

Humans are finite and fallen—and that's another excellent reason to study history. C. S. Lewis points out that people share "a great mass of common assumptions" simply because they live together at the same time and place. This is true even among people who vehemently disagree with each other.[6] But pick up a book from a bygone era, or begin to study the thought of another time and place, and you'll find yourself in a different world of thought—so different, sometimes, that it can be hard to grasp.

Uncovering your own assumptions is very hard work. Culture is at its strongest when it's most invisible. Breathing the air of another century is one of the best ways to expose your own presuppositions and to force you to evaluate them. You'll find that some of the assumptions of previous eras were healthier than those of the present.

telos: *the ultimate end of a goal-oriented process (borrowed from the Greek)*

Previous eras, for example, didn't all make reason the source and standard of truth; they made it a tool—among other tools—for finding truth. Previous eras, even non-Christian ones, saw a **telos*** in created things. Where the spirit of this age sees an undirected process of evolution guiding everything to nowhere in particular, past eras have seen inherent purposes in created things.

People of the past also got some things wrong that we get right. They were no less intelligent than people today, but they were just as fallen and finite. Many of them saw a purpose in created things because they lived in what they considered an "enchanted" world where spirits or gods were in the rocks, trees, and rivers.

Mere history—simple description of what people have done and thought—does not really distinguish between old worldviews and newer ones. The Bible is the only ultimate standard for determining what's true and false. That's why Scripture ends up being the key evaluative instrument in the toolbox of a Christian historian.

History can provide insight into the consequences of ideas and actions. Today's bright ideas may have already failed (or succeeded) many times before, and that's worth knowing. History, then, is a well of wisdom. But only when it's interpreted through the lens of the Christian worldview.

ESTABLISHING A CULTURAL IDENTITY

The assumptions, values, and practices of the cultures we live in all have histories. Why do Americans value freedom, individualism, equality, and growth? They value these things in large part because of the history of the development of America.

We can value the economic growth that enabled entrepreneurial Americans to raise the standard of living for millions of others around the world. We can value the equality that allows those from humble backgrounds to develop their God-given abilities and rise to prominence so that they can benefit their community, state, or nation. We can value a culture in which people take responsibility for their actions, in which people are willing to step out and take risks that bring significant gains for themselves and others. We can value a culture in which we have the freedom to worship God as Scripture commands us. And history helps us understand where these values came from—and it gives us Abraham Lincolns, Booker T. Washingtons, and William Bradfords who exemplify these virtues.

But history, when read through a scriptural lens, can also serve as a warning to keep us from making our culture an idol. It can caution us about the pursuit of growth that seizes land unlawfully, about the danger of an equality that refuses to submit to God-given authorities, about an individualism that cares little for family or community, about a liberty that stands on its right to do wrong.

Even though the Fall affects the values of every culture, history can at the same time reveal the positive characteristics of other cultures (perhaps those with longer histories) that may value different things. They may value conformity to the group, social class stratification,* and the stability of tradition. There is value to be found in every culture because each is constructed by God's image-bearers making something of His good creation.

social class stratification: *the establishment of higher and lower classes*

History, then, should play a vital role in everyone's life. While Scripture is the norm that must be applied to all of life, history gives us a clearer vision of the life that Scripture is being applied to. For this reason, the rest of this chapter will explore how the discipline of history should be pursued.

THINKING IT THROUGH 22.2

1. What are three worldview reasons for studying history?
2. What often gets exposed when you study a different group of people from a different time period with a different worldview?
3. How can history challenge unfounded contemporary assumptions?
4. What powerful force entrenches assumptions, values, and practices in a specific group of people?
5. Why should a Christian historian seek to carefully discern God's purposes in history?

22.3 CHRISTIAN FOUNDATIONS FOR HISTORY

Given that history is so important and that God built history into the way His world works, how should a Christian practice the discipline of history? Another way of asking this question is "What creational norms must the historian conform to?" If God designed His world to unfold historically and if He intends humans to make sense of this historical unfolding, then it is likely that the very nature of the world and the very nature of the human person would require historical investigation to proceed according to a certain structure (see page 123).

But as we noted in the previous unit on science, determining the norms for disciplines such as science and history is not as straightforward as determining the norms of marriage and family life. The norms for studying history are not spelled out in the Bible. Instead, the Christian recognizes that God built the world according to the blueprint of His wisdom (Prov. 8:22–31). To learn the creational norms for wisdom a person needs to bring together fear of the Lord (Prov. 1:7) and observations about the world (cf. Isa. 28:26) and view them through the corrective lenses of Scripture.

Wisdom is God's creation, and it is God who teaches through general revelation. Those who reject God are going to miss some of the basics of how life works. Thus, the Christian historian should expect his approach to historical study to be distinct from the approaches of unbelievers. But since general revelation is given to all people, the Christian should expect unbelieving historians to have discovered much that is right about studying history. Since the Christian is finite and fallible, the unbeliever will in some cases have discovered things that the Christian can learn from. As he does this, however, the Christian needs to continue to run all of this teaching through the filter of a Christian worldview.

FOUNDATIONAL ESSENTIALS

A historian can arrogantly assume (or pretend) that he has a "neutral" perspective, or he can fall in the opposite ditch, despairing that he'll never do justice to his subject matter because of his **situatedness*** within history. Neither option is healthy. Instead, a historian would do well to acknowledge to himself his basic commitments and nonetheless work to be fair and thorough. The Christian historian, in particular, will come to history with some fundamental presuppositions.

situatedness: *the inescapable truth that every human views the world from a particular historical, geographic, and intellectual point of view*

In contrast to a **cyclical view of history**, the Christian believes that history had a beginning described by Genesis 1. The Christian believes that history also has a

CYCLICAL VIEW OF HISTORY

Historian David Bebbington proposes that cyclical views of history developed as people observed either the generational cycle of birth, growth, and death or the annual cycle of the seasons. These cycles were then applied to history as a whole. Not all cyclical views are the same. Bebbington identifies three.

> In the first, the circular pattern is restricted to particular dynasties or civilizations. Each in turn rises to prosperity before falling to defeat, disaster or decay. The second variation holds that the whole inhabited earth or even the universe is passing through a cycle, which usually extends over a vast period of time. The conclusion of a cycle may mean the end of all things, or else be the prelude to a fresh cycle of a new earth and sometimes a new heaven. In the third, the past is a time of steady decline from a lost golden age to the decadence of the present. This view, often called primitivism because it idealizes primitive times, concentrates on only a section of a cycle, its downward curve. The three variations interacted with each other, but it is broadly true to say that, while the third has coloured thought throughout the world, the first was specially characteristic of China and the second of India.[7]

this-worldly culmination: "Then comes the end, when [Christ] delivers the kingdom to God the Father after destroying every rule and every authority and power" (1 Cor. 15:24). At the end of earthly history, "the kingdom of the world has become the kingdom of our Lord and of his Christ, and he shall reign forever and ever" (Rev. 11:15). Though human history had a starting point, it will never end because the age to come is an eternal age (Luke 18:30).

The Christian view of history, though linear, is not simply the Enlightenment (and evolutionary) view of continual progress. Christian historians would not agree with what one prominent sociologist said:

> The human march forward has been filled with wrong turns, backsliding, and horrible crimes. But taken in its grand sweep, it has indeed been a march forward. On every dimension, the last half-dozen centuries in particular have brought sensational improvement which, with qualifications, continues to this day.[8]

Christians can certainly acknowledge and praise all the progress that humans as God's image-bearers have made in medicine, science, engineering, and the arts (and in many other fields), but Scripture also reveals that the righteous will suffer persecutions and that evil people will grow worse and worse (2 Tim. 3:12–13). The Enlightenment view is a defection from the Christian view because it replaces the coming kingdom of Christ with scientific and technological advances as the measure of progress.

Christians also know something of their location in history. We live at the end of the ages (1 Cor. 10:11) and in the last days (Heb. 1:2). God hasn't told us how much longer these last days will extend. But this much is clear: Christ's death, resurrection, and ascension make up the defining moment in human history. The kingdom of God has come in salvation, and it is going to come in judgment. It could happen at any time.

CREATIONAL NORMS FOR HISTORY

Nailing down your basic commitments as a historian is essential, but a Christian historian cannot stop there. He must seek out the best practice for his discipline—its creational norms. This section outlines seven such norms.

1. Studying Source Materials

Historians necessarily begin their work by looking at sources. Sometimes these sources are artifacts that archaeologists have recovered. Historians can gain some knowledge of how people lived by looking at the pottery they used, the kinds of houses they lived in, even the kinds of animal bones found in their garbage dumps.

Sometimes sources are traditions that have been handed down from generation to generation or oral histories collected from the participants in historical events. But often the sources are written records that have somehow survived the centuries. The best sources—**primary sources**—are the letters, diaries, official records, and such that provide first-hand accounts of historical events.

Sifting through sources is central to the work of the historian, and that work often looks pretty much the same whether it's done by a Christian or a non-Christian. And yet, even here worldview makes a difference. It can influence a person's evaluation of what source material is significant and worthy of tracking down or of what topics are significant for study.

Historians gather primary sources; they then necessarily evaluate the material and seek to judge the reliability of those sources. These are the pieces of information they use to construct a readable story.

2. Making Models

But when a historian writes a history, he is never simply writing "what happened" because "what happened" is complex, contains many factors, and may not be fully knowable. Even the divine Author in writing Kings and Chronicles or Matthew, Mark, Luke, and John is not simply telling us "what happened." In one sense we get less than what happened:

> Now there are also many other things that Jesus did. Were every one of them to be written, I suppose that the world itself could not contain the books that would be written. (John 21:25)

But in the Gospels we also get more than what happened: we get interpretation of the events that even the people who witnessed them may not have had. This is true both of histories in the Bible and of those outside it. Historians identify and interpret evidence, and, on the basis of this, construct narratives. This is a complicated business because human historical actions are themselves always complicated and impossible to reduce to single causes, intentions, or motivations.[9]

Any time a limited human being tries to summarize or package a large set of complex information, he necessarily forms a model—like the scientific models discussed in the previous unit. Because historians are not inspired, they make their models with limited information (to varying degrees) and with limited understanding (to varying degrees) of the significance of the events they study and write about. A recognition of this human finitude, along with the realization that their own fallenness can affect their judgment, should make Christian historians humble as they make models.

3. Selecting What's Significant

Have you ever read a transcript of a real-life conversation? You can tell immediately that you're reading transcribed speech and not written discourse. Real-life dialogue is full of *ums* and *uhs*, run-on sentences, and awkward pauses that simply don't show up in formal writing. Even if it were possible, no one would ever want to read literally *everything* that was said by every participant in the Battle of Hastings in 1066, for example. It would take forever to read, and it would be impossible to grasp. Nor would anyone ever want to read a precise account of every step, every sword swing, every longbow shot, every horse, every outfit, every blade of grass trampled.

The records we have from that fateful battle already demonstrate one of the key principles of historiography (the practice of history as a discipline): selection. The people who wrote accounts of the battle in letters or books *selected* the stories and events and themes they felt were most important. And so does every historian.

Selectivity is unavoidable, and what a historian deems significant will depend to a great extent on his worldview.

Christian historian Timothy Larsen, for example, noticed a problem with selection in many histories of Victorian England. All historians recognize that this time period was a very religious one. "Yet, somehow all of that religion too often does not find a place in what is written in Victorian studies textbooks, or works of reference, or taught in courses. In such places, although there are laudable exceptions, one not infrequently learns simply that Victorians lost their faith."[10]

Why would secular historians tend to select stories of lost faith when writing about a highly religious age? Perhaps those historians could identify more with people who lost their faith; these people's experiences seemed more rational and normative. Secularism is the direction the world was going at the time they were writing, and therefore it seemed to deserve emphasis in their accounts of the past.

But Larsen, a Christian, was more attuned to the value of Christianity in the Victorian era. There certainly were people who abandoned their profession of faith in Christ in England during the nineteenth century, and their stories are worth telling. But Larsen noticed something secular historians were not interested in: a significant number of these ex-Christians came back to faith in Christ. What secular historians relegated to footnotes Larsen wrote a whole book about. He called it *Crisis of Doubt: Honest Faith in Nineteenth-Century England*. In this case Larsen's Christian perspective enabled him to see what many others were missing.

This does not mean, however, that the Christian historian seeks to make history as Christian as possible. The Christian historian's worldview should include the belief that all people are made in the image of God. Therefore, he should expect to find amazing achievements in non-Christian societies. The Christian worldview also teaches that the Fall has had pervasive effects. So the Christian should expect to find these effects in all cultures. But the Christian also believes that God is working out His redemptive plan throughout history. The Christian historian will be careful not to neglect the historical advance of the gospel. His Christian principles will lead him to select the most valuable information about the period he's studying, and what could be more valuable than the work of God?

4. Making Moral Judgments

Historians not only recount what happened in the past, but they also often evaluate what happened. Sometimes they're able to do this by pointing to minority voices who raised moral objections at the time the events unfolded. For instance, a historian may point to the resistance that American missionaries gave to the seizure of Cherokee land by Andrew Jackson and the state of Georgia. Or a historian might note that pastor James Waddell Alexander was concerned that the Mexican-American War might provoke God's judgment on the nation,[11] or that the American diplomat tasked with negotiating the treaty at the end of that war sought the fewest concessions possible from Mexico on account of "the iniquity of the war, as an abuse of power on our part."[12]

Sometimes there are no contemporary figures who speak out against moral wrongs because they all share the same moral blind spots. Christians can treat historical figures with moral blind spots fairly by positioning them within the context and assumptions of their times. But Christian historians also have in Scripture a moral standard by which to evaluate the conduct of any time period.

5. Discerning History as Divine Providence

Let's consider now the question introduced earlier. Can historians see God's hand in history?

Scripture teaches that the same God who spoke the universe into existence maintains that existence (2 Pet. 3:5, 7). He controls the clouds, the wind (Ps. 104:3–4), and even the ocean waves (Ps. 107:25, 29). When people or animals eat, the Bible says God is the one who has provided food (Ps. 136:25). Children are born according to God's providence (Ps. 113:9). Not even a sparrow dies apart from God's control (Matt. 10:29). That sovereign rule extends to individual lives and the affairs of nations (Prov. 16:1–9, 33). God determines the boundaries of those nations (Acts 17:26). He sometimes frustrates the plans of nations (Ps. 33:10–11). God looks down from heaven as the King of all the earth. When a king is successful in battle, it's not due to his own power or superior military equipment; it's due to God (Ps. 33:13–17). And God's rule extends so deep that it even shapes the intentions of people's hearts (Prov. 21:1).

So the answer of the Bible is "Yes, God's hand is evident in history because everything that happens is the work of God in some way." Joseph said basically the same thing to his brothers after their father Jacob died: "You meant evil against me, but God meant it for good, to bring it about that many people should be kept alive" (Gen. 50:20). The same event had two distinct sets of planners: (1) the brothers and (2) God Almighty.

Of course, non-Christians cannot accept the existence of two planners or two authors. As the *Stanford Encyclopedia of Philosophy* puts it, "The assumption that there is a divine author of history takes the making of history out of the hands of humanity."[13] But the Bible everywhere insists that God's rule is real and that people's choices are as well. Both shape history and are yet somehow compatible. This is a great mystery, but it must be affirmed by the Christian historian. It means, for instance, that the Christian historian studying the Great Awakening will discount neither the Spirit's working in hearts nor the roles played by the social and political conditions of the time and by powerful personalities.

Another objection—and a powerful one—to God's rule over history is that Christians are sometimes selective in their appeal to providence. Christians often point only to instances in which their points of view are favored; they tend to neglect instances in which the tide turns against them. You've heard Christians do this in prayer request time: People praise the Lord for preserving their lives in a car accident, but they generally fail to acknowledge that God allowed the accident in the first place.

At its worst, a selective reading of providence like that can be used to justify wrongdoing. The success of a revolution may lead certain Christians to justify their rebellion against rightful authority—even though the Bible says that "whoever resists the authorities resists what God has appointed" (Rom. 13:2).

Many Americans appealed to the idea of Manifest Destiny to justify the seizure of Mexican and Indian lands in the westward expansion of the United States. Though some Christians opposed this expansion, others argued that it was part of God's providential plan to spread liberty and Protestant Christianity[14]—as if stealing people's land is OK as long as you give them a gospel tract in the process.

But since God is providentially ruling over all, then everything that happens is providential. Sometimes the workings of providence may, with humility, be discerned by comparing events with God's revealed will in Scripture. If the gospel was preserved in England by the defeat of the Spanish Armada, the Christian historian may suggest that God used that military event to preserve the gospel witness in England—a gospel witness that would centuries later spread around the world. Often, the matter is more mixed. Christian missions was aided (though often hindered as well) by the spread of the British Empire. The empire itself brought both benefits (e.g., infrastructure) and problems (e.g., racist treatment) to the peoples it conquered. The purposes of God in such complex situations are most likely varied. Christians shouldn't doubt God's control when evil seems to triumph or when Christianity suffers setbacks. Why did God permit Christianity to take firm root in Europe but to be subdued in North Africa and halted in its early spread into China? To questions like these the Christian must simply answer, "The secret things belong to the Lord" (Deut. 29:29).

The Christian historian, then, must not neglect the providence of God, but he must proceed in such matters with dependence on what God has revealed and with great humility.

6. Clarifying Causation and Chronology

Historical models typically relate events to one another. So whether a historian is writing a history of the Battle of Gettysburg or of the entire Civil War, he's seeking to order events and to see if he can determine causation. These can be complex tasks. For instance, American Civil War expert Allen Guelzo notes how difficult it is to order the events of the Battle of Gettysburg given that the participants had watches set by dawn, dusk, and church bells—and many had no watches. Thus reports about the timing of events varied widely. Guelzo had to weigh the varying reports and organize them into the most coherent model that he could develop.[15]

Another historian points out that there are numerous proposed causes for that same Civil War, from states' rights versus nationalism, to divisions over the morality of slavery, to differing cultural ideals and economic systems. The plural in the title of his book, *The Causes of the Civil War*, points to the idea that complex events have complex causes. Though slavery stands at the nexus of these causes, that doesn't mean that culture, economics, and politics played no role. Slavery was tied into all of those things, and yet different people may have had very different primary motivations for joining the war effort on either side.[16] In the case of the Crimean War, one historian makes the case that both religious and political concerns provoked the conflict.[17] Causation is complex. The potential causes that stand out to a particular historian as interesting and worth discussing will very likely have a lot to do with his worldview.

7. Communicating Historical Truth

Finally, just as in science, the findings of historians must be communicated in order to benefit others and advance the historical discipline. Sometimes this is done in detailed journal articles that focus on the specifics of a particular incident or aspect of history. Sometimes historians write scholarly monographs* for the benefit of other historians. Sometimes they will instead write for the average interested reader. They might build upon the work of many other historians and put together a sweeping survey that looks at the history of a region, a nation, or even the world.

monograph: *a detailed, scholarly book on one specific topic*

HISTORY AND WORLDVIEW

Historians all do their work looking through worldview lenses. But this doesn't mean that historical research and writing leave a person unchanged. Though the Christian historian should not change his views on biblically rooted matters of doctrine and practice, his historical study should give him a richer view of the world. He should be developing a deeper understanding of how precisely God has worked in the world, a better understanding of the intractability* of sin through a myriad of examples, and a greater ability to understand and evaluate his own culture biblically.

intractability: *difficulty in resolving or eliminating*

Historical research doesn't alter the fundamentals of the faith, but it may alter our evaluations of history. For instance, some think that the Puritans were hypocrites for seeking religious freedom for themselves and then denying it to others. But a student of history will know that modern ideas of religious liberty came later. The Puritans were always looking for the freedom to worship and live in a society governed by Scripture, not simply for "religious liberty" as an abstract value.

Or some might have thought that the American founders were all Christians (since they were clearly not modern secularists). But closer examination reveals that between the First and Second Great Awakenings there was a religious decline in America. Unitarianism and "rational" religion spread, especially among the educated classes. Thomas Jefferson predicted that by the time he died evangelical Christianity would be extinct in America. In reality, even as he spoke, the Second Great Awakening was under way.[18]

Christians who study history ought to look at everything through the lenses of the biblical worldview. But they're looking at something; they aren't just looking at the lenses. They're studying source material, tracking down witnesses, and looking at archaeological evidence. They're doing the work of historians. But they do it as Christians.

WRITING HISTORY

Humans are story-telling creatures. We can't help it. We view even the objects we run across in our day-to-day lives as parts of tiny stories. That coffee cup on the shelf has no meaning—it's just a blob—until it's part of a story: "Once upon a time, I poured coffee into that mug, put it to my lips, drank it down slowly, and placed it in the dishwasher." Certain coffee cups mean more because they're part of more significant stories, such as "Once upon a time, my best friend left for Germany and gave me this cup as a parting gift."

The power to tell the story of more significant things—such as a person, a city, a college, or even a nation—is the power to give meaning to those things. History is a powerful tool for bringing glory to the God of history and for helping our neighbors better see the world as He sees it. Only the history in the Bible can give us a true God's-eye view, of course, but history books written according to creational principles can do a great deal to shape God's image-bearers.

THINKING IT THROUGH 22.3

1. Since Christians believe that human history begins at creation and culminates at Christ's return, what philosophy of history must be rejected?
2. Restate in your own words the seven creational norms for conducting historical research.
3. What are generally the best kinds of sources?
4. Why should the Christian historian appeal to God's providence in history? What danger must he avoid when doing so?
5. Why are models necessary for the study of history?

22 CHAPTER REVIEW

TERMS TO REMEMBER

telos
situatedness
cyclical view of history
primary sources

Scripture Memory

Acts 17:26–27

Making Connections

1. How does the fact that God took a week to create the world demonstrate that God works His will through history?
2. How does God's plan of redemption demonstrate that God works His will through history?
3. What are three primary sources that historians use in their research? How does their worldview impact this research?
4. What makes determining causation difficult for historians?

Developing Skills in Apologetics and Worldview

5. How would you explain to an unbeliever why Christians follow some laws from the Old Testament and not others?
6. How could you persuade someone if you disagree with his moral judgments about a historical event?

Examining Assumptions and Evidence

7. What significant difference between the Old Testament and New Testament demonstrates the historical progress of God's people from child to adult?
8. Why is it controversial to claim that historians should connect God's purposes with the historical events they study?
9. How can you prevent your cultural identity (assumptions, values, practices) from becoming an idol?
10. Why is history always more than simply retelling what happened?

Becoming a Creative Cultivator

11. Write a brief history about a significant person or event in your town during the last thirty to sixty years. Conduct an interview of at least one eyewitness to gather oral history.

Chapter Twenty-Three **FALLEN HISTORY**

You are of your father the devil, and your will is to do your father's desires. He was a murderer from the beginning, and does not stand in the truth, because there is no truth in him. When he lies, he speaks out of his own character, for he is a liar and the father of lies. But because I tell the truth, you do not believe me.

Scripture Memory
John 8:44–45

23.1 THE FALL, HISTORY, AND IDEOLOGIES

In John 8:44, Jesus calls the devil "the father of lies." The first lie Satan told was about history. And the first lie Adam told was too. When God asked Adam if he had eaten from the forbidden tree, Adam responded with a historical narrative: "The woman whom you gave to be with me, she gave me fruit of the tree, and I ate" (Gen. 3:12). In one sense, this historical narrative is true. God did give the woman to be with Adam. The woman did give Adam the fruit from the tree. And Adam did eat. But Adam selected and arranged the details to tell a story that wasn't true: "This sin isn't my fault; it's God's. He's the one who gave me this woman."

Adam omitted some key information: Eve was created to be Adam's helper; he was given the authority to lead (1 Tim. 2:13). Eve was deceived when she took and ate the fruit; Adam's guilt was greater than Eve's because he was not deceived when he ate (1 Tim. 2:14). But Adam failed to mention the part of the story in which he let the serpent undermine the order of authority in his family. Adam's historical account didn't include his own intentional rebellion against his Creator.

This first historical lie reveals the complex way that the Fall has affected the study of history. Historians today can do the same thing Adam did: they can communicate facts about things that really happened. But they can select and organize those facts to present a false picture.

Historians also never write from a neutral perspective; they're influenced by ideologies similar to those we discussed in the government chapter. Historians can fasten on to truths and exalt them to a role in their theories that distorts their work. Other truths can easily be left out.

This section will focus on four significant ideologies that distort the work of historians. The first one you should recognize from the science unit: it's naturalism. The second is nationalism. The third is postmodernism. The fourth is a fixation on the issues of class, race, and gender.

NATURALISM

Remember that scientism exerts its influence beyond the sciences; it has claimed authority even in the humanities, in disciplines such as history. One proponent of scientism even asked in a major American newspaper, "[When] will the humanities . . . gratefully accept the peace imposed by science?"[1]

Scientific naturalism has definitely put pressure on the practice of writing history. This pressure is an obvious result of naturalism's view of humanity. According to this worldview, humans and their civilizations are merely the products of nature operating according to physical laws of cause and effect.[2]

Why Certain Cultures Dominate History

Jared Diamond's *Guns, Germs, and Steel* is an excellent example of the naturalistic approach to history. This 1997 book is an impressive attempt to bring many disciplines together—geography, archeology, botany, zoology, and others—to tell the history of the world and all its major civilizations. The book won a Pulitzer Prize shortly after it was published and still remains a bestseller today.[3]

One of the opening stories in Diamond's book describes the impressive army of the Inca king Atahualpa and its incredible defeat even though it vastly outnumbered the Spanish forces under the command of Francisco Pizarro. Diamond asks why Atahualpa didn't cross the ocean and conquer Spain rather than the other way around. Diamond notes rightly that people around the world are equally intelligent. So why have certain cultures dominated world history while others have remained undeveloped or even primitive?

Why didn't Inca forces cross the ocean and conquer Spain instead of the other way around?

Diamond's answer focuses on environmental conditions. Cultures with fruitful land (and easily domesticated animals and crops) can start towns and cities because not everyone has to be a farmer. They can establish political organizations and develop writing systems for their languages, giving these societies further advantages over hunter-gatherers and subsistence farmers. Diamond notes that these were precisely the conditions in Eurasia, so those peoples had a head start in developing the technologies—like guns and steel—that would eventually help them conquer the world.

A Christian Critique of Naturalism in History

The Christian historian can agree with Diamond that the environment does have an effect on human civilization. For instance, the sophisticated Nubian culture (called "Cush" in the Bible) was destroyed by the encroaching Sahara Desert. The Bible itself affirms the effect of the environment on civilizations. The very way God described the Promised Land to the Hebrews focused on its natural richness: it was "a land in which you will eat bread without scarcity, in which you will lack nothing, a land whose stones are iron, and out of whose hills you can dig copper" (Deut. 8:9). Israel's location at the intersection of continents and bodies of water was also advantageous for trade.

But even though the environment has an effect on civilizations, the environment itself doesn't determine human history. One reviewer said of *Guns, Germs, and Steel,* "Much more powerfully than any other species, we change the environment around us. . . . Human beings do indeed often 'approach limits imposed by environmental constraints' only to find a way to overcome and escape those constraints, as the history of technology repeatedly illustrates."[4] A Christian reading these comments should immediately think of the Creation Mandate. The environment does not determine human history because humans have been given the responsibility to rule over creation and not the other way around.

determinism: *the philosophical view that everything that happens in nature or society is caused by previous events and conditions, not by human choices or divine will*

There is a **naturalistic determinism*** in Diamond's theory that doesn't fit with the Bible's emphasis on the real impact of human choices. "By justice a king builds up the land, but he who exacts gifts [bribes] tears it down," Solomon said (Prov. 29:4). In other words, a just king can make a major difference in his environment—and so can a greedy one. Human righteousness and wickedness change the world and the future of nations. For instance, Mao Zedong's attempt to bring about a cultural revolution in China in the late 1960s and early 1970s brought wide-scale environmental devastation to his country.

Diamond thinks naturalism will prevent racism by showing that all peoples are fundamentally equal—and that is a good desire. But accomplished Christian historian George Marsden notes that naturalism also leads to major problems. Naturalism teaches that humans are the result of evolution and that their cultures result from "natural evolutionary processes." But if cultures have simply evolved naturally, there are no moral absolutes by which to judge cultures. In a naturalistic worldview, morals also evolve; morality evolved as a way for different cultures to survive. If different cultures evolve different moralities, Marsden asks, what right does the historian have to say one method of survival is superior to another? He concludes, "Some sort of moral relativism seems the only consistent option."[5] But this isn't an acceptable option. What if the morality of one culture develops into a form of eugenics*? The Christian has a standard by which he can judge this to be wrong; the naturalist will have difficulty doing so with intellectual consistency.

eugenics: *the "science" of improving the human race by improving its genetic stock and pruning off undesirables*

NATIONALISM

Nationalism is the attitude of lifting up the independence of a nation or ethnic group as a kind of ultimate good. The great evil, in this view, is to be ruled over by another nation. In nationalism, a person's greatest loyalty is to be given to the nation or ethnic group—loyalty even to the point of death. Nationalism is often supported with quasi-religious ceremonies, symbols, and even holy days.

Like other flawed ideologies, nationalism has picked out certain aspects of truth. It recognizes that humans do not live merely as individuals but as communities. They develop shared memories, customs, and values, which bind them together and enable them to do more as a group than they ever could have done as a loose collection of individuals. Often the combination of values in particular cultures is worthy of high praise. Germany, for example, has developed a reputation for highly skilled manufacturing and attention to detail that makes people around the world value its products. Other cultures have developed a respect for close family life and a determination to always do the honorable thing even when that means sacrificing self-interest. The preservation of these cultures is a good thing. People who love their nation's cultural heritage are often worried when immigrants with different cultures threaten to change something they value highly. As a result, the concern to preserve one's culture can be twisted, but the desire for cultural preservation is not in itself bad. Also, when a country is threatened by a military invasion, it's typically considered heroic to defend one's nation with one's life.

Nationalistic Idolatry

But nationalism tends toward idolatry, and this idolatry becomes evident when people of other ethnic groups are demonized simply for being culturally different. Nationalist movements tend to evaluate other cultures more negatively than honesty and fairness would allow. In the past, many Americans claimed that immigrants from Ireland, Germany, Italy, and Eastern Europe were drunken, shiftless foreigners who would debase American culture. In fact, most of these immigrants proved to be hard-working folk who assimilated into American life while holding on to the best of their own traditions. The genuine value of other ethnic groups is forgotten when nationalism ignores the fact that all humans are made in God's image and have received His creation blessing. There is something we can appreciate in every culture on earth.

In an effort to preserve something good in its own culture, a nationalist group may do truly wicked things against another culture, from persecution to lynching to outright war.

Nationalistic Salvation

Nationalism is also a powerful force offering an attractive prize to larger minorities within certain nations. The Tibetans in China, the Kurds in the Middle East, the Chechens in Russia, and the South Sudanese in Sudan are all ethnic groups that have sought in various ways to break free and form their own independent nations. The Kurds have achieved some measure of success; they have self-rule within Iraq. The South Sudanese won full independence in a bloody civil war.

But the salvation promised by nationalism is usually hollow. Independence rarely achieves what revolutionaries hope to gain. The great conflicts of the twentieth century, as well as many of the smaller ones, were fueled by nationalism. Nationalism was the flint that created the spark in the powder keg of Europe, leading to World War II. German and Japanese nationalism spawned World War II. And the postwar nationalism fueled various revolutions against colonial powers around the world. While in most if not all cases there was good reason to grant these countries independence, national independence rarely brought salvation. One particularly sad case is Eritrea, which fought for freedom from Ethiopia for many years, only for the revolutionary leader to establish himself firmly as a dictator once his people achieved independence.

German nationalism was one of many nationalisms that shaped the twentieth century.

Nationalism in Japan was a major contributing factor to the deadliest war in the history of mankind, WWII.

Nationalistic History

Every nationalist movement necessarily tells a story about itself—a history. And the temptation such movements face is obvious: to spin that history to favor the nation.

Nineteenth-century historians such as Thomas Macaulay in Britain, George Bancroft in the United States, and others in France and Germany wrote national histories that extolled the virtues of their countries and their political views. They selected events to frame a story that made their respective nations look good. They tended to turn history into a story about a progressive march toward the bright day when their nations arrived to grace the universe.

These kinds of boastful nationalist histories largely fell out of favor in the twentieth century as the dangers of nationalism became apparent, especially in light of the role German nationalism played in the two world wars. Historian Herbert Butterfield, in his 1931 book *The Whig Interpretation of History*, famously warned against any view of history that "studies the past with reference to the present"[6] and tends "to praise revolutions provided they have been successful, to emphasize certain principles of progress

THOMAS MACAULAY: A WHIG AND HIS STORIES

Thomas Macaulay (1800–1859) wrote an influential five-volume history of England from the reign of James II through the reign of William III. Macaulay was associated with the Whig party, which favored a constitutional monarchy in England (instead of an absolute monarchy), a strong Parliament, and religious freedom for dissenters from the Church of England. Macaulay wrote as though the history of England was the history of the triumph of the Whigs' ideas. He presented anyone who opposed Whig ideas in a bad light and anyone who supported them in a good light.

It's important to understand that a Whiggish approach to history doesn't necessarily have anything to do with the Whigs as a political party. Anybody with any strong partisan view can write a Whiggish history.

in the past and to produce a story which is the ratification if not glorification of the present"[7]—what he called a **Whiggish** view of history.

Butterfield warned that the Whiggish approach to history viewed past events through the eyes of present concerns. For example, if people today are concerned about individual liberties, the historian will choose to write about the events that seemingly led to today's conceptions of liberty. But the people of a particular time and place may have had very different interests. Perhaps they focused more on religion or kinship, not liberty. The Whig historian fails to really understand the concerns of people who lived in other times and places. Whig history neglects what people of the past thought was significant and how and why they thought differently from people in the present. Butterfield was also concerned that Whiggish historians made moral evaluations based on a current moral consensus—and then used their moral evaluations to further promote their vision of how life ought to be.

A Christian Critique of Whiggish and Nationalistic Histories

Christians can certainly fall prey to ultranationalist and Whiggish views, but at the very heart of the Bible is a command that ought to keep us away from them: "Love your neighbor as yourself" (Lev. 19:18). You like your nation? Great! Allow others to like theirs. Don't let the value you place on your culture blind you to the values of other cultures; admit it when Germans have cleaner homes, better highways, and a greater mastery of engineering. Admit it when the Chinese and the Brazilians and the South Africans have better food or folk songs or any of a thousand things, huge or almost invisible, that cause cultures to differ from one another.

The people of the past are your neighbors, too, in a sense. And they ought to get the same benefit. They had weaknesses that your culture doesn't have, but they had strengths your culture doesn't have too. It's a very Christian thing to seek to understand others as they saw themselves, to try to put yourself in their shoes and feel their concerns. As a Christian, you have a clear moral standard that sometimes requires you to disagree with the actions and beliefs of others. But to lie about those actions or beliefs by failing to present them accurately isn't biblical.

For instance, the Christian historian may find that he sympathizes with the Puritans rather than with Charles I and the Church of England prelates. But when he tells this part of history, the Christian historian must try to help the reader understand King Charles, his motivations, and his aims. Likewise, though he may be sympathetic to Cromwell and the Puritans, his duty as a historian is to portray them truthfully, warts and all.

"Christian America"

One area in which this is especially pertinent for American Christians is US history. In the face of rising secularism, many Christians have argued for a "Christian America" approach that claims to demonstrate that the United States has always been "a Christian nation." It's true that Christians from the time of the Pilgrims onward have played significant roles in American history. Nor was the United States founded as a secular nation. American political leaders have consistently spoken in religious terms throughout our history. Secularists are wrong to ignore these aspects of the American story.

THEISTIC RATIONALISM

Theistic rationalism is a term coined by Gregg Frazer to describe a moderate form of deism. **Theistic rationalists** tended to believe in a God who did answer prayer and act providentially in the world. They also tended to believe that the Bible contained some revelation from God. But they believed that reason was the judge of what was true revelation and what was myth. They did not believe that Jesus was God, but they tended to believe that he was "a great moral teacher."[8]

HOW CHRISTIAN WERE THE FOUNDERS?

Champions of the Christian America approach are often not careful enough about determining the actual beliefs of early American leaders. The American Founders did believe that religion should play an important role in public life, and they did not hesitate to use religious language in their speeches and writings. Yet, while there were orthodox Christians among the founders, many held to "theistic rationalism." While affirming belief in a god and his providential control, they denied the Trinity, the deity of Jesus, substitutionary atonement, and the inerrancy of Scripture. When Christians today appeal to such figures in support of a "Christian America" view of history, they diminish the vital importance of fundamental doctrines of the faith.

But not all Americans who spoke of God were Christians. Some—such as Jefferson and Adams—were "theistic rationalists" who denied the fundamental doctrines of the faith (see sidebars above). When Christians try to claim them as brothers in Christ, they're not only inaccurate but they may also be unintentionally signaling that those doctrines are unimportant for Christianity.

Another danger of the Christian America approach is that it sometimes seeks to justify immoral national acts. Andrew Jackson, in this view, becomes a hero of democracy; Manifest Destiny is celebrated as God's will; and negative aspects of US history are minimized. This approach to America's past dishonors the memory of faithful Christians who worked hard to prevent or rectify national sins. It also undermines the Christian responsibility to evaluate the events of history from a scriptural perspective. America is not a new and perfect Promised Land; Americans have always been capable of sin.

THINKING IT THROUGH 23.1A

1. Summarize the naturalistic view of history.
2. According to the naturalistic view of history, why did Spain conquer the Inca Empire rather than the other way around?
3. What do nationalists view as the ultimate good? What do they view as the ultimate evil?
4. How do nationalists write history to favor their own country or ethnic group?
5. How does Genesis 1:26–28 undermine nationalism?

POSTMODERNISM

French philosopher Jean-François Lyotard is famous for defining *postmodernism* as "incredulity toward metanarratives."[10] *Incredulity* means "skepticism, an unwillingness to believe," and *metanarrative*, as you learned in Chapter 1, means "an all-encompassing story." Postmodernists are skeptical whenever anyone tries to tell a big story that shows how all the little stories relate. Whiggish history provides a perfect example: postmodernists are quick to point out that it seems more than a little suspicious that Whig history manages to make all the little stories in American history point to the vision of America that the writer happens to hold himself.

The opposite of a metanarrative is a "local" narrative. A historian might write the history of a particular West African village, for example. Postmodernists would want the local narrative to stand on its own rather than being brought into a larger, all-encompassing metanarrative. Postmodernists think that no such narrative exists (or that if it does, no human has reliable access to it[11]). Instead, they want to see multiple viewpoints expressed, especially the viewpoints of the marginalized and oppressed. Nobody gets to take charge and make all the little stories fall in line. Postmodernism reacts to naturalism the same way we did in the science unit—by noting that there are no uninterpreted facts. Truly "neutral," "objective," "impartial" histories are impossible. In a fallen world, this is undoubtedly true. Even primary sources—personal letters, official records, etc.—come with a bias and are not fully reliable.[12]

In a postmodern view of history, there's no way to get at what "really happened." As Alan Muslow says, "The past is not discovered or found. It is created and represented by the historian as a text."[13]

A Christian Critique of the Postmodern View of History

Postmodernists are correct to note that there are often multiple viewpoints about historical events. Consider a historian studying the "Great Game" between Russia and Great Britain over spheres of influence in central Asia in the nineteenth and twentieth centuries. It will likely matter a great deal whether the author is Russian or British—or Afghan.

And yet postmodernists take their skepticism further than a biblical worldview allows.

Even unfallen humans were limited; if Adam and Eve had never eaten of the forbidden tree, their perspectives on life in the garden would still have been different. If an unfallen Eve at age two hundred, say, had written *A History of Eden* (published by Mesopotamian Books), her history might have focused more on the things that interested her, whether botany or childrearing or artisan guilds. She would have seen things and known things that Adam didn't. And the reverse is true: Adam's history would have been different from Eve's, though not contradictory to it.

There are as many perspectives on a historical event as there are people who know anything about it. Postmodernists tend to throw up their hands and say, "So we can never know what *really* happened; we're lost in this sea of perspectives." And the Christian grants that, unless God reveals some history to be true—as He does in the countless historical records in the Bible, culminating in the history of Christ's incarnation and resurrection—then we can't know that history. But our lack of full knowledge doesn't mean that the work of history is pointless. If human finiteness and fallenness kept us from knowing anything about history, they would also keep us from knowing anything about anything.

God's grace—common grace to all humans and special grace to His children—makes it possible for historians to listen to other people with care, diligence, and respect, even and especially if those people are long dead. The creational norms for the work of history suggested in the previous chapter are the tools Christian historians can use to push back against their own fallenness and finiteness. In other words, the Christian historian studies source materials, makes models with humility, selects significant events according to a Christian worldview, makes moral judgments, looks for God's hand, and carefully considers the possible "causes" for historical events—and then he writes it all down and publishes it. Even if this doesn't seem to work in (postmodern) theory, it pretty clearly works in practice.[14]

For example, several US historians have set out to construct a historical model that fits the evidence better than the one used by the Christian America movement. Daniel Dreisbach, one of these historians, argues that if American Christians sometimes claim too much Christianity for the American founders, secularists generally claim too little. Secularists take Thomas Jefferson's famous phrase about the "wall of separation" between church and state to mean that all religion should be excluded from public life: no prayers before governmental meetings, no religious symbolism on government buildings, and no public funding for religious charities.[15]

Dreisbach conducted a careful historical study of Jefferson's "wall of separation" phrase. It comes, in fact, from a letter Jefferson wrote to the Danbury Baptist Association in 1802. Dreisbach makes the case that Jefferson was reaffirming that since the states were in charge of religious matters, the national government wouldn't interfere with the free exercise of religion. Dreisbach is a Christian, so he's not neutral when it comes to this issue. But Dreisbach makes use of the tools of historiography* to keep him—as much as possible—from prejudice and bias and to help him listen faithfully to what Jefferson actually said. Other historians, even those who have different biases, recognize the merits of Dreisbach's work.

historiography: *the methods and principles historians use in researching and presenting their findings*

Anyone who expects the work of history—outside the Bible—to do more than listen carefully to the past and establish models to understand it all will be disappointed. But someone who's willing to do hard work with the available tools of historiography will still be doing something valuable.

Even the Gospel writers used the tools of the historical discipline. In the first verse of the Gospel of Luke, the writer comments that "many have undertaken to compile a narrative of the things that have been accomplished among us." In other words, there were written sources that Luke had read. And then he even mentions primary sources: "Just as those who from the beginning were eyewitnesses and ministers of the word have delivered them to us, it seemed good to me also, having followed all things closely for some time past, to write an orderly account" (Luke 1:1–3). Luke's main purpose in this preface is not to teach how the work of history ought to be done, but these statements show that he worked hard at being a responsible and careful historian of the earthly life of Jesus.

The four Gospels, taken as a group, also teach us something about history: the existence of multiple different perspectives shouldn't make us throw up our hands and give up on the possibility of true reports. The Gospels give accounts of Jesus' life from four perspectives. Every perspective is absolutely true, and yet each is different—not contradictory, but different. Each writer sees and emphasizes details that the others don't. Matthew tells stories from Jesus' childhood that no one else includes (2:13–23). Luke highlights the place of women in Jesus' entourage (e.g., 23:55). John focuses on Jesus' deity in a unique way (1:1–3). Mark even notes the color of the grass (6:39)!

Of course, apart from Scripture no human perspective on an event will be absolutely true. Historians must constantly evaluate perspectives, including their own. Even postmodernists do this evaluating; they just don't always admit it. Christian historian Carl Trueman notes that the list of marginalized groups to whom postmodernists try to give a voice somehow fails to include "members of the Ku Klux Klan, Holocaust deniers, serial killers, and collectors of other people's toenail clippings"—all of whom have been "written out of the dominant narratives of this world; but none . . . enjoys the support of a significant postmodern lobby group."[16]

Postmodernists, who say they wish for all local narratives to be heard, don't listen to the KKK's narratives. But they have difficulty giving a reason for this choice. The Christian has one: all stories are not equal because the moral standard of Scripture condemns some perspectives.

CLASS, RACE, AND GENDER

Postmodernists want to bring the oppressed "other" into the mainstream of history. In the Western world, ruled as it has generally been by rich white males, the "other" includes the lower classes, racial minorities, and women. As a result, many historians today focus on class, race, and gender in their studies.

But not all of the focus on these themes arises out of postmodernism—especially the focus on class. Marxist historians have always emphasized the role of class because it's essential to their big story about the world that the lower classes will rise up and conquer the upper ones.

These approaches have brought some genuine benefits. Historian Gordon Wood notes,

> Many historians have absorbed from theories no more than the desire to write about issues of race and gender. And this desire has led to many stimulating and worthwhile contributions to our understanding of the past. Our knowledge of slavery in America, for example, has been greatly amplified over the past forty years; and no one can deny that our appreciation of women's history has been similarly enhanced.[17]

But there are dangers in focusing on race, class, and gender in the work of history. For instance, early-twentieth-century historian Charles Beard—influenced both by relativism and Marxism—wrote an influential book, *An Economic Interpretation of the Constitution of the United States*. Beard argued that the framers of the Constitution weren't motivated by the public interest when writing the document. Rather, as property owners, they wrote a constitution that would protect and benefit their own interests. Beard concluded that the Constitution was thus an instrument of class warfare, or conflict between classes based on differing economic interests.

Later critiques of Beard's work explained that since the majority of American men of the time did, in fact, own property (most were farmers), the interests of the common man and those of the framers were not sharply at odds. In addition, primary sources indicate that average citizens often expressed the opinion that the Constitution would benefit them. Finally, a close look at the Constitution itself reveals that the Founding Fathers were just as concerned about providing protections to persons as about maintaining protections of property. People at that time wanted both.

Thus one critic concluded: "Whether Beard had his thesis before he had his evidence, as some have said, is a question that each reader must answer for himself. Certain it is that the evidence does not justify the thesis."[18] Beard's work illustrates a problem with all strictly Marxist history. The pattern for how history must unfold is already determined by the theory. Yet often the historical evidence simply doesn't fit.[19]

Writing about recent Marxist historian Gary Nash, Gordon Wood observes, "Nash is so bound up in the Marxian categories of class warfare that he can make little sense of what happened." Because of his Marxism, Nash must believe that revolutions arise from dissatisfied lower classes. Wood notes, however, that this stands at odds with the fact that "the white colonists in British North America enjoyed the highest standard of living of any people in the Western world" and that they "had the broadest ownership of farm land of any place in the Western world." Nash's Marxist theories force him to see "American society [as] a poverty-stricken, class-ridden place where rich and poor were at each other's throat."[20]

Wood also highlights another problem with these single-issue emphases:

> So suffocating has been the stress on "race, class, gender" issues that sometimes beginning graduate students hesitate to write about anything else. A female historian who wanted to study the eighteenth-century founders told me that she was criticized by other female scholars for wasting her time working on those "dead white males."[21]

The Christian historian should, by contrast, seek to understand, praise, and critique all of God's image-bearers by the standard of Scripture. Studying the plight of slaves and researching the life of George Washington are equally legitimate endeavors for the Christian.

A Christian Critique of the Race, Class, Gender Emphasis

Historical ideologies are dangerous because they tend to find the Fall concentrated all in one place, and they find redemption in the wrong place. Studies that focus on race, class, or gender tend to locate the evil in the world in economic differences, gender roles, or racial divisions. Without a doubt, the wealthy have oppressed the poor, men have oppressed women, and those of European descent have oppressed Africans and Indians. Christian historians must expose these wrongs for what they are—sin.

But Christians also recognize that sin is not just a problem that runs through one certain class, race, or gender. It runs through all people. And trying to remove all inequalities of class, race, and gender won't bring true redemption. Fallen people and cultures will twist any good gift of God.

It was possible for a slave owner such as James Madison to have real moral insight when writing the US Constitution. And it was possible for freed American slaves to go to Liberia and create a stratified society that prospered in certain ways and yet treated indigenous Africans unjustly. Good and evil are found in all races, every class, and both genders—because they're found in every person.

THINKING IT THROUGH 23.1B

1. Explain the meaning of Lyotard's definition of postmodernism as "incredulity toward narratives."
2. What limitations do fallenness and finiteness place on the Christian historian?
3. Which group of historians especially emphasize the role of class?
4. Which group of people should the Christian historian seek to understand, praise, and/or critique by the standard of Scripture?
5. Why is the following statement by Alan Muslow false? "The past is not discovered or found. It is created and represented by the historian as a text."

23.2 SELECTION AND MORAL JUDGMENTS

Every small child understands the principle of selection in the work of history. "He hit me" is almost always the item selected from the list of events in a recent altercation. "I pushed him" is rarely mentioned—unless a perceptive parent prods the child for that information. "He hit me" is most likely true. But why don't four-year-olds tend to mention their own role in fights? Because to do so would violate their principles of selection, which are designed to (1) make themselves look good and (2) make their enemies look bad. By selecting only certain details, even ones that really happened, little kids end up giving histories that aren't really "true."

This is why witnesses in court promise to tell not just the truth but "the whole truth." They can be held in contempt of court if it comes out later that they have omitted certain key details. The legal principles of selection require you to tell the court (1) anything you're asked to tell and (2) anything else that is relevant to the purpose of establishing the innocence or guilt of the defendant.

Historical Selection

Historians look at lots of fights and lots of court cases and countless other events. They, too, must use principles of selection, as discussed in the previous chapter. They can't list *everything* that happened—that would take longer than the events took to happen because so much is always going on at once.

The principle of selection is very clearly at work throughout the Bible. The Gospel of John ends with this comment: "Now there are also many other things that Jesus did. Were every one of them to be written, I suppose that the world itself could not contain the books that would be written" (John 21:25).

But selection can lead to errors—like when certain political and historical ideologies affect selection. For instance, a historian who sees history through the lens of race, class, and gender may tell the story of the American Revolution from the eyes of Indians, women, and the poor to the neglect of the contributions of George Washington, John Adams, and Benjamin Franklin. This wouldn't be a problem if the historian were writing a narrow study investigating neglected aspects of Revolutionary War history. It would be a problem in a general survey of the war, such as you find in a textbook. Likewise, an advocate of the "great men" approach to history may focus so much on Washington, Adams, and Franklin that the significance of average men and women to the war is not mentioned as it ought to be.

Sometimes faulty selection can be a much more personal matter, one perhaps invisible to the historian doing the selecting. We mentioned in the previous chapter Timothy Larsen's book, *The Crisis of Doubt*. While researching that book, Larsen, a twenty-first-century Christian historian of Victorian

The Victorian era was "the golden age of church attendance."

DOUBTER IN CRISIS

One Victorian who had a crisis of doubt was John Henry Gordon. Once a Sunday school teacher, Gordon became one of the "more abusive and blunt anti-Christian lecturers."[22]

But a preacher that his mother convinced him to hear simply used the Bible, and Gordon was cut to the heart. After he reconverted, he admitted that his unbelief—he was a strict materialist—had never brought him any satisfaction.

He had also noticed that his atheist friends couldn't agree on morality. He questioned "whether or not Secularism provided the intellectual resources for making . . . moral judgments."[23] He began to see atheistic secularism as a "just-what-you-like-ism" in which the ultimate moral authority was self. Gordon called it "a recipe for immoral self-indulgence."[24]

Finally, Gordon came to realize that he had idolized reason to such a degree that almost nothing could be determined to be true.[25] His solution wasn't to dismiss reason or to accept things contrary to reason, but to recognize reason's limitations and to trust reason's Creator.

England, noticed that existing histories of that era (including encyclopedia entries, books, articles, etc.) give heavy coverage to the "crisis of faith" that many Victorians experienced. The discussions center on how Darwinism led to these crises.[26] He further noted that key encyclopedias on the era included entries for the "doubters" but lacked entries about Charles Spurgeon, Thomas Chalmers, or other leading Christian figures. Larsen found one encyclopedia that included entries on "Babism, Bahaism, Spiritualism, the Theosophical Society, Transcendentalism, and Zionism, but none on Baptists, Congregationalists, Dissenters (or Nonconformists or Free Churches), Evangelicalism, or Methodism."[27]

Larsen isn't claiming that these works have an overt bias against Christians, but he says that it can occur. For example, historian A. N. Wilson assumes that atheists are "honorable," that doubters who remain in church are "dishonorable," and that believers have sinned "against the Intellect."[28] But more often, Larsen says, the personal interests and views of scholars in the historical discipline are leading them to a misconception about the Victorian era.[29] They see doubt as a major theme and fail to see the Christian religion in its place in the times.

Larsen notes in his study that doubt is a major theme in the Victorian era *precisely because of the importance of religion*. The Victorian era could be called "the golden age of church attendance."[30] Furthermore, the evangelical emphasis that true religion brought together head, heart, and action (rather than just being something you show up to do as a matter of course on Sundays) was actually an essential part of the reason there were so many doubters. If the dominant religion of the time had been different, the challenges to that religion would not have been intellectual.[31]

Larsen's principles of selection—formed by his Christian faith—allow him to see things that non-Christian historians didn't care to see: not just the reconversions to Christianity of some of the Victorian era's famous doubters, but the reasons for those reconversions. Larsen noticed that the skeptics fell out of love with skepticism because it never offered a positive worldview, one that explained and promoted morality and gave life significance beyond the physical realm. Larsen also noticed that skeptics often found the Bible more compelling when they came to it for a purpose other than trying to find problems in it.[32]

Historical Moral Evaluation

Another area in which the Fall affects historians is that of moral evaluation. A now widely recognized example of this is the early-twentieth-century view of the Puritans. The Puritans were often dismissed as dour, strict, fun-hating people who always dressed in black. These misapprehensions may have lasted so long among scholars and nonscholars alike because many of them disapprove of Puritan beliefs. It took the diligent work of Harvard professor Perry Miller to bring Puritans some respect among scholars.

A more recent example would be popular treatments of Muslims from both sides of the political spectrum. The American left makes a multicultural effort to avoid criticism of Muslim culture. In order for this view to work, they have to translate offensive concepts such as *jihad** into inoffensive ones. Jihad, in their view, becomes a merely spiritual struggle—despite the lack of historical evidence for the claim that this is what the term has meant.[33] The American right, on the other hand, tends to lump together the ancient doctrine of jihad with modern terrorism despite the fact that careful study reveals some important differences.[34] Moral evaluation can bias historical study.

jihad: *(gee HOD) the Islamic concept of holy war against non-Muslims*

And yet moral evaluation is necessary. A historian's first responsibility in writing about the mass slaughter of Armenians in Turkey in 1915 is to accurately describe the conditions, motivations, and actions of the people in that place and time. He must understand them on their own terms first. But he fails if he never arrives at a moral evaluation—and if he does give a moral evaluation, it should be based ultimately on Scripture and not on other grounds.

COMPLEXITIES AND LIMITATIONS

Understanding past events is a complex task. Humans are so limited that we often make little effort to see things from someone else's perspective. And we're so fallen that we often turn around and exalt our own perspective to an ungodly height. We select the facts that further our own agendas and evaluate actions in history from a perspective other than the one God gives in Scripture. The Fall deeply affects the work of history.

THINKING IT THROUGH 23.2

1. What major influences often guide a person's choices in historical selection?
2. What did Larsen's principles of selection allow him to see that non-Christian historians didn't care to see?
3. Why have many historical scholars erroneously dismissed the Puritans as dour, strict, fun-hating people who always dressed in black?
4. Why is moral evaluation necessary in the work of history?

23 CHAPTER REVIEW

TERMS TO REMEMBER

naturalistic determinism
nationalism
Whiggish
theistic rationalists

Scripture Memory

John 8:44–45

Making Connections

1. Which ideology writes history to favor one's own nation?
2. Which ideology denies that the past can really be known?
3. Which ideology allows single-issue emphases to commandeer the interpretation of history?
4. Which ideology teaches that favorable environmental conditions determine a culture's advancement?

Developing Skills in Apologetics and Worldview

5. How could you demonstrate whether political and historical ideologies are inappropriately affecting the selection of historical data?
6. How would you defend the necessity of moral evaluation in the work of history?

Examining Assumptions and Evidence

7. Why is the ideology of naturalism flawed?
8. Why is the ideology of nationalism flawed?
9. Why is the ideology of postmodernism flawed?
10. Why is the fixation on class, race, and gender a flawed approach to history?

Becoming a Creative Cultivator

11. Write a brief history of the school year. Why did you select the details that you did?

Chapter Twenty-Four HISTORY IN LIGHT OF REDEMPTION

Remember the former things of old; for I am God, and there is no other; I am God, and there is none like me, declaring the end from the beginning and from ancient times things not yet done, saying, "My counsel shall stand, and I will accomplish all my purpose."

Scripture Memory
Isaiah 46:9–10

24.1 FINDING RELIABLE SOURCE MATERIALS

The brilliant Samuel Johnson (1709–1784) wrote the first major English dictionary practically by himself. It took him only nine years. He was a committed Christian and has been called "arguably the most distinguished man of letters in English history."[1] Besides that, he was a real wit. Once Johnson was conversing with a similarly clever man who argued that matter didn't really exist. Someone else told Johnson, "Though we are satisfied his doctrine is not true, it is impossible to refute it." Johnson immediately kicked a large stone with "mighty force"—kicking so hard that he bounced back when the rock didn't move—and said, "I refute it *thus*."[2] That refutation of an erroneous philosophy appears to have worked, at least in the minds of most people, since the story keeps being repeated nearly three hundred years later.

But refutations of erroneous history are not so simple. Astronaut Buzz Aldrin, the second human to ever set foot on the surface of the moon, once tried to use an argument similar to Johnson's. One day a moon-landing skeptic, conspiracy theorist Bart Sibrel, confronted Aldrin in public and demanded that he swear on the Bible that he really did land on the moon. (Sibrel has made documentaries claiming that the moon landing was cleverly faked.) Aldrin refused to swear, so Sibrel called him "a coward, and a liar, and a thief." Aldrin, who was seventy-two at the time, refuted Sibrel *thus*: he punched him in the jaw.

This action is not the biblically recommended way of dealing with historical disputes, and though it made the news, it doesn't appear to have worked. There are still many active groups of people online who don't believe that the moon landings ever happened—or that the Holocaust occurred (to name just two prominent groups of history skeptics). Despite all our scientific, archaeological, and information-retrieval capabilities, people still make false and outlandish historical claims all the time.

> **"HISTORY IS NOT SIMPLY A COLLATION OF FACTS WHICH CAN ONLY BE RELATED TOGETHER IN ONE VALID NARRATIVE."[3]**
>
> —CARL TRUEMAN

How can you spot—and refute—false claims about history? You can't kick a rock or punch a conspiracy theorist every time you hear false claims. So what can you do?

A Christian worldview is essential to the answer. It provides assurances that we can know certain things about history, and it gives us the basic shape of that history. We know that the history of the world is the history of what God is doing to glorify Himself by redeeming His fallen creation—and judging His enemies. Without such a framework, the work of studying and writing history becomes aimless—or aims at the wrong targets.

But a Christian worldview by itself doesn't tell you whether the Holocaust happened or whether Neil Armstrong really took "one small step for a man." A biblical worldview provides the necessary framework, but the Christian worldview also calls on you to act. There really is only one way to build reliable historical models: hard work with the sources. If you want to know history—and especially if you yourself are called to be a historian—you need to learn how to find, sift, and process historical evidence until you have a model to communicate to others.

HISTORICAL EVIDENCE

The fundamental task of the historian is to study the basic source materials of history. Sometimes these sources are artifacts uncovered by archaeology. Historians have to know enough about archaeology to make accurate assessments of that evidence. They have to understand the careful systems used by archaeologists and the complex nature of interpreting evidence from archaeological digs. Ancient cities were often built on top of even more ancient cities; historians who work in ancient eras have to understand the art and science of figuring out what artifacts belong to what historical layer. They have to interpret evidence, such as the fact that some clay pottery in a city appears to have come from somewhere else. Could this mean that there was active trade going on in that place?

And, of course, written materials are often uncovered in archaeological digs—coins, inscriptions, tablets, and (in some dry places in the world) papyri, documents written on an ancient form of paper. The research of some historians means reading countless letters and scraps from which they build a picture of the ancient world. Here's what a wife wrote her husband a century and a half before Jesus was born:

> Isias to . . . Hephaestion; greetings. . . . I am displeased because after having piloted myself and your child through such bad times—and having been driven to every extremity owing to the price of corn—I thought that now at least, with you at home, I should enjoy some respite. But you have not even thought of coming home nor given any regard to our circumstances![4]

On the one hand, this short letter (and so many others like it) provides tantalizing hints about how different life was in ancient times. It's the historian's job to breathe that ancient air and describe it to the rest of us. On the other hand, clearly husbands and wives way back then were people, just like they are today. There is a simple humanity in the letter; wives today still want their husbands to come home.

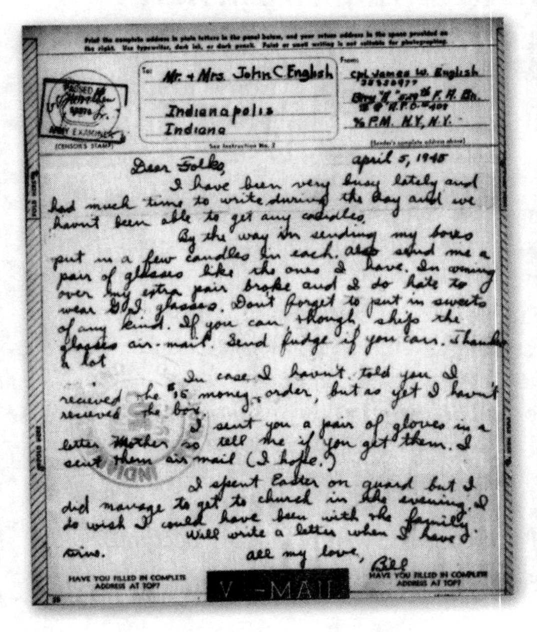

To: Mr. + Mrs. John C English
Indianapolis
Indiana

From: Cpl. James W. English
% P.M. N.Y., N.Y.

Dear Folks, April 5, 1945

I have been very busy lately and had much time to write during the day and we havn't been able to get any candles.

By the way in sending my boxes put in a few candles in each. Also send me a pair of glasses like the ones I have. In coming over my extra pair broke and I do hate to wear G.I. glasses. Don't forget to put in sweets of any kind. If you can, though, ship the glasses air-mail. Send fudge if you can. Thanks a lot

In case I havn't told you I received the $15 money order, but as yet I havn't received the box.

I sent you a pair of gloves in a letter Mother so tell me if you get them. I sent them air mail (I hope.)

I spent Easter on guard but I did manage to get to church in the evening. I do wish I could have been with the family.

Will write a letter when I have time.

All my love,
Bill

HAVE YOU FILLED IN COMPLETE ADDRESS AT TOP?

V-MAIL

HAVE YOU FILLED IN COMPLETE ADDRESS AT TOP?

Letters provide a good example of primary sources.

A good historian enters into his source materials, trying to listen to them faithfully as a neighbor should do—even if that neighbor lives far away in time and space.

Primary Sources

Historians use two major kinds of written sources, whether they study ancient eras or modern times—primary sources and secondary sources. A **primary source** is simply a source that comes from the period being studied. If a historian is studying World War II, then primary sources would include maps laying out guerrilla plans from the French resistance, letters from American generals to US politicians (or from soldiers to their girlfriends), and technical memoranda used by the Nazis to effect the final solution.[5] A biography of General Dwight D. Eisenhower or of

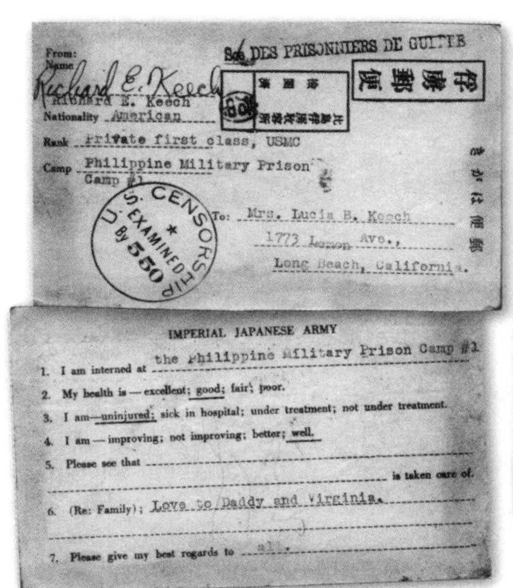

From:
Name Richard E. Keech
Nationality American
Rank Private first class, USMC
Camp Philippine Military Prison Camp #1
SERVICE DES PRISONNIERS DE GUERRE
U.S. CENSORSHIP EXAMINED By 550
To: Mrs. Lucia B. Keech
1773 Lemon Ave.,
Long Beach, California.

IMPERIAL JAPANESE ARMY

1. I am interned at the Philippine Military Prison Camp #1
2. My health is — excellent; good; fair; poor.
3. I am — uninjured; sick in hospital; under treatment; not under treatment.
4. I am — improving; not improving; better; well.
5. Please see that ________ is taken care of.
6. (Re: Family); Love to Daddy and Virginia.
7. Please give my best regards to all.

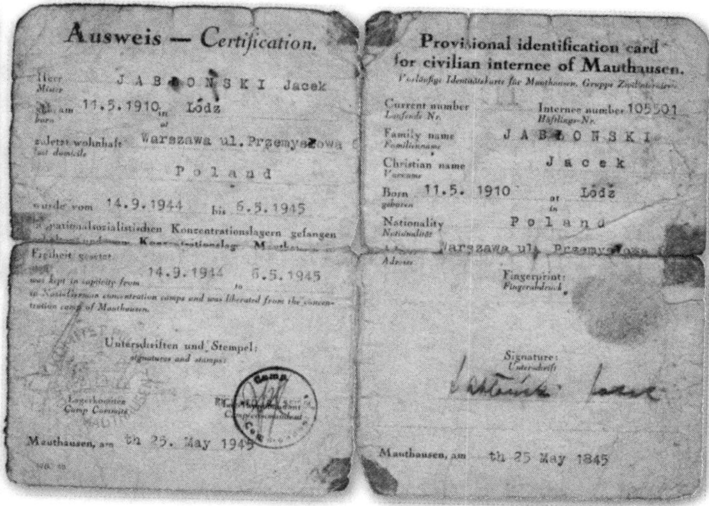

Ausweis — Certification.

Herr / Mister JABŁONSKI Jacek
geb. am / born 11.5.1910 in / at Lódz
zuletzt wohnhaft / last domicile Warszawa ul. Przemysłowa
Poland
wurde vom 14.9.1944 bis 6.5.1945
nationalsozialistischen Konzentrationslagern gefangen
was kept in captivity from 14.9.1944 to 6.5.1945
Unterschriften und Stempel: / signatures and stamps:
Mauthausen, am th 25. May 1945

Provisional identification card for civilian internee of Mauthausen.
Current number
Internee number 105501
Family name JABŁONSKI
Christian name Jacek
Born 11.5. 1910 at Lódz
Nationality Poland
Address Warszawa ul. Przemysłowa
Fingerprint:
Signature:
Mauthausen, am th 25 May 1945

Official documents are primary sources for historians.

Hitler himself wouldn't be "historical" if it didn't delve into archives and ferret out old letters, telegrams, and pay stubs. Such a biography is not itself a primary but a **secondary source**.

Secondary Sources

There are historians whose work it is to take mostly secondary-source material and construct a bigger narrative out of it all. No one could possibly read all the documents written by World War II generals, let alone those by soldiers and mothers and villagers and everyone else affected by the war. But a historian who reads secondary sources such as specialized studies by scholars who have focused on the letters of soldiers or the archives of war departments can make use of that research to write a history.

History textbooks pull together the work of many primary and secondary sources to create new secondary sources.

WORLDVIEWS AND HISTORY

Scholarly historical work is to be done primarily on the level of primary sources. This means that the historian has to know the language that the documents are written in. He has to read them for himself. He has to weigh the accuracy of each source. He has to make sure that the document is not a forgery. He may need to compare two primary sources that give conflicting accounts. For all of this work, a Christian worldview is essential. Ideally, having an accurate view of humanity's fallenness should help Christians make careful judgment calls about the validity of someone's statements. Wives missed their husbands in ancient Greece, just like they do today. And, just like today, husbands sometimes lied.

Glorifying God Through History

Even non-Christian historians would agree with us about the value of research in the primary sources. Virtually all practicing historians, whatever their worldview, engage in this kind of research. So what's distinctive about the way a historian with a biblical worldview works?

On one hand, a Christian historian will be working, ultimately, for a greater purpose than big sales or academic prestige. So he or she ought to work in a truly excellent and diligent way, "as for the Lord, and not for men" (Col. 3:23).[6] Christians shouldn't be sloppy or lazy in their historical work because when they study history, they are—in a very real way—studying the outworking of the plan of God over the course of history:

> Remember the former things of old; for I am God, and there is no other; I am God, and there is none like me, declaring the end from the beginning and from ancient times things not yet done, saying, "My counsel shall stand, and I will accomplish all my purpose," calling a bird of prey from the east, the man of my counsel from a far country. I have spoken, and I will bring it to pass; I have purposed, and I will do it. (Isa. 46:9–11)

If God rules over flying eagles and calls rulers from far countries to fulfill His purposes, then the plan of God lies underneath the surface of every good history book. Christian historians work to glorify God. Many non-Christian historians are careful, diligent practitioners of their craft, but they do not have this highest of motivations.

Benefiting Others Through History

On the other hand, the work of the historian is for other people, not just for the Lord. It's a work of service to one's neighbors, including dead ones. It lets them speak. It also serves living neighbors, of course; history provides wisdom for them. It broadens our understanding so that we're freed from the cultural nearsightedness we have from simply living in our own time and place. It helps free us from conformity to the spirit of the age. The biblical worldview of Christian historians will guide them as they write history. It will shape not only their moral evaluations, but also their principle of selection. They will ask themselves, "What stories do my neighbors need to hear?"

Researching and writing for the good of others is one area where the Christian worldview is pushing back against the direction of the historical disciplines today. In the previous chapter we noted that historians can be so caught up in discussions of race, class, and gender that they miss other important discussions—or twist the historical evidence to fit what they consider to be the flow of history. Ultimately, only your worldview can tell you what's important enough in history to warrant research. Race (or rather, ethnicity), class, and gender *are* important themes. But ideally, a Christian historian will be so rooted in what's truly important that he won't be knocked over by passing fads within his discipline.

THINKING IT THROUGH 24.1

1. What provides a basic historical framework, assuring that we can know some basic things about history and make some basic moral judgments?
2. What is the fundamental task of the historian?
3. Identify and explain the two major kinds of written sources that historians use.
4. What two motivations should direct a Christian's engagement in rigorous scholarly historical study?
5. Of the two types of sources identified and explained in question 3, which is more reliable? Explain why.

24.2 PROPOSING HISTORICAL MODELS HUMBLY

A bunch of pottery shards buried in dirt don't make a history. Nor do a bunch of ancient letters, or a cache of war plans in a national archive. Somebody—a historian—has to sit down and combine all of the available raw information into a model that explains the data. And that model itself will be built on the backbone of a story the historian tells about what's going on in that period of history.

Human actions don't make any sense unless they're placed in some sort of context. But having a context—or an overarching story—doesn't necessarily make the work of interpretation easy. Christian historian Carl Trueman points out that "human historical actions are themselves always complex and impossible to reduce to single causes, intentions, or motivations."[7]

Think about last Friday night. Why did you spend your time the way you did? Can even *you* give a full explanation for that choice? We like to think we have full control over our choices, but our influences and our opportunities and our desires—and a thousand other factors—play into those choices.

Archeologists have developed systematic ways to analyze the various layers of an ancient archeological site.

Trueman says, "It is important to realize that forces far larger than any individual agent are at play in the world, and that human beings are not simply shaped by what they read or what they hear, but also by hidden forces of which they themselves might be unaware, such as economic and ethnic factors."[8]

An archaeologist's report will explain what was found in a dig and where. And he will attempt to explain the findings. He will propose, perhaps, that different layers of the dig be dated to the third century BC based on the pottery shards found in those layers. He might suggest that trade with a neighboring region picked up during the fifth century BC based on the artifacts found in another layer. Or he might note that at a certain period the site appeared to be destroyed and abandoned. All of this is a model the archaeologist is constructing from the available information.

EXAMPLES OF FAULTY MODELS

Like archaeologists, historians who work from primary sources also make models. They look at the primary source data and construct a narrative from it. Models should be revised as new information comes to light.

Victorian Religion and Skepticism

In Chapter 23, we pointed out that many historians studying the Victorian era have constructed a model that presents that time period as one of a crisis of faith. However, a Christian scholar working on that same time period noted that this thesis excluded some key primary sources. He constructed a model to explain more of the data, arguing that the Victorian era was a highly religious time in which, nonetheless, certain basic tenets of religion were being challenged. Some religious people lost their faith in Christianity, but some of the most prominent doubters actually came to doubt their doubts and returned to faith in Christ.[9]

Missionaries and European Colonialism

Another example is the common historical model of the European colonization of Africa, Asia, and the Americas that portrays missionaries as key *partners* in the colonization project. In this model, missionaries sought protection from the European powers, and in exchange, they helped destroy the various native cultures they found—by participating in the "civilizing" project the great European nations were engaged in. Missions, according to this model, was a significant part of the oppression and injustice that nineteenth-century powers like England inflicted on nations such as Kenya.

But sociologist Robert Woodberry has proposed a different model based on extensive research. His research began with the observation that some countries that emerged from colonization were democratic while others were totalitarian. Some of these countries were very similar in natural resources and even in ethnicity. What made the difference in political outcomes?

Woodberry noticed that in some colonies the missionaries were part of state churches. These missionaries did often work closely with the colonial powers. But, he pointed out, many other missionaries served churches that were not state churches. He found that these missionaries tended to oppose injustices practiced by the colonial powers. For instance, it was missionaries of this sort that smuggled pictures of horrible abuses out of the Congo. And missionaries in South Africa spearheaded an agreement that protected the peoples in what is now Botswana from further European land grabs. In addition, Woodberry found that these missionaries invested a great deal of time and effort in teaching the people they ministered to how to read and write. The net effect, Woodberry concluded, was that the countries where these missionaries worked are now more stable and democratic. Those missionaries weren't trying to be social reformers or to lay the foundations for democracy. They were protesting injustices against the people they loved and educating those people in the basics that they needed to read and understand Scripture. But there were unintended, unforeseen positive results. Woodberry's model is a better explanation of the data.[10]

THE NEED FOR HUMILITY

In these two examples Christians come out looking better after a historian and a sociologist made more reliable models, using more of the data. But Christians doing historical research have to remain humble: the best model could result in Christians looking worse than they did before. And a model itself is just a fallible human construction—another reason for humility. Other historians may find gaps, logical problems, or alternative explanations. Christians cannot simply reject alternative models as attacks on their faith (they may be or they may not). Christians have to seek to substantiate their models with the best research available.

In Woodberry's case, he constructed a statistical model to test whether the case studies he had gathered would be confirmed. He then tested other factors, such as "climate, health, location, accessibility, natural resources, colonial power, disease prevalence."[11] These did not statistically correlate to stable democracy the way that the presence of independent missionaries did. Only God knows precisely what role missionaries in Tanzania, Vietnam, and other places played in bringing positive change. But Woodberry presented a useful model with appropriate humility and yet with appropriate confidence because he had followed the best practices of his discipline.

THE NEED FOR HONESTY

What if Woodberry's research had ended up not supporting his thesis? What if he had found that countries with independent missionaries in the nineteenth century, even controlling for other factors, all ended up being totalitarian dictatorships with abysmally low literacy rates? What should he have done?

This brings us to the important historical concept of **objectivity**, which is not the same as neutrality. As historians use the term *objective* today, they don't mean that people should be neutral—without biases or presuppositions—when they do their research. They don't even mean that historians should put aside their basic worldview commitments. A Christian historian cannot set aside his fundamental belief in the existence of God, God's sovereign control over all things, the accuracy of Scripture, or the work of the Holy Spirit in human hearts. But objectivity does mean that the historian doesn't try to marshal support only for the position he wants to be true. He tries, by God's grace, to find the truth.

> *It is actually the duty of a historian, when he postulates a certain thesis . . . to make a special effort to find evidence that would call his theory into question."*[12]
>
> —CARL TRUEMAN

For instance, a Baptist church historian might be looking for evidence that in the early centuries of the church baptism was practiced exclusively by immersion. A Presbyterian church historian may be looking for evidence that infants were baptized in the early church. It's not wrong for these historians to look for historical support for their church's doctrinal position. But they have to be sure that they're not selecting only facts that support their case to the neglect of contrary facts. They will actually want to look for evidence that goes *against* their expectations. And they'll want to be sure that they don't interpret texts in ways that support their position while neglecting that alternative readings are possible or even more likely. What is at stake here for the Christian historian are the virtues of honesty and integrity. In fact, Christians haven't always lived up to Scripture's standard. A historian shouldn't distort his model of history to make the facts fit the story he wants to tell.

THINKING IT THROUGH 24.2

1. Once a historian has gathered all of the raw data from source materials, what must he use to explain that data?
2. How did Robert Woodberry demonstrate that his model is superior to existing popular models?
3. Give two reasons why humility is essential in historical work.
4. What is the difference between objectivity and neutrality?
5. Why is the work of historical interpretation difficult—even when you have an overarching biblical worldview through which to filter the evidence?

24.3 SEEING GOD'S HAND IN HISTORY

One of the benefits of studying history is the exposure it brings to other ways of thinking. C. S. Lewis noted that even authors of the past who considered each other enemies actually agreed on a great many assumptions simply because they lived in the same time period.[13] For instance, contemporary American views about democracy, free speech, separation of church and state, and many other topics are views common to many people living in the United States. But these views would seem foreign to people in most other places and other times in world history. Likewise, the ideas that democracy is subversive, that free speech is dangerous, that the state has the responsibility to protect true religion, and that divine law should regulate behavior are foreign to many Americans—but these ideas used to be simply assumed in many places and times in world history.

MAKING MORAL JUDGMENTS

Moralities and political views have differed significantly over time, and this ought to lead to more humility on the part of the historian. It's important to judge historical figures within the context of their times. For example, today someone who favored sending African Americans to Africa or denying them the right to vote would rightly be called a racist. But Abraham Lincoln himself held such opinions even as he signed the Emancipation Proclamation.[14] Yet given the intellectual and political climate of his day, Lincoln clearly deserves great charity for pressing for a position that more closely aligned with Scripture despite retaining some unbiblical views common for his time.

But the Christian historian has a more definite standard than the shifting views of contemporary cultures. A biblical worldview roots all moral evaluations, of course, in Scripture. That standard never changes, and it is applicable at all times and places.

Christian historians share the blind spots of their own eras. They, too, fall short of the standards of Scripture. So the Christlike thing to do when a sinner writes about other sinners, living or dead, is to give as much grace to people as possible. And one way a historian does this is by acknowledging the cultural and intellectual forces that shaped figures of the past. Christian historians should write with the biblical virtues of grace and kindness.

DISCERNING DIVINE PROVIDENCE

providence: *the theological term designating God's control over and directing of human affairs*

How to view divine **providence*** is one of the most controversial topics among Christian historians. Virtually all Christians accept the doctrine of God's providence, however they might define it. The Bible teaches that God is in control of every event in history. He directs all human affairs (Ps. 22:28; Prov. 16:33; Acts 17:26), particularly for the good of His people (Rom. 8:28; Eph. 1:11). Nonetheless, not even the persecution and suffering of God's people are outside the bounds of His providence (2 Tim. 3:12), and the goodness the Lord shows to non-Christians is also included (Matt. 5:45). Sometimes the Bible lets its readers see God at work "behind the scenes" of world history. For instance, God motivated King Cyrus to send some of the exiled Israelites back to Judea. God didn't use a miracle to do this. He worked silently within Cyrus's heart (Ezra 1:1–2). We would not know about this except that God first predicted that He would do it and then did it. But some Christian historians think that, for various reasons, a Christian should avoid discussing providence in histories outside of the Bible.

Problems with Saying Certain Events Are Providential

Carl Trueman raises two objections to discussing divine providence in history. First, he says, God's providence stands over all things. *Everything* that happens in the world is providential. Therefore, claiming that providence is the reason something happened doesn't really explain anything. Second, he notes that those who do appeal to providence often do so to promote their own point of view or to claim God for their side in some argument. To say "God did this" ends the argument, often unfairly.[15] John Fea points out the way that this is often done in American history. Some historians point to anything that promotes American freedoms and interests as an example of God's providence, thereby attempting to justify the rightness of the American Revolution or some other event.[16] Fea notes that such claims presuppose the position they're seeking to support; they assume that God approves of their causes. As Christian historian Mark Noll observes, whether you see the Reformation as an act of God for purifying the church depends on whether you're Protestant or Catholic.[17]

C. S. Lewis also raises an objection to finding God's providential hand in history. He warns of the danger of ascribing "our calamities (or more often our neighbours' calamities) to divine judgment."[18] Lewis asks how anyone can possibly know whether a certain calamity is a divine judgment unless God explicitly says so. Lewis also notes, however, that unbelievers are even more prone to this error than Jews and Christians are.

Guidelines for Saying Certain Events Are Providential

There is wisdom in the objections these writers raise. Certainly, we have no right to claim God for our side, while we do have a responsibility to be on His side. But there are also some answers to those objections that we need to think through.

Imagine a prayer meeting at a church when a member stands up and says:

> Last week I was taking a big road trip when my car broke down in the middle of nowhere. I don't have much mechanical expertise, but I got out and started to poke around under the hood. I didn't know what I was looking for, so I started to pray for help. Fifteen minutes later a car pulled over behind me. The driver knew a lot about fixing cars, and he was able to get me going well enough for me to get to a garage for a more permanent fix.

Someone who gives a testimony like this will usually end by praising God for answering prayer and providing help. If you've grown up in church, you've probably heard testimonies like this—or even given them.

But suppose that, instead of praising God, the person who gave the testimony concluded with a statement like this: "I'm not certain this was an answer to prayer; it may just have been a coincidence." Most Bible-believing Christians would think that saying this is somehow wrong because they believe that prayer matters (James 5:16), that God is our Father and cares about what we need, and that He wants us to ask Him for those needs and delights to meet them (Matt. 7:9–11). If God providentially sent the help, He also providentially sent the car trouble itself. He could have kept the water pump temperature sensor from wearing out, but He didn't. Christians' cars break down just as much as non-Christians' cars (maybe even more). And yet Christians are still right to see God's hand behind their automotive experiences.

Given all this discussion of divine providence, what do you think of the following comment in an actual history book about Henry VIII?

> Had this makeshift political match [between Henry VIII and Katherine of Aragon] not taken place, and prince Henry taken instead a younger, more fertile consort (such as his father's former choice for him, Katherine's niece Eleanor), his subsequent break with Rome almost certainly would not have occurred, in which case any tender young English reformation must have faced the wrath of a ruthless, orthodox monarch and his equally Catholic heirs.[19]

How is a conservative Protestant Christian to respond? To say, "That's a mighty big, world-changing coincidence," doesn't seem to be the right response.

We don't know all of God's purposes in the world. And it's hard or impossible to figure out exactly what God is doing through every situation in your own life—or what He's doing in others' lives through you. Sometimes, you figure out after a decade why God gave you certain experiences. But there's a lot you won't know about even your own life until that day when we shall "know fully" even as we have been "fully known" (1 Cor. 13:12).

Nonetheless, the Bible does reveal quite a number of God's purposes. And when, broadly speaking, those purposes get fulfilled, it's right to point to God's good and powerful hand of providence. If you're convinced that the Protestant Reformation rescued the biblical gospel and other precious biblical doctrines, rooting the church once again in Scripture—if you're convinced that the health of Christ's church depended in large measure on the success of the Reformation—then how could you fail to see God's hand in Henry VIII's choice of a wife? Think of the wide-ranging consequences of that choice. Could it be that one of them was the modern missionary movement launched from English-speaking lands? God says it's not His desire "that any should perish, but that all should reach repentance" (2 Pet. 3:9). He wants the gospel to go to the ends of the earth (Matt. 28:19–20).

In the final chapter of Genesis, Joseph told his brothers,

> As for you, you meant evil against me, but God meant it for good, to bring it about that many people should be kept alive, as they are today. (Gen 50:20)

We don't need special revelation from God to conclude that, though Henry VIII meant to do evil (to divorce his lawful wife), God meant it for good, to bring it about that many people should be evangelized, as they are today.

Of course, if our understanding of biblical doctrine or of God's purposes in Scripture is incorrect, then our interpretation of God's providential purposes in history is bound to be incorrect too. This is why it is the Christian's responsibility to rightly understand Scripture and the purposes of God as stated in Scripture. Given that understanding, it cannot be wrong to examine whether those purposes are actually being worked out in history.

This is the answer to Carl Trueman's argument that since everything is providential, providence is not a worthwhile category for the historian: some events clearly promote God's purposes as stated in Scripture. Since God is providentially in control of all things, as Trueman acknowledges, it is appropriate to point out the connection between God's stated purposes and the events that promoted them. And when events go against God's purposes, it is right to see the hand of the evil one. As in the case of Job, God sometimes gives Satan a long leash.

Dangers to Avoid in Discerning Providence in History

We should note that a "providence" is different from a "miracle." God providentially works through the ordinary operation of human thought and action. He uses what theologians call "secondary causes." He doesn't have to use His own finger, as it were, to crush His enemies. When the Spanish Armada—a military offensive launched by Roman Catholic Spain—suffered defeat in 1588, keeping Protestant England permanently out of the hands of the pope, the immediate causes for that naval victory included the fact that the English had superior firepower. They had developed a more efficient way of repeatedly firing their cannons.[20] The Christian historian would be irresponsible to simply call the defeat of the Spanish Armada a providential act of God while ignoring the secondary causes at work to bring about its defeat.

Christians should also refrain from appealing to providence to justify the rightness of their own actions. For instance, what if the English appealed to the Armada's defeat as an example of their national righteousness compared to that of the Spanish? What if Henry VIII justified his divorce by pointing to the spreading of the gospel that resulted?

This kind of thinking gets everything precisely backwards. God sometimes uses crooked sticks to draw straight lines. For instance, the assassination of France's leading Protestants in the Saint Bartholomew's Day Massacre didn't mean God favored the Catholics and their doctrine. Nor did it mean that God was more in control of the events in England than of the ones in France. One of the purposes of God in the world, according to the Bible, is that His people will sometimes suffer (Matt. 5:12–13; Heb. 12:7–11; 1 Pet. 1:6).

Saint Bartholomew's Day Massacre: A providential reading of history doesn't look at those who are successful and presume that they're the ones God favors. It looks at Scripture to see what God favors, and then it is justified in making interpretations of history.

Not all possible historical examples of divine providence are clear-cut. In fact, most are not. This means once again that Christian historians must be humble. In many cases, they will not know what God's purpose—or, more accurately, His purposes—might be. Historians shouldn't be afraid to confess their ignorance or offer mere suggestions. But neither should this limitation prevent historians from considering the providence of God. God really is providentially controlling all things.

WRITING AND TEACHING

A historian's task is not complete when he has researched an event, of course. That research must be communicated to others. The two most common ways for a historian to communicate his research are through teaching and writing. Writing can be published in scholarly journals or in books—whether those books are scholarly or popular, that is, written for people who aren't specialists. Some historians look down on writing for a general audience, but the Christian shouldn't. If all people should have a Christian perspective about God's world, then Christians should write histories that are accessible to a wide readership. On the flip side, some Christians are suspicious of scholarly histories. They may think that scholarship is elitist or detracts from more directly gospel-related work. But if Christian scholars aren't doing excellent work in the primary sources, then they will be dependent on the work that non-Christians do.

God calls Christian historians to view—and do—their work through the lenses of a biblical worldview. And He calls all believers to view history through those same lenses.

THINKING IT THROUGH 24.3

1. What is divine providence?
2. Give a biblical example of God's providence in human history.
3. Explain two reasons why some historians believe that Christians should avoid discussing providence in histories outside of the Bible.
4. Even though humans can't know all of God's purposes in the world and won't figure out exactly what God is doing through every situation, why should Christians still point to God's providence in history?
5. Why shouldn't a providential reading of history look at those who are successful and presume that they are the ones God favors?

24 CHAPTER REVIEW

TERMS TO REMEMBER

primary source
secondary source
objectivity
providence

Scripture Memory

Isaiah 46:9–10

Making Connections

1. What should provide the framework for historical study?
2. What must a historian do before he can communicate a historical model to others?
3. What is a historical model?
4. What can cause a historical model to be faulty?

Developing Skills in Apologetics and Worldview

5. How would you evaluate the claim that the attack on the Twin Towers on 9/11 was an act of God's divine judgment on the United States?
6. How would you respond to someone who denies that the Protestant Reformation was an act of God's divine grace in world history?

Examining Assumptions and Evidence

7. Why should Christian historians seek to benefit their neighbors through their historical work? Give an example of how they could do this.
8. Why are humility and honesty necessary in the work of model-making?
9. Why is the discernment of divine providence in human history one of the most controversial topics among Christian historians?
10. Why wouldn't it be right to settle the debate over discerning divine providence in human history by viewing all historical events as merely inexplicable coincidences?

Becoming a Creative Cultivator

11. Read a section from a Christian history textbook; then read a section from a secular textbook about the same historical era. Identify ways a model influences each excerpt—affecting the selection of data from sources, the moral judgments expressed, or the discernment of divine providence.

ARTS & CULTURE

Chapter Twenty-Five TRUTH, GOODNESS, AND BEAUTY

Whatever is true, whatever is honorable, whatever is just, whatever is pure, whatever is lovely, whatever is commendable, if there is any excellence, if there is anything worthy of praise, think about these things.

Scripture Memory
Philippians 4:8

25.1 BEAUTY AND CULTURE

A man in jeans and a ball cap stands in a Washington, D.C., metro station playing a violin as passersby rush off to their various appointments. A few people toss coins into the open case in front of him. A camera up on the wall catches the action—and the sound, the beautiful sound. If you know music, you know this isn't the kind of sound usually produced by street musicians. It's exquisite.

As it happened—though precisely one out of the hundreds of people passing by recognized it—the music was coming from a 3.5-million-dollar Stradivarius and a world-class violinist, Joshua Bell. Very few people stopped, a few more gave money, and Bell's total take for an hour of Bach and Schubert was $32.17.[1]

It's such a fascinating story. And everybody who reads it seems to realize that it has to be some kind of parable. It has to mean something. Dozens of books have mentioned the event. Some use it to make points about marketing. A Buddhist writer uses it to urge everyone to slow down. But what parable did the original writer of the story, the *Washington Post*'s Gene Weingarten, see in the free-but-ignored Joshua Bell concert?

Weingarten saw a parable about beauty. "What is beauty? Is it a measurable fact . . . or merely an opinion?"[2] If beauty is a fact, then it's a kind of personal defect that almost everybody rushed past this particular beauty. People are busy, especially at subway stations, but surely more people could've—should've—spared three minutes.

That's especially true if Joshua Bell was right about the music he was playing—"Chaconne" from J. S. Bach's Partita No. 2. The nonreligious[3] Bell described the piece as "one of the greatest achievements of any man in history . . . a spiritually powerful piece, emotionally powerful, structurally perfect."[4] Bell told one interviewer, "A great piece of music gives one the sense of divine order."[5] Bell said,

> Everyone's definition of what God means can vary. But music is something that really takes you to that . . . thing that is greater than we are—the beauty, the magic of the universe. Bach, for instance, [is] probably one of the

Joshua Bell

great recruiters to religion . . . because it's when you listen to Johann Sebastian Bach, the music . . . you can only think that there is something, something great out there. There is no other explanation for his music.[6]

SECULAR AND POSTMODERN VIEWS OF BEAUTY

But the secular postmodern West isn't eager to admit that there is something greater than we are, especially if that something makes demands on us. The leading worldviews of our time deny that beauty really exists, or at least that we can reliably recognize it.

For naturalistic materialists, beauty is just an accidental byproduct of evolution. Music, for example, may be an unintended effect of language formation. Or maybe musical males attract more females.[7]

According to postmodernists, for you to make an **aesthetic*** judgment—to call something "beautiful" or "ugly"—is to say something about your individual feelings and not necessarily about any reality outside yourself. For a postmodern, beauty is so deeply stuck in the eye of the beholder that it cannot get out. Beauty is decidedly not fact; it's mere opinion.

aesthetic: *relating to beauty or the experience of beauty*

A Cultural Triad: Truth, Goodness, and Beauty

Christian philosopher Ron Horton has observed that "our age attempts to separate goodness and beauty, but the Bible ascribes both to God."[8] "How great is his goodness, and how great his beauty!" (Zech. 9:17). God unites goodness and beauty—and, of course, truth. Truth, goodness, and beauty make up a **triad**, a collection of three concepts that seem to flow necessarily together. Modern Western worldviews doubt and weaken all three.

This chapter makes a fairly simple argument: modern Western attacks on beauty sound an awful lot like modern Western attacks on truth and goodness. And that similarity is not accidental. Truth, goodness, and beauty stand together. If you don't accept **relativism** when it comes to truth (knowledge) and goodness (morality), why would you agree that beauty is merely in the eye of the beholder?

Perhaps you are, in fact, nervous about ever claiming that someone else's aesthetic judgment is wrong. If your friend loves "Bang Yer Head" by an earsplitting screamo band, but you find it distasteful, who are you to judge?

This relativistic perspective about beauty would surprise people of past ages, especially Christians. Our secular age is the first in history in which people find it easy to believe beauty is what we make of it, and hard to believe that "beauty" is something that exists independently of human judgment.[9]

But we'll discover as we explore culture and the arts that Joshua Bell was right. Beauty points to a **divine order**, and what's more, beauty is part of that order. The arts are full of creational norms. **Art** is a work of discovery and imitation as much as it is a work of creation. A culture that denies that beauty exists outside the eyes of its beholders is a culture that is "revolting against reality itself."[10]

Subcreators of Truth, Goodness, and Beauty

As we've seen in various portions of this book, the Creation Mandate is a call for—and a blessing to—humans to be "creative cultivators." "We take the stuff of creation and shape artifacts and institutions," says Ken Myers. "We build things from stone and steel. We make art by arranging colors and textures, sounds and words." Myers is right: "Culture is what we make of creation."[11] And that's the way God designed things to be.

Humans are "subcreators"—creators under God.[12] The best art—whether it's realistic or abstract painting, comic or tragic theater and film, intense or subtle music—captures the beauty of God's creation and helps us see the beauty of God. The best stories capture something of the great story that that the divine Author is writing, and they help us see that story with clearer eyes.[13]

Good subcreation can't help but glorify the ultimate Creator. When colors, sounds, and words are arranged beautifully, they point beyond themselves as all created things are supposed to. They point to a divine order and a divine Orderer.

Culture is far bigger than the arts, of course. Culture includes science, engineering, business practices, academic research, food preparation, marriage customs, and much more. But in this unit we'll focus on the arrangement of colors and textures, sounds and words. Though we'll reference multiple areas of culture, we'll focus mainly on music, the visual arts, literature, and drama. These are such large categories that we will be able to speak in only a general way.

THINKING IT THROUGH 25.1

1. Identify the aesthetic errors of scientific naturalism. Identify the aesthetic errors of postmodernism.
2. What three concepts fit together in a cultural triad?
3. Identify the source of the triad, which demands that the triad be objective and transcendent.
4. What does it mean to be a subcreator?
5. If cultural creativity is a matter of subcreation, then what purpose should good art seek to fulfill?

25.2 TRUTH, GOODNESS, AND BEAUTY IN THE EYE OF THE BEHOLDER

Without ever reading a philosophy book, average Western people still absorb the doubt in the air about truth, goodness, and beauty. Sociologist Christian Smith, the scholar who coined the term *moralistic therapeutic deism* to describe the religion of American teenagers, recorded comments from many interviews with those teens that demonstrate this doubt about what's moral. One teen said,

> I think morals are just a social tool to keep us not killing each other, to keep us in line with our culture, so it can function as a unit.[14]

Another said,

> Well, a lot of the times it's personal, it changes from person to person. What you may think is right may not necessarily be right for me, understand? So it's all individual.[15]

Yet another:

> You can't say, you feel that something is absolute. You can be like, man, I feel that's ridiculously wrong, you know, you have the right to choose, that's your choice. But, I don't know, *absolute*'s such a strong word. Um, I don't know, I really don't. . . . I mean, in today's society, sure, like to murder someone is just ridiculous. I don't know, in some societies, back in time, maybe it's a good thing.[16]

And one more:

> I guess it kind of depends on the situation. Like taking an extra vacation day, for me it's not going to hurt anyone. In my job, it's not really going to hurt anyone. Is it morally right? Probably not, no. What's a moral rule, though? A personal thing? Well then I would say that sometimes breaking a moral rule might be all right, depending on the situation.[17]

People have been justifying and rationalizing their sin ever since Adam, of course. That's not new. What's new is the "relativistic" rationalization that has become popular in the modern West. The teens quoted above see morality as relative, not to an absolute standard, but to an individual or cultural or situational one. "It's personal" or "that's your choice." "It kind of depends on the situation." Only "in today's society" or "in our culture" is murder bad—or porn, or gossiping online, or software piracy.

Straight-up moral relativism is—one would hope—not as likely to afflict Bible-believing teens. They know there are moral absolutes given by their Creator. And Smith's statistics (he surveyed hundreds of teens in various religious groups) bear this out. Conservative Christian churches generally do a pretty good job of convincing their teens that moral rules are set by God and accessible in the Bible. The same goes for the concept of truth; teens raised in Christian homes mostly accept that the Bible is really true and whatever disagrees with the Bible is false.

But truth and goodness are tied not just to each other but also to beauty. Weakening one of the three weakens the other two. A biblical worldview rests all three on a firm foundation in the triune God. Let's discuss truth, goodness, and beauty in order to cement the relationship among them and, ultimately, build a Christian view of the arts. If Christians do not accept relativism when it comes to truth and goodness, why would they accept relativistic visions of beauty?

TRUTH IN THE MIND OF THE BEHOLDER

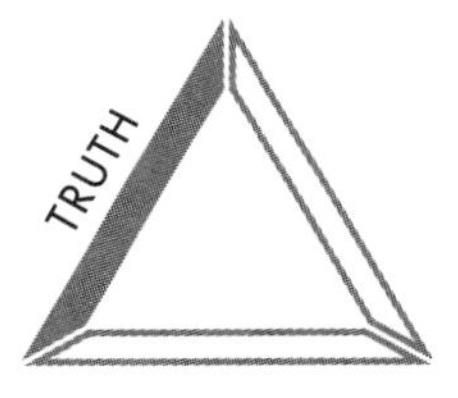

"What is truth?" The question is as old as Pontius Pilate and, of course, older than that. Influential thinkers in the West have tended to move in two different but related directions on this question.

- **The scientistic direction:** As we discussed in the science unit, "It is a tenet of scientism that only certifiably scientific knowledge counts as real knowledge. All else is mere opinion or nonsense."[18]
- **The postmodern direction:** "Postmodernism tends to hold that there is no all-embracing, 'totalizing' viewpoint, no 'God's-eye view,' no pure objectivity. . . . There are, according to most postmodernists, only interpretations."[19]

These two directions seem opposed because scientism claims objectivity, but postmodernism, if it's consistent, has to regard science as only one viewpoint among many. But in practice, educated people in the West tend to hold both of these contradictory approaches to truth together. They assume that science is the only way to answer certain questions, and that the answers to other questions are culturally relative. For them evolution is true, but ideas outside science vary culture by culture. They hear biblical truth claims as one person's opinion (and a long-dead person at that) rather than as the testimony of the only Person whose opinion truly matters. Truth outside science is in the mind of the beholder, in this view.

Some Christians respond by insisting that "all truth is objective!" And it is. There *is* a God's-eye view. But we need to be very careful what we claim because we don't have access to the divine view on the specifics of every issue. God hasn't revealed to us His precise viewpoint on the minimum wage in early twenty-first-century America. God knows what the wisest and most successful approach to the issue is, and He has spoken to the issue in a general way in the Bible ("the laborer deserves his wages," Luke 10:7). But there's no Bible with a chart in the back giving us dollars-and-cents figures.

We are finite, and we are fallen. Objective truth really exists, but our access to it is unavoidably **subjective**. You are a "subject." All that means is that you think and feel; you are "subjected" to stimuli from various "objects." You can't stop being a subject because God made you one. You can't detach yourself from reality and become a totally **objective**, neutral, fact-processing machine. Subjective factors color the human apprehension of truth.

The Bible teaches as much. The Bible says that if you want true understanding, you must be a certain kind of person. "The fear of the Lord is the beginning of knowledge," Solomon says (Prov. 1:7). God "stores up sound wisdom for the upright" (Prov. 2:7). You cannot be wise if you will not be good. And Jesus makes this astonishing claim to some of His hearers: "Because I tell you the truth, you do not believe me" (John 8:45). In contrast, Jesus goes on to say, "Whoever is of God hears the words of God" (John 8:47). Of course, in this context, *hears* refers not to properly functioning ear drums but to spiritual understanding (cf. John 8:43). This is why Paul distinguishes between the "wisdom of this age" and the "wisdom of God" (1 Cor. 2:6–7). To those "of this age," God's wisdom seems foolish (1 Cor. 1:18–25). Indeed, they're "not able to understand" it (1 Cor. 2:14). But people who have the Spirit of God can understand God's wisdom (1 Cor. 2:10–14).

So postmodernism is correct about one thing: you aren't born with a God's-eye view of truth. And yet scientism is right about one thing too: there is real truth out there to discover. The Christian view unites these two realities in a way that manages not to be self-contradictory. The Bible says that if you fear God, then you have access to God's view on everything He thinks you need to know to live a wise and faithful life. You have access to all the divine revelation you need. You have truth.

So what is truth? It is a gift of God. The Christian view of truth gives us genuine confidence because truth is not relative to cultures or individuals. But the Christian view also gives us genuine humility because we have to admit we can only know the truth if God opens our eyes.

GOODNESS IN THE HEART OF THE BEHOLDER

As with truth, the major Western worldviews of our time have a particular take on goodness.

- **The scientistic take:** "Morality is a collective illusion, genetic in origin, that makes us good cooperators. . . . Morality is purely emotions, although emotions of a special kind with an important adaptive* function."[20]
- **The postmodern take:** "There is no standard, not even a divine one, against which the decisions of a free people can be measured."[21]

adaptive: *able to adjust to differing conditions*

Neither of these views of goodness and morality is new. Both were alive and well when C. S. Lewis was invited to give religious radio talks to the British during World War II. The very first matter Lewis addressed to a nation at war was moral relativism (although it would not have been called a "postmodern" idea at the time). The second was an evolutionary view of morality.

(Postmodern) Moral Relativism

"I know that some people say the idea of a Law of . . . decent behaviour known to all men is unsound, because different civilisations and different ages have had quite different moralities," Lewis said.[22] That's basically the postmodern argument against the objective reality of goodness.

Lewis used a counterargument that was very relevant at that moment. There was no sense in saying Hitler was wrong, he said, "unless Right is a real thing which the Nazis at bottom knew as well as we did and ought to have practiced."[23]

"There are thousands of cultures, [so] it is hard," said one young American who was recently asked to define morality. "But I am not living in that culture, like here the way we are taught and stuff, I mean there are rights and wrongs, and there are definites in every culture. They may be different in every culture."[24]

But people who proclaim that different cultures are allowed to have different views of morality still generally end up condemning those other cultures when it suits them. For example, when the Iranian leader Ayatollah Khomeini issued a *fatwa*, a formal Islamic death sentence, against author Salman Rushdie, "enlightened," tolerant Western governments rushed to condemn Khomeini's act. Never mind that the *fatwa* was entirely defensible from an Iranian point of view since Rushdie had deeply insulted the prophet Muhammad and therefore all Muslims. "Multiculturalism" never lasts long.[25] People can't live as if morality is entirely relative.

Materialist Moral Illusion

Lewis's second talk on the BBC was about another denial of the objective reality of goodness and morality—the evolutionary, materialist denial. This is the idea that "morality is a collective illusion . . . that makes us good cooperators."[26]

Lewis called this the "herd instinct." And he didn't deny that there is such a thing. We all have instincts to love our offspring or to eat. But that's not the moral law, Lewis said. In order to demonstrate this, Lewis asked his listeners to think about times when their instincts conflict:

> Supposing you hear a cry for help from a man in danger. You will probably feel two desires—one a desire to give help (due to your herd instinct), the other a desire to keep out of danger (due to the instinct for self-preservation). But you will find inside you, in addition to these two impulses, a third thing which tells you that you ought to follow the impulse to help, and suppress the impulse to run away. Now this thing that judges between two instincts, that decides which should be encouraged, cannot itself be either of them.[27]

The moral law, Lewis argued, is that feeling that you ought to choose one instinct over the other, whether you feel like it or not. Everywhere in history and in the world we see evidence that people feel beholden to a moral law, even when they disobey it.

The Bible explains why: God wrote the moral law on the heart of every person (Rom. 2:14–15). These norms are part of the creational or natural law that God has established for His universe and revealed in Scripture, though fallen people suppress them. Different moral systems exist because cultures don't all suppress the same truths (Rom. 1:18).

Subjective and Objective Morality

One of the moral problems people today have is "the inability to distinguish between objectively real moral truths or facts and people's human perceptions or understandings of those moral truths or facts."[28] It's just like truth: because people don't have a God's-eye view of goodness, they think goodness isn't really real.

But this kind of relativism gives rise to injustice. If every culture gets to set its own morality, what right did Britain have to declare war against Hitler's Germany? And moral relativism fails to grasp something else that Lewis argued—there really is basic agreement about morality around the world.[29] "Men have differed as to whether you should have one wife or four. But they have always agreed that you must not simply have any woman you liked."[30]

The Bible says that if you want to find true goodness, you must be a certain kind of person. It requires wisdom to apply moral truth to particular situations in your culture (Col. 1:9–10). "Honor your father and mother" applies everywhere in the world, but in some cultures it means saying "Yes, ma'am," and in others, even within the same country, it doesn't. A foolish person can't make these applications (Prov. 17:24). You've got to refuse to conform to the world before you can discern God's will (Rom. 12:2).

And Christians recognize that the demands of divine morality aren't merely external. Right actions are actually immoral if they're done with a sinful motive (Matt. 6:1–8; 1 Cor. 13:3). The goal of Christian ethics is not simply change in behavior but change in character.

So, as with truth, the apprehension and practice of goodness has a subjective element to it, but what's good or bad is objective, factual, real—a divine norm.

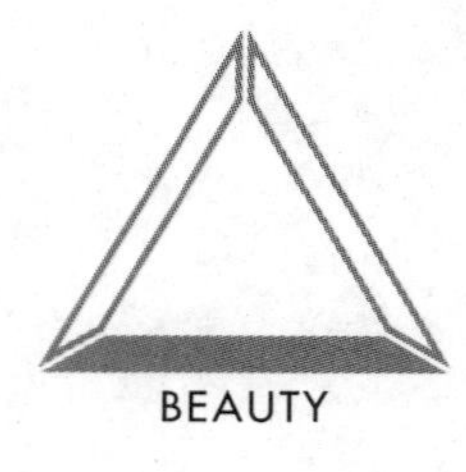

BEAUTY

BEAUTY IN THE EYE OF THE BEHOLDER

And now to beauty. "Beauty," says a Christian art and music textbook, "is what makes art, art." To call something "art" at all is to say, "first, that somebody made it (for we don't call accidents 'art'), and, second, that its appearance has the potential to reward those who pay attention to it. That is, it can be appreciated for its beauty."[31]

How do scientism and postmodernism, the main intellectual currents of our time, regard beauty? Basically the same way they regard truth and goodness.

- **The scientistic view:** "The sense of beauty has emerged through the process of sexual selection. . . . By making himself beautiful the man is doing what the peacock does when he displays his tail: he is giving a sign of his reproductive fitness, to which a woman responds as the peahen responds, claiming him . . . on behalf of her genes."[32]
- **The postmodern view:** Beauty is in the eye of the beholder.

just-so story: *a fanciful and unfalsifiable explanation of how something originated*

The scientistic view should be recognized immediately for the "just-so story"* that it is. What evidence could possibly confirm or falsify such an idea? Evolutionists who favor group-level selection offer a second fanciful explanation, the idea that beauty unites the community around special objects, conferring on that group an evolutionary advantage over other groups.[33] But recall what Joshua Bell said about the power of music to point to "divine order." And think of your own experiences with beauty—are you willing to write them off as accidental neuron firings? Beautiful things are, to us, significant things: we admire them, we gather them, we treasure them. Materialism strips all significance and meaning from beauty, just as it does with everything else in the universe. But it doesn't work. You can't act as if the beautiful things you treasure are beautiful only by evolutionary accident.

The postmodern view is only slightly different, really. It, too, removes ultimate meaning from beauty by insisting that one person's idea of beauty has no authority over any other person's view.

Once again, you know better. Your experience and, more importantly, your Christian worldview both tell you beauty isn't merely subjective.

A man goes to the Louvre* in Paris to see a famous work of Renaissance art. He stands for some time with furrowed brow, studying the master painter's work. Finally, he comments to a nearby guard: "I don't like it." The guard replies, "Sir, these paintings are no longer being judged; the viewers are."[34]

Louvre: (loov) the most prominent art museum in the world

The guard is exactly right: beauty stands over us and not just in us. It confronts us. And it calls us. That's one big reason sunsets and galaxies and moonscapes were made. "The heavens declare the glory of God" (Ps. 19:1).

> The beauty in creation is all the time saying, "There is a great God of glory and power and generosity behind all this awesome universe; you belong to him; he is patient with you in sustaining your rebellious life; turn and bank your hope on him and delight yourself in him, not his handiwork."[35]

Cultural Variation

As with truth and goodness, beauty has to enter through your senses for you to perceive it. There is a subjective element to beauty. Whole cultures perceive it in characteristically different ways. Even within the boundaries of Western music, Rachmaninoff sounds unmistakably Russian, and Vaughan Williams sounds quintessentially British. But both composed utterly beautiful music. Think, too, of Arabic and Hindi microtonal music: it's almost incomprehensible to Westerners, but it would be arrogant to say that such music is not beautiful—at least without first trying to understand it.

Nonetheless, we must not conclude from looking at the cultural landscape that beauty is culturally relative. There are elements of beauty common among cultures, of course: "Symmetry and order; proportion; closure; convention; harmony, and also novelty and excitement: all these seem to have a permanent hold on the human psyche."[36] But it's OK if two cultures see beauty in different hues: beauty is so massive that new angles of vision are always waiting to be explored.

> [Beauty] is an object bigger than we [are]—infinitely bigger than we [are]—so we all see different aspects of it. And, as we do so, more of God's glory is [seen] than if we all saw the same things. As it turns out, the Christian doctrine of beauty provides the only true basis for diversity.[37]

No Basis for Taste?

If beauty is something real, something solid, then it's wrong to deny it, just as it's wrong to deny truth or goodness. It may even be wrong for you, depending on your gifts and opportunities, to fail to explore avenues of beauty made available to you. You can educate your taste, and you should. To do so is to take dominion and learn more of God at the same time.

And there is an explanation for taste. It can be difficult, but humans made in the beautiful image of God can justify their judgments about beauty by using critical reasoning.[38] If two people disagree over whether or not something is beautiful, the possibility must be left open that one of them may be wrong.

(POST)MODERN ART

British philosopher Roger Scruton has said,

> Imagine now a world in which people showed an interest only in replica Brillo boxes, in signed urinals, in crucifixes pickled in urine, or in objects similarly lifted from the debris of life and put on display with some kind of satirical or "look at me" intention—in other words, the increasingly standard fare of official modern art shows in Europe and America.[42]

Scruton points out that a world like that would be totally different from the world of the Old Masters.* The only similarities would be that in both cases works of art are put on display and that people view them through aesthetic lenses. He concludes, "It would be a world in which human aspirations no longer find their artistic expression, in which we no longer make for ourselves images of the transcendent, and in which mounds of rubbish cover the sites of our ideals."[43]

Old Masters: *distinguished European artists of the Renaissance period*

And it isn't necessarily the art critic who has good taste and the common man who lacks it. Much of modern art is an exercise in charging more and more money to give the emperor ever-changing styles of invisible clothes. Sometimes Christians may feel like following in the footsteps of artist Jacqueline Crofton, who marched into an empty room at the Tate Modern Gallery in London and defaced a minimalist artwork by throwing two eggs at it. The mess was easily cleaned up, and all went back to normal because the "artwork" consisted of nothing more than an empty room with the lights turning on and off every five seconds.[39] The minimalist artist had once created a work in which "some Blu-Tack [was] kneaded, rolled into a ball, and depressed against a wall."[40]

cartel: *a group of elites who have taken over control of the production of some good or service*

"What I object to fiercely," said the egg thrower, "is that we've got this cartel* who control the top echelons of the art world in this country and leave no access for painters and sculptors with real creative talent."[41]

Of course, it can only be "real creative talent" as opposed to counterfeit creative talent if there's some standard of beauty by which some pieces of art can be said to reflect God's creativity and not others.

The Purpose of Beauty

Beauty thrills you, it calls you to God, but it isn't just for you. One Christian writer, an experienced hiker, is among the relatively few people on the planet who have climbed all fifty-four of the peaks over fourteen thousand feet in the Colorado Rocky Mountains. "I've spent a lot of time up there above the tree lines," he says.

> So what do I see? I see a carpet of wildflowers, and I'm thinking, "Why is this here?" At most, 200 people have seen this site—or perhaps the Great Barrier Reef. . . . There's nothing more beautiful on Earth than these unbelievable tropical fish. For most of history we didn't even know they were there until Jacques Cousteau invented scuba gear, which was in 1950. Nobody even knew the greatest art in the world was already there just swimming around. Why is that there? Well, God didn't put it there just for our enjoyment, or He would have made it a little more accessible! There's something about His own enjoyment, His pride in artistic creation.[44]

The fact is that beauty—like truth and goodness—is in the eye of the Beholder. All things (including beauty) are "from him and through him and to him" (Rom. 11:36). The ultimate standard of beauty is God Himself.[45]

Of course, the way God's own beauty can serve as the standard of all human-created beauty will take some explaining. But for now the important point is that, like truth and goodness, beauty is both subjective and objective. The fact that human eyes often miss beauty doesn't mean beauty is not really there to be seen. You must be a certain kind of person to truly appreciate beauty.

THINKING IT THROUGH 25.2

1. Why is relativism attractive to contemporary people?
2. Why shouldn't believers embrace a relativistic view of truth, goodness, and beauty?
3. What justifies Christian confidence in the apprehension of objective truth, goodness, and beauty?
4. Why should Christians be humble when they evaluate the truth, goodness, and beauty in art?
5. Respond to the following statement: "Beauty is in the eye of the beholder."

25.3 NORMS FOR THE ARTS

One of the ways you know you're growing as a Christian is that familiar verses and stories from Scripture come to mean more to you. You memorized them, perhaps, as a small child, and they were just words on a page in an activity book. But then they came to your mind when you faced a particular temptation in seventh grade, and suddenly they took on a deeper significance.

Let's try to see that happen with one particular verse (the one you're supposed to memorize for this chapter)—Philippians 4:8.

> Whatever is true, whatever is honorable, whatever is just, whatever is pure, whatever is lovely, whatever is commendable, if there is any excellence, if there is anything worthy of praise, think about these things.

Maybe you learned this as a verse about watching TV and movies—and it most definitely applies to those things. But it's much richer and deeper than that.

This is an important statement in God's Word about a vocation some readers of this book are even now being called to. It's a command that all Christians, whatever their calling, ought to embrace their whole lives long. This verse underpins a Christian view of the arts. It provides a biblical reason to take truth, goodness, and beauty as norms.

Lists of virtues like these—truth, honor, justice, purity, loveliness, and so on—are found in the Bible and elsewhere. But Paul doesn't commend just any kind of justice or purity; he's promoting the specifically Christian practice of these virtues. In fact, "truth," "justice," "loveliness," and the other virtues mean something different when they're viewed through non-Christian lenses.

And one of the reasons we know this is that the virtues qualify and modify each other in specifically Christian ways. Not everything that is "true" is also "honorable." If you've ever watched a movie you regret seeing, it's probably because things that truly do happen in this world—graphic violence and sexual immorality—were made even more dishonorable by being turned into entertainment for people in easy chairs. It dishonors sex to take it out of the marriage bed and put it on a plasma screen (Heb. 13:4). It disrespects the sad necessity of the sword in a fallen world (Rom. 13:4) when people watch blood and gore for kicks.[46] The Bible describes sin truthfully, but it does so with respect for its readers, not in a vulgar, base, corrupting way.

Christians are typically alert to questions of truth in the movies or in popular books. They're ready to point out the pantheistic worldview in the *Star Wars* films or voyeuristic: *taking pleasure in watching the pain of others*

the voyeuristic* violence in *The Hunger Games*, but some Christians are so eager to point out what's true (or not) in art that they fail to give sufficient weight to the honor and purity a work of art is supposed to have. We instinctively cringe at the thought of drinking polluted water but eagerly quench our thirst with clean water. That's the way a Christian should respond when contemplating works of art—recoiling at the impure and being refreshed by the pure.

Truth heads Paul's list in Philippians 4:8. **Goodness** comes next (think on whatever is "honorable," "just," "pure"). **Beauty** follows: we are supposed to think on "whatever is lovely" and "whatever is commendable." By *lovely* Paul appears to mean something that is visually beautiful; *commendable* probably refers to beautiful, well-chosen speech.[47]

Teens who grow up with rules about what they can and cannot watch or read or listen to or play sometimes fixate on the many pleasures they are denied by their parents. "But Sarah's mom lets her watch it!" is one of the more common arguments used by aggravated teens. (And you will always be able to find a Sarah whose mom is not as strict as other moms.)

TRUTH
GOODNESS
Phil. 4:8
BEAUTY

But don't miss the repeated *whatevers* in Paul's list: whatever is true, whatever is honorable, whatever is lovely. Yes, there are things that don't fit in those categories because of the Fall. But there's a lot that does fit, more than you could experience in a lifetime.[48] This is a big world with lots of artistic and cultural good in it. "Of every tree of the garden you may freely eat," God told Adam and Eve (Gen. 2:16, NKJV); don't repeat their mistake by fixating on the one tree that's off-limits.

What Paul has given in Philippians 4:8 is a set of creational norms by which all cultural pursuits can be evaluated, and they boil down to truth, goodness, and beauty. This triad provides a biblical norm for evaluating all cultural endeavors. Let's look at examples of truth, goodness, and beauty in culture and the arts.

TRUTH

Christ identifies himself as the truth (John 14:6). Satan stands directly opposite to God. There is no truth in him, and his followers don't listen to Jesus precisely because He is telling the truth (John 8:44–47). God's Word is truth (Ps. 119:160). And God exhorts us to delight in the truth (Ps. 51:6). Truth is to be sought after diligently; it's an aspect of wisdom to connect the truth of God's Word with the truth of God's world in a way that enables you to live wisely (Prov. 23:23).

Literature

Good literature helps us do that. The criterion of truth doesn't rule out fiction. Often fiction can help a reader see reality more clearly than plain exposition of the facts can. When Nathan confronted David about his sin with Bathsheba, he first told him a story (2 Sam. 12). The story stunned David with the truth of what he had done—a truth he had until then rationalized away.

Jesus' own parables were, in one sense, fiction. There probably never was a servant who owed his master ten thousand talents but was forgiven his debt—and then went out and choked somebody else who owed him only a hundred denarii (Matt. 18:21–35). But nothing could be more true-to-life than this and the other parables Jesus told. Our sin debt to God really is like a huge bill we could never pay off, and our failure to forgive others really is shameful by comparison.

Or consider the lessons about the appropriate balance of reason and emotion in Jane Austen's *Sense and Sensibility*, or of the dangers of rash vows in Shakespeare's *King Lear*, or the follies and dangers of sudden wealth in Dickens's *Great Expectations*. Stories should be experienced as stories before we try to reflect on the truths they contain; stories are narratives and not lists of truths. But all stories undoubtedly communicate truth, and a great many of them communicate falsehood too.

Music

Music, by contrast, may not seem to be either true or false. But music does communicate at a deep level. And that communication can be true or false. Two Christians who have thought deeply about art and music have observed,

> Ugly music is ugly because it lies. It suppresses . . . the truth and goodness of creation and providence. Sad music pleases us by speaking truthfully (in tones and rhythms) about the effect of the fall and the law's curse on creation. . . . Happy music moves us the way it does by speaking truthfully about grace and hope in a new creation. Only music's potential for communicating the good and the true explains why we find such succor [assistance, relief] in it.[49]

Visual Arts

Visual arts can clearly communicate truth too—as well as lies. Jacques-Louis David's *Death of Marat* was full of artful lies that served his political cause. Leni Riefenstahl, widely regarded as the greatest female filmmaker of the twentieth century, made her film *Triumph of the Will* as a piece of Nazi propaganda, with Adolph Hitler as the star.

The truth that the visual arts convey may be obvious in the case of realist painting, but even abstract art serves up truth and falsehood to its viewers. Compare, for example, the "drip paintings" of Jackson Pollock to the Nihonga paintings of Christian artist Makoto Fujimura. Both are abstract, but Pollock's work implies that chance rules the universe while Fujimura's art points to a divine order.[50]

Jackson Pollock's famous drip paintings imply that chance rules the universe.

The Death of Marat tells several lies that served the artist's political cause.

GOODNESS

There is no one good but God alone, Jesus told the rich young ruler (Mark 10:18). And yet nonbelievers can truly do good, as we discussed in the common grace chapter. And Christians are expected both to do "good works" and to grow in "goodness" over time (Gal. 5:22).

Works of art can express goodness, and they can encourage us to pursue it. A beautiful landscape or melody may cause you to so delight in the beauty of God's creation that your heart wells up with a desire to please Him. Every branch of the arts can display goodness.

Poetry

"Poetry is the art of using words charged with their utmost meaning," says Dana Gioia, a poet and the former chairman of America's National Endowment for the Arts.[51] Think of the good that can be done through such words, the comfort people can enjoy in sorrow, and the sharp insights people can share to enrich their neighbors.

Fiction

Novels explore human morality with a depth that only God can exceed. Few if any other kinds of writing can make you feel the weight of a moral dilemma the way a novel can or explore the possibilities of human personality or sense the call of goodness. Even insight into human fallenness can be good (and true as well as beautiful) if it is treated the way the Bible treats it.

ART AND WORLDVIEW IN *LES MISERABLES*

In Victor Hugo's novel *Les Miserables*, Fantine is perceived as morally blameless even though she sold her body for money—because the author assumes a world in which she had no choice. The reader swallows a view of sin as a problem with society (which it is in part) but brushes aside a view of sin as a problem with the self (which it always is). This all happens without the distraction of an argument. It happens because Hugo's story assumes a false view of the world, and the (careless) reader absorbs the assumption.

Drama and Film

American poet Carl Sandburg said in an interview that some people

> think motion pictures, the product Hollywood makes, is merely entertainment [and] has nothing to do with education. That's one of the darnedest fool fallacies that is current . . . . Anything that brings you to tears by way of drama does something to the deepest roots of our personalities. All movies, good or bad, are education, and Hollywood is the foremost educational institution on earth.[52]

Films combine some of the most viscerally powerful artistic methods known to man—close-ups, a swelling musical score, sweeping vistas, emotionally charged acting, romance, action—in the service of whatever story and values the movie exists to spread. If those two things are righteous and if truth and beauty are also present, a film can do powerful good. But if you diminish any member of the triad, the others suffer. If the film isn't true, it's not as beautiful. If it's not good, it's not true. If it's not beautiful, it's neither good nor true. Truth, goodness, and beauty are most fully themselves when they harmonize together. They aren't three independent pillars; they're three strands of a braid.

The classic theater drama *Our Town* by Thornton Wilder braids them well. The play is an insightful and entertaining reminder of the brevity of life—one that's very consistent with the message of a biblical book like Ecclesiastes. *The Winslow Boy* by Terrance Rattigan demonstrates a family's love of truth in their desire to protect their son's reputation against false charges in Edwardian England. Skillful dramas like these can press truth and goodness into human hearts. Those hearts may resist, but they can hardly help but be swept up into the story.

BEAUTY

It's time we clarify something: by "beauty" we do not mean "prettiness." Beauty salons and beauty aids all have their place, and a truly beautiful woman is a marvel of divine design that almost no human being can fail to notice. But beauty is deeper and broader than the female cosmetics industry. Dana Gioia, quoted earlier in this chapter, has observed that beauty means something particular in the Christian tradition. "Beauty," he says, "is the pleasure we get in recognizing the particular manifestation of a broader, universal order."[53]

It's our connection with "the essential harmony of creation," he explains. "The world and the cosmos are intrinsically beautiful. And as God's creation, we have been made to recognize this order."[54] All humans, not just Christians, can recognize this order by virtue of having been created in the image of a Creator.[55] No healthy person is wholly incapable of distinguishing beauty from ugliness or order from chaos.

Music

Leonard Bernstein was one of the most gifted musicians of the twentieth century. He was a creative composer who could write both classical and popular music. His "Chichester Psalms" is a beautiful setting of multiple biblical psalms in the original Hebrew (Bernstein was ethnically Jewish).

Bernstein is also known for a series of videotaped lectures on music he delivered at Harvard, his alma mater. In them he brilliantly demonstrates some of the "laws"—his word—underlying Western music. He shows how one musical interval, the fifth, developed into the full chromatic scale used all throughout the Western tradition.[55]

Bernstein describes that scale as a discovery, not an invention. And this particular discovery of a beautiful creational order for sound is all the more remarkable because it's not the only one. Other musical scales exist besides the Western one. There's a beauty even in the simplicity and mathematical precision of these scales, but so much more beauty is experienced in the apparently infinite variety of musical compositions that can be built on them.

Art

Art likewise relies on the beautiful structures God built into creation, from physical structures like pigmentation to much deeper and more complex aesthetic laws regarding form, proportion, and line.

We need look no further than our Bibles to learn that mere beautiful forms, even without words, can communicate truth. As we've had reason to observe several times in this book, "the heavens declare the glory of God" (Ps. 19:1) and "what can be known about God is plain . . . in the things that have been made" (Rom 1:19–20).

Art communicates through form. Beauty was created to be a medium for communicating truth. And people were created to receive it. But people aren't all healthy; fallen people suppress the beautiful just as they suppress the good and the true.

> *"For a Christian, beauty is truthful, pleasurable, revelatory, and transformative. It's our recognition of the deepest tendencies of forms in the universe, the highest and most complete level of understanding."*[57]
>
> —DANA GIOIA

So the structures of art are regularly twisted in wrong directions. There is no "art for art's sake." Art always serves one worldview or another.[58] Art is the discovery of beauty in the laws of creation, but it's also human communication, with all the possibilities for truth or falsehood and goodness or evil that entails. Art lets you look at some aspect of the world through someone else's eyes. The view can be enlightening or damning.

CREATION COMMUNICATES THROUGH FORM

Paul Munson and Robert Drake write,

> We know that God speaks through the Bible. But that same Bible tells us that God speaks through his creation too. How is it, for instance, that the meadows and valleys of Psalm 65:13 "shout and sing together for joy" except through the way they look? Or how is it that in Psalm 148 the sea creatures and deeps and fire and hail and snow and mist and all the other things there listed are to praise the Lord? They can only do so by their forms, since they have no other language. We know that God speaks through design as well as through words. So do artists and composers.[59]

The Divine Standard

Just as God is the ultimate standard of truth and goodness, so also with beauty. This may seem strange since God is invisible. But God's beauty is not invisible. It's a beauty that becomes apparent as His people meditate on His perfections (Ps. 27:4). When God acts, He reveals His beauty (Ps. 90:17, KJV). When He reveals Himself, His beauty shines (Ps. 50:2).

Though God is invisible, He created a visible world. Think of the flaming colors of a sunset sky streaked with clouds of orange, purple, and pink or of the great clear blue dome on a summer's afternoon or of the gossamer grey texture of an autumn evening, low against the red-orange-yellow treetops (cf. Job 26:13). Or consider trees—some of them tower above us like gigantic pillars that seem to hold up the vault of heaven, spreading their branches to create a green-roofed cathedral (cf. Ezek. 31:2–9). Or consider the smell of cedar or pine (cf. Hos. 14:6). Think of walking through a forest carpeted with small white-and-purple wildflowers. Or imagine strolling through a field of waist-high grass that bends under the gentle breeze (cf. Isa. 28:4; 40:6; James 1:11).

God also describes humans as beautiful (Isa. 44:13). And though beauty, when divorced from truth and goodness, can be dangerous (Pro. 6:25; 31:30), within the bounds of truth and goodness, the bright eyes, flowing hair, glowing smile, and the forms of male and female bodies are beautiful (Song of Sol. 1:15–16; 4:1–7; 5:10–16).

What's more, humans can enhance their beauty with clothing and jewelry. A sparkling necklace, a golden ring, a sharp suit, a beautiful gown, hair curled or braided—all can enhance human beauty (Exod. 28:2; Isa. 3:18; Zech. 9:16; 2 Chron. 3:6; 1 Pet. 3:3). Of course, this adornment can be inordinate (1 Pet. 3:3–4). But in cautioning us about elevating external beauty over internal beauty, God is not dismissing the reality of either.

CREATIVE CULTIVATORS

A studied opinion about art or music, and one worth sharing, is hard to come by. It's (ideally) why we look to art, film, and music "critics" to help us know what pieces of art to spend our time and money on.

And we keep bothering about this because of something Dana Gioia, a contemporary poet in the Christian tradition, describes this way: When we see beauty, we "see this beautiful and meaningful pattern unfolding . . . like a vision of redemptive order in a fallen world."[60]

No artistic creations in this world are perfectly true, good, or beautiful. But for a piece of art to be truly redemptive and truly worthy of Christian contemplation, no member of the triad can be deeply violated.

When truth, goodness, and beauty come together, we glimpse the God we were all created to love and serve. We gain a vision of how this world is supposed to be. And that is attractive to people, even fallen people. By God's grace they see something in a good story, a good movie, a good painting—they see something good that they can't help but want, at least a little.

This means that true beauty is a powerful message from God. No wonder, then, that sinful people don't want to acknowledge that any ultimate standard for beauty really exists. Munson and Drake, in their book on the Christian view of the arts, argue that people's inherent "attraction to aesthetic relativism suggests an aversion to God's glory." They ask, "Could it be that we hate beauty because we hate God? That we hate real pleasure?"[61]

Christians ought to love real beauty because they know the only real, lasting pleasures available in this world. Christians, who live under the blessing of God's original mandate to mankind (Gen. 1:26–28), ought to cultivate the traditions of beauty they've inherited. And they ought to create more beauty. By doing so, they're displaying something of God's truth and goodness to their neighbors.

THINKING IT THROUGH 25.3

1. When Christians defend a false, bad, or ugly cultural artifact, what common error do they tend to make?
2. Why doesn't fiction violate the *truth* element of the triad?
3. How can drama and film promote goodness?
4. When does beauty become dangerous?
5. Why does art always serve one worldview or another?

25 CHAPTER REVIEW

TERMS TO REMEMBER

aesthetic
triad
art
relativism
divine order
subjective
objective

Scripture Memory

Philippians 4:8

Making Connections

1. Which view denies that beauty truly exists by arguing that what we call beauty is merely accidental or useful?
2. Which view of beauty denies that humans can reliably recognize it, arguing that what we call beauty is merely subjective opinion?
3. What are the three objective and transcendent creational norms for evaluating human subcreations?
4. What is the source of the three creational norms for art? How does that source ensure that the norms are objective and transcendent?

Developing Skills in Apologetics and Worldview

5. How should you respond to Christians who claim that beauty is entirely culturally relative or personally subjective?
6. How should you respond to a Christian who says, "I can see how some people wouldn't be able to handle the *Texas Chainsaw Massacre* films, but they don't affect me"?

Examining Assumptions and Evidence

7. Since humans are subcreators under God, what should their artistic products seek to do?
8. If truth, goodness, and beauty are objectively real, what keeps people from seeing them?
9. If beauty is objectively real, why is beauty viewed differently in different cultures?
10. Why must all three creational norms stand together in harmony in order to be truly redemptive?

Becoming a Creative Cultivator

11. Analyze a picture of a famous work of art or a recording of a famous piece of music. Write three paragraphs of critical analysis explaining how the artistic work conforms either to the triad of creational norms or violates one or more of them. Explain why your tastes are or are not drawn to it and defend that response.

Chapter Twenty-Six **THE FALSE, THE BAD, AND THE UGLY**

Therefore God sends them a strong delusion, so that they may believe what is false.

Scripture Memory
2 Thessalonians 2:11

26.1 UNRAVELING TRUTH, GOODNESS, AND BEAUTY

It takes countless colored threads to produce a beautiful tapestry—such as the imposing, five-hundred-year-old "Hunt of the Unicorn" tapestries that John D. Rockefeller once bought for $14 million.[1] And, obviously, it takes a creative intelligence to design such a piece of art. The threads have to be placed into a relationship with each other—woven, stitched, clipped—every thread in its place.

When God created the world, everything just fit in proper relationship to everything else. With God at the heart and all things properly in submission, the whole creation was rightly ordered. This perfection brought glory to God and joy to mankind. Each molecule and atom of God's creation, every blade of grass and drop of water, was intertwined and woven together into a fabric, and God made the whole into something far more than the sum of its parts. Just as a tapestry is far more valuable than piles of thread, Creation is more valuable than piles of matter.

In the Fall, one of the threads in God's tapestry, mankind—which was, in fact, the chief thread—began yanking itself out of the weave, damaging other threads and marring the picture in the process. In Adam's effort to assert his independence, he caused the creation to begin to unravel. The beautiful tapestry became tangled, marred, and diminished.

Truth, goodness, and beauty form a tapestry in which each thread is necessary.

ART THAT WORSHIPS TRUTH, GOODNESS, OR BEAUTY

If you really love God, then you will feel defensive when God's image-bearers worship His handiwork instead of worshiping Him. You'll be upset when they unweave His beautiful tapestry. (And, of course, you'll want to become an expert re-weaver; but that's the topic of the next chapter.)

In this unit we've been discussing three interwoven things in particular that fallen people are always in the process of unraveling in culture and the arts. Those three things are truth, goodness, and beauty. Ultimately, in the triune God, these three things are united. And just as the personality of an artist always shows up in the style of his work, God imprints truth, goodness, and beauty on His creation. To unweave these three things is to attack the unity of the one, tri-personal God they flow from.

Idolizing Truth

If, for example, truth gets detached from goodness and beauty, the results will be disastrous. People will worship a sort of disembodied reason, mere "facts" disconnected from moral considerations.

Consider the medical experiments of the so-called Unit 731 of the Japanese military during World War II. The Japanese abused Chinese and Russian prisoners for the sake of scientific advancement and medical knowledge. They offered exactly one justification for their painful and immoral research methods: they said they were just following where the pursuit of truth led.

This is truth without goodness or beauty. Yes, the Japanese doctors and scientists, using their God-given faculty of reason, discovered some truths through their work (and Allied governments gave the "researchers" immunity from prosecution for war crimes to get that information). But it was barbaric work, work that led to the degradation of the very thing it pretended to exalt. Who could possibly call it "reasonable" to maim and murder infants, even and especially in the name of knowledge?

The war crimes of World War II are considered sufficiently despicable today that just about no one would defend them. The whole Western world is united, for now, in opposition to conducting medical experiments on unconsenting children and adults. But plenty of educated people are happy to affirm that the pursuit of truth should not be "contaminated" by moral (or aesthetic) considerations.

Embryonic stem cell research (scientific use of human embryos) is another good example: does it destroy human life or not? Many Westerners are impatient with this question. Embryos don't experience pain, they say, and if getting rid of some of them brings medical benefits to others, then religious considerations shouldn't stand in the way.

But biblical religion does and *must* stand in the way when voiceless, powerless people are victimized. No truth is worth having if you must give up goodness to get it.

But TV personality Bill Maher, an atheist, disagrees:

> The plain fact is religion must die for mankind to live. The hour is getting very late to be able to indulge in having key decisions made by religious people—by irrationalists.[2]

Maher is wrong: goodness and beauty don't contaminate reason. In fact, when one of them is unraveled from the others, the result is ugliness and evil.

Idolizing Goodness

Goodness can also get yanked out of the cultural weave. It can be made to stand on its own, without truth and beauty.

Of course, people don't generally think of themselves as doing this yanking. They think that their definition of what's good is true, or they wouldn't adopt it. But think carefully: the very definition of *good* has been adjusted a great deal in Western culture over time. Sexual morality may be only the most obvious realm in which that's the case.

It was in 1996 that a Democratic president, Bill Clinton, signed the Defense of Marriage Act limiting legal marriage to heterosexual, monogamous couples. Ten years later, then-senator Barack Obama wrote in his autobiography, *The Audacity of Hope*, that he was opposed to "gay marriage" though he admitted he might prove to be "on the wrong side of history."[3]

By 2012, President Obama had decided that history had spoken, and he officially announced his support for gay marriage in a *Good Morning, America* interview. The argument that Christian conservatives are, in fact, on the "wrong side of history" has since become increasingly common. Such an argument assumes a great deal, however. As one writer put it,

> Upon inspection, "X is on the right side of history" turns out to be a lazy, hectoring* way to declare, "X is a good idea," by those evading any responsibility to prove it so.[4]

hectoring: *bullying, harassing, intimidating through force*

Lots of people—the majority of a culture—can sign on to a view of "good" that isn't true. America is doing this kind of thing with gay marriage; many in the US South did it with their racist views. People who didn't accept phrenology* were on the wrong side of history for thirty years or so during the nineteenth century, but today the idea that bumps on your head predict your personality type is, to say the least, unpopular. Any doctor who used phrenology today could be sued for malpractice; he could do real harm to a patient by missing the truth of his condition. What is good (like marriage or medicine) cannot be divorced from what is true, or it becomes evil. Truth, goodness, and beauty are most themselves when they are together.

phrenology: *the "science" of feeling bumps on people's heads and thereby describing their personalities*

Idolizing Beauty

Truth is distorted when it's in isolation; goodness is too. And when beauty gets unwoven from truth and goodness, we get **romanticism**. Romanticism prizes intense emotion and seeks it in ever-concentrated doses. Sensualism, eroticism, and anti-intellectualism generally result.

Nineteenth-century writer and poet Oscar Wilde, whose plays are still performed and whose books are still read today, was an "aesthete." He was a devotee of artistic beauty.[5] One of his characters, the "New Hedonist" Lord Henry, expressed what appears to have been Wilde's own view:

> Beauty is a form of genius—is higher, indeed, than genius, as it needs no explanation. . . . It cannot be questioned. It has its divine right of sovereignty.[6]

Can you draw a connection between what Lord Henry said here and this next quotation from him?

> The only way to get rid of temptation is to yield to it.[7]

If this chapter is correct—that beauty can become an idol, making truth and goodness drop away—then there is a connection between these two Oscar Wilde quotes. Someone who pursues beauty at all costs, who gives it divine authority separate from truth and goodness, can't hold on to truth and goodness for long. You can't have beauty by itself, or truth by itself, or goodness by itself.

To love God is to love reality as He has ordered it—a reality where truth, goodness, and beauty share a unity in His person. These three things are a tapestry. Trace any one thread, and it will lead to the others—and ultimately to God.

ART THAT ATTACKS TRUTH, GOODNESS, AND BEAUTY

Fallen art and culture can isolate truth, detach goodness, and unweave beauty from the unity they are meant to maintain. Culture can separate three things that were designed to be together. But, of course, art and culture can also attack these three things individually and directly in this fallen world. For this segment of our discussion about fallen arts, we'll focus on one artistic medium: the theater. It's certainly capable of great good, but the following three plays—all winners of major theater awards—attack truth, goodness, and beauty, respectively.

Attacking Truth

You may never have heard of the play *Equus*, by Peter Shaffer, but you may have heard of its biggest star. Daniel Radcliffe, who played the title role in the *Harry Potter* films, took a role in *Equus* in the middle of the filming of the Potter series. *Equus* means "horse" in Latin; in the play, Radcliffe's character, seventeen-year-old Alan Strang, is undergoing psychotherapy for having blinded six horses.

The psychiatrist assigned to help the young man discovers that Alan actually worships horses. But some horses were present while Alan committed immorality with a stable girl. Riddled with guilt and convinced that the horses had witnessed his sin, Strang blinded the animals.

The play ends with the psychiatrist voicing frustration over his job. He feels reluctant to take away Alan's horse-god even though he recognizes the god as false. He fears that treatment will strip Alan of the emotional power of his pagan worship.

The Bible records the lives of messed-up people such as Samson who, today, might wind up in a psychiatrist's office—and who committed heinous sins like Alan Strang's. So *Equus* is not objectionable simply for telling a story about fallen people committing sin; the play is wrong because it promotes an untruth. Whereas the Bible never leaves readers with any doubt that the truth is the only way to lead a good human life, *Equus* ends by shrugging its shoulders: if a big lie makes someone happier, why force the truth on him? The play even goes a step further and suggests that Alan's pagan mental derangement actually makes him more human. The psychiatrist, in contrast, seems to imply that conventional morality makes people less human, somehow emptier.

Attacking Goodness

Sometimes art attacks goodness as well. In *The Real Thing*, a play by British playwright Tom Stoppard, which was recently revived on Broadway, an actress (Annie) and a playwright (Henry), who have an adulterous affair, leave their spouses and marry each other. Annie has taken up the cause of a political prisoner named Brodie, who himself writes a play, but one so obviously terrible that Henry is asked to fix it up.

In one scene, Henry insists that Brodie's play is horrendous and unusable. He uses an illustration to argue the point with Annie. He tells his wife that a good cricket bat will knock the ball two hundred yards while a bad one will barely make it go ten feet. He points to a well-made bat:

> This [bat] isn't better because someone says it's better. . . . It's better because it's better. You don't believe me, so I suggest you go out to bat with this [script from Brodie] and see how you get on.[8]

Good writing makes ideas travel like a cricket ball (American translation: like an out-of-the-park home run). Bad writing, not so much.

Then Annie gets the part of the female lead in a production in another city, where she promptly begins another adulterous affair, this time with her young co-star, Billy. Even though Henry finds out, Annie refuses to leave either Henry or Billy. Henry manages to accept the new arrangement and reconciles with Annie at the end. The audience is left with the feeling that in the search for love, you have to go after "the real thing" at all costs, even it if means sacrificing your marriage or your dignity.

In writing the script for this play, real-life playwright Tom Stoppard marshalled his considerable literary skill to hit a homer with the immoral idea that extramarital affairs are justified if one is in search of true love. You can say it's all just art—that it's all in good fun. But in the original London production, Annie was played by an actress who ended up having an affair with Tom Stoppard in real life. The affair broke up his marriage to Dr. Miriam Stoppard. Sadly, the play was dedicated to Miriam.

Attacking Beauty

Art can also attack beauty, of all things. Some "art" is truly ugly. *Pillowman*, a play by Martin McDonagh, focuses on Katurian, a writer whose short stories frequently describe violence against children. Two detectives arrest Katurian because his stories bear a striking resemblance to some actual child murders that have taken place in his area.

The title *Pillowman*, is taken from one of the stories Katurian tells. The Pillowman is a creature made of pillows, and his job is to help suicidal people. He "helps" them, however, by traveling back in time to when they were children and persuading them to commit suicide early. This way they don't have to suffer so much in life. Such a task takes an emotional toll on the Pillowman, so he goes back in time and convinces his own younger self to commit suicide.

This is not the most gruesome of Katurian's stories. The *New York Times* reviewer offered this "advisory note" to potential theatergoers: "Severed fingers and heads, electric drills, barbed wire and premature burial all figure prominently."[9] And don't forget the crucifixion of a child.

One reviewer was critical of *Pillowman*: "The supreme and only unquestioned good in the play is the preservation of Katurian's stories from censorship and police destruction."[10] But what if those stories are twisted, evil, and ugly?

Pillowman suggests that because we can't know truth, goodness, and beauty, the only way to measure art is to experience its power over us. Whether it makes our flesh crawl with horror or our hearts sing with joy, it's art if it makes us feel.

GLAMORIZING SIN

All three of these plays won mainstream awards. They represent the art of drama today—and that means that attacks on truth, goodness, and beauty are going to be difficult to avoid for anyone who lives on the cultural grid. You will run into fallen pieces of art in one way or another.

Paul instructed the Corinthians,

> I wrote to you in my letter not to associate with sexually immoral people—not at all meaning the sexually immoral of this world, or the greedy and swindlers, or idolaters, since then you would need to go out of the world. (1 Cor. 5:9)

Every reader of this textbook has been exposed to fallen culture. We have been entertained by works of human art which have unwoven truth, goodness, and beauty from the tapestry. Sometimes we've done this on purpose, sinning "with a high hand" (Num. 15:30). But sometimes we were misled by someone else's recommendation or saw something in a store window we never intended to see. Those images and themes made it into our heads and into our hearts, where sin already lives.

Now what? Try some analysis and evaluation using the categories of truth, goodness, and beauty. If you have seen a film (or listened to music or read a book) you now object to, sit down and think through—even write out—why you object to it. Analysis is a way of distancing yourself from something emotionally, trying to view it from another perspective, hopefully a biblical one. And biblical evaluation measures what you find by God's standards. Ask yourself questions: Was this work of art true? Was it good? Was it beautiful? Did it unite all three qualities, or was one of the three either attacked or worshiped?

Analysis is hard mental work, but what's the alternative? Being swept away by the powerful forces of your culture. "The unexamined life is not worth living"[11] isn't a Bible verse, but it's certainly consistent with Scripture. One of the goals of a Christian should be to have his or her "powers of discernment trained by constant practice to distinguish good from evil" (Heb. 5:14).

THINKING IT THROUGH 26.1

1. What's the problem with trying to keep goodness and beauty from "contaminating" the pursuit of truth?
2. How should goodness be defined?
3. What results when beauty is disconnected from truth and goodness?
4. Instead of idolizing truth, goodness, or beauty, what do some artists explicitly do to undo God's tapestry?
5. Analyze and evaluate the most recent cultural artifact you watched, read, or listened to. Was it true? Was it good? Was it beautiful?

26.2 THE GREAT UNRAVELING OF HUMAN NATURE

People are tapestries too. For a temporary period at some point in the future, our bodies and souls will be unwoven: bodies in the grave, souls with the Lord. But at the beginning of eternity God will weave us back together like He wove His Son. David says we are "fearfully and wonderfully made." He says to God, "You knitted me together in my mother's womb" (Ps. 139:13). We run into difficulties when we try to unweave the knitting—to separate the different "parts" of man. Some people talk as if we humans are controlled by little, separate beings called "mind," "will," and "emotion," each of which is vying for supremacy in our brains . . . or our hearts . . . or whatever organ you want to pick.

You can't see your inner person, but God can. And God's Word teaches that all our actions arise out of an indivisible mixture of all our faculties. We do have minds, we have wills, and we have emotions, but the Bible never separates them. God never commands our minds to think, our wills to choose, or our emotions to feel. God through Scripture simply gives us commands—as whole beings.

One of the proofs of our fallenness is that we perceive a conflict inside ourselves over what we ought to think, choose, and feel. Sometimes we don't really *feel* what we *think*—we don't feel deep gratitude for the death of Christ or deep hatred for the sin we know is harming us. Sometimes we don't really *think* our *feelings* are right—like when we feel a strong pull to sin, or when we feel no love for God. Sometimes we *choose* something we *think* and *feel* is wrong.

No aspect of man is more fallen than the others. The Fall has tainted every part. So one of the goals of the Christian life is to bring our thoughts, choices, and feelings into righteous unity—to think the truth, choose the good, and feel the beautiful. Psalm 86:11 says:

> Teach me your way, O Lord,
> that I may walk in your truth;
> unite my heart to fear your name.

"Teach me your way, O Lord"—that's our thinking. "That I may walk in your truth"—that's our doing, our choosing. "Unite my heart to fear your name"—that's our feeling. Like a three-note chord, our thinking, choosing, and feeling should harmonize. Our understanding of God's way should lead us to choose to walk in that way with emotions that resonate with the fear of God and love for Him.

The Fall of Adam and the Curse on creation mean that our ability to think, do, and love God's way is impaired. And there are curse-compliant elements in every culture that make thoughtful, loving, obedience to God more difficult. Said one wise pastor:

> There is something more impacting on the soul of a Christian than being tied to a stake and put on fire. And that is to be systematically pressured over his whole lifetime by a culture intent on slowly drawing his heart away from God.[12]

One of the ways fallen culture puts that pressure on us is by unweaving *people*: treating them as if they are just truth-, goodness-, or beauty-receptors.

NOT JUST TRUTH-RECEPTORS

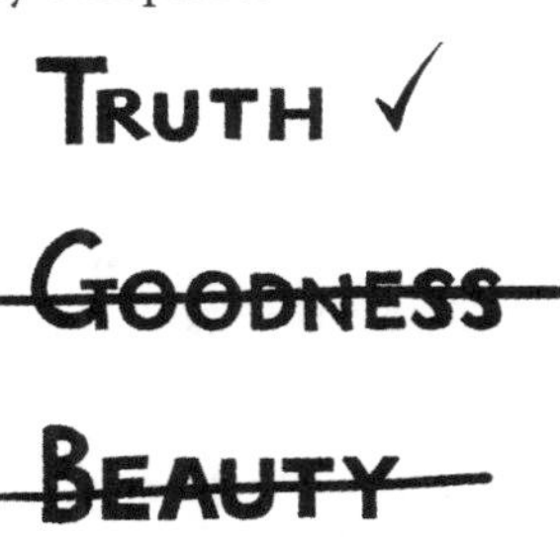

The Rationalist

But people are more than truth-receptors or fact-processors. Art woven with truth, goodness, and beauty will reflect this fact.

Pieces of culture that flatten people into mere truth-receptors might be defined by their willingness to look evil and other hard truths in the face. Telling hard truths is regarded as the primary virtue of Cormac McCarthy's 2006 novel *The Road*, for example. *The New York Times* review of the Pulitzer-Prize–winning book ends this way: "*The Road* offers nothing in the way of escape or comfort. But its fearless wisdom is more indelible than reassurance ever could be."[13]

The plot follows a father and his young son as they try to survive in a post-apocalyptic wasteland. The new humanity of that era includes "good guys"—like the father and son—who are "carrying the fire" by trying to hold on to civilization. But the world that the main characters stumble through is full of bad guys that commit murder and even cannibalism. At the end of the book, the father dies after being shot with an arrow. As he dies, he urges his son to keep carrying the fire, and the boy does find another family. They claim, at least, to be "good guys," but it turns out that their goal is the same as his father's was: to avoid brutality for as long as possible and then succumb to it.

The book lends some nobility to the idea of carrying the fire of civilization, but it also argues that that decision is irrational. The lives of those who resist the darkness end in the same futility as the cannibals.

Cormac McCarthy is known for his lean prose; this makes the book feel honest. It's true that destruction flows with the current of the world; civilization is always swimming upstream. But the Christian knows that the Fall isn't the end of the story. Redemption has come in Jesus Christ, and the Good Guy will win in the end. He will carry the fire, launching an everlasting civilization and banishing all darkness.

People in court swear to tell the truth, and McCarthy has told it: people really are as bad as he shows. But people in court also swear to tell the whole truth. By lopping off the end of the story, omitting redemption, McCarthy has actually told a falsehood. It would be like cutting off the end of Joseph's story in the Bible. Joseph is the favorite son of his father, and he is given a wonderful coat, which makes his brothers jealous. They throw him in a pit and sell him into slavery. The end. The critics might praise the story as "uncompromising" and "gritty." They might admire the author for resisting the temptation to produce a happy ending. But there was a happy ending, and every little salvation in the Bible—and in the world—is a picture of the big salvation God has brought to His creation.

There is one book in the Bible that, at first glance, seems to say, "Let's be honest. Everything is futile." It's Ecclesiastes. But Ecclesiastes itself doesn't end in despair; it ends with a promise that God will bring justice to the world (Eccles. 12:14).

On the flip side, Christian movies are often too propositional—too preachy. (This sin is not unique to Christian movies; secular ones regularly do it, too). Certain Christian end-times films of the 1970s, for example, were so obvious—and corny—in their attempts to get out the truth that you'd have a hard time watching them without cringing. When a movie features long stretches of dialogue uninterrupted by action, people sense that something is wrong; movies aren't supposed to be sermons. Christian movie reviewer Paul Asay says, "Evangelicals demand so much from their Christian movies: authenticity, biblical accuracy and, often, a clear altar-call at the end. The one thing we're not so much of a stickler for is artistic quality. If we get it, great. If not, well, maybe next time." Asay points to some movies, such as the 1981 Best Picture winner *Chariots of Fire*, which were all about faith but still managed to honor film as a medium.

Many truths in Scripture can be illustrated well in film, but some of those truths are too complex; they need to be *explained*, something movies are not made for. Good movies appeal to people as more than just truth-receptors, but also as image-bearers of a God of goodness and beauty. Truth is most itself when it is interwoven with goodness and beauty. Rationality disconnected from your emotions and ethics is irrational.

THE FOOLISHNESS OF PREACHING

Evangelistic films are often defended by a statement like this: "People won't listen to a sermon—but they will watch a film." Movies can and do communicate truth. But the complex truths of the gospel require explanation, something movies aren't good at. God already ordained an "art form" appropriate for communicating the gospel: preaching. God says that the "foolishness of preaching" is a powerful method for transforming people's lives (1 Cor. 1:21).

NOT JUST GOODNESS-RECEPTORS

People are more than goodness-receptors too. They're more than their consciences.

Journalist Sabrina Erdely writes frequently on themes of bullying and assault. Her work has appeared in some of America's most widely read magazines—*GQ, Self, New Yorker, Mother Jones, Glamour*.

And *Rolling Stone*. It was an article in that magazine that catapulted Erdely to national prominence. Entitled "A Rape on Campus," it told the horrendous story of a conspiracy to commit a violent rape at a frat party at the famed, historic University of Virginia.[16] Erdely also accused the UVA administration of sweeping sexual assault accusations under the rug in order to keep up its public image.

The Moralist

UVA is a national symbol of respectable American academia. The story was so terrible, and the actions so criminal, and the accusations so damning that the story exploded into the American twenty-four-hour news cycle.

But the rape never happened, at least not as described. As the story gained prominence, other investigations (including those by the police and by the *Washington Post*) turned up evidence that Erdely's story was largely fabricated. Two weeks after the story ran, it fell apart. She defended herself, saying, "I am convinced that it could not have been done any other way, or any better."[17] But she had not followed ethical journalistic practice. Her article was condemned by the prominent *Columbia Journalism Review* as the worst journalism of the year.[18]

Some people still defended Erdely's piece. They said, "Even if it didn't happen here, it's happening elsewhere." But here's the point: this is journalism asking a reader to be a raw conscience, unwoven from the truth. It's asking people to be outraged over something that didn't happen. A conscience is good. And rape is bad. (And rape does happen.) But by making wildly false accusations, Erdely actually hurt her conscience-raising cause. Now a true victim of on-campus rape may be more likely to be perceived as a girl who's just crying wolf.

Christian art can be guilty of turning people into mere goodness-receptors too. Some Christian artists and writers seem to believe that the Fall never happened and that people can be inspired to be good by viewing pictures or hearing stories in which only good things happen. Thomas Kinkade was the torch-bearer among painters for this sentimentalized view of the world. His paintings were idyllic, meaning they portray an idealized place where every light seems to shine extra bright and everybody is happy, happy, happy. Christian books, too, sometimes take a Pollyannaish view, which—like the best-selling 1913 novel *Pollyanna*—is simply naive about the extent of the Fall.

> "SENTIMENTALITY IS LOVING SOMETHING MORE THAN GOD DOES."[19]
>
> —R. H. BLYTHE

It's difficult to write a book in which goodness looks truly good, evil looks truly evil, and yet the evil doesn't defile the reader and the good doesn't make him feel like he's eaten too much sugar. The Bible does it (think of the Gospels). And that's the high calling of the Christian writer. The Bible sets an artistic standard or norm, not just a moral one.

NOT JUST BEAUTY-RECEPTORS

On February 24, 1970, Mark Rothko was arguably America's most important living painter. On February 25, he was dead. His assistant found his body on the floor of his New York studio. After overdosing on antidepressants, the painter had committed suicide. Rothko, a brainy and articulate theoretician who wrote multiple articles discussing his artwork, left the world with no explanation. There was no note.

Rothko created paintings that the critics labeled "color field" paintings. After casting about unsuccessfully in modernist art, Rothko finally found his niche. He painted large patches of color on canvas. Mark Rothko was an ardent Marxist who felt like people in the 1950s and '60s were vacillating between the threat of the Cold War and consumerist distraction. In order to connect people with their humanity, he sought to give them deep emotional experiences. Instead of painting subjects, Rothko painted only areas of color on his canvases. Rothko said:

> I'm not an abstractionist. . . . I'm not interested in relationships of color or forms. . . . I'm interested only in expressing basic human emotions—tragedy, ecstasy, doom and so on—and the fact that lots of people break down and cry when confronted with my pictures shows I communicate those basic human emotions. . . . The people who weep before my pictures are having the same religious experience I had when I painted them.[20]

One art critic said that if there is a spiritual dimension to Rothko's work, it is aestheticism—devotion to beauty (like Oscar Wilde).[21] These paintings were, in Rothko's view, color and texture harnessed to present raw emotion. Rothko flattened people into beauty-receptors, purely emotional beings. But beauty and emotions without truth are meaningless.

If you shuffle through his paintings, you notice that his palette choices become increasingly dark toward the end of his life. Many of his final paintings were charcoal-colored paint on black backgrounds.

Beauty without truth or goodness leads to its insignificance. As one *New York Times* art critic observed, "Beauty can attach itself to the sublime ([as in painters such as] Titian [and] Rembrandt) or to the merely decorative, and Rothko's pictures have always looked alarmingly good hanging over sofas in [New York City] apartments."[22]

As a Marxist, Rothko, took aim at capitalist consumerism, but even during his lifetime he couldn't protect his paintings from becoming another commodity to buy and sell. (His "Orange, Red, Yellow" sold for nearly $87 million in 2012.) And without truth, Mark Rothko could not direct his own emotions away from the darkness. His depression mirrored his paintings; deep feeling that wasn't *about* anything, just feeling for feeling's sake. Rothko ultimately left the world with nothing to say to us all.

WHY BOTHER?

Some readers of this book are called to be carpenters or mothers or salespeople, and it may not seem apparent to you why careful analysis and evaluation of the truth, goodness, and beauty in drama, art, and literature is worthwhile for you.

But think about it: carpenters, mothers, and salespeople are all creators. Your creations will shape the people those creations touch. This may be most obvious for mothers: the family culture—of food, of bedtime rituals, of cleanliness—that you create will shape your children. What you make of your world will be their world, their entire world. Will it be a world of truth, goodness, and beauty?

Or will you shape your children (or your customers) with a stunted or idolatrous view of the world?

THINKING IT THROUGH 26.2

1. What part of a human receives truth, goodness, and beauty?
2. What's wrong with making the explicit realism of evil into a virtue by "transparently telling the hard truth"?
3. What's wrong with crusading for some good cause if the crusade isn't rooted in the truth?
4. What is the end result of an artist creating something beautiful while ignoring truth and goodness?
5. Why is analysis of the arts and culture important for everybody?

26.3 POP GOES THE CULTURE

So far in this chapter on fallen culture and arts, we've analyzed (1) a few offerings of high culture that most people your age don't care about and (2) a few plays that your parents won't let you see anyway. But now we'll use the concepts we discussed—truth, goodness, and beauty—and apply them to the cultural artifacts you actually like (or are *tempted* to like). Let's talk about pop culture.

Popular culture is the commercially driven culture of media and entertainment shaped by the tastes of ordinary people. It is "a culture of diversion" driven by novelty.[23] Pop culture is whatever sells. That doesn't mean it's all bad; it depends on the quality of the culture doing the buying.

If you think this section is going to be a rant about sex, language, and violence on TV, you're about 2 percent right. Somebody needs to rant; Christians just *can't* make peace with a popular culture that entertains people with sins Jesus died to eradicate, or our Christianity offers nothing to anyone. There was a time in American culture, at least, when conservative Christians generally said a unified "no" to vulgar movies and music, but no longer. As Andy Crouch, the evangelical Christian leader we quoted in Chapters 5 and 8, has said, "Evangelical Christians . . . seem to be more avidly consuming the latest offerings of commercial culture, whether *Pirates of the Caribbean* or *The Simpsons* or *The Sopranos*, than many of my non-Christian neighbors."[24]

Attacks on truth, goodness, and beauty are attacks against the God who created them; so the content of the songs, films, magazines, books, and shows of popular culture really does *matter*. And the fact that Christians are consuming as much or more popular culture than their non-Christian neighbors isn't just problematic or unwise. It's sin. Have you ever in your life stopped watching a movie or listening to a song, not because your parents commanded you to but because God did?

SENSIBILITIES

So that was your 2 percent, and we're done with critiques of content. Christians need to dig deeper than the level of content, down to the level of **sensibilities**—your ability (or inability) to appreciate some artistic or cultural work, your affections and expectations when it comes to art and culture. Listen again to this comment from another Christian leader you read in Chapter 8:

> I rarely meet the young Christian who needs to be exhorted to engage their culture. They seem to consume what everybody consumes, and are in general agreement with the zeitgeist that a steady stream of entertainment is the Fifth Freedom that our forefathers fought for.[25]

Zeitgeist refers to the spirit of the age, and in our age that spirit makes it not just a right but practically a duty for people to consume the products of pop culture at every available moment. It's top-forty radio in the morning while getting ready, streaming music in the car, TV after school, YouTube and games (or both at the same time) after dinner, and a Netflix binge on the weekend. And your peers expect you to sing along with the top hits and spout the latest catch-phrases. Just listen to how people at school talk, all the way down to the kindergarteners. Pop culture will come up *a lot*. It has become something of a shared religion, the one experience most people in America can relate to.

Some reviewers complained that Emma Thompson was too old to play Elinor Dashwood in *Sense and Sensibility*, but they failed to level the same complaint at her male co-star.

Maybe at your house it's Christian radio, Christian music, Christian TV, God-Tube, and a David and Goliath video game. The content may be different (and that's a step in the right direction), but the sensibilities formed are the same: you begin to expect to be entertained all the time. You don't develop the patience necessary to be rewarded by more difficult artistic forms like painting and poetry and literature. You're never just quiet. Your mind wanders when you read. And you think kids who make it through three years of piano lessons ought to get a medal or something.

A life full of diversion that focuses on immediate pleasure and whatever's cool is not a life of truth, goodness, and beauty. Let's bring out CFR again: diversion is good, and so is immediate pleasure—but not when they're twisted and inflated to fill your life, crowding out better things.

THE POWER OF CULTURE

"The power of culture is the power to define reality,"[26] says Christian sociologist James Davison Hunter. In Chapter 5 we quoted Andy Crouch's observation that culture defines "the horizons of the possible."[27] Your expectations and assumptions and sensibilities are molded largely by the culture you land in as an infant. "All [cultural] institutions are character shaping," says Hunter. And "today, entertainment [is] especially important."[28] The high culture and the pop culture you "consume" both shape your character. But the high culture stuff typically isn't playing in the background at the mall and isn't getting shared by your friends online. Pop culture is influential if only because it's everywhere. Is it shaping your reality with the truth?

Actress Emma Thompson spent five years writing the screenplay for a movie adaptation of Jane Austen's classic novel *Sense and Sensibility*. It became one of her biggest hits, but some reviewers complained that she was too old for the role of Elinor Dashwood. At thirty-five, she was indeed a good deal older than the nineteen-year-old Elinor in the original story. But oddly enough, no one seemed to have the same complaint about Thompson's male love interest in the film, who in the book was twenty-three but in the movie was played by an actor (Hugh Grant) the same age as Thompson.

The arts both reflect and enforce a cultural narrative in which women are supposed to live up to certain youthful ideals. These ideals, good or bad, affect the sensibilities of the viewers.

Have you ever noticed that pictures of Eve painted in the 1500s to the 1800s make her look, well, a little fat by contemporary standards? In Albrecht Dürer's five-hundred-year-old woodcuts, she's positively corpulent.* But Eve lost a good deal of weight in the twentieth century, as any recent kids' Bible storybook will show.

corpulent: *very large; overweight*

Maybe you've seen one of those videos that demonstrates how Photoshop can be used to alter a woman's picture. Something is wrong with the sensibilities of a culture in which photos of the women admired as truly attractive are doctored by computers.

Television isn't the sole reason that the ideal of feminine beauty has changed over time. We could point to a complex of factors. But what does it do to a culture's sensibilities when its TV shows and movies almost never feature unattractive people—except when gawking at a hoarder or one of the "biggest losers" is the whole point of the show?

Watching one TV show won't make you believe that all dads are stupid and premarital sex has no consequences. And pop culture in the West isn't all lies. But even "reality" TV is heavily edited by producers to tell stories and make points that shouldn't be taken as gospel. Pop culture "ain't necessarily so." It isn't all true. It isn't all good, and it can skew your view of (feminine) beauty.

Your Best Life Now

Christian culture watcher Ken Myers has a great deal of wisdom to offer in his book *All God's Children and Blue Suede Shoes: Christians and Popular Culture*, a book that thinking Christians can profit from. One of his most penetrating insights is that popular culture lulls us into thinking that we can have everything worth having immediately. If you've got the cash (or a credit card that's not maxed out) along with the self-confidence and sex appeal that come from using the right products, then there's no need to delay until you're more mature, wiser, or more perceptive to experience the feelings, think the thoughts, or imagine the fantasies you desire. "There is no distance between you and any good thing."[29]

Pop culture, then, offers a drastically limited definition of good—because, in its view, anything that takes a massive time investment isn't good, or (at least) isn't a good worth having for most people.

And where is the *goodness of God* in American popular culture? Once again, let's set aside content (like the way God gets mocked and cursed on the TV show *South*

Park) and let's think again about the sensibilities pop culture tends to form. Pop culture doesn't blaspheme God as much as it ignores Him. Living in a pop culture world forms a sensibility, a pervading sense that God doesn't really matter, that someone can live just fine without Him. God does get trotted out to approve of NASCAR races—but then He gets shoved back in His box as soon as the opening prayer is done. The world of pop culture is a secular one where it's assumed we can all, as John Lennon famously sang, "imagine there's no heaven."[30]

And what about the good of heaven itself—if there's no distance between us and any good thing? Jesus said, "The way is hard that leads to life" (Matt. 7:14). So why bother?

Soon, your parents may not have any direct influence over what pop culture you take in. Whether they have been permissive or strict, before too long you're going to have to decide for yourself what role popular culture will play in your life—and in your kids' lives.

One silly pop song, an episode of a sitcom, or a YouTube video won't turn you or your future kids into atheists, but a steady diet will give your sensibilities an atheistic shape. Rather than asking yourself, "What's wrong with this movie/song/show?" ask yourself, "What's right with this?" In other words, "How will exposing myself to this bit of culture help me achieve Christian goals for my life?" Your choices in life aren't always going to be between good and evil but will sometimes involve deciding between what's permissible and what's best. Myers says, "Popular culture . . . specializes in instant gratification. But like most instant things, it may spoil your taste for something better."[31]

High culture, ideally, offers something better, but high culture is still a mixture of good and bad just like pop culture is. But one thing you can say about "the best which has been thought and said"[32] in high culture is that it often stretches you in ways you can't appreciate until after the stretching operation. It takes the purposeful cultivation of your sensibilities, not just passive exposure, to be able to enjoy it. You can't help admiring someone who stuck with piano lessons and now clearly relishes the music he or she has become capable of producing. But the only way you can have that good thing is by recognizing that there's a big distance between you and it, and patiently taking a step or two in that direction each day.

> ***"Pop music, largely created by and for commercial purposes, resists serious analysis. . . . Commerce, then, has an enormous interest in our not taking such questions seriously."[34]***
>
> —T. DAVID GORDON

Soaking and Vegging

Everybody's busy. We're tired. We turn to TV or movies because we want to veg, "to relax to the point of complete inertia."[33] And not just physically but mentally. We don't want to have to critically analyze and evaluate; we just want to soak. It takes effort to probe beneath the surface of your entertainment.

Don't soak or veg. (Soaked vegetables tend to get corpulent.) Analyze, using truth, goodness, and beauty. Ask questions like these: Is it true that sports are worth what Americans pay to watch them? Is it good that American news programs focus so much on celebrities? Is the singing on the latest competition show truly *beautiful*?

True, good, beautiful art is worth a lifetime of practice and study. Bad art is simply not worth spending your life on. And neither is mere diversion. The billions of hours Americans spend on it every year isn't *true*. It doesn't give an accurate picture of what diversion is worth and what human lives are for. Diversion *is* worth something: "Popular culture . . . is a part of the created order, part of the earth that is the Lord's, and thus something capable of bringing innocent pleasure to believers," says Ken Myers. "But not everything that is permissible is constructive."[36]

"WHO IS SLAIN WHEN TIME IS KILLED?"[35]

—ERNEST VAN DEN HAAG

What, after all, are you trying to construct in your life? What's your goal? To make it to death without too much pain? Or to lay up treasures in heaven, treasures no moth or rust can ever get to, treasures that will pay out interest for eternity? Good art is entertaining, but it isn't mere diversion—just killing time. It forms the sensibilities in you that are necessary for good dominion over God's world. We are not called to inertia.

THE THINGS WE DELIGHT IN

The stories about early Scottish missionary John G. Paton are amazing—both the stories of failure and of success. On the South Pacific island of Tanna, the cannibals went along with some of Paton's instructions for a while. But they finally drove him off the island, and he was rescued by a ship just in time. The natives of Tanna explained to Paton why they hated him so much:

> We have taken everything your house contained, and would take you too if we could; for we hate the Worship, it causes all our diseases and deaths; it goes against our customs, and it condemns the things we delight in.[37]

The Bible condemns many things American popular culture delights in. It condemns the unspoken assumption of pop culture that a life of diversion and novelty is a good life in the first place. Ken Myers says that attempting to free ourselves from enslavement to pop culture's sensibilities doesn't mean we have to become ascetics, but it does mean that we should get more rather than less out of our experience of culture, namely more of what's true, honorable, just, pure, lovely, and commendable.[38]

There are so many true, good, and beautiful pieces of art, music, and literature available, especially in the Western tradition, and for English-speakers. The category of things that are "true, honorable, just, pure, lovely, commendable, excellent, and praiseworthy" (Phil. 4:8) is not a small one. Whatever you give up to gain these things will not really be a sacrifice.

The 1997 film *Titanic* was one of the most lucrative cinematic productions ever made. Drawing its storyline from one of the twentieth century's most famous events, the movie features beautiful cinematography and beautiful people. It catapulted at least one member of the cast, Leonardo DiCaprio, to international stardom.

The gist of the story is that a young artist saves his rich female counterpart from an arranged marriage. The two unmarried characters commit immorality. The heroine survives the marine catastrophe, but the hero dies. The director, James Cameron, sets before the audience a "savior," whose affection for a young woman impels him to rescue her relationally and physically.

Part of the message seems to be that precluding a conventional but unwanted marriage is reason enough to take moral liberties. In fact, *Titanic* offers an inadequate salvation and does so in God-condemned fashion. The sexually immoral who do not repent cannot inherit the kingdom of God (1 Cor. 6:9). This wildly successful film romanticizes a teenage affair in a way that pits beauty against truth and goodness. It strives to capitalize on a disharmony between our emotions, our ethics, and our intellect. Such an endeavor should make us feel the way we do when we look at a false equation: 2 + 2 = 5. Cameron's movie may have been cinematically impressive, but its morally inverted storyline should seem just as dangerous as basing one's checking account on faulty arithmetic.

THINKING IT THROUGH 26.3

1. Why can't Christians just make peace with pop culture?
2. In addition to content, what else should Christians be aware of when analyzing culture and the arts?
3. Why is culture so powerful?
4. Why does pop culture offer a drastically limited definition of goodness?
5. Why do people tend to react negatively to any criticism of their consumption of pop culture?

26 CHAPTER REVIEW

TERMS TO REMEMBER

romanticism
popular culture
sensibilities

Scripture Memory

2 Thessalonians 2:11

Making Connections

1. What major event damaged God's tapestry of the world, making it necessary to critique artistic and cultural creations?
2. What's ultimately being attacked when truth, goodness, and beauty are unraveled?
3. What three components of human nature, woven together to make us who we are, should never be separated into isolated compartments?
4. What drives popular culture?

Developing Skills in Apologetics and Worldview

5. How would you describe the dangers of cultivating exclusive pop culture sensibilities?
6. How would you respond to someone who argued that as long as Christians are communicating truth, aesthetic considerations don't matter?

Examining Assumptions and Evidence

7. Christians can't avoid sin in a fallen world—it's already inside them; so why bother avoiding fallen elements of human culture?
8. What is it about the medium of film that makes preaching the gospel through a movie difficult?
9. Why are sensibilities important to evaluate in addition to the actual content of an artistic product?
10. Name one thing about high culture sensibilities that is morally superior to the sensibilities typically formed by popular culture.

Becoming a Creative Cultivator

11. Create a chart with three questions across the top: Is this cultural product true? Is it good? Is it beautiful? List down the side five specific cultural artifacts from a variety of artistic media (movies, literature, painting, music, etc.).
    - Check each box in which the artifact conforms to standards of truth, goodness, and beauty.
    - Below the chart, provide a brief sentence or two defending your choices for each of the five.
    - If the class evaluates the same five artifacts, discuss why your answers differ from those of your classmates.

27.1 GESTURES & POSTURES

Babies aren't born knowing how to make all the gestures they need for day-to-day communication. In India, especially in Gujarat State, babies need to learn a little side-to-side head wobble you'll see all over the place. It means something like "yes" or "OK" or "good," depending on the context. The Western equivalent would be a head nod. [1]

If you want to communicate effortlessly with a Gujarati, you have to pick up this gesture, just like Gujarati babies do. And you have to know when to use it. As a gesture, the head wobble is good. As a posture, not so good—you don't just keep doing it and doing it. Likewise, the gesture of bowing in Japan is an important gesture to master, but it shouldn't become your permanent posture; you'll kill your back if you go around stooped like that all the time.

Christian thinker Andy Crouch has suggested that gestures and postures make a good analogy for Christian approaches to culture and the arts. He suggests four *c*'s that are appropriate gestures, but not good postures:

- Condemning culture
- Critiquing culture
- Consuming culture
- Copying culture

Sometimes you must *condemn* certain cultural artifacts.* That's the appropriate gesture toward child pornography, for example. But condemnation is not an appropriate posture—you can't condemn every **cultural artifact**. You have to *critique* some things, *consume* others, and maybe *copy* yet others.

Since you're an image-bearer tasked with dominion by your Creator, there are two postures you do need to make permanent, two more *c*'s: you need to *cultivate* and *create*. (But we'll talk about those in the next section.).

cultural artifact: *almost anything made by a human being, embedded within a certain culture*

MATURE DISCERNMENT

You're more than old enough to recognize that there is a gray area between the good stuff and the bad stuff in culture and the arts.

- Some cultural artifacts are truly excellent, totally worth your time. The "classics" in art, literature, and music generally achieved that status because so many people over time have considered them to be worthwhile.
- Some products of human culture are less valuable but still worthy. You might read a sci-fi trilogy or watch a Hercule Poirot mystery for the fun of it.
- And some cultural artifacts may be righteous choices for someone else but not for you—or not now. Some of the significant works of the twentieth century—such as *Brave New World* or *1984*—shouldn't be read by high schoolers for the fun of it. They contain sexual and other themes that shouldn't provide entertainment for Christians. And yet these writings are significant enough in Western thought that some Christians believe that they ought to read them with a guarded heart. Other Christians, knowing the weakness of their flesh, know that they ought not to read such works, whatever value they might have. Scripture recognizes that godly Christians, knowing their own hearts, can make different, but correct, choices (1 Cor. 9:1–22; Rom. 14:5).

Choosing among available cultural options in our consumer society can be difficult or even overwhelming. Being a Christian in the modern West involves having to make some tough calls about culture. And you'll never be able to make those tough calls if you won't make the easy ones. **Discernment** is gained through a process of training:

> Solid food is for the mature, for those who have their powers of discernment trained by constant practice to distinguish good from evil. (Heb. 5:14)

And that training is not something you do by yourself. The Bible calls on young people to gain wisdom by listening to their elders (Prov. 2:1–2), by searching for truth like you would for buried treasure (2:3–5), and by becoming the sort of person God grants wisdom to (2:6–7). You're also called to be part of a church community that helps you—and puts pressure on you—to make wise choices (Heb. 10:24; Matt. 18:19–20).

When (by the wisdom of God through His Word and His people) you spot evil, your obligation is clear: you've got to condemn it. But the Bible not only calls you to spot evil and avoid it but also *to discern the good and pursue it.* Peter says that "whoever desires to love life and see good days" (is that you?) should not only "turn away from evil" but also "do good" (1 Pet. 3:10–11).

APROPOS RESPONSES

So don't hear the previous chapter ("The False, the Bad, and the Ugly") as a call to pull out of all the joys of human culture. Music is fundamentally *good*, a gift of God. Painting is good. Journalism is good. Architecture, novel-writing, cinematic production, literary criticism—every legitimate vocation that arises out of the human need to make something of our world (Gen. 1:28) is fundamentally good. Enjoy them. Use them. Create new things yourself within the tradition of your calling. The Bible calls you to get more out of your cultural life, not less—as Ken Myers said—"at least more that is true, noble, right, pure, lovely, and admirable."[2]

Condemning Culture

And yet, we can't forget the Fall. Sexual trafficking is a significant element within human cultures around the world. The various institutions complicit in this trafficking make a lot of money for their national economies. They employ a lot of people. And many people use their "services." The porn that accompanies this trafficking is also a perverse form of artistic expression. But it is all unequivocally wrong, in every way imaginable. It all ought to be stopped. If only it could be—it seems only Jesus has that power. But that shouldn't stop us from condemning the selling and using of God's image-bearers and from doing what we can to stop it.

Likewise, certain pieces of art are fit only to be *condemned*. When Marcel Duchamp took a urinal in 1917, flipped it over, wrote "R. Mutt" on it, and called it "Fountain," he was purposefully expanding the definition of "art" past the breaking point. "Fountain" was not art; it was not beautiful; it wasn't good or true. It was a slap in the face of Western culture and ultimately of the God who created beauty. Of all places for beauty to be attacked, you'd think the art world would be the last. But it's not.

Christian artist Makoto Fujimura, head of the International Arts Movement and an expert in a shimmering and colorful form of traditional Japanese painting called Nihonga, says, "When I began to exhibit [my art] in New York City . . . 'beauty' was a taboo not to be spoken of in public. . . . The art world still resists this word."[3] Fujimura observes that Western artists of the twentieth century shied away from beauty and instead "produced work aimed at shocking people into recognizing and decrying the horrors of the age."[4] Fujimura actually sees some genuine value in this kind of work. The prophet Isaiah himself was told by God to use a shocking bit of "performance art" to communicate truth to Israel—he was told to walk around almost naked and barefoot as a sign of what would happen to the people of Israel if they didn't repent (Isa. 20; cf. Jer. 13:1–11).

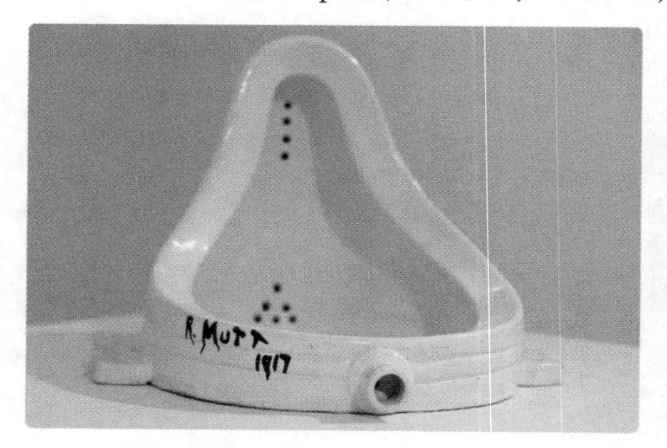

Marcel Duchamp's "Fountain" (left), and Tracy Emin's "My Bed" (right)

But, Fujimura says, today the mission of artists has been twisted. "Artists have been conscripted . . . as frontline soldiers to defend 'freedom of expression' against tradition and conformity."[5] In other words, now artists shock people for no purpose other than to exercise their freedom to shock people. The result is more and more shocking and degrading pieces of art, such as English artist Tracy Emin's "My Bed," an unmade bed surrounded with trash and stained clothing. Even the non-Christian British public condemned Emin's work and said "good riddance" when a good deal of it went up in flames in a warehouse fire. Sometimes the most redemptive thing you can do is to condemn a particular work of human culture.

Condemning culture can go too far: you're not free to condemn something merely because you don't like it. There is great diversity among beautiful things, and another person or culture may see genuine beauty that you can't (yet) see. To justify condemning a piece of art or other artifact of culture, you've got to do some work to explain to yourself and others how that thing violates truth, goodness, and beauty.

The Christian faith is meant to exist in all cultures. Jesus told His followers to "make disciples of *all* nations" (Matt. 28:19), and that means that dress, music, and other aspects of culture will rightfully differ between Filipino Christians and Canadian ones. The early church recognized that Jesus didn't put Jewish cultural expectations on Gentiles (Acts 15:22–29). But biblical faith also condemns parts of every culture in existence—and it calls them to a divine standard.

That call is why you can't make this particular *c*, condemnation, a posture—only a gesture. You *need* art and music like you need water and food and love. To be human is to love and need beauty. Dogs don't hire interior decorators.

Critiquing Culture

Sometimes the appropriate Christian gesture toward a particular artistic creation will be to *critique* it.

The label "**critic**" is not always a nice one. But, especially in a world full of more cultural experiences than you have time for, critics are necessary for several reasons. They can help you know what to watch or listen to or read so that you don't waste time on comparatively worthless options. And then they can help you process what you just saw or listened to or read.

Help is the key word here. A good critique helps the critic's neighbors. A truly good critique holds up various cultural artifacts to divine standards of truth, goodness, and beauty, something a non-Christian will generally have trouble doing. But even a non-Christian movie reviewer can help his neighbors analyze and understand the message of a particular film, book, play, or painting. And when even non-Christian critics are saying, "This is hyper-sexualized" or "This is luridly violent," what should Christian movie watchers conclude? That the time for critique is over, that condemnation is the only appropriate Christian response.

THE MEDIUM IS THE MESSAGE

When critiquing culture, you may find it helpful to use one key intellectual tool, the famous observation of media theorist Marshall McLuhan: "The **medium** is the message."[6] What he means is that the way one communicates a message significantly affects its meaning. Imagine that there's a romantic comedy about how an unlikely couple gets together. At the climax of the movie, when the man and woman look into each other's eyes and realize that they are meant for one another, the music softly rises.

Then it blares: "Ding dong, the witch is dead!" It's the song from *The Wizard of Oz*. What does a romantic scene *mean* when accompanied by that music? Something confusing. Movies don't use Sousa marches—or Gregorian chants or "Twinkle, Twinkle, Little Star"—during romantic scenes because the mediums of march music, chant, and nursery songs carry messages, messages that don't fit with romance. *Star Wars* would be a different movie if you switched John Williams's Darth Vader theme and his Princess Leia theme.

Music *means*, cinematic genres *mean*, graphic design *means*—everything humans make carries meaning.

You yourself may need to become a critic of sorts in order to help your neighbors or your family. There may be times when it will be appropriate for you to read a book you disagree with simply to be able to discuss it with your Muslim coworker or your agnostic college roommate. Several years ago when Dan Brown's *The DaVinci Code* reached the bestseller lists, some Christians held their noses and read the novel just because it was actually persuading a lot of people that Jesus had a wife and children, despite the fact that it was simply bad literature.

Not all non-Christian literature is bad, of course. Good literature in general "clarifies the human situation to which the Christian faith speaks."[7] The best of human art provides insights into the human condition that we all find ourselves in. The ability to read a book that you have objections to and come out wiser—that's "critiquing."

The only way you can critique something from the standpoint of a biblical worldview is to have a thorough, head-heart grasp of that worldview yourself. Until then, the more difficult the critique, the more likely you should stay away. Or wait. Tony Reinke, author of *Lit! A Christian Guide to Reading Books*, says that some books demand a certain maturity before they can be read with profit. Reinke and his wife evaluated their own nine-year-old son and decided he wasn't old enough to handle certain books. You don't send boys into battle, says Reinke. They have to develop the instincts of a solider first. Reinke says, "So, too, our children—and those who are children in the faith—need time to grow the deep roots of a biblical worldview before being called to exercise that worldview against the force of culture displayed in non-Christian books."[8]

Reinke says this doesn't necessarily stop him from reading a non-Christian book out loud to his children; when he does that, he has a chance to stop and have discussions along the way. But when his child reads on his own, "choosing what books to read is often not a yes/no decision but a now/later decision. . . . Be cautious of reading literature that you are ill-equipped to read with discernment. Sometimes the proper Christian approach to literature is humble postponement."[9]

Sensitive to the effects of the Fall in his children, Reinke is aware that "critique" is a demanding task not every Christian (no matter his or her age) is ready for. God has probably placed parents and other spiritual leaders in your life—pastors, teachers—who *can't* articulate precisely how a certain cultural artifact twists truth or goodness or beauty. Nonetheless, they've seen the effects of fallen culture on fallen young

A MOVIE THAT TEACHES ABOUT TOTAL DEPRAVITY

Many contemporary American Christians have the impression that past generations of believers were "isolationists" who failed to "engage culture." This criticism contains significant elements of truth. Some American Christians have, in practice, denied the goodness of God's created world and acted as if creation were only a stepping stone to heaven. But recognition of this fact has led to many overcorrections. One particular Christian magazine seems to write the same movie review over and over: "This is a culturally significant film you need to know about. Yes, it has plenty of sex and violence, so kids shouldn't see it without their parents' permission and presence. But the on-screen sins help us learn about the fallenness of man and provide bridges for you to talk to your non-Christian neighbor." One church actually showed the sexually-explicit film version of *Les Miserables* to the congregation in a service, presumably because Victor Hugo's story does contain a memorable illustration of grace.

Admittedly, such films have created a bridge between the Christian community and the world—but which direction are most people on that bridge going? Christian leaders and thinkers such as David Wells have noted that the world's entertainment has had a lot more influence on the church than vice versa. There's a reason for this: Christians still have to contend with their flesh (Gal. 5:13, 17), and the sins portrayed in entertainment too often please the flesh.

people for a long time. The Bible tells us to listen to wise people even if their critiques aren't professional.

Critique is an important gesture available to Christians. If cultures are truly a mixture of good and evil, they're all ready for critique. But you can't make "critique" your full-time posture. Some Christians use cultural critique as an excuse to watch movies they really should just condemn. Then again, there will be many times when it is appropriate for you to simply "consume" the offerings of your culture.

THINKING IT THROUGH 27.1A

1. What is the biblical means for training young people in discernment?
2. According to Proverbs 14:16, how must you respond when you spot evil?
3. What makes condemning a cultural artifact an absolutely necessary response for a Christian? When shouldn't condemnation be the response?
4. For what two reasons is critique a bad posture?
5. Why are both maturity and a biblical worldview prerequisites for critiquing art?

Consuming Culture

You eat food, don't you? You use toothpaste, right? The food you eat and even the toothpaste you use are very much products of your culture. A newspaper once published pictures of the breakfasts kids around the world got from their parents; it turns out that kid breakfasts in Japan really are different from kid breakfasts in Brazil and Greece.[10] Even toothpaste differs in various cultures; tea-flavored toothpaste is popular in China.[11]

If your mom puts a plate of steak in front of you, don't condemn it. Don't critique it. Those are bad gestures when it comes to mom's cooking. Just consume it. And if she buys you a tube of Crest, smear it on your teeth, rinse, and spit.

There is a time for critique, even of food. You should be generally aware of the calories and sugars you ingest, and you'll want to critique your own eating habits on a regular basis. But once you've set up healthy guidelines, you're free to simply enjoy the countless culinary creations available to you inside those lines.

"The earth is the Lord's," Psalm 24 says. God's kids are allowed to open up His fridge and forage for stuff, whatever's in there. If they ask for bread, they don't get stones (Matt. 7:9). "Everything created by God is good, and nothing is to be rejected if it is received with thanksgiving" (1 Tim. 4:4).

Especially since you're a student, trusted people will regularly tell you, "This piece of art is good. Look at it." Or, "This book is good. Read it." You can't know what effect the painting or novel will have on you, but you jump in anyway and "consume" it—because you trust. Maybe you don't feel fully capable of judging the piece of art. You're just taking it in. That's OK sometimes. Good ideas in art can still plow up soil in which truth can later grow.

The classic Western film *Big Country* (and this is one of the few times in this book when *Western* means cowboys) holds profound lessons and a great example of someone "turning the other cheek" out of strength, not weakness. But you may not get that on first watch. And if you stop the movie every time one of those lessons comes up, you'll lose some of the power of the experience of just consuming it.

C. S. Lewis's Chronicles of Narnia are full of insightful points about human nature, such as the scene when Digory starts to tell Aslan that he sinned because he was under a magic spell—only to have Aslan growl. But the author of *What I Learned in Narnia*, a book exploring those moral lessons, encourages readers to simply consume the stories first, then worry about the lessons later.

> "BY APPRECIATING THE BEAUTY OF LITERATURE, WE HONOR GOD, THE GIVER OF ALL BEAUTY."[12]
>
> —TONY REINKE

Some people view consuming fiction and fantasy stories like Lewis' Narnia books as escapism. But as Lewis pointed out, the people who are normally concerned about escape are jailers—and what matters is what you're escaping from and what you're escaping to.[13] The arts can lead you away from the pain you're facing and into beautiful and complex worlds created by gifted minds imitating their Creator. Sometimes you just go to those places and enjoy them, without too much focus on critique.

Nonetheless, in a world touched everywhere with poison, you can't live in a constant mode of consumption. We can't take a Pac-Man posture and consume anything that comes within the span of our always-chomping mandibles.

Copying Culture

Humans, made in the image of a creative God, often need to put aside the gestures of condemnation, critique, and consumption and adopt another gesture: making things of their own. And that's not easy; it's a process requiring training and growth—a process in which you have to start somewhere. So a fourth necessary *c* is *copying*. If you go to the National Gallery in Washington, DC, you'll often find someone there with an easel copying a masterwork. If you're learning to sculpt, there's hardly a better way to do it than to copy the masters. You'll copy their work and their methods—and even their tools. It probably won't be necessary to reinvent the pottery wheel. But once you've mastered the artistic or cultural tradition you've received, you'll be able to do some creating on your own.

Every act of human creation involves a degree of copying because we can't create completely out of nothing. We are subcreators. We have to use existing materials. When humans tried to copy the flapping motions of bird wings, we failed to fly. But we still ended up using design elements from birds. An airplane wing is very different from a bird wing, but there's some necessary copying in the airfoil design.

Nonetheless, copying can quickly go astray. A kindergartener may prefer tracing a flower to the hard but educationally necessary work of drawing it himself. And though there are many skillful and beautiful things worth copying in culture and the arts, American Christians don't tend to get as excited about those things as they do about copying pop and celebrity culture.

Evangelical Christians have a "deeply neurotic relationship with popular culture,"[14] says secular journalist Hanna Rosin. She says evangelicals in America are like the Old Testament Israelites who began fitting into the culture of the pagans around them so much that it became difficult to tell them apart. It's like we inhabit our own gigantic parallel universe where an evangelical "can now buy books, movies, music—and anything else lowbrow to middlebrow—tailor-made for his or her sensibilities."[15] That's copying at its worst. It's purposefully being "conformed to the world" despite the command of Romans 12:1–2.

At one point Christians were known for boycotting offensive offerings from popular culture, says Rosin, but in more recent years they've moved from boycotting to co-opting and have begun trying to "enlist America's crassest material culture in the service of spiritual growth."[16] Every artifact of American popular culture seems to have a Christian version, regardless of how incongruous* it may be. Rosin, a secular Jew, compares this phenomenon to living on a different planet where everything's the same as on earth except that it's synthetic and the wrong color.

incongruous: *inappropriate; not fitting in with the surrounding context*

Her article mentions, for example, "Christian" chick lit and "Christian" Harlequin or "Christian" rappers and "Christian" raves. (Rosin wonders how techno music can be called "Christian" when it has no lyrics; she says that her personal favorite is the "Christian" version of professional wrestling.)[17]

Rosin asks two penetrating questions of this parallel culture: "What does commercializing do to the substance of belief, and what does an infusion of belief do to the product?"[18] In her opinion, when your love song for Jesus sounds just like a ballad for your boyfriend, both your faith and your music may be damaged. By sanitizing the rock lyrics of Jay-Z or Nirvana, you force "a message that's essentially about obeying authority into a genre that's rebellious and nihilistic, and the result can be ugly, fake, or just limp."[19]

Copying can be a worthwhile gesture for Christians to make but a horrible posture for them to maintain.

GESTURING WITHOUT POSTURING

If you were marooned by yourself on a desert island with no technology, you wouldn't need any skills in analyzing and evaluating culture and the arts. But as soon as you add other people, you've got a culture. And you're going to need to develop the ability to detect good and evil—structure and direction—in that culture. Some things you see or read or hear will need to be condemned, others critiqued, others just consumed, and some copied. Never will one of these first four *c*'s be your permanent posture, but a well-educated Christian will know when and where to gesture in these ways.

THINKING IT THROUGH 27.1B

1. List four possible gestures or responses to cultural artifacts.
2. Once healthy guidelines have been set up, what should Christians feel free to do with the cultural artifacts within those guidelines?
3. What's one prerequisite for creating a cultural artifact yourself?
4. What gesture have evangelical Christians tended to overuse, prompting secularists to criticize them? Is the criticism valid or not?
5. Can humans create anything that is untouched by the Fall? Why or why not?

27.2 CREATING AND CULTIVATING

Every senior in high school gets "The Question." Some have a ready answer for it; some grow to dread it: "What are your plans?" Never mind that a large percentage of college freshmen have no major, another large percentage change their major after declaring one, and less than half of college freshmen graduate in four years anyway.[20] How are you supposed to know what your plans are? A lot of things are going to change for you—and *in* you—during the next few years.

But you still have to make some sort of choice, and your options are narrowing. Kids in elementary school are told, "You can be anything you want to be." But by now a career requiring good spelling or calculus skills may no longer be available to you. You've discovered you're not gifted in those areas.

But there are still many options. And in order to choose wisely, you need to know about a raging debate in higher education over two of them: the liberal arts (or the humanities) versus the sciences.

College costs a lot more money than it used to. And it provides less of a guarantee than it used to that you'll actually get a job that pays well enough to justify the expense. The fields where you are most likely to make money at the moment are the so-called STEM fields: science, technology, engineering, and mathematics. Many parents nowadays aren't too excited about laying out tens of thousands of dollars for you to major in art or literature. The return on investment just isn't as likely.

Or is it? Art and literature professors can't deny that their grads typically don't make the cash that engineers and doctors and software developers do, so they tend to point to other values of the liberal arts. One such professor, who teaches literature, tried to distill those values into a list:

> Every defense of liberal [arts] education . . . makes one or more of the following arguments:
>
> - Studying the liberal arts makes you a better citizen.
> - Studying the liberal arts makes you more empathetic and compassionate.
> - Studying the liberal arts teaches you critical-thinking skills.
> - Studying the liberal arts makes you a capable communicator, in speech and writing.
> - Knowledge is good for its own sake.[21]

These are all good justifications, but they may not be very comforting for parents looking at a $60,000 tuition bill. And none of them is particularly Christian.

Created to Create

Is it worthwhile, from the perspective of a biblical worldview, to study the liberal arts and humanities? Some readers of this book are about to spend four years—or six, or ten, or sixty—doing it. Is it a good idea?

The answer is a definite *yes*. The humanities are *vital* in the most literal sense of the term: necessary to life. The arts are a glorious part of what makes us human. This is not to put down the sciences. They, too, are blessings God gave to mankind in the Creation Mandate. And this is not to say that every single reader of this book should major in the humanities. Some aren't called to college; others are called to the sciences.

But the arts, even when they don't carry clear practical or monetary value, provide you the opportunity to do something truly God-like. They let you *create*.

This is the ultimate *c* in the Christian approach to culture. Condemn and critique when you must, consume when you can, copy when appropriate. But your goal as a created being should be to turn around and do some creating of your own. *Creating* (and, as we'll see, *cultivating*) shouldn't just be a gesture but should be a life-long posture.

American culture, especially, is at war. You will have to battle the fallen elements of culture your whole life. But you weren't created for condemnation and critique. You were created to create.

Think yet again about Genesis 1:26–28:

> Then God said, "Let us make man in our image, after our likeness. And let them have dominion over the fish of the sea and over the birds of the heavens and over the livestock and over all the earth and over every creeping thing that creeps on the earth."
>
> So God created man in his own image, in the image of God he created him; male and female he created them.
>
> And God blessed them. And God said to them, "Be fruitful and multiply and fill the earth and subdue it, and have dominion over the fish of the sea and over the birds of the heavens and over every living thing that moves on the earth."

By the time you get to these verses in Genesis 1, just about the only thing you know about God is that He is explosively creative. Inventing one animal is hard enough, let alone multiple kinds, some of which can fly—*fly*! Would you have thought of that? Some animals can eat four tons of food in a day (the blue whale). Some make light from their bodies (the anglerfish). And at least one eats sunshine (the sea slug[22]). And that's only the beginning of the list of amazing things animals can do.

The only earthly creature that can do more amazing things is man. And one of the things that most sets humans apart from animals is the very creativity first modeled by God. You were created to create.

STEM AT A LIBERAL ARTS COLLEGE

The sciences and the liberal arts don't have to be mutually exclusive. You can study both—if you're called to a scientific career, beginning it at a liberal arts college may be a great educational path for you. It will give you an opportunity to develop all your gifts, and sometimes it's the gifts you'll never make a dime off of that you wouldn't trade for all the money in the world. How much is the ability to sing well—and to enjoy and appreciate choral music—really worth, exactly? How much is it worth to have a lifelong friend who was a philosophy major?

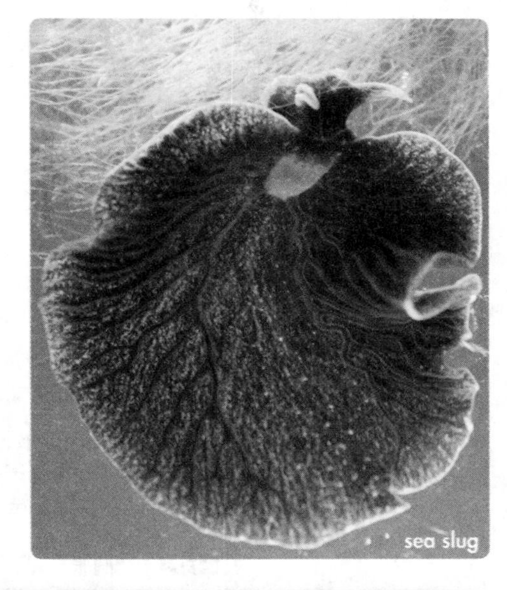
sea slug

blue whale

anglerfish

Created to Do

Over the years since worldview thinking has become more common in American Christian circles, a number of people have noticed that the term itself—*worldview*—can emphasize a posture of mere evaluation, of thinking without feeling or doing.[22] That's why we defined *worldview* in part as a head-heart system—to bring in feeling and loving. That's also why we defined *worldview* as action—to bring in doing. Every one of the redemption chapters in this book (Chapter 15 on gender, Chapter 18 on government, Chapter 21 on science, Chapter 24 on history, and now this chapter on culture) is meant to blaze a path for you to do something positive with your knowledge of the world's created structure, to take the world in the direction its true Ruler wants it to go.

"We could tear that down in a day."

In Albania, a land long under the thumb of a communist dictatorship, a man once heard of all the incredible work that went into constructing the Empire State Building. "We could tear that down in a day," he said. And indeed, in order for Christians to "take every thought captive to obey Christ," they will have to "destroy arguments and every lofty opinion raised against the knowledge of God" (2 Cor. 10:5). Destruction is a necessary part of rebuilding something marred by sin. But destruction and construction are not of equal weight. Construction—positive, beneficial work—in all fields of human culture weighs more.

This world was meant to be full of building, improving, constructing—creating. Creating is a way to rebel against the rebellion of God's highest creation. It's a positive way of pushing the world back to the way it ought to be. Every time you mow your lawn, you are at war against the forces of the Fall, creating order and beauty in a place of disorder and detritus. And if that's true of lawn mowing, think how much more significant your future vocation will be. Moms, if they are to survive their children's time between birth and kindergarten, have to be some of the most creative people on the planet. Teachers likewise. God has given us a huge world to "work and keep"—to develop and preserve. Whatever your calling, take it up and go to it!

CREATIVITY AND LOVE

Moms and teachers provide a great example of where creativity ought to come from because their callings are generally—and rightly—associated with love. What drives a mother to lose sleep every night for months, changing diapers and wiping noses and cleaning spills? (Hint: It's not the money.) What drives teachers to put in seventy-hour weeks and endure the same questions year after year ("Why do I have to learn this stuff?")? Ideally, at least, what motivates teachers is love.

The desire to destroy and protest and undermine and question things does sometimes have to be one of the drivers of art, literature, and music. Flannery O'Connor, the great twentieth-century short story writer, said, "To the hard of hearing you shout, and for the almost-blind you draw large and startling figures."[24] Accordingly, her stories are shocking at times. But her readers still get the sense that her points are driven by love. Love drives the best art, as it drives the best of everything.

Love—and the gratitude and joy and hope that spring from it—is the affection best suited to drive Christian creativity, just as truth and goodness and beauty guide and shape that creativity. It's out of the abundance of the heart that the mouth speaks, Jesus said (see Luke 6:45).

Culture and the arts aren't exempt from the two great commandments driving everything: love for God and love for neighbor. That love for neighbor is why sculptor Frederick Hart said,

> I believe that art has a moral responsibility, that it must pursue something higher than itself. Art must be a part of life. It must exist in the domain of the common man. It must be an enriching, ennobling, and vital partner in the public pursuit of civilization. It should be a majestic presence in everyday life just as it was in the past.[25]

SKILL

Frederick Hart (1943–1999) was a sculptor in the Western classical tradition who took that tradition to new heights. Many would say that his *Ex Nihilo* at the National Cathedral in Washington, DC, is utterly astounding. Hart could make life out of stone. But the art world did worse than reject him; it ignored him.[26] Hart sculpted a bronze statue for the Vietnam memorial; same result. Tom Wolfe, one of the critics of the world of art, summarized their view of Hart. Artists like Hart, "used a devious means—skill—to fool the eye into believing that bronze or stone had turned into human flesh. Therefore, they were artificial, false." Wolfe says that the art world created a climate in which "no ambitious artist was going to display skill, even if he had it."[27]

It is peculiarly appropriate, then, that Hart's masterwork was about God's creation of man. We were given our creative skills in order to use them for the glory of God and the good of mankind.

In other words, our neighbors need our creativity. Some thinkers who've explored art have called this others-oriented principle "**hospitality**." When a hostess invites a guest over for dinner, she usually prepares a meal she has made before (new recipes don't always turn out to be "hospitable"). But regardless of whether the lasagna is novel or not, no true hostess tosses in bizarre ingredients—gum drops, walnuts, tea bags—to express her culinary creativity. Her goal is to please her guests, not break their teeth or sour their stomachs. She also sets the table, lights the candles, and plays the background music for the same reason she takes care with the lasagna ingredients—for the good of her guests. Likewise, a carpenter makes doorways the new homeowners don't have to stoop to walk through. A knife maker crafts blades that are sharp and handles that fit smoothly in the hand. One significant measuring stick of worthy art is whether this piece of culture moves beyond mere self-expression to the benefit of others.

THE GREAT WAR IN ART

When a gifted young Christian artist attended the prestigious Savannah College of Art and Design for her Master of Fine Arts degree, she heard about a "great war" between what many there sneeringly called "decorative art" (the kinds of things you would hang in your living room) and "**conceptual art**" (as if decorative art—both realistic and abstract—didn't have any concepts behind it). By "conceptual," they meant "activist." Art was expected to make disturbing statements in support of some cause such as environmentalism or feminism. If art didn't disturb, it wasn't art. There was a definite Marxist theory behind this view. Art had to oppose established ruling norms in order to foster conflict—and therefore, progress.

Christian art is permitted to disturb (the Bible's own literary art is sometimes disturbing, such as in the book of Judges), but Christian art must be driven by love.

The irony is that works of merely "decorative" art produced by that Christian MFA student—driven by love—sold for $5,000 to $7,000 each while nobody would buy the "conceptual art." She paid off her grad school bill with her creativity.

"The greatest motivator to artistic expression is to enjoy something. And you want to share what you enjoy. That should be the governor that shapes your art. If somebody's not feeling what you feel, you try to tailor your efforts in order to get them to feel what you feel. That's hospitable. You think, 'I like this, and I think you should, and I'm going to do whatever I can to help you feel this with me.'"[28]

—ZACH FRANZEN

O. Henry illustrates this self-giving artistry in his short story "The Last Leaf,"[28] in which a budding artist who lives in Greenwich Village catches pneumonia and becomes disillusioned with life. Her roommate tells an older neighbor and fellow artist that the sick woman believes she will die when the last leaf falls off the ivy vine outside their window. In response, the older man secretly spends the next night out in cold rain, painting a permanent leaf on the brick wall. Two days later he succumbs to pneumonia, whereas the younger, temporarily depressed artist eventually recovers. Rarely is the sacrificial nature of artistry so dramatic, but this brief piece of literature demonstrates the power of art to show hospitality, to make a home for people.

Think about the common art form of photography. Many photographs, such as Ansel Adams' famous black-and-white photos of Yosemite National Park, capture a frame of God's glorious creativity. Others, like the ones hanging in your hallway, represent your family's nostalgic past. Such art isn't self-absorbed. It points away from itself to our Creator God or to the importance of human relationships. Its beauty pictures truth and goodness for the enjoyment of others. Even selfies can be used to send Grandma a smile.

Ansel Adams created famous photographs of American landscapes.

TO CHANGE THE WORLD

This is the final section of a long book (congratulations if you've made it this far; extra points if you've read all the sidebars). This section isn't so much making an argument as weaving a spell. The argument has already been made throughout the book: you were created to create in all legitimate aspects of human culture, and by doing so to live redemptively in God's world. You may not be called upon by God to change the whole world, but the good cultural creations you come up with *will* make a difference in the circle of "neighbors" God gives you to love: your family, your church, and your community.

American Christians are pretty enamored with the idea of making a big cultural splash. They flock to see celebrities and sports stars who are Christians. They're thrilled when a song by a Christian music group hits the secular Top 40. A lot of Christians were positively ecstatic when Mel Gibson's *The Passion of the Christ* made it to theaters. They were practically ready to build additions onto their churches to prepare for the influx of converts they expected. *Hollywood is evangelizing for us!* But the conversions didn't materialize. The Narnia films didn't bring them in either.

Positive cultural change on a grand scale is possible, but take a lesson from Jesus: He invested in precisely twelve disciples, and only three of them were really close. He didn't make all that big a splash. The great majority of the world's population had no idea that He lived or died. Or resurrected. But that resurrection was a tiny seed that grew into a massive tree. Nothing in the history of the planet has ever had a greater cultural impact. Don't assume that you have to change the world in obvious ways for your life to be faithful and worthwhile.

A homeschooling mother of six started producing a regular podcast that aims to revive the practice of family reading time.[30] No one but God will ever know the good she has done for other families. A dad who didn't care for soccer started a soccer league for his sons so they'd have a place to play and grow. A group of Christian young adults discovered a mutual passion for well-designed board games, and they thought they could do better. So they started their own game-design company, launched a website, and got an online video series going.[31] It's hard to look at these cultural artifacts, these good works, and pinpoint the direct benefits they bring. In a hundred years, no one will ever have heard of them, most likely. Christians don't create because they have the power to bring *permanent* good. Only God can do that. We create because we are created in the image of a good Creator.

CULTIVATING

CULTIVATE

All those who create art and other cultural artifacts have to go through a period of being horribly bad at their chosen craft before they can make any progress. Every world-famous concert pianist begins by plunking out three-note melodies. Every legendary artist starts with scribbles. Every carpenter starts out bending nails and cutting lumber too short. Every novelist starts with wooden prose. And every artist or musician or writer—every sort of cultural creator—has to take the art he or she has inherited and *cultivate* it before adding to it. The etudes pianists play are "studies," exercises in the craft of music-making with that particular instrument. Cultural creators all have to toil in fields others have plowed before they can grow something new.

You can't be a successful writer, for example, unless you read a lot:

> How do you cultivate an "ear" [for language]? . . . Wide reading. You cannot memorize rules, you will not even want to try, until you have an intuitive knowledge of language, until you have cultivated some taste.[32]

Some upperclassmen in high school, a few, have begun to truly *create* in their fields—they can make utterly beautiful and original paintings or poetry or pastries. But most young people need more time cultivating their skills and studying their disciplines before their God-given creative powers can be given full display. Some skills take almost a lifetime to cultivate.

But when you've toiled in the field, cultivating, and when you've put in your time to gain a creative skill, there's almost no feeling on earth like exercising that gift for God's glory.

In *Babette's Feast*, a 1987 Danish film, a French refugee named Babette arrives in a rural part of Jutland in Denmark. Never revealing her past, she works for fourteen years—for free—as the cook for a pair of spinsters who are members of an austere religious sect. She cooks the bland meals these two buttoned-up sisters expect.

Then she wins ten thousand francs in the lottery—a fortune at that time. She decides to stage a grand meal for the ladies and the small group of graying congregants in their tiny religious assembly. The old folks are afraid that the exotic ingredients Babette is shipping into the tiny seaside town will cause them to sin; will she feed them a decadent meal, leading them into sensuality? They agree not to express any pleasure over the meal but to merely consume it dispassionately, the way they eat their normal pabulum.

One guest at the meal, however, is an outsider who knows good cooking when he tastes it. Astounded by the quality of the food and drink, he regales the other guests with stories of a legendary meal he once enjoyed at the Parisian restaurant Café Anglais.

Babette's amazing culinary artistry wears away the distrust of her austere guests, and "a mystical redemption of the human spirit settles over the table."[33] The power of creativity, borne of love and gratitude, overcomes even the most abstemious* objections as Babette shares her joy through her creative work. It turns out that Babette was once the chef at Café Anglais and that a dinner for twelve at her restaurant used to cost ten thousand francs.

abstemious: *refusing to be self-indulgent*

The simple, rural folk assume Babette will return to Paris, but she has spent every bit of her lottery winnings on the extravagant meal. One of the sisters says, in tears, "Now you will be poor the rest of your life." Babette replies, "An artist is never poor."[34]

CHRISTIAN CREATORS

Christian creators, such as contemporary classical composer Dan Forrest, can express their love for God, for neighbor, and for their art with hearts full of joy. Forrest's work has achieved worldwide recognition. His choral work *Requiem for the Living* has been particularly popular—you can find it online. Forrest's website carries his statement of beliefs, which shows how the Creation-Fall-Redemption worldview drives his work:

> All good things, including any beauty that we encounter, are from God, through God, and ultimately to God. All beauty is God's beauty, wherever it is found.

> Our world was designed to be a place of beauty and goodness, but was marred by sin, and continues to struggle with evil. But one day God will make things fully right again; and in the meantime, beauty and goodness are not totally lost—they still shine through, and point us toward the way things ought to be.
>
> Whatever abilities I have, for creating beauty, are gifts from God. So I will make the most beautiful music I can, not because music making is my ultimate end, but because I want to press my gifts to their maximum potential toward the true ultimate end: glorifying God. This is equally true of my "secular" music and "sacred" music, of my concert music and church music.
>
> Jesus Christ is Lord, to the glory of God the Father. "He must increase, and I must decrease."[35]

Just as going on the offensive and doing good science is one of the best defenses of the Christian faith in the scientific arena, doing good art (including literature, music, and all forms of culture—even if that culture never goes beyond the confines of your immediate family) is one of the best defenses of the Christian faith in the cultural arena.

Christians will never quite feel comfortable in this fallen world until Christ makes all things new. But this is still our Father's world. "He shines in all that's fair."[36] Christians should be on the forefront of creative work, cultivating a culture of transcendence attractive to a broken world.

THINKING IT THROUGH 27.2

1. What posture toward culture should be the ultimate goal of Christians?
2. In addition to critical thinking, what other two elements must be included in a biblical worldview?
3. Why can't the biblical worldview stop with simply destroying those things that are raised up against God?
4. What ought to motivate creativity?
5. Why must every subcreator begin with cultivation?

27 CHAPTER REVIEW

TERMS TO REMEMBER

cultural artifact
discernment
critic
medium
conceptual art
hospitality (in art)

Scripture Memory

Genesis 2:15

Making Connections

1. List the six possible gestures/postures a person can use with regard to culture and the arts.
2. How can a person gain discernment according to Hebrews 5:14?
3. Is the primary goal of a biblical worldview to be destructive or constructive? Explain your answer.
4. Should you try to change the whole world? Why or why not?

Developing Skills in Apologetics & Biblical Worldview

5. Assuming it's true that "the medium is the message," how would you differentiate between the biblical portrayal of immoral acts (e.g., Gen. 19:30–38 or 2 Sam. 13:1–20) and a movie with scenes depicting similar situations?
6. Based on Romans 12:1–2, how would you differentiate between legitimate copying of and illegitimate blending into the surrounding heathen culture?

Examining Assumptions & Evidence

7. In order to justify condemning a cultural artifact, what must you demonstrate beyond merely disliking it?
8. By what standard should a Christian critique a cultural artifact?
9. When was the last time you simply consumed a cultural artifact without critiquing or condemning it? Do you support or regret that choice?
10. Why is cultivation a prerequisite for creativity?

Becoming a Creative Cultivator

11. Think of the last cultural artifact you created. This could include poetry or a short story, instrumental or vocal music, a painting or a sculpture, a meal or a craft (e.g., woodworking). Write a paragraph explaining how or whether your cultural artifact demonstrates the principle of "hospitality."

ADDITIONAL RESOURCES

ENDNOTES

Frontispiece

1. Theodore Roosevelt, "Chapters of a Possible Autobiography," *The Outlook: Volume CIII* (New York: The Outlook Company, 1913), 403.

Chapter 1: Worldviews

1. Glenn Branch, "The Kilosteve," *Reports of the National Center for Science Education* 29, issue 3 (2009): 35.

2. Bill Maher, interview with Conan O'Brien, *Late Night with Conan O'Brien*, NBC, January 4, 2008. http://www.nationalreview.com/node/155715/print.

3. Stephen Jay Gould, *Leonardo's Mountain of Clams and the Diet of Worms* (Cambridge, MA: Harvard University Press, 2011), 269–84.

4. Real Science 4 Kids (website), http://www.gravitaspublications.com/.

5. Albert Wolters, *Creation Regained: Biblical Basics for a Reformational Worldview* (Grand Rapids: Eerdmans, 2005), 3.

6. Gregg L. Frazer, *The Religious Beliefs of America's Founders* (Lawrence: University of Kansas Press, 2012), x.

7. Kitty Ferguson, *Stephen Hawking: His Life and Work* (London: Transworld, 2011), 129.

8. Brian J. Walsh and J. Richard Middleton, *The Transforming Vision: Shaping a Christian World View* (Downers Grove, IL: IVP Academic, 1984), 35.

9. Based on a comment by Bradlee Dean, quoted in Matt Labash, "What Would Jesus Rap?" *Weekly Standard* (website), May 15, 2006.

10. Richard Dawkins, *The God Delusion* (New York: Houghton Mifflin Harcourt, 2006), 19.

11. Stanley Fish, *The Trouble with Principle* (Cambridge, MA: Harvard University Press, 2001), 33.

12. Brian Swimme, *Journey of the Universe*, PBS, June 11, 2011.

13. Ibid.

14. Carolyn Weber, *Surprised by Oxford* (Nashville: Thomas Nelson, 2011), 124–26.

15. Neil Postman, "Science and the Story We Need," *First Things* 69, January, 1997.

16. Nathan Wilson, *Death by Living: Life Is Meant to Be Spent* (Nashville: Thomas Nelson, 2013), 6.

17. Richard Dawkins, quoted in "The Reading File," *New York Times* (website), November 9, 2003.

Chapter 2: Presuppositions

1. J. Warner Wallace, *Cold-Case Christianity* (Colorado Springs: David C. Cook, 2013), 29.

2. Gary Habermas, William Lane Craig, Paul D. Feinberg, Kelly James Clark, and John M. Frame, *Five Views on Apologetics*, ed. Steven B. Cowan (Grand Rapids: Zondervan, 2000), 95.

3. Ibid., 100.

4. Stanley J. Grenz, David Guretzki, and Cherith Fee Nordling, *Pocket Dictionary of Theological Terms* (Downers Grove, IL: InterVarsity Press, 1999), 48.

5. Stephanie Pappas, "What Preserved *T. Rex* Tissue? Mystery Explained at Last," *NBC News*, November 27, 2013.

6. Thomas Nagel, *Mind and Cosmos: Why the Materialist Neo-Darwinian Conception of Nature Is Almost Certainly False* (New York: Oxford University Press, 2012), 5.

7. Bertrand Russell, quoted in Emily Eakin, "So God's Really in the Details?" *New York Times* (website), May 11, 2002.

8. Thomas Nagel, *Mind and Cosmos: Why the Materialist Neo-Darwinian Conception of Nature Is Almost Certainly False* (New York: Oxford University Press, 2012).

9. Tim Keller, *The Reason for God* (New York: Dutton, 2008), xviii.

10. Richard Dawkins, Richard Dawkins Foundation for Reason and Science (website), http://old.richarddawkins.net/quotes?page=4.

11. C. S. Lewis, *Mere Christianity*, revised edition (New York: HarperCollins, 2009), 62.

12. A. Viberg, "Job," *New Dictionary of Biblical Theology* (Downers Grove, IL: IVP Academic, 2000), 201.

Chapter 3: The Two-Story View

1. Gary Gutting, "Is Atheism Irrational?" *New York Times* (website), February 9, 2014.

2. Lesslie Newbigin, "Certain Faith: What Kind of Certainty?" *Tyndale Bulletin* 44, no. 2 (1993): 340.

3. Adapted from Nancy Pearcey, *Total Truth: Liberating Christianity from Its Cultural Captivity* (Wheaton: Crossway Books, 2004), 20–21.

4. Barack Obama, "Remarks by the President at the National Prayer Breakfast," The White House (website), February 2, 2012.

5. Abraham Lincoln, "Second Inaugural Address of Abraham Lincoln" (March 4, 1865), http://avalon.law.yale.edu/19th_century/lincoln2.asp.

6. "Moving America Forward: 2012 Democratic National Platform," http://www.panly.net.

7. Ibid.

8. Michael J. Sandel, *Justice: What's the Right Thing to Do?* (New York: Farrar, Straus and Giroux, 2009), 261 (emphasis added).

9. Nancy Pearcey, *Total Truth: Liberating Christianity from Its Cultural Captivity* (Wheaton: Crossway Books, 2004), 19.

10. *The Incredibles* (DVD), directed by Brad Bird (Burbank, CA: Walt Disney Home Entertainment, 2005).

11. Herman Bavinck quoted in Jan Veenhof, *Nature and Grace in Herman Bavinck* (Dordt College Press, 2006), 29–30.

12. James D. Bratt, ed., *Abraham Kuyper: A Centennial Reader* (Grand Rapids: Eerdmans, 1998), 488.

13. Stanley Fish, "Why We Can't All Just Get Along," *First Things*, February 1996, 10.

14. List of disciplines adapted from Albert Wolters, *Creation Regained: Biblical Basics for a Reformational Worldview* (Grand Rapids: Eerdmans, 2005), 3.

15. Bob Jones Sr., sermon, September 14, 1948, J. S. Mack Library archives, http://www.markandlauraward.com/blog/2014/01/27/dr-bob-jones-srs-first-use-of-all-ground-is-holy-ground/.

Chapter 4: God the Creator

1. N. D. Wilson, "Myth Wars: C. S. Lewis vs. Scientism" (video), Desiring God Conference, September 27, 2013, http://www.desiringgod.org/conference-messages/myth-wars-c-s-lewis-vs-scientism#full-video.

2. Michael Reeves, *Delighting in the Trinity* (Downers Grove, IL: InterVarsity Press), 21.

3. Ibid., 31.

4. Quoted in J. N. D. Kelly, *The Athanasian Creed: The Paddock Lectures for 1962–3* (London: Adam and Charles Black, 1964), 17.

5. "Muhammad Ali," Wikipedia, en.wikiquote.org/wiki/Muhammad_Ali.

6. Roy Sorensen, "Nothingness," in *Stanford Encyclopedia of Philosophy*, ed. Edward N. Zalta (Winter 2012).

7. Jonathan Edwards, "A Dissertation Concerning the End for which God Created the World" as cited with updated language by John Piper, *God's Passion for His Glory* (Wheaton: Crossway Books, 1998), 247.

8. Roy Sorensen, "Nothingness," in *Stanford Encyclopedia of Philosophy*, ed. Edward N. Zalta (Winter 2012).

9. Michael Reeves, *Delighting in the Trinity* (Downers Grove, IL: InterVarsity Press), 28.

10. Quoted in James R. Boyd, *The Westminster Shorter Catechism with Analysis, Scriptural Proofs, Explanatory and Practical Inferences and Illustrative Anecdotes* (Philadelphia: Presbyterian Board of Publication, 1884), 19.

11. Diagrams based on Wayne Grudem, *Systematic Theology* (Grand Rapids: Zondervan, 1995), 267ff.

12. Carl Sagan, *Cosmos* (DVD), Cosmos Studios, 2002, http://www.cosmolearning.com/documentaries/cosmos/.

13. Ann Druyan, quoted in Brit Mandelo, "Exploring Carl Sagan's *Cosmos*," Tor.com (blog), November 9.

14. Neil deGrasse Tyson, *Cosmos: A Spacetime Odyssey* (DVD) (Los Angeles: 20th Century Fox, 2014).

15. Herman Bavinck, *Reformed Dogmatics*, ed. John Bolt, trans. John Vriend, *God and Creation* (Grand Rapids: Baker Academic, 2003), 2:412.

16. "Are You a Pantheist?" Universal Pantheist Society (website), http://www.pantheist.net/.

17. Christian Smith and Melinda Lundquist Denton, *Soul Searching: The Religious and Spiritual Lives of American Teenagers* (New York: Oxford University Press, 2005), 162.

18. Ibid., 162–63.

19. Robert Bellah, "Civil Religion in America," *Dædalus, Journal of the American Academy of Arts and Sciences* 96, no. 1 (1967): 1–21.

20. Voltaire, quoted by J. I. Packer in *Still Sovereign*, eds. Thomas R. Schreiner and Bruce A. Ware (Grand Rapids: Baker Academic, 2000), 277.

21. Terri Gross, "Seth Macfarlane: TV's 'Family Guy' Makes Music, Too" (interview), NPR (website), October 17, 2011.

22. C. S. Lewis, *The Four Loves* (San Diego: Harcourt Brace Jovanovich, 1960), 127.

Chapter 5: Man and His Mandate

1. "Prime Directive," Wikipedia, http://en.wikipedia.org/wiki/Prime_directive.

2. People for the Ethical Treatment of Animals (website), http://www.peta.org.

3. Brian May, "Life Is Evolution," *New York Times* (website), March 28, 2007.

4. Jeri Taylor, "Nothing Human," *Star Trek Voyager* (season 5, episode 8; DVD), directed by David Livingston (Los Angeles: Paramount, December 2, 1998), http://www.amazon.com/gp/product/B005HEVKSA/ref=dv_dp_ep8#.

5. "Threshold," *Star Trek* episode, http://en.memory-alpha.org/wiki/Threshold (episode).

6. "Carl Linnaeus," Wikipedia, http://en.wikipedia.org/wiki/Carolus_Linnaeus.

7. G. K. Chesterton, *The Everlasting Man* (Radford, VA: Wilder Publications, 2008).

8. C. S. Lewis, *Prince Caspian: The Return to Narnia* (New York: Harper Collins, 1951), 218.

9. Stephen Hawking, televised interview with Kenneth Campbell, *Reality on the Rocks*, 1995.

10. Stanley Horton, *Systematic Theology* (Springfield, MO: Gospel Publishing House, 2013), 373.

11. Gregory Berns, "Dogs Are People, Too," *New York Times* (website), October 5, 2013.

12. Robert Krulwich, *Morality*, NPR radio podcast

(season 2, episode 3), http://www.radiolab.org/story/91508-morality/.

13. Christian Smith and Melinda Lundquist Denton, *Soul Searching: The Religious and Spiritual Lives of American Teenagers* (New York: Oxford University Press, 2005), 173.

14. Gilda Sedgh, "Induced Abortion Incidence and Trends Worldwide from 1995 to 2008," *The Lancet* 379 (2012).

15. Larry Bumpass, "The Measurement of Public Opinion on Abortion," *Family Planning Perspectives* 29 (July/August 1997): 177–80.

16. Janine Latus, "Self-Esteem: The Repair Kit," *O Magazine*, January 2008.

17. Roman Price, lifepulp.com, http://bit.ly/QdAoyZ.

18. Centers for Disease Control and Prevention (website), http://www.cdc.gov/nchs/fastats/leading-causes-of-death.htm.

19. Jonathan Last, *What to Expect When No One's Expecting* (New York: Encounter Books, 2013), 7.

20. "Combined Oral Contraceptive Pill," Wikipedia, http://en.wikipedia.org/wiki/The_pill.

21. "The World Factbook," Central Intelligence Agency (website), https://www.cia.gov/library/publications/the-world-factbook/rankorder/2054rank.html.

22. See "China's Achilles' Heel," *The Economist*, April 2012.

23. Nina Fedoroff quoted in Steven Duke, "Earth Population 'Exceeds Limits,'" *BBC News* (March 31, 2009).

24. Bryan Smith, "BJU Press BI—Story," conference presentation April 12, 2011, http://prezi.com/xxsnfdf17mic/bju-press-bistory/.

25. John Frame, *Systematic Theology* (Phillipsburg, NJ: P&R Publishing, 2013), 1034.

26. "Naples Waste Management Issue," Wikipedia, http://en.wikipedia.org/wiki/Naples_waste_management_issue.

27. Victor P. Hamilton, *The Book of Genesis: Chapters 1–17*, New International Commentary on the Old Testament (Grand Rapids: Eerdmans, 1990), 171.

28. Malcolm Gladwell, *Outliers: The Story of Success* (New York Little, Brown and Company, 2008).

29. Carina Chocano, "The Chef at 15," *New York Times Magazine* (website), March 28, 2014.

30. Ed Panosian, Church History class, Bob Jones Seminary.

31. See Jared Diamond's evolutionary and materialistic, but still valuable, account of human history, *Guns, Germs, and Steel: The Fates of Human Societies* (New York: W. W. Norton, 1997).

32. Based on Andy Crouch, *Culture Making: Recovering our Creative Calling* (Downers Grove, IL: InterVarsity Press, 2009), 41.

33. See Brian J. Walsh and J. Richard Middleton, *The Transforming Vision: Shaping a Christian World View* (Downers Grove, IL: IVP Academic, 1984), 55.

34. Andy Crouch, *Playing God: Redeeming the Gift of Power* (Downers Grove, IL: InterVarsity Press 2013), 35.

35. Andy Crouch, *Culture Making: Recovering our Creative Calling* (Downers Grove, IL: InterVarsity Press, 2009), 23.

36. John Frame, *The Doctrine of the Christian Life: A Theology of Lordship* (Phillipsburg, NJ: P&R Publishing, 2008), 866.

37. Andy Crouch, *Playing God: Redeeming the Gift of Power* (Downers Grove, IL: InterVarsity Press 2013), 201.

38. Peter Gutmann, "The Sounds of Silence," Classical Notes (website), 1999; see also Alex Ross, *The Rest Is Noise: Listening to the Twentieth Century* (New York: Farrar, Strauss and Giroux, 2007), 364ff.

39. This argument about John Cage is based on Andy Crouch, *Culture Making: Recovering our Creative Calling* (Downers Grove, IL: InterVarsity Press, 2009), 73-74.

40. Ibid., 22.

Chapter 6: Everything God Made Was Very Good

1. Albert Wolters, *Creation Regained: Biblical Basics for a Reformational Worldview* (Grand Rapids: Eerdmans, 2005), 48–49.

2. Gregg R. Allison, "Toward a Theology of Human Embodiment," *Southern Baptist Journal of Theology* 13, no. 2 (2009): 4.

3. Frederica Mathewes-Green, "The Subject Was Noses: What Happens When Academics Discover That We Have Bodies," *Books and Culture* (January/February 1997): 14.

4. Zachary G. Smith, "Gnosticism," ed. John D. Barry and Lazarus Wentz, *The Lexham Bible Dictionary* (Bellingham, WA: Lexham Press, 2012).

5. Christian Smith and Melinda Lundquist Denton, *Soul Searching: The Religious and Spiritual Lives of American Teenagers* (New York: Oxford University Press, 2005), 189.

6. Erik Lundegaard, "Truth, Justice, and (Fill in the Blank)," *New York Times* (website), June 30, 2006, A23.

7. Andy Crouch, *Playing God: Redeeming the Gift of Power* (Downers Grove, IL: InterVarsity Press 2013), 45.

8. Rob Lister, *God Is Impassible and Impassioned: Toward a Theology of Divine Emotion* (Wheaton: Crossway, 2012), 163–64 (especially the Feinberg quote).

9. "Making Data Dance," *The Economist*, December 9, 2010, emphasis added.

10. Ibid.

11. "About Abby," Abby Johnson (website), http://www.abbyjohnson.org.

12. Ibid.

13. Albert Wolters, *Creation Regained: Biblical Basics for a Reformational Worldview* (Grand Rapids: Eerdmans, 2005), 50.

14. See Stephanie Coontz, *Marriage, a History: From Obedience to Intimacy or How Love Conquered Marriage* (New York: Viking, 2005).

15. James Fincannon, "Six Flags on the Moon: What Is Their Current Condition?" NASA (website), April 2012.

16. David T. Koyzis, *Political Visions and Illusions* (Downers Grove, IL: IVP Academic, 2003), 185.

17. See review of Carl Trueman's *Republocrat* (Phillipsburg, NJ: P&R Publishing, 2010) at http://byfaithweunderstand.com/2010/10/11/confessions-of-a-christian-conservative/.

18. See Albert Wolters, *Creation Regained: Biblical Basics for a Reformational Worldview* (Grand Rapids: Eerdmans, 2005), 38.

19. "'Nones' on the Rise," Pew Research Center (website), October 9, 2012.

20. Alice Chasan, "On the Frontline of the Mommy Wars" (interview with Linda Hirshman), Belief.net (website), October, 2006.

21. Ibid.

22. Ibid.

23. Brian J. Walsh and J. Richard Middleton, *The Transforming Vision: Shaping a Christian World View* (Downers Grove, IL: IVP Academic, 1984), 156.

24. Ibid.

25. Barba Demick, *Nothing to Envy* (New York: Spiegel 7 Grau, 2010), 220. See also "Famine in North Korea," Wikipedia, http://en.wikipedia.org/wiki/Famine_in_North_Korea.

26. David T. Koyzis, *Political Visions and Illusions* (Downers Grove, IL: IVP Academic, 2003), 197.

27. Colin Kidd, *The Forging of Races: Race and Scripture in the Protestant Atlantic World, 1600–2000* (Cambridge: Cambridge University Press, 2006), 3.

28. Robert Benne, *Good and Bad Ways to Think about Religion and Politics* (Grand Rapids: Eerdmans, 2010), 58.

Chapter 7: Far as the Curse Is Found

1. John Frame, *Systematic Theology* (Phillipsburg, NJ: P&R Publishing, 2013), 851.

2. John Piper, "Nudity in Drama and the Clothing of Christ," Desiring God (website), November 20, 2006.

3. Gregg R. Allison, "Toward a Theology of Human Embodiment," *Southern Baptist Journal of Theology* 13, no. 2 (2009):9.

4. Jeffrey Kluger, "The Evolution of a Narcissist," *Time*, September 1, 2014.

5. Alan Jacobs, *Original Sin* (New York: HarperCollins, 2009), 92.

6. "Fall," MormonWiki, http://www.mormonwiki.com/Fall.

7. J. R. R. Tolkien, *Return of the King: Being the Third Part of the Lord of the Rings* (New York: Houghton Mifflin Harcourt, 1988), 924.

8. "Lun Lun the Giant Panda Gives Birth to Twins!" Zoo Atlanta (website), July 15, 2013.

9. Natalie Angier, "One Thing They Aren't: Maternal," *New York Times* (website), May 9, 2006.

10. Alfred Lord Tennyson, in "In Memoriam A. H. H.," *The Works of Alfred Lord Tennyson* (Ware, Hertfordshire, England: Wordsworth Editions Ltd., 1998), 338.

11. Abraham Kuyper, *Calvinism: Six Stone-lectures* (Charleston, SC: BiblioBazaar, 2009), 174.

12. Gilda Sedgh, "Induced Abortion Incidence and Trends Worldwide from 1995 to 2008," *The Lancet* 379 (2012): 2.

13. Alfred Lord Tennyson, in "In Memoriam A. H. H.," *The Works of Alfred Lord Tennyson* (Ware, Hertfordshire, England: Wordsworth Editions Ltd., 1998), 339.

14. Richard Dawkins, *The Selfish Gene* (Oxford: Oxford University Press, 1976), 2.

15. Carl Sagan, "One Voice in the Cosmic Fugue," *Cosmos* (TV series), season 1, episode 2.

16. John Frame, *Systematic Theology* (Phillipsburg, NJ: P&R Publishing, 2013), 858.

17. Bruce Waltke, *Genesis: A Commentary* (Grand Rapids: Zondervan, 2001), 92.

18. Derek Kidner, *Genesis*, Tyndale Old Testament Commentary (Downers Grove, IL: InterVarsity, 2008), 71.

19. Bruce Waltke, *Genesis: A Commentary* (Grand Rapids: Zondervan, 2001), 95.

20. "Maternal Mortality," World Health Organization (website), May 2014.

21. Nik Ripken with Greg Lewis, *The Insanity of God: A True Story of Faith Resurrected* (Nashville: B&H Books, 2013), 63.

22. Ibid., 118.

23. Ibid., 60.

24. Charles Murray, *Coming Apart: The State of White America, 1960–2010* (New York: Crown Forum, 2012), 167.

25. Stephanie Coontz, *Marriage, a History: From Obedience to Intimacy or How Love Conquered Marriage* (New York: Viking, 2005), 5.

26. "The Holy Virgin Mary," Wikipedia, http://en.wikipedia.org/wiki/The_Holy_Virgin_Mary.

27. Deb Richardson-Moore, "Help, Don't Hurt, the Homeless with Your Gifts," Greenville Online, March 2, 2014.

28. See Steve Corbett and Brian Fikkert, *When Helping Hurts* (Chicago: Moody, 2014).

29. Herman Ridderbos, *Paul: An Outline of His Theology* (Grand Rapids: Eerdmans, 1975), 91.

30. John Frame, *The Doctrine of the Christian Life* (Phillipsburg, NJ: P & R Publishing, 2008), 866.

31. W. B. Yeats, "The Second Coming," in *The Classic Hundred Poems*, ed. William Harmon (New York: Columbia University Press, 1998).

32. Nik Ripken with Greg Lewis, *The Insanity of God: A True Story of Faith Resurrected* (Nashville: B&H Books, 2013).

Chapter 8: Common Grace, the World, and You

1. C. S. Lewis, *Mere Christianity* (New York: Harper Collins, 1980), 56.

2. C. S. Lewis, *The Screwtape Letters* (New York: Harper Collins, 1942), 8.

3. Examples adapted from John Frame, *Systematic Theology* (Phillipsburg, NJ: P&R Publishing, 2013), 863.

4. Herman Bavinck, "Calvin and Common Grace," Princeton Theological Review 7 (1909): 437–65.

5. Kenneth Myers, "Is 'Popular Culture' Either?" *Modern Reformation* 6 (January/February 1997): 9–12.

6. T. M. Moore, *Redeeming Pop Culture* (Phillipsburg, NJ: P&R Publishing, 2003), 9.

7. Kenneth Myers, *All God's Children and Blue Suede Shoes: Christians and Popular Culture* (Wheaton: Crossway, 1989), xiii.

8. Ibid.

9. Ibid., xii–xiii.

10. John Frame, *The Doctrine of the Christian Life: A Theology of Lordship* (Phillipsburg NJ: P&R Publishing, 2008), 866.

11. Cornelius Platinga Jr., *Engaging God's World: A Christian Vision of Faith, Learning, and Living* (Grand Rapids: Eerdmans, 2002), 63.

12. Ibid.

13. Fred Sanders, "They Quit Making Good Music When I Turned 30," *First Things* (blog), October 21, 2009, http://www.firstthings.com/index.php?permalink=blogs&blog=firstthoughts&year=2009&month=10&entry_permalink=they-quit-making-good-music-when-i-turned-30.

14. Andy Crouch, *Culture Making: Recovering Our Creative Calling* (Downers Grove, IL: IVP, 2013), 89.

15. Richard Mouw, *He Shines in All That's Fair: Culture and Common Grace* (Grand Rapids: Eerdmans, 2002), 28.

16. Nancy L. Segal, "The Closest of Strangers," *New York Times* (website), May 23, 2014.

17. Fernando Garibay, Paul Blair, Stefani Germanotta, and J. B. Laursen, "Born This Way," http://www.metrolyrics.com/born-this-way-lyrics-lady-gaga.html.

18. "Born This Way (song)," Wikipedia, http://en.wikipedia.org/wiki/Born_This_Way_(song).

19. John Piper, *When I Don't Desire God: How to Fight for Joy* (Wheaton: Crossway, 2004), 47.

20. Bruce Waltke, *The Book of Proverbs, Chapters 1–15*, New International Commentary on the Old Testament (Grand Rapids: Eerdmans, 2004), 180–81.

21. Ibid., 100–101.

22. M. J. Stephey, "What Came Before the Big Bang?" *Time*, August 13, 2009.

23. Ibid.

24. Ibid.

25. Sinclair Ferguson, ed., *New Dictionary of Theology* (Downers Grove, IL: IVP Academic, 1988), 328.

26. Douglas Wilson, *Collision* (DVD), 2009, http://www.collisionmovie.com/.

Chapter 9: Structure and Direction

1. C. S. Lewis, *Perelandra* (New York: HarperOne, 2012), 161.

2. Albert Wolters, *Creation Regained* (Grand Rapids: Eerdmans, 2005), 66–67.

3. Ibid., 91.

4. C. S. Lewis, *Christian Reflections* (Grand Rapids: Eerdmans, 1967), 33.

5. Laura Sessions Stepp, "Books—*Unhooked: How Young Women Pursue Sex, Delay Love, and Lose at Both*," *Washington Post* (website), February 14, 2007.

6. Ross Douthat, "Conservative and Affirmative Consent," *New York Times* (website), October 16, 2014.

7. Rachel Slick, "The Atheist Daughter of a Notable Christian Apologist Shares Her Story," The Friendly Atheist (blog), July 15, 2013.

8. Albert Wolters, *Creation Regained* (Grand Rapids: Eerdmans, 2005), 57.

9. Laura Sessions Stepp, "Books—*Unhooked: How Young Women Pursue Sex, Delay Love, and Lose at Both*," *Washington Post* (website), February 14, 2007.

10. "Materialism, n." OED Online, December 2014, Oxford University Press.

11. "Affluenza," Wikipedia, http://en.wikipedia.org/wiki/Affluenza.

12. Lily Rothman, "Kids TV Survey: How Much TV Kids Watch," *Time*, November 20, 2013.

13. See Andy Crouch, *Culture Making* (Downers Grove, IL: InterVarsity Press, 2009), 29–30.

14. Vern Poythress, *In the Beginning Was the Word* (Wheaton: Crossway, 2009), 9.

15. Stephen Anderson, *Doctor Dolittle's Delusion: Animals and the Uniqueness of Human Language* (New Haven, CT: Yale University Press, 2006).

16. Vern Poythress, *In the Beginning Was the Word* (Wheaton: Crossway, 2009), 353ff.

17. Jay Hathaway, "NPR Pulled a Brilliant April Fools' Prank on People Who Don't Read," Gawker (blog), April 3, 2014, http://gawker.com/npr-pulled-a-brilliant-april-fools-prank-on-people-who-1557745710.

18. Ronald Horton, *Christian Education: Its Mandate and Mission* (Greenville, SC: BJU Press, 1992), 66.

19. Ibid.

Chapter 10: An Everlasting Kingdom

1. Albert Wolters, *Creation Regained: Biblical Basics for a Reformational Worldview* (Grand Rapids: Eerdmans, 2005), 72.

2. Isaac Backus, *An Appeal to the Public for Religious Liberty Against the Oppressions of the Present Day* (Boston: John Boyle, 1773), 6.

3. Albert Wolters, *Creation Regained* (Grand Rapids: Eerdmans, 2005), 45–46.

4. Bruce Riley Ashford, quoted in Justin Taylor, "An Interview with Bruce Ashford on Christian Cultural Engagement," The Gospel Coalition (website), May 5, 2015.

Chapter 11: Redeemed for Good Works

1. J. R. R. Tolkien, "On Fairy Stories," in *Tree and Leaf* (London: George Allen & Unwin Unlimited, 1964), 62.

2. J. R. R. Tolkien, *The Two Towers*, Part 2 of *The Lord of the Rings*, 2nd ed. (New York: Del Rey Books, 2012), 362.

3. Ibid., 362–63.

4. Ibid., 363.

5. Ibid.

6. C. S. Lewis, *The Last Battle* (New York: HarperTrophy, 1994), 228.

7. D. A. Carson, "Editorial: The Hole in the Gospel," *Themelios* 38 (2013): 354.

8. Cornelius Plantinga Jr., *Not the Way It's Supposed to Be: A Breviary of Sin* (Grand Rapids: Eerdmans, 1995), 16.

9. "Colombia: Pastor Martyred," Voice of the Martyrs (website), October 12, 2009.

10. Personal communication with the lead author of this textbook, March 2013.

11. Richard Lee, ed., *The American Patriot's Bible: The Word of God and the Shaping of America* (Nashville: Thomas Nelson, 2009).

12. "Births: Final Data for 2013," *National Vital Statistics Reports 64* (January 15, 2015): 6.

Chapter 12: The Mission of the Church and Your Vocation

1. Gregg R. Allison, *Sojourners and Strangers: The Doctrine of the Church*, ed. John S. Feinberg (Wheaton: Crossway, 2012), 89, fn 60.

2. Christopher J. H. Wright, *The Mission of God's People: A Biblical Theology of the Church's Mission*, ed. Jonathan Lunde (Grand Rapids: Zondervan, 2010).

3. Kevin DeYoung and Greg Gilbert, *What Is the Mission of the Church? Making Sense of Social Justice, Shalom, and the Great Commission* (Wheaton: Crossway, 2011), 232–33.

4. Alan Jacobs, "Gardening and Governing," *Books & Culture* (March/April 2009): 18.

5. Tim Keller, *Every Good Endeavor* (New York: Dutton, 2012), 70.

6. Martin Luther, *Sermons I*, ed. John W. Doberstein, Luther's Works, ed. Helmut T. Lehmann (Philadelphia: Fortress, 1959), 177.

7. *The Incredibles* (DVD), directed by Brad Bird (Burbank, CA: Walt Disney Home Entertainment, 2005).

Chapter 13: The Man and the Woman in Creation

1. Christin Milloy, "Don't Let the Doctor Do This to Your Newborn," *Slate* (June 26, 2014).

2. Ibid.

3. Ibid.

4. Sarah Wright, "Society Needs to Look Beyond Marriage," *New York Times* (website), July 24, 2014.

5. Wayne Grudem, "Does Kephale Κεφαλη Mean 'Source' or 'Authority Over' in Greek Literature? A Survey of 2,336 Examples," *Trinity Journal* 6:1 (1985): 38–59.

6. Andreas Köstenberger, *God, Marriage, and Family: Rebuilding the Biblical Foundation*, 2nd ed. (Wheaton: Crossway, 2010), 24.

7. Rachel Held Evans, "The False Gospel of Gender Binaries," (blog), November 19, 2014.

8. Michael Reeves, *Delighting in the Trinity* (Downers Grove, IL: InterVarsity Press), 28–29.

9. Andreas Köstenberger, *God, Marriage, and Family: Rebuilding the Biblical Foundation,* 2nd ed. (Wheaton: Crossway, 2010), 25.

10. Thomas Schreiner, in *Women in the Church*, ed. Andreas Köstenberger, Thomas Schreiner, and Scott Baldwin (Grand Rapids: Baker, 1995), 151; Philip Towner, *The Letters to Timothy and Titus*, New International Commentary on the New Testament (Grand Rapids: Eerdmans, 2006), 235; Howard Marshall, *The Pastoral Epistles*, International Critical Commentary (New York: T & T Clark Ltd., 2004), 470.

11. Amy Richards, "When One Is Enough," *New York Times* (website), July 18, 2004.

12. Ibid.

13. Ibid.

14. "Core Beliefs," Council on Biblical Manhood and Womanhood (website), http://cbmw.org/core-beliefs/.

15. "What Is CBE," CBE International (website), http://www.cbeinternational.org.

16. "Core Beliefs" and "Statement of Faith," Council on Biblical Manhood and Womanhood (website), http://cbmw.org.

17. "About CBE," CBE International (website), http://www.cbeinternational.org/content/about-cbe.

18. Rachel Held Evans, "For the Sake of the Gospel, Let Women Speak," (blog), June 7, 2012.

19. Philip H. Towner, *The Letters to Timothy and Titus*, New International Commentary on the New Testament (Grand Rapids: Eerdmans, 2006), 219–20.

20. Rachel Held Evans, "For the Sake of the Gospel, Let Women Speak," (blog), June 7, 2012.

21. C. S. Lewis, *The Lion, the Witch and the Wardrobe* (New York: HarperCollins, 2002), 119.

22. *The Lion, the Witch and the Wardrobe* (DVD), Buena Vista Home Entertainment/Disney, 2005.

23. Andrew Adamson, quoted in Eric Brady, "A Closer Look at the World of Narnia," *USA Today* (website), December 2, 2005, http://usatoday30.usatoday.com/life/movies/news/2005-12-01-narnia-side_x.htm.

24. Marvin Olasky, quoted in David Wegener, "The Impact of Feminism," *Journal for Biblical Manhood and Womanhood* 3 (Winter 1998): 4.

25. Council on Biblical Manhood and Womanhood, *Recovering Biblical Manhood and Womanhood: A Response to Evangelical Feminism*, eds. John Piper and Wayne Grudem (Wheaton: Crossway, 1991), 35–36.

26. Jonathan Parnell in David Mathis, John Piper, et al., *Good: The Joy of Christian Manhood and Womanhood*, eds. Owen Strachan and Jonathan Parnell (Minneapolis: Desiring God, 2014), 4.

27. Rachel Held Evans, "For the Sake of the Gospel, Let Women Speak," (blog), June 7, 2012.

Chapter 14: Marriage Twisted

1. "The Trivializing of Dan Quayle," *Chicago Tribune* (website), May 28, 1992.

2. "I Love the 90's Murphy Brown" (video), https://www.youtube.com/watch?v=pmFTeVNPk1g.

3. "'Murphy Brown' Reunion" (video), https://www.youtube.com/watch?v=KSmY96A6ADA.

4. See Barbara Dafoe Whitehead, "Dan Quayle Was Right," *Atlantic Monthly*, April 1993.

5. William Arndt, Frederick W. Danker, and Walter Bauer, *A Greek-English Lexicon of the New Testament and Other Early Christian Literature*, s.v. *pornos* (Chicago: University of Chicago Press, 2000), 855.

6. Joseph Carroll, "Society's Moral Boundaries Expand Somewhat This Year," Gallup News Service, May 16, 2005.

7. Christopher Ash, *Marriage: Sex in the Service of God* (Vancouver, BC: Regent College Publishing, 2005), 249–52.

8. Andreas J. and Margaret E. Köstenberger, *God, Marriage, and Family*, 2nd ed. (Wheaton: Crossway, 2010), 50–51.

9. William J. Bennett, "Why Men Are in Trouble," CNN (website), October 4, 2011.

10. *Child Maltreatment 2012* (Washington, DC: Children's Bureau of the US Department of Health and Human Services, 2013), 21, http://www.acf.hhs.gov/sites/default/files/cb/cm2012.pdf.

11. John Inchley, *Kids and the Kingdom* (Wheaton: Tyndale House, 1976), 95–105.

12. "Mandatory Reporters of Child Abuse and Neglect," Children's Bureau of US Department of Health and Human Services, 2013, https://childwelfare.gov/pubPDFs/manda.pdf#.

13. "Teenager, n.," OED Online, December 2014, Oxford University Press.

14. Patricia Hersch, *A Tribe Apart: A Journey into the Heart of American Adolescence* (New York: Ballantine Books, 1998), 14.

15. Rosaria Butterfield, *The Secret Thoughts of an Unlikely Convert: An English Professor's Journey into Christian Faith* (Pittsburgh: Crown & Covenant Publishers, 2012).

16. Matt Hastings, "Tampa Students Protest Homophobic Speaker," *FightBack! News* (website), October 12, 2013.

17. "Community Covenant," Wheaton College, http://wheaton.edu/about-wheaton/community-covenant.

18. Anna Morris, "Students Hold Demonstration Before Chapel Speaker," *Wheaton Record*, February 7, 2014. See also http://arealrattlesnake.com/2014/02/20/more-than-a-single-story-at-wheaton-college/.

19. "Gay and Lesbian Rights," Gallup (website), http://www.gallup.com/poll/1651/Gay-Lesbian-Rights.aspx.

20. Brian Ward et al., "Sexual Orientation and Health Among U.S. Adults," *National Health Statistics Reports* 77 (July 15, 2014): 1.

21. Peter Westen, "The Empty Idea of Equality," *Harvard Law Review* 95 (January 1982): 537–96.

22. See, for example, soulfource.org, gaychristian.net, and similar sites.

23. Anna Morris, "Q&A with Dr. Rosaria Butterfield," *Wheaton Record* (website), February 7, 2014.

24. Derek Brown, "Review of *Making Gay Okay*," The Gospel Coalition (website), October 1, 2014.

25. Mel White, *What the Bible Says—and Doesn't Say—About Homosexuality,* http://soulforce.com/wp-content/uploads/2013/09/whatthebiblesays.pdf.

26. See James V. Brownson, *Bible, Gender, Sexuality: Reframing the Church's Debate on Same-Sex Relationships* (Grand Rapids: Eerdmans, 2013), 275.

27. John Allen Jr., "Interview with Anglican Bishop N. T. Wright of Durham, England," *National Catholic Reporter* (website), May 21, 2004.

28. Michael Hannon, "Against Heterosexuality," *First Things* (March 2014).

29. Mel White, *What the Bible Says—and Doesn't Say—About Homosexuality*, 2nd ed. (Lynchburg, VA: Soulforce, 2005?), 18, http://drops.forwarddesigner.net/SAS.

30. One example of current standard pro-homosexual readings of the Bible is James Brownson, *The Bible, Gender, and Sexuality* (Grand Rapids: Eerdmans, 2013), which dismisses the very passage Jesus appeals to when discussing marriage, Genesis 1, saying it has nothing negative to tell us about homosexuality.

31. Luke Timothy Johnson, "Homosexuality and the Church," *Commonweal* (website), June 11, 2007.

32. Albert Mohler, "The Bible Condemns a Lot, but Here's Why We Focus on Homosexuality," The Briefing (podcast), May 22, 2012.

33. Supreme Court of the United States (blog), April 7, 2014, http://www.scotusblog.com/case-files/cases/elane-photography-llc-v-willock/.

34. Richard B. Hays, *The Moral Vision of the New Testament: Community, Cross, New Creation: A Contemporary Introduction to New Testament Ethics* (New York: HarperOne, 1996), 402.

35. John Paulk, "To Straight and Back: My Life as an Ex-Ex-Gay Man," *Politico Magazine* (website), June 19, 2014.

36. Anna Morris, "Q&A with Dr. Rosaria Butterfield," *Wheaton Record* (website), February 7, 2014.

37. Stephanie Coontz, *Marriage, a History: How Love Conquered Marriage* (New York: Penguin Books, 2006), 4.

38. Ibid., 5.

39. Ibid.

40. David Popenoe and Barbara Dafoe Whitehead, "Should We Live Together? What Young Adults Need to Know About Cohabitation Before Marriage," 2nd ed. (Piscataway, NJ: National Marriage Project, 2002), 1.

41. Robert Lauer and Jeanette Lauer, *Marriage and Family: The Quest for Intimacy*, 5th ed. (New York: McGraw-Hill, 2004), 135.

42. Casey Copen et al., "First Premarital Cohabitation in the United States: 2006–2010 National Survey of Family Growth," *National Health Statistics Reports* 64 (April 4, 2013): 1.

43. Sheela Kennedy and Steven Ruggles, "Breaking Up Is Hard to Count: The Rise of Divorce in the United States, 1980–2010," *Demography* 51 (April 2014): 596.

44. David and Amber Lapp, "Alone in the New America," *First Things* (website), February 2014, 30–31.

45. Anjani Chandra et al., "Sexual Behavior, Sexual Attraction, and Sexual Identity in the United States," *National Health Statistics Reports* 36 (March 3, 2011): 26.

46. Mark Pattison, "Study Finds Cohabitation Even More Harmful to Children than Divorce," Umatuna Si Yu'os (website), 2011, http://umatuna.org/study-finds-cohabitation-even-more-harmful-to-children-than-divorce.

47. Ben Wattenberg, "The First Measured Century," PBS program, http://www.pbs.org/fmc/timeline/ddisruption.htm.

48. "Cohabitation," Wikipedia, http://en.wikipedia.org/wiki/Cohabitation.

49. Christopher Ash, *Marriage: Sex in the Service of God* (Vancouver, BC: Regent College Publishing, 2005), 224.

50. Noah Smith, "Liberals Are Rescuing Marriage," BloombergView (website), July 15, 2014.

51. Ted Olson quoted in Jennifer Rubin, "Why Gay Marriage Opponents Have Lost," *Washington Post* (website), October 13, 2014.

52. Steven Petrow, "Civilities: The President Made History with Three Words Last Night," *Washington Post* (blog), January 21, 2015.

53. Wilcox, W. Bradford. "The Evolution of Divorce," *National Affairs* 1 (2009): 81.

54. Sheela Kennedy and Steven Ruggles, "Breaking Up Is Hard to Count: The Rise of Divorce in the United States, 1980–2010," *Demography* 51 (April 2014): 596.

55. Christopher Ash, *Marriage: Sex in the Service of God* (Vancouver, BC: Regent College Publishing, 2005), 40.

56. Ashley McGuire, "The Feminist, Pro-Father, and Pro-Child Case Against No-Fault Divorce," Witherspoon Institute (website), May 7, 2013.

57. Ibid.

58. Marcia Pappas, "Divorce New York Style," *New York Times* (website), February 19, 2006.

59. Anne-Marie Slaughter, "Why Women Still Can't Have It All," *The Atlantic*, July/August 2012.

60. John Piper, "A Vision of Biblical Complementarity: Manhood and Womanhood Defined According to the Bible," in *Recovering Biblical Manhood and Womanhood: A Response to Evangelical Feminism*, eds. John Piper and Wayne Grudem (Wheaton: Crossway, 1991), 27.

61. Ruth Padawer, "When Women Become Men at Wellesley," *New York Times Magazine* (website), October 15, 2014.

62. Steven Douglas Smith, *The Disenchantment of Secular Discourse* (Cambridge, MA: Harvard University Press, 2010), 29.

63. Rod Snyder, "Love Wins: The Shifting Landscape on LGBT Issues in the Evangelical Church," *Huffington Post* (blog), July 22, 2014.

64. Dashka Slater, "The Fire on the 57 Bus in Oakland," *New York Times Magazine* (website), January 29, 2015.

65. Anthony Esolen, "A Requiem for Friendship," *Touchstone*, September 2005, 27.

66. Ryan T. Anderson, "Marriage: What It Is, Why It Matters, and the Consequences of Redefining It," Heritage Foundation (website), March 11, 2013.

67. "*The Brady Bunch*," Wikipedia, http://en.wikipedia.org/wiki/The_Brady_Bunch.

68. "The Trivializing of Dan Quayle," *Chicago Tribune* (website), May 28, 1992.

69. "Candace Bergen Agrees with Quayle," CNN Entertainment (website), July 11, 2002, http://web.archive.org/web/20080126033326/http://archives.cnn.com/2002/SHOWBIZ/News/07/11/showbuzz/index.html.

Chapter 15: Marriage Redeemed

1. Kurt Eichenwald, "The Bible: So Misunderstood It's a Sin," *Newsweek* (website), December 23, 2014.

2. David Platt, *Counter Culture: A Compassionate Call to Counter Culture in a World of Poverty, Same-Sex Marriage, Racism, Sex Slavery, Immigration, Persecution, Abortion, Orphans, and Pornography* (Carol Stream, IL: Tyndale House, 2015), 152.

3. John Piper, "To a Spouse Considering Divorce," Desiring God (website), July 31, 2014.

4. Katherine Schulten, "How Do You Define 'Family'?" The Learning Network (a *New York Times* website), February 24, 2011.

5. Ibid.

6. Andy David Naselli, "Training Children for Their Good," *Journal of Discipleship and Family Ministry* 3 (2013): 50.

7. http://www.endcorporalpunishment.org/.

8. Paul D. Wegner, "Discipline in the Book of Proverbs: 'To Spank or Not to Spank?'" *Journal of the Evangelical Theological Society* 48 (2005): 715–32.

9. C. S. Lewis, *God in the Dock* (Grand Rapids: Eerdmans, 2014), 301.

10. Stanley Fish, "Two Cheers for Double Standards," *New York Times* (website), March 12, 2012.

11. Thomas R. Schreiner, in *Two Views on Women in Ministry*, eds. John Piper and Wayne Grudem, rev. ed. (Grand Rapids: Zondervan, 2010), 184.

12. Andreas J. and Margaret E. Köstenberger, *God's Design for Man and Woman* (Wheaton: Crossway, 2014), 103–4.

13. Roger W. Gehring, *House Church and Mission: The Importance of Household Structures in Early Christianity* (Peabody, MA: Hendrickson, 2004), 210–11.

14. Ibid., 211.

15. Andreas J. and Margaret E. Köstenberger, *God's Design for Man and Woman* (Wheaton: Crossway, 2014), 16.

16. Doug Wilson, "Sexual by Design," lecture and question/answer session at Indiana University, April 2012, http://www.canonwired.com/bloomington/.

17. Raymond C. Ortlund, in *New Dictionary of Biblical Theology*, eds. T. Desmond Alexander and Brian S. Rosner (Downers Grove, IL: InterVarsity Press, 2000), 652.

Chapter 16: Foundations of Government

1. George M. Marsden, *The Twilight of the American Enlightenment: The 1950s and the Crisis of Liberal Belief* (New York: Basic Books, 2014), 92–95.

2. Ronald Reagan, quoted in Steven Weisman, "Reagan Takes Oath as 40th President," *New York Times* (website), January 21, 1981.

3. James G. March and Johan P. Olsen, "Elaborating the 'New Institutionalism,'" in *The Oxford Handbook of Political Institutions*, eds. R. A. W. Rhodes, Sarah A. Binder, and Bert A. Rockman (New York: Oxford University Press, 2006), 3; Douglass C. North, *Institutions, Institutional Change and Economic Performance* (Cambridge: Cambridge University Press, 1990), 3; Philip Selznick, *The Moral Commonwealth: Social Theory and the Promise of Community* (Berkeley: University of California Press, 1992), 232–33.

4. Charles Dickens, *Great Expectations* (New York: James G. Gregory, Publisher, 1861), 1:86.

5. "Revenge," Wikipedia, http://en.wikipedia.org/wiki/Revenge (disambiguation).

6. Michael J. Sandel, *Justice: What's the Right Thing to Do?* (New York: Farrar, Straus, Giroux, 2009), 19, 261.

7. Ibid., 31ff.

8. Ibid., 37.

9. Michael Slote, "Utilitarianism," *The Oxford Companion to Philosophy*, ed. Ted Honderich (Oxford: Oxford University Press, 1995), 890.

10. This discussion of utilitarianism also drew on Frederick Copleston, *A History of Philosophy* (London: Burns and Oates, 1966), 8:11–42; Richard Norman, "Happiness," *The Oxford Companion to Philosophy*, ed. Ted Honderich (Oxford, OUP, 1995), 332–33; Alan Ryan, *On Politics* (Liverlight, 2012), 696–721; Robert C. Solomon and Kathleen M. Higgins, *A Short History of Philosophy* (New York: Oxford University Press, 1996), 230–31.

11. See also Nicholas Wolterstorff, *Justice: Rights and Wrongs* (Princeton, NJ: Princeton University Press), 93–94.

12. Arifa Akbar, "Mao's Great Leap Forward 'Killed 45 Million in Four Years,'" *The Independent*, September 17, 2010.

13. Frank Dikötter, *Mao's Great Famine: The History of China's Most Devastating Catastrophe, 1958–1962* (New York: Walker Publishing Company, 2010).

14. Carl R. Trueman, *The Creedal Imperative* (Wheaton: Crossway, 2012), 178.

15. Edmund Burke, *Burke's Speeches*, ed. F. G. Selby (London: MacMillan and Co., 1897), 311.

16. Otto von Bismarck, *Bismarck: The Man and the Statesman, Vol. 1* (New York: Cosimo Classics, 2013), back cover.

17. Fred Miller, "Aristotle's Political Theory," *Stanford Encyclopedia of Philosophy*, ed. Edward N. Zalta (Fall 2012), http://plato.stanford.edu/archives/fall2012/entries/aristotle-politics/.

Chapter 17: Political Perspectives

1. Nancy S. Love, *Dogmas and Dreams: A Reader in Modern Political Ideologies*, 3rd ed. (Washington, DC: CQ Press, 2006), 7.

2. David T. Koyzis, *Political Visions and Illusions: A Survey and Christian Critique of Contemporary Ideologies* (Downers Grove: InterVarsity, 2003), 8.

3. Ibid., 13–41.

4. Ibid., 42–68; Nancy Love, *Understanding Dogmas and Dreams*, 2nd ed. (Washington, DC: CQ Press, 2006), 21–47; David Boaz, *Libertarianism: A Primer* (New York: Free Press, 1997), 1–58.

5. See Jonathan Haidt, *The Righteous Mind: Why Good People Are Divided by Politics and Religion* (New York: Pantheon, 2012), 282.

6. David Koyzis, *Political Visions and Illusions* (Downers Grove: InterVarsity, 2003), 60–61.

7. Ibid., 63–64.

8. David Boaz, *Libertarianism* (New York: Free Press, 1997), 28.

9. Murray N. Rothbard, *For a New Liberty: The Libertarian Manifesto*, rev. ed. (New York: Collier, 1978), 46.

10. David Boaz, *Libertarianism* (New York: Free Press, 1997), 57.

11. Murray N. Rothbard, *For a New Liberty: The Libertarian Manifesto*, rev. ed. (New York: Collier, 1978), 23.

12. Nancy Love, *Dogmas and Dreams* (Washington, DC: CQ Press, 2006), 7.

13. Michael J. Sandel, *What Money Can't Buy: The Moral Limits of Markets* (Farrar, Straus and Giroux, 2012), 9–11, 47–51, 113–14, 125–27; Nicole Gelinas, "Review of *What Money Can't Buy: The Moral Limits of Markets*," in *City Journal* (May 2012), http://www.city-journal.org/2012/bc0511ng.html.

14. Jonathan Edwards, *Sermons and Discourses, 1730–1733*, ed. Mark Valeri, in *Works of Jonathan Edwards*, ed. Harry S. Stout (New Haven, CT: Yale University Press, 1999), 17: 403.

15. Isaac Backus, *An Appeal to the Public for Religious Liberty* (Boston: John Boyle, 1773), 8.

16. David Koyzis, *Political Visions and Illusions* (Downers Grove: InterVarsity, 2003), 126; Robert P. Kraynak, *Christian Faith and Modern Democracy: God and Politics in the Fallen World* (Notre Dame, IN: University of Notre Dame Press, 2001), 25.

17. Mark A. Noll, *America's God: From Jonathan Edwards to Abraham Lincoln* (New York: Oxford University Press, 2002), 54.

18. John Cotton quoted in *A Source Book in American History to 1787*, ed. Willis Mason West (Boston: Allyn and Bacon, 1913), 204; Robert Kraynak, *Christian Faith and Modern Democracy* (Notre Dame, IN: University of Notre Dame Press, 2001), 67.

19. Kraynak, 124–27.

20. Hugh Helco, *Christianity and American Democracy* (Cambridge, MA: Harvard, 2007), 7.

21. Mark Noll, *America's God* (New York: Oxford University Press, 2002), 57–58; Helco, 8, 13.

22. Noll, 54.

23. Ibid., 57.

24. Helco, 13.

25. C. S. Lewis, *The Weight of Glory* (New York: Macmillan Company, 1949), 113.

26. C. S. Lewis, *Present Concerns* (New York: Houghton Mifflin Harcourt, 1987), 18.

27. *Inaugural Addresses of the Presidents of the United States* (Bedford, MA: Applewood Books, 2009), 2:182.

28. Mark Henrie, "War Without End," *First Things* (February 2013): 47.

29. Summary based on David Koyzis, *Political Visions and Illusions* (Downers Grove: InterVarsity, 2003), ch. 6;

Nancy Love, *Understanding Dogmas and Dreams* (Washington, DC: CQ Press, 2006), ch. 4; R. N. Berki, *Socialism* (London: Dent, 1975); Joshua Muravchik, *Heaven on Earth: The Rise and Fall of Socialism* (New York: Encounter Books, 2003).

30. Nancy Love, *Understanding Dogmas and Dreams* (Washington, DC: CQ Press, 2006), 89.

31. Analysis largely based on David Koyzis, *Political Visions and Illusions* (Downers Grove: InterVarsity, 2003), ch. 6.

32. H. Evan Runner quoted in David Koyzis, *Political Visions and Illusions* (Downers Grove: InterVarsity, 2003), 93.

33. See Melvin J. Thorne, *American Conservative Thought Since World War II: The Core Ideas* (New York: Greenwood, 1990), 11–13; Ethan Fishman and Kenneth Deutsch, *The Dilemmas of American Conservatism* (Lexington, KY: University Press of Kentucky: 2010), 2–4; Irving Kristol, "American Conservatism 1945–1995," *Public Interest* 121 (Fall 1995): 80–89.

34. Edmund Burke, *The Works of the Right Honourable Edmund Burke*, 5th ed. (London: George Bell and Sons,1886), 2:555.

Chapter 18: The Goal of Government

1. Hugh Heclo, *Christianity and American Democracy* (Cambridge, MA: Harvard, 2007), 20.

2. Ronald Beiner, *Civil Religion: A Dialogue in the History of Political Philosophy* (New York: Cambridge University Press, 2011), 1.

3. Ross Douthat, *Bad Religion* (New York: Free Press, 2012), 6–8.

4. Gregg L. Frazer, *The Religious Beliefs of America's Founders: Reason, Revelation, and Revolution, American Political Thought*, eds. Wilson Carey McWilliams and Lance Banning (Lawrence, KS: University Press of Kansas, 2012), 16–17, 227–31.

5. Hunter Baker, *The End of Secularism* (Wheaton: Crossway, 2009), 124.

6. This section draws on ibid.; Greg Forster's *Starting with Locke* (New York: Bloomsbury Academic, 2011) and *The Contested Public Square* (Downers Grove, IL: IVP Academic, 2008); and Steven Smith's *Disenchantment of Secular Discourse* (Cambridge, MA: Harvard University Press, 2010).

7. Ronald Dworkin et al., "Assisted Suicide: The Philosophers' Brief," *New York Review of Books* (website), March 27, 1997.

8. Steven D. Smith, *Disenchantment of Secular Discourse* (Cambridge, MA: Harvard University Press, 2010), 53–59.

9. Ronald Dworkin, *Life's Dominion: An Argument About Abortion, Euthanasia, and Individual Freedom* (New York: Knopf, 1993), 13, 88.

10. John Locke, *Second Treatise of Government* (Seaside, OR: Watchmaker Publishing, 2011), 9.

11. Michael J. Sandel, *Justice: What's the Right Thing to Do?* (New York: Farrar, Straus and Giroux, 2009), 243.

12. See Daniel Walker Howe, *What Hath God Wrought: The Transformation of America, 1815–1848* (New York: Oxford University Press, 2009), 349–51.

13. Facebook.

14. Alexander Solzhenitsyn, *The Gulag Archipelago, 1918–1956: An Experiment in Literary Investigation* (New York: Collins Harvill, 1986), 312.

15. Greg Bahnsen, *By This Standard: The Authority of God's Law Today* (Nacogdoches, TX: Covenant Media Press, 2008), 3–6.

16. Ibid., 4.

17. Edwin C. Darden, "The Law Trends Toward Transgender Students," *Phi Delta Kappan* (October 2014):76–77.

18. See Greg Forster, *The Contested Public Square* (Downers Grove, IL: IVP Academic, 2008).

19. See D. A. Carson, *The Intolerance of Tolerance* (Grand Rapids: Eerdmans, 2012).

20. David Koyzis, *Political Visions and Illusions* (Downers Grove: InterVarsity, 2003), 78.

21. See Edward M. Panosian, "A Church Historical View of a Christian's Responsibility Before Caesar," in *The Providence of God in History* (Greenville, SC: Bob Jones University Press, 1996), 27–35.

22. Martin Luther, *Luther's Works*, ed. Walther Brandt (Philadelphia: Fortress, 1962), 45:62–64; cf. William Tyndale, *The Obedience of the Christian Man* (New York: Penguin Classics, 2000).

23. Justin Martyr, *First Apology*, chs. 11, 12, 17.

24. David W. Hall, *The Genevan Reformation and the American Founding* (New York: Lexington, 2003), 191, 194.

25. Winthrop S. Hudson, "John Locke: Heir of Puritan Political Theorists," in *Calvinism and the Political Order* (Philadelphia: Westminster, 1965), 108, 113; Greg Forster, *Starting with Locke* (New York: Bloomsbury Academic, 2011), loc. 1661.

26. Greg Forster, *Starting with Locke* (New York: Bloomsbury Academic, 2011), loc. 1661; Alan Ryan, *On Politics* (Liveright, 2012), 139–40.

27. Edward M. Panosian, *The Providence of God in History* (Greenville, SC: Bob Jones University Press, 1996), 4.

Chapter 19: Science Is Something God Created Humans to Do

1. *New Oxford American Dictionary*, s.v. "scientism."

2. Richard Dawkins, Richard Dawkins Foundation for Reason and Science (website), http://old.richarddawkins.net/quotes?page=4.

3. Neil deGrasse Tyson, *Cosmos: A Spacetime Odyssey* (DVD) (Los Angeles: 20th Century Fox, 2014), episode 1.

4. Lawrence Principe, *The Scientific Revolution: A Very Short Introduction* (New York: Oxford University Press, 2011), 37.

5. Ibid.

6. Ibid., 57.

7. Donald Petcher and Tim Morris, "Well Done, Good and Faithful Scientific Servant," in *Science and Grace: God's Reign in the Natural Sciences* (Wheaton: Crossway, 2006), 243–78.

8. "Fierce Curiosity About the Fundamental Nature of Things," Milliken, http://www.milliken.com/en-us/Innovation/Pages/innovation-deep-science.aspx.

9. Alvin Plantinga, *Where the Conflict Really Lies: Science, Religion, and Naturalism* (New York: Oxford University Press, 2011), ix.

10. Lesslie Newbigin, "Can the West Be Converted?" *Princeton Seminary Bulletin* 6 (1985): 32–33.

11. Ibid, 33.

12. Lawrence Principe, *The Scientific Revolution: A Very Short Introduction* (New York: Oxford University Press, 2011), 19.

13. Vern Poythress, *Redeeming Science: A God-Centered Approach* (Wheaton: Crossway, 2006), 28.

14. Rob Dunn, "Painting with Penicillin: Alexander Fleming's Germ Art," Smithsonian (website), July 11, 2010.

15. Prince Philip, as reported by Deutche Presse-Agentur, August 1988, quoted in "His Royal Virus," *American Almanac*, August 25, 1997.

16. Paul Davies, "Taking Science on Faith," *New York Times* (website), November 24, 2007.

17. Ibid.

18. Ibid.

19. Ibid.

20. "Armstrong 'Got Moon Quote Right,'" *BBC News* (website), October 2, 2006.

21. Karen Kaplan, "Did Neil Armstrong Really Say, 'That's One Small Step for a Man'?" *Los Angeles Times* (website), June 5, 2013.

22. Gene Cernan, *In the Shadow of the Moon* (DVD) (Los Angeles: Mirage Productions, 2008), 1:30:00.

23. Chris Krycho, "Speak the Truth in Beauty: A Review of *Echoes of Eden*," Mere Orthodoxy (website), February 11, 2015.

24. Paul Spencer Sochaczewski, *An Inordinate Fondness for Beetles* (Singapore: Editions Didier Millet, 2012), 195.

25. *Owls: Silent Hunters* (video), Incredible Nature Birds Documentary, World of Nature, 2014, https://www.youtube.com/watch?v=19DfrkRECDY.

26. David C. McClelland, *The Achieving Society* (New York: Free Press, 1961).

27. Donald Petcher and Tim Morris, "Well Done, Good and Faithful Scientific Servant," in *Science and Grace: God's Reign in the Natural Sciences* (Wheaton: Crossway, 2006), 6.

28. Duane A. Garrett, *Proverbs, Ecclesiastes, Song of Songs*, New American Commentary, ed. E. Ray Clendenen (Nashville: Broadman, 1993), 108.

29. Thomas Kuhn, *The Structure of Scientific Revolutions* (1962; repr., Chicago: University of Chicago Press, 2012), 17–18.

30. Vern S. Poythress, "Three Modern Myths in Interpreting Genesis 1," *Westminster Theological Journal* 76 (2014): 321–50.

31. Thomas Kuhn, *The Structure of Scientific Revolutions* (1962; repr., Chicago: University of Chicago Press, 2012), 10.

32. Buckminster Fuller, *Critical Path* (New York: St. Martin's Press, 1982).

33. David Russell Schilling, "Knowledge Doubling Every 12 Months, Soon to Be Every 12 Hours," *Industry Tap into News*, April 19, 2013, http://www.industrytap.com/knowledge-doubling-every-12-months-soon-to-be-every-12-hours/3950.

34. "Prototype Kilogram 20, Replica," National Institute of Standards and Technology, http://museum.nist.gov/object.asp?ObjID=38.

35. "History of the Meter," Wikipedia, http://en.wikipedia.org/wiki/History_of_the_metre#International_prototype_metre.

36. Terrance Egolf and Rachel Santopietro, *Earth Science*, 4th ed. (Greenville, SC: BJU Press, 2012), 11.

Chapter 20: Fallen Science

1. *Encyclopædia Britannica Online*, s.v. "Émile Coué."

2. National Institute on Aging, "Prevalence of Alzheimer's Disease," *2011–2012 Alzheimer's Disease Progress Report*, National Institutes of Health (website).

3. Hugh Lofting, *The Story of Doctor Dolittle* (1920; repr., Mineola, NY: Dover Publications, 1997), 39.

4. "Bill Nye: Creationism Is Not Appropriate for Children" (video), August 23, 2012, https://www.youtube.com/watch?v=gHbYJfwFgOU.

5. *CBS News*, *60 Minutes*, and *Vanity Fair*. CBS News/60 Minutes/Vanity Fair National Survey, January 2, 2013. ICPSR34992-v1. Ann Arbor, MI: Inter-university Consortium for Political and Social Research [distributor], 2014-03-20.

6. "83% Say Measles Vaccine Is Safe for Healthy Children: No Partisan Differences in Views of Vaccine Safety," Pew Research Center (website), February 9, 2015.

7. Richard Dawkins, *The Magic of Reality: How We Know What's Really True* (New York: Free Press, 2011), 19.

8. Kurt Vonnegut, *Fates Worse than Death* (New York: G. P. Putnam's Sons, 1991), 117–18.

9. Ibid., 118.

10. Ibid.

11. Richard N. Williams, *Scientism: The New Orthodoxy* (New York: Bloomsbury Academic), 6.

12. "Metaphysical Naturalism," Wikipedia, http://en.wiki pedia.org/wiki/Metaphysical_naturalism.

13. http://www.quora.com/Religion-and-Politics/Why-do-some-people-think-Its-in-the-Bible-is-a-valid-argument/answer/Mark-Ward-11/comment/9138897

14. Ibid.

15. Mark Regnerus, "New Research on Same-Sex Households Reveals Kids Do Best with Mom and Dad," Public Discourse (website), February 10, 2015.

16. Steven Pinker, "Science Is Not Your Enemy," *New Republic* (website), August 6, 2013.

17. Robert Ingersoll, *The Works of Robert G. Ingersoll: Lectures* (New York: Dresden Publishing, 1915), 290–91.

18. Richard Dawkins, *The Blind Watchmaker* (New York: Norton, 1986), 1.

19. Alvin Plantinga, *Where the Conflict Really Lies: Science, Religion, and Naturalism* (New York: Oxford University Press, 2011), ix–x.

20. "Missa Charles Darwin," Gregory W. Brown (website), http://www.gregorywbrown.com/missa-charles-darwin/.

21. Gregory W. Brown quoted in Jan McCoy Ebbets, "We Sing the Theory of Evolution," *Insight*, April 15, 2011, 1.

22. Charles Darwin, *The Descent of Man and Selection in Relation to Sex* (London: John Murray, 1882), 2.

23. Charles Darwin, *The Origin of Species* (New York: P. F. Collier and Son Company, 1909), 297.

24. "Terence McKenna Pokes Fun at the 'Big Bang' Theory" (video), https://www.youtube.com/watch?v=BWv02kYyvo4.

25. Terence McKenna, quoted in Chris Twomey, "Words with the Sham Man," Eye Weekly (website), July 7, 1994.

26. "Terence McKenna Pokes Fun at the 'Big Bang' Theory" (video), https://www.youtube.com/watch?v=BWv02kYyvo4.

27. Ibid.

28. *New Oxford American Dictionary*, s.v. "myth."

29. https://twitter.com/sapinker/status/258350644979695616.

30. Jennifer Schuessler, "An Author Attracts Unlikely Allies," *New York Times* (website), February 6, 2013.

31. Alva Noë, "Are the Mind and Life Natural?" NPR (blog), October 12, 2012.

32. "Terence McKenna Pokes Fun at the 'Big Bang' Theory" (video), https://www.youtube.com/watch?v=BWv02kYyvo4.

33. Elizabeth Kolbert, "The Big Question: What's the Point?" *Intelligent Life* (website), September/October 2014.

34. Charles Darwin, *The Origin of Species* (New York: P. F. Collier and Son Company, 1909), 529.

35. Ibid.

36. Lawrence Krauss quoted in Cara Santa Maria, "Lawrence Krauss: 'A Universe from Nothing,'" *Huffington Post* (website), July 18, 2012.

37. Ibid.

38. Thomas Nagel, *Mind and Cosmos: Why the Materialist Neo-Darwinian Conception of Nature Is Almost Certainly False* (New York: Oxford University Press, 2012), 12.

39. Julian Barnes, *Nothing to Be Frightened Of* (New York: Knopf, 2008), 1.

40. "Neil deGrasse Tyson on the New *Cosmos*" (video), https://www.youtube.com/watch?v=da3G2ezt9R0.

41. Steven Pinker, "Science Is Not Your Enemy," *New Republic* (website), August 6, 2013.

42. Rebecca Grambo, *Eagles* (Stillwater, MN: Voygeur Press, 2003), 32.

43. Kurt Vonnegut, *Breakfast of Champions* (1973; repr., New York: Dial Press, 1999), 266, 270.

44. John Gray, "What Scares the New Atheists," *The Guardian* (website), March 3, 2015.

45. Ibid.

46. Ibid.

47. Ibid.

48. N. D. Wilson, *Death by Living: Life Is Meant to Be Spent* (Nashville: Thomas Nelson, 2013), 20.

49. See page 11.

50. Quoted in Sabrina Tavernise, "Warning: That Tan Could Be Hazardous," *New York Times* (website), January 10, 2015.

51. "Take Me to Church," Wikipedia, http://en.wikipedia.org/wiki/Take_Me_to_Church.

52. Andrew Hozier Byrne, "Take Me to Church," https://www.musixmatch.com, © The Evolving Music Company.

53. "Hozier Is 'Thrilled' to Be Performing at the Grammys," Grammy.com (video), February 5, 2015.

54. N. D. Wilson, *Death by Living: Life Is Meant to Be Spent* (Nashville: Thomas Nelson, 2013), 20.

55. Steven Pinker, "Science Is Not Your Enemy," *New Republic* (website), August 6, 2013.

56. Richard Dawkins, *The God Delusion* (New York: Houghton Mifflin Harcourt, 2006), 266.

57. John Gray, "What Scares the New Atheists," *The Guardian* (website), March 3, 2015.

58. "Documentary: John Nash, A Beautiful Mind" (video), https://www.youtube.com/watch?v=ctV1C0YpyTU.

59. John Nash, in Mark Samels and Randall MacLowry, "A Brilliant Madness" (transcript), PBS (website).

60. Steven Pinker, "Science Is Not Your Enemy," *New Republic* (website), August 6, 2013.

61. Richard N. Williams, in *Scientism: The New Orthodoxy*, ed. Daniel N. Robinson and Richard N. Williams (New York: Bloomsbury Academic, 2015), 6.

62. Armand Marie Leroi, "One Republic of Learning: Digitizing the Humanities," *New York Times* (website), February 13, 2015.

63. Peter Markie, "Rationalism vs. Empiricism," *Stanford Encyclopedia of Philosophy*, ed. Edward N. Zalta (Spring 2015), http://plato.stanford.edu/archives/spr2015/entries/rationalism-empiricism/.

64. Richard Dawkins, *The Magic of Reality: How We Know What's Really True* (New York: Free Press, 2011), 18.

65. "United in Godlessness: The 2012 Reason Rally" (video), https://www.youtube.com/watch?v=4iiXobOUtEU.

66. Ibid.

67. Ibid.

68. Ibid.

69. "Liberals Are Stifling Intellectual Diversity on Campus" (debate), Intelligence Squared U.S., http://www.intelligencesquaredus.org/images/debates/past/transcripts/022415%20Liberal%20Stifling.pdf.

70. Ibid.

71. Stanley Fish, "Citing Chapter and Verse: Which Scripture Is the Right One?" *New York Times* (blog), March 26, 2012.

72. Jonathan Haidt, *The Righteous Mind: Why Good People Are Divided by Politics and Religion* (New York: Vintage Books, 2013), 292–317.

73. Ibid., 224–25.

74. C. S. Lewis, *The Weight of Glory and Other Addresses* (1949; repr., New York: HarperCollins, 1980), 135.

75. Ibid., 134–35.

76. Ibid., 135.

77. Ibid., 135–36.

78. Francis Beckwith, "What's Upstairs," *First Things* (website), November 2004.

79. John Nash, in Mark Samels and Randall MacLowry, "A Brilliant Madness" (transcript), PBS (website).

80. Walter Hooper, ed., *The Collected Letters of C. S. Lewis* (New York: HarperCollins, 2004), 1:977.

81. Layton Talbert, "The Trustworthiness of God's Words: Why It's Important to God" (Sunday school class), Mount Calvary Baptist Church, Greenville, South Carolina, January 11, 2015, http://www.mountcalvarybaptist.org/Pages/Sermons/Default.aspx?SpeakerID=393.

Chapter 21: Reading Genesis and Doing Science

1. David Brooks, "I Am Not Charlie Hebdo," *New York Times* (website), January 8, 2015.

2. David Brooks, "The Prodigal Sons," *New York Times* (website), February 17, 2014.

3. Christopher Beam, "A Reasonable Man," *New York* magazine (website), July 4, 2010.

4. George Lakoff and Mark Johnson, *Metaphors We Live By* (London: University of Chicago Press, 2003), 7–8.

5. George Lakoff and Mark Johnson, *Metaphors We Live By* (Chicago: University of Chicago Press, 1980), 107–8.

6. Timothy H. Heaton, "Review of *Mapping the Origins Debate*," *Reports of the National Center for Science Education*, November/December 2013, 1–2.

7. Gerald Rau, *Mapping the Origins Debate: Six Models of the Beginning of Everything* (Downers Grove, IL: IVP Academic, 2013), 28.

8. Ibid., 30.

9. Ibid., 38.

10. Ibid., 41 (adapted from Rau's chart).

11. Stephen Hawking quoted in Alison George, "Stephen Hawking's Bedtime Stories," Signs of the Times (website), March 19, 2009.

12. Stephen Hawking, *A Brief History of Time* (New York: Bantam, 1998), 191.

13. Gerald Rau, *Mapping the Origins Debate* (Downers Grove, IL: IVP Academic, 2013), 189.

14. Georgia M. Green, *Pragmatics and Natural Language Understanding* (New York: Routledge, 2012), 96–97.

15. Peter Enns, *The Evolution of Adam: What the Bible Does and Doesn't Say About Human Origins* (Ada, MI: Brazos Press, 2012), xvi.

16. Ibid., xvii–xviii.

17. John H. Walton, *The Lost World of Adam and Eve: Genesis 2–3 and the Human Origins Debate* (Downers Grove, IL: InterVarsity Press, 2015), 50.

18. Raymond C. Van Leeuwen, "ארב," in *New International Dictionary of Old Testament Theology and Exegesis*, ed. Willem VanGemeren (Grand Rapids: Zondervan, 1997), 1:731; Andrew Steinmann, "Lost World of Genesis One: John H. Walton, American Evangelicals and Creation," *Lutheran Education Journal*, May 9, 2012.

19. John H. Walton, *The Lost World of Genesis One: Ancient Cosmology and the Origins Debate* (Downers Grove, IL: InterVarsity Press, 2010), 181–82.

20. Richard E. Averbeck, "A Literary Day, Inter-Textual, and Contextual Reading of Genesis 1-2," in *Reading Genesis 1-2: An Evangelical Conversation*, ed. J. Daryl Charles (Peabody, MA: Hendrickson, 2013), 13.

21. Peter Enns, *The Evolution of Adam: What the Bible Does and Doesn't Say About Human Origins* (Ada, MI: Brazos Press, 2012), 139.

22. Ibid., 95.

23. Augustine of Hippo, "Reply to Faustus the Manichaean," in *St. Augustine: The Writings Against the Manichaeans and Against the Donatists*, ed. Philip Schaff, trans. Richard Stothert (Buffalo, NY: Christian Literature Company, 1887), 4:178.

24. Stephen Wellum, "Debating the Historicity of Adam: Does It Matter?" *Southern Baptist Journal of Theology* 15, no.1 (2011):3.

25. "Did Death Occur Before the Fall?" BioLogos (website), July 9, 2012.

26. Michael Wines, "Though Scorned by Colleagues, a Climate-Change Skeptic Is Unbowed," *New York Times* (website), July 15, 2014.

27. M. J. Stephey, "What Came Before the Big Bang?" *Time* (website), August 13, 2009.

28. "Bill Nye Debates Ken Ham" (video), February 4, 2014, https://www.youtube.com/watch?v=z6kgvhG3AkI.

29. Chandler Burr, "The Geophysics of God," *U.S. News & World Report*, June 16, 1997, 55–58.

30. Robert L. Hill, et al., "Photometric Study of the Solar Type Pre-Contact Binary, V2421 Cygni," *American Astronomical Society Meeting Abstracts* 222 (June 2013): 115.

31. "Steve Figard" (faculty information page), Bob Jones University (website).

32. "Dr John Hartnett," Creation Ministries International (website).

33. "Mark F. Horstemeyer" (faculty information page), Mississippi State University (website).

34. "D. Russell Humphreys, Ph.D.," Creation Ministries International (website).

35. Todd Purdum, "High Priest of the Pasture," *New York Times* (website), May 1, 2005.

36. Ibid.

37. "Dr John Sanford, Ph.D.," Creation Ministries International (website).

38. Richard Dawkins, "Sadly, an Honest Creationist," Scepsis (website), 2005.

39. "Bill Nye: Creationism Is Not Appropriate for Children" (video), August 23, 2012, https://www.youtube.com/watch?v=gHbYJfwFgOU.

40. Peter Harrison, *The Territories of Science and Religion* (Chicago: University of Chicago Press, 2015), 22.

41. James Copeland, ed., *The London Medical Repository, Monthly Journal, and Review* (London: Thomas and George Underwood, 1825), 258.

42. Blaire Briody, "Real Genius: Eight Brilliant Inventors Still in High School," *Popular Science* (website), August 24, 2009.

43. John Ioannidis, "Why Most Published Research Findings Are False," PLOS Medicine (website), August 30, 2005.

Chapter 22: Foundations for History

1. Augustine, *On Genesis*, ed. John E. Rotelle, trans. Edmund Hill (Hyde Park, NY: New City Press, 2006), 266–77.

2. Alasdair MacIntyre, *After Virtue: A Study in Moral Theory*, 3rd ed. (Notre Dame, IN: University of Notre Dame Press, 2007), 216.

3. See T. D. Bernard, *The Progress of Doctrine in the New Testament* (London: Macmillan, 1864), 154, 157–58; Albert M. Wolters, *Creation Regained: Biblical Basics for a Reformational Worldview* (Grand Rapids: Eerdmans, 2005), 40–41.

4. George Santayana, *The Life of Reason or the Phases of Human Progress* (New York: Charles Scribner's Sons, 1906), 284.

5. Geerhardus Vos, *Redemptive History and Biblical Interpretation* (Phillipsburg, NJ: P&R, 1980), 7–8.

6. C. S. Lewis, "Introduction," in Athanasius, *On the Incarnation* (1944; repr., Crestwood, NY: St. Vladimir's Seminary Press, 1996), 5.

7. David Bebbington, *Patterns in History: A Christian Perspective on Historical Thought* (Vancouver: Regent College Publishing, 1990), 21–22.

8. Charles Murray, *Human Accomplishment: The Pursuit of Excellence in the Arts and Sciences, 800 B.C. to 1950* (New York: Perennial, 2004), xviii–xix.

9. Carl Trueman, *Histories and Fallacies: Problems Faced in the Writing of History* (Wheaton: Crossway, 2010), 106.

10. Timothy Larsen, *Crisis of Doubt: Honest Faith in Nineteenth-Century England* (New York: Oxford University Press, 2006), 1.

11. John Hall, ed., *Forty Years' Familiar Letters of James W. Alexander* (New York: Charles Scribner, 1870), 2:74.

12. Virginia Trist correspondence, *Nicholas Philip Trist Papers, 1765–1903* from the Southern Historical Collection, Wilson Library, University of North Carolina at Chapel Hill, collection 02104, folder 225, scan 24, http://dc.lib.unc.edu/cdm/singleitem/collection/02104/id/56196.

13. Daniel Little, "Philosophy of History," *Stanford Encyclopedia of Philosophy* (website), ed. Edward N. Zalta (Winter 2012).

14. Daniel Walker Howe, *What Hath God Wrought: The Transformation of America, 1815–1848*, Oxford History of

the United States, ed. David M. Kennedy (New York: Oxford University Press, 2007), 704–5.

15. Allen C. Guelzo, *Gettysburg: The Last Invasion* (New York: Knopf, 2013), xii.

16. Kenneth M. Stampp, *The Causes of the Civil War* (Englewood Cliffs, NJ: Prentice-Hall, 1965).

17. Orlando Figes, *The Crimean War: A History* (New York: Metropolitan, 2010), 1–60.

18. Gordon S. Wood, *Empire of Liberty: A History of the Early Republic, 1789–1815* (New York: Oxford University Press, 2009), 587–88.

Chapter 23: Fallen History

1. Armand Marie Leroi, "One Republic of Learning: Digitizing the Humanities," *New York Times* (website), February 13, 2015.

2. George M. Marsden, "What Difference Might Christian Perspectives Make?" in *History and the Christian Historian*, ed. Ronald A. Wells (Grand Rapids: Eerdmans, 1998), 17.

3. "*Guns, Germs, and Steel*," Wikipedia, http://en.wikipedia.org/wiki/Guns,_Germs,_and_Steel.

4. William H. McNeill, review of *Guns, Germs, and Steel* in *New York Review of Books* (website), June 26, 1997.

5. George M. Marsden, "What Difference Might Christian Perspectives Make?" in *History and the Christian Historian*, ed. Ronald A. Wells (Grand Rapids: Eerdmans, 1998), 17.

6. Herbert Butterfield, *The Whig Interpretation of History* (London: G. Bell and Sons, 1931), 11.

7. Ibid., v.

8. Gregg L. Frazer, *The Religious Beliefs of America's Founders: Reason, Revelation, and Revolution* (University Press of Kansas, 2012), 19–20.

9. David Barton, Liberty University Convocation (video, 2:30–3:09), September 9, 2011, http://youtube.com/watch?v=dybHrSi4Now.

10. Jean-François Lyotard, "The Postmodern Condition," in *The Postmodern History Reader*, ed. Keith Jenkins (New York: Routledge, 1997), 36.

11. Stanley Fish, *There's No Such Thing as Free Speech* (New York: Oxford University Press, 1994), 7–8.

12. Keith Jenkins, ed., *The Postmodern History Reader* (New York: Routledge, 1997), 1–30.

13. Alun Munslow, *Deconstructing History* (New York: Routledge, 1997), 190.

14. Carl R. Trueman, *Histories and Fallacies: Problems Faced in the Writing of History* (Wheaton: Crossway, 2010), 27–28.

15. For example, see Ian Millhiser, "The Supreme Court Just Blew a Gaping Hole in the Wall of Separation Between Church and State," ThinkProgress (website), May 5, 2014.

16. Carl R. Trueman, *Histories and Fallacies* (Wheaton: Crossway, 2010), 53, fn 16.

17. Gordon S. Wood, *The Purpose of the Past: Reflections on the Uses of History* (New York: Penguin, 2008), 5–6.

18. Robert E. Brown, *Charles Beard and the Constitution: A Critical Analysis of "An Economic Interpretation of the Constitution"* (Princeton, NJ: Princeton University Press, 1956), 196; cf. 195–200.

19. Cf. Mark T. Gilderhus, *History and Historians: A Historiographical Introduction*, 5th ed. (Upper Saddle River, NJ: Prentice Hall, 2003), 56–60.

20. Gordon S. Wood, *The Purpose of the Past* (New York: Penguin, 2008), 281, 286–87.

21. Ibid., 292.

22. Timothy Larsen, *Crisis of Doubt: Honest Faith in Nineteenth-Century England* (New York: Oxford University Press, 2006), 113.

23. Ibid., 122.

24. Ibid., 123.

25. Ibid., 124.

26. Ibid., 1–9.

27. Ibid., 5; cf. 2–5.

28. A. N. Wilson quoted in ibid., 245.

29. Ibid., 5.

30. Ibid., 1.

31. Ibid., 11–13.

32. Ibid., 15–17, 242–43.

33. David Cook, *Understanding Jihad* (Berkeley and Los Angeles: University of California Press, 2005).

34. Ibid.

Chapter 24: History in Light of Redemption

1. *Oxford Dictionary of National Biography*, s.v. "Samuel Johnson."

2. James Boswell, *The Life of Samuel Johnson, LL.D.*, (Philadelphia: Claxton, Remsen, and Haffelfinger, 1878), 1:375.

3. Carl R. Trueman, *Histories and Fallacies: Problems Faced in the Writing of History* (Wheaton: Crossway, 2010), 17.

4. From Charles Barrett, ed., *New Testament Background: Selected Documents*, rev. ed. (New York: HarperOne, 1995), 28 [translation slightly adapted].

5. Mark Ward Sr., *Deadly Documents: Technical Communication, Organizational Discourse, and the Holocaust* (Amityville, NY: Baywood Publishing, 2014).

6. Andreas J. Köstenberger, *Excellence: The Character of God and the Pursuit of Scholarly Virtue* (Wheaton: Crossway, 2011), 33–54.

7. Carl Trueman, *Histories and Fallacies* (Wheaton: Crossway, 2010), 6.

8. Ibid., 107.

9. Timothy Larsen, *Crisis of Doubt: Honest Faith in Nineteenth-Century England* (New York: Oxford University Press, 2006).

10. Andrea Palpant Dilley, "The Surprising Discovery about Those Colonialist, Proselytizing Missionaries," *Christianity Today* (website), January 8, 2014.

11. Ibid.

12. Carl Trueman, *Histories and Fallacies* (Wheaton: Crossway, 2010), 99.

13. C. S. Lewis, "Introduction," in Athanasius, *On the Incarnation* (1944; repr., Crestwood, NY: St. Vladimir's Seminary Press, 1996), 5.

14. Allen C. Guelzo, *Fateful Lightning: A New History of the Civil War and Reconstruction* (New York: Oxford University Press, 2012), 375.

15. Carl Trueman, *Histories and Fallacies* (Wheaton: Crossway, 2010), 166–67.

16. John Fea, *Why Study History? Reflecting on the Importance of the Past* (Grand Rapids: Baker, 2013), 76–78.

17. Mark Noll quoted in Tim Stafford, "Whatever Happened to Christian History?" *Christianity Today* (website), April 2, 2001.

18. C. S. Lewis, "Historicism," in *God, History, and Historians: An Anthology of Modern Christian Views of History*, ed. C. T. McIntire (New York: Oxford University Press, 1977), 226–27.

19. James McDermott, *England and the Spanish Armada: The Necessary Quarrel* (New Haven, CT: Yale University Press, 2005), xii.

20. Colin Martin and Geoffrey Parker, *The Spanish Armada*, rev. ed. (New York: Palgrave, 1999), 184–205.

Chapter 25: Truth, Goodness, and Beauty

1. Gene Weingarten, "Pearls Before Breakfast," *Washington Post Magazine*, April 8, 2007.

2. Ibid.

3. George Robinson, "Violinist Joshua Bell Walks in the Footsteps of Masters," *Jewish Journal*, October 12, 2006.

4. Gene Weingarten, "Pearls Before Breakfast," *Washington Post Magazine*, April 8, 2007.

5. Blair Howell, "Concert Preview: Music of Violinist Joshua Bell 'Feeds Both Brain and Heart,'" *Deseret News*, November 9, 2013.

6. Bob Faw, "Interview with Joshua Bell," *Religion & Ethics Newsweekly*, October 10, 2014, www.pbs.org.

7. Paul Munson and Joshua Farris Drake, *Art and Music: A Student's Guide*, ed. David Dockery (Wheaton: Crossway, 2014), 83.

8. Ronald Horton, "Aesthetics" (class lecture), Bob Jones University, September 1, 2011.

9. James K. Smith, *How (Not) to Be Secular: Reading Charles Taylor* (Grand Rapids: Eerdmans, 2014), 22–23.

10. Paul Munson and Joshua Farris Drake, *Art and Music: A Student's Guide*, ed. David Dockery (Wheaton: Crossway, 2014), 22.

11. Kenneth Myers, *Mars Hill Audio* 78, audio journal, January/February 2006 (00:08–00:57).

12. J. R. R. Tolkien, "On Fairy Stories," in *Tree and Leaf* (Boston: Houghton Mifflin, 1965), 37.

13. Ibid., 71.

14. Quoted in James K. Smith, *How (Not) to Be Secular: Reading Charles Taylor* (Grand Rapids: Eerdmans, 2014), 28.

15. Ibid., 22.

16. Ibid., 29.

17. Ibid., 30.

18. Richard N. Williams and Daniel N. Robinson, *Scientism: The New Orthodoxy* (New York: Bloomsbury Academic, 2014), 6.

19. Robert C. Solomon and Kathleen M. Higgins, *A Short History of Philosophy* (New York: Oxford University Press, 1996), 300.

20. Gary Gutting, "Does Evolution Explain Religious Beliefs?" *New York Times* (website), July 8, 2014.

21. Richard Rorty, *Achieving Our Country: Leftist Thought in Twentieth-Century America* (Cambridge, MA: Harvard University Press, 1998), 16.

22. C. S. Lewis, *Mere Christianity* (San Francisco: HarperSanFrancisco, 2009), 5.

23. Ibid.

24. James K. Smith, *How (Not) to Be Secular: Reading Charles Taylor* (Grand Rapids: Eerdmans, 2014), 36.

25. Stanley Fish, "Boutique Multiculturalism, or Why Liberals Are Incapable of Thinking About Hate Speech," *Critical Inquiry* 23 (Winter 1997): 383–84.

26. Gary Gutting, "Does Evolution Explain Religious Beliefs?" *New York Times* (website), July 8, 2014.

27. C. S. Lewis, *Mere Christianity* (San Francisco: HarperSanFrancisco, 2009), 9–10.

28. James K. Smith, *How (Not) to Be Secular: Reading Charles Taylor* (Grand Rapids: Eerdmans, 2014), 61.

29. R. W. Hepburn, "Relativism, ethical," in *The Oxford Companion to Philosophy*, ed. Ted Honderich (New York: Oxford University Press, 1995), 758.

30. C. S. Lewis, *Mere Christianity* (San Francisco: HarperSanFrancisco, 2009), 6.

31. Paul Munson and Joshua Farris Drake, *Art and Music: A Student's Guide*, ed. David Dockery (Wheaton: Crossway, 2014), 15.

32. Roger Scruton, *Beauty: A Very Short Introduction* (New York: Oxford University Press, 2011), 31. [See also Charles Darwin, *The Descent of Man, and Selection in Relation to Sex* (1871; repr., New York: Penguin Classics, 2004), 114–15.]

33. Ibid., 29.

34. Story told by Mike Bullmore, "Feeding on God: Cultivating a Fruitful Life in the Word" (sermon), New Attitude Conference, 2006.

35. John Piper, *The Pleasures of God: Meditations on God's Delight in Being God*, rev. ed. (Colorado Springs: Waterbrook Multnomah, 2000), 86.

36. Roger Scruton, *Beauty: A Very Short Introduction* (New York: Oxford University Press, 2011), 119.

37. Paul Munson and Joshua Farris Drake, *Art and Music: A Student's Guide*, ed. David Dockery (Wheaton: Crossway, 2014), 26.

38. Roger Scruton, *Beauty: A Very Short Introduction* (New York: Oxford University Press, 2011), 6.

39. "Tate Egg Protester Faces Life Ban," BBC News (website), December 12, 2001; Martin Creed, "Work No. 227," Museum of Modern Art, New York, 2000, http://martincreed.com/site/works/work-no-227.

40. Martin Creed, "Work No. 79," 1993, http://martincreed.com/site/works/work-no-79.

41. "Tate Egg Protester Faces Life Ban," BBC News (website), December 12, 2001.

42. Roger Scruton, *Beauty: A Very Short Introduction* (New York: Oxford University Press, 2011), 85.

43. Ibid.

44. Philip Yancey, interview with Steven Curtis Chapman, "Listening In . . . ," Today's Christian Music (website), n.d.

45. Paul Munson and Joshua Farris Drake, *Art and Music: A Student's Guide*, ed. David Dockery (Wheaton: Crossway, 2014), 35.

46. Mark Minnick, "Characteristics of a Christlike Mind" (sermon), Mount Calvary Baptist Church, Greenville, SC, August 25, 2013.

47. Markus Bockmuehl, *The Epistle to the Philippians*, Black's New Testament Commentary (Grand Rapids: Baker Academic, 1998), 253.

48. Gordon D. Fee, *Paul's Letter to the Philippians*, New International Commentary on the New Testament (Grand Rapids: Eerdmans, 1995), 416.

49. Paul Munson and Joshua Farris Drake, *Art and Music: A Student's Guide*, ed. David Dockery (Wheaton: Crossway, 2014), 85.

50. Francis A. Schaeffer, *The Complete Works of Francis A. Schaeffer: A Christian Worldview* (Westchester, IL: Crossway Books, 1982), 5:200.

51. Dana Gioia, "Can Poetry Matter?" *Atlantic Monthly*, May 1991, 94.

52. Carl Sandburg, quoted in Robert Konzelman, *Marquee Ministry* (New York: HarperCollins, 1971), 13.

53. Dana Gioia, "Beauty's Place in the Christian Vision" (chapel sermon), Biola University, La Mirada, CA, February 8, 2012, www.youtube.com/watch?v=xmEbg36_IDY.

54. Ibid.

55. Kenneth Myers, *All God's Children and Blue Suede Shoes: Christians and Popular Culture* (Wheaton: Crossway, 1989), 35.

56. Leonard Bernstein, *The Unanswered Question: Six Talks at Harvard* (DVD), Kultur Video, 2001.

57. Dana Gioia, "Beauty's Place in the Christian Vision" (chapel sermon), Biola University, La Mirada, CA, February 8, 2012, www.youtube.com/watch?v=xmEbg36_IDY.

58. Douglas Wilson, *Wordsmithy: Hot Tips for the Writing Life* (Moscow, ID: Canon Press, 2011), 20.

59. Paul Munson and Joshua Farris Drake, *Art and Music: A Student's Guide*, ed. David Dockery (Wheaton: Crossway, 2014), 40.

60. Dana Gioia, "Beauty's Place in the Christian Vision" (chapel sermon), Biola University, La Mirada, CA, February 8, 2012, www.youtube.com/watch?v=xmEbg36_IDY.

61. Paul Munson and Joshua Farris Drake, *Art and Music: A Student's Guide*, ed. David Dockery (Wheaton: Crossway, 2014), 30.

Chapter 26: The False, the Bad, and the Ugly

1. "*The Hunt of the Unicorn*," Wikipedia, http://en.wikipedia.org/wiki/The_Hunt_of_the_Unicorn (adjusted to 2014 dollars).

2. Bill Maher, *Religulous* (DVD), director Larry Charles, 2008.

3. Barack Obama, *The Audacity of Hope: Thoughts on Reclaiming the American Dream* (New York: Crown, 2006), 350.

4. William Voegeli, "The Redskins and Their Offense," *Claremont Review of Books*, Spring 2014, 17.

5. Leonard Cresswell Ingleby, *Oscar Wilde* (New York: Mitchell Kennerley, 1907), 335.

6. Oscar Wilde, *The Picture of Dorian Gray* (1891; repr., Mineola, NY: Dover Publications, 1993), 16.

7. Ibid., 13.

8. Tom Stoppard, *The Real Thing* (London: Faber & Faber, 1984), 52.

9. Ben Brantley, "A Storytelling Instinct Revels in Horror's Fun," *New York Times* (website), April 11, 2005.

10. John Simon, "Exquisite Corpses," *New York* magazine (website), April 25, 2005.

11. Plato, *Apology* 37e–38a.

12. Mark Minnick, sermon at Mount Calvary Baptist Church, Greenville, South Carolina.

13. Janet Maslin, "The Road Through Hell, Paved with Desperation," *New York Times* (website), September 25, 2006.

14. Nick Schager, "*Courageous*: Subtle as a Chastity Ring," *Village Voice* (website), September 28, 2011.

15. Frank Scheck, "Courageous: Film Review," *Hollywood Reporter* (website), September 30, 2011.

16. Sabrina Rubin Erdely, "A Rape on Campus: A Brutal Assault and Struggle for Justice at UVA," *Rolling Stone* (website), November 19, 2014.

17. Ravi Somaiya, "Magazine's Account of Gang Rape on Virginia Campus Comes Under Scrutiny," *New York Times* (website), December 2, 2014.

18. David Uberti, "The Worst Journalism of 2014," *Columbia Journalism Review* (website), December 22, 2014.

19. R. H. Blythe, quoted in Kenneth Myers, *All God's Children and Blue Suede Shoes: Christians and Popular Culture* (Wheaton: Crossway, 1989), 85.

20. Mark Rothko, in Selden Rodman, *Conversations with Artists* (New York: Capricorn, 1961), 93.

21. Michael Kimmelman, "Rothko's Gloomy Elegance in Retrospect," *New York Times* (website), September 18, 1998.

22. Ibid.

23. Kenneth Myers, *All God's Children and Blue Suede Shoes* (Wheaton: Crossway, 1989), 56.

24. Andy Crouch, *Culture Making: Recovering Our Creative Calling* (Downers Grove, IL: IVP, 2013), 89.

25. Fred Sanders, "They Quit Making Good Music When I Turned 30," *First Things* (blog), October 21, 2009, http://www.firstthings.com/index.php?permalink=blogs&blog=firstthoughts&year=2009&month=10&entry_permalink=they-quit-making-good-music-when-i-turned-30.

26. James Davison Hunter, "The Backdrop of Reality: James Davison Hunter in Conversation with James K. A. Smith," *Comment* (Fall 2013): 37.

27. Andy Crouch, *Culture Making: Recovering Our Creative Calling* (Downers Grove, IL: IVP, 2013), 28.

28. James Davison Hunter, "The Backdrop of Reality: James Davison Hunter in Conversation with James K. A. Smith," *Comment* (Fall 2013): 39.

29. Kenneth Myers, *All God's Children and Blue Suede Shoes* (Wheaton: Crossway, 1989), 114.

30. John Lennon, "Imagine," Chappell Music, 1971.

31. Kenneth Myers, *All God's Children and Blue Suede Shoes* (Wheaton: Crossway, 1989), xiv.

32. Matthew Arnold, *Culture and Anarchy: An Essay in Political and Social Criticism* (1896; repr., New York: Cambridge University Press, 1993), viii.

33. *New Oxford American Dictionary*, s.v. "veg."

34. T. David Gordon, *Why Johnny Can't Sing Hymns* (Phillipsburg, NJ: P&R, 2010), 26.

35. Ernest van den Haag, *Passion and Social Constraint* (New York: Stein and Day, 1963), 332.

36. Kenneth Myers, *All God's Children and Blue Suede Shoes* (Wheaton: Crossway, 1989), xiii.

37. John Gibson Paton, *John G. Paton D.D.: Missionary to the New Hebrides: An Autobiography*, ed. James Paton (London: Hodder and Stoughton, 1891), 218.

38. Kenneth Myers, *All God's Children and Blue Suede Shoes* (Wheaton: Crossway, 1989), 183.

Chapter 27: Creative Cultivators

1. Devdutt Pattanaik, "East vs. West—The Myths That Mystify," Technology, Entertainment, Design (TED) website, November 2009.

2. Kenneth Myers, *All God's Children and Blue Suede Shoes: Christians and Popular Culture* (Wheaton: Crossway, 1989), 183.

3. Makoto Fujimura, *Culture Care: Reconnecting with Beauty for Our Common Life* (New York: International Arts Movement, 2015), 9.

4. Ibid., 18.

5. Ibid., 19.

6. Marshall McLuhan, *Understanding Media: The Extensions of Man* (1964; Cambridge, MA: MIT Press, 1994), 8.

7. Tony Reinke, *Lit! A Christian Guide to Reading Books* (Wheaton: Crossway, 2011), 128.

8. Ibid., 61.

9. Ibid.

10. Maria Wollan, "Rise and Shine: What Kids Around the World Eat for Breakfast," New York Times Magazine (website), October 8, 2014, http://www.nytimes.com/interactive/2014/10/08/magazine/eaters-all-over.html.

11. "Tea-Flavored Toothpaste Is Helping Chinese Brands Edge Out the Competition," Shanghaiist (website), July 29, 2014.

12. Tony Reinke, *Lit! A Christian Guide to Reading Books* (Wheaton: Crossway, 2011), 122.

13. C. S. Lewis, On Stories and Other Essay onLiterature (Orlando, FL: Harcourt, Inc., 1982), 63.

14. Hanna Rosin, "Pop Goes Christianity," *Slate* (website), May 5, 2008.

15. Ibid.

16. Ibid.

17. Ibid.

18. Ibid.

19. Ibid.

20. "Why Create a College and Career Plan?" http://www.mymajors.com.

21. Alan Jacobs, "On Defending Liberal Education," *The New Atlantis* (website), September 25, 2014. Used by permission.

22. Catherine Brahic, "Solar-Powered Sea Slug Harnesses Stolen Plant Genes," *New Scientist* (website), November 24, 2008.

23. Stephen Altrogge, "A Solid Worldview Won't Save My Kids," The Blazing Center (blog), January 2015.

24. Flannery O'Connor, *Mystery and Manners: Occasional Prose* (New York: Farrar, Straus and Giroux, 1970), 34.

25. Frederick Hart quoted in "Hart Cathedral Collection," Angela King Gallery (website).

26. Tom Wolfe, "The Artist the Art World Couldn't See," *New York Times Magazine*, January 2, 2000, 16.

27. Ibid., 17.

28. O. Henry, "The Last Leaf," in *The Trimmed Lamp, and Other Stories of the Four Million* (Garden City, NY: Doubleday, Page & Company, 1907), 198–208.

29. Zach Franzen, personal communication, June 17, 2015.

30. "Read-Aloud Revival," http://amongstlovelythings.com.

31. Tantrum House, http://www.tantrumhouse.com.

32. Richard A. Lanham, "The Abusage of Usage," *Virginia Quarterly Review* 53, no. 1 (Winter 1977):32–54, http://www.vqronline.org/essay/abusage-usage.

33. Mark O'Connor, "The Kingdom Is a Feast," *Kairos* 24, issue 20 (October 27, 2013): 19, http://www.cam.org.au/Portals/0/kairos/kairos_v24i20/files/assets/basic-html/page19.html.

34. Kim Hammond and Darren Cronshaw, *Sentness: Six Postures of Missional Christians* (Downers Grove, IL: InterVarsity Press, 2014), 88–89.

35. Dan Forrest, "What I Believe," http://www.danforrest.com/bio/what-i-believe. Used by permission.

36. Maltbie Babcock, "This Is My Father's World," *Rejoice Hymns* (Greenville, SC: Majesty Music, 2011), 147.

MEMORY VERSES

1: Worldviews

1 Corinthians 10:4–5 And all drank the same spiritual drink. For they drank from the spiritual Rock that followed them, and the Rock was Christ. Nevertheless, with most of them God was not pleased, for they were overthrown in the wilderness.

2: Presuppositions

Hebrews 11:3 By faith we understand that the universe was created by the word of God, so that what is seen was not made out of things that are visible.

3: The Two-Story View

Colossians 1:19–20 For in [Christ] all the fullness of God was pleased to dwell, and through him to reconcile to himself all things, whether on earth or in heaven, making peace by the blood of his cross.

4: God the Creator

John 1:1–3 In the beginning was the Word, and the Word was with God, and the Word was God. He was in the beginning with God. All things were made through him, and without him was not any thing made that was made.

John 17:24 "Father, I desire that they also, whom you have given me, may be with me where I am, to see my glory that you have given me because you loved me before the foundation of the world."

5: Man and His Mandate

Genesis 1:26–28 Then God said, "Let us make man in our image, after our likeness. And let them have dominion over the fish of the sea and over the birds of the heavens and over the livestock and over all the earth and over every creeping thing that creeps on the earth."

So God created man in his own image,
in the image of God he created him;
male and female he created them.

And God blessed them. And God said to them, "Be fruitful and multiply and fill the earth and subdue it, and have dominion over the fish of the sea and over the birds of the heavens and over every living thing that moves on the earth."

6: Everything God Made Was Very Good

Proverbs 3:19 The Lord by wisdom founded the earth; by understanding he established the heavens.

7: Far as the Curse Is Found

Romans 8:19–21 The creation waits with eager longing for the revealing of the sons of God. For the creation was subjected to futility, . . . in hope that the creation itself will be set free from its bondage to corruption.

8: Common Grace, the World, and You

1 Peter 2:11–12 Beloved, I urge you as sojourners and exiles to abstain from the passions of the flesh, which wage war against your soul. Keep your conduct among the Gentiles honorable, so that when they speak against you as evildoers, they may see your good deeds and glorify God on the day of visitation.

Proverbs 1:7 The fear of the Lord is the beginning of knowledge; fools despise wisdom and instruction.

9: Structure and Direction

Ephesians 5:10–11 And try to discern what is pleasing to the Lord. Take no part in the unfruitful works of darkness, but instead expose them.

10: An Everlasting Kingdom

Genesis 3:15 (NKJV) And I will put enmity between you and the woman, and between your seed and her Seed; He shall bruise your head, and you shall bruise His heel.

11: Redeemed for Good Works

Matthew 5:14–16 You are the light of the world. A city set on a hill cannot be hidden. Nor do people light a lamp and put it under a basket, but on a stand, and it gives light to all in the house. In the same way, let your light shine before others, so that they may see your good works and give glory to your Father who is in heaven.

12: The Mission of the Church and Your Vocation

Acts 2:42 And they devoted themselves to the apostles' teaching and the fellowship, to the breaking of bread and the prayers.

13: The Man and the Woman in Creation

Genesis 2:18 Then the Lord God said, "It is not good that the man should be alone; I will make him a helper fit for him."

14: Marriage Twisted

Genesis 3:16–17 To the woman he said, "I will surely multiply your pain in childbearing; in pain you shall bring forth children. Your desire shall be for your husband, and he shall rule over you." And to Adam he said, "Because you have listened to the voice of your wife and have eaten of the tree of which I commanded you, 'You shall not eat of it,' cursed is the ground because of you; in pain you shall eat of it all the days of your life."

15: Marriage Redeemed

Proverbs 18:22 He who finds a wife finds a good thing and obtains favor from the Lord.

16: Foundations of Government

2 Samuel 23:3*b*–4 When one rules justly over men, ruling in the fear of God, he dawns on them like the morning light, like the sun shining forth on a cloudless morning, like rain that makes grass to sprout from the earth.

17: Political Perspectives

Psalm 82:1–4 (NASB) God takes His stand in His own congregation; He judges in the midst of the rulers. How long will you judge unjustly and show partiality to the wicked? Vindicate the weak and fatherless; do justice to the afflicted and destitute. Rescue the weak and needy; deliver them out of the hand of the wicked.

18: The Goal of Government

Revelation 11:15*b* The kingdom of the world has become the kingdom of our Lord and of his Christ, and he shall reign forever and ever.

19: Science Is Something God Created Humans to Do

Psalm 111:2 Great are the works of the Lord, studied by all who delight in them.

20: Fallen Science

Romans 1:25 They exchanged the truth about God for a lie and worshiped and served the creature rather than the Creator, who is blessed forever! Amen.

21: Reading Genesis and Doing Science

Genesis 1:31 And God saw everything that he had made, and behold, it was very good. And there was evening and there was morning, the sixth day.

22: Foundations for History

Acts 17:26–27 [God] made from one man every nation of mankind to live on all the face of the earth, having determined allotted periods and the boundaries of their dwelling place, that they should seek God, and perhaps feel their way toward him and find him. Yet he is actually not far from each one of us.

23: Fallen History

John 8:44–45 You are of your father the devil, and your will is to do your father's desires. He was a murderer from the beginning, and does not stand in the truth, because there is no truth in him. When he lies, he speaks out of his own character, for he is a liar and the father of lies. But because I tell the truth, you do not believe me.

24: History in Light of Redemption

Isaiah 46:9–10 Remember the former things of old; for I am God, and there is no other; I am God, and there is none like me, declaring the end from the beginning and from ancient times things not yet done, saying, "My counsel shall stand, and I will accomplish all my purpose."

25: Truth, Goodness, and Beauty

Philippians 4:8 Finally, brothers, whatever is true, whatever is honorable, whatever is just, whatever is pure, whatever is lovely, whatever is commendable, if there is any excellence, if there is anything worthy of praise, think about these things.

26: The False, the Bad, and the Ugly

2 Thessalonians 2:11 Therefore God sends them a strong delusion, so that they may believe what is false.

27: Creative Cultivators

Genesis 2:15 The Lord God took the man and put him in the garden of Eden to work it and keep it.

SCRIPTURE INDEX

TOPICAL INDEX

D

E

F

T

U

V

W

XYZ

PHOTO CREDITS

Key: (t) top; (c) center; (b) bottom; (l) left; (r) right

Unit 1

7 Karwai Tang/Getty Images Entertainment/Getty Images; **25** © iStockphoto.com/harmatoslabu; **29** John Chillingworth/Stringer/Picture Post/Getty Images; **34** (sky) © 2006 Jesse Larson, (church) © iStockphoto.com/stu99, (house) Norman Pogson/Shutterstock.com

Unit 2

53 Library of Congress; **56** "Selznick Kimball Young"/Wikimedia Commons/Public Domain; **64l** Ultima_Gaina/iStock/Thinkstock; **64r** Agency-Animal-Picture/Getty Images News/Getty Images; **66l** © iStockphoto.com/Avatar_023; **66cl** © iStockphoto.com/Britta Kasholm-Tengve; **66cr** © iStockphoto.com/SensorSpot; **66r** © iStockphoto.com/afhunta; **69t** lightphoto/iStock/Thinkstock; **69b** © iStockphoto.com/Fenykepez; **79t** Hulton Archive/Getty Images; **79b** "Vietnam Protestors" by US Army/National Archives/Wikimedia Commons/Public Domain; **85t** tupungato/iStock Editorial/Thinkstock; **85b** Guido Koppes / age fotostock / SuperStock

Unit 3

97 kursaltunsal/iStock/Thinkstock; **99** AP Photo/Atlanta Journal-Constitution, Jason Getz; **103** AP Photo/Jerome Delay; **111** © iStockphoto.com/Tarzan9280; **115** JACQUELYN MARTIN/AFP/Getty Images; **119** © iStockphoto.com/Pauline S Mills; **130l** "Abraham Lincoln Caricature" by DonkeyHotey/Flickr/CC By-SA 2.0; **130r** "George Washington - Caricature" by DonkeyHotey/Flickr/CC By 2.0

Unit 4

139 © iStockphoto.com/Sasha Radosavljevic; **157l** © iStock-photo.com/georgi1969; **157r** © blickwinkel / Alamy; **158** AP Photo/Juan Bautista Diaz; **164** © iStockphoto.com/trekandshoot; **177t, b** © iStockphoto.com/ZU_09

Unit 5

189 Dr. Najeeb Layyous / Science Source; **192** © iStockphoto.com/RonTech2000; **205** AP Photo/Mark Humphrey

Unit 6

240 "Mich. Guardsmen inspect water wells in need of repair in Iraq" by Petty Officer 1st Class Carmichael Yepez, Joint Combat Camera Center Iraq/Flickr/CC By 2.0; **242** AP Photo/File; **245t** Universal Images Group / SuperStock; **245b** Keystone-France/Hulton Archive/Getty Images; **253** © iStockphoto.com/TarpMagnus; **257** Architect of the Capitol; **260l** © Alan Wylie / Alamy; **260r** The Granger Collection, New York; **261** © Georgios Kollidas - Fotolia; **263l** Royal Albert Memorial Museum, Exeter, Devon, UK / Bridgeman Images; **263r** Bachrach/Archive Photos/Getty Images; **269l** AP Photo/Mary Ann Chastain; **269r** jhans/Bigstock.com

Unit 7

287 © iStockphoto.com/ookawa; **293tl** © iStockphoto.com/Grafissimo; **293tr** © iStockphoto.com/Volodymyr Goinyk; **293bl** © iStockphoto.com/MajaPhoto; **293br** © iStockphoto.com/kuch3; **308** Cover art for Gregory W. Brown's Missa Charles Darwin. Design and Illustration by Brett Picknell (2013). Courtesy of Navona Records, LLC.; **317** "Illustration at Cover of Just So Stories (c1912)"/Wikimedia Commons/Public Domain; **332t** Courtesy of Dr. John Baumgardner; **332b** BJU Photo Services; **333t**, **334l** © AnswersinGenesis; **333b** Greg Kahn/The Washington Post/Getty Images; **334r** Creation Ministries International (US) CREATION.com

Unit 8

343 DEA / S. VANNINI/De Agostini/Getty Images; **355** "Millais, John Everett (Sir) - Pizarro Seizing the Inca of Peru - Google Art Project"/Wikimedia Commons/Public Domain; **357** Past Pix / SSPL / Science and Society / SuperStock; **358** © TopFoto / THE IMAGE WORKS, INC.; **365** North Wind Picture Archives via AP Images; **370** "Vmail letter" by NathanBeach/Wikimedia Commons/Public Domain; **371l** "Dad-pow-postcard-wwII" by Steven Keech/Wikimedia Commons/CC By-SA 3.0; **371r** "Mauthausen Ausweis from WWII - front"/US Army/Wikimedia Commons/Public Domain; **373** imageBROKER / SuperStock; **379** Private Collection / © Look and Learn / Bridgeman Images

Unit 9

384 Joe Kohen/WireImage/Getty Images; **395l** Fine Art Images / SuperStock; **395r** "The Death of Marat" by Jacques-Louis David/Royal Museums of Fine Arts of Belgium/Wikimedia Commons/Public Domain; **401** AP Photo/Paola Crociani; **412** © AF archive / Alamy; **420l** Geoff Caddick/PA Wire URN:8988422 (Press Association via AP Images); **420r** Rex Features via AP Images; **427t** "Elysia-chlorotica-body" by Karen N. Pelletreau et al./Wikimedia Commons/CC By 4.0; **427bl** Mark Carwardine/Barcroft Media/Getty Images; **427br** Peter David/The Image Bank/Getty Images; **428** © iStockphoto.com/Lisa-Blue; **429** Raymond Boyd/Michael Ochs Archives/Getty Images; **430** "Adams The Tetons and the Snake River" by Ansel Adams/National Archives/Wikimedia Commons/Public Domain